STALIN

STALIN

A Critical Survey of Bolshevism

By Boris Souvarine

Alliance Book Corporation

LONGMANS, GREEN & CO.

New York

TRANSLATED BY C. L. R. JAMES

Copyright 1939 by Alliance Book Corporation

FIRST PRINTING, SEPTEMBER 1939
SECOND PRINTING, SEPTEMBER 1939
THIRD PRINTING, OCTOBER 1939

MANUFACTURED IN THE UNITED STATES OF AMERICA

CONTENTS

FOREWORD   ix

Chapter I   SOSSO   I

Birth of Stalin—His family, his native country—Childhood and youth—The
Caucasus and Georgia—The social environment—Bandits and gentry—Economic
and social conditions—The Tiflis Seminary—The Transcaucasian railway—The
first Social-Democrats of Georgia—Stalin joins the Socialist Movement.

Chapter II   THE YEARS OF APPRENTICESHIP   18

Socialism in Russia—Workers and peasants—Industry under Tsarism—Backward
capitalism and an impotent bourgeoisie—The Intelligentsia—The Pioneers of the
revolution—Theoreticians and policies—Herzen, Bakunin, Nechayev, Tkachev—
Populism and terrorism—Enter the proletariat—Marxism—Plekhanov—Workers'
and Socialist circles—First Congress of the Social-Democratic Party—Stalin at
Tiflis—Autobiography in perspective—Lenin—Iskra—Origins of Bolshevism—
The professional revolutionaries—Stalin as militant—Arrest, first exile—Trotsky
—The fundamental ideas of Lenin.

Chapter III   PROLOGUE TO REVOLUTION   50

Stalin and Lenin—Second Congress of Social-Democracy—The "hards" and the
"softs"—Bolsheviks and Mensheviks—The split—Lenin the Jacobin—Stalin the
Bolshevik—Internal struggles in the Party—Lenin's isolation—Discussions and
polemic—Rosa Luxemburg—Plekhanov's prophecy—The first Leninists—The
Russo-Japanese War—The Social Revolutionary Party—Strikes and the working-
class movement—Bloody Sunday at St. Petersburg—The Revolution of 1905—
The Third Social-Democratic Congress held by the Bolsheviks—The Soviet of
Workers' Deputies—Disagreements between Socialists—Lenin as seen by Stalin.

Chapter IV   A PROFESSIONAL REVOLUTIONARY   83

After the first revolution—Social-Democratic unity—The Stockholm Congress—
New dissensions between Bolsheviks and Mensheviks—The Duma—Lenin and
the boycott of the elections—The Boyeviki—Expropriations and banditry—
Guerilla warfare—The Bolshevik Centre—Krassin—The Tiflis affair—Kamo—
Stalin and Bolshevik terrorism—Tsintsadze—Pilsudski—The London Congress
—Stalin at Baku—Stalin in prison—Stalin at St. Petersburg—Definitive split in

the Social-Democracy—Bolshevism and Menshevism—Dislike of the revolution—
Tendencies, fractions and groups—The question of money—Bogdanov—The
Bolshevik Party—Stalin member of the Central Committee—Lenin and Trotsky
—The national question—Stalin in Austria—Malinovsky—Stalin deported to
Siberia—Police and provocateurs.

Chapter V THE REVOLUTION 139

The war of 1914—Defencism and defeatism—Lenin against all—The February
Revolution—Provisional Government and Petrograd Soviet—Stalin at liberty—
Bolshevik confusion—The return of Lenin—The April Theses—"All power to
the Soviets"—Trotsky with Lenin—Hopes of the world revolution—The July
days—The question of the Soviets—The Kornilov episode—The Sixth Party
Congress—Stalin's rôle—The great Bolshevik wave—Trotsky president of the
Petrograd Soviet—Lenin advocate of complete democracy—State and revolution
—Divergences of view on the date of the insurrection—Lenin demands the coup
d'état—Trotsky directs the military operations—The October Revolution—
Achievements and prospects.

Chapter VI THE CIVIL WAR 188

The morrow of victory—Discussions between the Bolsheviks—Lenin at work—
The liberty of the press—Gorky against Lenin—The Council of People's Com-
missars—Stalin, Commissar for Nationalities—The rights of nations, theoretical
and practical—Evolution of Lenin—Rosa Luxemburg's warnings—Georgia—
Insoluble contradictions—The agrarian question—Rosa Luxemburg's advice—
Lenin's waverings—The dictatorship of the proletariat—War and Peace—Brest-
Litovsk—Disagreements among the Bolsheviks—Lenin and peace at any price—
Trotsky's attitude—The fraction of the Left—Acute crisis in the Party—The
Seventh Congress—The Communist Party—Trotsky War Commissar—The Cheka
—Stalin at the front—The Red Army—Treasons, risings and rebellions—The
military opposition—Tsaritsyn—Terror—Stalin against Trotsky—Armistice and
revolutions—The civil war of Russian versus Russian—Stalin as military chief—
The Communist International—The Eighth Party Congress—Stalin Commissar
of Inspection—Lenin's colleagues.

Chapter VII THE SOVIET REPUBLIC 255

The evolution of Bolshevism—Lenin and the dictatorship—The ruling oligarchy
—The death penalty—Militarisation of the regime—The labour armies—Stifling
of the Soviets—Lenin's contradictions—The Politbureau of the Party—The Secretariat of the Central Committee—The Ninth Party Congress—The democratic
opposition—Discussion on the Trade Unions—Lenin versus Trotsky—The
Workers' Opposition—The Tenth Party Congress—Kronstadt—The New Economic Policy—Thermidor—Stalin Secretary of the Party—Soviet reality—The
machine—Personal antagonisms—The Eleventh Party Congress—Lenin's praise
of Stalin—Lenin's illness—Stalin in action—The bureaucracy—Lenin's projects
for reform—The National policy—Stalin and Georgia—Lenin against Stalin—

Lenin's last advice—The Testament—The question of the economic plan—Split
between Lenin and Stalin—The Republican Soviet State.

Chapter VIII   THE HERITAGE   321

The troïka—Trotsky in expectation—The Union of Soviet Republics—The
Twelfth Party Congress—The economic crisis and the "scissors"—Trotsky and
the peasants—Tendencies and groupings in the Party—The clandestine fractions
—The dictatorship of the triumvirate—Strikes and workers' demonstrations—
Trotsky against the troïka—The Forty-Six—Stalin and the German revolution—
The triumvirate and democracy—The New Course—Stalin against Trotsky—Defeat of the Opposition—Trotsky's responsibility—Lenin's death—Leninism the
state religion—Bolshevism and Leninism—The Thirteenth Party Congress—The
bolshevisation of the Communist International—The persecution of the Trotskyists—Stalin as prophet—The Georgian insurrection—Stalin's declaration—Cheka
and G.P.U.—Suicides—New conflict in the Party—Defeat of Trotsky—Split in
the triumvirate—The Leningrad Opposition—The dictatorship of the Secretariat
—Face to the country—"Enrich yourselves"—The Left and the Right—Stalin as
theoretician—Socialism in a single country—The Fourteenth Party Congress—
Stalin and statistics—Defeat of the new Opposition—Stalin, irremovable secretary.

Chapter IX   THE INHERITOR   412

Stalin seen by Trotsky—Variations on Thermidor—Trotsky's optimism—The
Opposition bloc—Condition of the working class—The vagabond children—
Stalin's foresight—The industrialists—The Plan—Settlement of accounts between
Leninists—The "English Question"—Stalin at the helm—Discords, disputes and
quarrels—Stalin totally opposed to industrialisation—The Chinese question—
Stalin's mortification—Communist disaster in China—The imminent war—Dis-
location of the Opposition bloc—Trotsky's contradictions—The tenth anniver-
sary of October—The Five Year Plan—Trotsky excluded from the Party—The
Opposition outlawed—The Fifteenth Party Congress—Stalin the industrialist—
The "capitulators"—The Canton Commune—Deportation of the Opposition—
Trotsky in Siberia—Contradictions and responsibilities of the Opposition—
The Shakhty trial—Stalin and the collectivisation of agriculture—The Right
against Stalin—New internal struggles—Bukharin's revelations—The Right dan-
ger—Trotsky in exile—Stalin and the Plan—Dekulakisation—Defeat of the Right
—Stalin's regime—The "knouto-Soviet State"—The "year of the great turn"—
End of the N.E.P.—Stalin's fiftieth birthday.

Chapter X   STALIN   512

Stalin's plan—Promises and conditions—Public Education—Bureaucratic machine—Stalin's dictatorship—The Sixteenth Party Congress—Rural collectivisation—"Dizzy with Success"—Industrialisation—Draconian measures—Decrees and
circulars—The interior passport—Food shortage—Suppressions, arrests, deportations—Riazanov—Stalin's silence—The famine—The balance-sheet of the Five

Year Plan—Appearances and realities—The Plan, results and consequences—
Historic precedents—The memory of Peter the Great—Parallels and comparisons—The lessons of Russian History—Soviet society—Socialism or State-Capital-
ism—The new privileges—Possibilities of war—Neo-patriotism and neo-defeatism
—Socialism and Communism reversed—Political and social inequality—Letters
and the arts under Stalin—Suicides—The Seventeenth Party Congress—Stalin
supreme—The greatest chief of all times and all peoples—The Second Five Year
Plan—Evolution of Stalin—The U.S.S.R. and the League of Nations—Stalin
pacifist—The Soviet youth—International discredit of Communism—What is
Stalin—Suicide of Alliluieva—The assassination of Kirov, the reply of terrorism
to terror—Stalin's courage—Lenin's last words.

Postscript   THE COUNTER REVOLUTION   597

Historic dates—The Kirov murder—Diversion and repression—Stalin's Consti-
tution—Deportations and purges—Transferences and disappearances—Nicholas
Yezhov—The end of the Old Guard—Suppressions and liquidations—The
Great Retreat—Economic measures—Morals and customs—Stakhanovism—"The
offensive on the Cultural Front"—"The Happy Life"—Discovery of Patriotism—
Stalin and Hitler—Hierarchy and Honours—Public Education—The revision
of history—The Tradition—Stalin's volte-face—The end of the Soviets—
Unanimity—Suicides and suspicious deaths—The Trial of the Sixteen—The
Trial of the Seventeen—The Fall of Yagoda—Mass arrests and executions—
Decapitation of the Red Army—The Year of Terror—Numerous suicides—The
Trial of the Twenty-one—Mussolini and Stalin—The Great Mass Murder—A
Communist St. Bartholomew—Trial by Statistics—The "Democratic" elections—
A new Sixteenth Century—Ivan the Terrible—The meaning of the Trials—"Men
of no political importance"—Communist youth—Riddles of history—Military
plot?—Stalin's motives—Apologies and dithyrambs—Failure of totalitarian economy—The 1937 census—Balance sheet of disaster—Foreign policy—Stalin's
regime.

INDEX   677

FOREWORD

Djugashvili, J.V., peasant of the province and district of Tiflis, from the village of Didi-Lolo, orthodox, clerk. By decision of the Ministry of the Interior, exiled under surveillance for two years, dating from the 29th September 1908, to Solvychegodsk, province of Vologda, whence he escaped. Exiled again to the province of Vologda, he again escaped on February 29, 1912. By decision of the Ministry of the Interior, exiled under surveillance for three years dating from June 8, 1912, to Narym district, whence he again escaped on September 1, 1912.

These few lines contained, at the beginning of the Russian Revolution, all that was known of an obscure Bolshevik answering to the surname Stalin; it was found in the archives of the Moscow Police Department, and published in 1918 at Moscow. General A. I. Spiridovich, one of the heads of the Okhrana (secret political police) of the old regime, reproduced it almost verbatim in 1922 in his *History of Bolshevism in Russia*. But no one at that time paid any attention to it. Stalin's name was still lost in a semi-anonymity, unknown not only to the people of Russia but even in the ranks of the Bolshevik Party and, obviously, still more so abroad.

This police chit may be supplemented by a note of the local gendarmerie relating to the year 1903 and published by close associates of Stalin in *Zarya Vostoka* of Tiflis, official organ of Bolshevism in Georgia:

According to information recently received from our agents Djugashvili was known in the Organisation under the nicknames of "Sosso" and of "Koba"; he has been working in the Social-Democratic Party since 1902, Menshevik first and then Bolshevik, as propagandist and director of the first section (railways).

ix

The first biographical notice of Stalin by the Communist
Party, less obscure but as brief as that of the Okhrana, is to be
found in the explanatory or documentary notes added to the
Complete Works of Lenin:

J. Stalin, born in 1879, member of the Party since 1898, one of
the most notable organisers and leaders of the Bolsheviks. Frequently imprisoned, six times deported; member of the Central Committee uninterruptedly since 1912; editor of *Pravda* in 1917; after
the October Revolution, People's Commissar for Nationalities; in
1921-1923 People's Commissar for Workers' and Peasants' Inspection; member of the All-Russian Central Executive Committee,
Secretary of the Central Committee of the Communist Party.

During Lenin's lifetime it appears that comparatively little
attention was paid to the future master of Russia, although
Stalin was already Secretary of the Bolshevik Party. His name
did not figure in any authoritative history of socialism, of the
workers' movement, or of the Russian Revolution. In the first
ten volumes of Lenin's works treating of the events, the ideas
and the men of a whole epoch, he is never once mentioned; very
rarely in the other ten, and then only as a lay figure. There is
no word of him in the innumerable memoirs and recollections
published in the course of ten years. In the *Great Upheaval*,
a work in which Lunacharsky sketches a series of *Revolutionary Silhouettes*, afterwards collected under this name in a
small volume, Stalin is not taken into consideration. There is
not a trace of him in the publications of the Party and hardly
any in the local press. His early career resembles that of hundreds of other revolutionaries of different schools: arrest, deportations and escapes under the old regime; high political and
administrative functions under the new. At first sight, it is
duller than many others; devoid of any outstanding, of any
memorable episode, of any notable event in the revolutionary
calendar; it offers no contribution to the body of socialist
thought. In another volume of Lenin's *Works* there are some
supplementary details in the appendices, of no particular interest
to the outsider:

Stalin, J. V. Djugashvili, revolutionary name "Koba," of peasant origin in the province of Tiflis. Frequently arrested and deported. Participant in a number of congresses and conferences. One of the most notable organisers and leaders of the Bolshevik Party. Co-opted at the beginning of 1912 to the Central Committee of the Russian Workers' Social-Democratic Party; after the general conference at Prague he entered the Russian Bureau of the Central Committee, and was active illegally in Russia, where he was soon arrested, and then deported to Turukhansk. Returned from exile after the February revolution. Close collaborator of Lenin at the time of the preparation and achievement of the October Revolution. Member of the Central Committee uninterruptedly from 1912 onwards and of the Council of People's Commissars since 1917.

Identical notes are to be found in other volumes of Lenin's *Works* and in the *Works* of Gregory Zinoviev. Stalin's peasant origin is noted in each case. The article *Djugashvili*, in the unfinished work of V. Nevsky: *Material for a Biographical Dictionary of Social-Democrats*, is more complete and detailed but contains inaccuracies. After Lenin's death, a new revised and augmented edition of the *Complete Works* was undertaken, but the official historians, in spite of their zeal for the new master, could give him little more, after ten years of revolution, than a dozen lines (Vol. XX). Some of the variants may be quoted:

Militant Social-Democrat from 1896 onwards. Organised in 1902, at Baku, various workers' demonstrations, was exiled to Eastern Siberia, escaped in 1904, and began illegal activity. . . . Exiled in 1912 to the Narym district; exiled in 1913, after another escape and return to St. Petersburg, to Turukhansk. . . .

But in the next volume, published in 1928, the tone changes. The account of Stalin's life is modified and becomes more detailed. It is still documentary in form, but the propagandist element is apparent. Bolshevism was then engaged in merciless intestine struggles, and the personal record of every important figure became a weapon in the struggle. Each of them searched the past of his adversary in the hope of discovering some instance of weakness, some error or mistake. And each accentuates his own title to the confidence of the ruling party and the new dominant class. This time Stalin dictated the notice himself:

Stalin, J.V. (Djugashvili), born in 1879. Son of a boot operative in Tiflis, militant from 1897 onwards, one of the original Bolsheviks; imprisoned in 1901 for having directed strikes at Baku, deported to Eastern Siberia, escaped and returned to the Caucasus to take part in the Party's illegal activities. Was present in 1905 at the Tammersfors Congress; delegate to the Stockholm and London Conferences of the Russian Social-Democrats; in 1907 made the Baku organisation the stronghold of Bolshevism in the Caucasus. Arrested and deported in 1908 and 1910; militant in illegal activity at Petersburg, again arrested, elected to the Central Committee in 1912. Took part in editing the legal Party organs in 1912-13, deported in 1913 to Turukhansk, where he remained until the time of the Revolution. Member of the Political Bureau of the Party from May 1917, directed the central organ of the Party, when Lenin was outlawed after the events of July 1917, with Sverdlov managed the Sixth Congress of the Party, was a member of the Committees of Five and of Seven which organised the October insurrection. People's Commissar for Nationalities, then for Workers' Inspection, served in the Red Army in the Civil War (defence of Tsaritsyn, on the Polish front, in the Wrangel campaign, etc.). From 1920 to 1923, member of the Revolutionary War Council. General Secretary of the Party since 1922. Member of the Executive Committee of the Communist International from 1925 onwards. Author of a series of works on Leninism and the question of nationalities.

Thus the Didi-Lolo peasant had become a boot operative of Tiflis, and his son Sosso, as he was familiarly called in Georgia, later "Koba," and finally Stalin, made known his merits as writer, politician, soldier, statesman, and even as thinker and theorist. This account was to serve as a basis for the article compiled by his secretary for the dictionary and encyclopaedia *Granat*, and reproduced *ad nauseam* in Russian brochures and periodicals.

But this is nothing compared with the remarkable demonstration of December 21, 1929, Stalin's fiftieth birthday. The whole Soviet press displayed vast headlines, large portraits and articles of enormous length. The eulogies of the Dictator were not less portentous. According to the incense-burners of his entourage, all human and some superhuman virtues were incarnate in Stalin. His modesty, courage and devotion were paralleled by his knowledge and wisdom. He was the organiser of the Bolshevik Party, the leader of the October Revolution, the head of the Red Army, and victor in the Civil War as well as in foreign war. He was, moreover, the leader of the world proletariat. The man of action proved himself as great as the theorist, and both are infallible; there is no instance of a mistake made by Stalin. One *leitmotiv* recurs constantly in the dithyrambs: man of iron, steeled soldier, allusions to the name he had adopted, with variations on the invariable theme of steel and iron: "iron Leninist," "granite Bolshevik." The same formula, the same exaggeration, the same extravagant expressions of admiration and submissiveness, in strict conformity with models sent down from Moscow, recur in thousands of addresses, messages and telegrams from all parts of Russia, which fill whole pages of the newspapers, and then several columns daily for weeks. The State publishing-houses issued thousands of copies of collections of these tributes in which panegyrics filled over 250 pages, in addition to innumerable messages simply indicated by the names of the senders. An official portrait bust was manufactured by mass production and distributed officially. The name of Stalin, already given to several towns, was again given to factories, electricity stations, rural undertakings, barracks and schools. . . .

Under the title of "Stalin the Enigma," a contributor to *Pravda*, the Bolshevik official organ in Moscow, set out (December 21, 1929) the terms used outside Russia to describe the man of the day: "Stalin, the mysterious host of the Kremlin"; "Stalin, dictator of a sixth of the world"; "Stalin, victor over all opposition"; "Stalin, Impenetrable Personality"; "Stalin, the Communist Sphinx"; "Stalin, the Enigma." "Insoluble mystery," "indecipherable enigma" were the most frequently used tags, no doubt because Stalin emerged quietly from an obscure past and an apparently banal present, and because none but a few of the initiated could explain his access to unlimited power.

One of Stalin's oldest comrades, of Caucasian origin and resembling him also in his rise to power, Sergo Ordjonikidze, wrote naïvely on the same anniversary: "The whole world is writing to-day about Stalin," as if the orders of the Bolshevik dictatorship had the force of law for the press of all countries, as if the circulars of the Secretariat of his party were propagated and could be imposed beyond the Soviet frontiers like waves of light. He adds, this time with more justification: "Much will also be written in the future," and further, "His enemies will write with hatred and his friends with love," forgetting that it may be possible to write "without hate and without fear," conscientiously and with some degree of critical spirit, in an attempt at impartial investigation and historical truth.

Ten years earlier, on April 23, 1920, Moscow celebrated the jubilee of Lenin, the real initiator of Bolshevism, the actual founder of the Communist Party, the authentic victor of October, the true creator of the Soviet State. It was practically an intimate gathering of the Moscow Committee of the Party. Old friends exchanged their recollections. The record is a modest pamphlet of thirty pages. Between 1920 and 1930 a profound change had come over the Russian Revolution. The Bolshevism of to-day is no longer what it was. It is this which lends a special interest to the personality of Stalin, wielder of a dictatorial power unparalleled in the world of to-day and unprecedented in history.

Chapter 1

SOSSO

STALIN, his real name Joseph Vissarionovich Dju-gashvili, was born in 1879 at Gori, Georgia, and not at Didi-Lolo (in reality Didi-Lilo), his grandfather's native place. Trotsky (Leon Davidovich Bronstein) was born in the same year. Most of the leaders of the Russian Revolu-tion of 1917 belong to the generation of the '80's of the last century; Lenin (Vladimir Ilyich Ulianov) was older by a decade.

Stalin's father, Vissarion, was a peasant like his grandfather, but a handicraftsman as well, as were innumerable *kustari* peasants in the various provinces of the former Empire. In the Djugashvili family the shoemaker's trade was hereditary, though they remained attached to the soil; and little Joseph would have continued the family tradition but for his father's premature death. According to the official biographer, Vissarion worked at the small Adelkhanov boot factory, at Tiflis, the only town in the neighbourhood. The peasant shoemaker died, leaving an only son of eleven years old. Three other children had died before his birth. His mother, Catherine, died in 1937 at the age of 78, and had lived during her last years at Tiflis in a modest apartment in a socialised mansion, once the residence of the former Viceroy. She was devoted to her only son, and sent him to the church school at Gori, with the idea of making him a parish priest. There young Sosso acquired the rudiments of education, and learned many prayers.

He was Sosso, in accordance with the equalitarian and simple Georgian custom, which transforms names from the calendar

1

into endearing diminutives, and makes general use of the familiar second person singular. A Georgian retains his pet-name all his life, and many friends would be incapable of saying what were the real Christian names of a Chito or a Zakro, a Valico or a Kote. Among his relatives and friends Stalin therefore remained Sosso.

Gori was a big township on the left bank of the Kura (Greek, Kuros; French, Cyrus), seventy versts from Tiflis, the capital of Georgia and of Transcaucasia. The stream is rapid and abounds in fish; in the Turki language its upper reaches are romantically called "Coral Waters" or "River of Pearls." The "town" had 5,000 inhabitants when Stalin first saw the light of day there; the population is now about twice that figure. When Dubois de Montpéreux visited the place he noted that there was an Armenian majority, "almost all of them artisans and traders," but the proportion diminished substantially later on. There is a Tartar admixture in the Georgians of the valley. Gori lies in the centre of a lacustrine plain, with a fertile soil and a climate favourable to agriculture; its peasants produce good wine and the best wheat in the Caucasus. "Nothing could be more picturesque," writes a traveller, "than the two thousand year old fortress, dominating the town from the summit of an isolated hill in the centre of a plain surrounded by high mountains, among which may be discerned in the distance the snowy summit of Mount Kasbek." The slopes are forest clad. There is no local industry. Eight kilometres away is the troglodyte city of Uplis-Tzikhe, attributed by Greek legend to Ulysses, with the relics of an ancient civilisation in its caves.

Sosso grew up among the Georgian and Tartar peasants of Gori until he was fourteen. In 1893 he entered the Seminary at Tiflis, where the curriculum corresponded roughly to that of a Russian High School, except for the large share allotted to instruction in the Greek Orthodox religion. The seminarists were usually destined for holy orders or for the lower ranks of the clergy. There, apparently, he acquired his knowledge of Old Slavonic, and the ritual phraseology which appeared later in some of his most characteristic writings.

His friend B. Bibineishvili, in memoirs published at Tiflis in 1930 under the title *A Quarter of a Century*, has devoted a short chapter to him. For Stalin's school-days he uses articles written by old boys of the seminary, Bakuradze and Parkadze, printed in the review *Drosha* (The Flag) in 1924. From these, however, he gets very little. He says he remembers seeing him riding on the back of their fellow-student Davitashvili and shouting *"Ya stal, ya stal"* (I am steel). If this story, which cannot be authenticated, is true, then Stalin was very early conscious of his strength. Catherine Djugashvili maintains, erroneously, that her son received his name of Stalin from Lenin. It appears also that Sosso wrote verses of which some were printed under the pseudonym of Sosselo, in *Iveria*, a local nationalist journal edited by I. Chavchavadze, but the verses have never been reprinted.

There is hardly any reliable information to enable us to judge of his childhood and youth—no recollections of relatives or memoirs of acquaintances, no family papers or private letters, no school notes or boyish essays. All that is available is the guarded confidences of some of his comrades of those days. The brochure of I. Iremashvili, *Stalin und die Tragödie Georgiens*, published in Germany, is too suspect to be accepted by serious persons without confirmation of the contents. There is little scope in such a case for the art of the self-styled psycho-analysts who seek the origin of great historical and social events in the adolescence of great men.

Once only, his mother made a statement, a serious one, for publication. "He was always a good boy. . . . I never had to punish him. He worked hard, was always reading and talking, and tried to understand everything. He went to school when he was eight." This maternal account is flatly contradicted by the accounts already referred to of Bolshevik Georgians who were his school-fellows. They found Sosso hard, insensitive, without consideration for his mother, and adduce rather unpleasant facts by way of proof. But a mother is a mother, and indiscreet boyhood comrades are in prison or in exile.

Sosso did read, but in Georgian, that is to say, folk-lore,

fabulous tales which are the foundation of the literature of his native land and no doubt the great epic and lyric poem of Rustaveli, *The Knight in the Panther Skin*. Georgia obstinately resisted Russification, and the people maintained their original language. Even to-day Stalin speaks Russian incorrectly, with a strong Caucasian accent which arouses the rather scornful irony of "real" Russians. Except with a Georgian interviewer his mother required an interpreter. One cannot help thinking of the Corsican Bonaparte, whose mother tongue was Italian and who hated France before he came to govern it, just as the Georgian Stalin was to govern the Russia whose imperial rule he had detested.

His reading and the teaching at school provided him with the rudiments of education; neither have left visible traces in his writings and speeches. In that he is unlike any other notable revolutionary of modern times. The speeches of the outstanding men of the French Revolution constantly reveal their spiritual ancestry by quotations from Montesquieu, from Rousseau and Mably, by references to the heroes and famous stories of Sparta and Rome. The revolutionary idiom of our own day is impregnated with the ideas of Karl Marx and Friedrich Engels, with here and there formulae taken from Lassalle and Blanqui, from Proudhon and Bakunin, and their successors, and with references to historical precedents—to Jacobinism, Babouvism, Chartism, the Revolution of 1848, the Commune of 1871. Nothing of the kind with Stalin. The age-long tradition which revives to-day the name of Spartacus finds no expression in his words, even though it is continued in his deeds. Nevertheless from a given moment he neither spoke nor wrote without quoting Lenin at every point, as if he owed everything to one book, a work in twenty volumes—just as Cromwell seems to have read only the Bible. If he should happen to quote another writer it is at second hand, as if to create the impression, unwillingly revealed, of a modicum of erudition.

His compatriot, A. Yenukidze, a high official devoted to his service, says: "Stalin, while still a seminarist, read books on science, sociology, and the working-class movement, but in secret, like a conspirator. In spite of all precautions, his reading was discovered by the vigilance of his monastic directors, and Djugashvili was expelled from the Seminary." It seems very strange that the reading of purely scientific books, all of which had in any case been submitted to the strict Russian censorship, should at that time be considered a crime, even at the Tiflis Seminary; the zealous but clumsy friend here seeks to prove too much. Moreover, Sosso's mother explicitly denies his expulsion: "He was not expelled. I brought him home on account of his health. When he entered the Seminary he was fifteen and as strong a lad as could be. But overwork up to the age of nineteen pulled him down, and the doctors told me that he might develop tuberculosis. So I took him away from school. He did not want to leave. But I took him away. He was my only son." Catherine Djugashvili insists again and again: "He was not expelled; I took him away."

Thus the little information we have about his youth is inexact or contradictory. For those who seek historical analogies at any price, here is one more slight resemblance to Cromwell. One may assume, in both cases, that probably this obscurity hides nothing very important. Stalin's character is comprehensible without a knowledge of its early indications; his work can be estimated without knowing his childish impressions, his early desire for knowledge or any precocious ideas he may have had. He was certainly not haunted by Plutarch's heroes, by the great historical figures which some leaders of men have sought to follow as their model. The work he was one day to do was not the fruit of early meditation, nor the execution of a great premeditated plan. The first factors in his life demanding attention are the peasant psychology of his family and friends; and the basic theological education. The other factors we must seek in the general conditions of the country and the period, in the half-light of the historic past, before tracing more direct influences on his character.

2

THE Caucasus was known in legend before it entered upon the stage of History. But mythology, geography, ethnology and linguistics were merely a confused and distant memory when the World War shattered established national relations, brought into play the interests of States and coalitions, raised frontier questions once more, and with them interest in the nationality of the inhabitants of the districts involved.

For the purpose of the peace negotiations, rival propagandists hastily improvised instruction for the general public in the past records of forgotten races, raising historical claims that had lain dormant for centuries. As the Russian Revolution brought Caucasian, and especially Georgian, problems to the forefront, short courses of history and geography in pamphlets reinforced current knowledge of legendary history. And of all this, in the minds of the contemporaries of Stalin, what remains?

This is the mythical country of Colchis whither Jason led the Argonauts to secure the Golden Fleece. Some see in this a symbol of the riches of the country, others an allusion to the particles of metal in the sheepskins used to wash the auriferous sands of the Ingur and the Rion. In earlier times the Hebrews had believed that Noah's Ark came to rest on Mount Ararat. The Greeks, more especially Aristotle, seem to have been fascinated by the mighty mountain chain of the Caucasus, raising its crests of over 16,000 feet like a natural rampart between two worlds. In it they saw the cradle of their race, the birthplace of civilisation. The Caucasus is the home of the Prometheus myth, the symbol of humanity in revolt handed down the centuries; its adoption by modern revolutionary thought presaged the storm about to break between East and West.

Is the Caucasus part of Europe or Asia? Historians and geographers as far back as Herodotus and Strabo have raised the question. In saying that "It can no longer be doubted that the Caucasus belongs to Asia," Elisée Reclus follows Humboldt, and Humboldt, Pallas. History and ethnography confirm the geological fact. The indigenous races, settled mainly on the southern slopes, belong to the Asiatic world; before the Russian conquest they were linked in every way with Asia Minor and Persia. "By her fauna and flora Transcaucasia belongs to subtropical Asia," writes Reclus, summing up earlier scientific observation. The epithet *Asiatic* spontaneously applied to Stalin in Russia is correct, apart from the special sense sometimes attached to the word.

The physical geography of the country has been exhaustively described: high mountains and narrow valleys, except for the basin of the Kura which opens out more and more until it reaches the Caspian Sea; steep slopes, rugged escarpments, ravines and precipices, torrents fed by the eternal snows from the glaciers. Magnificent vegetation, especially in the eastern regions, and forests of great variety cover more than half the country in spite of barbarous deforestation. Possibly the vine originated in this region where, according to Jewish tradition, a patriarch first pressed the grapes, and was the first to be drunk with wine. The walnut is said to have originated in the valleys of Imeretia. In no country of the world is there to be found so great a variety of fruit and nut-bearing trees. Hunting has not exterminated a fauna stretching back to far distant times; there formerly could be found the aurochs, lynx, tiger, panther, hyena, brown bear, antelope, eagle, the bearded vulture, and rare birds such as the rosy starling and the blue thrush.

Strabo counted seventy races in the Caucasus, speaking as many languages. According to Pliny there were a hundred and thirty languages in use in the marches of Colchis. The Arabs gave the name *Mount of Languages* to the great rocky massif whose folds shelter the residue of prehistoric migrations. Even in his time Reclus put the number of dialects and local patois at seventy, but classified them under a few main groups. This variety of language reflects the differentiation of the population into tribes isolated by physical obstacles and the configuration of the country. The common assertion that mountain districts encourage conservatism can be verified in the Caucasus better than anywhere else. For the ethnologist and philologist there is

inexhaustible material for controversy. It is agreed that the
Georgians (or Kartli), the race to which Stalin belongs, are of
Iberian origin; they are sub-divided into Gurians proper, Svan-
etians, Imeretians, Mingrelians, Khevsurs, Pshavs, Tushes, Lazis,
with some Chechens, Ossetes, and Lesghians; yet they have maintained for two thousand years their ethnological entity and
the purity of their language. Recent philological studies have
attempted to throw light from Georgian sources on the tale of
Tristan and Iseult, thus linking the Caucasus with Brittany.

The mixture of races makes it unnecessary to seek for pure
racial characteristics in Stalin. The Georgians, surrounded by
various remnants of Mongol, Slav, and Aryan populations, have
an admixture of Tartars, Persians, Armenians, Kurds and various
Mediterranean peoples. On the authority of Herodotus, Maspero
mentions the presence in Colchis even of descendants of Egyp-
tians brought there by Sesostris. Summarising the observations
made by writers on the Georgians, Reclus has written, in words
pregnant with meaning for anyone who knows Stalin: "They
are said to have a lower average intelligence than the other
Caucasian peoples; sitting side by side in the schools with Tartars
and Armenians, they show less facility than these in the study
of foreign languages, science, and elocution." But, if we are to
accept literally the descriptions of the Georgians as friendly,
frank, care-free, straightforward, sociable and peaceable, then
it must be supposed that Stalin has a strong infusion of Turki
blood, through Kurd or Tartar ancestry. Old socialist militants
in the Caucasus assure us that Catherine Djugashvili is an Osse
(Ossetinka) and attach great importance to this detail: not only
are the Ossetes less subtle and more crude than the Georgians,
but Russia has always recruited among them a strong proportion
of gendarmes and of convict-guards.

The history of Georgia yields to no other in horror. Twenty-
five centuries ago Georgia had reached a higher degree of civilisation than the greater part of Europe. Her Euxine shore had
been colonised by the Greeks; then in turn the Jews, the
Romans, the Persians, and later, the Genoese left their traces on
the country from the Black Sea to the Caspian. As the main land

route to Central Asia, the Caucasus was frequently invaded, was conquered by Alexander the Great, was subjected by Mithradates Eupator, and later experienced the destructive tidal wave of the Huns. Christianity became the dominant religion there almost at the same time as in Greece, much earlier than in Europe generally. The Iberian Church formed a point of contact with Byzantium. ". . . There arose a highly civilised society based on a curious synthesis of Byzantine culture and Arab and Persian influences." This civilisation reached its highest point in the twelfth century, in the reigns of King David and Queen Tamara, during the short respite Georgia enjoyed while the Persians and the Turks were at war. Then the Mongol hordes of Genghiz Khan, followed by those of Tamerlane, put the country to fire and the sword; towns and villages were completely devastated and the inhabitants almost exterminated.

In the next five centuries Georgia was coveted and fought for by her warlike neighbours, invaded many times, dismembered, pillaged, sacked and her population decimated by Persian and Turkish armies, and by raids followed by razzias of human cattle (especially of women intended for the harem). She appealed in vain for Russian protection. Annexation by the Tsars in 1801 put an end to her age-long misfortunes by enabling her to share the unenviable, but relatively endurable, lot of the other peoples of the Russian Empire. Her population had fallen from seven million to one million. For half a century longer a guerilla war was maintained in the higher mountain regions, where Georgian rebels against Russification by force defied the Tsar's troops from their inaccessible retreats, and carried out audacious surprise attacks.

This long series of terrible calamities, alternating with periods of torpor following on massacres, left Georgia poor in spite of her rich natural resources and backward in spite of the antiquity of her civilisation. For strategic reasons the Russians built roads, thus facilitating trade and travel; they encouraged wine-growing, which was not competitive with Russian agriculture, and contributed to repopulation by sending to Georgia soldiers, officials, traders, tourists, and political and religious exiles. A century of peace brought back life to the unhappy country without, however, substantially raising either the standard of education or of living, or improving technical methods.

At the time of Stalin's birth, Reclus wrote: "The ancient method used in the construction of Georgian houses has been maintained for two thousand years. There are whole villages composed of nothing but holes made in the ground and in the rocks, only indicated from the outside by heaps of brushwood on their mud roofs, on which the women sit out in the cool of the evening." In most Georgian towns many houses still have only the traditional mud roofs.

Agricultural implements were rudimentary and ineffective. In 1900 an official report stated: "The Georgian plough is a very large, costly and heavy contrivance, which does not give satisfactory results and demands enormous labour power . . . it must be drawn by from three to four pairs of oxen or buffaloes according to the nature of the soil and other considerations." To provide a team of this kind the peasants form a temporary *artel,* putting into the common stock one man's plough, another's harness, others' cattle. Their harrow is simply a plank; everywhere the sickle is used for harvesting, and often the harvest is carried on men's backs.

Industry was practically non-existent, mineral riches neglected, transport archaic. The extraction of manganese in the Kutais province and of petroleum at Baku were only just beginning. Domestic industry on a small scale by local artisans covered domestic needs, and sufficed for clothing and weapons. The railway had not yet replaced the ruts of the road dug deep by the heavy *arbas* drawn by oxen. Tools remained primitive.

The past weighed heavily on the family and social life of the Georgians. Stalin's parents had been serfs, the system not having been abolished in Transcaucasia until about 1865. Some of "the nobility, who have remained great landlords, have not yet lost the habit of treating the peasants as animals subject to their caprice, and the manners engendered by serfdom among the people themselves have not disappeared." The same author, Reclus, in describing the condition of the countryside, says: "In spite of the fertility of the soil of Georgia and the relatively small population occupying the land, the peasants in the Kura valley are mostly very poor, and they possess wretched cattle, scurvy cows, and sheep with wool almost like bristles." Marshy ground and absence of sanitation made vast stretches of country unhealthy.

Even the favoured coast region, the "Caucasian Riviera," was wretchedly poor, and a former Minister of Agriculture, A. Yermolov, wrote in 1907: "To see this lovely country the traveller must journey for hundreds of kilometres through virgin forests and waste land, spend nights in the poor huts of the peasants complaining of their poverty and sometimes dying of fever, listen to the howling of the jackals, hear the complaints of the inhabitants on the ravages of bears and wild boars in their maize fields . . . in fact see a country poor and desolate in the midst of luxuriant vegetation." At the other end, descending towards Tiflis, the valley of the Kura, like that of the Lower Araxes, is rendered arid by the scorching winds from Asia; its poverty is not less.

Such was Stalin's environment in his earliest years. He was surrounded by remnants of barbarism, by ruin, desolation, and sometimes famine (there was scarcity in 1891-2 and in 1897-8). Patriarchal traditions and many a mediaeval custom still persisted. Religion laid its powerful hand on a population of which more than three-quarters in all, and a higher proportion outside the towns, were illiterate. "No country in the world is richer in churches," wrote Dubois de Montpéreux. Gori, he adds, "has two large modern churches, a Catholic Church and an Armenian, and other smaller Greek Orthodox Churches, making eight in all." Among other survivals from the Middle Ages, little Sosso would be accustomed to meeting in the mountains Khevsurs, a curious people who wore coats of mail, buckles, arm-pieces, and a whole equipment which induced the belief long held that they were descendants of the Crusaders. There was a feudal touch about the local costume, borrowed from the Cherkesses; it resembled a miniature walking arsenal complete with pistols, dagger, sabre and cartridge belt, now more decorative than use-

ful. The practice of brigandage, kept up by the natural inclination of armed mountaineers to prey on the products of the plain,
was maintained in various forms, from highway robbery to
political banditry. Gori, says Dubois de Montpéreux, lay at the
centre of a district where brigandage was rife. Young Stalin was
witness of racial hatreds between Armenians and Georgians,
between Tartars and Armenians, fostered by the Russian
colonisers in their own interests.

The population, twenty-three to the square kilometre according to the census of 1897, was five parts rural to one urban. The
majority were landless peasants, and small farmers on a *métayage*
system, who were exploited by a rural gentry numerous but by
no means rich. Narratives of travel in the Caucasus always express the amazement of Western observers at the multitude of
the poor landed gentry—a Mingrelian nobleman as inn-waiter,
an Imeretian prince as stable boy. In this country princes are
as plentiful as game, noted von Thielmann. Another traveller
says of the Georgians: "Most of them are at once noble and
poor, and this is not the only trait in which they resemble the
Spaniards," and to this rather summary estimate he adds some
just remarks on the idleness of the indigenous population, their
immoderate indulgence in Khaketian wine and their propensity
to brigandage: "Young men belonging to the most ancient
families have earned on the highroad a reputation which does
not injure their standing in society but often ends in Siberian
exile." The ownership of five or six hectares of land might
carry with it the title of Prince. Artisans, ranking with the
peasantry in the country or in the mountains, and with the small
shopkeepers in the towns, did not form a well-defined class.
Workmen properly so called, few in number, remained attached
to their native village. There was neither industrial proletariat
nor capitalist bourgeoisie, in the modern sense of those terms. A
small intelligentsia and the rank-and-file of the clergy were in
close relations with the common people. The handful of nobles
of higher rank, the great landed proprietors, attached themselves to the Court at St. Petersburg or became officers in the

army. The whole structure of society was dominated by the Russian bureaucracy.

Tiflis, when Stalin began his studies there, was a rapidly growing oriental city of some 150,000 inhabitants, with a commonplace European quarter built by the Russians. The Georgians were in a minority, the population including Armenians, Northern and Southern Slavs, Tartars, Persians, Germans, Jews, Greeks and Ossetes. The principal centres of activity were the Persian, Armenian and Tartar bazaars, whose alleys were thronged with a motley Asiatic crowd, through which water-carriers, camels, and donkeys laden with wine-skins and bales of goods pushed their way; on sale were carpets from Persia and Kurdistan, bright-coloured woollens and cottons, pottery and inlaid work, sabres from Daghestan and arms made on the spot. Large-scale trade in the town was in the hands of the Armenian middle-class. The ancient Georgian Tiflis, bearing the stamp of Persian domination, was an unchanged mass of grey terraced houses, intersected by a maze of steep streets with refuse drying in the sun.

3

YOUNG Stalin certainly could not imbibe new ideas or be subjected to European influence in this mediaeval agglomeration of Western Asia with its manifold religions and national superstitions, in a backward society, with a continuous infiltration of nomads; nor in the administrative and military quarters of the city where the despotic Tsarist bureaucracy was housed in buildings European in style. But he entered a new sphere in the Seminary where, in the course of his clerical studies, he came for the first time into contact with the spirit of revolt.

For the beginning of a tradition of insubordination existed, even under the stern rod of religious discipline, among the students at Tiflis, as elsewhere in "All the Russias." The resistance of the rising generation to the oppression of the old regime, which long retained a purely national character among the population, gradually assumed a liberal and then a socialist colour. As early as the beginning of the nineteenth century, that is from the date of the Russian occupation of Georgia, subversive ideas had been brought into the country by exiles who had been compelled to live in the confines of the Empire. The policy of brutal Russification adopted by Yermolov, Viceroy of the Caucasus, aroused a popular movement of protest, violently suppressed by Cossack troops. Down to the date of the emancipation of the serfs there were incessant and sanguinary peasant revolts. The Tiflis Seminary became an intellectual centre of the opposition to Russian rule. Finally there appeared the new and decisive factor which was to change the social centre of the revolutionary struggle. In 1867 the first railway in the Caucasus was begun, from Tiflis to the Black Sea.

Capitalism began to penetrate into the Caucasus. In the workshops Georgian peasants who had become unskilled labourers and skilled Russian workmen were fused under the hand of the same management and formed the beginnings of a proletariat. At this period begins the exploitation of manganese at Chiaturi, and of naphtha at Baku. Transcaucasia emerged from its provincial isolation, and was dragged from the rut of primitive economic life into the highway of capitalist production.

In 1873, twenty years before the arrival of Stalin at Tiflis, there had been trouble at the Seminary, where the students felt their national pride was offended. Many students, expelled in consequence, returned to their villages to become propagandists of advanced ideas. Ten years later there was a revolt on a small scale in the same school. The Rector spoke in contemptuous terms of the Georgian language, and a student rose and struck him. This youth, Sylvester Djibladze, was conscious of the support of his fellow-students and even of the Georgian teachers. He was condemned to three years in a disciplinary corps, and the Seminary was closed. In 1886 the Rector, the arch-priest Chudnietsky, was stabbed to death by a seminarist aged nineteen. "Scarcely half the students condemn the crime, and many hardly conceal their wicked delight," wrote the Exarch of Georgia to Pobiedonostsev, the Procurator of the Holy Synod.

"The Russian teachers are demoralised; the Georgian teachers assume a fierce manner. Some go so far as to excuse the assassin; all in their heart of hearts approve." The Seminary was closed once more. Each time more students were scattered among the villages, propagating their burning convictions.

At this point the second section of railway was completed, from Tiflis to the Caspian Sea. The line crossed Caucasia from west to east, by the valleys of the Rion and the Kura, parallel with the main mountain chain, connecting the Black Sea with the Caspian, Baku with Batoum. The petroleum industry, provided with new means of transport, received a great impetus; a production of 800,000 metric tons in 1883 increased to 1,370,000 metric tons in 1885, and continued to increase. The proletariat of the petroleum wells and the railway grew in proportion. That same year the first socialist groups were constituted, under the leadership of pupils of the Seminary, and composed mainly of Georgian or Russian intellectuals in exile; among the foremost were Sylvester Djibladze, Noah Jordania, Nicholas Chkheidze and Ninoshvili. This was the first "cell" of Georgian Social-Democracy. The *Communist Manifesto* of Marx and Engels was translated; the Caucasian rebels set themselves to study European ideas.

On arriving at Tiflis in 1893, therefore, Stalin found the germ of a revolutionary socialist movement, and before long faint echoes of ferment among the workers penetrated the thick walls of the Seminary; the first railwaymen's strike at Tiflis occurred in 1896. The class struggle became more important than the national struggle. The Georgian question gave way to the social question. Tiflis railwaymen, Baku oil-workers and Chiaturi miners were all directed from one centre. Moreover, the general unrest among the proletariat throughout Transcaucasia was now not merely a local incident. The gigantic massif of the Great Caucasus, which had in the course of centuries prevented so many invaders from reaching the steppes, and had retained so many migrant peoples in its hollows, could no longer resist the solidarity created by the bonds of capital and the workers' lot. By force of circumstances Caucasian revolutionaries became a detachment of the great army of revolutionary socialism taking shape in Russia in the school of struggle.

Speaking of the origin of his conversion to socialism, Stalin one day said: "I became a Marxist thanks so to speak to my social position—my father was a worker in a shoe-factory and my mother was also a working-woman—but also because I could hear the murmurs of revolt among the people who lived at the social level of my parents, finally on account of the rigorous intolerance and jesuitical discipline so cruelly crushing me in the orthodox Seminary where I passed some years." And he added: "The atmosphere in which I lived was saturated with hatred against Tsarist oppression and I threw myself with all my heart into revolutionary activity."

In 1898, when Catherine Djugashvili took her son away from the Seminary, which was seething with councils and clubs of all shades of opinion, Sosso was caught in the current which swept with it the more active of his contemporaries. Like other self-taught socialists, he read propagandist pamphlets, abstracts, drafts, schemes. That was sufficient for membership in the Tiflis Social-Democratic group. In the workshops of the railway where had laboured the manual worker, Alexis Peshkov, to be one day celebrated under the name of Maxim Gorky, Stalin came into contact with the proletariat. Some years earlier he might have met among them the locksmith, Sergo Alliluyev, and two years later, the lathe-worker, Michael Kalinin. This was the time when the pioneer workmen's clubs, the clandestine *krujki*, which had been springing up throughout Russia in the last twenty years, were taking steps to form a general organisation, with a single directing centre. In that year there was a small meeting of nine delegates at Minsk, who boldly called themselves a "Congress of the Russian Workers' Social-Democratic Party." In one of the Ukrainian provinces, near Nicolayev, a youth of Sosso's age had already been arrested, transferred from prison to prison and was awaiting deportation to Siberia; this was the future Trotsky. And in Eastern Siberia an exile aged twenty-nine was engaged on a learned work on the development of capitalism in Russia; he was writing an essay on the "economic romanticism" of Sismondi and his followers and translating the *History of Trade Unionism* by Sidney and Beatrice Webb; this was the future Lenin.

Nascent Russian Social-Democracy had embarked on its life and death struggle with Tsarism. And with the quiet resolution of the volunteers for civil war, Sosso had enrolled himself in the ranks of the new party, the Russian section of the international working-class movement; this was the future Stalin.

Chapter II

THE YEARS OF APPRENTICESHIP

SIDE by side with the formation of the industrial proletariat, socialism developed in Russia toward the middle of the last century on a somewhat confused and complex basis of ideas, and grew steadily stronger by its diversity. But from the beginning, both the socialist movement and the proletariat showed certain fundamental characteristics which were to give them a future unparalleled in history.

It is essential to glance at the origins of the Russian Social-Democratic movement, its precursors and its notable exponents, in order to understand Bolshevism and its representatives at different stages of its evolution from Lenin to Stalin.

In Russia a poverty-stricken working class grew up slowly around the earliest spinning mills, iron-works and factories. The first rudimentary strikes caused by the cruel labour conditions occurred at Moscow, Kazan, Yaroslavl, Tambov, Kaluga, Voronezh and Tula. Under Alexander I about half the 200,000 persons employed in industry remained serfs, bound to the works or the factory by their master's orders; the rest, with the "freedom" to work sixteen hours and more a day, overwhelmed by fines, privation and persecution, were hardly better treated. Nicholas I, sometimes called the "Iron Tsar"—for in its political regime Russia experienced the iron age before the steel—even promulgated a law making it a crime at common law to go on strike. The peasants, transferred by force from the village to the factory, generally remained peasants, passing part of the year at work on the land. All of them preserved close links with the village and retained their peasant psychology long after the change in their work.

Industry, aided by foreign capital and technique, made rapid and continuous progress; in less than forty years after the abolition of serfdom it recruited more than a million and a half peasants. The mass of the Russian proletariat, therefore, derives directly from the countryside, whereas the proletariat of the West had for its basic nucleus the descendants of mediaeval guild workers, from whom it inherited urban culture and its own traditions. This is its most distinctive characteristic.

The early revolutionary tradition of the Russian working class bore the imprint of peasant influence. From the sixteenth century onwards, declares M. Pokrovsky the historian, Russia was perhaps the most rebellious country in Europe. Each of the other great countries had its peasants' civil war; Russia had four in two centuries—those of the "Time of Trouble," of Bogdan Khmelnitsky, of Stenka Razin and of Pugachev. Peasant revolt was not entirely crushed out, in spite of implacable repression. And since the freeing of the serfs in 1861, some two thousand local risings have been counted, down to the insurrection on a large scale in 1905. "Revolution," wrote Leroy-Beaulieu, "is latent in the Russian people." Such is the past which has left its mark on contemporary events. Strong characteristics of peasant mentality were transmitted to the workers' movements: passive resignation interspersed with violent rebellion, individual mistrust and collective credulity, simplicity of ideas, mystical feeling and fanatical prejudice—all have come down to the Russian workers from this little developed class which, according to Karl Marx, represents barbarism in the heart of civilisation.

Russia, where capitalism developed late and inadequately, possessed no bourgeoisie capable of becoming a ruling class. Peter the Great himself created the first factories; Catherine II followed his example, and later on Imperial initiative was required for the construction of the first railways. Nowhere in the world did the Government control so many productive industries, of which the distillation of vodka was not the least important. Industry advanced slowly at first, sheltered by protective duties. A bourgeoisie feeble in economic activity could not claim the political rôle of a Third Estate. Russia never had any equivalent of the English Magna Carta or the French Declaration of Rights. Thus the intelligentsia, consisting of the generous and learned *élite* of the aristocracy and the landed gentry, cadres of the army and the cultivated bourgeoisie, after attempting single-handed a desperate and vain struggle against absolutism, was to provide skeleton cadres for the workers' and peasants' revolution.

In spite of certain national characteristics, there was nothing exclusively Russian about Tsardom. "The type of domination exercised by the Romanovs is absolutely identical with that of the Valois and the Tudors," remarks Pokrovsky. The pioneers of liberalism came for the most part from free-masonry, which was twice dissolved. Novikov and Radishchev, the earliest, expiated their humanitarian anticipations, the one in prison, the other in exile, thanks to Catherine II, friend of Voltaire and of the encyclopaedists. The attempt at a revolution made by the Decembrists (1825) was merely a conspiracy against the domination of the nobility, and had no links with the people. But the most resolute leaders were already thinking in terms of republicanism with slightly socialist tendencies. The Decembrists, members of lodges and other secret societies, had among them officers who had come into contact with the French Revolution through the Napoleonic armies, and intellectuals in charge of capitalist enterprises. The torture of the ringleaders, Pestel, Ryleyev, Kakhovskoi, Muraviev-Apostol, Bestuyev-Riumin, and the deportation of one hundred and fifty conspirators put an end for a long time to dreams of liberty, equality and fraternity. The reign of Nicholas I began under the auspices of the executioner.

Despotism grew yet stricter under the Iron Tsar, but even so a varied and intense spiritual life found some expression. Driven from politics, free thought sought a refuge in literature and philosophy. The great writers of Russia, from Pushkin to Tolstoy, gave lustre to this epoch. Lermontov was followed by Nekrassov, Gogol by Dostoievsky; Goncharov and Turgenev were succeeded by Ostrovsky and Shchedrin. Thus literature took the place of the public platform; poetry and the novel, satire and the drama combined to discredit serfdom, to ridicule bureaucracy, and to outwit the censorship. Bielinsky raised literary criticism to the height of a criticism of society and founded the tradition which Dobroliubov, Chernishevsky, and Pissarev were to follow. Enlightened youth passionately embraced the doctrines of Fichte and Schelling, Hegel and Feuerbach, later of John Stuart Mill and Spencer, Büchner and Darwin. Petrashevsky's circle studied Saint-Simon and Fourier, Cabet and Proudhon, Louis Blanc and Lamennais, which earned for its members prison and exile, after a condemnation to capital punishment commuted to forced labour at the last minute. It was only by a very narrow margin that the pen of Pushkin was not broken in the adventure of the Decembrists; and by even less was Dostoievsky to escape death on the scaffold in 1849, with the *petrashevtsy*, before enduring the long torments of the *House of the Dead*.

In the 'forties two currents of earlier origin divided the intelligentsia into "Slavophils" and "westerners." Reacting against the brutal reforms of Peter the Great, introduced with violence in order more quickly to imitate European evolution, the slavophils, hostile to exterior influences and the imitation of the foreigner, idealised the Russian past, argued that the backwardness of "Holy Russia" was superior to the "decadent West," and insisted on the jealous and mystical conservation of the aristocracy, the Orthodox Church and the national characteristics. They repudiated rationalism, science and democracy as the products of an exhausted civilisation. The westerners wished to raise their country to the level of cultivated Europe, to secularise Russian life, to liberate the genius of the people and to introduce the rights of man. But with Alexander Herzen a new tendency arose, a purely Russian form of socialism which attempted a synthesis. Later, under the varied influences of his successors, this was destined to assume a very different form and finally to become the movement known as Populism *(narodni-chestvo)*.

Herzen reconciled in one eclectic doctrine his faith in the universal subversive mission of the Slav peasants with his borrowings from the revolutionary theories of the West, above all from Proudhon. He elaborated a conception which would resolve at the same time "the Russian question and the social question," predicted the end of bourgeois Europe on the morrow of a devastating war, and foretold the advent of communism in the world at a signal from Russia, where the peasants would set an example to all humanity. For the Russian people, so Herzen and his disciples, influenced by the slavophils, believed, had the advantage above all others of its ancient institutions: the village community (*obshchina* or *mir*) had by its very nature a tendency towards socialism and constituted the embryo of the federalist and co-operative organisation of the future. Rural Russia, then, would initiate the era of social revolution and the march towards communism.

Through Haxthausen in Germany, Mackenzie Wallace in England and Leroy-Beaulieu in France, much is already known outside Russia of the system of collective property and agricultural exploitation of the *mir*, to which Herzen, his rival Bakunin, and his followers and critics Chernishevsky and Lavrov, genuine theoreticians of Populism in the 'sixties, attached such hopes. Populists of all colours, whether disciples of direct action like Bakunin or propagandists like Lavrov, believed that bourgeois evolution is not progress but regression, and that the backward Russian economy was an ideal to be brought to perfection. On the original basis of the *mir*, completed by *artels*, or associations of artisans, a unique civilisation could be built up, avoiding all the evils of capitalism, provided only that the land was handed over to the communes, and the factories to the workers. But from the general tendency of Populism, various different schools, based on natural science, political economy, or sociology, were developed. There is a great gulf between the radical and explosive peasant anarchism of Bakunin and the balanced and educative evolutionary socialism of Lavrov. Herzen's successors repudiated his pan-Slavic messianism, his mysticism and utopianism, while adopting his slogan: *Land and liberty*, and his famous advice: *Go to the people*. Many also followed his example of emigration to the West, where he published *Polarnaya Zviezda* (The Pole Star) and *Kolokol* (The Bell), as weapons in the struggle against Tsarism.

Bakunin, "the apostle of universal destruction," believed that the desires of the Russian people tended spontaneously towards a seizure of the land by those who tilled it, and to communal autonomy in opposition to any form of government. He preached a permanent peasant revolt, even though it must be partial and doomed to checks, while he dreamed of a universal uprising of which Stenka Razin and Pugachev were the precursors. He also held a high opinion of brigands, those "instinctive revolutionaries." It was he who issued to the young students the urgent slogan: *Go to the people*, originated by Herzen and repeated by Lavrov. In effect he said to them: "You must abandon at once this world which is destined to perish, these universities, these academies and schools. . . . You must go among the masses. . . . All science must be submerged along with the world of which it is the expression." A new Stenka Razin was approaching, he added, but this time in numbers, multiplied and therefore invincible. . . . The final revolt was to bring about an anarchist federation of free communes without a central power and without a State.

In readiness for the great day when the irresistible conflagration would break out, helped on by local riots, Bakunin sought to prepare his tools, that is to say persons who were fore-armed and ready for anything. For their instruction he drew up a book of rules from which they were to derive inspiration—a strange document which contrasted with the high morality of the young Populists and was more likely to repulse than to attract them. This *Catechism for a Revolutionary*, introduced into Russia by his disciple Nechayev, contained many sections. In the first, *Attitude of a Revolutionary towards Himself*, Bakunin advocated the renunciation of every interest, sentiment and personal bond; a break with the civilised world, its laws and conventions; to know only one science, that of destruction; to despise public opinion; to hate accepted morals and customs;

to be ruthless, expecting in return no mercy, but to be always ready to die and prepared to bear torture; to stifle in one's self all family sentiment, friendship, love, gratitude, and honour; to find no other satisfaction than that of the success of the revolution, and to this end to destroy all obstructionists. In the second part, *Attitude of a Revolutionary to his Comrades*, the writer recommended solidarity between the brethren in so far as each one was useful to the cause; every comrade should have one or two second or third class revolutionaries at his disposal, as a sort of capital to be used with economy; in case of misfortune a comrade should only be saved from danger if his revolutionary value was such as to justify the necessary expenditure of forces. In the third, *Attitude of a Revolutionary to Society*, Bakunin urged the need to penetrate into every milieu, including the police, the Church and the Court; to make out a list of those who must be condemned to death in the order of their importance, and another of those who might be spared until such time as their wicked conduct incited the people to revolt; to exploit rich and influential persons, discovering their secrets in order to blackmail them; to enter into pretended conspiracies with liberals in order to deceive them, make use of them and compromise them; to lead on and inveigle the doctrinaires and garrulous conspirators so that the majority might more rapidly be ruined and the rare few might be trained and tempered for the struggle; to make use of women according to their quality—the lives of the mediocre might be sacrificed, but the best were to be looked on as "the most precious treasure." Finally, in the fourth, *The Attitude of the Association towards the People*, the author urges that the misfortunes and sufferings under which the people labour must be aggravated by all possible means, to exhaust their patience and drive them to universal revolt; for this the revolutionaries must unite with bandits, "the only genuine revolutionaries in Russia," and form an irresistible force capable of destroying everything in its way. . . . No *résumé* can give any idea of the tone of cold hatred and explicit cynicism of the famous anonymous *Catechism*, which no study of the origins of Bolshevism can afford to neglect.

Herzen had said: "We lack all the riches and all the inheritance of the West. We have no heritage from Rome, from antiquity, from chivalry, from feudalism, nothing Catholic, hardly anything bourgeois in our traditions. Therefore no regrets or relics, no respect for the past can hold us back." Bakunin showed this in his writings without taking responsibility for it, and Nechayev demonstrated it later by his actions, from which even Bakunin himself recoiled in horror or disgust. By lies and impostures, tricks and intimidations, intrigues and blackmail—since all means are justified—but also by hard and obstinate work and extraordinary energy, the confidential bearer of the *Catechism* succeeded in forming and directing a secret society, called the *Narodnaya Rasprava* (the People's Avenger), which was destined to come to a bad end; one of the members was assassinated by the others at the instigation of Nechayev, who had spread false rumours of his treason, in order to get rid of him. The affair resulted in hundreds of arrests and a prosecution that resounded throughout the country. This incredible drama is known in Europe and America through Dostoievsky's book, *The Possessed*. The *Catechism*, when it was revealed, scandalised revolutionary circles, and Bakunin refrained from laying claim to the authorship, which, for a long time, was attributed to Nechayev. The latter took refuge in Switzerland, where he accorded to Bakunin just that revolting treatment laid down in the rules for a perfect revolutionary, summed up in the formula: "Drag him as deeply as possible through the mire." The master broke with his fanatical and perverse pupil, whose unlimited devotion to the cause of the people he could not but admire, but whom even he considered too devoid of scruples. The term *Nechayevshchina* is still used to describe a pseudo-revolutionary lack of morality. But it must not be forgotten that Nechayev was the first genuine "practitioner" of subversive organisation in Russia, and the first professional revolutionary for whom the desired ends justified the use of any means. Many imitators were to follow in his steps.

The realists of the 'sixties succeeded the idealists of the 'forties, and were succeeded in their turn by the men of action of the

'seventies. In contrast to the Bakuninists, believing in riot and
anarchism, and to the Lavrists, believing in propaganda and
education, a very small group grew up around Peter Tkachev,
in 1875, believing in a quite different ideology, that of Russian
Jacobinism, whose symptomatic importance was not seen until
the following century. By his belief in the *mir* and his reliance
on the creative faculty of the peasant, Tkachev ranks as a
Populist, but his conception of the path of the revolution and
the means of attaining it, showed him to be a Jacobin and
intellectually close to Blanqui. He explained in *Nabat* (The
Tocsin) that a revolution must first of all seize the power, since
this is an indispensable step to achieving final success. Propaganda
can only give results after the power has been taken over: it
must follow the *coup d'état* and not precede it. The *coup d'état*
will be achieved by a conspiracy carried out by a small, disciplined minority. It must be carried out by violence, which
necessitates a centralised, carefully chosen, disciplined and
hierarchic Party, which would watch over the safety of its militants, carry out reprisals against its executioners and avenge its
martyrs. "Neither now nor in the future can the people achieve
the social revolution if left to itself. We alone, the revolutionary
minority, are capable of rapidly carrying out this task. . . . The
people cannot save itself . . . it cannot give expression to its real
needs, nor breathe life into the idea of social revolution." The
fewer revolutionary elements there are among the people, the
smaller will be its rôle in the upheaval, and the greater the authority which will revert to the thinking minority, who will
introduce communism. "The people, deprived of leaders, is not
fit to build up a new world on the ruins of the old. . . . This rôle
and this mission belong only to the revolutionary minority."
Tkachev foreshadowed the terrorism which was soon to come,
and the Bolshevism of the future.

Already in 1866 a first attempt had been made on the life of
the Emperor, an isolated gesture by the student Karakozov.
Towards the end of the 'seventies, the violence of the tyranny
began to give rise to violent opposition. Revolvers, bombs and
daggers replied to persecutions, deportations, executions and

long prison sentences. The Populists, disillusioned with their peaceful movement "towards the people," began to defend themselves against the police with arms, and declared war against the Government which ruled by terror. In 1876 they created, at the instigation of Alexander Mikhailov, the first revolutionary Socialist Party in Russia, the *Zemlya i Volya* (Land and Liberty) group, which absorbed the existing circles of intellectuals and the various scattered revolutionaries, and which staged at St. Petersburg the first workers' demonstration in the streets where a student addressed the crowd. The members of Chaikovsky's circle, founded a few years earlier, joined the group, as did also Mark Natanson, Sophia Perovskaya, Stepniak and Kropotkin. The organisation had a Central Committee, sections for work and a section of fighters. In 1878, Vera Zasulich fired at General Trepov, who had ordered a political prisoner to be whipped, and Stepniak stabbed Mesentzev, the Chief of Police. In 1879, a Prince Kropotkin, cousin of the foregoing, and Governor of Kharkov, was assassinated, but Soloviev just failed in his attempt on Tsar Alexander II. This series of attacks was quite open; "Land and Liberty" claimed full responsibility. Under the redoubled blows of the repression, the terrorists elaborated their technique, preparing a bloody revenge. But the best men, such as Ossinsky, Lizogub and Vittenberg were sacrificed. Opinion among the *zemlievoltsy* became divided on the question of tactics, some believing, with Alexander Jeliabov, in systematic terrorism, others preferring, with George Plekhanov, the use of persuasive propaganda. In 1879, at the secret Congress of Voronezh, the party split into the *Narodnaya Volya* (The People's Will) and the *Chorny Perediel* (The General Distribution).

The Executive Committee of the *People's Will* at once took up the struggle, and a few months later, Sophia Perovskaya, daughter of the Governor-General of St. Petersburg, attempted, with Mikhailov's and Hartman's assistance, to blow up the Imperial train. Her friend, Jeliabov, and her comrades, Kibalchich and Vera Figner, made similar attempts at other points on the railway line, but without success. In 1880, the worker Khalturin succeeded in exploding a charge of dynamite in the Winter Palace, narrowly missing the Tsar. Finally, in 1881, Sophia Perovskaya directed the attempt in which both Alexander II and Grinevetsky, his murderer, were killed, but which cost the lives of all the regicides, Perovskaya, Jeliabov, Mikhailov, Ryssakov and Kibalchich, all of whom were hanged a month later. Contrary to their expectations, the event did not provoke the smallest reaction from the peasant population, who remained inert. Following the advice of Pobiedonostsev, the new Tsar refused to listen to the demands of the *People's Will*, which, through the pens of Mikhailovsky and Tikhomirov, promised to cease all terrorist activity if he would grant a Constitution and certain liberties. The *Okhrana* was created following the death of Alexander and a period of crushing reaction set in, during which the desperate efforts of the *Narodovoltsy*, "the advance-guard without arms," gradually weakened under the blows of the autocracy. Tikhomirov's retraction, Degayev's treason and Lopatin's arrest hastened the decline. The later conspiracies miscarried and the *People's Will* was brought to the point of death by the execution of five students, implicated in a plot against Alexander III. Among them was Alexander Ilyich Ulianov, whose younger brother, Vladimir, was later to be known as Lenin.

The lessons of this tragedy were not to be forgotten, and the example of the *Narodovoltsy* has become a part of the national revolutionary tradition. Karl Marx was right when he wrote to his eldest daughter, in the very year in which the *People's Will* was crushed:

These are admirable men, without any melodramatic pose, full of simplicity, real heroes. Making an outcry and taking action are two things completely opposite which cannot be reconciled. The Executive Committee in St. Petersburg, although it acts with such decision, publishes manifestoes of an extreme moderation. . . . The Executive Committee is endeavouring to convince Europe that its *modus operandi* is a specifically Russian form of action, which in any case is historically inevitable, and on which one can no more moralise, for or against, than on the catastrophe of Chios.

"A specifically Russian form of action"—this is certainly the characteristic which must be underlined in the attitude of those men who regarded terrorism as a "painful and terrible necessity," and who protested with eloquence against the assassination of President Garfield, declaring: "Violence is only justifiable against violence."

The lassitude and pessimism which followed on the voluntary sacrifice of the revolutionary *élite* could not prevent the growth and strengthening of that force which was truly capable of overthrowing Tsarism. Under the pressure of war and the requirements of the world market, a primarily agricultural State was impelled in the process of economic evolution towards capitalism and modification of its social system.

Big industry supplanted small rural industry, giant works the domestic workshop, and both drew labour from the enfranchised and poverty-stricken serfs; there was no transition stage. For a long time army requirements made the State the main customer of industry. A definite stimulus was given to metallurgical industry in the 'sixties by the railways, which advanced from 2,000 kilometres in 1860 to 10,000 in 1870, and then went on increasing at an average rate of 1,500 kilometres a year. Moreover the advance in transport stimulated trade of every kind in an immense country without roads fit for traffic. The 'sixties have been called by some a "brief eighteenth century"; they saw the initiation of a privileged minority of the bourgeoisie into intellectual life. At that time only ten per cent of the population was urban, and less than one per cent attended school. The proletariat was massed together in the industrial centres, where a primitive form of capitalism made profits of sixty per cent with poor equipment, by monstrous excesses and cruel spoliation of the workers, who were herded in barracks or crowded into cellars; and simultaneously the peasants, overwhelmed with charges on their steadily decreasing plots of land, fell into indescribable poverty. Tsarism suppressed by force strikes in the town and revolts in the country. But while the intellectuals exhausted themselves by individual actions which were doomed to defeat, a new movement was being born. From St. Petersburg to Odessa, workers' circles sprang up, putting forward political demands which conformed more and more to the programme of European socialism. As the antagonism between capital and labour gradually became more important than the struggle of the peasants against the landlords, the proletariat crystallised and the elements of a new party were prepared. During the 'eighties, and the years that followed, the signs become more marked, foreshadowing the Social-Democracy. Many Populists of yesterday, having learned from their failures, were converted to Marxism.

2

THE most important pioneer was George Plekhanov, who, as a student, took part in the St. Petersburg demonstration of 1876, in front of the Kazansky Cathedral, where two hundred and fifty workmen ventured for the first time to demonstrate in the streets. He separated himself from the *Narodovoltsy* to constitute the ephemeral group of *Chorny Perediel.* In 1882 he translated the *Communist Manifesto*, adding a preface of his own; in a letter to Lavrov he roundly criticised the Proudhonism of Stepniak, one of the surviving Populist terrorists, and declared himself ready to make Marx's *Capital* "a bed of Procrustes for all the contributors to the *Messenger of the People's Will.*" In 1883, with Axelrod, Leo Deutsch and Vera Zasulich, former Bakuninists, he founded at Geneva soon after Marx's death the professedly Marxist group of the Emancipation of Labour. His pamphlets: *Socialism and the Political Struggle*, and *Our Discords*, caused a sensation, and made him famous as a theorist even before his incomparable power as a polemist in writing and in speech made him the central figure of the Russian Social-Democracy. In 1889, at the International Socialist Congress, he boldly declared that the Russian Revolution must conquer through the agency of the working-class or fail.

Socialist clubs became more numerous in Russia, strikes more frequent. An economic crisis in the 'eighties fed the class struggle. The workmen secured the first laws restricting the exploitation of labour. The great famine of 1891, followed by a fresh impetus to industry, accentuated the movement. Some groups amalgamated, others formed *fighting alliances*. A new generation of revolutionary intellectuals, among them men of powerful mental calibre, appeared: at St. Petersburg, Lenin and Martov; at Odessa, Riazanov; at Nicolayev, Trotsky. In 1898 the first Social-Democratic Congress was held at Minsk and adopted the text of a manifesto drawn up by Peter Struve; a year earlier had appeared the *Bund*, the Jewish workers' Socialist party. The nine members of the Congress were arrested or compelled to disappear, but the first step had been taken.

It was into one of these workmen's clubs guided by intellectuals working for the people's interests that Stalin entered at Tiflis. What part did he play in it, while the leaders of the Party were developing their first theoretical and practical controversies abroad? We have his own testimony on this point.

In 1926, Stalin, addressing the workers of Tiflis, delivered a speech in which he put in their place the servile officials who were already offering him incense to secure power and place for themselves.

I must, in all conscience, tell you, comrades, that I have not deserved half the eulogy that various delegates have here given me. It appears from them that I am one of the October heroes, the director of the Communist Party of the Soviet Union, the head of the Communist International, a peerless knight and all sorts of other things. This is mere fantasy, comrades, and a perfectly useless exaggeration. That is the way one speaks at the grave of a revolutionary. But I am not preparing to die. Therefore I must give you a true picture of what I once was and say to whom I owe my present position in the Party. Comrade Arakel (Okuashvili) has said that he once considered himself as one of my masters and me as his pupil. That is absolutely correct, comrades. I have been and still am a pupil of the pioneer workmen of the Tiflis railway workshops.

Even if this apparent modesty were affected and homage to the railway workers an astute demagogic device, the tone is none the less worthy and it is very possible that at that moment Stalin was expressing a genuine sentiment. In his autobiographical speech he went on to say:

Allow me to revert to the past. I remember the year 1898, when for the first time the workers in the railway workshops put me in charge of a club. That is twenty years ago. I remember how, at Comrade Sturua's rooms, in the presence of Sylvester Djibladze (he was then also one of my teachers), of Zakro Chodrishvili, of George Chkheidze, of Mikha Bochorishvili, of Ninua, and other advanced workers of Tiflis, I learned *practical* work. In comparison with these comrades I was then a tyro.

Perhaps I had a little more book-learning than many of these comrades. But in the practice of revolution I was certainly a beginner. Here, among these comrades, I received my first baptism of fire in revolution. Here, among these comrades, I became an apprentice of revolution. As you see, my first teachers were the workers of Tiflis. Allow me to express to them now the sincere gratitude of a comrade.

Then I remember the years 1905 to 1907, when at the desire of the Party I was *thrown* into the work at Baku. Two years of revolutionary work among the oil workers made me a *practical* fighter and a *practical* leader. In the society of the advanced section of workers at Baku such as Vatsek, Saratovetz and others, on the one hand, and on the other in the stormy conflicts between the oil workers and the oil masters, I learned for the first time what the leadership of great masses of workmen really meant. I had my second *baptism* of fire in revolution. Then I became a journeyman of revolution. Let me now express my sincere gratitude as a comrade to my Baku teachers.

The speech, deliberately unpolished, with its sometimes clumsy phrases, its naïve metaphors and monotonous repetitions, reveals the characteristics of the speaker: a religious turn of mind finding expression in a style like a litany, the insistence on the metaphor of "baptism" and humility in public testimony. There is a repeated allusion to "practical" work, the real strength of a leader able to impose himself without being either orator or writer. Finally there is the anxiety to place himself on the low level of the mass of the people without attempting to raise his audience or to rise intellectually himself; he is careful to describe his past life as spent exclusively among the proletariat as he was later to try to pass for the son of a workman. The last part of the speech emphasises the picture:

I remember 1917, when by the decision of the Party, after prison and deportation, I *was thrown into* Leningrad. There, among the Russian workers, in close contact with the great educator of the proletariat throughout the world, Comrade Lenin, in the storm of the mighty struggle between the proletariat and the bourgeoisie, during the World War, I learned for the first time to understand what it meant to be one of the leaders of the great working-class Party. There, in the midst of Russian workmen, liberators of oppressed nations and fighters in the proletarian struggle in all countries and among all nations, I received my *third baptism of fire* in revolutionary warfare. There, in Russia, under Lenin's direction, I became a master-worker in revolution. Let me express to my Russian teachers my sincere gratitude as a comrade and bow my head before the memory of my master Lenin.

From apprentice at Tiflis, to journeyman at Baku, to masterworker in our revolution at Leningrad—such, comrades, is the course of my apprenticeship to revolution. Such, comrades, is the true picture, honest and without exaggeration, of what I was and what I have become.

If it be true that an individual cannot be judged by the notion he has of himself, still less on the view of himself he desires to present, nevertheless certain aspects of Stalin's individuality are involuntarily revealed in this case. In so far as "style is the man," Stalin is presented in a fairly crude light. As for any facts illustrating or illuminating the opening of his political career, they are almost entirely lacking in the literature relating to this period—historical documents, contemporary publications, party literature and polemics. To explain this gap in information is less important than to indicate its existence by way of explanation.

From his earliest steps in Social-Democracy Stalin showed the qualities which were later to attract the attention of the Party leaders and procure uninterrupted advancement. Devotion to the cause, the desire to be useful, and self-surrender, did not distinguish him from thousands of other revolutionaries of the same temper; but the sense for practical work, the power of acting when others prefer talking, a rare composure and exceptional firmness made him an executive agent of the first rank.

Practical activity meant the obscure and ungrateful task, effective but inglorious, of the hunted conspirator; it meant patient, meticulous organisation, continually countered or destroyed by the police but continually renewed, propaganda and agitation conducted by means of clandestine newspapers and pamphlets; it was what the world calls "doing the dirty work," specially difficult in Russia at that time. Stalin was in his element.

He had the defects of his qualities. With small aptitude for intellectual work, either theoretical or scientific, he was apparently absorbed in a thousand local details, in subterranean tasks and in the risks of open action. His outlook remained provincial, there was nothing in his employment as a tool of revolution to enlarge his views or mature him. Happily, if one may say so, for him as for all revolutionaries his imprisonment was, later on, to provide him with the enforced leisure to complete his studies.

Nevertheless some of his weaknesses even served his purpose in his original environment. To be understood by Georgian and Tartar peasants, even if they had donned the workman's blouse, recently emancipated serfs or sons of serfs, inaccessible to abstract ideas and ground down by poverty, what was needed was simple, rather coarse speech, appealing to immediate interest and suited to the mentality of the race and to local circumstances. Stalin spoke that language. Railwaymen, tobacco workers, shoemakers and navvies understood him. But he took no part in theoretical discussion, important at that time for the future of Social-Democracy and for the direction of the movement. There is not a trace of him to be found in this sphere, for he left none.

At that period, at the turn of the century, Plekhanov's party still had its inconsistencies; its theory was halting and ill-defined.

Marxism was making its way against the influence of earlier systems of thought, and was being transformed by new interpretations. Karl Marx was read and highly esteemed by intellectuals in Russia before Marxism became a cult, and the *People's Will* had paid him public homage. The very first translation of *Das Kapital* was published in St. Petersburg in 1872, and was the

centre of discussion in the controversies between the different
schools of socialism. The opinion of Marx and Engels on the
agrarian community was a matter of never-ending discussion.
Plekhanov and the *Emancipation of Labour* published abroad
literature on Marxism which aroused livelier attention in Russia
than anywhere else. "Marxist works appeared one after another,
Marxist reviews and newspapers were founded, there were mass
conversions to Marxism, Marxists were flattered and courted,
and publishers were enthusiastic over the extraordinary sales of
Marxist books . . ." wrote Lenin.

"Legal Marxism" (so called because the censorship did not
understand economic studies written in learned terminology,
and allowed them to be published without suspecting their
significance, seeing in them merely a criticism of Populism)
satisfied for some time the eager thirst of the intelligentsia for
new knowledge, but it soon gave way to revolutionary and
illegal Marxism. Modern socialist thought and the spontaneous
workers' movement developed simultaneously and independently, until the time of their union.

Lenin called the interval between the foundation of the
Emancipation of Labour group down to the accession of
Nicholas II the "intra-uterine" period of the Party; there were
then but few skilled exponents of the Social-Democratic programme. The next period, up to 1898, was "infancy"; there
was elemental movement among the masses of the people, and
strikes were frequent; the intellectuals mixed with the workmen and a new generation studied Marxism and gained strength
by fighting. Then the Party was founded; according to its
historian, V. Nevsky, it may have had about five hundred
members. Next came "adolescence," and growing pains; "the
adolescent's voice breaks," said Lenin, "and so did that of
Social-Democracy."

The "Legal Marxists," under Peter Struve, Berdiayev, Bulgakov, Tugan-Baranovsky, developed rapidly, some in a liberal
and bourgeois direction, some towards spiritualism and religion.
Others, Social-Democrats, like Martinov and Krichevsky, abandoned revolutionary politics and became syndicalists (or trade

unionists) under the name of "Economists." Long drawn out
controversy developed between the spokesmen of the various
camps. The working classes naturally could neither follow their
arguments nor understand the points at issue, and sought their
own road.

Those Social-Democrats who were most conscious of the
requirements of revolution and most determined on methodical
action now began seriously to organise the Party and to provide
it with a directing brain. Lenin and Martov, on their return
from exile in Siberia, where they had been thinking out the
problems of the hour, went abroad for this purpose; together
with Potressov they joined the veterans of the *Emancipation of
Labour*. "The revolutionary struggle is often impossible without a revolutionary emigrants' group," thought Lenin, inspired
by the example of Herzen and of Bakunin, of Tkachev and of
Lavrov. In 1900 the three young men, with Plekhanov, Axelrod
and Vera Zasulich, founded at Munich *Iskra* (the Spark), the
journal of the Workers' Social-Democratic Party. The editors,
to affirm the continuity of the Russian revolutionary tradition,
adopted as a motto the phrase addressed by the martyred Decembrists to Pushkin: *"The spark will kindle a flame."* The
prefatory declaration and the first article were by Lenin.

The best sketch of the situation at this time is given by the
future leader of the revolution in words which reveal at this
early date the keenness of his vision and his analytical ability:

The past few years have been marked by an astonishingly rapid
spread of Social-Democratic ideas among our intelligentsia, and
this tendency of educated thought is echoed by the independent
movement of the industrial proletariat which is beginning to unite
and to fight against its oppressors and is eagerly striving towards
socialism. Circles of workers and Social-Democratic intelligentsia
are springing up everywhere; local agitation leaflets are beginning
to appear; the demand for Social-Democratic literature is increasing
and is far outstripping the supply, while the intensified persecution
of the Government is powerless to restrain this movement. The
prisons and the places of exile are filled to overflowing. Hardly a
month goes by without our hearing of socialists being "discovered"

in some parts of Russia, of the capture of literature and printing presses—but the movement goes on and grows. . . .

As for Social-Democracy, Lenin criticises its lack of concentration, its division into groups often ephemeral, disconnected and without tradition, with ideas often confused and contradictory. "Before we unite and in order to unite, resolute differentiation is essential."

In its prefatory announcement *Iskra* denounced the purely reformist Social-Democrats, who were influenced by the German revisionist, E. Bernstein. It demanded "the spirit of a clearly defined tendency," that is, of revolutionary Marxism, and envisaged "controversy among comrades" in its columns. It set out to provide a common programme for the whole Party, to create means of communication, of information, and for the spread of socialist literature. For these purposes it appealed not only to the workers and to the socialists, but "to all who are oppressed and crushed by our political system," to "all democratic elements."

But the most striking ideas of the Social-Democratic organ were contained in the very first number, in Lenin's comprehensive article. The anonymous author did not pretend to add anything new on the general ideas of socialism. His exposition is in agreement with classic Marxism, of which Karl Kautsky had been the recognised exponent since the death of Engels, but with a specially clear understanding of Russian conditions. Following Plekhanov's example he refutes especially the Syndicalist thesis, with its tendency to restrict the worker to the economic struggle, condemning it as contrary to the general interests of the proletariat. He approves the unity of the socialist and the workers' movements, insisting on its absolute necessity from the national point of view: *"Unity has in every case arisen from historical conditions and has been carried out by methods varying with the circumstances of time and place."* Finally he emphasises the urgent necessity of a fighting political organisation under strict control: "No class has ever attained power

without having found within itself political leaders, pioneers able
to organise and direct the movement."

Axelrod, the able tactician of the first generation of Russian
Social-Democracy, of which Plekhanov was the theorist, wrote
that this article had affected him like "a vivifying stream of
clear water." The newcomer showed the stature of a great
leader. From 1900 to 1903 he was to play an increasingly important part among the Iskraists. "It was precisely during those few
years," said Trotsky, "that Lenin became Lenin."

Before he left St. Petersburg, he had earned from his friends
the name of the "old man," because of his assurance and his
early won authority. His knowledge, already considerable, grew
continually. Whether on economic and historical questions or
on current matters of policy and tactics, he would always make
a serious contribution showing personal and persistent effort to
understand and develop the subject. Moreover, he excelled all
others in his gift of bringing out the main lines in a mass of
facts and figures, of emphasising the essential. His work on *The
Development of Capitalism in Russia* shows how conscientiously
and scrupulously he examined, scrutinised and compared statistics, what pains he took to draw from them conclusions for the
future.

Like all the socialists of his time, he was above all a fervent
democrat. His socialism aimed at conquering political democracy
in order to complete it by economic democracy. "The difference
between the political demands of the workers' democracy and
those of the bourgeois democracy is not one of principle but of
degree," he was to write in *Iskra*. Such reflections were to
abound both from his pen and from that of others. For example:
"Without political liberties, all forms of workers' representation
will remain a miserable deception, the proletariat will continue
imprisoned as heretofore, deprived of the air, the light, and the
space which are indispensable to its complete emancipation."
As for the nationalisation of the land, demanded by the descendants of the Populists, he predicted that it would lead to an
"absurd experiment in State socialism" in the absence of "deeply
rooted and firmly established democratic institutions."

He regarded himself as a pupil of Plekhanov, especially in theoretical and philosophical problems; he took respectful counsel of Axelrod, and he frequently exchanged views with Martov and Potressov. But at the same time he could not help being conscious of his superior ability as a commander; he thought, rightly or wrongly, that the moment was approaching when he must go beyond his masters, and he foresaw his destiny as organiser of the advance guard and leader of the masses in the coming social struggle. His whole effort was bent towards battle and victory, and that soon. He began prudently to think out his personal tactics in the hard tasks before him.

His writings in *Iskra* and in the review *Zarya*, his pamphlets and correspondence reveal glimpses of the ideas which were to detach him from the foremost phalanx of Social-Democracy and lead him to originate new paths. In 1902 he published a little book, *What is to be Done?*, in which his strength as a leader in civil war is shown with extraordinary force; it contains, among many germs of the doctrine which was to bear his name, his perfected and specifically Russian conception of the "professional revolutionary."

In a passage from Stalin's speech already quoted the expressions "*I was thrown* into the work at Baku," "*I was thrown* into Leningrad" were emphasised. He meant that the Party had been able to dispose of him like a soldier at the disposition of his superior officers, available, according to circumstances, for any place and any task. This was the method in which one section of the Party was eventually organised, in conformity with Lenin's view of the necessity of opposing the army of absolutist repression by an army of "professional revolutionaries." The police, in the document already quoted, attributed to the recidivist Djugashvili the trade of "clerk," and it is possible that Sosso practised it after leaving the Seminary, or after having worked for a few months at the Tiflis Observatory, for he had to live without counting on support from his relatives. But, as political action became more and more absorbing, he had to give himself up to it more and more until he became a "professional revolutionary" in the full sense of the term. It is important to examine the definition given by its initiator.

"We must educate men who devote to the revolution not only their free evenings, but their whole lives," wrote Lenin in the first number of *Iskra*. There lay the root principle of his organisation of the Party. In *What is to be Done?*, the same idea is driven home with characteristic insistence by repetition and by turning his opponents' arguments against themselves. "The struggle with the political police demands special qualities, professional revolutionaries"; it must be organised "in accordance with all the rules of the art." Parallel with mass action, there must be action by men selected, trained and prepared with a definite object in view. "It matters little whether they are students or workmen; they will be able to make themselves professional revolutionaries." The distinction between intellectuals and proletarians disappears in the close, secret association "which must include first and foremost men who adopt revolutionary action as a profession," whereas trade union organisation is necessarily on a large, public scale. It is not claimed that the argument is valid in all times and places; he is talking of Russia under the autocracy, where any workman's demonstration is forbidden.

Lenin sums up by asserting that there can be no serious revolutionary movement without an established directing organisation to ensure its continuance; the larger the fighting force, the more need there is of this directing group; it will consist mainly of professional revolutionaries, limited in number; it will accept none but militants who have served their apprenticeship in the struggle with the police, and are consequently able to evade them. "*There are many people, but no men*," that is to say, many discontented persons, many rebels, but no "directing minds, political leaders, men of talent." These must be educated. "Without the 'dozen' of tried and talented men (and talented men are not born by hundreds), professionally trained, schooled by long experience, and working in perfect harmony, no class in modern society is capable of conducting a determined struggle." It is a conception very near to Tkachev's, originating with Blanqui, but more precise and deepened in its application.

But this does not exhaust the question, and nothing escapes Lenin. How is the professional revolutionary to secure bread and butter? "We must arrange for him to live at the Party's expense, so that he can pass at will to secret action, move from place to place, as otherwise he will not acquire great experience, enlarge his horizon, or survive, for several years at least, the struggle with the police." The struggle demands thoroughly drilled specialists. "When we have detachments of revolutionary workers specially prepared by a long training (of course 'in all the arms' of revolutionary warfare), no police in the world will be able to master them."

An organisation of this kind could not be democratic, Russian autocracy permitted neither publicity nor elections, essential conditions of democracy, effectively and rightly used by socialist parties enjoying political liberty. "Rigorous secrecy, a minutely careful selection of members, and lastly complete fraternal confidence among revolutionaries," were essential in Russia. Here were the traditions of the *Zemlievoltsy* and of the *Narodovoltsy*. There are many objections, for which Lenin has an answer. "It is far more difficult to catch ten clever men than it is to catch a hundred fools," he replied to those who pointed to the ease with which a movement led by a handful of intellectuals could be decapitated. "The concentration of all secret functions in the hands of the smallest possible number of professional revolutionaries by no means signifies that they will do the thinking for everyone," that the mass will not take part "actively in the movement." It is a question of division of labour. And finally, categorically and frankly, he says point blank "*What we need is a military organisation.*"

3

THUS, in view of the coming revolution, Lenin provided for the formation of a real army, strong by its military discipline and practised in tactics. Stalin was one of the first recruits, and it was soon evident that he had the qualifications needed for a non-commissioned officer. Like his companions, he was busy with strikes, demonstrations, and the distribution of leaflets and of pamphlets drawn up by others. A radical democrat, George Tseretelli, at that time published in Tiflis a Georgian review of the extreme "left," *Kvali* (The Track) with the collaboration of N. Jordania, Ph. Makharadze, etc., who converted it into a socialist publication. From propaganda the Social-Democrats passed to agitation, that is, to use Plekhanov's words, that instead of instilling many ideas into a few individuals, they spread less ideas among more individuals. Mass action began to develop.

On May 1, 1900, the workers of Tiflis assembled for the first time in the suburbs with a red banner bearing the names: Marx, Engels, Lassalle. The penalties in the form of dismissals which followed sent into the countryside earnest agitators who began to convert the peasants to socialism. Next year on May 1 the workers demonstrated in the streets of Tiflis; there was a Cossack charge, and casualties, both killed and wounded. The Social-Democratic Committee was broken up, the militants prosecuted, and Sosso, whose lodgings were searched, became an outlaw, and changed his name several times: he was "David," "Nijeradze," "Chijikov," and for a long time "Koba," as he is sometimes still called. Some have seen in this last choice a borrowing from the novels of the Georgian poet, Alexander Kazbek, denoting a keen nationalist sentiment, but that is not certain for "Koba" is a name common enough in Georgia. Finally, he used to attend congresses under the name of Ivanovich before he definitely adopted the name "Stalin."

Brief reports have been discovered in the archives of the local police: "Joseph Djugashvili, employed at the Tiflis Observatory, intellectual, has connections with the railwaymen," a communication made on March 28, 1901, to the department of police. "On Sunday, October 28, at nine in the morning, Station Road, there was a meeting of advanced railwaymen, in which the intellectual, Djugashvili, took part." Other denunciations relate to his goings and comings and show his extreme prudence. His closest friend, R. Kaladze, has found nothing to write relating to this period. Bibineishvili notes that at this time "Comrade Sosso" made the acquaintance of a young Armenian Ter-Petrossian, a revolutionary of no particular opinions, and got him to serve the Party. The new recruit was later to gain a certain celebrity under the name of Kamo.

At the end of 1901 Sosso suddenly left Tiflis. Of this unexpected migration the Georgian Social-Democratic review *Brdzolis Khma* (The Echo of the Struggle) provides the only known explanation:

From the earliest days of his activity among the workmen, Djugashvili attracted attention *by his intrigues* against the principal leader of the Social-Democratic organisation, S. Djibladze. He was warned, but took no notice, and continued to spread slanders with the intention of discrediting the authorised and recognised representatives of the movement and of thus succeeding to the management of the local organisation. . . . He was brought before a Party tribunal, found guilty of unjust slander of S. Djibladze, and was excluded unanimously from the Tiflis organisation.

According to this version of the affair, he showed his greed of power and intrigues for its satisfaction at the very beginning of his career; the exclusion would explain the necessity of his betaking himself elsewhere. He went to Batoum, a port on the Black Sea.

Batoum is a small town of about 35,000 inhabitants in an unhealthy situation; it was formerly a fishing village and a nest of pirates. The population had increased tenfold in twenty years, thanks to the transit of petrol from Baku, and it had become the principal commercial port of the Caucasus and the terminus of the railway. The strongest workers' units were in the Rothschild and Mantashev works. Stalin worked among them, encouraged strikes, and took part in a street demonstration in 1902. The disciplinary measures taken against him at Tiflis did not prevent him from militant action elsewhere in the then primitive state of Social-Democratic organisation. But he had little inclination to measure himself against N. Chkheidze, I. Ramishvili, and other leading spirits at Batoum, and he created a separate group where he would not be overshadowed. From the recollections of the printer S. Todria it appears that C. Kandelaki was the only outstanding individual of this circle. The recent arrest of the principal representatives of the Party left the ground clear for the time being. Stalin seized the opportunity to incite unarmed workmen to attack the prison, an adventure which cost several of the assailants their lives. The workers of Batoum never forgave the useless shedding of the workers' blood.

This sanguinary affair led to the arrest of most of the militants, Kandelaki and Stalin among them. The latter passed eighteen months in prison. The following details on the prisoner Djugashvili were provided by the Colonel of Gendarmerie, Shabelsky, on June 17, 1902: "Height 2 *archins*, 4½ *vershoks*. Body medium. Age 23. Special features: Second and third toes of the left foot attached. Appearance: Ordinary. Hair dark brown. Beard and moustaches: Brown. Nose straight and long. Forehead straight but low. Face long, swarthy and pockmarked." The police called him "the Pockmarked." According to certain doctors, the malformation of the foot, and the semi-impotence of the left arm, which the police did not remark, seem to confirm the alcoholic heritage on the paternal side mentioned by various persons.

Side by side with this information, B. Bibineishvili also gives (1930) a personal account of Stalin's bearing. He was, he says, calm, resolute and above all "implacable" (the word is several times repeated), very severe in matters of discipline and punctuality. At a committee meeting he once addressed an "implacable" rebuke to a comrade who was late, ending with: "You should not keep us waiting, even if your mother were dying."

Condemned to three years "administrative exile" in Siberia, Stalin was sent by stages to the little village of Novaya Uda, in the Irkutsk province. All the revolutionaries gifted with some character and devoted to their cause had the same alternatives, the same experience and the same fate.

While new arrivals were constantly reaching the colonies of exiles, the road back to Russia by a thousand secret routes restored to the revolution its most active members. Among those who escaped was a young Marxist who hastened to attach himself to the *Iskra* organisation, with which he came into direct contact at Samara. Having learnt much in prison and in exile, Leon Trotsky had begun his career as a publicist and his socialist faith was clarified and strengthened. At the end of 1902 he arrived in London; he visited Lenin; on the way he had made acquaintance with Victor Adler at Vienna, and with Axelrod at Zurich.

Iskra found in the twenty-three-year-old member a brilliant contributor and propagandist, an eager student, an impassioned theorist, and a writer and orator who immediately made an impression in émigré centres. Lenin soon proposed that he should become a seventh member of the editorial board. "He is incontestably a man of the greatest ability, convinced, energetic, and will certainly go far," he wrote to Plekhanov. Foreseeing the coming discord in the Party, Lenin was anxious to secure an assured majority of the younger men against the veterans of the movement. Plekhanov scented the manœuvre and opposed it. Preparation was then being made for the Second Congress of the Social-Democrats and, as the approach of great events demanded active intervention, concealed dissensions were developing in the background.

It was not only a matter of difference of temperament, of divergences on certain methods of application of common principles, or on the questions of organisation and tactics. Up to the time of the Congress no sign of the differences appeared in *Iskra*. The paper suddenly rose to a superior intellectual level, and its editorials, by dint of strenuous effort, showed a united front to its readers. Hence its prestige and influence on the Russian revolutionaries of the time. Off the stage Plekhanov and Lenin were discussing the draft programme of the Party with acerbity, but yet no one suspected irreducible differences.

But Lenin, with that sixth sense which warned him of the imminence of a great political and social battle, wanted to accelerate the transformation of the Social-Democratic groups into fighting units. "*Give us an organisation of revolutionaries,*

and we will turn Russia upside down," he would say, paraphrasing Archimedes. No one was so obsessed as he was with
the necessity and urgency of this practical measure, and his
whole heart was fixed on advancing as far as possible in this
direction, without knowing exactly how far. As far as theory
was concerned, he was at one with the other Iskraists. The
contrast lay in the clearness, the categorical tone, and the
combative spirit of his view.

In his first writings there are certain key ideas, which, without being peculiar to him, reveal the lucidity of his thought
and express his convictions. His attention was especially directed
towards the understanding of Russian realities: "Hopeless
poverty, ignorance, the inequality and the humiliation of the
peasant give our whole regime an Asiatic stamp." He looked on
Tsarism as the "most powerful rampart of European reaction,"
a thought borrowed from Karl Marx, but he added: "and of
Asiatic reaction." He saw in Russia "a State politically enslaved
in which ninety-nine per cent of the population is completely
perverted by political servility." These views were in keeping
with his notion of the management and organisation of men—
fierce reaction against the servility and perversion engendered
by serfdom. A social system which was the outcome of two and
a half centuries of serfdom largely accounted for political inertia. Lenin, like Karl Marx, knew that "the tradition of all the
past generations weighs like a nightmare on the thought of the
living."

In connection with the importance of the social system in
historical development, it is necessary here to recall Kropotkin's
words:

... A whole series of habits is born of domestic servitude, outward
scorn of the individual personality, despotism by fathers, hypocritical submissiveness of wives, sons and daughters. At the beginning
of the century domestic despotism prevailed everywhere in Europe
—witness the writings of Dickens and Thackeray—but nowhere so
much as in Russia. The whole of Russian life, in the family, in the
relations between heads of departments and their subordinates, between officers and soldiers, employers and employed, bore the stamp

of despotism. A whole system of habits and methods of thought, of prejudices and of moral baseness, of manners engendered by an idle life had gradually grown up. . . .

What Turgenev called Nihilism, a movement erroneously confused in the West with terrorism and anarchism, and which Mikhailovsky considered to be the "infantile malady" of the revolutionary movement, was, in the 'sixties, a negation of this social system, a reasoned reaction, specifically Russian, against conventional falsehood, family and social hypocrisy, politeness and fashion, prejudices and tradition, dogmas and religion. But the nihilism of which Pissarev was the theoretician, the doctrine of "the thinking realist," nourished on the physical and natural sciences, positivist and materialist, iconoclastic and atheistic, remained an unmixed current of intellectual individualism, lacking contact with the people.

Lenin gave the workers a preponderant part in the liquidation of this burdensome past: "The industrial proletariat alone is able to fight the autocracy *en masse* and unhesitatingly." But he did not forget the claims of the peasant, "so that the cause of democracy and the political struggle for freedom may profit from the connection which many intellectuals and workers devoted to Social-Democracy have with the countryside." "The peasant," he wrote, "suffers as much, if not more, from the pre-capitalist regime, from survivals of feudalism, as from capitalism itself." This is why he demanded the expropriation of the landlords and nationalisation of the land. At the same time he reminded the workers that they needed the guidance of the intellectuals. Like Blanqui, he assigned an essential place to those who had left their class. "Demagogues are the worst enemies of the working class," he told the syndicalists. He fought against sham plebeian ignorance: "Without revolutionary theory there is no revolutionary movement." He inveighed against the narrowness of nationalism: "Our young movement can only bear fruit by assimilating the experience of other countries."

His conception of the relations between workers and intellectuals is worth attention:

The history of all countries shows that *the working class, left to its own resources, can develop only trade-union consciousness;* that is, it may itself realise the necessity for combining in unions to fight against the employers, and to strive to compel the government to pass necessary labour legislation, etc. The theory of socialism, however, grew out of the philosophic, historic and economic theories that were elaborated by the educated representatives of the propertied classes, the intellectuals. The founders of modern scientific socialism, Marx and Engels, themselves belong to the bourgeois intelligentsia. Similarly in Russia the theoretical doctrine of Social-Democracy arose quite independently of the spontaneous growth of the labour movement; it arose as a natural, inevitable outcome *of the development of ideas* among the revolutionary socialist intelligentsia.

It is true that the workers may contribute to this development: "but they do not contribute in their capacity as workmen, but in their capacity as a Proudhon or a Weitling," that is to say "in the degree in which they acquire the knowledge available in their time and increase it," by assimilating general culture. "There are some wretched intellectuals who think it is enough to speak to the workers of factory life and to go on repeating what they have known for a long time." Marxists must inoculate the people with the "bacillus of revolution."

He has this idea at heart and insists on it repeatedly: "The *spontaneous* development of the workers' movement leads to the domination of bourgeois ideology." Why? "For this simple reason, that bourgeois ideology is far older in origin than Social-Democratic ideology, and far more fully developed. . . ." Consequently: "The workers can acquire political class consciousness *only from without,* that is, only outside of the economic struggle." It can only be found in the relations of all classes with one another and with the State. He quotes a whole page from Karl Kautsky, whose words are "profoundly true and important." Thus: "Socialism and the class struggle arise side by side and not one out of the other." The proletariat can create neither economic science nor modern technique. "The vehicles of science are not the proletariat, but the *bourgeois intelligentsia* (K.K.'s emphasis). It was out of the heads of members of this stratum that modern socialism originated. . . ." This should be borne in mind by anyone who desires to judge Lenin's disciples by the tenets of their master.

The political realism, the supple tactics, which were later to be praised even by his enemies, are already visible: "Social-Democracy does not tie a man's hands, is not limited to one plan or one fixed method once for all; it admits all means so long as they lie within the resources of the movement and permit the maximum results under the given conditions." He is anxious to use the university movement, then in the vanguard, and to associate it with working-class action. He thinks that the liberal opposition against the reactionary State should be supported, "to help forward all democratic opposition," to carry "to all classes of the population" the activities of Social-Democracy. Without allowing himself to be influenced by mistaken trade union purism, he envisages alliances with the bourgeois liberals. "Only those fear temporary alliances, even with uncertain elements, who lack confidence in themselves." His masterly intuition is perfectly shown in the words: "The whole of political life is an endless chain composed of an infinite number of links. The whole art of the politician consists in finding and taking firm hold of the link that it is most difficult to take from you, the most important at the given moment and the one which best guarantees to you the possession of the whole chain."

On the eve of assuming the responsibility of a revolution in his Party and pending the revolution in his own country, Lenin attained perfect mastery over his means. His confidence in himself was reinforced by his confidence in Marx and Engels, by his intellectual agreement with Plekhanov and Kautsky, especially with his immediate master, the Plekhanov who had thrown out in *Iskra* the prophetic warning: "In the great socialist movement two different tendencies are emerging and—who knows?—perhaps the revolutionary struggle of the twentieth century will bring a rupture between the *Mountain* and the *Gironde* of Social-Democracy." For Plekhanov such visions were an intellectual exercise; for Lenin realism in ideas was to be translated into serious action.

Chapter III

PROLOGUE TO REVOLUTION

"I FIRST made Lenin's acquaintance in 1903. The acquaintance, it is true, was not personal but by correspondence, but there remained with me an indelible impression which has never left me during the whole of my work for the Party. I was then in Siberia, an exile." These words, spoken after the death of Lenin, are Stalin's only personal allusion to his first period of exile.

There seems to be no documentation on this first short stage of his adventurous life; the person most interested has taken pains that it should disappear. Nothing about it is to be found in the prolix memoirs of former prisoners or political exiles, nor in the voluminous accounts of the Social-Democratic Party. In the police archives, where valuable material on revolutionary history is preserved, all traces of Stalin have been removed, though various reviews have published all that can be found about the more or less remarkable or noteworthy Bolsheviks. Are we to conclude, with Trotsky, that the writings of the Stalin of that period, of "Koba," would compromise his reputation? The reply is to be found in the statement of the facts and analysis of documents.

The rest of Stalin's speech gives the measure of its veracity:

Knowledge of Lenin's revolutionary activity from the end of the 'nineties, and especially after 1901, after the publication of *Iskra*, had led me to the conviction that we possessed an extraordinary man in Lenin. He was not then merely a director of the Party in my eyes; he was its effective creator, for he alone understood its internal substance and its urgent needs. When I compare him with

50

other Party leaders, it always seems to me that his companions in arms—Plekhanov, Martov, Axelrod and others—all of them a head below Lenin, were such that in comparison with them Lenin was not simply one of the directors, but a director of a higher type, a mountain eagle, knowing no fear in the struggle and boldly leading the Party forward by the unexplored paths of the Russian revolutionary movement. I was so profoundly moved by this conviction that I felt I must write on the subject to one of my nearest friends, then an émigré, asking him for a reply.

This is obviously a version prepared after the event for a special purpose. In fact the writings of Lenin in the 'nineties were anonymous or signed by names still unknown. In *Iskra* the articles were unsigned; no one except a few of the initiated in London and in Switzerland, no one in Russia except very close friends, and certainly no one in the Caucasus, knew exactly Lenin's share in the paper. Martov was the principal stand-by of the paper because of his prolific output, Plekhanov for the extent of his knowledge and his authority in the International. In *Zarya*, except for a refutation of the criticisms of Marx on the agrarian question, Lenin used various initials, but never his own. His book on the development of capitalism in Russia, inaccessible to a young seminarist ignorant of the alphabet of economics, revealed the author's learning and powers of analysis, but not the foresight and audacity of the future leader. Nothing but immediate contact with Lenin in his daily work could give an idea of his quality or reveal his importance, and that is why it was possible for a thoroughly experienced revolutionary, Alexeyev, visiting Lenin in London, to say to Trotsky: "I think that as far as the revolution is concerned, Lenin is more important than Plekhanov." In order to appreciate—and that after twenty years' delay—Lenin's personal contribution to the anonymous Social-Democratic press, the complete edition of his works was required, and even then it was impossible for his wife, his sisters, and his closest fellow-workers to attribute with certainty the paternity of certain articles. The clairvoyance of which Stalin boasts ought not therefore to create any illusions, but rather to be taken as an indication of the intention by which it was inspired.

Some time afterwards [continued Stalin] while I was an exile in Siberia—it was at the end of 1903—I received an enthusiastic reply from my friend, and a letter, simple but profound in substance, from Lenin, who had been informed of my letter by my friend. Lenin's note was relatively short, but contained a bold and fearless criticism of the tactics of our Party and a remarkably clear, brief exposition of the work of our Party in the immediate future. Lenin alone could write about the most complicated matters so simply and clearly, so briefly and boldly, that each phrase hit the bull's eye. This simple, courageous letter strengthened my conviction that we had in Lenin the mountain eagle of our Party. I cannot forgive myself for having burned this letter of Lenin's, with many other letters, in accordance with the instinct of an old conspirator.

(A literal translation leaves to Stalin the responsibility for the metaphors as well as for the thought.)

The improbability of this account becomes clear from the statement, in his official biography, that Stalin remained only one month in Siberia at the time of his first exile. The exchange of correspondence by clandestine ways between the West and Baikal would have taken much more time. Furthermore, he escaped before arriving at his destination, at least if one can trust Nevsky's dictionary; he could therefore neither give any address nor receive any letter. As to the pretended instinct of the old conspirator, it has not deprived the Lenin Institute of thousands of manuscripts, letters, copies, drafts, fragments, etc. —an inheritance jealously guarded. What emerges is that Stalin thought it necessary to antedate his relations with Lenin as if to parry an expected attack.

Though it may seem pedantic, outside a small circle of experts, to examine a detail apparently so unimportant, it is really necessary, for it concerns one of the pretexts which have served as an excuse for the bitterest internal quarrels at Moscow. Besides, the by no means fortuitous disappearance of essential biographical material about Stalin, the absolute impossibility for those living in Russia of supplying information and of establishing the facts in a sense contradictory to Stalin, compel the biographer to put scraps together and to interpret them in the light of knowledge. Stalin, like many other people discussed by their contemporaries or by posterity, cannot be believed on his word alone, nor invariably contradicted. Historical accuracy demands the verification of his statements and, in case of need, the motives for his modifications.

Social-Democracy did not really exist in Russia at the moment when Koba underwent his first months of imprisonment. Its formal foundation by the little committee at Minsk, five years before, was necessarily only a pioneers' gesture, whose symbolic value did not supply the realities of a party. But steady progress in industry, the development of the proletariat, repeated strikes, and the multiplication of clubs, emphasised the necessity of a central organisation which should embrace all the isolated groups and co-ordinate their scattered effort—a party able to draw the masses after it, and to mould their elemental action. Such a party was about to appear.

2

The real Constituent Congress of the "Workers Social-Democratic Party of Russia," preceded by long preparatory conversations, opened at Brussels in July 1903, but, owing to the action of the police, was compelled to move to London. Of fifty-eight delegates, fourteen of them with consultative voice, there were only four workmen and there was some difficulty in arranging for their presence. The fact is important, for, as the principal leaders afterwards admitted, the plethora of intellectuals largely explains the exhausting subtlety of the interminable discussions of the Social-Democratic émigrés.

The Congress held no less than thirty-seven sessions, as well as innumerable supplementary meetings. Twenty subjects were on the agenda, several of them—such as the Party programme, for example—involving many others and requiring different votes, without counting the votes on procedure. The infinite complexity of these controversies—sometimes on a high plane—and the often transitory classifications, make it difficult even for the initiated to comprehend the situation. A subsequent historico-polemical literature, considerable (in quantity), has still further confused and obscured it by a thousand variants, errors or omissions. The lack of an accurate stenographic report and the abundance of hidden meanings and unavowed motives increase the difficulty. Nevertheless, we must try to disentangle the bare essentials in order to understand the sequel.

The Iskraists were in a majority and at first formed a bloc directed particularly against the *Bund* which wished to preserve its independence in a federative organisation. But in voting on the first article of the Statutes, they divided into almost equal sections, 28 supporting Martov, and 23 Lenin. For want of an available definition, the latter were called "hards" and the former "softs," as characteristic of the two temperaments. The majority oscillated by the margin of a few votes between Left and Right. Finally when the personal question arose over the election of central organs, Lenin, thanks to the departure of the more moderate members of the Congress, secured 19 votes against 17 and 3 abstentions; but the minority declined to give way. There was a virtual schism in the Party. Henceforward Social-Democracy was divided into two main sections, that of the majority, the "Bolsheviks," and that of the minority, the "Mensheviks," without counting those who, like Riazanov, stood outside both.

Although Lenin was to play the decisive rôle in the issue of the Congress and its consequences, Plekhanov dominated its debates from the intellectual standpoint. In the Party Programme Committee, over which he presided, he "illuminated the big meeting like a burning, blazing firework of knowledge and wit," says Trotsky in *My Life*. "*The safety of the revolution is the supreme law,*" he said in plenary session, commenting on the Party programme, in which were included such essential demands as a Constituent Assembly elected by universal suffrage, liberty of conscience, of speech, of the press, of meeting, the right to strike, and inviolability of the person. "If the safety of the revolution demanded the temporary limitation of such and such a democratic principle, it would be criminal to hesitate. . . . It is an admissible hypothesis that we, Social-Democrats, might be against universal suffrage. . . . The revolutionary proletariat might limit the political powers of the upper class just as they limited ours in the past." As though he foresaw the fate of the future Constituent Assembly, he declared: "If the people, in a moment of revolutionary enthusiasm, elected a very good parliament, we should try to make it a Long Parliament, but if the elections should turn out ill, we should have to try to dissolve it, not at the end of two years, but, if possible, at the end of two weeks." These words engraved themselves on Lenin's memory. On the question of the death penalty, Plekhanov warned the Congress against taking up too absolute a position, suggesting the possibility that the revolution might have to get rid of the Tsar and some of the nobility.

At one of the first meetings Trotsky had made a very successful speech, following the general policy of *Iskra;* Riazanov called him "Lenin's big stick." Later on, though temperamentally one of the real "hards," he inclined more and more to the side of the "softs." Probably Plekhanov's instinctive dislike of him had something to do with this. His attachment to the old staff of the journal, especially to Axelrod and Vera Zasulich, kept him on the side of the minority. But the simple explanation is no doubt that a politician of twenty-four cannot be what he will be when he reaches maturity. Plekhanov was then forty-seven; Lenin thirty-three. Wisdom and experience strengthened the ascendancy of their distinguished personalities. It was no small thing to be able to meet them in argument with original views.

The Party programme already envisaged the dictatorship of the proletariat, thus defined: "The dictatorship of the proletariat is the pre-requisite of the social revolution, *that is to say the conquest by the proletariat of power which will permit them to crush all resistance on the part of the exploiting class.*" For Trotsky this dictatorship would only become possible if Social-Democracy and the working classes were ready to unite. "It will not be a case of the seizure of power by conspirators, but the political reign of the organised working class, forming the majority of the nation"—a conception evidently inacceptable to the "hards." In looking forward to tactical co-operation with the liberals, Trotsky was opposed to Lenin, and supported the wider formula of Potressov.

When the line of demarcation between Bolsheviks and Mensheviks was drawn, Trotsky gave energetic support to the latter. The first article of the Statutes proposed by Lenin admitted as Party members "all who profess its programme and support the Party not only with money but by personal participation in its organisations." Martov put forward a text with the modification: "and give regular personal assistance under the direction of one of the organisations." Controversy grew round these formulæ. Axelrod referred to the example of the *People's Will* in support of the argument that the most devoted elements of the Party should be surrounded by a category of less active members. That is to say the Party might include sympathisers not formally affiliated to the organisation. "We are the conscious interpreters of an unconscious process," said Martov in defining the Party. "The more people there are called Party members, the better it will be. We shall have reason for rejoicing if every striker and every demonstrator pleading his case can call himself a member of the Party."

Plekhanov took the side of Lenin. "I have no preconceived idea," he said in substance, "but the more I reflect on what has been said here, the stronger is my conviction that 'the truth lies with Lenin.' There is no insurmountable obstacle to the entry into the Party of a real revolutionary. 'As for the gentlemen who do not want to join, we have no need of them.' The intellectuals alone will hesitate for individualistic reasons to join the Party, but so much the better, for they are generally opportunists." Trotsky, in agreement with Martov, replied: "I don't know that you can put a statutory exorcism on opportunism—I do not give the statutes any sort of mystical interpretation."

In replying to his opponents, Lenin began by reassuring them: "I do not consider our differences to be so vital as to be a matter of life or death for the Party. We certainly will not perish because of a bad clause in the rules!" But nevertheless he stuck firmly to his text. "Trotsky has completely misunderstood the fundamental idea advanced by Comrade Plekhanov," he said, giving further precision to his ideas: "Does my formula restrict or broaden the term, member of the Party? My formula restricts this conception while Martov's broadens it." In the same way Trotsky "completely misinterpreted the main idea of my book *What is to be Done?* when he said that the Party is not a conspirative organisation. . . . He forgot that in my book I propose a number of types of organisations; from the most secret and the most exclusive to the comparatively broad and 'free' (loose) organisations." The working class, he added, should work "under the control and direction" of the Party and not identify itself with it. *"Our task is to form a clandestine group of leaders and to set the largest possible mass in motion."*

To Axelrod and Martov he replied: "It is exceedingly difficult, and almost impossible, for us to distinguish talkers from workers. And there is hardly another country in the world in which the confusion of these two categories is as common, causes such boundless confusion and does so much damage as in Russia. We suffer severely from the presence of this evil, not only among the intelligentsia, but also in the ranks of the working class; and Martov's formula legitimatises it." In conclusion he said: "Each member of the Party is responsible for the Party, and the Party for each member."

Defeated by five votes, Lenin was not discouraged for a moment; he pursued his plan tenaciously and at last succeeded in obtaining a majority of two votes for the reduction of the *Iskra* editorial board to three members. Martov refused to join Plekhanov and Lenin in this triumvirate; the minority took no part in the election of the Central Committee; the breach was irreparable. Lenin was reluctant to acquiesce in it. For him, as for all, the schism was a surprise and a disaster. But his intransigence, really fundamental, left no hope of reconciliation. People began to talk of a state of siege in the Party, of seizure of the leadership, of dictatorship. To which Lenin coldly replied that he was not afraid of big words: "In regard to unstable and wavering elements, it is not only our right but our duty to create 'a state of siege.'" To the elders of the Party, astounded and indignant at the audacity of their emancipated disciple, Plekhanov said: *"It is of such stuff that Robespierres are made."*

How did Koba react in his prison at Batoum to the news of the rupture in London? The police note quoted above from *Zarya Vostoka* placed him among the original Mensheviks; Stalin having never denied it, Trotsky used it against him. The supposition does not at first seem very plausible, for the three delegates of the Caucasus at the Congress, Topuridze (Tiflis), Zurabov (Batoum), Knuniantz (Baku) were ranged on the Bolshevik side. Jordania, one of the original Mensheviks, was present at the London Conference, with consultative powers, but stayed for two years abroad. But Koba, with his slow and prudent temperament, may possibly have been influenced by Kandelaki, his close companion, who was always a Menshevik, or he may have hesitated momentarily before joining the camp of the "hards" to which his character predestined him. In any case ordinary militants were very slightly informed. And perhaps the doubtful story of the letter from Lenin may have been an unverifiable fiction chosen to cover up a difficulty. In any case the hesitation was of very short duration.

Extraordinary stress, for no real reason, is laid by the Bolsheviks on details of this kind. In 1903 no one understood the exact nature of the conflict, and Lenin himself, in striving to reunite the divergent sections, in seeking to associate them with himself in work and in action, showed plainly enough that he did not regard the rupture as definitive, or the positions taken up as irremediable. The history of the Party, indeed, saw numerous reconstructions of the directing personnel, unexpected separations, and unforeseeable rapprochements. The controversies among the émigrés seemed confused and meaningless in Russia. In the Caucasus especially the schism was for a long time incomprehensible. Everywhere an external unity concealed the truth from the average Social-Democrat. The real touchstone—revolution—was not there to try men, to test ideas. Is it not an arbitrary proceeding, in any case, to pretend to compare individuals without taking account of their age, origin, environment, acquired education, and the divers influences to which they are submitted?

Historical examples show the meaninglessness of these retro-spective criteria, especially among those precedents which the Bolsheviks claim as their own. Marat did not enter the French Revolution as a Republican; before the fall of the Bastille, he shared the general illusions, and hoped for an enlightened, limited despotism; the first numbers of the *Ami du Peuple* advocated a liberal monarchy; up to the middle of 1790 he still had confidence in the King; then he denounced the hereditary principle, and in 1791 advocated a restriction of the prerogatives of the Crown; on the 10th August, he still favoured an elective monarchy; finally he accepted the Republic as an accomplished fact. Robespierre, also, admitted in 1792 different forms of sovereignty: "I should prefer to see a popular representative assembly, and citizens free and respected under a king, than a nation enslaved and degraded under the rod of an aristocratic senate and a dictator. I do not like Cromwell any better than Charles I, and I could not endure the yoke of the Decemvirs any better than that of Tarquin." A year before the armed rising in North America against England and the War of Independence, Washington wrote (1774): "Independence is neither desired, nor is it in the interest of this colony, or of any other on the Con-tinent...." And Jefferson (1775) said: "There is not in the whole of the British Empire a man who esteems more warmly than I do the union with Great Britain." Cromwell, before the second Civil War, was still an advocate of constitutional monarchy with Charles as sovereign. It is the course of events, the endless chain of cause and effect, which determines the solutions of problems that have to be resolved, and reveals men of a stature to deal with them. Lenin knew this and was fond of quoting the Napoleonic formula, "First engage, then see."

It matters very little then, whether Stalin was a Menshevik at first or whether Trotsky was always a Bolshevik. Both under-took responsibilities later on by which they can be better appreciated than by the hesitations of their youth. Moreover there are many ways of taking sides: as master or disciple, for practical reasons or by conviction. Koba could only be a disciple. Everything points to the conclusion that he took a decision not *for* something but *against* someone. When he followed Lenin it would have been difficult for him to give straightforward reasons for his position.

3

IN JANUARY 1904, Stalin escaped from Siberia and returned to Tiflis. He lay low and spent a long time there unobserved, working in the provincial organisation of Transcaucasia. A whole series of panegyrists now give him credit during this period for a "bitter struggle against Menshevism." In fact, Menshevism was then non-existent, and the Georgian Social-Democracy "maintained its unity and had neither internal quarrels nor splits," so writes P. Makharadze the communist historian of the revolution in the Caucasus. The assertion is very imprudent for other reasons, for, if judged by its results, Koba's effort had purely negative results. The Mensheviks obtained their greatest successes in Georgia; they won over without a contest the greater part of the population.

In any case it is only necessary to consult the memoirs, narratives and documents concerning socialism in Transcaucasia to ascertain that Stalin, whether present or absent, never exercised any influence at all on the course of events. Never at any time did he play a part of the slightest importance. Especially significant is the detailed "report" of A. Yenukidze to the Old Bolsheviks' Club in 1923 on the illegal printing presses in the Caucasus. Stalin is mentioned once in sixty pages and without eulogy. Six years later, the same Yenukidze was to write *Fragmentary Recollections*, especially intended to affirm that his superior in the hierarchy "literally carried on his shoulders the whole struggle against the Mensheviks in the Caucasus from 1904 to 1908." The *Recollections* of S. Alliluyev, a militant workman active in Transcaucasia and Stalin's future father-in-law, mention him incidentally only once and that in a list. Many of Stalin's subordinates, in their Memoirs, hardly mention the name of their chief, and cannot impute to him a single original idea, a single notable act; one would seek in vain any characteristic statement about him. The copious *Histories* of the Party, each more official than the last, relating to this time and place, are absolutely silent about him.

At that time there were Bolsheviks and Mensheviks, in many ways comparable to the "chartists of physical force" and to the "chartists of moral force," but there was neither Bolshevism nor Menshevism as yet. A disagreement, even an insoluble one, on the editorial board of a paper, was not sufficient to establish incompatible doctrines. Principles were held in common, and the programme had just been adopted in common. But the antagonism would soon become envenomed, the divergences deeper, and the respective ideas of the two sides more differentiated.

The Congress had been the starting-point of infinitely complicated dissensions and disputes. For more than fifteen years, ruptures, unions, resignations and combinations criss-crossed one another. A specialised work would be required to relate the changes, if only to indicate them in their main outlines. Only real experts can disentangle the committees, councils, sectional bureaux, dissident groups, leagues, unions, co-optations, conferences where the Minority Party were in a majority, subdivisions of sections, Bolsheviks of the Right, Mensheviks of the Left, advocates of unity, conciliators, extreme Right, extreme Left, adhesion or defection of national parties (Polish, Lett, Jewish), birth and disappearance of journals of various shades and similar titles, and innumerable sobriquets. For the purposes of this study we must deliberately put aside detail for the main essential outlines.

At first sight the subdivision of the Party into so many sections seemed to condemn it to impotence. But this subdivision was an effect rather than a cause, and could be terminated under new circumstances. "A party declares itself a victorious party by subdivision, and by its ability to survive it," wrote Engels thirty years earlier, in explaining how "the solidarity of the proletariat is realised everywhere by groupings of different parties which are waging a life and death conflict, like the Christian sects in the Roman Empire during the worst persecutions." No section of the Socialist International suffered so many fratricidal struggles as the Russian section, doubtless because no other was so ripe for passing from theory to practice.

This internal struggle was not undertaken light-heartedly, and its champions, moved by an impersonal force, were the first to suffer from it. Lenin, especially, was profoundly affected by the results of his tactics. The end of his friendship with Martov was very painful, and the subsequent breach with Plekhanov caused him real grief. His wife, Krupskaya, says that even his health was undermined. He persisted, however, certain of the rightness of his case, and faced the adversary, consenting occasionally to political compromises to gain time without giving way on essentials. He had his hours of discouragement, and even thought at one time of leaving for America. To-day Bolsheviks never allude to episodes of this kind, as if Lenin's reputation would suffer thereby. It is unnecessary to seek historical justification for individual weariness, but, if it were necessary, two precedents at least come to mind. Marat, in the full tide of revolution, thought the cause was lost, and left France, and nearly left a second time. Cromwell intended, if the Grand Remonstrance had not been voted, to leave England.

How the majority became a minority and vice versa, is easy to explain. The Mensheviks were more numerous among the émigrés; the Bolsheviks had more supporters in Russia. The proportions were to be modified later on. Lenin had to live through many difficult moments at Geneva in the committees where he soon stood alone in his opinion. He had wished to re-establish an understanding between the two parties. Plekhanov was eager for the same thing, as were Martov and Trotsky. But, as each understood the peace after his own fashion, their attempts merely widened the breach: and Lenin, weary of the affair, resigned from *Iskra*, which passed into the hands of the Mensheviks, temporarily reinforced by Plekhanov. "*Robespierre has fallen*," said the latter. Between the old and the new *Iskra*, there is an "abyss," wrote Trotsky. Plekhanov left the Bolsheviks, as Trotsky was to separate himself from the Mensheviks a year later. This was the attitude of Riazanov and other less known men, called simply Social-Democrats. Plekhanov considered himself "above the divisions," and Trotsky, more modest, "outside" them.

Martov wanted a party "strictly centralised" but not composed of men who had *"resigned, whether of their own free will or not, the right to think."* He thought Lassalle's ideas on organisation were implicit in Lenin's and would lead to an occult dictatorship of theorists, he denounced "mechanical obedience" in his pamphlets, the state of terror and of siege in the Party and accused Lenin of bureaucratic formalism, of absolutism, of Jacobinism, of Bonapartism. Axelrod, in his articles in *Iskra* and elsewhere, rehearsed these arguments, spoke of autocratic centralism, and imputed to Lenin "the systematic stifling of individual initiative," reproaching him with turning men into the "cogs and screws" of a machine. Lenin replied in his pamphlet *One Step Forward, Two Steps Backward*, in which he defends himself by taking the offensive.

According to him, the bureaucratic method as opposed to the democratic is centralism against autonomy, it is the principle of revolutionary organisation as opposed to opportunist organisation; all the accusations of the Mensheviks were so much cover for anarchist and opportunist degeneration. For, he said, quoting Kautsky, his favourite author after Marx and Engels: "Democracy by no means connotes the absence of power; it is not anarchy; it is the supremacy of the mass of the electorate over its representatives, while under other forms of power, the so-called servants of the people are really its masters." Jacobinism? "If Axelrod assails the Jacobins, is it not because he has been consorting with Girondins?" And Lenin is not afraid of the epithet, for he is ready to give it content: "The Jacobin, bound indissolubly to the organised proletariat, and class-conscious—that is the revolutionary Social-Democrat."

This definition provided food for controversy for a long time, and that beyond the national field. Rosa Luxemburg, one of the strongest personalities of the socialist movement, wrote a refutation which appeared in the new *Iskra* (No. 69). Rosa Luxemburg took an active part in the workers' movement in Germany and Russia, and she was also the inspiring force in the Polish and Lithuanian movements. The importance of her works on political economy, historical criticism, and revolutionary strategy and tactics, her strength of purpose, her ability as a writer and propagandist, gave her weight as a controversialist. In criticising Lenin's formula, she accused him of entertaining a conception of the Jacobin Social-Democrat outside the proletarian organisation, whereas *"Social-Democracy is itself the working-class movement."* Opportunism cannot be routed by a regulation however severe: "Nothing so surely and easily puts a workers' movement in its early stages at the mercy of the intellectuals as its imprisonment in the strait-jacket of bureaucratic centralisation." Kautsky, always keenly interested in Russian questions, supported Rosa Luxemburg's view, as did Parvus, one of the most distinguished Marxists of the time.

But the most violent, if not the most effective blows, were dealt by Trotsky in the pamphlet, *Our Political Tasks*, in which he described Lenin as "head of the reactionary wing of our Party" and the "dull caricature of the tragic intransigence of Jacobinism." Leninist methods, said Trotsky, would lead to a situation in which *"the organisation of the Party takes the place of the Party itself, the Central Committee takes the place of the organisation, and finally the dictator takes the place of the Central Committee."* They would in the end impose on the Party the discipline first of the barracks, and then of the factory. "Rigour of organisation as opposed to our opportunism is simply another form of political stupidity." Lenin's ex-"big stick" struck with vigour him who had formerly guided it.

According to Trotsky all questions of the organisation of the proletriat find their own solution in the course of the political struggle. "The Jacobins," he wrote, "were Utopians, and we mean to be exponents of objective tendencies. They were thoroughgoing idealists; we are thoroughgoing materialists. They were rationalists; we are dialecticians. . . . They cut off people's heads—we illuminate them with class-consciousness." Lenin would guillotine instead of convince. *"Under Jacobin-Bolshevik tactics, the whole international proletarian movement would be accused of moderatism before the revolutionary tribunal, and the lion head of Marx would be the first to fall under the knife of the guillotine."* Trotsky protests against intimidation in matters of theory, against any preconceived idea of orthodoxy: "Those who deny it are to be rejected. Those who doubt are near rejecting it. Those who question are near doubting. . . ." As for the dictatorship of the proletariat, "Maximilian Lenin" and the Bolsheviks represent *"a dictatorship over the proletariat."*

This controversy, in which Koba would have been embarrassed at having to take part, and of which Lenin took charge alone against a galaxy of brilliant doctrinaires and writers, is just as pertinent to-day; the same arguments have been exchanged and developed for a quarter of a century and recur in recent discussions, many controversialists having changed camps. From the very beginning the Bolsheviks were obsessed by the French Revolution to which they have continued to refer, whether as an example to be followed or a precedent to be avoided. The germ of the tendency which constituted at once the strength and the weakness of Lenin's party was already discernible—the ability to organise and to act as a disciplined army capable of carrying out orders, but always at the mercy of an error on the part of their leader and in danger of sinking into an intellectual passivity contrary to their theoretical mission as vanguard and model.

Plekhanov in the end definitely took sides against Lenin. Not that he would have chosen to be the spokesman of a Menshevik section; the choice did not take shape as a dilemma; the difference being between generals without troops, so that there was no open schism, though the two principal groups—whose distinctive ideas were still ill-defined and the result mainly of personal affinities—were already acting in complete independence of one another. But he thought he saw in Lenin a theorist vowed to isolation, dangerous because of his narrow and rigid interpretation of Marxism. Looking beyond their agreement at the recent Congress, he foresaw an extreme accentuation of centralisation by the Bolsheviks, as disastrous as the contrary excesses on the Menshevik side. After having shared the direction of *Iskra,* first with Lenin, then with Martov, he proceeded to edit alone his *Journal of a Social-Democrat,* and to criticise severely both the rival factions, the "enemy brothers." In that *Journal* he predicted the evolution of Bolshevism to the *"final end, when everything would revolve around one man who will,* ex providentia, *unite all power in himself."*

4

LENIN, sorely tried by a separation which he did not think definitive, had gained fresh confidence after securing fresh support. The most important new supporter was Alexander Bogdanov, writer and scholar, a highly cultured and scrupulous economist and philosopher, who brought with him his friends Bazarov, Stepanov and Lunacharsky. Among the faithful were also Leonid Krassin, brilliant organiser of illegal action and audacious conspirator under the mask of his profession of engineer, and valuable for many reasons, especially for his connections among the liberal bourgeoisie, from whom he extracted subscriptions for the Party; also Vorovsky, Olminsky, and Litvinov, less brilliant but devoted auxiliaries. With their assistance Lenin decided on a prolonged struggle. He created the periodical *Vperyod,* appealed to the humble militant workers in Russia against the brilliant émigré leaders, and demanded a new Congress. He had already seen former Marxists, notably Peter Struve, author of the first Manifesto, leave socialism; he had seen the *Bund,* the first Social-Democratic organisation in Russia, detach itself from the body of the Party; he had seen the whole staff of *Iskra* turn against him. He felt that he was not understood in the International. But he could and must get back to work; there were immense reserves among the people, there were incalculable possibilities for the future; symptoms of the coming storm recurred in Russia, where the proletariat, regardless of the laboratories of social science, passed from resistance to the offensive, and demonstrated more and more frequently in the streets.

The strike at Batoum, in which Koba took part in 1902, and its violent sequels of demonstrations and repressions, had had reverberations in many towns as far north as Nizhni-Novgorod. A serious industrial and commercial crisis accompanied by severe unemployment fanned the fire of revolution. Every economic event took on a political aspect, and aroused republican and socialist demands. At the end of the year a strike of unprecedented dimensions broke out at Rostov, involving all the workers. In the summer of 1903 the petroleum workers at Baku left work, and their example was followed by all the workers from Tiflis to Batoum; there were strikes at Odessa, at Kiev, and in all the southern centres. Everywhere there were conflicts with police, soldiers and Cossacks. The workmen's societies, formed by the police agent Zubatov for the purpose of turning the movement away from opposition to the existing regime, broke their leading strings and rushed to join in the struggle, as Lenin had predicted in *What is to be Done?*. Social-Democrats of the rank and file, in spite of the quarrels among the leaders and ignoring Article I of the Statutes of the Party, began to take part in social conflicts; sometimes they gained control and gave them a political orientation. In the rural districts arson threw its tragic light on the increasing distress of the peasants, weighed down with taxes and imposts, condemned to permanent undernutrition and periodically decimated by famine. The emancipation of the serfs had been carried out by methods which in practice retained the dependence of the freed serfs on the great landowners; a special kind of feudal system still existed. There was periodical rioting by the despairing peasants, savagely repressed by the army. Corporal punishment was still practised in the villages as in the army. The level of agricultural technique allowed no hope of better crops without the restoration to the peasantry of the lands owned by the privileged classes. The extreme poverty of this mass of consumers and their low purchasing capacity restricted the home market and was a further obstacle to the expansion of an industry already hampered by heavy fiscal burdens.

In this way Tsarism paralysed the productive power of the nation and, with the exception of the small castes dependent on the Crown, all classes had an interest in its overthrow. The State, which with its banks, its railways and its vodka monopoly, was the chief employer of labour, was in constant need of foreign loans and new sources of revenue. Interest on the debt and military expenditure absorbed more than half the Imperial revenue. Torn by contradictions, Russian economy, backward in spite of superiority of plant due to its recent origin, and more concentrated than in any other country, could advance no further without a new impulse. Hence the Russo-Japanese War.

In the past the autocracy had solved many difficulties by conquest. But after having encountered the English in Central Asia, in the Far East it ran up against the Japanese, who were, moreover, allied with England. The war imposed a short respite on the revolutionary movement, but it soon exposed the barbarism of the old regime, its impotence and its corruption. *Defeatism*, which had already shown its head in the Crimean War, asserted itself this time on a large scale among the liberal bourgeoise, the oppressed nationalities, and the socialist parties, and among the workers and peasants. By comparison with Imperial Russia, suffering one defeat after another, Japan appeared almost as a champion of civilisation. This view, widespread in Europe, found singular expression in the International in articles by the Englishman, H. M. Hyndman, who described the Japanese victory as one of the greatest events in history and as an event decisive for the future of socialism. . . .

The Manchurian disaster shook Russian "society," that is the bourgeoise, to its foundations. The democratic movement, emboldened by great workmen's demonstrations, sought expression in the *Zemstvos* (consultative provincial councils), in congresses and banquets. The powerful evangelical criticism of Tolstoy threatened the ancient despotism. But liberalism in Russia, lacking a solid social basis and represented by an intelligentsia that had lost its courage, confessed defeat before going into action. The radical intellectuals and courageous students rallied to the workers' movement, the one real coherent force with which Tsarism had to reckon.

Social-Democracy was not alone in claiming the organisation of the people. A party known as the Social Revolutionaries, constituted abroad in 1901, and composed of various groups, leagues and autonomous unions, was about to hold its first congress. Its general tendency was that of the earlier Populism brought up to date by Lavrov and Mikhailovsky, somewhat influenced by western socialism, and its characteristic feature was terrorism. In 1902, its "Fighting Brigade" had begun a series of individual assassinations, decried in principle by the Social-Democrats, advocates of mass action, but which nevertheless maintained the revolutionary atmosphere, and stimulated opposition against the Tsarist regime. Michael Gotz, Gershuni, Natanson, among its representative figures, and terrorists like Karpovich, Balmashev, Sazonov and Kalyayev, were worthy exemplars of the resuscitated *narodovoltsy* tradition. Marxists looked on these Social-Revolutionaries as disgruntled liberals, democrats armed with bombs. The most energetic of them developed in opposite directions, a Savinkov to the Right, a Spiridonova to the Left.

In Poland, a "Polish Socialist Party" of national struggle grew more rapidly than the Social-Democratic Party of the class struggle; it was closely akin to the Russian Social Revolutionaries in the vagueness of its philosophy and its terrorist methods. In the different nationalities subject to the Empire, nationalist revolutionary groups supported the workers' and peasants' movement. These were *activists* in Finland, *federal socialists* in Georgia, as later on there were *dachnakists* in Armenia and *mussavatists* in Azerbaijan. The Japanese Government offered money and arms to all the subversive parties in order to weaken Russia in the rear of the armies by domestic disturbances. The only ones who accepted were the Finnish Activists, the Georgian Federal Socialists and the most nationalist section of the

Polish Socialist Party, whose leader, Pilsudski, even went to Japan to ally himself with the enemies of the Russian oppressor.

In December 1904, again at Baku, a strike broke out which made the Social-Democrats masters of the situation for several weeks and caused a recrudescence of the workers' militancy. In January 1905, an incident at the Putilov works led to a sympathetic strike of the whole of the workers in St. Petersburg. There again Zubatov's legal association had gone further than its founder intended. On January 22nd, 200,000 workmen followed Father Gapon to lay before the Tsar a petition stating their demands. This loyalist and peaceful demonstration, met by machine-gun fire and Cossack cavalry charges, ended in a massacre, and turned to revolt. There were thousands of victims. "Bloody Sunday" provoked a general rising, a great strike in over a hundred towns. The revolution hoped for by many generations, so often prophesied, on the altar of which so many lives had been sacrificed, had begun without waiting for a signal from the professional revolutionaries.

5

SOCIAL-DEMOCRACY was caught unawares, and the learned calculations of its adepts were upset by the spontaneity of the popular explosion. The Russian militants, without distinction of creed, threw themselves into the movement, seeking to organise it and to instil into it a socialist programme. The theorists of the emigration embarked more vigorously on their controversies.

Lenin said that the immediate objective was the preparation of an armed insurrection, even the date of which was to be fixed. Martov's reply in substance was that a man may prepare himself for insurrection, but an insurrection is not prepared. For Lenin the revolution could not be prepared beforehand, but the insurrection could, "if those who arranged it had influence on the masses and knew how to choose the right moment." To the abstract reasoning of the Mensheviks he opposed a concrete slogan, "Arms!" His paper, *Vperyod*, published prac-

tical advice for the insurgents, by Cluseret, General of the
Paris Commune of 1871, giving technical instructions for the
erection of barricades. By his reading and his thorough studies
Lenin was well-versed in the art of war, in the strategy of
insurrections and the tactics of street fighting. Even before
him, Plekhanov, who had studied at the Military College of
Voronezh and then at the Cadet School at St. Petersburg, had
published an article on the subject. Both were indebted to
Marx, and especially to Engels, for their ideas on civil war.
The Mensheviks also, thanks to the assistance of Mikhail Pav-
lovich, printed in the *Iskra* plans for barricades and trenches,
supplemented by full explanations. Trotsky bidding good-bye
to theory and conjecture, had crossed the frontier to be in the
fighting.

At that time, when unknown socialists were lavishly expend-
ing their energies in Russia, in strikes, meetings and demonstrations of protest, the general staff beyond the frontier continued
their battles. In April and May, 1905, the Bolsheviks held a
little congress in London attended by twenty qualified delegates of the "hards"; the Mensheviks had a conference at
Geneva. Both assemblies attacked each other and claimed the
right to represent the Party. "There was not a single worker
at the Third Congress, at any rate not one in any way remarkable," says Krupskaya, in her *Recollections of Lenin*. Krassin
made a move in consort with Trotsky, which shows how arbitrary the lines of demarcation still were. Koba was not a
member of the Caucasus delegation, which included Kamenev
and Nevsky, and the Georgians Tskhakaya and Djaparidze; if
he had played the part that is belatedly attributed to him by
Yenukidze, his absence would be inexplicable. The Congress,
under Lenin's influence, adopted the project of the general strike
transformed into armed insurrection, and the installation of a
democratic revolutionary government in which the Bolsheviks
might take part. It recognised implicitly the factitious, or at all
events the premature, nature of the schism by its conclusion as
to the necessity of uniting the Social-Democratic sections and
groups into a single party.

The reunion of the fragments of the Party would have been all the easier, in that Lenin had never abandoned his uncompromising democracy. In 1904 he wrote: "We are prepared to support even a bourgeois democrat in the degree that he conforms to democracy; we are prepared to expose any democrat, even a Social-Revolutionary, who abandons democracy." One reads in his pamphlet, *Two Tactics*, which was dated 1905: "Anyone who attempts to achieve socialism by any other route than that of political democracy, will inevitably arrive at the most absurd and reactionary deductions, both political and economic." In the same year he defined his conception thus: "Everyone is free to say and to write what he believes without the slightest restriction. . . . Liberty of speech and of the press should be complete." Even the Mensheviks could not have gone further; but the divergence over ways and means was stronger than the agreement on principles.

The immense reserves of revolutionary energy long suppressed in Russia broke out everywhere without plan or system. Strike after strike in the towns, rioting and pillage in the country, mutinies in the Army and Navy, small armed outbreaks everywhere. The workmen organised defensive and offensive detachments against the reaction and its patriotic unions, nationalist bands, and anti-Semitic *Black Hundreds*, who incited pogroms and massacred women and children. Among the mass of revolutionaries who bore no label, Social-Democrats, Social-Revolutionaries, Bundists and Anarchists preached by their example without any opportunity of concerting their activities, and helped one another in spite of differences in principle, in chance encounters and in the instinct of defence against the common enemy. The Social-Democrats formed mixed or federative committees without asking permission of their fraction leaders.

The Government, powerless to deal with all the attacks against it, concentrated its forces on fortifying the main positions of the existing regime. The Army on the Far Eastern front, though defeated there, was still strong enough to crush an unarmed people. Strikes ceased in some industrial centres, only to break out in others. Spread over an unlimited field, the peasants did not take action beyond their own village. A military mutiny at the Nova Alexandria camp, in which the Menshevik Antonov-Ovseënko came into prominence, was quickly crushed, as were the mutinies at Sebastopol, where a leader chosen on the spot, Lieutenant Schmidt, a moderate socialist, paid the penalty with his life. The revolt on the cruiser *Potemkin* in the Black Sea, organised by the Mensheviks, remained an isolated action, and was quelled, as was the later outbreak at Kronstadt. The revolution allowed itself to be beaten in detail.

The insurrection stimulated by the sentiment of oppressed nationality reached its highest point in Poland at the beginning and the Caucasus at the end of the movement. The Warsaw strike, which was a reply to the shootings in January at St. Petersburg, cost more than a hundred dead on the barricades, and about a thousand wounded and prisoners. At Lodz, later on, five hundred were killed in street fighting. Pilsudski's *Bojowka* (fighting organisation), consisting of squads of five determined men, harried police and Cossacks, and carried out assassinations.

In Georgia the general strike organised as a reply to "Bloody Sunday" dragged in all classes of people, and developed into revolt in the villages. The Tsarist authorities only held their own in the garrison towns and along the railway line. There the Social-Democratic Party guided the movement. Under the direction of its committees, the peasants were able to create their local committees, confiscate land, replace the officials, organise a police force and arm their militia, the *"Red Hundreds."* At Tiflis, the workers met the provocation of Cossack violence by organised bomb-throwing on dates fixed by the Party. In December the whole of the province of Guria, Stalin's small fatherland, was in the power of the revolutionaries. Social-Democracy, the only force enjoying popular confidence, was able to intervene between the fanatical Armenians and Tartars, incited to mutual destruction by the Russians, and to prevent carnage at Tiflis as the Party had done at Baku in February.

In these memorable events of the revolution in Transcaucasia there is always difficulty in finding any trace of Koba. There is no mention of him in most of the specialised works on the subject. In the rare cases where his name occurs it is in lists, where there is nothing to distinguish him from the other names. From the monograph by P. Makharadze, for instance, published by the State Georgian press in 1927, where the Bolshevik historian had at his disposal the *Revoliutsiis Matiane* (Revolutionary Annals) of Tiflis and the unpublished State archives, it appears that in 1905 Koba was still in the background. His pamphlet, *Sketch of the Divergences within the Party*, a mere paraphrase in Georgian of Lenin's formulas, passed unnoticed and has not since been reprinted. This fact, in a country where those in power are fond of collecting their most insignificant writings, leaves no doubt of the author's own opinion.

Moreover, the Mensheviks, for lack of opponents of any mark, dominated Georgia. Makharadze admits it in bitter terms. "At the beginning of 1905 the Social-Democratic organisation, united up to that time, underwent a schism as it did in Russia. But that was only half the evil, for the directing organs of the Party passed entirely into Menshevik hands. This circumstance made the rally of the masses to the Menshevik position inevitable. And that is what happened." The pro-Lenin attitude of the Caucasus delegates at the 1903 Congress had no result. Following the example of Topuridze, the "hards" Zurabov and Knuniantz became Mensheviks one after the other. Stalin had nothing to show for his time and his trouble. When Jordania returned the whole of the Party adopted his course.

Before the schism in the Party, Lenin had sent to the Caucasus a fellow-exile named Kurnatovsky, a good propagandist whose useful work was stopped by a fresh sentence of exile. Kurnatovsky escaped, crossed the frontier, and died abroad. Contemporaries are unanimous in his praise, but in the recollections we have quoted, Stalin does not mention him, as if he never knew him. Neither does he mention Ketzkhoveli, an energetic militant killed in the Baku prison by a sentinel, nor Postalovsky of Tiflis. He never alludes to Krassin, who however spent several years at Baku, where he rendered valuable service, maintained the principal clandestine press, and fostered the Bolshevik "cell" with literature and money. As at Tiflis and Baku, so at Kontars and Batoum he pretends not to know most of the Social-Democrats who personified the movement. Stalin's silences have their significance.

In 1905 the Mensheviks were in a majority in the Social-Democratic organisation throughout the Empire. According to Nevsky they numbered about 15,000, a third of whom were in the Caucasus, as against 12,000 Bolsheviks. Martov (*History of Russian Social-Democracy*) puts Lenin's followers at a substantially lower figure, and Bubnov, the most recent and perhaps the most official of the Bolshevik historians, puts them at 8,000. In an industrial proletariat of about three millions the Social-Democrats according to the most favourable calculations were about one per cent, if the intellectuals are left out of account.

Nevertheless, Bolshevism and Menshevism began to develop divergence in politics and tactics, if not yet in theory. New problems in an extraordinarily rapidly-changing situation demanded solutions. Parties and groups were judged by deeds, not words.

Confusion in the Russian administration gave opportunity for a relatively free press. Liberal and socialist pamphlets abounded, and there were many popular meetings in the universities. Conspirators of all sorts emerged from their subterranean hiding-places to make use of the possibility of open agitation, now tolerated in fact though not in law. Trade unions were openly organized for the first time. An effervescent public opinion gave opportunity for all sorts of efforts and discussion outside the small traditional clandestine clubs.

In September a printers' strike at Moscow inspired sympathetic action in other organisations, and new revolutionary potentialities were opened up. By October the strike had extended to the railways, then to the whole country, and developed into a general strike such as the world had never seen. In many towns the proletariat erected barricades, and defied police and soldiers. It was the culminating point of the revolution. Under this enormous pressure, the Tsar finally retreated and promulgated the Constitution of October 1905. Plekhanov's prediction was realised; the first victory over the autocracy had been won by the working class.

6

IN THE course of the St. Petersburg strike the Mensheviks had proposed the constitution of a body representing the fighting forces of the workers and had invited them to elect one delegate for every 500 workers. In the June and July numbers of *Iskra*, the idea of the formation of "representative organs of revolutionary autonomy" was put forward, especially by Dan. The Bolsheviks were hostile, opposing the notion of a "revolutionary Government" to that of "revolutionary municipalities." Local organs of that kind, said Lenin, might prove to be the epilogue and not the prologue of revolt. But the Menshevik suggestion satisfied the latent desire for a "large class organisation independent of party," the *Iskra* formula. The strikers hastened to nominate their representatives, who formed the "Soviet of Workers' Deputies." Its first President was the Menshevik Zborovsky. After him Khrustalev-Nosar, a non-party socialist who afterwards joined the Mensheviks, held the position until he was arrested. A bureau of three members, of whom Trotsky was one, was then nominated. There were similar bodies of soviets in the provinces, usually ordinary strike committees enlarged, but these were of less importance.

In the absence of Lenin, who all this time was in exile, the Bolshevik organisations in St. Petersburg failed to grasp the significance of the political and social phenomenon which was being accomplished under their eyes. Their one-track mind admitted no virtue outside the "Party," that is to say, outside their narrow group, and every workmen's organisation appeared to them as a revolutionary competitor. Also they regarded the trade unions with indifference, if not with disdain. They demanded from the St. Petersburg Soviet an explicit adhesion to Social-Democracy which would have deprived it of any reason for existence. The Mensheviks, clearer-sighted on this point and in closer touch with the masses, worked zealously in the soviets and in the trade unions, and acquired incontestable influence in both. It needed Lenin's return to induce his followers to change their attitude. His polemic with *Iskra* did not prevent Lenin from renouncing his formula in order to seize a new chance in the changing situation.

It is a remarkable illustration of the fundamental vice of the Bolshevik Party: without Lenin there would have been no Bolshevism. Not that his section had never attracted eminent men, but the Bogdanovs and Krassins were in turn to detach themselves from it as Trotsky and Plekhanov had done in the past, leaving Lenin with comrades incapable of meeting an unforeseen situation unaided.

Lenin's isolation reminds one to some extent of that of Washington, who also had to rely exclusively on himself, and whose lieutenants, left to their own initiative, would have compromised the common task.

Before returning to Russia, in October 1905, Lenin had written to Plekhanov: "Our revolution sweeps away tactical divergences with surprising rapidity. Here is a field in which forgetfulness of the past and a mutual understanding in face of a piece of live work will always be made easy." At St. Petersburg he founded, with Bogdanov and Kamenev, a new paper, *Novaya Zhizn*, edited by an actress, Marie Andreyeva, with the collaboration of well-known writers, Gorky, Balmont, Leonid Andreyev. On their side the Mensheviks published *Nachalo*, in which Trotsky and Parvus defended a special idea—the "permanent revolution." "We have always said that a revolution would strengthen and not weaken the bourgeoisie, and would provide the indispensable conditions for a victorious struggle for socialism," Lenin had declared at a recent Congress of his fraction. In *Two Tactics* he speaks of the same idea:

Marxists are absolutely convinced of the bourgeois character of the Russian Revolution. What does this mean? That the democratic changes in the political system and the economic and social changes which have become indispensable in Russia, do not of themselves signify the destruction of capitalism or the downfall of the reign of the bourgeoise. On the contrary they will, for the first time, really throw open the field to the development of a European, not an Asiatic capitalism, thus making possible for the first time, the reign of the bourgeoise as a class.

All the Social-Democrats agreed on the general definition. But disagreements soon arose. Trotsky and Parvus thought the working class to be the only one capable of seizing and holding power, with the more or less active support of the peasants. Social-Democracy must then claim the succession to Tsarism; but in the exercise of power it would necessarily engage in socialist enterprises which could only be consolidated by an international revolution; therefore revolution must be uninterrupted, permanent and universal, and must be maintained by the dictatorship of the proletariat.

But for the Mensheviks, haunted by the scheme of European revolutions, the bourgeoisie alone could and must seize power. If the Social-Democracy attempted it, it would meet with the fate of the Paris Commune, Russia being as yet insufficiently developed for transformation into a socialist State. The proletariat would therefore have to support from outside the party of the advanced bourgeoisie, that of the Constitutional Democrats or Kadets, created in 1905. The Mensheviks quoted Engels in support of this proposal. *"The worst possible thing for the leader of an extreme party is to be compelled to assume power at a time when the movement is not yet ripe for the domination of the class which it represents and for the measures required for that domination."*

Lenin's view was that it was the autocracy, not the bourgeoisie, that had to be overturned, and that they had to establish, not the dictatorship of the proletariat, but "the democratic dictatorship of the proletariat and the peasants." For there was in Russia "an enormous peasant and lower middle class population capable of supporting the democratic but not yet the socialist revolution." Lenin reproved "the absurd half-anarchist conceptions on the immediate realisation of the maximum programme and the conquest of power for the socialist transformation." A revolutionary dictatorship could only endure if it had the support of the overwhelming majority of the people; the proletariat being in a minority in Russia, Trotsky and Parvus were merely phrase-making when they foretold its accession to political power. The true perspective was the foundation of "a democratic republic as the last form of bourgeois domination, and the most appropriate for the struggle of the proletariat with the bourgeoisie." With this end in view, the Bolsheviks should participate with the liberal bourgeoisie in a provisional revolutionary government.

Martov said he differed very little from this general point of view, and he praises its "realism" in his *History*, but he repelled, on grounds of theoretical orthodoxy, the suggestion of "participation in a bourgeois government" as compromising. Thus Lenin figured as an opportunist, Martov as an intransigent, and Trotsky as a utopian of the extreme Left. . . . Rosa Luxemburg inclined towards the thesis of the "permanent revolution," which was severely criticised by Franz Mehring, the historian and theoretician of German socialism. Twenty years later A. Joffe, a former Menshevik who had joined hands with Lenin, wrote to Trotsky from his death-bed: "I have often declared that I heard with my own ears Lenin say that you, not he, were right in 1905. A man face to face with death does not lie, and I repeat the statement now. . . ." History will give the deciding vote to the survivors of a debate which still continues in the logomachy engendered by deceptive appearances.

The Government of Nicholas II interrupted brutally for a time the dissertations and speculations on the "motive forces" of the revolution by exercising the power it still retained in December, when the workers' movement declined after a year of civil war in which the front ranks were always occupied by the same vanguard. At St. Petersburg the Soviet, of which Trotsky had been the indefatigable mouthpiece, was suppressed after an existence of fifty-two days, and its members imprisoned. Before his disappearance Trotsky had launched his *Financial Manifesto* repudiating in advance the loans made to the Tsar "then at open war with his people." At Moscow an insurrection begun, organised and inspired this time by the Bolsheviks, was crushed after nine days of fighting in which less than 2,000 workmen, 500 of whom were Social-Democrats, resisted the garrison which had received strong reinforcements. In the Caucasus strong reinforcements of all arms vanquished the insurgents, and artillery put an end to the "Guria Republic." Such were the main stages of a defeat presaging a victory to come. "Without the general rehearsal of 1905," wrote Lenin, "our victory in 1917 would have been impossible."

The revolution died down without being able to strike the decisive blow because attack was not simultaneous everywhere, because there was no consciousness of solidarity between town and country, no co-ordination of the elemental forces unchained, because there was no general organisation or direction. Its scattered efforts were broken by an army in the main faithful to the old regime. But absolutism had tottered under the shock. An embryo constitution, a sort of parliament had been gained. The political impotence of the bourgeoisie as a class had been revealed. Its revolutionary intellectuals had thrown in their lot with the proletariat in the course of the struggle. All the socialist parties emerged from the fight greater in prestige if not in numbers. Anarchism had failed under the test of experience. Finally, the October strike left a great example, the unforgettable lesson of the St. Petersburg Soviet.

No theorist had foreseen the Soviets or the rôle they were to play in the future. The Mensheviks could claim the largest share in their creation, but did not make use of them to the full extent. The Bolsheviks found difficulty in adapting themselves to the accomplished fact, with the exception of Lenin, who, on reflection, glimpsed the possibilities of the future. "The transfer of the leadership of the Soviet from Khrustalev to Trotsky will be an immense step forward," he said, not stinting his admiration of an adversary who had shown his real stature. The provincial Soviets of Moscow, Rostov, Novorossiisk, Baku, Odessa, etc., were most of them under Menshevik influence. That of Novorossiisk deserves special mention for having put itself at the head of a short-lived local republic. (Similar local republics were formed in Latvia.) Only one, the Bielostok Soviet, was in the hands of Social Revolutionaries and Anarchists. The forces of reaction swept away the soviets, but their memory remained vivid in the consciousness of the working class.

Lenin kept in the background during the 1905 revolution. He was not the man for showy achievements; his business was persevering, effective work for the future settlement. Moreover, the Bolsheviks in general lagged behind except in the final episode at Moscow. The Social Revolutionaries and Mensheviks showed themselves quicker and more energetic, more supple and more enterprising, perhaps because less encumbered with dogmatic theory. Plekhanov, who had become a Western European, removed from the actual struggle, did not know what to make of the revolutionary happenings in Russia. The fact that he did not return to Russia and his remark after the Moscow insurrection, "that Moscow should not have taken up arms," are sufficient indication of his attitude of detachment from "living work," to which Lenin had invited him. One may say, with Lunacharsky, that of all the Social-Democratic leaders "Trotsky undeniably showed himself, in spite of his youth, the best prepared, the most exempt from a certain émigré narrowness, which affected even Lenin at that time. He advanced in popularity during the revolution, when neither Lenin nor Martov did. Plekhanov lost much ground. . . . From that time Trotsky was in the foreground." In Georgia traditional Social-Democracy had acquired and exercised an authority everywhere acknowledged, and a new generation, among them I. Tseretelli, had arisen to carry on the work of the group founded by Jordania.

Of Stalin there would be nothing to say if he had not been summoned, for the first time, to a Bolshevik Conference at Tammerfors. "Summoned," for he could not be strictly speaking the delegate of a Menshevik organisation. It was then that he really made acquaintance with Lenin. No minutes of the Conference exist, and there is no mention of any part, or any speech of his. In his recollections on Lenin he makes some characteristic comments.

I met Lenin for the first time in December 1905 at the Bolshevik Conference at Tammerfors, in Finland. I expected to see the mountain eagle of our Party a great man, not only politically but physically, for I had formed for myself a picture of Lenin as a giant, a fine figure of a man. What was my disappointment when I saw the most ordinary looking individual, below middle height, distinguished from ordinary mortals by nothing, literally nothing. A great man is permitted to be generally late at meetings so that those present may be apprehensive at his non-arrival, and so that before the great man's appearance there may be cries of "Hush—silence—he is coming." This ceremony seemed to me useful for it creates respect. What was my disappointment to find that Lenin had arrived before the delegates and was carrying on the most ordinary conversation, with the most ordinary delegate, in a corner.

He continues in the same tone, on the same level, in the same sense. The reader is none the wiser for it. The matter, worthy of the style, requires no comment. One wonders how Koba could have won Lenin's esteem but for the fact that he was able to render remarkable service and to show his real capacity during the years following the 1905 Revolution, years of political reaction and socialist retrogression.

Chapter IV

A PROFESSIONAL REVOLUTIONARY

THE Revolution of 1905, says Trotksy, showed that Russia provided no exception to the laws of history. This country with its slow and retarded social development passed in turn through the same stages as the most advanced capitalist States. The Slavophile theory, exclusively based on the special characteristics of Russia, seemed to be refuted. But, in spite of analogies throwing light on the present and to some extent, thanks to western experience, on the future, it is still necessary to study distinctive national traits; and especially to consider the influences which have determined the particular historical course followed by contemporary Russia.

Nowhere else was the State so centralised; nowhere else did it play so important a rôle in economic development. "In Russia the State is all-powerful," wrote Combes de Lestrade in 1895; he compared the social organisation of the country to "a vast factory centralising in its workshops the activity and working power of all its inhabitants without exception."

The intervention of the State was looked upon as the mainspring of industrial progress. "Peter the Great's real achievement was to make our country, already rich in land, in men and in cereals, a country rich also in industries"; this is the opinion of Professor D. Mendeleyev. In the progress of industrialisation more was expected from State aid than from private initiative.

Foreign finance, by its large investments, helped in the development of the most concentrated industry in the world.

83

Beside the milliards lent to the State, eighty per cent of capital came from foreign countries. The statistics of the time show a proportionately higher percentage of works employing 1,000 workers than in the United States or in Germany. From an extremely low original level, production increased by fits and starts, more rapidly in Russia than in America. A close parallel can be traced between the "greatest Republic and the vastest Empire in the world," says C. de Lestrade. Industrial concentration demanded a corresponding concentration of the working classes, whose peasant origin and rapid growth in numbers offered virgin soil for revolutionary theories.

The proletariat had sacrificed about 15,000 dead, 20,000 wounded, and 80,000 prisoners for its first political victories— shorter hours of work, higher salaries, and a *de facto* if not a *de jure* right to form trade unions. More especially, its leaders had learned its strength and its weakness, and understood the pressing need of party and trade union organisation. All varieties of socialism flourished and won over practically the whole working population. N. Rubakin says that in 1905-7, there were some sixty million copies of socialist works in circulation.

Social-Democracy became a great party, attaining more than 150,000 adherents in 1906, of whom half were in national groups, in spite of the semi-illegal situation. In contrast with the "generals" who were eager to seize on their points of difference, the working army of the revolution exacted Social-Democratic unity, at least on the surface. The previous year Lenin had evaded a suggestion made by August Bebel on behalf of German Socialism and the International for fusion of the sections, but he was obliged to swim with the stream. Experience showed that Bolshevism could not yet claim independent existence either as a body of theory or as a party. A Unity Congress was held at Stockholm in 1906, where the Mensheviks, with a clear majority, assumed the official direction of the movement.

Stalin, under the name of Ivanovich, represented the province of Tiflis at the Congress. By what subterfuge had he secured election in a district practically entirely in Menshevik hands? In reality, he represented only the tiny handful of local Bol-

sheviks, too weak in every respect to stand up against the traditions of Georgian socialism, but clever enough to constitute an
obscure group and claim a place in the Congress, taking advantage of the temporary spirit of conciliation. He intervened in
debate three times, with brief remarks of elementary simplicity,
which he has never dared to reprint. The first proposal on the
agrarian question, refuted by Dan in a few words, advocated
division of the land in agreement with the peasants' wishes (the
Bolsheviks advocated nationalisation of the land, the Mensheviks
municipalisation). The second, on general tactics, passed unnoticed and concluded with the dilemma, "either the hegemony
of the proletariat or the hegemony of bourgeois democracy,"
quite contrary to Bolshevik views; the third, on the parliamentary problem, advised against any participation in the elections
for the Duma, at a moment when Lenin was revising his tactics
in the opposite sense.

Nothing could show more clearly the non-existence of Bolshevism as a doctrine except in Lenin's brain; every Bolshevik
left to himself wandered from "the line" of his fraction. But
Koba's three short speeches, assured, even cocksure, did not
hinder Stalin from voting with his friends, except on the last
point, when he abstained, for these men were bound together
by their temperament and by the ascendancy of Lenin rather
than by ideas. Years of action in common and many crises were
required to acquire even a degree of unity in the opinions of the
"Jacobins" of the proletariat.

Nevertheless the fractions survived with their own rules and
their intermittent press, each with its interior differences, its
diverging tendencies and its dissidents. Generally speaking the
Right was inclined to adapt itself to the spontaneous popular
movement, the Left to capture it in order to direct it. Both
hoped for a revival of the workers' and peasants' offensive in the
near future. The Mensheviks were the first to admit the decline
of the revolution; consequently, they wished to initiate legal
action, to support the most advanced of the bourgeois parties
and strengthen the influence of the Duma. The Bolsheviks, on
the other hand, expected an immediate revival of the revolution

—the classic error of revolutionary optimism. They calculated on a general strike followed by insurrection, aiming at the overthrow of the autocracy and the summoning of a Constituent Assembly. Both saw the necessity of political alliances for a proletariat which was still weak, but the Mensheviks relied above all on the liberal bourgeoisie, the Bolsheviks on the landless peasants.

Throughout the controversy, frequent references were made to the Revolution of 1848, and the respective positions of the parties were defined by the dates: 1847 or 1849? That is to say, the eve or the morrow of the revolution? The Bolsheviks thought they were on the eve of a decisive attempt (1847), the Mensheviks that they were on the morrow of a semi-defeat (1849). The Mensheviks began to work "by European methods," the Bolsheviks persisted in their *"specifically Russian"* methods, that is to say, the methods demanded by the circumstances of time and place, as interpreted by themselves.

In the Russian Revolution Lenin distinguished "two separate and heterogeneous social wars; one within the existing autocratic-feudal regime, the other within the future bourgeois-democratic regime." It was necessary, he thought, to wage a triple war on the theoretical, political and economic fronts. In view of the approaching revolt, he studied and criticised in detail the December fighting in Moscow, how the barricades were used, what part was played by artillery, and by the new weapons revealed by the Russo-Japanese war, such as the hand grenade. He recalled Marx's aphorism, *Insurrection is an art*, and therefore an art to be studied, and he urged the workers to form groups of three, five and ten volunteers, and gave them instructions and advice.

"The battle is near at hand," he assured them, deceiving himself as to the proximity of the date. He emphasized the necessity of "creating a *military organisation* side by side with the soviets, for their defence and for the organisation of the insurrection without which all the soviets and all the delegates of the masses would remain powerless." This idea was to be realised, but not till ten years later. He was untiring in keeping his followers up to the mark.

Remember [he said] that the day of the mass struggle is approaching. It will be armed insurrection. It should be as far as possible simultaneous. The masses must know that they are engaging in an armed, sanguinary, and merciless struggle. They must be animated by scorn of death, which will bring victory. The attack must be pressed with the utmost energy; the offensive, not the defensive, must be the order of the day, and the objective, the implacable extermination of the enemy. . . .

Meanwhile he occupied himself first with the prosaic question of participation in parliament. The first Duma scheme, boycotted by all the revolutionary and democratic Parties, came to nothing. The second, based on a restricted and indirect franchise in three stages, was applied. The various socialist Parties boycotted the elections, thus assuring the victory of the Kadets (Constitutional Monarchists). The Mensheviks, who were disposed to take part in the electoral campaign for purposes of agitation and propaganda, at any rate in the first two stages, had not opposed the general feeling, but their preponderance was so great in the Caucasus that five of their candidates, Social-Democratic, were elected there. The Georgians were already carrying on their own policy. Jordania and his comrades thus became the mouthpieces of the whole Social-Democratic movement in the first Duma.

The Georgian political success made the Mensheviks regret their abstention, and they began resolutely to advocate participation in the elections. Lenin agreed with them. At Tammerfors he had agreed to the boycott, but under pressure of the Conference. In one of his speeches Stalin reports this episode:

The debate opened, and the provincial members, Siberians and Caucasians, led the attack. What was our astonishment when, after our speeches, Lenin intervened, and declared himself in favour of participating in the elections, but then saw his mistake and took his stand with the section. We were stupefied. The effect was electric. We gave him a great ovation.

Lenin rarely allowed himself to be influenced by his followers. But there were cases when local information on the temper
of the people might be allowed, for tactical reasons, to influence
his judgment. On this occasion, as was usually the case, he had
reason to regret it. "We all erred," he wrote fifteen years later
in alluding to the boycott. But at the time he refused to admit
it; in giving his reasons for a change of attitude under new
conditions, he justified his past attitude. Stalin was among those
who incited the Party to commit this "error."

On the dissolution of the Duma, Lenin felt it necessary to
oppose the boycott. At Stockholm he had indicated his point
of view by voting for the proposal of the Caucasus Mensheviks
for participation in the primary elections, without any hesitation about separating himself from comrades like Stalin, obstinate in the "error." He wrote several persuasive articles on the
subject, then carried on a fierce controversy in an attempt to
convince his section of the Party; so great an importance did he
attach to legal action, without at the same time renouncing
clandestine work. As opposed to this, conspiracy, underground
plots, terrorism, and the most dangerous armed operations
showed unprecedented development. In this new scheme Stalin
found employment for his natural gifts.

Repression had not broken revolutionary energy. While the
authorities shot rebels in the army and the navy without mercy,
crushed rural rioting by punitive expeditions on a considerable
scale, the intrepid *drujiny*—fighting squads of the various revolutionary parties—continued their activities all the more
boldly as the masses began to show signs of lassitude. From
their original defensive mission the *boyeviki* (armed militants,
sharpshooters, guerillas) turned to the offensive, following the
example of the Caucasian bomb-throwers and the Polish *bojowci*.
Murderous attacks on policemen, Cossacks and government
agents, armed expropriations of public and private funds began
to multiply.

The "expropriations," forcible confiscation of funds belonging to banks, post-offices, and store-houses, in transit by road
or rail, and sometimes of money belonging to private persons,

became frequent in 1906 and 1907. The word, abbreviated as *"ex,"* even passed into the language. Operations of this kind were rarely executed without shooting, with victims on both sides. But the revolutionaries had the advantage of the offensive, of surprise attack, and of extreme mobility, and generally succeeded in getting off scot-free from these attacks and ambuscades. Many civil and military officials perished in surprise attacks by the guerillas. On the other hand the *boyeviki* prisoners ran the risk of the gallows as the penalty of brigandage.

The object of these expropriations was to provide funds for the revolutionary groups. The smaller "ex'es" provided for the maintenance of the expropriators. But the matter passed more and more out of the control of the organisations. The flying squads were mixed up with mischievous elements which were not disinterested but indisciplined and operating on their own account. Signs of degeneration, cases of common assault, acts of terrorism against the inhabitants, soon threw great discredit on the movement. Robbers and bandits, who made it their business to hold the population to ransom rather than to annoy the authorities made the "war of the partisans" suspect. It became difficult to distinguish between "ex'es" of all sorts and various forms of brigandage. The Social-Democratic Party could not overlook this unforeseen danger.

A special resolution was passed at the Stockholm Conference condemning robbery, the expropriation of private property and the deposits of private banks, forced contributions, the destruction of public buildings and railways, but admitting, under Bolshevik pressure, confiscation of State moneys on the order of a revolutionary authority in districts where such an authority existed. For Lenin approved the "ex'es" while condemning their "Apache deviation," provided that they were carried out under strict Party control. The Congress had recognised "the inevitability of active struggle against Governmental terror and the violence of the *Black Hundreds*," the aim of which was to kill the enemy, while avoiding any attack on the "private property of peaceful citizens."

Thus Social-Democracy partially borrowed from the Social

Revolutionaries' tactics, which the Social Revolutionaries had themselves abandoned after the constitutional rescript of October. The London Congress of 1903 had voted for a motion of Axelrod's against the Social Revolutionaries, among other things denouncing their terrorist proceedings as adventurism. Two years later Plekhanov proposed to associate himself with their activities and adopt their methods, but was confronted with unyielding opposition by Martov. The Mensheviks, careful to observe "European" methods, objected to systematic violence and to attacks on individuals. The terrorist tradition of the *narodovoltsy* and of their successors was continued and exacerbated in the extreme Left wing of the Social Revolutionaries, the Maximalists, who formed an independent league, which distinguished itself by audacious exploits. Anarchists and Bolshevists vied with them.

"A great part of the innumerable thefts and robberies on private persons which passed like a muddy wave over this period of depression when the revolution was temporarily on the defensive," said Rosa Luxemburg, "were committed in the name of anarcho-communism." This is an erroneous statement, for all sorts of revolutionaries furnished their contingents to the *boyeviki* and the expropriators. In the Caucasus, where Social-Democracy was in the ascendant, 1,150 acts of terrorism were committed between 1904 and 1908, according to statistics published by P. Makharadze; the Federalist Socialists and the Bolsheviks, not numerous but very active, had a large share in them. In Latvia the Social-Democratic Party methodically organised "ex'es," and gave receipts for the proceeds. In Poland Pilsudski's Socialist Party, a rival of the Social-Democrats, acted in the same way.

The anarchists had a certain number of groups and clubs but only in a few places. "Bakunin's native country was to be the tomb of his theory," said Rosa Luxemburg when she was demonstrating the thesis that the Russian Revolution was "the historical winding-up of anarchism"; but her definition of anarchism as "the ideology of the mob" is a piece of rhetorical exaggeration. Kropotkin, the anarchist theorist of the general expropriation of the bourgeoisie, of the seizure of the means of production by the people, notably in the *Notes of a Rebel* and in the *Conquest of Bread*, disavowed partial and individual expropriation. Lenin, on the other hand, approved of them under certain circumstances. At St. Petersburg an anarchist group preached terror and the pillage of shops under the name of "direct action," but the Bolsheviks required no influence to induce them to act as they wished. The accusations of Anarcho-Blanquism, launched against them by the Mensheviks, did not dissuade them from following their own methods.

Lenin admitted that "these methods of social struggle have been adopted by preference, even exclusively, by the most wretched elements of the population, by tramps, the lumpen-proletariat, and by anarchist groups." But that seemed to him inevitable at that time. "They tell us that the 'war of the partisans' brings the class-conscious proletariat into touch with the lower strata, with rogues and drunkards. That is so. But the only conclusion to be drawn from the fact is that these means should be subordinated to others, and employed within reasonable limits proportioned to the main methods of action, and ennobled by the educating and organising influence of socialism."

He practically said that Marxism admitted the most various fighting methods, did not invent them, but rationalised them, gave conscious expression to spontaneously developed procedure. Hostile to doctrinaire formulas, to the proposals of "paper-scheme makers," Marxism does not disavow any form of struggle, and, far from *lecturing the masses*, it is a student in their school of *practice*. Therefore the "war of the partisans" arose spontaneously as a counter-move to the exactions of the *Black Hundreds*, the army and the police. Everything that is spontaneous is necessary, would fairly sum up Lenin's meaning.

Under cover of this theoretical justification and in spite of the Stockholm decisions, the Bolsheviks tried, at their own risk, to derive advantage from the circumstances, from the warlike enterprise of the *boyeviki* and sometimes by complicity with those of another camp. Their section, organised in complete independence of the regular Party institutions, was secretly directed by a Bolshevik Centre, in accordance with Lenin's known views on the subject of "professional revolutionaries." Under the clandestine instructions of the *troïka*, Lenin, Krassin and Bogdanov, it sought to procure the maximum of money and arms.

The "Technical Bureau" of the Central Committee at St. Petersburg could supply as many as 150 bombs a day; soldiers on their way home from Manchuria sold their rifles to the railwaymen. That was enough. An organisation of "professional revolutionaries" preparing an insurrection in the near future needed immense supplies of war material. Party subscriptions were insignificant. Krassin and Gorky were the principal purveyors of funds, thanks to their connections with the liberal bourgeoisie and with literary and artistic circles; through them certain textile capitalists, among them S. Morosov, contributed substantial subsidies. But the revolutionary *profession*, extended to a Party, or at all events to its officials, required more funds, and the "ex'es" were the main source of supply for the Bolshevik Centre.

Krassin was not only Finance Minister of the Section. He was in charge of the manufacture of explosives, the purchase and transport of arms, the courses of bombing instruction, and he inspired and supplied the fighting squad in the Caucasus. He was arrested in Finland, and had a narrow escape from the gallows. Later on he entered the service of the firm of Siemens-Schuckert in Germany as a highly qualified engineer. He was equally highly qualified for the Bolshevik illegal conspirators' service, and with inexhaustible energy and coolness he took part in the most "delicate" enterprises to ensure for the Party the indispensable resources for carrying on clandestine rebel activity. Bogdanov, historian, philosopher and economist, was closely concerned in the *boyeviki* operations in the Urals. Lenin directed the whole from his distant eminence.

The year 1906 was memorable as regards "ex'es" and terrorism. At Moscow a group of twenty Socialist Revolutionaries forced a bank in March, and carried off 875,000 roubles in booty. At Dushet, in the province of Tiflis, six Federalist Socialists disguised as soldiers seized in March 315,000 roubles which the Bolsheviks confiscated by a stratagem. In Poland Pilsudski's *bojowci* in August made a simultaneous attack in several towns on the soldiers and the police, killing several dozen. Polish Social-Democracy felt it necessary to protest against mass destruction of innocent recruits. In concert with the Maximalists, the Bolshevik "Technical Bureau" at St. Petersburg connived at the blowing up of Stolypin's villa in August; and also at pillaging in October a van belonging to the State Bank. The Maximalists had carried out a resounding "ex" against a Mutual Credit Bank at St. Petersburg, the famous coup of the *Fonarny pereulok*, which was talked about in the press for a long time. The month of October alone witnessed 121 terrorist deeds, 47 fights with the police, and 362 expropriations. In the space of four months 2,118 Government agents and officials were killed and wounded, following on 2,000 casualties in the preceding eighteen months. The General of Police, Spiridovich, described the pillage of the State Bank at Helsingfors as an operation "only comparable with the Tiflis expropriation in 1907."

The mysteries of these legendary exploits have not yet come fully to light. Twenty years after, on the death of Krassin, one of the Old Bolsheviks, the engineer G. Krizhanovsky was to write: "Even now the time has not come fully to expose the underground activities of Leonid Borissovich . . ." But in another article, after alluding to the secret printing presses and sapping of the Butyrky prison, he makes veiled references to the links which bound Krassin, alias Nikitich, to the Caucasian *boyevik*, Kamo, famous for "the pillage of a bank at Tiflis" and certain "experimental explosions of Macedonian bombs among the rocks of Finland." A less discreet communist historian, M. Liadov, ascribes to Krassin-Nikitich the establishment of the laboratory where the Bolsheviks prepared their various explosives; "it is enough to say that the contrivance which blew up Stolypin's villa in the isle of Aptekarsky and the *Fonarny pereulok* bombs were made under Nikitich's supervision" . . . The same writer also says: "The plans of all the expropriations organised by the latter (Kamo), at Kvirilli, at the Treasury Dushet, in Erivan

Square, were drawn up and concerted with Nikitich." The so-called Erivan Square affair is the same as that of Tiflis which Spiridovich treats as a record.

The Tiflis "ex," the most "grandiose" of all, to use the current phrase, was a masterpiece of its kind, and eclipsed all earlier efforts by its dramatic scale and its perfect success. It constituted Stalin's principal claim to the consideration of the leaders of the section. An obscure provincial militant acting under the direction of the mysterious triumvirate, a "professional revolutionary" par excellence, incapable of promotion for brain-power in the Party hierarchy, but ready to serve its cause by playing a steadily increasing part, Koba had found circumstances in which he could show the temper of his steel.

Nevertheless, the obvious tendency of the "ex" to degenerate into banditry, and the increase of corruption, led to categorical condemnation, by a new general Congress of Social-Democracy held in London in 1907, at which the Bolsheviks were in the majority, of "all participation in or assistance to the operations of the 'partisans' and 'expropriations' as disorganising and de-moralising." Orders were also given that all the fighting squads connected with the Party should be disbanded. Many Bolsheviks, alarmed at the turn the minor civil war was taking, had separated themselves from Lenin on this issue to support the Mensheviks. Koba was present in a consultative capacity at the Congress. But for the "professional revolutionaries" of Bolshevism, the orders of the section took precedence of those of the Party, and Lenin's instructions supplanted political morality. A few days after the return of members of the Congress from London, the Tiflis affair exploded (the word is justified) like a bomb.

2

Tiflis, June 26.

To-day in Erivan Square in the middle of the town, and at a moment when the Square was swarming with people, ten bombs were thrown in succession. They exploded with great force.

Between each of the explosions there were rifle and revolver shots. Chimneys, doors and windows were broken or shaken down. The

Square was covered with débris. There were many killed and wounded. The authorities immediately cleared the Square and forbade access to the scene of the catastrophe.

THIS confusing telegram (very badly written) appeared on June 27, 1907, in the supplementary edition of the *Temps* and to it was added the next day the following lines, no less obscure:

Robbery was the motive of the Erivan outrage, related in yesterday's *Petit Temps*. The authors of the outrage got away with 341,000 roubles in a Treasury van.

The *Novoye Vremya* of the following days reported the affair with more detail, but still in vague terms mixed with angry comments against "heroes of the bomb and the revolver." Eight bombs, followed by repeated shots, were said to have been hurled on two carriages under Cossack escort which were carrying a large sum to the State Bank (341,000 roubles, that is about $170,000 at par, more than 4¼ million francs). There were three killed and more than fifty wounded, soldiers and innocent peasants, for the Square was full of people at 10.45 a.m.; the panic was indescribable and was accentuated by the flying pieces of glass from the windows of shops and houses. The crowd rushed to the shops where the doors were promptly closed. Two suspicious-looking carriages had been noticed, one occupied by two women, the other by "an individual in officer's uniform." The aggressors, perhaps fifty in number, had disappeared without leaving any trace. "The devil knows how this robbery of unheard-of boldness was carried out," sighed the *Novoye Vremya*. Shortly afterwards the police notified all countries of the numbers of the "expropriated" series of 500 rouble notes.

Two women actually took part in the coup, both comrades of the Social-Democratic Party, Patsya Goldava and Annette Sulamlidze. The pseudo-officer was the leader of the *boyeviki* squad in person, Ter-Petrossian, known as Kamo. Second in command would be the more correct description, for district operations were in charge of Koba, who in turn obeyed the orders of the supreme *troïka*.

The extraordinary existence led by men such as Kamo illustrates the inestimable devotion to which the Bolshevik Party in the hands of a Lenin owed its strength. Simon (Senko) Ter-Petrossian was born, like Stalin, at Gori, the son of Armenian parents. He was the faithful assistant of Stalin, to whom he owed his nickname. A communist historian might find a parallel in Rob Roy, Walter Scott's mediaeval hero: a counter-revolutionary might compare him to Rocambole.

Before the revolution he served Social-Democracy by accepting the most repugnant tasks, the most difficult and perilous missions. He was arrested, escaped, took part in insurrection, and was then captured and tortured by the Cossacks, one of whom threatened to cut off his nose; he was made to dig his own grave, was twice brought to the foot of the gallows. Imprisoned, set free by a stratagem, always on the run, he conspired incessantly and was one of the pioneers in the "war of partisans." In December 1906 he took part in the successful expropriation at Kvirilli, he organised fighting *drujiny*, then, at Lenin's suggestion, he went to the Balkans in search of arms but failed, and after many tribulations he returned to the Caucasus where he created a formidable squad of *boyeviki*.

At that time there were groups of "forest brothers" hidden in the forests and in the mountains in revolt against authority; these men had no principles and were a danger on the roads. The time was favourable for the recrudescence of the ancient brigand traditions of the Caucasus. From among these outlaws Kamo recruited the better elements, inspired them with his own revolutionary spirit, drilled them and put them under discipline. He himself lived on fifty kopecks a day and gave them no more, though the Kutais "ex" brought in 15,000 roubles. But their technique was still only mediocre. Kamo, disguised as an officer, went to Finland to meet Lenin and Krassin, and brought back arms and explosives to Tiflis. In a collection of reminiscences published about Krassin it is stated that "nearly all the *coups de main* brought off by our famous Kamo were planned and executed under Krassin's direction. The Tsar's cleverest spy would have had difficulty in associating Krassin's physiognomy with a friendship for the bold and famous Caucasian revolutionary Kamo."

On his return to Georgia an attempt was made to secure at once a large sum for the Bolshevik Centre. The coup failed. Kamo was seriously wounded by the detonation of a bomb, and almost lost the sight of the left eye. But in a few weeks the indefatigable fighter was about again, and undertook a new expedition which began well but, owing to the defection of an accomplice, ended badly. The comrades returned to Tiflis in great distress. "The bombs," says Kamo's wife, "were only serviceable for two or three days; they had to be used at once or there could be no practical action for many months. . . . Happily, that very evening a message was received that 250,000 roubles were to be transferred to the State Bank."

On the following day [writes S. Medvedyeva Ter-Petrossian, whose narrative is worth recording, with the omission of some superfluous details], the cashier K. and the clerk G., accompanied by two policemen and five Cossacks, went to the Bank, conveying the 250,000 (?) roubles. From Pushkin Square, from which the Post Office could be seen, Patsya Goldava gave the signal agreed with Stepko Kitskirvelli: They are starting!

The latter immediately communicated with Annette Sulamlidze, who in turn, passed on the message to the *boyeviki* who were waiting in the Tilipuchuri Restaurant. Bachua Kupriashvili walked round Erivan Square unfolding a newspaper. This was the signal for preparing the attack awaited by comrades posted at various points—Datiko Chibriashvili, Arkady Elbakidze, Vano Shimshanovi, Vano Kalandadze, Ilico Chachiashvili and Ilico Ebrialidze. Also Akaki Dalakishvili and Theophilus Kavriashvili were in readiness to hold up the Cossacks stationed before the doors. Finally Elisso Lominadze and Serapion Lomidze waited at the corner of the Armenian Bazaar and V. . . . . Street, defending the road by which the expropriators were to carry off the money.

Surrounded by horsemen the carriages drove rapidly through clouds of dust. The Cossacks in front were already turning into S. . . . . Street. At that moment Datiko stepped forward a few paces. All the conspirators hurled their bombs with all their strength.

Two explosions, and then another two. Two policemen and a Cossack lay on the pavement. The horses dashed through the escort.

But the carriage in which the money was loaded was not blown up, and the horses dashed with it towards the S. . . . Bazaar.

This was the decisive moment, and Bachua alone kept his head. He dashed forward to cut off the horses, and caught the carriage at the end of the Square. Unhesitatingly and with no thought for his own safety he threw a bomb between the horses' legs. The force of the explosion threw him to the ground. The money might once more have been saved from the bold *boyeviki* but Chibriashvili came up just in time. Without paying any attention to Bachua, he dragged the bag of money from the carriage and made off in the direction of V. . . . Street.

Where was Kamo, organiser and inspirer of the whole business? Dressed as an officer, still pale and hardly recovered from his wounds, he had been walking about the Square all the morning, keeping the public away by clever, mysterious remarks (his uniform prevented suspicion), so as to avoid useless shedding of blood. Kamo was in a carriage when the explosion occurred. His business was to receive the money and place it in safety. When he came out of G. . . . Street into the Square, in accordance with the plan of campaign, he thought the attempt was another failure.

In any case he had to help the comrades to get away before the soldiers arrived—that was Kamo's first instinct. Rising in his seat, shooting with his revolver, uttering shouts and oaths like a real captain, he urged his horse towards V. . . . Street. And there by chance he encountered Datiko. The money was taken to the house of Mikha Bocharidze and hidden under a divan. Then it was taken to an absolutely safe place, the private office of the Director of the Observatory.

When the soldiers surrounded the Square they found no one there. Luckily all the persons engaged escaped arrest. Only certain indirect accomplices, changing the notes abroad, were discovered with small sums, but the Governments refused to extradite them.

This version of the affair, authenticated by the Bolshevik Party, completes and corrects the earlier one, but it may also need examination and correction. There is another by Dzvali, one of the participants, in a book by B. Bibineishvili on Kamo, with a police report and the deposition of a witness: several statements are contradictory and the proper names sometimes vary. It is very unlikely that a conspiracy of these dimensions could be improvised in a few hours, and there are no indications of the personal part played by Stalin, or of the share of his colleague

Sergo Ordjonikidze, who had just arrived on the scene. Trotsky, alluding to this famous affair, admits that it "reflects honour on Stalin's revolutionary determination," but in answer to the inquiry why it should be omitted from the official biographies of that personage he says that in this affair Stalin displayed his lack of political sense, for the "ex'es," compatible with a mass offensive, were degenerating into adventurism in a period of revolutionary retreat. If the criticism was justifiable, it applied to Lenin, not to a subordinate. Moreover if the money requirements of the Party or the fraction justified such methods at all, considerations based on the ebb and flow of the revolution and brought forward after a delay of twenty years are not very convincing.

The end of the story is to be found in an article by Martov on *The Mysterious Unknown*. At the beginning of 1908 Kamo, arrested in Berlin under the name of Mirsky, succeeded in evading extradition by simulating madness. At the same time the Paris police arrested Litvinov, who was in possession of a considerable quantity of 500 rouble notes derived from the Tiflis "ex." Various other Bolsheviks were arrested at Munich, Stockholm and Geneva for attempting to change these notes, Semashko and Olga Ravich among others.

The Mensheviks demanded an impartial inquiry, and the Central Committee, under Lenin's direction, entrusted the matter to a commission presided over by Chicherin. The latter, making rigid inquiry, found that Kamo was preparing to pillage the Mendelssohn Bank in Berlin by bomb throwing. Chicherin also discovered that the Bolsheviks had placed an order for special paper for the manufacture of bank notes. A certain quantity had already been sent through the dispatch agency of *Vorwärts* to Kuokkola in Finland, where Lenin and Zinoviev were living in secret at the time. Naturally *Vorwärts* was ignorant of the contents of the package. The man who provided the paper recognised Krassin as the customer from photographs. Lenin put a stop to these discoveries by persuading the Central Committee to transfer the inquiry to the "Bureau for foreign countries." But the Transcaucasian Committee, having made its own investigations, decided to exclude from the Party all the authors of the Tiflis coup, Stalin included. No name was mentioned in public, for fear of giving indications to the police; the same consideration prevented any open mention of false money.

Kamo had as a companion in arms a *boyevik* of remarkable personality, Alipi Tsintsadze, familiarly known as Koté. The latter was in prison at the time of the great exploit and therefore could take no part in it. But he had many others to his credit. His memoirs on this period are not without interest.

After the defeat of the revolution, an era of reaction set in at the beginning of 1906. Comrade Arsenius Djordjiashvili was entrusted with a mission to kill General Griaznov, a terrible reactionary, charged by the Government with the suppression of the revolutionary movement in Georgia. There was delay in carrying out the terrorist deed. Koba-Stalin sent for me and said: "If within the next week Djordjiashvili does not succeed in murdering Griaznov, we will give you the job, and for this purpose you must organise selected terrorists." But Djordjiashvili fulfilled his mission.

These lines show what sort of business Koba conducted and help to make his rôle clear: he did not himself execute operations, but directed those who did. Koté Tsintsadze proceeds as follows:

At this time the two sections worked in one organisation and were preparing for the "unity" Congress at Stockholm. Except for the Baku representatives the overwhelming majority of Transcaucasian delegates were Mensheviks. After the Congress it became clear that we Bolsheviks could not continue to work in one organisation with the Mensheviks. For my part I decided to create a purely Bolshevik club for expropriating State funds. Our advanced comrades, and particularly Koba-Stalin, approved my suggestion. In the middle of November 1906, the expropriators' club was organised and at the railway junction at Chiaturi we attacked a post office railway car, and took 21,000 roubles, of which 15,000 were sent to the Bolshevik fraction and the rest to our own group to provide for a series of expropriations later on. . . .

Stalin's line of conduct gradually becomes clearer. Sometimes he would give a free hand so as to take advantage of success without being compromised in the event of failure; sometimes he would urge on others without directly exposing himself. Generally speaking he would take no direct responsibility, but maintain a certain effective authority by delegation of powers to intermediaries between the head and the lower ranks of the organisation. He had plenty of physical courage, but it was better to live for the revolution than to die for it.

As for Kamo his troubles were not ended. His incredible story must be shortly told, not for its romantic interest but because of his close association with Stalin's political career. Moreover the life of this rebel illustrates the specific characteristics of revolutionary action in Russia; no other Party affiliated to the Socialist International could have produced a rebel of this type. Comparison of this "professional revolutionary" of the Leninist school with any other European Social-Democrat, any representative of English labour or of trade unionism in the Latin countries shows how violent is the contrast created by social environment and historical circumstances. It is true that we are dealing here with an Armenian from Georgia, but one could find the same type of men in St. Petersburg and in Moscow, in Poland and in the Urals.

Kamo was a refugee in Berlin, and was then denounced by one of the principal militant Bolsheviks, Jitomirsky, an agent of the Russian secret police, and arrested after search of his lodgings; the police found explosives and an electrical apparatus "discovered to be an infernal machine." Imprisoned in the Alt Moabit jail, not speaking German and pretending he understood Russian with difficulty, he was zealously defended by the Social-Democratic lawyer Oscar Cohn, who communicated to him a note from Krassin advising him to feign mental disease. He carried out the incredible feat of keeping up pretended violent madness for four years, and submitting to the treatment imposed for it. He stamped, shouted, tore his clothes, refused food and struck his keeper. He was shut up naked in an icy cell, but did not yield. Put under observation in the infirmary and subjected to horrible tests, he stood upright for four months, refused food, was forcibly fed at the expense of several broken teeth, tore out his hair, hanged himself, counting on intervention at the last moment, opened blood vessels with a sharpened bit of bone, and lost consciousness in a flood of blood. The doctors gave in, and Kamo was transferred to an asylum where his tortures recommenced.

In order to test his pretended insensibility, needles were stuck under his nails and he was touched with red hot irons. He bore his torments stoically. The professors concluded that his malady was real. In 1909, the administration handed him over to Russia, rather than provide for a foreigner. *Vorwärts* at Berlin, *L'Humanité* at Paris and other journals roused public opinion. Brought before the Council of War at Tiflis, he took from his blouse a bird he had tamed in prison, and began to feed it with crumbs. He was again placed under observation; and underwent new tests sufficient to drive a sane man mad. At last, in August 1911, thanks to Koté Tsintsadze, he achieved a marvellous escape after having spent three months in sawing through his chains and the window bars, nearly killing himself by falling on to a rock in the Kura (the rope had broken), but escaped, outwitted the search for him, and reached Batoum, where he stowed away in the hold of a ship. In the end he reached Paris and "Vladimir Ilyich" (Lenin).

Lenin thought Kamo's health much shaken (sic), and prescribed rest. The "Caucasus brigand," as Lenin humorously called him, set out for the "South." At Constantinople he was arrested, but was set at liberty through the intervention of Georgian monks of Notre Dame de Lourdes! He dispatched arms to Russia, was again arrested in Bulgaria, but the socialist Blagoyev helped him to escape. Arrested once more on board the boat, with luggage filled with explosives, he was released by the Turks and went to Greece. "Some months afterwards, by agreement with Vladimir Ilyich, Kamo returned to Russia to procure money for the Party, which was at that time in considerable straits."

In the Caucasus he gathered round him once more the survivors of his old squad, and in September 1912 occurred the unsuccessful attempt on the Kodjorsky road. Bachua Kupriashvili and Koté Tsintsadze, both of them brilliant shots, covered the retreat by shooting down seven Cossacks, but in vain. The *boyeviki* were captured. Imprisoned once more in the Metekh fortress, four death sentences were passed on Kamo.

Tsintsadze, who occupied the next cell, got a note through to him in a lamp, and received the following reply:

> I guessed, found the letter, resigned to death, absolutely calm. On my grave there should already be growing grass six feet high. One can't escape death for ever. One must die some day. But I shall try my luck again. Try any way of escape. Perhaps we shall once more have the laugh over our enemies. . . . I am in irons. Do what you like. I'm ready for anything.

The plan could not be carried out. Kamo was doomed. But the magistrate had a secret sympathy for this astonishing criminal, and prolonged the formalities until the tercentenary of the Romanov dynasty. Then came the Imperial Rescript commuting the death penalty for prisoners under conviction to twenty years' hard labour. A vile penitentiary regime was slowly killing the martyr to Bolshevik finance. In 1917 he was saved by the revolution, brought back to life and a new career.

It is difficult to imagine such a man in a western industrial environment, and it is hard to think of him as a contemporary. It is not fortuitous that the old Bolshevik Lepeshinsky should call him a mediaeval hero. The Russian people, wrote Leroy-Beaulieu, "may have received a visit from Diderot, they may own Voltaire's library, but they are still living in the age of theology. . . . For the great mass of the people the Middle Ages are still a reality." The unchanging fervour of a Kamo, his consistent passion for sacrifice, his resignation under suffering and in the face of death derive from a mysticism which is plainly an anachronism by any comparison with the rationalism of more developed countries, whatever the view taken of rationalism itself. "Marxism" has nothing whatever to do with his inextinguishable ardour.

There was a religious mentality about the little Bolshevik group at Tiflis of which Kamo was the leading spirit. It had voluntarily separated from the Party for form's sake after the Stockholm Congress, which forbade expropriations. Russian socialists recalling past times can still make its environment and its atmosphere live again. The town in state of siege, the streets patrolled night and day, the perpetual menace of raids by soldiers and police—these were the conditions under which the seven comrades led a community life, a separate "cell," but still maintaining their personal connections with Social-Democracy. Their lodging was open to all comers, in a typical Georgian house with doors and windows opening on to a long balcony; it consisted of two rooms furnished in a primitive way, the men occupying the larger and the two women the smaller room. They possessed a very rudimentary knowledge of socialist theory, several of them rarely read anything, but their devotion to the cause was boundless. Lenin, the incarnation of the Party in their eyes, was the object of a regular cult, and they burned with desire to distinguish themselves by some signal service. Full of kindliness in their relations as between comrades, they could be ferocious if they thought the interests of the Party were at stake. Wretched conditions of life undermined their bodily health; those who survived the repression died of tuberculosis.

Moral and social criteria of other places and other times are not always applicable to terrorists and expropriators, whose methods could not be grafted on a modern State. The crossed cheque, the bank transfer, more and more in use, and the means of coercion perfected by a strong Government, to a large extent eliminate the picturesque violence of the methods in vogue in peasant countries. The barbarity of the Tsarist regime engendered cruel methods of opposing it. In the shadow of Russo-Asiatic despotism the inevitable revolutionary conflagration is preluded by the glare of explosions. A story of Leonid Andreyev's *Sashka Yeguliov*, giving a picture of the "ex," reflects the sympathy felt in educated society for the rough avenging *boyeviki*. Violence answered violence; the end desired by a whole nation seemed to justify the means. It is hard to understand why Stalin has taken pains to obliterate all signs of his responsibility in this matter, unless the reason is a tardy regret for having sacrificed the lives of comrades while he himself stood aloof. Pilsudski does not blush for the part he played as leader of the Polish *bojowka*, and he plunged sword in hand into terrorism.

The "fighting organisation" of the Polish Socialist Party carried out a hundred "ex'es" on a large or small scale: Rogow, Mazowieck, Bezdany are the most important. Only in the last did Pilsudski personally take part, the rule of the *bojowka* being that each member must take part in at least one armed attack. The affair took place in the night of September 27, 1908, on the St. Petersburg-Warsaw line at the little station of Bezdany, where the *bojowci* cut the telephone and telegraph wires, seized a post-office car, terrorised the staff of the station and the car, and were able to "work" at their ease, carrying off 2,400,000 roubles according to an official biographer, though the figure is doubtful. From the confused accounts given in the *Novoye Vremya* it is impossible to extract a brief and comprehensible story. But it is true that Pilsudski made his will before the expedition; the precaution was unnecessary, for Bezdany was child's play compared with the Tiflis "ex."

The dissolution of the *bojowka* was one of the reasons for the schism of the Polish Socialist Party in 1906. The Nationalist Right, with Pilsudski and Daszynski, were more and more absorbed in secret military organisation. Similarly the "ex" deepened the gulf between Bolsheviks and Mensheviks in Russian Social-Democracy. But in this case it was an international Left which attached a fundamental importance to military and "technical" work. On both sides the men of action tended towards practical preparation, looking for tangible means of securing victory in imminent civil war. The Polish Social-Democrats, opponents of the Pilsudski Party because of their hostility to nationalism, had no objection whatever to his lucrative proceedings, and their reputed organiser, Leon Tyshko, employed them on mutual account with Lenin.

The money question, the invariable corollary of the idea of professional revolutionaries, gradually assumed a disproportionate place in the life of the Social-Democratic émigrés, which had undergone changes after the defeat; it envenomed the relations between the two sections of the Party. If the Bolsheviks were able to secure a majority in 1907 it was largely due to the enormous resources obtained by the "ex'es" which made it possible for them to maintain a legion of militants, to send emissaries to all quarters, to found journals, to distribute pamphlets, and to create more or less representative committees. The Caucasus was not the sole source of revenue. An ex-*boyevik* from the Urals, Sulimov, relates in his memoirs that his group paid to the Bolshevik Central Committee 60,000 roubles; 40,000 roubles to the Regional Committee, providing, among other things, for the publication of three newspapers; and in addition subsidised the journeys of delegates (certainly Bolsheviks) to the London Congress, paid for the course for instructors in fighting at Kiev, the school for bomb throwers at Lemberg, the traffic in contraband, etc. Although the revenue of the Party central organisation did not exceed a hundred roubles a month in bad years, the Bolsheviks had considerable sums at their disposal, though never enough for their needs. They sent, for example, a thousand roubles a month to their St. Petersburg organisation, and five hundred to Moscow. The Mensheviks, obstinately attached to European legalism, reduced to relying on the infinitesimal subscriptions, could not fight on equal terms with competitors who had no scruple; nor submit to the rule of a factitious majority. There was no discipline, and two parties wore one another down within the Party, which was doomed to break up anew into new fractions and sub-fractions.

3

STALIN had seen Lenin for the second time at the Stockholm Congress, but his recollections of the meeting contain nothing worth quoting. The third meeting was at the London Congress in 1907, and there is nothing interesting in Stalin's narrative of that; he confines himself to expressing unbounded admiration for Lenin, who was unperturbed by his success. There was nothing to be excited about in a precarious majority of a few votes, when one knew at what price and by what means it had been secured. If Lenin had only merited praise of this kind, his name would long since have been forgotten.

The Party had undergone great changes during the revolution; it had developed in numbers, in experience, and in political maturity. At the Stockholm Conference there were 36 workmen and 108 intellectuals, who represented 343 prosecutions for political crime, and 286 years of prison and deportation. At London there were 116 workmen, and 196 intellectuals and others. The statistics state that these included 56 "professional revolutionaries" and 118 delegates "living at the expense of the Party" (without indicating how many militants of this class there were in Russia). The delegates had against their names 710 prosecutions, 834 years in prisons, fortresses, and deportation, of which 597 years had actually been served, and 210 escapes. Finally, in a single year the Mensheviks had increased their membership from 18,000 to 43,000; the Bolsheviks from 13,000 to 33,000; the total number of Bundists (33,000), Poles (28,000), Letts (13,000) had doubled.

The London Church in which the Congress held its thirty-five sessions was the scene of stormy debates. Trotsky, escaped from Siberia, took up a "centrist" position, and was almost the only conciliator between the two nearly equal sections (the Bolsheviks supported by the Poles and Letts, the Mensheviks by the Bundists). "What has the schism done for you?" he asked the two sides. "To do the same thing side by side, to march on common ground and mutually tread on one another's toes. And what is the result? You are compelled to reunite, first on a federative basis, and then in a congress of unity." He proceeded to conjure up the danger of a future schism with a succession of alternating unions and separations. His relations with the Left were still strained (the President even had to call him to order for having accused Lenin of hypocrisy), but there appeared to be a basis for a political rapprochement. He had the satisfaction of hearing a speech from Rosa Luxemburg which came very near his own conception of the "permanent revolution."

A new feature in the Congress was the appearance of a "parliamentary section," who criticised the Bolsheviks severely. After the brusque dissolution of the first Duma, followed by the Vyborg Manifesto, by which all the democratic parties repudiated in advance the debts contracted by Tsarism without the assent of the national representatives, the Party had taken part in the electoral struggle in spite of the unfavourable conditions created by the electoral property qualification. Internal discord at once appeared on the question of the tactics to be followed with regard to the Kadets. "Strike together, but march separately," Marx's formula, rediscovered by Plekhanov and adopted by Lenin, did not quite solve the problem.

Martov proposed to support liberalism in cases where the choice lay between it and reaction, and to conclude an electoral agreement, even in the primary elections. Lenin consented to understandings of this kind *except* in the primary elections, advocating as more advantageous a left bloc, with the *Trudoviki* (Labour), or with the Social Revolutionaries as occasion offered. The Central Committee, and also a Party Conference held in Finland (November 1906) had adopted the Menshevik view. A "Red" Duma succeeded the Kadet Duma; fifty-four Social-Democrats entered Parliament, of whom two-thirds were Mensheviks and one-third Bolsheviks. In Georgia Social-Democracy triumphed over all its adversaries and rivals.

Under the perpetual menace of dissolution and in the absence of real parliamentary immunity, the parliamentary fraction had a difficult task, and their courage and goodwill failed to solve all the difficulties. In their illusions about the Kadets, "His Majesty's Opposition," and their prudent language, they ill-reflected the combative state of mind of the active majority of the Party. Lenin criticised them severely. Tseretelli, Leader of the Duma, and Rapporteur to the Congress, had declared: "The struggle for freedom cannot be conducted without some sort of coalition with bourgeois democracy." Lenin accused him of reformism, and reproached the deputies with inclination to bourgeois parliamentarism. Trotsky, who agreed to some extent with the Bolsheviks on the principle but objected to their tone, spoke against them, and drew down on himself the reply from Lenin: "It is not wise, nor worthy of a working-class party, to conceal differences."

The majority of the Bolsheviks voted against Axelrod's proposition for a "workers' congress," for summoning all the socialist parties and workers' groups in one large assembly, a first step possibly towards a kind of Labour Party on the English model. They secured the adoption of a motion which gave Social-Democracy a directing rôle in the trade unions (only recently formed in Russia and usually by socialists), and established organic connection between them and the Party. But on questions of internal management they could not secure a majority; in the new Central Committee they had a majority of only one vote, and that an uncertain one. The Bolshevik Centre continued to exist in secret, directing the "war of partisans," and the expropriations which the Congress had just forbidden.

Stalin saw Trotsky for the first time in London but Trotsky probably did not notice him. The leader of the St. Petersburg Soviet did not make chance acquaintances, or make friends except on the basis of real affinities. Outside of the Caucasus, Koba was unknown except by a very small circle of Bolsheviks. He did not speak at the Congress. He had succeeded in getting a seat as representative of the Borchalo district, where no branch of the Party existed, but with less success this time; the authorised delegation from the Caucasus protested against this fabrication, and Koba remained only on tolerance and without the right to vote. A "true Bolshevik" did not bother about a detail like that. The Tiflis affair soon showed how much Koba cared about the Congress, its orders and its resolutions.

The official biography relates that Koba directed the *Dro* (Times) at Tiflis in 1906, and in the following year the *Bakinsky Rabochi* (Baku Workman) at Baku. He also wrote a series of articles on *Anarchism and Socialism* which have remained unknown. These small local journals, whose editors simplified and diluted Lenin's writings, had an ephemeral existence of a few weeks; as for the articles in question they are not reprinted. Stalin did not then pretend to any rank as a theorist and writer. His more modest aim was to procure control of the Bolshevik group at Baku, outside Georgia, where he felt he could get no further. After so notorious a defiance of a decision of the Congress, his exclusion from the Party at Tiflis was inevitable; prudence counselled a speedy change in his field of action. Baku was the nearest place, and one of steadily increasing importance.

The ancient Perso-Tartar town, now blackened with naphtha, grew like an American city. Its population rose from 14,000 in 1865 to 112,000 at the 1897 Census, and it now numbers 446,000. In odd contrast with the petroleum wells, it has kept its mosques and minarets, its vast oriental bazaar, and labyrinth of sordid streets crowded with Muslims, and its temple of the Fire Worshippers, guarded by a Parsee. The petroleum wells, which produced 340,000 *poods* in 1862, were already yielding 636,000,000 in 1902 and attracted a wretched and illiterate proletariat of Turks, Persians, Armenians and Russians, whom the two opposed Social-Democratic groups each sought to dominate.

After the departure of Krassin and then of Knuniantz, who joined the Mensheviks, the outstanding militants of Lenin's fraction were S. Shaumian and P. Djaparidze. The latter (who must not be confused with his namesake, Artshil, deputy to the Duma), devoted himself to trade union work. Stalin, who competed with Shaumian for pre-eminence in the Party, determined to oust him. The two men were soon at daggers drawn. "Between the two there began a long struggle, pushed to such length that the Baku workmen *even suspected Djugashvili of having denounced Shaumian to the police* and wanted to bring him up before a Party tribunal. He was saved by arrest and exile in Siberia." This episode, known to old militants and related in the article in *Brdzolis Khma*, already quoted, has never been cleared up. The dates are uncertain, but it is a fact that Shaumian's arrest was attributed in Party circles to denunciation and that Koba was suspected.

There is nothing to prove the accusation. Such proofs hardly ever exist. But are the moral presumptions sufficient to support the terrible suspicion? Accumulated indications may perhaps lead to certainty. What is certain and significant is that Stalin's own comrades should have thought him capable of giving up a brother-in-arms to rid himself of a rival. For the second time he was accused of intrigue and greed of power, and the accusation does not come from the enemy, but from the ranks of the Party and the fraction. Whether deserved or not, the assumption was made.

To this period also belong certain special practices only vaguely referred to by Bolsheviks to-day—manœuvres for the extortion of funds (vymogatelstvo) for the Party treasury by various methods of pressure on the employers in the petroleum industry. For the same reason it would be premature to seek to verify certain stories put about by those who saw much of Stalin at Baku, among others those relating to the Sakvarelidze false money affair. To note them even without mentioning names would be to reveal the sources and jeopardise the liberty of those who committed the indiscretions. The silence imposed on Stalin's former fellow-workers in prison or in exile is eloquent enough in a country where the most detailed and unreserved memoirs are published.

Even Koba's own writings are systematically suppressed. Trotsky has stated that "During the whole period of the reaction, from 1907 to 1911, there is not a single document available, whether article, letter or resolution, in which Stalin has expressed his opinion on the actual situation or on the future. It is impossible that such documents should not be in existence. It is impossible that they should not have been preserved, if only in the police archives. Why are they not published?"

More interesting information on the Koba of these days has been published abroad by the Social Revolutionary Vereshchak, who presided over the Soviet of soldiers of the Tiflis garrison. How much confidence can be placed in it? Simon Vereshchak had a faultless moral reputation in various revolutionary circles; the Bolsheviks themselves gave indisputable proof of it by reproducing his recollections, in their own fashion, in Pravda, the official Party organ. Under the heading of "Certified Correct," and, exceptional circumstance, twice over, on

February 7, 1928, and December 20, 1929, the paper published a feuilleton by Demian Biedny, a close friend of Stalin's, in which extracts from Vereshchak alternate with a commentary by the Bolshevik writer. "Certified Correct," said *Pravda*, by way of emphasising and confirming the passages which seemed to them likely to enhance their master's reputation. But a simple comparison of Vereshchak's memoirs with Demian Biedny's feuilleton reveals a clever, deceptive selection, which gives an inexact impression of the document in question. The source only has to be consulted to re-establish the truth and learn more about the real Koba.

He had been arrested in March 1908, after Shaumian, then imprisoned in the Bailovskia jail before being exiled for two years under surveillance to the province of Vologda, north of Moscow. He spent eight months in prison, where Vereshchak knew him well. Prison was a good place for estimating character for many reasons. In the Baku jail, intended to accommodate 400 prisoners, but at that time occupied by more than 1,500, the "politicals" had their own economic commune and a doyen assisted by a commission on which Bolsheviks, Mensheviks and Social Revolutionaries had equal representation. Vereshchak was a member of the commission, and was thus able to collect biographical information about Stalin which at all events reflected current opinion. It is easy to discriminate between facts and comments.

According to Vereshchak, the young Djugashvili had been excluded from the Seminary for being a member and leader of a clandestine socialist club: "His comrades in the club say that soon after his expulsion, they were in turn expelled. After an interval it was ascertained that the expulsions were the result of a *denunciation conveyed by Stalin* to the Rector. In the subsequent explanations with his comrades he did not deny the accusation, but *justified the action* by saying that the expelled students, who lost their claim to the priesthood, would become good revolutionaries." A parallel is suggested between the two denunciations, for Vereshchak evidently knew nothing of the

Shaumian affair, which he does not mention. If this is a coincidence of error, it is a disturbing one.

In prison Stalin was admitted without difficulty to the prisoners' commune. The jail, says Vereshchak, "was a revolutionary school for propaganda and fighting purposes. Among the leaders of groups and clubs Koba professed his Marxian principles." The newcomer was cautious in speech and not very communicative. "While the 'politicals' tried not to mix with ordinary criminals, and specially warned their younger members against doing so, Koba was always to be seen in the company of murderers, blackmailers and robbers. . . . He was always impressed by men who had brought off an 'affair.' He looked on politics as an 'affair' requiring dexterity. He shared a cell with the two forgers of 500 rouble notes, Sakvarelidze and his brother Niko, then a Bolshevik." Vereshchak describes Koba as given to formal controversies.

The agrarian question was at that time exciting hot discussions, in which the antagonists sometimes came to blows. I shall never forget an agrarian debate organised by Koba at which his comrade, Sergo Ordjonikidze . . . brought home his conclusion by striking his fellow speaker, the Socialist Revolutionary Ilya Kartsevadze, in the face, for which he received a thorough thrashing from the Social Revolutionaries.

Koba's personal appearance and his rudeness in controversy made him an unpleasing speaker. His speeches lacked wit and his statement of his case was dry. His mechanised memory was astounding.

He was always ready to quote Marx, and so impress the young and ignorant. In Transcaucasia he seemed a sort of local Lenin. . . . "His remarkable lack of principle and his practical cunning made him a master of tactics." He hated the Mensheviks, whose arguments he was incapable of meeting. "*All means are justified against them,*" he said.

When the whole prison was nervously excited on account of a midnight execution, Koba would sleep or quietly recite in Esperanto, the future language of the International, he thought. As for solidarity among the prisoners, "he never proposed any measures of protest, nor did he resist the most extreme or ridiculous treatment. . . . He did not instigate revolt, but he supported the instigators. That made the prisoners look on him as a good comrade." One day (Vereshchak is certainly wrong here in his date), the politicals were thrashed by a company of soldiers. "Koba walked along under the blows of the butt ends of rifles with head unbent, with a book in his hands." This is the phrase to which *Pravda* paid homage.

Another point, "partly explaining perhaps why Stalin remained so long obscure," was "his capacity of secretly urging others to action while himself remaining aloof." This confirms the description given of his conduct during the "expropriations." One day a young Georgian was cruelly struck down in a corridor of the prison on account of a rumour accusing him of being an *agent provocateur;* the body covered with blood was taken away on a stretcher. It was asserted that no one knew anything of the victim or of the accusation. "A long time after, it became clear that *Koba had originated the rumour*." How can one help recalling the two earlier anonymous denunciations?

On another occasion the ex-Bolshevik Mitka G—— stabbed to death a young workman, unknown to him, in the belief that he was a spy. Now the execution of a traitor or a spy on the initiative of an individual has never been permitted in revolutionary circles; there is a rigid rule requiring group responsibility. For a long time the affair remained obscure. "At last Mitka let it be known that he thought he had been led into error. *The instigation came from Koba*." A fourth incident of this kind, which justifies the following remarks by Vereshchak, and confirms many other statements.

This aptitude for striking secretly by the hands of others while remaining in the background himself showed Koba as an astute intriguer, using all means to gain his end and escaping the penalties and the responsibility for the actions in question. This characteristic of Stalin's was displayed in all his "affairs." In the organisation of forgers issuing 500 rouble notes, in the notorious robberies of State funds, Koba's hand was felt, but he was never implicated in the prosecutions, although forgers and "expropriators" had been imprisoned with him. Moreover he insolently assailed the Social Revolutionaries for terrorism and expropriation.

Such were the essential data which *Pravda* was so imprudent as to "certify correct," under the censor's scissors, thanking the author for "having in spite of himself traced, though in faint lines, the living portrait of a true Bolshevik." These data, indeed, complete and confirm the observations already made. Certain characteristics emerge from the picture. The first is a "will to power" disproportionate to the will to know, almost attenuating the Nietzschean conception of the end of man to material and practical requirements, ignoring the various forms of intellectual activity, analysis and synthesis and aesthetic appreciation, serving the instinctive rebelliousness of a man who had never been reconciled to his environment (the spirit of revolt not always finding expression in the concept of a loftier humanity or of a rational organisation of society). The second characteristic is a narrow realism, efficacious within strict limits; and with it a lack of appreciation of theory or of general ideas—a temper of mind inherited from his peasant ancestors. The third is a religious education overlaid with a travesty of Marxism consisting of elementary formulae learned by heart like a catechism, and lastly oriental dexterity in intrigue, unscrupulousness, lack of sensitiveness in personal relations, and scorn of men and of human life. Koba, more and more a professional revolutionary, felt himself to be hard and cold as the steel from which he adopted his name.

In July 1909 he escaped from Solvychegodsk, in the province of Vologda, where he had been sent to live under surveillance, and lived in hiding at St. Petersburg with Savchenko, quartermaster of the regiment of Horse Guards. Flight was easy for exiles of this category, only subjected to obligatory residence in a certain place, and to report periodically to the authorities. A month later he returned to Baku, and resumed his subterranean political activity until March 1910, when he was again arrested and, after some months in prison, sent back to Solvychegodsk for five years. There, in a sparsely populated forest region where there were many exiles, "he helped to form a Social-Democratic organisation, delivered lectures, and trained propagandists," if one can trust the account of V. Nevsky. In fact nothing is known of his existence in exile, and the vague statement in the dictionary adds nothing to the original sources of information. A police dossier shown at an exhibition at Veliky-Ustiug under the heading "conduct," notes to his advantage, "rude, insolent, disrespectful to the authorities."

The period of his activity in the Caucasus was at an end; exclusion from the Party practically drove him from Georgia, and Baku was too hot for him. What did he leave behind him in the town? "A citadel of Bolshevism," replies his official biographer. A flagrant inexactitude. The "citadel" dissolved rapidly into fusion with the Mensheviks. Another revolution was required to reconstitute a Bolshevik group at Baku.

In the spring of 1911, Koba fled again, and went to St. Petersburg, where he went by the name of Ivanov, spending his nights at the lodgings of his friend Todria. On September 10th of that year, he was arrested, spent some weeks in prison, and was exiled for the third time, on this occasion for three years, to Solvychegodsk. Shortly afterwards he escaped again; at the end of 1911 he returned to St. Petersburg. The official biographies are not in detailed agreement, but the errors and contradictory statements are unimportant. It is only necessary to note the relatively light sentences and the slightness of the surveillance, indications that the police did not regard Koba as very dangerous. The revolutionaries in the "dangerous" category were more severely treated and better watched.

In February 1912, a decision taken by a small committee abroad made Koba a member of the Central Committee of the Party. What explanation is there for the rapid advance to the supreme controlling organ of the Party of a man who had been expelled from it? It is that the Party at this moment was not one, but two. Trotsky's fears were justified; a new schism had thrown the "enemy brothers," henceforward not brothers at all, into violent opposition. Lenin had gathered round him his "professional revolutionaries" and had chosen the most faithful of them as his "group of clandestine organisers." Stalin filled his requirements. There were as yet no definitive boundaries, and many Social-Democrats crossed the line from one to the other, but

Bolshevism and Menshevism were crystallising into irreconcilable systems.

4

IMMEDIATELY after the London Congress, the Red Duma had been dissolved, the Constitution derided, and the Social-Democratic deputies, with Tseretelli at their head, imprisoned and deported. This *coup d'état* of June 1907 may be said to indicate the end of this phase of the revolution. The country made no protest. Lenin, who had up till then insisted on keeping armed rebellion on the programme, could no longer hope for an immediate union of workmen, peasants and soldiers in victorious insurrection, and resigned himself to the reality; reaction was general and profound, and would be more so. He recognised the fear and apathy of the masses. All the socialist parties were exhausted, disorganised and disabled. Repression hastened the decline of the workers' movement; journals were suppressed, printing offices closed, trade unions prohibited and persecuted. Social-Democracy was not the least seriously affected. Zinoviev admits that "it may be said plainly that at this unhappy period the Party as a whole ceased to exist."

Tsarism enjoyed a respite largely due to the international situation. In the game of European alliances, Imperial Russia, in spite of the disastrous war in the Far East, was an important, though over-estimated, factor. Loans made by French capitalism, deaf to the warning of the St. Petersburg Soviet and to the Vyborg Manifesto, contributed substantially to the consolidation of the autocracy. The Prime Minister, Stolypin, though he kept the gallows busy, also prepared his agrarian reform, facilitating the formation of a class of small rural proprietors in the hope of disarming the simmering peasant revolt. "Agrarian Bonapartism," said Lenin. After two years of famine the harvest of 1907 and the exceptional plenty of the two following years gave a strong impulse to agriculture, in the midst of the industrial crisis.

The revolution, conquered, did not admit defeat, but resistance was maintained only by the conscious few. Socialist organisations of all shades lost members in less time than it had taken to enrol them. Retreat, discouragement, decadence and disintegration are the terms which recur on each page of this chapter of social history. Indifference in political matters, a renaissance of religious mysticism, eroticism in literature, scepticism and pessimism, all of them phenomena caused by the disorder following defeat and despair, created an atmosphere unfavourable to Social-Democracy. In addition to losses in physical strength, the Party was entering on an era of demoralisation and disintegration of its forces and its central organisation.

Lenin, in choosing his "professional revolutionaries," had sought courage rather than intellectual gifts. This enabled him to create a skeleton organisation, carefully graded and disciplined, to use for his own ends energy such as that of the fighting squads which the Mensheviks were neglecting; he was able to summon to Helsingfors a conference of his technical and military experts, who formed the embryo of a Red Guard. But any such "active" militant, useful to some extent in the hands of an experienced chief, tended to become "passive" when left to deal on its own initiative with a situation requiring political intelligence and an historic sense. So long as the "best man" was not definitely imposed on his subordinates, to handle the instrument in the best interests of the cause, he wasted his energies in securing recognition of his authority, and waging a constant struggle to maintain it. Without him the phalanx was a body without a head. To leave it to lieutenants was to invite disaster.

Shortly after the London Conference, Lenin found himself in opposition to his own fraction, and his success at the recent Congress was shown to be illusory. At the Party Conference held at Vyborg in July there came up again the question of participating in the elections, this time to a Parliament in which representation of the workers would be practically wiped out under the altered laws. The Bolsheviks wanted a boycott, with the exception of Lenin, who did not hesitate to vote with the Mensheviks in favour of participation, and had no support; he was alone in his group, says Kamenev, or almost alone. Koba, a fervent "boycottist," was not present, but Zinoviev and Kamenev were there to voice a pseudo-revolutionary intransigence on the morrow of the revolution. The most serious aspect of the matter for Lenin was the conflict with his closest colleagues, Bogdanov and Krassin, members of the secret Bolshevik Centre known as the "Little Trinity." It was the beginning of a bitter internal struggle among the Bolsheviks.

The "Black Duma," the third, only included fifteen Social-Democrats, most of them Mensheviks. The Georgians had once more surpassed all expectations, and their deputies, Chkheidze and Gueguechkory became the most prominent spokesmen of socialism in Russia. The character of this Duma is well described in the famous words of the Minister Kokovtsev: "Thank God, Parliament is no more." But, said Lenin, that was no reason for not trying to get into it. The "boycottists" became either "ultimatists," advocating the dispatch to Social-Democratic deputies of an ultimatum imposing on them the orders of the Central Committee, or "otzovists," advocating their withdrawal. Lenin, at odds with this Left of the Left, manœuvred carefully before deciding on open war. Martov notes in his *History* that Lenin associated himself with the "ultimatists" twice, in 1907 and in 1908. Finally he made a stand, refusing even to recognise "ultimatumism" as a legal form of Marxism. He called its adherents "Mensheviks turned inside out," while they accused him of Menshevism pure and simple and called him a renegade.

On the Menshevik side the position was no better. The majority, with Potressov and Larin, wanted to "liquidate" the Party as moulded by pre-revolutionary circumstances, to make an end of "illegal" action, to found a new Party adapted to new conditions, and to keep it on "legal" lines at all costs. They were the Right of the Right. Martov and Dan, attracted at first by this tendency, sought to put "legal" action first, without categorically condemning "illegal" work, which would, they thought, die a natural death. Plekhanov represented a third Menshevik position, the nearest to Lenin's, definitely favourable to the maintenance of the clandestine Party.

Lenin, logical in his own standpoint, wanted to combine

"legal" with "illegal" action, laying most stress on the second. The Left, inspired by Bogdanov, demanded a return to the earlier conspiratorial methods and abandonment of trade union-ism as well as of Parliament. Trotsky, at the head of an inter-mediate group, professed himself to be "neither Bolshevik nor Menshevik, but revolutionary Social-Democrat," and aimed at reconciling the irreconcilable. Lenin was soon confronted in his section of the Party with a Right Wing, unionist and concilia-tory, advocating any sort of compromise with the Mensheviks and acting on the advice of Nogin, Rykov and Sokolnikov. In addition to all these divisions there were the national groups—Poles, Letts, Bundists—leaving out of account minor complica-tions; such was the situation among the leaders of a Party which claimed to be the natural guide of the proletariat in matters of theory. Under the circumstances it is comprehensible that a man like Riazanov should stand aside and prefer to devote himself to editing the posthumous works of Marx and Engels.

It is impossible here to follow up the divisions of Social-Democracy in their various proceedings, general conferences and sectional meetings, learned theories and transcendental con-siderations—a theme arduous for specialists. The essential is to watch those of the leaders who influenced the events which transformed the unknown Koba into the surprising Stalin, and to know what were the results of their agreements and disagree-ments. For the same reason we shall abstain from recalling the changing fortunes of competing papers and reviews. In this mass of detail there is nothing valuable for future generations.

In 1908 Lenin had asked Trotsky to collaborate in the *Proletarian*, a Bolshevik paper, and had been met with a refusal. In a letter to Gorky he called this attitude a *pose*. In later con-troversies he called Trotsky a *poseur* and a "phrasemaker," words expressing his dislike of fine words and magniloquence, so alien to his own sober diction. Trotsky thought he was more useful outside the Party divisions, and played a lone hand in his *Pravda*, waiting for an opportunity of reunion. At the end of the year, a Party conference had condemned both the Right and the Left wings, acting under the influence of Lenin, who was determined to "liquidate the liquidators" and to fight those of his old disciples who had become "liquidators of the Left." A Bolshevik committee in 1909 confirmed the tactics of "war on two, fronts." Moreover, while the Left demanded the continuance of conspiratorial and terrorist methods, Lenin secured the disavowal of "fighting methods degenerating into pure adventure," the dissolution of the last fighting units, and the exclusion of belated "expropriators." When he thought tactics and methods were out of date he did not hesitate to strike hard if he failed to convince those who moved too slowly; he sometimes ignored his own earlier instructions. That did not prevent him, as we have seen, from sending Kamo in 1912 to the Caucasus, to risk his life on the road to Kodjor. . . .

This attitude meant rupture with the Left. Lenin lost not only Krassin, but Bazarov, the economist, Pokrovsky, the historian, Gorky, the great writer, and lesser auxiliaries, Alexinsky, Liadov, Menzhinsky, Lunacharsky and Manuilsky. But he was not the man to shrink from losses entailed by hopeless disagreement with his ideas. It was essential, to use his own expression, to show "steadfastness in the struggle not only on the holidays of revolution but on the ordinary week-days of counter-revolution." He reproached the Left with "repeating a formula divorced from the series of circumstances which had produced it and assured its success, and applying it to conditions essentially different." During the revolution, he said, we learned to "speak French," now we must learn to "speak German," that is to say, to follow up the heroism of the revolutionary period by patient organisation appropriate to the new situation.

He remained an impenitent "Jacobin" of the proletariat, with an unreserved admiration for the "great French Revolution whose vitality and powerful influence on humanity is demonstrated by the wild hatred which it still provokes"; he was haunted by the French national tradition of 1793, "perhaps the final model for one order of revolutionary methods." But the hour for Jacobin methods had not yet sounded in Russia. Meanwhile, after having "spoken French," and advised "speaking German," he never ceased "speaking Russian," sounding all possibilities, weighing opportunities, calculating the chances of keeping the Party on the right track, avoiding alike belated or premature insurrection inspired by romantic motives, and constitutional and parliamentary illusions.

Always to "speak Russian," even when borrowing theory and practice from other revolutionary movements, this was the secret of his superiority over his adversaries. He was a disciple of Marx, but undogmatic, eager in the pursuit of science and knowledge, always alive to the teachings of experience, capable of sincerely recognising, surmounting and making good his errors, and consequently of rising above himself. Endowed with the temperament of a leader, and with a sure sense for the real and the concrete, he had in addition Russian intuition. When Trotsky, Axelrod, Martov and Dan, impressed by the continuous growth of socialism and the numerical strength of the trade unions in Germany, advocated the "Europeanisation" of Russian Social-Democracy, a radical change in mentality, Lenin, who had earlier told the Mensheviks enamoured of parliamentarism *not to copy German models*, replied that the character of any Social-Democracy was determined by the economic and political conditions of a country. No one had more respect for the original methods of a workers' party, and he did not wish to model the Russian revolutionary movement on any other, but was willing to learn something from all schools. He took part in the International Socialist congresses at Stuttgart in 1907, and at Copenhagen in 1910, but abstained from laying down the law to anyone, reserving his criticisms for the "Girondins" of his Party.

In the common parlance of political topography, Trotsky belonged to the Centre, from which point of vantage he reproved Right and Left extremists; his standpoint bore apparent similarity to Lenin's; in reality it was quite different. The latter opposed both Wings, and ran the risk of detaching them from the Party, while the former dreamed of conciliating all groups, directing his main attack on the Bolsheviks as being the most serious obstacle to unity. Trotsky denounced Lenin's "sectarian spirit, individualism of the intellectual, and ideological fetichism." He maintained that Bolshevism and Menshevism had not struck deep root and were rivals for *"influence over a proletariat still politically immature."* Martov compared the Leninists to the American socialist sect of Daniel de Leon and regarded the Russian experiment as a "victory of Blanquist and anarchist ignorance over Marxian science"; he ascribed to the Bolsheviks the responsibility for Russian Social Democracy's having learnt "to 'speak Russian' too exclusively and of neglecting to 'speak European.' "

Lenin's reply was: "Yes, the Russian proletariat is much less mature politically than the western proletariat. But of all classes of Russian society, the proletariat showed the highest degree of political maturity in 1905 to 1907." He held his ground against his two opponents, developing the following argument: "Martov and Trotsky confound different historical periods in comparing Russia, which is only now completing its bourgeois revolution, to Europe where it is long since over." But above all he concerned himself with Trotsky, whom he condemned. To summarise Lenin's own words, Trotsky's sonorous and empty phrases were those of a Tartarin de Tarascon, he was accused of hole and corner diplomacy, of the methods of a procuress, and of wishing to stifle discord instead of searching out its causes, of following the principle of "live and let live." At the International Congress at Copenhagen, in alliance with Plekhanov, always hostile to Trotsky, he tried to induce the Russian delegation to censure him as guilty of harsh criticism in *Vorwärts* (August 1910), of both Mensheviks and Bolsheviks, the latter for the expropriations; but Riazanov and Lunacharsky intervened with success to prevent it.

Thus relations between the strongest personalities in the Party were envenomed, in spite of their agreement on the faults of the Left and Right Wings. In January 1910, the Central Committee met to make a final attempt to secure internal peace. Eight fractions were represented, without counting minor groups. The principal personages achieved a compromise on the basis of repudiating the faults of the "liquidators" on both sides, of reorganising the central organisation and the press. The Central Committee was to be transferred to Russia, with a bureau abroad, and Trotsky's *Pravda* became its official organ. But these decisions were violated by all sections who resumed their liberty of mutual attack. An inexplicable state of things if only the arguments exchanged in public are taken into account, but quite comprehensible to anyone knowing the real reasons kept secret outside the Party. These are to be found especially in a pamphlet of the time, *Saviours or Destroyers,* in which Martov recapitulates a long series of grievances against the Bolsheviks, and sets out the facts too long unknown except to a few initiates.

Martov's views are disputable, and have been abundantly discussed, but no doubt has been cast on his veracity, even by his most impassioned opponents. Krupskaya, in her *Recollections,* testifies to the great esteem which Lenin always had for him, even in the midst of the fiercest factional disputes. Martov was an extremely sensitive man, who, "thanks to the delicacy of his perceptions, could comprehend Lenin's ideas and develop them with great ability," she wrote, and Lenin "renewed relations with him whenever he came into line at all." During the War of 1914, Lenin said in public that the *Goloss,* in which Martov wrote, "is the best socialist journal in Europe" and often expressed the desire of coming to an understanding with his old comrade of St. Petersburg. Trotsky calls him "one of the most tragic figures of the revolutionary movement, a gifted writer, a resourceful politician, a man with a mind brilliant but not sufficiently virile, clear-sighted, but lacking in will-power." However that may be, the sincerity and truthfulness of his testimony cannot be contested. Moreover, other sources provide details and facts which confirm his allegations.

The pamphlet reports incidents arising inside the Central Committee which made even a minimum of harmony impossible. Discord began over the "Anarcho-Blanquism" of the Leninists, "the product of the contradictory conditions of development of the Russian working-class movement," the advantageous effect of which during open civil war as stimulating revolutionary energy is not denied by Martov. But the infractions of the resolutions passed by Congress on the terrorist activity had fatal consequences in the end. Expropriation developed into brigandage, and compromised the Social-Democratic Party, introducing the seeds of failure and disintegration. The funds seized were not used only for arms, but in the interests of a faction and sometimes even for personal ends. The pro-Bolshevik committees in Russia, accustomed to live on funds provided by their organisers, disappeared as resources declined. The Bolshevik Centre exercised a regular occult dictatorship, thanks to its unauthorised ramifications and its funds, behind the back of the Central Committee, even though that Committee had a Leninist majority. Lenin was the centre of "an Order of Jesuits" within the Party, professing the cynical amoralism of Nechayev. The money question was disastrous. The Bolshevik Centre went so far as to "expropriate the Central Committee" of an immense sum earmarked for the Party. A series of scandals occupied the Party leaders. A Bolshevik named Victor defrauded the trustees of a considerable legacy, the possession of which was disputed between the two sections after the testator's death. The division of the money between the relatives of the testator and the Party was made the occasion of fresh threats from Victor, who wanted to deprive the heirs of their share. The affair had to be submitted to a commission nominated by the Social Revolutionary Party, as being neutral. The Bolshevik Centre was accused by the *boyeviki* of the Ural District (the Lbovtsy, from the name of their leader Lbov) of having taken their money improperly; the detachment of partisans at Perm had made an agreement with the Bolshevik "Technical Military Bureau" for a consignment of arms, paid for in advance, while the Central Committee had dissolved the said Bureau, which did not deliver the arms and refused to refund the money. Then there was the Tiflis "ex" and its repercussions, the difficulties raised in the Party by the *camorra* of those who changed the expropriated 500 rouble notes, and the arrest of various accomplices (Litvinov and Semashko), and the discovery at Berlin of Kamo's infernal machine. The Central Committee had to decide to destroy the remaining notes to circumscribe the danger. On top of this came the forgery affair, for which the paper bought by Krassin had been detected by the Reichsbank. There was also a case of an *agent provocateur,* many other suspicious cases, and a story of falsifications by Zinoviev. Added to all this were personal quarrels pursued to the point of folly, requiring investigation committees, juries of honour, and party tribunals.

These interminable discords, which had nothing to do with differences on theory, assumed alarming proportions in a period of political and social depression in which incidents took on the aspect of events. The quarrel over the inheritance, with its unexpected complications, attracted excessive attention, and aggravated misunderstanding. Private correspondence of this period, some of it published, gives evidence of this. Later writings by Trotsky frequently quoted in controversy, allude to "an expropriation within the Party," and to "dirty money" extracted from Kautsky and Clara Zetkin by the Bolsheviks. It is always the old tale.

The matter might be dismissed, if the eternal and disgusting question of cash had not acquired so much importance for international Bolshevism. A student, Nicholas Schmidt, the son of a rich furniture manufacturer, who had joined the Social-Democracy, died in prison, leaving to the Party a large fortune which he had inherited from V. Morosov. The Bolsheviks, as interested persons, sent to Moscow to supervise the transfer; one of their members, a lawyer, who betrayed his trust, entered into relations with the testator's eldest sister and secured for the Bolsheviks only a third of the estate. Another emissary, Victor (Taratuta), married the younger sister, and threatened her pro-Menshevik relations with energetic action by the Caucasian *boyeviki* if the whole sum was not paid over. There followed a complaint to the Central Committee, intervention by Martov, arbitration, conflicting claims, etc. The last slice of the booty, entrusted to Kautsky, Clara Zetkin and Franz Mehring pending a final settlement, fell into the hands of the Bolsheviks, always more successful than their rivals in this sort of thing.

Other issues arise in this doubtful business. The Social-Democrat Voytinsky relates, at second hand, that Lenin was supposed to have justified the employment of this man Victor by remarking: "He has this advantage, that he stops at nothing.

. . . Would you for the sake of money have been capable of allowing yourself to be kept by a rich bourgeois woman? No. Nor would I, it would have been beyond me. But Victor did it. That man is irreplaceable." These words are unconfirmed but they are none the less plausible for that. In an article on the elections Lenin had written, paraphrasing Chernishevsky: "A man who is afraid of soiling his hands should not go into politics. The simpletons with white hands only do harm in politics. . . ." Nevertheless, his political amorality was always subordinated to a higher social morality, expressed later on in his formula: "Morality is that which helps to destroy the former society of exploiters." He did not admit *any* kind of action under *any* pretext: "Would it be sufficient to allege an excellent aim or a good reason to justify participation in any abominable deed?" His criterion was the *efficiency* of any course from the point of view of the general interests of the proletariat and the progress of the socialist revolution. He never lost sight of his principles, and when he broke with Bogdanov, it was because philosophical differences seemed to him more important than the practical utility of work in common. But as he was not infallible, and as he was alone in his group in considering temporary expedients in their historical framework, his example was pernicious to mediocre imitators. Hence the reprobation of Trotsky, Martov and others and the frequent allusions to Nechayev, forerunner of the expropriators and comrade of Bakunin, whose strange *Catechism* might have served the Bolsheviks as a manual for pseudo-revolutionary immorality.

5

OPEN differences in theory ran parallel with dissensions behind the scenes. The Left, under the direction of Bogdanov, had its own paper, *Vperyod*, supported by an anonymous group who cherished the hope that they were creating an art, science and philosophy of the proletariat. They even evolved a project for utopian religion "without God," which Lenin undertook to fight as a materialist, following Plekhanov. On this occasion

Plekhanov, with his great reputation in Russia as a controversialist, resumed his pen to refute Bogdanov's "empirio-criticism." Lenin, who was inadequately versed in philosophical questions, began to study them with enthusiasm, even neglecting his paper, in order to find a reasoned basis for his criticism. This scrupulous conscientiousness in intellectual work was an essential characteristic, and differentiated him from his immediate associates. Bogdanov and Gorky had founded a school of socialism for Russian workmen at Capri, then at Bologna; Lenin created one at Longjumeau, near Paris, one pupil of which had a successful career, Sergo Ordjonikidze.

In spite of profound tactical differences, and after having declared Plekhanov to be beneath consideration as a political leader, Lenin tried to come to an understanding with his former master, who replied: "I also think that the only means of bringing the present crisis in the Party to an end is a rapprochement between the Marxist Mensheviks and the Marxist Bolsheviks"—but he deferred the interview. Plekhanov clearly divined the real intention. He said: "Lenin wants the unity of the Party, but he understands it as a man understands unity with a piece of bread; he swallows it." Trotsky had his own ideas about unity, allying himself both with Right and Left to bring the Bolsheviks to a compromise. Rosa Luxemburg demanded a general conference called at the request of the two principal sections.

In Russia the militants, and especially the workers, hardly understood these complications at headquarters. A letter from Koba written in 1911, interprets their attitude with good sense:

We have heard talk of the storm in a teacup abroad, the Lenin-Plekhanov bloc on the one hand and the Trotsky-Martov-Bogdanov bloc on the other. So far as I know the workers favour the first. But, generally speaking, they begin to look with scorn on doings abroad. Let them do what they like; as for us, if a man has the interests of the movement at heart and does his work the rest can be arranged. That is the best way in my opinion.

Such was the view of the ordinary Bolshevik, weary of seeing hairs quartered. Trotsky tried in vain, after the event, to define this state of mind as "indifference to theory," and the "myopia of the practical man." Other statements of Stalin's may be set against this, but it would be an error to take the political quarrels of the emigration for serious controversies or demand from the rank and file a contribution to the investigation of "empirio-monism."

Nogin's biographers say that he went in 1910 to Baku to ask Koba to enter the reorganised Central Committee; there is no indication of the result. It was evidently impossible for an expelled member of the Party to become a member of the Central Committee without being readmitted, at least so long as the façade of unity was maintained.

This deceptive appearance was about to disappear. Life in common was becoming intolerable; the two sections paralysed one another. Moreover, the situation in Russia was developing rapidly. Signs of effervescence appeared, as at Tolstoy's funeral. There were indications of new life. The industrial crisis came to an end and the renewal of production stimulated the working classes. There were new opportunities for socialist activity. Trotsky, always looking forward, had written some months earlier: "To-day, through the veil of the black clouds of reaction, we can discern the victorious gleam of a new October." Lenin, with his finger on the political pulse of Russia, wrote in his turn: "The Russian people are awakening to a new struggle, and are going forward to a new revolution." Each of them took the initiative in calling a Social-Democratic Conference. Lenin's was held at Prague in January 1912; it unceremoniously assumed Congress powers, and nominated a Central Committee. The Bolshevik Party was constituted at last.

The new "usurping" Central Committee consisted of seven members, among whom were Sergo Ordjonikidze, and immediately enlarged itself by adding two members by co-optation; Stalin was one of these. The Mensheviks had excluded this "professional revolutionary," the Bolsheviks advanced him. Unknown to the Party of which he was the instrument, he became one of the leaders solely by the decision of the other leaders. He was never elected; at all stages from the local and provincial committees in the Caucasus, up to the supreme All-Russian Committee he rose patiently and gradually in the hierarchy of the organisation without requiring the confidence of the masses or thinking of responsibility to them. He belonged exclusively to the "clandestine group of organisers" who imposed him on the organised. The Party knew nothing about him at the time of his nomination and was to remain in ignorance for a long time. Lenin tried in his editorial note to attract attention to Koba's contributions in his *Social-Democrat,* but only a few dozen copies penetrated into Russia. In contrast to a Trotsky, independently developed, ripened in dispute and in controversy with Plekhanov, Lenin, and Martov, and associated with the representatives of international socialism, Stalin was a product of the Party, grown up under its tutelage; but this was only a section of the Party which was itself incorporated in the directing organisation.

The Central Committee, which was to sit abroad, at once appointed an "executive bureau" for Russia. Koba and Sergo, fellow-workers in the expropriating operations, were members, "with allowances of fifty roubles a month," says a police report. They showed themselves apt in the execution of the orders which Lenin, himself practically the Central Committee, was authorised to give them. Stalin sometimes wrote in the St. Petersburg *Zviezda,* and brought some obscure assistance to the foundation of *Pravda* when the opportunity arose for the legal publication of a Bolshevik paper. The awakening perceived by Lenin was clearly evident after the massacre of the Lena strikers, which gave rise to protests and sympathetic strikes. The following First of May was the occasion of a great demonstration. The new *Pravda* appeared at a good moment. Supported by workmen's contributions, it met a real need for a daily socialist paper; its existence was better assured by humble voluntary sacrifices than was the case in earlier enterprises based on the proceeds of expropriations or the gifts of capitalists.

It is significant that histories of the Bolshevik Party by Zinoviev, Nevsky, Shelavin, Yaroslavsky and Bubnov do not mention Stalin in connection with *Zviezda* and *Pravda.* A specialist work by Olminsky on these two papers does not attribute to him any part in their foundation or management. There is only one trace of his hand, with a note indicating occasional contribution by him. The part assigned to him by the official biography prepared by his own secretary under his dictation is therefore pure fiction. On the tenth anniversary of *Pravda,* out of about forty articles commemorating its editors and various militants, two or three only mention Stalin, and that without saying anything of interest about him. He may have been useful in circulating the paper, though he was occupied with subordinate tasks and unable to write in an interesting fashion. "Editing" with the Bolsheviks has always meant management rather than editorial work; a good "editor" in their parlance means a man who sees to the strict execution of the instructions of the "clandestine group of management." Stalin was in hiding at St. Petersburg in the house of the Duma Deputy, Poletayev, whose recollections give no important information. In April of the same year he was arrested, condemned to three years in Siberia, and sent to the Narym district, in the Tomsk province, whence he escaped in September.

During this period several Social-Democratic fractions hostile to the Bolsheviks, answering a summons from Trotsky, had held a "unity" conference at Vienna in August 1912. The "August bloc," heterogeneous and negative in character, had no vitality and no future. Its effect was to exacerbate the relations between Lenin and Trotsky. Their most virulent controversies belong to this period. They do not contribute anything to the intellectual content of Bolshevism, but to ignore them altogether would be to suppress an element necessary for the comprehension of later crises in the Party.

Lenin denounced Trotsky for a policy of self-advertisement, for lack of principle and for adventurism. These were his actual expressions:

People like Trotsky with their resounding phrases about Russian Social-Democracy, are the plague of our time. . . . Trotsky to-day plagiarises the ideology of one fraction, tomorrow of another, and then declares himself above all the fractions. . . . It is impossible to discuss principles with Trotsky, for he has no definite conceptions. One can and should discuss with convinced adherents of the Right and the Left, but not with a man who plays at concealing the faults of one to the others; he is to be unmasked as a diplomat of the basest metal. . . . Trotsky has never had any political colour; he comes and goes between the liberals and the Marxists, with shreds of sonorous phrases stolen right and left. Not all is gold that glitters. Trotsky's phrases are full of glitter and noise but they lack content.

Trotsky's views on Lenin were not less drastic: "professional exploiter of all the backward elements in the Russian workers' movement" and past master in "petty squabbling." In the letter to Chkheidze containing these words, Trotsky foresees the destruction of the very foundations of Leninism, which is "incompatible with the organisation of the workers into a political party, but flourishes on the dungheap of sectionalism," after having stated that "the whole edifice of Leninism to-day is founded on lies and falsifications and carries within itself the poison germ of its own decomposition."

This exchange of compliments went on simultaneously with professions of mutual tolerance, whose sincerity is only on a par with their absolute inanity. "*A Party may include a whole spectrum of colours, in which the extremes may be absolutely contradictory*," said Lenin, when he parted with Bogdanov, whom he would not have in his fraction, but whom he did not wish to drive out of the Party. He thus transposed into the socialist movement his democratic convictions, which he summed up in the concise axiom: "Outside democracy, no socialism." And after the definitive schism, Trotsky was to write:

In a large Marxist community embracing tens of thousands of workmen, it is impossible that divergences and discords should not exist. Every member of the community has not only the right but the duty of defending his point of view on the basis of the common programme. But in fulfilling that duty none should forget that he is dealing with differences among a band of brothers. . . . Discipline and cohesion in the struggle are inconceivable without an atmosphere of mutual esteem and confidence, and the man who fails to observe these moral principles, whatever may be his intentions, is undermining the very existence of Social-Democracy.

As for passing from words to deeds, no one took the step. Attempts at general unification were futile. Trotsky recognised the fact, and went to the Balkans as war correspondent for a Kiev newspaper. There he studied military questions, not without profit for the future, and formed a close friendship with Christian Rakovsky, the leader of Roumanian socialism, and one of the most attractive figures in international socialism. Lenin, foreseeing the approach of a revolutionary upheaval in Russia, left Paris for Cracow, where communications across the Austrian frontier were easier and more rapid. Stalin, escaped from Siberia, joined him there in December, 1912, for the Bolsheviks were to hold a meeting of the Central Committee.

Nothing would be known of Koba's brief sojourn in the Narym district, but for the opportune chance that Vereshchak met him at the village of Kolpashovo. Among the exiles there were Sverdlov, Lashevich and Ivan Smirnov. There was one escape after another, and Koba in his turn departed by boat, "almost openly, via the province of Tobolsk." In Siberia he had as a comrade a Social Revolutionary, Surin, who was later discovered to be an *agent provocateur*. In a Shanghai paper the singer Karganov, a former Social Revolutionary, published some Siberian reminiscences in which Stalin appeared as defending a common thief, as an anti-Semite, and as friend of the local commissar of police. For the latter connection he is said to have been brought before an exiles' tribunal. The article is wrong in its chronology at all events, but it confirms information already collected on Koba's personal predilections, though it adds little that is new.

After the meeting of the Central Committee he spent some months at Cracow and Vienna in 1913. Lenin, anxious to educate his co-workers, and to specialise them, provided him with the outline of a study on *The National Question and Social-Democracy*, and helped him in the work which was published in the review *Prosvyeshchenye (Instruction)*. This is the first

article signed Stalin. Having become a politician on the Russian scale, Koba adopted, with secret satisfaction, a name with
a Russian ending which expresses his master quality—hard as
steel. Rupert called Cromwell's men "Ironsides." Augustin
Robespierre drew his brother Maximilian's attention to the
young Bonaparte as "an iron soldier." Stalin did not wait for
anybody to confer his metallic pseudonym.

Lenin thought him a suitable person to deal with the question of nationalities, since he came from a country where
Georgians, Tartars and Russians ought to live at peace. "We
have here a wonderful Georgian who is writing for *Prosvyeshchenye,* a great article containing all the Austrian and other
material," wrote Lenin to Gorky. Stalin did not know any
foreign language (even his studies in Esperanto remained fruitless), and the "Austrian material," with the possible exception
of Otto Bauer's book in the Russian translation, was evidently
derived directly from Lenin, together with the general ideas.
His article is the work of a diligent pupil, good for a man of
his education, but it passed unnoticed; even in 1923 Saveliev took
no notice of it in the article he wrote on *Prosvyeshchenye.*

The question of nationalities, that is, the question of subject
peoples and the ruling races, was most important at that time
in Russia, where the revolutionary struggle was complicated
by claims for independence or for autonomy by subject peoples.
International Social-Democracy had no single definite opinion
on the subject. The very existence of national socialist parties,
Polish and so forth, while a single party grouped all the peoples
of the Caucasus, shows the complexity of the problem in
Russia. The Austrian Marxists, directly interested in the question,
merely demanded national cultural autonomy within the established territorial limits, including all classes, without imposing
on the workers any obligation to organise themselves as workers
without distinction of nationality. Lenin maintained the right of
self-determination up to and including separation, but at the
same time he inculcated in all workers the duty of organisation
for trade union or political purposes in a single group in each
country irrespective of nationality. This is the thesis he had

given Stalin to develop. Rosa Luxemburg thought it contrary to working-class internationalism, and considered Poland as too closely connected economically with Russia to think of separation.

On his return to St. Petersburg, Stalin, charged with the "direction" of the small group of Bolsheviks in the Duma, or more exactly with the transmission to them of Lenin's instructions, lived in hiding in the houses of the deputy Badayev and of the workman Alliluyev. The fourth Duma, elected in 1912, included thirteen Social-Democrats, of whom only six were Bolsheviks, but the latter certainly represented a majority among the workers. Identical programmes did not prevent schism between the two sections, as desired by Lenin—and by others, as they were one day to learn. The Prague Conference had adopted three essential demands: a democratic republic, the eight-hour day, confiscation of large estates—these were also the Menshevik demands. Chkheidze and Chkhenkeli, both Georgians, were the most popular orators in the Duma. The Bolshevik deputies, unable to take a line of their own or to formulate the Party programme, read from the tribune documents drawn up by Lenin at Cracow. . . . The strongfisted Stalin was there to keep them on "the line" traced by their leader. Lenin did the thinking for all of them.

Stalin's task was soon over. In February 1913, that is at the end of a few days, the police arrested the mentor at a "literary evening." After a few months in prison he was deported to the Turukhansk district, Martov's former place of exile, north of the Arctic Circle. This time the penalty was serious, Stalin was not to escape. His rank in the Party meant a correspondingly strict surveillance. He had been denounced by the Bolshevik leader in the Duma, the principal reader of Lenin's parliamentary speeches, the workman Malinovsky, a member of the Central Committee and at the same time agent of the Okhrana who submitted the speeches before they were read to the Police Department.

The Russian political police did not only maintain spies and *agents provocateurs* in the revolutionary organisations; they

controlled the parties, groups and men in different ways, sometimes upsetting their plans by encouraging quarrels over theory.
The break of Plekhanov and his comrades with the People's
Will had been encouraged by the secret agent Degayev, who
had been sent to persuade Tikhomirov to intransigence. The
priest Gapon, hero of the Bloody Sunday of 1905, became an
agent of the Okhrana, and was executed by order of the Social
Revolutionary Party. The "fighting organisation" of this party,
in the hands of the *agent provocateur* Azev, served police and
Government plans at the same time that it was preparing plots
for the assassination of grand-dukes and of the Tsar himself.
Stolypin was killed by a terrorist police officer. The Bolshevik
Party was infested with spies from top to bottom: Malinovsky,
Jitomirsky, Romanov, Lobov, Chernomazov, Ozol, the best
known, were "responsible militants." At the secret minor Bolshevik Conference in Prague of twenty-eight delegates present,
there were at least four identified afterwards as *provocateurs*.
The ample and detailed information supplied by police documents and circulars provide a remarkable historical documentation which no investigator can afford to miss. The varying
configuration of the fractions of Social-Democracy is pictured
in them with photographic accuracy. Spies had first-hand
information.

It was not only the wishes of Lenin which had split the
Social-Democratic Group in the Duma. General P. Zavarzin
writes in his *Memoirs of a Chief of the Okhrana:* "Malinovsky
continued his secret collaboration under the direction of the
Head of the Police Department, S. P. Bieletzky, who advised
him to provoke a split among the Social-Democrats sitting in
the Duma, in order to reduce this fraction which had thirteen
members. Malinovsky followed this counsel and obtained the
wished-for result, without awakening the least suspicion among
his comrades. . . ." But a suspicion more and more concrete
took shape in the minds of Bolsheviks like A. Troyanovsky and
among the Mensheviks who demanded an inquiry from the
president of the Bolshevik parliamentary fraction. Lenin replied
defending Malinovsky and calling on Martov to repeat his

"calumnies" in Switzerland so as to stand responsible for them before "the tribunal of the free Helvetian republic."

Lenin placed unlimited confidence in Malinovsky. In July 1913 at Poronino, in Galicia, where Lenin had hired a country house, there was a meeting of five members of the Central Committee: Lenin, Krupskaya, Zinoviev, Kamenev and Malinovsky. Malinovsky knew everything. In view of recent arrests of Bolsheviks of the foremost rank, a small committee of three members invested with full powers, was charged with selecting trustworthy persons. Krupskaya and Kamenev retired; Malinovsky remained in the supreme trio. Among the decisions reached was one relating to the proposed escape of Sverdlov and of Stalin, both of them in exile near Turukhansk. The Okhrana, immediately warned by Malinovsky, of course took steps to prevent it. In September-October a new conference of eighteen delegates and four invited members met near Poronino. Two reports found in the Ministry of the Interior give detailed minutes of it; Malinovsky, who was again present, was nominated as Lenin's deputy to the International Socialist Bureau. He had no opportunity of fulfilling his mission.

In July 1914 the International Socialist Bureau summoned all fractions to Brussels with a view to ending the multiplicity of fractions in Russian Social-Democracy. Plekhanov, Rosa Luxemburg, Axelrod, Martov, Trotsky, Chkhenkeli, Alexinsky, Zurabov, Lapinsky, etc., took part in the session, which Lenin avoided, though as usual he had a long memorandum read by Inessa Armand demanding the recognition of the Bolshevik Party as an authorised section of the International. Vandervelde and Kautsky had difficulty in soothing the indignation of the Russians present, and Plekhanov so far forgot himself as to speak of Lenin as a thief anxious to secure the cash-box, which made the President ask him to sit down (at least so it is stated in a note by the Okhrana); in any case this was certainly the tone of the disputes. If Malinovsky had not been kept in Austria to clear himself of early suspicions (Lenin saved him once more in 1917), he would have been chosen to read the Bolshevik document after first forwarding a copy of it to St. Petersburg.

Unanimously, with the exception of the Leninist and the Lett delegates, the Brussels Conference invited all Russian Social-Democrats to surmount their divisions and to achieve unity. That would not suit the Okhrana. A Police Department circular soon sent instructions enjoining "all the secret members of the various Party organs to defend urgently, with firmness and perseverance, the thesis of the absolute impossibility of any fusion of the Bolsheviks with the Mensheviks." Lenin, for reasons which the Okhrana could not understand, was apparently of a similar opinion. But he did not despair of reaching relative unity by his own means, by assembling under his command the scattered forces of the movement.

Stalin, silent and gloomy, relegated to the forsaken hamlet of Kureyka, hunted foxes in the Siberian *taïga* and wild duck in the monotonous *tundra*.

Chapter V

THE REVOLUTION

THE War broke the workers' revolutionary movement in Russia just as it was reviving. Its power and energy had been revealed by strikes and barricade fighting in St. Petersburg during M. Poincaré's visit in July 1914. As everywhere else, mobilisation and the state of war stifled at first all tendencies to open opposition. The policy of the great socialist parties of the belligerent countries in rallying to the "union sacrée" caused profound disturbance in the various strata of Russian socialism.

Nevertheless, Mensheviks and Bolsheviks in the Duma agreed without difficulty on a common declaration, though in equivocal terms, refusing to vote war credits. Their rapprochement was soon ended by the differences between the émigré theorists.

Plekhanov, influenced by Jules Guesde, adopted the patriotic point of view in favour of the Allies as champions of democratic progress against the reactionary Central Empires. Thus he broke irretrievably with the socialist revolution. This was also the attitude of many Social-Democrats, especially among the Mensheviks and Social Revolutionaries. Some Bolsheviks, won over by the general state of mind in France, joined the army as volunteers. Even anarchists, following the example of Kropotkin, to whom the heritage of the French Revolution appeared to be menaced by "German militarism," put the necessity of an *Entente* victory before their anarchist principles.

But Lenin, opposed to "defensism," immediately declared for "defeatism" in its extreme form, unconditional and pushed to its final consequences. In his *Social-Democrat*, his pamphlets, his manifestoes, he characterised the world struggle as a "war of capitalist brigandage," a "war between slaveholders for the division of the slaves and the strengthening of their chains," a "war betweeen slave-raiders in dispute over their 'cattle.' " From this standpoint he urged the socialists of each country to contribute to the defeat of their own Government, to encourage fraternisation on all fronts, to "transform the Imperialist War into a Civil War." With Rosa Luxemburg and Martov he had secured the adoption at the International Socialist Congress at Stuttgart in 1907 of a motion for "utilising the economic and political crisis engendered by war for agitation among the lowest stratum of the population and to precipitate the fall of capitalist domination"; he took the resolution seriously, not retreating from what he had then proposed. In any case the defeat of Russia, that is to say, of Tsarism, was in his eyes the "lesser evil."

Alone in holding a point of view so definite and so directly contrary to any other, he called the "defensists" the "Tsar's Socialists" as Marx had called the followers of Lassalle, "Socialists of the King of Prussia," and, joining battle on the European arena, he denounced the bankruptcy of the Workers' International, abused all the patriotic socialists as traitors, condemned the socialist pacifists and the platonic internationalists as being stained with chauvinism and more or less conscious accomplices of the former. For him real solidarity of the proletariat implied hostility to national defence under the given conditions, without distinction of camps, and demanded revolt both against war and the bourgeois regime. Finally he demanded the foundation of a new International. Throughout the War he continued to develop these themes, which separated him for ever from all other socialists. But he persisted no less in declaring himself an incorruptible democrat: "Socialism is impossible without democracy, in two senses; (1) the proletariat cannot accomplish the socialist revolution if it is not prepared for it by the struggle for democracy; (2) Socialism victorious cannot maintain its victory and lead humanity to the extinction of the State unless it fully realises democracy."

Between the two extremes of "defensism" and "defeatism" there were many intermediate stages of opinion. Trotsky and Martov, with most of the leading personalities in revolutionary internationalism—Rosa Luxemburg, Karl Liebknecht, Franz Mehring, Rakovsky and Riazanov—declared against national defence, but in favour of a peace without victors or vanquished; they had no intention of breaking with socialists like Kautsky, who remained verbally faithful to the common principles, while adopting a practical compromise with the partisans of the "union sacrée." Trotsky supported the demand for a peace without reparations or annexations, with national self-determination, and sketched the outline of a United States of Europe. Lenin mercilessly attacked these "Centrists" of all shades and harassed them with criticism and appeals; he reproached them with hesitation, equivocation, eclecticism, and compromise, though for tactical reasons he spared Rosa Luxemburg and praised the exemplary courage of Liebknecht. He was uncompromising in regard to Trotsky above all, precisely because Trotsky was politically so close to him.

As for Stalin, it was impossible to know what he was thinking during these years of exile. Deprived of Lenin's guidance, did he share the ideas of his leader? The gap in his biography, the complete absence of documentation, the disappearance of every vestige of correspondence or signs of intellectual activity on his part are significant. In this connection and from the Bolshevik standpoint which Stalin claimed to represent, Trotsky was justified in asking for a reckoning:

It is impossible that in four years Stalin should have written nothing on the essential question of the War, of the International, or of the revolution. . . . It is clearly true that if a single line of Stalin's had advocated the necessity of "defeatism" or the need for a new International, that line would long since have been printed, photographed, translated into all languages and enriched by learned commentaries by Academies and Institutes. But such a line is not to be found.

Stalin has not only suppressed his writings of this period, but sees to it that they are not brought forward by anyone else. In the voluminous collection *Katorga y Ssylka (Fortress and Deportation)*, a review devoted to former prisoners and political exiles, whose pages are open to the slightest recollections of the survivors of the Tsarist terror, especially if they can mention an important personage, Stalin's name does not occur.

Other historical publications, full of documents and memoirs, fail to mention him. The case is unique in Russia, and justifies the most unfavourable deductions.

In default of political indications, there is a reticent statement on Stalin in Siberia by his comrade in exile, Sverdlov, one of the principal non-émigré Bolsheviks. According to letters of his published before Stalin's rigorous personal censorship was imposed, relations soon became difficult between the two exiles at Kureyka. They lived in the same peasant's hut and hunted together. At first Sverdlov liked Stalin as "a good companion, but found him too individualist in daily intercourse." Soon "we knew one another too well," he wrote; "in exile and prison conditions the naked man appears in all his meanness." They ended by separating, and saw less and less of one another. Sverdlov got a transfer to another place in the district; without exactly formulating grievances against Stalin, his correspondence shows the latter as impossible to live with.

Stalin ended by being isolated, occasionally seeing, and that at long intervals, Spandarian, an Armenian Bolshevik who has not published any memoirs. One of his present subordinates, Shumiatsky, who was an exile in the same colony, describes him as a "defeatist" from the first, and in a pamphlet on Turukhansk he has described the solitary hunter and fisherman equipped with a variety of nets, hawks, guns, traps, snares and baskets. . . . "He cut wood, cooked his food, and found time to work at his writings." These must be the writings which Trotsky asked for so insistently. But Sverdlov says he does not even know whether Stalin did the least bit of intellectual work in exile.

A letter from Lenin in November 1915 which asks for Koba's real name shows that if Stalin's name was forgotten his strong personality was not. Perhaps the question concerned some scheme of escape. But a careful watch was kept on the Kureyka trapper. In 1917 Sverdlov mentions twenty exiles in the district who were called up for military service; Stalin was on the list but the infirmity in his left arm saved him.

Russia must have been in great straits for men before avowed revolutionaries were summoned to the army where they would certainly preach indiscipline. More than fifteen millions of men had been mobilised. But the losses were disastrous; want of arms and munitions, an inadequate munitions industry, disintegrated transport, fraud in provisioning the army, incapacity in the High Command, bureaucratic paralysis, and administrative corruption, drove the army to slaughter. In 1917 the dead already numbered two million and a half; there were three million wounded and prisoners. Hospitals and ambulance stations were overflowing with the sick. Waste of human life could not compensate for the moral and material inferiority of the troops, the disorder and debauchery in the rear.

The longer the War went on, the less comprehensible were its aims to the people who were its victims. Patriotic enthusiasm was dead, suspicion haunted the regiments renewed after each defeat, irritation and despair preyed on the exhausted soldiers, "blind martyrs," weary of fighting with bayonets against machine-guns and urged on by flogging; there were more than a million deserters and mutineers in 1917.

At home the position of the autocracy was no better; the fall in agricultural production due to the successive levies of millions of adult labourers, the deterioration of the railways, the requirements of the armies, profiteering and blockade little by little paralysed the provisioning of the towns. Fuel and raw material were lacking in the factories, most of which were on war work. Anarchy in the administration prevented any rational utilisation of resources. In the *Zemstvos* and in various charitable organisations, "enlightened society" tried in vain to make good the State failures. Depreciation of the rouble and the rise in prices reduced wages, and made life more and more difficult for the workers who were driven to strike in self-defence. Statistics show an increasing number of strikes; police reports give reiterated warnings of revolution. Exasperation in the army was matched with general hostility to Tsarism.

At the same time, Court scandals and the blind policy of the reigning *camarilla*, shook the last supports of the regime. The degenerate sovereigns, surrounded by adventurers, charlatans and madmen, dominated by a drunken and lascivious monk, discouraged their most faithful servants. In spite of the most disinterested advice and the most alarming symptoms, Nicholas II defended the stupid measures of his chosen Ministers against the wishes of a Duma, which was itself a reactionary body. In vain the parties of the Right loyally denounced "occult forces," corruption and treason in the ruling cliques. Even members of the Imperial family resigned themselves to participation in palace plots to depose the Tsar to save the monarchy. Grand-Dukes and generals were preparing *coups d'état*. The assassination of Rasputin was merely a sinister auxiliary operation. The intrigues of the Germanophile aristocratic clique in favour of a separate peace with Germany drove the nationalist bourgeoisie to carry out their preventive plan—the abdication of the Tsar and the installation of a regency.

But catastrophe was to overtake "His Majesty's Opposition" in their interminable preparations. At the beginning of 1917, cold and hunger brought popular discontent to a climax and forced events. Bread was scarce in St. Petersburg in February. The workers struck again and again, women provoked street demonstrations, the army hesitated to obey orders against the demonstrators, and then joined resolutely in the movement of protest, as the French Guard did in 1789; insurrection was in being. In "a hundred hours" absolutism, which found practically no defenders, was irresistibly swept away. The servile Duma, overwhelmed, was compelled to form a provisional government. On the same day the Workers' Soviet, soon extended by the admission of the soldiers, was improvised in the capital. Two rival authorities marshalled themselves simultaneously on the ruins of the old regime, which had tumbled to pieces almost without a struggle under the pressure of practically the whole population. The insurrection cost less than fifteen hundred victims, including wounded. The provinces unanimously followed the capital.

Of the Commune in 1871 Benoît Malon has observed: "Never had revolution surprised the revolutionaries more." Once more the revolution had begun without the help of professional revolutionaries. No socialist party had urged or guided the masses in revolt. The principal deputies, from Rodzianko to Chkheidze, with Guchkov, Miliukov and Kerensky between the two extremes, submitted in their various fashions to the accomplished fact. The Petrograd proletariat, left to its own devices, instinctively realised the first elements of success by fraternising with the peasant soldiery. Of their own accord they took by assault the police offices and forced open the doors of the prisons. Their *élite*, veterans of the 1905 struggle, though they were matured by continuous activity, had small training in socialism, and needed outside direction in the chaos. Deprived of their recognised leaders, either deported or in exile, they abandoned the nominal power to the privileged classes, to the partisans of constitutional monarchy preoccupied with the maintenance of the dynasty to safeguard their own privileges. Kerensky, a recent convert to the Social Revolutionary Party, a typical representative of the confused ideas of a transitional period, was the "hostage of democracy" in the Provisional Government of which Miliukov was the governing spirit. The Petrograd Soviet did not dare to assert its pre-eminence or even demand a republic. But this voluntary effacement did not deprive it of the effective hegemony which was assured to it by the confidence of the armed workmen and above all of the soldiers, its sworn defenders. *Prikaz* No. 1 had put the army at its disposal. The dyarchy, a singular combination of two powers, immediately developed into a sullen antagonism of irreconcilable forces.

The transformation of the imperialist War into civil war, was brought about, as Lenin said, by the logic of circumstances, not by propaganda. Neither Bolshevik appeals nor any other reached the Russian people. "Defeatism," widely spread during the Crimean War and still more in the course of the Manchurian campaign, found less direct echo this time in the people and in the army where it was vaguely latent. Seconded by his wife, Krupskaya, and by his adjutant, Zinoviev, Lenin inspired in Switzerland an intransigent isolated group, without offshoots. At the international conferences of Zimmerwald (1915) and Kienthal (1916) summoned by the Swiss and Italian Socialist parties, he formed a little group of intellectuals known as "the Left," opponents of all pacifism, and of any conciliation with the official International. No workers' group supported his effort, unknown outside a very narrow circle of international revolutionaries. Alone, he repudiated the appellation of Social-Democrat to substitute that of Communist. Alone, he wished to create without delay a Third International. Alone, in accordance with Clausewitz's maxim on war, "the continuation of politics by other means," and in agreement with the Marxian formula of force as the "accoucheur of society in labour," he regarded civil war as the inevitable prolongation of the policy of the class struggle. But his hopes dwindled and a month before the February Revolution he ended a speech at Zurich on this sad note: "We, the older ones, will not perhaps live to see the decisive battles of the coming revolution. . . ."

He was in correspondence with the docile group of Duma Bolsheviks, all five imprisoned or exiled. The Central Committee of the Party had only one representative, himself, at liberty, unless Zinoviev is included. Of seven members of the Bolshevik Committee at Petrograd, three were discovered to be police agents, who sabotaged all its work.

The *agent provocateur*, Malinovsky, was then in Germany in a prisoners' camp, where he was lecturing on the Erfurt socialist programme. A few copies of the works of Lenin and Zinoviev, afterwards published under the title *Against the Current*, were brought in through Scandinavia. Cut off from their master, his disciples were lost. They were hardly distinguishable from other revolutionaries in the first enthusiasms of the revolution. The Petrograd *Pravda*, edited by modest militants, Molotov and Shliapnikov, had difficulty in striking out a line of its own, though it tried to show how Left it was by printing old sayings of Lenin's dating from 1905. The *Social-Democrat*, at Irkutsk, published articles by Ordjonikidze, Yaroslavsky and Petrovsky, whose Bolshevism closely resembled Menshevism. In the provinces many Social-Democratic groups incorporated the two sections.

The revolution took the revolutionaries unawares, though they had long foreseen its imminence, just as war had surprised the socialists, though they had announced and denounced it long before. Lenin rapidly recovered his wits. At the beginning he telegraphed to his friends from Zurich to put forward the modest demand for immediate elections to the Petrograd municipality. His programme contained three fundamental demands: *a democratic republic, the eight-hour day, confiscation of the large landed estates*—identical with the Menshevik demands. He confirmed his 1914 utterance: "*We desire at all costs a Great Russia proud, republican, democratic, independent and free, which, in her relations with her neighbours, will apply the human principle of equality, not the feudal principle of privilege*." But he was soon adjuring his followers to refuse confidence to the Provisional Government, to oppose the policy of the leaders of the Petrograd Soviet in that matter. His *Letters from Afar*, sent from Switzerland, dealing with the "first stage of the first revolution" to issue from the War, speak of the Soviet as the "embryo of a Workers' Government" and conclude by urging the necessity of conquering the Democratic Republic, "as a step towards socialism."

Trotsky looked at the situation as it developed in much the same fashion. He was opposed to "defeatism," which he regarded as nationalism turned inside out, to the call for civil war, preferring a call for peace, and to the extreme policy of schism practised by the Bolsheviks, but he nevertheless foresaw the course of events dimly discerned by Lenin. He had broken with Martov, who was too hesitating for him. He had published in Paris, under various titles, an internationalist paper which came up against the censorship, and led to his expulsion from France. This was after he had been convicted in Germany for a revolutionary pamphlet and before he was forced to leave Spain, where the secret police pursued him vindictively. Many Bolsheviks saw no difference between his attitude and Lenin's: "The *Social-Democrat* published by Lenin and Zinoviev in Switzerland, the Paris *Goloss* suppressed by the French police and changed into *Nashe Slovo*, directed by Trotsky, will be for the future historian of the Third International the essential elements from which was forged the revolutionary ideology of the international proletariat," wrote Manuilsky, a Bolshevik of the Left, six years afterwards. After emigrating to America, Trotsky collaborated in the *Novy Mir* of New York, with a young Bolshevik then unknown, N. Bukharin, and a brilliant convert from Menshevism, Alexandra Kollontai, who had recently joined Lenin. For him, too, events in Russia were a stage towards the socialist revolution, a prelude to social revolution in Europe.

Bolsheviks in Russia had no such bold ideas. Absorbed in action, they shared the collective illusion of a mob drunk with easy victory. From Perm, Lenin received this telegram: "Fraternal greeting. Start to-day for Petrograd. Kamenev, Muranov, Stalin." The liberated exiles were on their way. Lenin was unaware that Kamenev had shortly before signed another telegram, in the name of a popular meeting held in Siberia, congratulating the Grand-Duke Michael on having renounced the throne, pending the decision of the future Constituent Assembly. On their arrival in the capital, Muranov, Kamenev and Stalin, the first three leaders restored to the Bolshevik section, took over the direction of *Pravda* on their own authority. Stalin, delegated by the Central Committee of his party, that is by himself and a few close comrades, entered the executive committee of the Soviet without election either by the workers or the soldiers. History drew him from his subterranean activity and gave him the opportunity of working in the light of day.

2

War incontestably played a great part in the development of our revolution. It materially disorganised absolutism; it disintegrated the army; it emboldened the mass of the inhabitants. *But, happily, it did not create the revolution, and that is fortunate, because a revolution born of war is impotent;* it is the product of extraordinary circumstances, rests upon exterior forces and shows itself incapable of maintaining the positions conquered.

THESE words of Trotsky's, in *Our Revolution*, referred to the Revolution of 1905 and to the Russo-Japanese War.

Lenin did not attribute to his Party any imaginary merit; he recognised in the War the determining factor of the revolt of 1917, but without deducing from that connection the impotence of the revolution: "The fire of revolution was fed by the ignorance and terrible sufferings of Russia, by all the conditions created by the War," he said, adding on another occasion: "Our revolution was engendered by the War; without it we should have all the capitalists in the struggle arrayed against us." Later he laid emphasis on the indifference of the mass of the population with regard to frontiers and on the absence of national sentiment: *"It was easy to begin the revolution in such a country. It was easier than lifting a pen. But it would be vain to hope to undertake a revolution in a country where capitalism is flourishing without hard work and preparation."*

The War made possible the co-operation between workers and peasants which was lacking in 1905. Moreover, it had developed certain industries and accentuated the concentration of the proletariat in Petrograd and Moscow. The gaps created by mobilisation and the immense slaughter were met by a flow of peasants into the large towns. This new uneducated working class, without settled or conservative traditions, but also without technical knowledge or political education, was a blank sheet of revolutionary temperament for any party capable of interpreting its aspirations, aspirations fundamentally clear but confused in their outward manifestations.

The workers had been claiming for a long time a better standard of living and democratic privileges; the peasants coveted land in the possession of parasites; the soldiers wanted peace. But these same soldiers were for the most part peasants greedy for land; the workmen were no less interested in peace, the peasants in liberty. Moreover, the oppressed nationalities of the Empire hungered for autonomy and national independence. The mass of the people, unanimous for certain imperious necessities, waited impatiently for the Constituent Assembly to satisfy these vital requirements.

The Provisional Government, representing the interests and ideas of an infinitesimal minority, without contact with the people or experience of power, proved incapable of comprehending the urgency of the popular demands, and still more of beginning to resolve the problems laid down. They neither assured bread for the workers, nor peace for the soldiers, nor the liberty of self-determination to the nationalities. The convocation of the Assembly was fixed for a vague and distant date under the pretext of first passing a model electoral law. The economic crisis grew more and more acute.

The Petrograd Soviet, regarded by the workers as the authentic organ of democracy in spite of its amorphous constitution, and invested by tacit gratitude with prestige over "all the Russias," sought a compromise between "demagogy" and "reaction." Mensheviks were in a majority in the executive. There were only a handful of Bolsheviks. Georgian Social-Democracy, with Chkheidze as President from the beginning, and soon with Tseretelli, back from Siberia, and the most influential of the leaders, took the first place once more. On the Executive Committee, unanimous in declaring themselves as Zimmerwaldians, the internationalists Sukhanov and Steklov formed the Left Wing together with little known Bolsheviks, before the advent of Kamenev and Stalin.

In his *Notes on the Revolution*, prolix but sincere and vivacious, and used by all historians who have dealt with this period, Sukhanov gives in these terms the impression made by Stalin:

Of the Bolsheviks, with the exception of Kamenev, only Stalin figured in the Executive Committee. He was one of the central figures of the Bolshevik Party, and consequently one of the few individuals holding (and still holding) in his hands the fate of the revolution and the State. Why this was so I do not undertake to say: strange are the influences among the higher circles, far removed from the people, irresponsible, and little known! But in any case, as far as Stalin was concerned, there was reason for perplexity. The Bolshevik Party, in spite of the low level of its "officers' corps," its ignorant and casual rank and file, possesses a number of notable personalities suitable for leadership in its general staff. Stalin, during his meagre activity on the Executive Committee, impressed me, and not me alone, as a colourless personage acting sometimes in a dull and evasive way. In fact there is little more to say about him.

Stalin's rôle in the Executive Committee left in fact no trace in its minutes or in its archives. But the part he played at the head of the Party is known from articles in *Pravda* and from the works of Shliapnikov, a Bolshevik militant turned memoir-writer.

After brusquely evicting the management of the paper without taking any notice of the organisation or of the cadres, solely on the strength of his membership in the Central Committee by simple co-optation, Stalin imposed on the Party organ the policy known as "conditional defensism." According to this point of view, the Provisional Government might count on Bolshevik support in so far as its policy conformed to the views of the Menshevik-Social Revolutionary Soviet. Kamenev served as theorist in this volte-face, Muranov defended it as a deputy, and Stalin held the *de facto* command. This minor *coup d'état*, very illustrative of "professional revolutionary" methods with regard to the Party, subject to the will of a clandestine clique of management, unknown to all and elected by nobody, roused great indignation among subordinates who had not yet acquired the habit of blind obedience. Shliapnikov describes its first repercussions as follows:

March 15th, the day of the appearance of the first number of the "reformed" *Pravda*, was a day of rejoicing for the "defensists." The whole of the Tauride Palace, from the members of the Committee of the Duma to the Executive Committee, the heart of revolutionary democracy, was full of the news—the victory of the moderate, reasonable Bolsheviks over the extremists. Even in the Executive Committee we were met with venomous smiles. It was the first and the only time that *Pravda* won the praise of "defensists" of the worst type.

In the factories, this number of *Pravda* produced stupefaction among the adherents of our Party and its sympathisers, and the sarcastic satisfaction of our enemies. In the Petrograd Committee, at the Bureau of the Central Committee and on the staff of *Pravda*, many questions were received. What was happening? Why had our paper left the Bolshevik policy to follow that of the "defensists"? But the Petrograd Committee was taken unawares, as was the whole organisation, by this *coup d'état*, and was profoundly displeased, accusing the Bureau of the Central Committee. Indignation in the workers' suburbs was very strong, and when the proletarians learnt that three former directors of *Pravda*, just come from Siberia, had taken possession of the paper, they demanded their expulsion from the Party.

Especially in the Vyborg quarter, the "reddest" in the capital, the expulsion of Stalin and his two associates was demanded. After violent debates, all three were disavowed and reproved by the superior Party tribunal, and the former staff were reinstated with the addition of some newcomers. The Bolshevik Party was not yet organised on the military model, and the opinion of the rank and file could make itself felt. Warned by his unfortunate first effort in high politics, Stalin thought it prudent to abandon Kamenev, author of the condemned article, and to take a position a little more to the Left, but still not far removed from Menshevism. The formation of a small group more frankly Right Wing made it possible to class him with the "centrists." The truth is that he was for conciliation, as against Bolshevism, before the arrival of Lenin.

According to his *On the Road to October* Stalin had written so far only three articles. The first, on the Soviets, "upheld the necessity of a democratic republic for all the inhabitants of Russia" (without distinction of class). The second, on the War, proposes "pressure on the Provisional Government" for the opening of peace negotiations (a Menshevik idea). The third, on the conditions of revolutionary victory, enumerates three: the formation of an All-Russian Soviet as the future organ of power, the arming of the workers, and the early convocation of the Constituent Assembly. A fourth article, against Federalism, which appeared immediately after Lenin's arrival, reflects

on the subject of nationalities the hesitations and contradictions of Bolshevism, which was definitely hostile to federalism
a very short time before imposing it as an indispensable solution.

In fact Stalin was in complete agreement with every statement which committed the Party, as much with the programme
article of *Pravda* repudiating "defeatism," as with the action of
the Bolshevik fraction in the Soviet, which joined in the unanimous voting on fundamental questions where their principles
demanded that they should keep their distance. The Bolshevik
representatives had even approved, at a Soviet Conference at
the beginning of April, a resolution supported by Dan, the
Menshevik theorist who had returned from Siberia, "not to
hamper the Provisional Government"—such was their line of
conduct. In the provinces, unified Social-Democratic Committees reconciled the "enemy brothers" in the general
confusion.

In Switzerland, Lenin raged at the confusion of his fraction
under this bad leadership. After his *Letters from Afar* he wrote
in a threatening tone: "Our Party would completely disgrace
itself, would commit political suicide if it were lured by such
deception . . . unqualifiedly condemn . . . any connection with
those inclining towards Social-Patriotism. . . ." He recalls to a
sense of duty Kamenev, his closest comrade and the strongest
representative of the state of mind which he condemns, and
warns him to be on his guard against all the conciliators, including Stalin. At last, just as his patience was exhausted, he succeeded in returning to Russia, crossing Germany with a group
of émigrés, whence the legend of the "sealed car."

The idea was not Lenin's but Martov's. In face of the refusal
of the Governments of London and Paris to allow the political
exiles to be repatriated after the revolution, the only possible
route was through Germany or Scandinavia. The Swiss Socialists negotiated the journey as an exchange of civil prisoners,
and all the proscribed Russian revolutionaries were able to
profit by it, including the patriots. Lenin's example was followed by many of his adversaries. Miliukov's journal at the
time said politely: "A socialist leader as universally known

as Lenin ought to enter the arena, and we can only hail his arrival in Russia, whatever may be our opinion of his political doctrine."

Lenin arrived in the middle of a Bolshevik conference and found his Party completely off the rails. He was "more Left than our Left" wrote Shliapnikov. Alone in his conception of the coming deepening of the Russian Revolution by the dictatorship of the proletariat, in correlation with European revolution, he had to win over to his ideas his own pupils before attempting to convince the masses (even Zinoviev was inclined to join Kamenev and Stalin in the group of "old Bolsheviks" opposed to the intransigent policy of their master). He immediately attacked the position of the provisional directors of the Party, and published, under his single signature, the *April Theses*, which became famous in Russia, and formed the point of departure for a new development of Bolshevism.

These theses declared the impossibility of a democratic peace without first overthrowing capitalism; proposed fostering fraternisation among the soldiers at the front; fixed the present moment as the transition towards the seizure of power by the proletariat and the poorer peasants; and advocated the future republic of soviets, the suppression of the police, of the standing army, of a professional civil service, the nationalisation of the land, control of production by the workers, and the fusion of the banks into one undertaking controlled by the State; within the Party itself they proposed a revision of the programme, a change of name and the foundation of a new International. Lenin expounded them at the Bolshevik Conference in session at the time of his arrival.

In this same assembly, Stalin had already defended an absolutely contrary point of view. He imagined a sort of division of functions between the Provisional Government and the proletariat:

Power is divided between two organisations, neither of which has complete power. . . . The Soviet of Workers' and Peasants' Deputies mobilises the forces, and exercises control; the Provisional Government, though reluctantly and with many deviations, consolidates the conquests already realised in fact by the people. Such a situation has its negative as well as its positive side; it is not now to our advantage to force events, or to accelerate the process of detachment from the bourgeois classes, which must inevitably separate themselves from us in the end. . . .

Like the Mensheviks he proposed support of the Provisional Government, "in so far as it consolidates the advance of the revolution." Krestinsky was able to state: "There is no practical difference between Stalin and Voytinsky." The latter was about to join the Mensheviks.

The Conference had before it a resolution of Tseretelli's in favour of Social-Democratic unity. Stalin approved. "We ought to accept. It is indispensable to settle the line of agreement. Unity is possible on the Zimmerwald-Kienthal principles." To the faint objections raised by Molotov, he replied: "We have neither to anticipate nor to prevent differences. *Without differences there is no life in the Party.* Within the Party we shall overcome our minor disagreements." Lenin appeared in time to upset these proposals by the uncompromising declaration:

Even our own Bolsheviks show confidence in the Government. This can be explained only by the dazing effect of the revolution. It is the death of socialism. You, comrades, have faith in the Government. In that case our ways must part. I would rather be in the minority. One Liebknecht is worth more than a hundred and ten "defensists" of the Steklov and Chkheidze type. If you sympathise with Liebknecht, and extend even one finger (to the "defensists") you are betraying international socialism.

Not only did Lenin refuse any understanding with the Mensheviks, but he resolutely took the offensive by proposing the adoption of the name of Communist Party. "But," he said, "in order to change one's linen one must take off the soiled and put on clean." He imagined socialism to be already in a state of schism in all countries; and thought that the Zimmerwald Left existed in every country. And he cut short the ceremony, congratulations and speeches: "We have done with compliments and resolutions; it is time to get down to work, to proceed to serious business."

He again explained his views to an audience composed of both Bolsheviks and Mensheviks. There was more laughter than hooting, more scorn than indignation, and the general opinion was that Lenin was ridiculous rather than dangerous. Some thought he was raving; others were glad to see Bolshevism discredited by its chief. Goldenberg, a former Bolshevik, exclaimed: "Bakunin's place has long been vacant in the Russian Revolution. Now it is occupied by Lenin. . . . We have just listened to the negation of Social-Democratic doctrine and of scientific Marxism. Lenin, leader of our Party, is dead. A new Lenin, an anarchist Lenin, is born."

Stalin stood aloof, but Kamenev, on behalf of the Old Bolsheviks, tried to refute the *April Theses*, unacceptable because they sought to rush the transformation of the bourgeois revolution into the socialist revolution, and were contrary to the classic formulas of Bolshevism. Lenin replied by indicating the unforeseen circumstances of the situation, especially the duality of power in Russia and the international situation, and by advising revision of the old catchwords. "We are not Blanquists, partisans of the seizure of power by a minority." They had to fight for preponderance in the soviets, to strive to win over the toiling masses.

In vain Kalinin, another supporter of the Kamenev-Stalin group, said shortly afterwards: "I belong to the old school of Leninist Bolsheviks, and I think that the Old Leninism has by no means shown itself inapplicable to the actual situation. I am astounded that Lenin should denounce the Old Bolsheviks as a hindrance to-day." Lenin did not hesitate to attack *"these 'Old Bolsheviks,' who more than once have played a sorry part in the history of our Party, stupidly repeating a formula learned by heart, instead of studying the peculiarities of new living reality."*

This formula was "the dictatorship of the workers and peasants," long opposed by Bolsheviks to the "permanent revolution" and the "workers' government" of Trotsky, Parvus and

Rosa Luxemburg. Without abjuring it after the event, Lenin thought the hour had come for a further advance: "Bolshevik ideas and slogans have been generally confirmed by history; but, as to the concrete situation, things have turned out to be different, more original, more unique, more multi-coloured than could have been anticipated by anyone."

The occasion seemed to him a suitable one to give the rigid "Old Bolsheviks" a lesson in applied Marxism:

The Marxist must take cognisance of living reality, of the actual facts of the time, and he must not continue clinging to the theory of yesterday, which, like every theory, at the best only outlines the main and general, only approximately embracing the complexity of life. He added: A Marxist must proceed not from the possible, but from the real.

Since the soviets were the organisation of the majority of the people, Lenin declared himself "against any adventurism in the seizure of power by a workers' government, against any Blanquist *coup*," and in favour of a "*conscious* intervention of the majority," in the sense of the coming dictatorship of the proletariat, the power of the soviets.

A fortnight later, a radical change of front had taken place, for Lenin's general plan corresponded closely to the rapid development of the situation. Resolutions passed at public meetings everywhere, demanding peace and land, and hostile to the Provisional Government, showed the strength of the popular current opposed to the half-measures, tergiversations, and theoretical subtleties of a temporising socialism. The surrounding atmosphere put an effective pressure on the Party from all sides. Moreover, the Old Bolsheviks were overwhelmed by new young adherents; the organisation had 80,000 members by the time of its conference in the early days of May. Lenin had got his men in hand, imposed his theses, and forced the Right to retreat. Kamenev, Kalinin, Rykov, and Tomsky were wasting their time in defending Old Bolshevism. Kalinin in vain demanded union with the Mensheviks. But Lenin was still absolutely alone in recommending rupture with any indecisive socialist tendency whatever, even with the internationalism of the Zimmerwald majority.

Stalin made haste to submit. At the May conference, he put in a report on the question of nationalities, his special subject, in agreement with Lenin's ideas, in which the main point formulated the recognition of the right of nationalities to separate from the dominating State; he had to meet opposition from the Left, inspired by Rosa Luxemburg, and represented by Dzerzhinsky, Pyatakov and Bukharin, who feared to see the Party declare in favour of regional chauvinism and encourage separatist reactionary tendencies. He confined himself to repeating what Lenin had said. There is nothing in the report to indicate his future.

Seven years later, in a preface to the collection, *On the Road to October*, Stalin thought it necessary to give retrospective explanations of his political relations with Kamenev, the most un-Bolshevik of the Bolsheviks, who, before the telegram to the Grand-Duke Michael, had already repudiated Leninism at the trial of the Bolshevik deputies to the Imperial Duma. "The first three articles," he wrote cautiously:

. . . reflect certain hesitations felt by the majority of our Party on the questions of peace and of the power of the soviets; they belong to the period March-April 1917. It was a time of rapid break with old traditions. The earlier platform of the direct overthrow of the Government no longer corresponded with reality. . . . A new orientation of the Party was required. It is not surprising if the Bolsheviks, dispersed by Tsarism in prisons and in exile and only just permitted to assemble from all parts of Russia to prepare a new programme, were not able immediately to determine their course. It is not at all surprising that, in seeking a new orientation, the Party was brought up against the questions of peace and the power of the soviets. It required Lenin's celebrated *April Theses* to enable the Party to move forward energetically on a new path. . . . This mistaken position I held with the majority of the Party, but I left them at the end of April to adopt the Lenin Theses. . . .

Fresh confirmation of an observation essential for the comprehension of the course of the revolution: Bolshevism was non-existent without Lenin.

3

THE Provisional Government, in a state of permanent crisis, impotent to disentangle the contradictory elements in the March Revolution, or even to diminish the tension, exhausted one by one the various expedients for prolonging its factitious life. Neither the Premiership of Kerensky after that of Prince Lvov, nor the successive resignations of Ministers after Miliukov's sensational departure, nor the pseudo-dictatorial Directory after the Liberal-Socialist Coalition, resolved the question of power. They were so many stages of attrition and discredit before the final catastrophe.

All the visible phenomena of economic decadence under the old regime persisted and developed in catastrophic fashion: scarcity of commodities, debasement of the currency, rising prices, paralysis of transport, closing of factories, with their social consequences—growing destitution, insecurity, strikes and unrest. The number of deserters from the disintegrated army was to be doubled before October. Reference of the agrarian question to an indefinitely postponed Constituent Assembly meant that vast areas were unsown—a certain menace of famine. The soldiers at the Front, fearing a division of land in their absence, returned en masse to the villages without permission. The peasants began to pillage the great estates, and to seize cattle. Everywhere alarming symptoms increased.

Nevertheless, the bourgeoisie persisted in its hopeless policy. In a country whose army, in process of dissolution, could hardly maintain the defensive and whose people were devoid, not only of desire of conquest, but of any patriotic sentiment, Miliukov's avowed intention was to annex Constantinople and Armenia, and dismember Austria-Hungary and Turkey — showing thereby the political immaturity of his class, so weak in Russia owing to the preponderance of foreign capital.

Tied to this bourgeoisie, the Social Revolutionaries and the Mensheviks did everything to lose the confidence of the proletariat and the army, the moving forces of the revolution, and to disappoint the rural districts. Their participation in a government which perpetuated a state of affairs universally execrated, and their repeated compromises with those immediately responsible for the existing chaos, gave the Bolshevik Party the monopoly of expressing the aspirations of the impatient masses.

The Party of Social Revolutionaries, less and less socialist and revolutionary, more and more rhetorical and sterile, became a "grandiose nullity," as it was currently called in allusion to its temporarily large numbers. An energetic Left detached itself from the main body to act on parallel lines with the Bolsheviks with a view to "deepening" the revolution. Traditional Social-Democracy, steeped in western ideas, sought an impossible equilibrium by parliamentary methods unsuited to the time and place; on its Left, Martov and the group of internationalist Mensheviks criticised severely the majority and its tacticians, Dan and Tseretelli. The Bolsheviks, more homogeneous and better disciplined, trained to collective action led by a chief who was a realist, at once pliable and firm, prompt in manœuvre and unwavering in principles, lost no time in taking advantage of an exceptionally favourable situation and of the repeated errors of their rivals.

Fighting under the simple and attractive slogan of "All power to the Soviets," a phrase which went home everywhere, they won day by day more support among the poor, the poor whom Kerensky in despair called the "populace" and the "soldiery," factory workers, Kronstadt sailors, Lett fusiliers and Finnish machine-gunners. In May, states Sukhanov, a third of the Petrograd proletariat were on their side. Their advance was continuous. At the first Congress of the Soviets, in June, they had only 105 delegates as against 285 Social-Revolutionaries and 248 Mensheviks; the provinces moved more slowly than the capital. But in the Petrograd Soviet, their fraction was strengthened at every by-election. The district soviets, beginning with that of Vyborg, passed into their hands. Entire military units, the principal factories, among them the Putilov works, with 50,000 workmen, answered their call.

By the return of Trotsky, and with the assistance of the

Social-Democratic organisation known as "Inter-District," grouping dissident Mensheviks and Bolsheviks, they had received new strength. Trotsky, who found it more difficult than Lenin to get back to Russia, had been arrested at sea by the English, was interned near Halifax and was only liberated on the demand of the Petrograd Soviet. He did not arrive until May. He still hoped for the unity of the Social-Democratic fractions, but changed his mind when he was on the spot. The gulf between Bolsheviks and Mensheviks was thenceforward impassable, in spite of a common theoretical programme. On the other hand his conception of the "permanent revolution" and Lenin's new strategy were convergent. Although he had feared the sectarian spirit of a fraction subject to the "Ilyich regime," he thought he could discern a "debolshevisation of Bolshevism." The old differences seemed to be smoothed down and identity of view on immediate aims complete. The "Inter-District" group was one with the Bolsheviks in action before merging with the Party in July 1917. Beside Trotsky, there were ex-Mensheviks such as Joffe, Uritsky, Volodarsky and Karakhan, with Old Bolsheviks of the Left such as Lunacharsky and Manuilsky. Other former Mensheviks, Alexandra Kollontai, Larin and Antonov, rallied to Bolshevism, an example followed later by Chicherin, Steklov and others. Riazanov, "outside of fractions," did the same.

The name of Trotsky was coupled with that of Lenin in the press and the minds of the public, both in and out of Russia. The two personified to the world the growing plebeian movement on the march. Lenin, rarely seen, handled the Party tiller surely and well, and made full use of the band of "professional revolutionaries," at the same time elaborating the theoretical justification of his tactics. Trotsky always present at meetings within doors or in the streets, untiring speaker and writer, galvanised the crowd and recruited the legions for the final struggle. The phrase "Lenin and Trotsky," as the embodiment of social purpose, engraved itself in memory and history. Ultimately people even wrote "Lenin-Trotsky."

The two former adversaries understood one another better

in the great day of civil war than in the *chiaro-oscuro* of the emigration and were mutually complementary.

In the way Trotsky spoke of Lenin the attachment of the disciple is visible. At that time Lenin had behind him thirty years of militant work in the service of the proletariat, and Trotsky twenty. All trace of the differences of the pre-war period had disappeared. There was no difference between the tactics of Lenin and Trotsky. This rapprochement, signs of which had appeared during the war, had become clearly defined from the moment of Leon Davidovich's arrival in Russia. Immediately after his first speeches we, old Bolsheviks, Leninists, felt that he was one of us.

These are the words of Raskolnikov, a Bolshevik of the old guard.

Lenin fully appreciated his rival: "No one would think of disputing a candidature such as that of L. D. Trotsky," he wrote with regard to the Bolshevik list of candidates to the Constituent. And on another occasion, in connection with the reconciliation of the various socialist parties: "Trotsky has been saying for a long time that unity is impossible. Trotsky grasped the fact, and, since then, there has been no better Bolshevik." This disinterested sentiment was probably not shared in Lenin's immediate circle by those, Stalin among others, who felt they were eclipsed by the newcomer. The ruling nucleus in the Party formed a close brotherhood, and the rise of Trotsky to the top was unprecedented. Possibly the germ of certain personal rivalries dates from this moment. But it could not mature in the atmosphere of the collective struggle for power. Lenin justified his adoption of the political and tactical formula of the speedy advent of the dictatorship of the proletariat by the imminence of the social revolution in the advanced countries of Europe. In his view the Russian Revolution was inseparable from the coming of European socialism. "The victory of Social-Democracy," he wrote as early as 1905, "will make it possible for us to rouse Europe to revolt, and the socialist proletariat of the West will throw off the yoke of the bourgeoisie, and in its turn will help us to achieve the socialist revolution." The World War, then recently stoked up by the intervention of the United States, confirmed him in his belief in the near approach of universal civil war, in which the Russian episode would only be the first stage.

Kautsky, in a study on *Slavs and the Revolution*, published in *Iskra* in 1902, pointed out the displacement of the revolutionary centre from the West to the East, and predicted the rôle of the Slavs as its vanguard: "Russia, which has in great measure received her revolutionary impetus from the West, is now perhaps ready to serve the West in her turn as a source of revolutionary energy." The Russian Revolution would cleanse the vitiated atmosphere in which the European workers' movement, handicapped by parliamentarism, stagnated. After 1905 the same writer predicted as a result of the Russo-Japanese War a revolutionary era in Asia and in the Moslem world; his prediction was verified two years later in Turkey, next year in Persia, and two years later still in China. Signs of revolt were evident in India and in Northern Africa. Lenin on the other hand expected the war to result in European revolution, without which socialism would be impracticable in Russia.

With the optimism characteristic of all pioneers, he had always over-estimated the revolutionary capacity of the Occidental proletariat at any given time, and miscalculated the resources and the capacity of capitalism to resist. In 1914 his illusions about German socialism were so strong that he refused to believe that the Social-Democrats in the Reichstag had voted war credits, and thought the number of *Vorwärts* containing the news was faked, until he was compelled to accept the evidence. He reacted the more violently in the opposite sense, alone even in the International, against the old socialist parties moulded by bourgeois legality; the conclusions he drew were the inevitability and the necessity of new workers' parties, of a new Communist International, whose rôle would be to end the War by the overthrow of capitalism. There can be no doubt that his tactics in Russia would have been less radical if he had not reckoned with such certainty on the aid of European revolution.

His war-cry, "All power to the Soviets," is not to be under-

stood as indicating a hasty ambition to seize the State organisation which he intended to destroy and replace, for reformist
socialism was then dominant in the soviets. But he looked further ahead, foreseeing the rise of his Party assisted by the bankruptcy of the "Louis Blancs" of the moment. Moreover, he
never lost sight of the danger latent in the enormous mass of
the peasantry, capable of submitting to the most extreme reaction: "Let us be on our guard against the possibility of the
alliance of the peasantry with the bourgeoisie," he said, facing
the worst. Her peasants "make Russia the most petit-bourgeois
country in Europe." Therefore he advocated, in vain, separate
soviets of poor peasants, formed to counterbalance the holders
of small and medium holdings. Far from desiring to force historical events, he advised the soviets not to "decree any reform
for which the time was not entirely ripe both in the concrete
economic circumstances and in the minds of the overwhelming
majority of the people."

He did not over-estimate the degree of development of the
Russian proletariat, numerically small, "less conscious, less mature
than that of any other country." On many occasions he repeated
in varying words: "Socialism cannot be victorious immediately
or directly in Russia." He ceaselessly exhorted his Party patiently to explain their interests to the ignorant masses. But,
attentive to the changing temper of opinion, he was careful to
keep pace with the main current: "The country is a thousand
times more Left than Chernov or Tseretelli and a hundred times
more Left than we are." He was convinced of the necessity of a
dictatorship, of a power resting not on law but on force, and
he had already amazed the Congress of Soviets by declaring
that he and his Party were ready to assume the whole power
without sharing it with anyone, at a time when other socialists
were shrinking from responsibility. To his mind the soviets
represented in a confused fashion the interests of the workers
and peasants, but his own Party was alone capable of giving
them conscious and logical expression.

After the "July days," when the proletariat and the garrison
of Petrograd demonstrated of their own accord in the streets,

by way of answer to the disastrous Galician offensive needed by the Allies but decided on by Kerensky with the approval of a majority in the Soviet, he suddenly reversed his tactics, and changed his slogans. The Bolsheviks had not provoked the demonstration, but, seeing it was inevitable, they had decided to make use of it. Severe repression, in which they were the sufferers, followed. Decisive action was premature, and its objective, "All power to the Soviets," was still impracticable. The reactionary parties feared revolt. The headquarters of the Party of the permanent revolution were sacked. Trotsky, Kamenev, Kollontai and others were imprisoned, and Lenin and Zinoviev were obliged to go into hiding. Pretended revelations, fabricated to represent the Bolshevik leaders as in the pay of Germany, though obviously false, made them suspect. The dark days had come.

A whole literature, superficially imposing, is devoted to presenting the spectacle of a nation of over a hundred million souls at the mercy of the venality of a few individuals and a handful of German marks. Quite apart from the incontestable incorruptibility of the principal person concerned, proved by the whole course of his life, the "proofs" in question refute themselves. No distribution of funds has required to be substantiated by such a mass of superfluous documentation, inconceivable except as a demonstration of the non-existent. Moreover Kerensky did not dare to make use of "incriminating documents" of which there is no trace in the archives of the German Reich, made public by the German revolution. Further, Masaryk has disposed of them in his *Memoirs:* "I do not know what the Americans, the English and the French paid for these documents, but to anyone accustomed to dealing with matters of this kind, their contents alone are sufficient to reveal that our friends had purchased forgeries. There was one proof *ad oculos:* these documents, alleged to come from different countries, had been typed on the same machine." Thus the machine betrayed the machination.

In his retreat Lenin meditated on the lessons of the failure, and deduced from it the fact that the cry "All power to the

Soviets" had ceased to be correct. Henceforward, they must demand the dictatorship of the proletariat executed through the medium of the Bolshevik Party. Peaceful development of the revolution was made impossible by the fault of the "Louis Blancs" and the "Cavaignacs"; what was required was a war-cry announcing the fight without quarter. He announced with his customary directness: "Not to understand that, is to under-stand nothing about the essential problems of the moment."

But this was just what the Party did not understand, and the future justified the retention of the old popular formula. In this instance conservative inertia carried the day over the quick mind of the Party chief, who had not time to win over more than the directing circles of the Party to his thesis. Events moved with increasing rapidity, upsetting all reasoned conclusions. In August, Kornilov's abortive coup gave an unhoped-for turn to affairs; the scorned and persecuted Bolsheviks were summoned to help in the struggle against the factious general, the hope of the counter-revolution. They had the tactical sense to accept a socialist coalition in defence of the threatened revolution, and were thus able to take up arms once more and to show them-selves in the open. The danger was overcome, but Kerensky's prestige was still more diminished by the suspicious part he had played in the affair and his manifest powerlessness. His socialist allies, who had been in favour of conciliation, lost ground vis-ibly, and the suburbs, the garrison and the crews of the fleet, stimulated by the alarm, went over to the Bolsheviks who had given warning of the event. One by one those imprisoned in July were set at liberty. A new wave of revolution arose in the sea of the masses. Trotsky especially emerged from the affair with increased personal prestige. The moving tale of how he had intervened with the raging mob to save Chernov from lynching was in all mouths. In contrast to the equivocal attitude of Lunacharsky, a Left Bolshevik, whose opportunist behaviour was commented on in the press, he had openly taken part with the vanquished: "I share the principles adopted by Lenin, Zino-viev and Kamenev. I have maintained them in *Vperyod* and generally in all my public speeches." According to the testimony of his fellows he bore himself heroically before the examining judge. In Lenin's absence the Bolsheviks regarded him as their most eminent exponent, even before his formal enrolment in the Party.

Lenin, who was inclined to attribute to the enemy a decision equal to his own, a similar sense for effective action, had said in July: "Now they will shoot us all. It is their moment." In the same way he had expected to be arrested when he arrived in Russia. He was soon reassured by the turn of events. After the Kornilov affair, he said: "We are extraordinarily near power, but at a tangent." And, by way of compromise, he resumed the old slogan which he had too hastily repudiated: "All Power to the Soviets," the last chance, he said, of securing the peaceful progress of the revolution. What this really meant was "the formation of a government of Social Revolutionaries and of Mensheviks, responsible to the Soviets."

As for Stalin, it is still difficult to assign to him any considerable rôle without ignoring proportion. Whether calculated or not, this reticence is perhaps characteristic. He assumed administrative work at the headquarters of the Party and of its journals, and was careful to say and do nothing which would commit him irrevocably. Demian Biedny relates with admiration the following example of his method. On the eve of the July demonstration, the Kronstadt sailors telephoned to *Pravda* to know if they should march with their rifles. Stalin replied: "Rifles? It is for you to decide, comrades. We scribblers always carry our arm, the pencil. As for you, with your arms, it is for you to decide." According to Trotsky, he kept prudently aloof, waiting for an opportunity to display his wisdom. At any rate he was looked upon as one of the principal militants but behind the stage and, lacking originality, he made himself useful by perseverance.

Without Lenin and without the accredited theorists of the Party, the semi-clandestine Social-Democratic Congress of the Bolsheviks was held in July-August under the firm and discreet direction of Sverdlov. It was an assembly which had to confirm past action and to dispatch current business. The work was done by the members of the Central Committee, policy was determined strictly by Lenin's letters and articles. Delegates felt they were executants rather than directing agents. In this restricted task, Stalin played a leading part as mouthpiece of the directing central organisation. Repeating Lenin's instructions he recommended the abandonment of the watchword "All Power to the Soviets." He secured the introduction into the resolution carried of a phrase which is indicative of the temporary hesitation of Bolshevik headquarters: *"The Soviets are reaching the end of an agonising struggle to the death, and are perishing through not having seized all power into their hands in time."* A serious error, the blame for which rests in the first instance with Lenin; it excludes the possibility of the bolshevisation of the Soviets. Later on, Stalin took undue credit to himself for having resisted the amendment he himself had formulated in the text of the resolution, vague enough in any case to allow of various interpretations: "Full liquidation of the counter-revolutionary bourgeoisie." This did not supply any practical policy and showed no clear way of attaining power.

At the end of the Sixth Congress, there was a brief, unimpassioned exchange of observations between Stalin and Preobrazhensky on the last words of the resolution. The revolutionary classes, it said, should seize power to advance "in unison with the revolutionary proletariat of advanced countries towards peace and the socialist reconstruction of society." Preobrazhensky suggested an alternative wording: "Towards peace and, on the advent of proletarian revolution in the west, towards socialism." Stalin opposed, declaring: "It is not excluded that Russia may be *the pioneer country in the advance to socialism.*" An apparently insignificant difference, but one big with future consequences.

For the first time Stalin was confirmed in his functions as a member of the Central Committee by a Congress (his position had been confirmed at the May conference). He was helped by the position he had acquired by co-optation during the mysterious phase of his activity. No one thought of contesting the accomplished fact or questioning the validity of the earlier choice made by Lenin. At that time the Party had more than 175,000 members, but its framework and central organisation were sufficiently hierarchical to assure continuity of direction and organisation. Nevertheless, Trotsky was elected in his absence to the Central Committee by more votes than Stalin, a fact which illustrates the exceptional character of his election.

The official biography does not attribute any remarkable rôle to Stalin between February and October of this memorable year, but merely praises him for his "complete agreement" with Lenin. As the documents show, the "complete agreement" began in profound divergence, and continued as passive submission. Trotsky in his *My Life* gives the following estimate of Stalin's personal part in Party politics during the revolution:

Not one of his articles written about that period shows that Stalin made any attempt to estimate his previous policy and win his way to Lenin's stand. He simply kept silent because he had been too much compromised by his unfortunate leadership during the first month of the revolution. He preferred to withdraw into the background. He never made any public appearance to defend Lenin's views; he merely stood back and waited. During the most responsible months of the theoretical and political preparation for the uprising, Stalin simply did not exist in the political sense.

This statement is accurate if by policy is understood general ideas, wide conclusions arising out of theory and programme, plans for the future. But in the narrower sense and on the lower level of daily political action, Stalin was one of the foremost agents in the execution of Lenin's designs. In this respect and within his limitations, he rendered incontestable service to the Party and Lenin appears to have made full use of Stalin's special aptitudes.

4

"In spite of great errors and frequent absurdities, the soviets have been the primitive moulds, political and social, in which the torrent of revolutionary lava has been cooled down." These were the words of Kerensky, who assured the British Ambassador that the soviets "would die a natural death." This was practically Stalin's point of view in the "death struggle" of the soviets. The *Izvestia* of the first Executive Committee also stated that "The soviets are nearing their end." Facts were to give the lie to all these prophets; instead of disappearing the soviets went Bolshevik.

In September the Petrograd Soviet by a majority passed over to the vanquished of July, and elected Trotsky as its President. Those of Moscow, Kiev and the principal towns took the same course. At the municipal elections there was a parallel movement towards Bolshevism and a still stronger one in the army and navy. The Leninists won over the trade unions and the workshop committees. Their party had organised the earliest detachments of Red Guards. In this country in process of dissolution, the only real, active force, determined and disciplined, was at Lenin's disposal.

He was not the man to neglect or to miss the psychological moment. His whole life had been a laborious and detailed preparation for the decisive struggle. He saw that the long-expected hour was approaching and from his hiding-place he studied the news, examined possibilities, and calculated chances and risks. The Bolshevik organisation, his creation, the product of twenty years of work and struggle, had absorbed the most virile and the best elements of the workers' revolutionary movement. Around him were grouped all those who seriously regarded socialism as an immediate necessity, all those who were burning to pass from theory to practice. The Social Revolutionaries of the Left supported him with their increasingly numerous fighting elements. The Menshevik Internationalists, through Martov, appreciated him and were not without hope of future union. His adversaries committed folly on folly, and helped his game. The denouement was undoubtedly at hand.

Provided that the Party, the instrument of his plans, was ready at the supreme moment, the revolution would achieve the last lap. "Counter-revolution or Jacobinism?" So Lenin laid down the historic alternative. The conquest of power became an urgent question. To what end? To realise a "completely democratic republic." Complete democracy was the essential point in the programme.

The soviets, said Lenin, were *"a superior type of democracy."* There was nothing abstract about the matter: "Power to the Soviets—this is the only thing that can secure further progress, *gradual, peaceful and smooth*, keeping perfect pace with the consciousness and the resolve of the majority of the masses of the people, with their own experience."

He insists especially on the pacific character of this conception:

The pacific character of the revolution would be possible and probable provided that all power rested with the soviets. The struggle of Parties for power may develop peacefully within the soviets on condition that the latter do not give a twist to democratic principles, as for example, by giving one vote to five hundred soldiers as against one for a thousand workers. In a democratic republic these distortions of principle must not be permitted.

This idea recurs repeatedly in his writings at this time, with varying emphasis:

If the soviets assumed power, they could still now—and probably it is the last chance—assure the peaceful development of the revolution, peaceful election by the people of its deputies, peaceful rivalry of the Parties within the soviets, the trying out of the programme of the different Parties, and the transfer of power from one Party to another.

As for the measures to be taken by the sovereign soviets to realise real democracy, they are comprised in the suppression of the police, of the permanent army, of bureaucracy. Invariably, and not once but a hundred times, Lenin reiterated the definite and categorical promise for the suppression of the police, the army and professional civil servants. The militia, a general arming of the people, with officers elected in all ranks, would replace the police and the old army. The functions of the State would be assumed by citizens elected for the purpose, liable to dismissal at all times, whose pay would not exceed that of the workers. "These democratic measures, simple and automatic, by the solidarisation of the interests of the workers and of the majority of the peasants, will serve at the same time as the bridge between capitalism and socialism." The example to be followed was that of the Paris Commune of 1871.

Such are the propositions advocated by him in the Bolshevik press and more strongly justified in his work, *The State and Revolution*, written in various retreats, where he worked with extraordinary ardour and courage. Simultaneously he examined the economic and political situation in a pamphlet, *The Threatening Catastrophe and How to Fight It*, in which he advocated workers' control of production, the nationalisation of banks and trusts, the obligation to work. This contains the warning:

War is implacable, it puts the question with merciless sharpness; either overtake the advanced countries and surpass them *also economically* or perish. It is possible to do this, for we have before us the experiences of a great number of advanced countries; we have available the results of their technique and culture. . . . Either full steam ahead, or perish. This is how history has put the question.

On the day on which he finished this essay, he addressed to the Central Committee of the Party a letter beginning with these words: "Having obtained a majority in the Soviets of Workers' and Soldiers' Deputies of both capitals, the Bolsheviks can and must take power into their hands."

He foresaw that "the Bolsheviks will form a government which nobody will overthrow." It must be done quickly for it was rumoured that Petrograd would shortly be abandoned to the Germans, and a separate peace between England and the Central Powers was also mooted. (There were many panicky rumours at the time.) They must not wait for the Constituent Assembly because, "by surrendering Petrograd, Kerensky and Co. can always destroy the Constituent Assembly. Only our Party, having assumed power, can secure the convocation of the Constituent Assembly." Finally, they must take to heart Marx's words "Insurrection is an art."

This letter was followed by yet another in which Lenin explains why and how insurrection is an art, supporting his argument by the teaching of Marx and Engels, and applies his method to the particular situation. He says notably: "Our victorious insurrection alone will secure the failure of the intrigues for a separate peace," and, if the worst comes, "If our peace offer (general peace) were refused, and we did not even obtain an armistice, we should become ardent partisans of national defence." Then follows practical advice on the creation of a general staff for insurrection, on the distribution of forces, the occupation of strategic points, and the indispensable preliminary operations. Now or never, was the time to use, for the purposes of civil war, the military science learned from the study of the "masters of war," of Clausewitz, and of the experience of 1905.

How did the Party respond to Lenin's hopes and appeals? The minutes of the Central Committee show that those leaders who were at liberty were far from thinking for themselves of the eventualities so clearly indicated. On receiving pressing messages of this kind, some were convinced by Lenin's arguments, some obeyed out of fidelity, others awaited events, and some took an opposite view. Stalin was one of those who held their hand, though following with the stream. Trotsky, in close agreement with Lenin on the course to be followed, was busy with providing legal cover for insurrection, a condition realisable because of the coincidence of the rising with the Second Congress of Soviets, already won over to the Bolsheviks. Zinoviev and Kamenev, with the tacit approval of some others, thought the seizure of power dangerous and premature, fearing isolation for the Party and the consequences of an adventurous policy.

But Lenin certainly reflected the sentiments of the masses in revolt, especially of the soldiers eager to escape from the nightmare of war. Delegations from the Front were demanding daily the saving intervention of the Soviet; they called on the Bolsheviks to work hard for peace and for the solution of the agrarian question. Rumours of movements in rural Russia caused universal alarm; confiscation of harvests, seizure of land, and armed resistance to Kerensky's measures of repression showed that the patience of the peasants was nearing its end.

The Bolshevik Party had now 240,000 members. Its Right, vague in outline and of varying strength, was inclined to the rôle of a parliamentary opposition in the representative institutions of the Republic, finally proclaimed in September. The Right secured a decision in favour of participation in the Democratic Conference, arbitrary in composition, summoned by the Government in the interim before the Constituent as a sort of provisional assembly from which the Pre-Parliament would emerge. Trotsky, supported by Stalin, proposed to boycott the latter, but was outvoted. Once more pressure from Lenin was required to drive the Party back to the path of insurrection.

"We should have boycotted the Democratic Conference," cried Lenin in his article "The Errors of our Party": "We all erred by not doing so"; and now they "must boycott the Pre-Parliament." He congratulated Trotsky and encouraged him, he demanded an extraordinary Congress of the Party if need be to reverse the "shameful" decision of the "directing circles." The Central Committee submitted, and the Bolsheviks left the Pre-Parliament after Trotsky had read a threatening declaration. Violent conflict was only a question of hours.

"The crisis is ripe," said Lenin in another article, asserting that "there is no doubt that the beginning of October has brought us to the greatest turning-point in the history of the Russian and, according to all appearances, of the world revolution." He thought he saw "the unimpeachable signs of the great change, indications preluding world revolution" in Italy and Germany. "There is no room for doubts," he wrote, "we are on the threshold of a world proletarian revolution." It is for us, he continued, to begin, because of the advantages, the liberty and the means at our disposal in Russia. The break-up of the reformist socialists and the dizzy progress of the Bolsheviks, indicated at all the elections, precluded hesitation: "With the Left Social Revolutionaries, we have to-day a majority in the Soviets, in the army and in the country."

But there was in the Central Committee of the Party a tendency in favour of "awaiting the Congress of Soviets, *against* the immediate seizure of power"; it should be overcome; "*otherwise the Bolsheviks would cover themselves with shame for ever, they would be reduced to nothing as a Party.*" The allusion to Trotsky is clear. To wait for the Congress would be "idiocy" or "treason." We must strike unexpectedly at Petrograd, Moscow, and in the Baltic Fleet. To delay is to lose all. . . . And in order to rouse his too passive principal supporters, Lenin resigned from the Central Committee. For he knew himself to be indispensable.

He did not merely urge them to action; he used the full force of argument in discussion and persuasion. His pamphlet, *Will the Bolsheviks Retain State Power?* brought over many waverers. In this he refutes one by one current prejudices that if the Bolsheviks seized power they would be unable to retain it. Under cover of replying to the enemy he was really seeking to convert irresolute partisans. In that pamphlet he borrows from the comminatory words of the gospel: "He that doth not work neither shall he eat," and he opposed with assurance the sophisms of his timid followers. If 130,000 landowners were able to govern Russia in the interests of the rich, 240,000 Bolsheviks could administer it in the interests of the poor. There were obviously immense difficulties to be met, but "you cannot make an omelette without breaking eggs." The Bolsheviks will win, for they incarnate "the workers' idea of justice" and "ideas become forces when the masses embrace them."

The Central Committee gave way to these arguments, but with a delay and a slowness exasperating to Lenin, haunted by the idea of losing all by missing the right moment. "*Delay becomes positively a crime,*" said another letter to the directors of the Party. "Temporising is a crime, to wait for the Congress of the Soviets is a childish formality, absurd and disgraceful, it is the *betrayal* of the revolution. . . . There must be immediate insurrection. . . . Victory is certain at Moscow, where no one can fight us. Petrograd can wait. The Government is powerless, its situation is hopeless; it will yield. . . . Victory is certain, there

are nine chances in ten that it will be won without bloodshed.
... To wait is a crime against the revolution."

Next day Lenin sent his *Advice from an Outsider* to repeat
once more that the seizure of power meant armed insurrection
and to recall the Marxist conception of insurrection as an art.
Conclusion: "The triumph of the Russian Revolution and of
world revolution both depend on two or three days' fighting."

Another letter on the same day to the Bolsheviks in the Re-
gional Congress of the Northern Soviets, urges the offensive:
"The hour is so grave that to temporise is really like death."
For mutiny in the German Fleet, after many other symptoms,
was heralding the world revolution. Three times he repeated:
"To temporise means death."

On October 23rd, he returned secretly to Petrograd, and took
part in the session of the Central Committee which finally decided on insurrection. The reasons given in support of the revolution were in the first place the "growth of world revolution,"
the "threat of peace between the Imperialist powers," the undoubted "intention of the Russian bourgeoisie and of Kerensky
and Co. to surrender Petrograd to the Germans." It is important to make it clear that the historic act was based on three
mistaken suppositions. But a just appreciation of the internal
situation in Russia was sufficient to ensure its success.

Kamenev and Zinoviev alone had openly resisted Lenin's lead,
although their anxiety was shared by many others. They did
not think the world proletarian revolution was either so near
or so ripe, and refused to stake the whole future on the insurrection card. In fear of "certain defeat," they committed a breach
of discipline by disavowing the Party instructions in Gorky's
paper, hostile to Bolshevism. Kamenev emphasised the gravity
of his disapproval by resigning from the Central Committee.
The defection of two of the principal Old Bolsheviks at the
very moment of preparation for attack was an ill omen.

But Lenin did not think the loss irreparable. To disciples of
this kind he applied Marx's bitter words: "I have sown dragons
and reaped fleas." After patiently refuting their thesis, he denounced them constantly as "traitors" when he learnt of their

open opposition, invited the Party to exclude the "deserters," these "yellow" men whom he accused of "unbounded infamy" in plain terms. Stalin was foolish enough to try to break the force of the blow by an editorial note in the central organ of the Party: "The sharp tone of Lenin's article does not alter the fact that we remain in agreement on the essential point. . . ." General reprobation compelled his resignation from the staff of the paper, but he knew that the endless difficulties of the moment would prevent its acceptance.

This was not Lenin's gravest cause of alarm. The Congress of Soviets, several times deferred before it was fixed for November 7th, was approaching, and the Central Committee seemed to be awaiting this date before giving the signal of insurrection. Trotsky wanted to associate the two events, but Lenin was anxious to secure the accomplished fact, to execute the technical operation, content to have it politically confirmed later on. Might not Kerensky forestall them, and with the help of a few dependable regiments, upset all his plans? But nothing of the kind happened; an accumulation of unprecedentedly favourable circumstances facilitated the victory of the new revolution.

Everything concurred, as John Reed said, to pour "oil on the Bolshevik fire." Confronted by the most urgent collective tasks, the authorities oscillated endlessly between half-way solutions and ineffective repression; they accumulated miscalculations and errors. The only hope of the disappointed masses found expression in the clear notes of Lenin's programme.

The Government, incapable of taking any step towards peace, responsible for the useless massacre of Galicia, had become an object of hatred to the soldiers. The Bolsheviks, while promoting fraternisation in the trenches, proposed to offer immediately to all belligerents "a democratic peace," without annexations or indemnities. "In case of refusal, we will wage a war of revolution," said Lenin, and Trotsky spoke in the same tone.

The Government persisted in putting off to the Greek Kalends the appeasement of the land hunger; in their absorption in statistics, studies, commissions, and plans, they had lost all authority in the rural districts. The Bolsheviks proposed the im-

mediate reversion of the land to the peasants' soviets, charged
with its distribution according to local circumstances—a gigantic
expropriation in which every tiller of the soil was interested.

The Government refused to accede to the more and more
insistent demands of the nationalities oppressed by Tsarism, and
were in open conflict with Finland and the Ukraine. The Bolsheviks proposed to give complete self-determination.

The Government seemed to be accessory to Kornilov's counter-revolutionary coup, and their suspicious conduct in this
affair set the military chiefs against them without conciliating
anyone else. They lost at one and the same time the support of
the forces of the Right and the confidence of the Left. The
Bolsheviks had foreseen the renewal of the offensive by the reaction and were foremost in the fight against it. The Government
put off the Constituent as if they feared it. The Bolsheviks demanded its immediate convocation. The Government were evidently trying to wreck the meeting of the Congress of Soviets.
The Bolsheviks went ahead with it.

As if to complete their unpopularity the Government reinstated the death penalty in the army, they allowed it to be
thought that the capital would shortly be transferred to Moscow,
and revealed their intention of sending to the front two-thirds
of the Petrograd garrison. The Bolsheviks, making clever use
of the triple opportunity of overwhelming their adversary,
promised to abolish the death penalty, to keep the capital at
Petrograd, and to retain the revolutionary garrison there. The
Government plans were reduced to vague threats; they merely
encouraged and strengthened the opposition. At the end of
October the Bolshevik Party numbered about 400,000 members.

The logic of facts worked in the same direction. Economic
disintegration imposed on the local soviets intervention in everyday life; they had to transform themselves into directing organisations especially in the provisioning of their districts by
means of taxation and requisitions. The Menshevik Soviet of
Tiflis, for example, presided over by Jordania, acted as a regional
government, and the smallest revolutionary municipalities did
the same within their own jurisdiction. The socialisation of cer-

tain enterprises seemed the only solution possible to the partial stoppages of production brought about by bellicose employers, to strikes caused by engineers which brought about industrial paralysis. The Soviets of Kaluga, of Tashkent, of Kazan, of Kronstadt and other places did not wait for the Congress of Soviets to decide the question of power.

The conflict with regard to the Petrograd garrison served as a pretext and a bait for the first *coup d'état*. The Soviet nominated on October 26th a Military Revolutionary Committee, and placed the movements of troops under its control. Trotsky, president of both committees, therefore held in his hands all the levers. On its side the Bolshevik Central Committee had formed a Political Bureau of seven members charged with the direction of the Party without formalities; Lenin and Trotsky were its brains, Zinoviev, Kamenev, Stalin, Sokolnikov and Bubnov its arms. There was also a "military centre" of five members —Sverdlov, Stalin, Bubnov, Uritzky and Dzerzhinsky—introduced into the Military Revolutionary Committee presided over by Trotsky. Thus he had a regular revolutionary general staff.

The final result depended on the army, about whose state of mind there was no doubt. At the beginning of October the officer Dubassov had declared to the Soviet: "The soldiers do not at this moment demand either liberty or land. All they ask is the end of the War. And whatever you may say here they will do no more fighting." At the end of the month, a series of delegates from the Front warned the Soviet Executive Committee: "It is impossible to continue the War in the circumstances of to-day. . . . The Front lives in feverish expectation of peace"; "Many units demand peace of any kind, even a separate peace"; one of them added: "If it is a disgraceful peace, give us that." At the beginning of November, General Verkhovsky, Minister of War, said in a secret session of the commissions of the Pre-Parliament: "No persuasion has any effect on people who don't see why they should face death and privation. . . . General disintegration. . . . Hopeless situation . . . there are at least 2,000,000 deserters; the army cannot be fed. . . . It cannot be sufficiently clothed or shod. . . . The Staff no longer exist. . . . Bolshevism continues to dissolve our armed forces. . . . These actual facts compel us to recognise frankly and openly that we can no longer wage war." The insurrection could count on the support of millions of soldiers.

The Military Revolutionary Committee made its dispositions openly. "The centre of the work of mobilisation was the Petrograd Soviet, which had acclaimed as President Trotsky, the most brilliant tribune of the proletarian insurrection," writes Bukharin.

At the Regional Conference of the Soviets of the North, Trotsky got the following resolution voted:

The country means to survive; the Government must disappear. The soviets have not only the right; they have the necessary force. The time for words is past. The hour has come when only decisive and unanimous action by all the soviets can save the country and the revolution and solve the question of the central power.

At the Petrograd Soviet, Trotsky, who was ubiquitous, declared: "They say we are preparing a general staff for the seizure of power. We make no secret of it." But at the same time he neglected no precaution to deceive and to lull the vigilance of the enemy. To inquiries in the Soviet as to Bolshevik activities, he replied promptly and skilfully: "We are hiding nothing. I declare in the name of the Soviet that we have given no instruction for armed action. But if the course of events should force the Soviet to order action, the workers and soldiers would march like one man." Meanwhile, representatives of the Party were negotiating a compromise with other socialists to gain time.

Kerensky let things slide, or acted without vigour. "The whole of Russia is on our side. There is nothing to fear," he said three days before the *coup d'état*. Yet for months attrition had been going on in the Centre parties, to the advantage of the extremes of Right and Left. In the south the reactionaries were beginning to use the Cossacks and to dissolve the soviets. The Kadets were rallying the active forces of social conservatism. Some of them were using wrecking tactics, hoping to dispose of the Bolsheviks easily, after the fall of Kerensky; others preferred German "order" to Russian "disorder." The Social Revolutionaries were no longer a party, but a noisy mob in perpetual confusion. Their Left, definitely detached, served as a prop to Bolshevism. The Mensheviks lost prestige by declaring for peace in principle, but for war in fact. "This policy," says their theorist Voytinsky, "was understood neither by the Allies, nor by Russia." Martov's proposal, supported by the Georgian Mensheviks, was to constitute a "homogenous Socialist Government," including all shades from the Populists to the Bolsheviks, but it came too late and was no longer compatible with the tendencies of the groups to be associated.

"We were certainly weak," writes Trotsky, "in technique and in organisation." But the Bolsheviks were confronted with an even weaker force and they were borne along on the current. According to the same competent authority "the issue of the Revolution of November 7th was already three quarters predetermined when we opposed the removal of the Petrograd garrison." Lenin, in hiding, was less well-informed; that is why he advised beginning with Moscow and was so impatient of delay. Trotsky's explanation is not decisive; in fact, Lenin desired to forestall any defensive measure by the authorities, to confront the Congress of Soviet with the accomplished fact, not with a plan for discussion. "Ever since the battalions, by the order of the Military Revolutionary Committee, refused to leave the city, we have had a scarcely veiled victorious insurrection. . . . The insurrection of November 7th had a complementary character." This is Trotsky's view.

This was never Lenin's opinion, as is proved by a last letter to the Central Committee, a unique document in which the intelligence and the will of the chief is concentrated on shouting the order to attack, on the eve of the Congress of Soviets:

It is as clear as can be that *delaying the uprising now really means death.* . . . With all my power I wish to persuade comrades that now *everything hangs on a hair*, that on the order of the day are questions that are not solved by conferences, by congresses (even by congresses of soviets!). . . . *We must at any price, this evening, to-night, arrest the Ministers,* having disarmed (defeated, if they offer resistance) the military cadets. *We must not wait! We may lose everything.* . . . Who should seize power? At present this is not important. Let the Military Revolutionary Committee seize it, or "some other institution". . . . The matter must absolutely be decided *this evening, or to-night.* History will not forgive delay by revolutionaries who could be victorious to-day (and will surely be victorious to-day), while they risk losing much to-morrow, they risk losing all. . . . *Seizure of power is the point of the uprising;* its political task will be clarified after the seizure. It would be disaster or formalism to wait for the uncertain voting of November 7th. *The people have the right and the duty to decide such questions not by voting but by force.* . . . The crime of the revolutionaries would be limitless if they let go the proper moment. The Government is tottering. We must *deal it the death blow* at any costs. To delay action is the same as death.

Now or never, said Lenin. At last the Military Revolutionary Committee acted without further delay, and passed from preparation to action.

"The most important points in the city were occupied by us during that night almost without fighting, without resistance, without casualties," writes Trotsky.

Lenin's foresight was justified; no blood was shed in Petrograd, but, contrary to his expectation, there was a sanguinary struggle in Moscow. On the whole the revolution met with no serious obstacles. It took place, as Trotsky says, on the date fixed. On the disputed question of putting off the moment until the Congress of the Soviets, Lenin said afterwards to his comrades of the Central Committee: "Yes, you were right"—this is related by Stalin himself three years afterwards in a commemoration address.

The regime of yesterday, represented by the transient figure of Kerensky, fell almost as easily as its predecessor, incarnate in the hereditary Tsar, and for reasons analogous, if not identical. "War gave the power to the proletariat," observed Gorky, following Lenin, "*gave* it, because none can say that the proletariat itself, with its own hands, seized power."

But even in an extraordinarily favourable situation, the Party had to have capable leaders if full use was to be made of it. Stalin, with a thousand others, said: "All the practical work of organising the insurrection was done under the immediate direction of Trotsky, the president of the Petrograd Soviet. It can be safely asserted that for the rapid desertion of the garrison to the side of the Soviet and for the clever organisation of the Military Revolutionary Committee, the Party is above all and primarily indebted to Comrade Trotsky." As for Lenin, he shines by his own light.

On November 7th, writes Bukharin enthusiastically, "Trotsky, splendid and courageous tribune of the rising, indefatigable and ardent apostle of the revolution, declared in the name of the Military Revolutionary Committee at the Petrograd Soviet, with thunders of applause from those present, that the Provisional Government no longer existed. And as living proof of this fact there appeared in the tribune Lenin, whom the new revolution had liberated from the mystery which had surrounded him." In about six months, the Russian Revolution had brought forth the republic, and in less than nine months the dictatorship of the Bolsheviks. The French Revolution had taken more than three years to install the republic and the dictatorship of the Jacobins.

5

THE "professional revolutionaries" this time had their part in the victory; without them Lenin would not have brought off the enterprise, nor even have conceived it. If the advent of Bolshevism required for its achievement a concourse of propitious circumstances, a policy of suicide on the part of the possessing classes and the tenacious aberrations of the socialists advocating social conciliation—the intervention of a consciously revolutionary party, relatively conscious of the aims to be reached, was not less necessary. And among these "professional revolutionaries" Stalin was incontestably a prototype. Before he did anything that distinguished him as a political personage he found himself in command of positions in the new State, by sole reason of his fidelity to the victorious group and of his qualities as a soldier—sufficient for the immediate task.

In the historical "literature" of documents and memoirs which has accumulated on the October revolution, it is rare to find the name of Stalin. Most of these works never mention him. Only in the minutes of the Party is he listed as member of the committees on which he sat for the daily political administrative work. In these committees, wrote John Reed, "only Lenin and Trotsky were for insurrection"—an assertion not to be taken literally but nevertheless containing an element of profound truth. Lenin would never have praised so ardently and unreservedly the now classic work of the American Communist writer, as "an exact and extraordinarily living picture" if he had seen in it any depreciation of the Party to which the "professional revolutionaries" such as Stalin belonged.

"Men make their own history, but not on their own initiative or in circumstances freely chosen." Thus Marx, claimed exclusively by Bolshevism, interprets the objective and subjective data of historical events. Looked at from this point of view, Lenin and Trotsky emerge above the growing mass of their Party to the point of dominating it. Between them and the Party, the "professional revolutionaries" were agents of transmission communicating the impulse and the orientation desired by "the clandestine group of directing minds." In October, Stalin was not yet somebody, but he was something; if his name was unknown, his weight was felt, though merged in the collective authority of the Party. In the unprecedented experience now beginning, the "professional revolutionaries" were to be submitted to the real test, that of the building of the socialist State, the transition to a classless society.

Among them neither Stalin nor any other could foresee the events even of the near future. For some socialists it goes without saying that the conquest of power is not an aim in itself but the indispensable means of realising a programme. In this matter the Party had no clear idea at all; they had to leave it entirely to the directing minds whose views were very uncertain.

Having placed his faith on the world revolution, and that in the immediate future, Lenin had to modify his conception, as a scrupulous theorist, by collaborating in the revision of the Social-Democratic programme, a few days before the *coup d'état*. Putting aside as too boastful Bukharin's proposal to suppress the "minimum programme," he wrote: "*We do not know how soon after our victory the revolution in the west will come. It is not impossible that we may be at the beginning of a period of reaction. . . . We don't know and we cannot know*." On this point Zinoviev and Kamenev were not wrong in their warnings against the imminence of international revolution. And Riazanov was right in saying, if his words are correctly reported by John Reed: "The European workers will not move."

But even in this event Lenin did not refuse power; what was necessary was to maintain it, while taking the transitional measures leading to socialism. "The definitive victory of socialism is impossible in one country alone," he said three months after the October Revolution, but he still hoped for external reinforcement. Recalling the words of Marx and Engels: "The French will begin it, and the Germans will complete it," he expressed his conviction with a variant: "Russia has begun, the German, the Frenchman and the Englishman will complete the work, and socialism will conquer." A month later, while affirming that "Our safety, in all difficulties, lies in the pan-European revolution," he went on to say: "The revolution will not come so soon as we expect it. History has proved that. We must admit the fact."

At least he was not under any illusion as to why "Russia had begun." In a speech to the Moscow Soviet, he was to say in April 1918: "It was the fact of our being a backward country that enabled us to be in advance, and we may perish if we do not hold on until the moment when our revolution receives effective help from the revolutions of other countries." This is not an isolated remark on his part. "We are," he said, "a revolutionary detachment of the working class, thrown into the attack not because we are better than other workers, not because the Russian proletariat is superior to the working class in other countries, but only because we were one of the most backward countries in the world." He insisted some months afterwards, in a letter to American workers: "Circumstances have put our detachment in the van, the Russian detachment of the socialist proletariat, not by reason of our merits, but because of the especial backwardness of Russia."

Very similar was the view held by Plekhanov, whose political career was over before the revolution but who was still in full intellectual vigour. In reply to his friends who were inclined to look on the Soviet regime as a short episode he said: "The strength of the Bolsheviks lies in the weariness and ignorance of our people and also in our backward economic conditions. Bolshevism will last many years, and our people will only attain consciousness after this hard lesson. Then there will be an end of Bolshevism. But that day is far off."

Trotsky remained convinced of his theory of the "permanent revolution." He declared to the Congress of Soviets on the morrow of the revolution: "Either the Russian Revolution will bring about a revolutionary movement in Europe, or the European powers will crush the Russian Revolution." The whole of the Central Committee shared this view. "Unless there is a socialist revolution in the west," said one of its members at the beginning of 1918, summing up the general opinion, "our revolution is threatened with disaster." To which Stalin replied: "We also bank on the revolution, but you count in weeks, and we in months." No one reckoned in years.

But the vain expectation of socialist revolution in the west involved tactical errors more and more dangerous for Bolshevism. Lenin, in the absence of any valid forecast of the date, was the first to attempt to explain the delay of other countries. "To pass from one victory to another with such facility," he said, "was easy only because the actual international situation protected us for the moment from imperialism." Elsewhere and under other conditions, things would go differently. "It is much more difficult to begin in Europe," he said: "with us it was infinitely easier to begin, but it will be less easy to continue. In Europe the contrary is the case; once revolution has begun, it will be much easier to go on with it. . . ."

And, recalling the obstinately optimist Bolsheviks of the Left to a sense of realities, he added: "Yes, we shall see the world revolution, but in the meantime it is only a fairy-tale, very attractive, very pretty. I quite understand that children like pretty fairy-tales, but I ask a serious revolutionary—Can he believe in them?"

Chapter VI

THE CIVIL WAR

BOLSHEVISM inherited a truly catastrophic situation, in which the outstanding factors were famine, reduction of the grainfields, ruined industry and transport, a fall in the value of paper money with a corresponding rise in the cost of living, boundless speculation in shares and in exchange, and spontaneous demobilisation. These were not favourable conditions for what Trotsky, in the enthusiasm caused by the victory of the revolution in October, called an "unprecedented experiment."

There was no magic solution for the problem. The era of violence and suffering inaugurated by the War of 1914 was merely entering on a new phase. Once more history demonstrated the impossibility of social transformation by peaceful means. The resistance of the propertied classes at home and the hostility of the capitalist world abroad dissipated any hope of escaping regular civil war. And the harsh regulations of a state of war were to take the place of the promises of the Lenin programme. Victory must come before conversion, blows before persuasion.

The Bolsheviks had promised the immediate convocation of a Constituent Assembly; they had to defer it, then to dissolve it. They protested against the death penalty in the army; they reinstated it after having suppressed it, and then instituted it for civilians as well as soldiers. They offered violent opposition to the transfer of the capital to Moscow; they themselves afterwards carried it out. They recognised the right of independence for nationalities; they encouraged separation only to reintegrate them by force of arms. They vehemently denounced a separate peace; they were constrained to sign one. They were on the other hand committed to a war of revolution; they could not keep their word. They demanded a "democratic" peace; they had to submit to a "shameful" peace. They promised the land to the peasants; they were to confiscate the products. As for the abolition of the police, of the standing army and of bureaucracy, it was indefinitely postponed; the institutions condemned by Lenin were to survive under other names: the Extraordinary Commission (Cheka), the Red Army, the Soviet bureaucracy.

In other words the Bolshevik programme, admittedly, could not be translated at the moment from theory into practice, however sincere its promoters might be. The only realisable and actually accomplished step, the seizure of power, was related to a unique combination of circumstances. "If we had not seized power in October, we should never have obtained it," admitted Trotsky. In Lenin's words the whole thing hung by a hair.

Diverted by the Civil War from the line of action they had laid down beforehand, the Bolsheviks could do no more than execute their plan of socialisation by stages, beginning with the control of production by the workers. The immediate vital necessities which drove them to the momentary sacrifice of principle, without committing themselves as to the future, also drove them to desperate improvisation in the economic field. The inevitability of this radical action had been foreseen by Jaurès:

Whenever unexpected events, similar to the historic disturbance of 1871, carry the socialist proletarians to power, they would be compelled to accomplish or at least to attempt a social revolution by the transformation of the system of private property. It would be useless to say that perhaps not the whole peasant class was prepared, that perhaps even in the working class there were too many inert and non-conscious elements; they would be compelled by the very logic of socialism to use the power which historical events had put into their hands for the complete transformation of property.

The February (March) Revolution failed in the eyes of the people because it had failed to realise the truth formulated in

Kropotkin's *Memoirs:* "A Revolution must from its inception be an act of justice towards the ill-treated and the oppressed, and not a promise to perform this act of reparation later on. If not, it is sure to fail." The October (November) Revolution thus failed to fulfil its engagements, though only after having at least demonstrated the intention and desire to keep them. And when growing popular discontent put it in peril, it succeeded in maintaining itself, not by words, but by combining, in opportunist fashion, vigorous repression with cleverly conceived concessions. The Jacobins among the proletariat had profited by some of the lessons of history.

In fact, with their decrees on the subjects of peace and land, approved at the Second Congress of Soviets, the Bolsheviks displayed their anxiety to carry out when in power the promises they had made in opposition. The decree on a democratic peace could not provide such a peace, which must be determined by international conditions and the relative strength of the belligerents. The decree on the land could not provide a socialist solution of the agrarian question by consolidating the capitalism which the new regime aimed at limiting and eventually abolishing. But illusions shared alike by the Bolsheviks and the masses were at first satisfied by symbolic gestures. As these illusions vanished, the young Soviet Government found new means of strength in breaking all opposition by force, without pursuing any particular course of action to the bitter end, and, before as after the *coup d'état*, by taking advantage of the colossal mistakes of their predecessors. But they had gradually to abandon their initial programme.

Five days after the October insurrection, Kerensky, with his customary foresight, had proclaimed that "Bolshevism is breaking up, it is isolated, and, as an organised force, it no longer exists, even at Petrograd." The whole of the "cultured classes," the socialist and other political parties, upper, middle and lower classes of the bourgeoisie, the Allied embassies and missions, all shared this opinion, which was voiced abroad by press correspondents and official and non-official news services.

The avowed reactionaries had refrained from active assistance to the Provisional Government; General Headquarters waited to see what would happen, and the Cossacks in the capital had declared neutrality, reserving the right to act on their own account. Troops, the strength of which was unknown, under General Krasnov, were marching on Petrograd, raising alarm in some quarters, hope in others. A general strike of State officials and employees paralysed public administration. The railwaymen's and the postal servants' unions demanded a Coalition Socialist Government, under the threat of depriving the new Government, the Council of People's Commissars, of transport and communications.

At this critical moment, Lenin saw arrayed against him in his own Party the Old Bolsheviks, who were also supporters of a "Socialist Government of all the Soviet parties," and of agreement between Bolsheviks, Mensheviks, Left and Right Wing Social Revolutionaries. Ten days after the *coup d'état*, while negotiations for the sharing of power were in full swing, eleven out of fifteen People's Commissars handed in their portfolios, saying: "There is only one other course, the maintenance of a purely Bolshevik Government by means of political terrorism." Rykov, Nogin, Miliutin, Shliapnikov and their colleagues added: "This policy diverts the organisations of the masses of the proletariat from the direction of political affairs, and leads to the establishment of an irresponsible Government, to the ruin of the revolution and of the country."

Kamenev, Zinoviev, Rykov, Nogin and Miliutin resigned from the Central Committee of the Party, accusing its directing group, that is, Lenin and Trotsky supported by Sverdlov, Dzerzhinsky, Stalin and Bukharin, of *"desiring at all costs a purely Bolshevik Government without counting the number of worker and soldier victims it may cost."* By their resignation they hoped to put a stop at the earliest moment to the *"bloodshed between the various democratic parties."* The "Left" Bolshevik, Lunacharsky, had preceded them by resigning from the Council of Commissars on hearing the false news of the bombardment of a church in Moscow. Shliapnikov signed the protest without resigning. Riazanov also protested, but he was not an inveterate

Bolshevik and protested because he felt obligations to the rail-waymen's union, which he had helped to found. At Gachina the People's Commissar, Dybenko, concluded a compromise with Krasnov's Cossacks, admitting the temporary removal of Lenin and Trotsky from the Government and even from the assemblies of the people.

In fact Bolshevik principles no longer committed anybody to anything. Strategy superseded political loyalty. Lenin and Trotsky especially were playing for time, which spelled victory.

With this end in view they agreed to send delegates to the congresses of conciliation convoked by the railwaymen, and they did not refuse to constitute a Coalition Government, though they continued to insist on irreductible fundamental conditions as against the personal political conditions formulated by the socialists, so as to prolong negotiations until the moment came to take another tone and saddle their rivals with the responsibility of the inevitable breach. The blindness of their opponents made the Bolshevik tactics easier. There was equal intransigence on both sides. The victors desired confirmation of their fundamental decrees on the questions of peace and land; the vanquished proposed to decapitate the revolution by removing only Lenin and Trotsky. But these two had long ago taken the measure of their talkative adversaries and were the cleverer tacticians.

They were still too optimistic over the prospects of international revolution, but they were not under any illusion about Russia, and, at this decisive moment, they surveyed the situation dispassionately. They saw the profound apathy in the urban population, proved by the recent municipal elections, in which in some places more than two-thirds of the electorate did not vote; a wave of anarchy in the country districts, taking shape in sanguinary riots, pillage, lynchings and pogroms; a peasant mass suspicious but kept quiet in the provinces by the sharing out of the land and at the Front by promises of peace; nationalism in Finland, Ukraine, the Baltic provinces and the Caucasus satisfied by the right to secede; town soviets bolshevised but elected less and less by the working-class majority; trade unions, weak and too recently formed to assume an independent rôle; and they saw their enemies, whether socialists, liberals or reactionaries, divided and disorganised, and incapable of quick action. The struggle was between small forces on either side. The soldiers and sailors were masters of the situation.

Trotsky did not hesitate to speak frankly of the soldier as the man "in whose hands power rests." The *coup d'état* had been an essentially military proceeding, carried out under the orders of a military committee against a government with no military protection. "The inhabitants slept peaceably," said Trotsky, "without realising that power had passed from one body to another." The former police force was dissolved, and no new force existed to thwart the conspiracy. The attackers were hardly more warlike than the attacked; they spent a whole day in capturing the Winter Palace which might have been taken in a few minutes. Two or three point-blank shots from a cruiser would have sown terror in the Democratic camp. In Moscow the struggle was uselessly prolonged by the indecisive character of the Bolshevik action. Elsewhere, in the provinces, a telegram was sufficient to secure a change of government. The "battle" in Petrograd between Reds and Whites, and the capture of Tsarskoye Selo, admirable themes for grandiloquent communiqués, were really only feeble skirmishes followed by the occupation of a village already evacuated.

Lenin was not wrong in saying: "*It was easy to begin revolutions in such a country, easier than lifting a feather.*" For its continuation a respite was necessary to create the machinery of coercion lacking under the preceding Government; the Red Guard and the sailors served as such pending the organisation of the Cheka, the revolutionary police. Lastly, "the primitive sheep instinct of the Russians," as Engels said, was a destined source of strength for the strongest. There was no longer any question of the "peaceful competition" of parties in the soviets (Lenin had already said so). The Bolsheviks were determined to keep power at all costs, if necessary by the means employed to seize it. The parallel drawn by Lenin between the 130,000 rural landlords of yesterday and the 240,000 Bolsheviks of to-day, now raised to 400,000, was verified beyond all expectation; in both cases, despite class differences, the political domination of an exiguous minority implies certain analogous consequences.

The negotiations for conciliation gave time to meet the most pressing difficulties and to forge an embryo mechanism of government. Among the negotiators on the Bolshevik side, Kamenev and Riazanov sincerely believed in the necessity of compromise. On the contrary Lenin and Trotsky foresaw the failure of any collaboration of this kind, without disdaining at least a temporary alliance with the Left Social Revolutionaries. Stalin took part in these diplomatic manœuvres as confidential agent of the "clandestine directing circle," with instructions to make concessions in form while conceding nothing in principle. His principal characteristics, astuteness and firmness, made him an efficient agent for such a task. Lenin understood how to make the best use of the qualities and the defects of his followers.

The Bolshevik Central Committee declared themselves ready, under certain conditions, to form "a coalition within the limits of the soviets," not only with the various socialists of the Left but with those of the Right. Before constituting the Council of Commissars it had, indeed, invited in vain three Social Revolutionaries of the Left to join it. The demands of the Moderates made agreement impossible, and left the leading rôle to the Bolsheviks, who thus gained appreciable support for their Government from the Left Social Revolutionaries.

Lenin, a past master in the art of "negotiating and fighting simultaneously," strengthened his position in all quarters under cover of the truce. He had directed the first military operations with Trotsky and Stalin as his lieutenants, Trotsky at the front, Stalin in the rear, each where his best qualities were most useful; Trotsky as leader because of his personal magnetism as a leader of men, his masculine power of initiative and his inspiring courage, and Stalin in the rear because of his worth as a punctual, diligent, rigorous organiser, and as an energetic and reliable executive. At the same time he himself faced the deserters from his old group of "professional revolutionaries," the Zinovievs, Kamenevs and Rykovs; in violent philippics he roused opinion in the Party against them, reducing them first to silence and at last to submission. In his anxiety to bring about preliminaries of peace with Germany he overthrew the obstacle of the Army Headquarters by wireless as it were, by appealing to the troops over the heads of their officers; here again he had assistance from Stalin in the manœuvre executed by Krylenko. Finally, heedless of democratic hesitations and scruples in the Bolshevik ranks, he tackled resolutely the primary conditions of every dictatorship, restriction of the freedom of the press. No one at that time dared to envisage total suppression.

Immediately after the *coup d'état* there arose the question of abolishing the "bourgeois monopoly of the press," an expression paradoxical enough in Bolshevik journals with large circulations. *"Every group of citizens should possess its own printing press and materials,"* declared Trotsky. Lenin himself asserted that "now that the insurrection is over, *we have no intention whatever of suppressing the journals of the other Socialist parties* except in case of incitement to armed rebellion or sedition." A press decree, drawn up by Lenin, gave the express assurance that *"immediately the new order is consolidated, all administrative pressure on the press will be at an end; complete liberty of the press will be established on the principle of legal responsibility, on the widest and most advanced principles."* Meanwhile the attack against democratic principles on which Lenin and Trotsky prided themselves, met with protests even in the camp of Bolshevism, which still bore the name of Social-Democracy. But he had an incontrovertible argument for his insistence—the Red Guard and the sailors.

The whole of the non-Bolshevik press abused and vilified the "usurpers." Only the journals of the Right had been suspended, but the others felt their interests assailed by the attack on the freedom of the press. Articles of Gorky, a former Left Bolshevik, give an idea of the general point of view, and sum up the average opinion held by the socialist revolutionary intelligentsia: "Lenin, Trotsky and their disciples are already intoxicated with the poison of power as is proved by their shameful attitude towards liberty of speech, personal freedom, and all the rights for which Democracy has fought." In the same *Novaya Zhizn*, in the pages of which he had defended the fugitive Lenin after the days of July, Gorky described the Bolsheviks as *"blind fanatics, conscienceless adventurers,"* and Bolshevism as a *"national disaster."*

He denounced the "vanity of Lenin's promises . . . the extent of his madness . . . his anarchism on the Nechayev and Bakunin model," and his government as an *"autocracy of savages."* He expressed passionate indignation over their first steps in dictatorship. "Lenin and his acolytes," he said, "think they have licence to commit every crime." "How," he asked, "does Lenin's conduct with regard to freedom of speech differ from that of Stolypin, Plehve and other caricatures of humanity? Does not Lenin send to jail all those who do not think as he does, just as the Romanovs did?"

Friend of Lenin as he was, he wrote of him in these terms: *"Lenin is not an all-powerful healer, but a cynical conjurer caring nothing for the honour or the life of the proletariat."* Lenin, he adds, has all the qualities of a leader, "especially the amorality essential to the part, and the *country gentleman's* scorn for the life of the masses." The Leninists are no better, for the *"working classes are for them what minerals are for the mineralogist."* He clings to the comparison with Nechayev. "Vladimir Lenin," he says, "is introducing the socialist regime into Russia by Nechayev's methods—*at full steam through mud*. Lenin, Trotsky and all the others who accompany them to destruction in the slough of realism are evidently, like Nechayev, convinced that *dishonour is the best way of persuading a Russian*. . . ." He takes pleasure in likening Bolshevism to Tsarism: "by threats of starvation and massacre for all those who do not approve of the Lenin-Trotsky despotism, these leaders justify the despotic power against which the best elements in the country have so long been struggling."

In reply to the reproaches of certain partisans of the new regime Gorky said: *"Novaya Zhizn* has asserted and will continue to assert that the requisite conditions for the introduction of socialism are non-existent in our country, and that the *Gov-*

ernment at the Smolny Institute treats the Russian workman as if he were a log; it sets light to the logs to see if the flame of European revolution can be kindled on the Russian hearth." He fearlessly warns the workers on repeated occasions and in varying terms: "*The Russian proletariat is being subjected to an experiment which it must pay for in blood, life, and, what is worse, in lasting disillusion with regard to the socialist ideal.*"

Another Bolshevik of the Left, Bazarov, a colleague of Gorky's, wrote of Lenin in the same paper: "He is an incurable madman, signing decrees as head of the Russian Government instead of undergoing hydrotherapeutic treatment under the care of an experienced alienist." Such is the tone of all representatives of traditional socialism in Russia and elsewhere, among them many of Lenin's former comrades-in-arms.

Lenin did indeed sign many decrees which remained a dead letter. He himself said later on: "For a considerable period our decrees were a form of propaganda." According to Trotsky, he attempted by these decrees to cover the whole field of economic, political, administrative and cultural life. "He was not animated," says Trotsky, "by a passion for bureaucratic regimentation but by a desire to develop the Party programme in terms of law." Nevertheless the programme day by day was losing its initial content and tending exclusively to a single aim, the maintenance in power of the Bolshevik Party.

2

THE Council of People's Commissars was, in the idea of its creators and in the letter of the Constitutional Law adopted by the Congress of Soviets, a *Provisional Government* pending the convening of the Constituent Assembly—a solemn undertaking forgotten, as so many others, before and after, were forgotten. Lenin considered it as necessarily subordinate *ipso facto* to the sovereign Party, that is to the Bolshevik Central Committee. Therefore he thought it unnecessary himself to become a member of it. This was not modesty on his part but in keeping with the division of labour. He proposed to nominate as

President of the Council Trotsky, as the person best fitted to vitalise the fundamental decisions of the Party, and did not himself finally accept the post except under the unanimous pressure of the Central Committee.

None of the leaders had any conception of the various organs of the revolutionary dictatorship. It was a period of extreme confusion, of groping, of improvisation in the domain of government. There was no historical precedent, no scientific recipe for reference, and the example of the Commune of 1871, so often mentioned, only offered vague and general indications. Neither Lenin nor Trotsky believed a commissariat of Foreign Affairs to be necessary. The departments of State were entrusted to administrators, not to representative men or to political heads. This partly explains why the majority of the Commissars found themselves in opposition to Lenin and Trotsky from the very beginning on the essential question of the division of power. But the fact that this opposition had no influence on the march of events and that Lenin was easily able to ignore it suffices to show where the real power lay. By formulating the idea of a homogeneous Bolshevik Government, after having for tactical reasons allowed a week's discussion, Lenin intimidated the advocates of an entente with the Right Wing Socialists by the significant remark: "If there is a breach, so much the worse: *we shall go to the sailors.*"

Gradually the Central Committee of the Party and the Council of Commissars ended by carrying out the same functions, and the latter became the instrument of the former. Only the presence of the Left Social Revolutionaries on the Council secured an appearance of respect for existing constitutional forms. But for some months the Council of Commissars, with Lenin and Trotsky as its principal members, had the semblance of power. During the Civil War, the same group of men, overwhelmed by the chaotic state of affairs and by their tasks, were to assume all responsibilty, to direct everything, and juridical distinctions lost all meaning. Effective power was concentrated in fact in the small directing group of which Lenin was the centre, in the Central Committee. For the settlement of urgent questions a Political Bureau of four members was nominated, but under the obligation to consult all the members of the Central Committee present at any given moment in the Smolny Institute. It was a quartet consisting of Lenin, Trotsky, Sverdlov and Stalin, and underwent modification from time to time in accordance with the course of internecine struggles in Russia. In the distribution of government work Stalin was entrusted with the Nationalities question. For this reason he took charge of the journal, *The Life of the Nationalities,* which was the organ of this commissariat. His colleague Pestkovsky has related how, in putting his services at the disposal of the Soviet power at the outset, he made Stalin's acquaintance:

"Comrade Stalin," I said, "you are People's Commissar for Nationalities?" "Yes." "And have you a Commissariat?" "No." "Then I will make you one." "Good, what do you need for that purpose?" "For the moment only a chit indicating concurrence." "Good!"

This dialogue reflects with exactitude the state of the governmental services at the time and one of Stalin's master qualities—his economy of words, so remarkable in a nation of talkers and above all during a general fever of oratory. Pestkovsky goes on to describe the installation of the Commissariat in a room in the Smolny Institute already occupied—a small table, two chairs and a sheet of paper fixed on the wall with the inscription: "People's Commissariat for the business of Nationalities." "Stalin agreed, glanced at the Commissariat, uttered a sound indicative either of approbation or the reverse, and went back to Lenin's room." The remark indicates Stalin's skill in concealing his views.

The sketchy character of the Commissariat of Nationalities corresponded with the general aspect of new institutions; in fact it was almost sufficient for the functions of the Commissariat. Indeed Stalin's activity was absorbed by the invisible labours of the Central Committee. In the ministerial scheme his job was to represent the Government either personally or by deputy at the Congresses, assemblies and people's committees of the different nationalities. The Commissariat exchanged messages with them, received delegations of Letts and Ukrainians, Jews and Tartars, Lapps and Bashkirs, classified claims and grievances which were soon lost in the torrent of such documents at this period.

At the Finnish Social-Democratic Congress in November, Stalin, as mouthpiece of the Council of Commissars, launched an appeal for decisive action in the seizure of power by the Helsingfors workers, promising them the fraternal assistance of the Russian proletariat; two months later the advice was followed, but, for want of the promised aid, the Finnish Revolution was literally drowned in blood and the workers' movement crushed by the White Terror. Stalin's signature accompanied Lenin's on the Declaration of Rights of the Russian People, asserting "willing and honourable union" and "complete and reciprocal confidence," and then, at the foot of the manifesto "To the Mussulman Workers of Russia and the Orient," repudiating Imperialist Russian aims in Persia and Turkey—documents which were then useful for purposes of agitation and propaganda and now have retrospective interest for the evolution of Bolshevism from theory to practice.

In this matter Lenin's doctrine, which Stalin had to carry out, was hesitant, confused and contradictory. In opposition to the Austrian Social-Democrats, defenders of "cultural national autonomy" within the frame of existing States, and in opposition to the Left Social-Democrats of his own Party in Russia and Poland who had no interest in particularist nationalisms, Lenin had maintained the old democratic formula of the right of peoples to self-determination, as if, for a Marxist that did not signify the right of the ruling classes to dispose of the ruled and, in some cases, the right of one country to involve the fate of its neighbour.

In 1913, in a letter to S. Shaumian, he repudiated federalism in these terms: "*We stand for unconditional democratic centralisation. We are opposed to federation. We are for the Jacobins against the Girondins.* We oppose federation on principle; it weakens economic bonds, and is not a desirable type of State. . . . Generally speaking, *we are against separation, but for the right of separation*, because of Great Russian reactionary nationalism. . . ." But in 1917, in *The State and the Revolution*, he admits, in conformity with the teaching of Marx and Engels, the necessity of federation by way of exception or as a transitional stage towards the "Republic one and indivisible." He preaches simultaneously separation as a right and federation as a duty. Next year he did not hesitate to declare, contrary to his former declaration, that *"the interests of socialism are indeed superior to the right of self-determination."* Stalin was content to follow these variations obediently.

After having, as opponents of federation, created a federal republic, the Bolsheviks saw the impossibility of maintaining it without trampling on the reactionary nationalisms they had themselves stimulated. The bourgeoisie of Finland and the Ukraine and later of other neighbouring countries, appealed to German imperialism against the revolutionary movement, and Soviet Russia had to reply by armed intervention. The same thing happened with regard to the rights of nationalities as to other parts of Lenin's programmes: in a very short time practice bore no relation to theory. And Stalin, the theoretical advocate of the right of peoples to independence, became the executant of the right of the Soviet State to impose itself by arms on reactionary nations.

Rosa Luxemburg had indicated the impasse into which Bolshevik policy had strayed. Lenin's motto, she said, was in gross contradiction with the democratic centralisation proclaimed elsewhere and with the glacial scorn showered on other democratic liberties. This "hollow phraseology" tended in reality towards the breaking up of Russia into fragments without any advantage to socialism; on the contrary it provided water for the counter-revolutionary mill. By suppressing the right of public meeting, the liberty of the press, and universal suffrage, the Bolsheviks refused the Russian people the right of self-determination advocated for other nations. At the same time they delivered over the masses to reactionary demagogy, and thus provided their own enemies "with the dagger which these were to plunge in the heart of the Russian Revolution." Their nationalist formula, whether utopian or mere mystification, helped forward bourgeois domination, for, under capitalism, each class seeks "self-determination" after its own fashion, and the bourgeoisie has a thousand means of influencing a popular vote, for the same reasons which make it for ever impossible to establish socialism by a plebiscite. Rosa Luxemburg concluded: "The tragic consequences of this phraseology introduced into the Russian Revolution, from the thorns of which the Bolsheviks were to receive bloody wounds, should serve as a warning to the international proletariat."

Neither Lenin nor Trotsky attempted to refute this argument of a revolutionary of their own school, who was, they admitted, one of the most eminent Marxists of the day. Still less did Stalin attempt any reply, though the national question was the principal theme of his writings at that time and had played an essential part in his life as a militant. The collection of his writings on the subject would be worth studying in detail if there were to be found in them anything but paraphrases of the opportunist views expressed by Lenin, in which theory is adapted to the tactical pre-occupation of the dislocation of the Empire and the discovery of temporary allies among the revolutionary classes —and if facts had not eventually annulled words.

There are certain indications, nevertheless, that Stalin, if left to himself, would have inclined to the "Left" position of Bukharin and Pyatakov, who were sometimes charged by the Leninists with Muscovite Imperialism for denying to the subject nations the right of secession. This was especially evident at the time of the drafting of the constitution of the Republic of Soviets and in the debates of Congress. But these matters are hardly worth detailed examination, because the final decision always lay with Lenin, and Stalin made no original contribution to the subject; his political action will provide occasion for judging him by his achievement.

Another section of Pestkovsky's recollections, eight years after the first, presents Stalin as Commissar for Nationalities. This differs from the earlier one in its tendencious nature, characteristic of many writings of the time intended to be useful in internecine struggles. In it Stalin appears as a friendly and tolerant advocate against his colleagues in the Commissariat afflicted with the "Leftness" which Lenin called an infantile disease of communism. When his patience was exhausted by interminable discussions, Stalin disappeared, saying he was "going out for a minute," and did not return; his colleagues had no alternative but to close the meeting. It was a typical Oriental method of avoiding a definite decision. Stalin spent the greater part of his time with Lenin first at the Smolny Institution, then at the Kremlin, but the Nationalities question was not the most absorbing topic of discussion. Lenin had innumerable problems to solve, and needed diligent men to execute his orders; Stalin was one of the most valuable of his immediate collaborators in this matter.

In the *Memoirs* of Koté Tsintsadze, Kamo's redoubtable comrade in the Caucasus, there is an illuminating passage on Lenin's actual practice on the national question, more valuable than the compact theses and the voluminous reports in which Stalin specialised. He said:

After the October *coup d'état*, I left Georgia for Petrograd with a letter from Shaumian in order to see Stalin and Lenin. I found Stalin alone in the office, but after a while Lenin came in, and Stalin introduced me with the words: "This is Koté, the former Georgian terrorist expropriator." "Ah! tell us about Georgia," said Lenin. When I got to the incident of the capture of the Tiflis arsenal by the Mensheviks, Lenin cut me short. "What, you surrendered the arsenal to the Mensheviks?" However much I tried to explain the causes of the capture of the arsenal, he kept on saying: "But you surrendered the arsenal to the Mensheviks???" Then Kamo came in. Lenin was in a hurry, took his leave, saying to Stalin: "Don't keep them waiting; take all the necessary measures without delay." We decided not to stay more than two days. We were provided with some millions of Tsarist roubles and they gave us Colonel Sheremetyev as military director of Transcaucasia, with special reference to Georgia. We left.

This needs no comment. The right of self-determination, a two-edged weapon, was turned in Transcaucasia against its advocates, and that classic ground of national antagonisms justified

Rosa Luxemburg against Lenin only too well. Class struggles complicated by racial struggles in a historic situation in which the rivalries of world powers intervened in the smaller conflicts was no matter for democratic solution. All the various parties in the Caucasus appealed for outside aid, and violent intervention was to provide the dénouement of the tragedy. The first secret Bolshevik manœuvres to sovietise his native land were taken by Stalin in person, and, by a fateful irony, against the Georgian Social-Democracy of which he was the offspring.

Georgia had not followed Russia in her evolution towards Bolshevism and revolution. Fear of Turkish invasion created circumstances unfavourable to defeatism by giving definite local meaning to the idea of national defence. For a long time the only influence the Bolsheviks had was among the soldiers, mostly Russian, who were war-weary and naturally anxious to get home. But the unwarlike garrison of Tiflis allowed the arsenal to be captured and disarmed by a few hundred determined socialist workmen who formed a "People's Guard," as Bolshevik workmen had formed a Red Guard in Russia. Both Guards filled their respective missions—the maintenance of order for the benefit of the ruling party, with different aims but by identical means.

The Georgian Mensheviks, uncontested masters of the country, regarded their Party as merely a regional section of the Pan-Russian Social-Democracy. At Petrograd, where Chkheidze and Tseretelli were their best known representatives in the first Soviet and in the Provisional Government, they stood firm for a Russian Republic "one and indivisible," even against the very legitimate claims of Finland. After the October Revolution, although they had no "centrifugal" tendencies and were hostile to Lenin's views on the national question, they retreated across the Caucasus to join an ephemeral grouping of Georgia, Armenia and Azerbaijan. When the Russian advocates of separation became country snatchers by revolutionary necessity, the Georgian advocates of Greater Russia became separatists in order to defend their democracy. Like Lenin, but in the opposite direction, Tseretelli felt himself driven, by the inexorable necessity of the political and the social struggle in time of revolution, to take action contrary to his programme.

"*Hatred of Bolshevism was the reason why Transcaucasia made itself independent of Russia,*" said the socialist, Albert Thomas. But the immediate cause of the Balkanisation of the Caucasus, and of the incessant disturbances and wars, which were to end in the negation of the pseudo-principle of nationalities, was less important than the distant causes. Elisée Reclus had already indicated them in his impartial, monumental work: "*The geographical situation of Georgia hardly permitted its peoples to maintain their independence and form a single nation with satisfactory boundaries.*" Since these words were written, the Baku oil-wells have reinforced the geographical reasons by economic considerations founded on the geological formation of the country. Neither neutrality nor independence was possible in the era of imperialism.

The bridge between Europe and Asia, as Jordania called her, Transcaucasia could not fix her own future without the help of one of the Great Powers whose interests were concerned. The national question, always a burning and acute one in these regions, merely multiplied pretexts for external intervention. The Armenians, in fear of the Turks, called in the Russians; the Mussulman Tartars, in fear of Russia, called in the Turks; the Georgians, in fear of the Turks and the Russians, called in first the Germans and then the English. Moreover, Armenians, Tartars and Georgians, in local competition, fought among themselves. The Russians on their frontiers were of two kinds, Reds and Whites. In the interior, Bolshevism was making headway and undermining fragile States. In spite of implacable repression, peasant insurrections followed one another. Foreign military and civil missions poured oil on the flames by mutually thwarting their intrigues. The theoretical Bolshevik solution of the national question then could settle nothing and itself propounded an insoluble question: whose right was it to determine what? "*Does the right of self-determination mean the right to injure one's*

neighbours with impunity?" This question addressed by Trotsky
to the Georgian Mensheviks was also an unconscious answer to
Lenin.

3

THE squaring of the national circle was insoluble without
belying theory in practice. The agrarian question also was
settled by a tactical expedient postponing difficulties instead of
overcoming them. The Land Decree abolished the big estates
in principle without laying the foundation of collective management. Cultivation by individuals gave the peasant a right to use
the soil, a perpetual usufruct equivalent to possession.

Rosa Luxemburg had said of the Leninist solution of the
national question: "It is analogous to the Bolshevik policy with
regard to the peasants, whose appetite for land it is proposed
to settle by permission to take direct possession of the great
estates, thus securing their adhesion to the revolution. . . . Unfortunately the calculation has been absolutely wrong in both
cases." Like the territorial dismemberment of the State, the
parcelling out of the land was diametrically divergent from the
natural tendency towards economic centralisation. Neither
Stalin, nor any Bolshevik of the second rank, in their blind following of Lenin and Trotsky, foresaw the future perils from
these large strategic plans.

The immediate seizure of land by the peasants has nothing
in common with socialism, wrote Rosa Luxemburg in substance:
*"Not only is it not a socialist measure; it cuts away the path
leading to socialism."* There was thus established not socialised
property, but a new property of individuals, which was tech-
nically backward compared with the relatively advanced great
estates. The apportionment of the land accentuated inequality
instead of tending towards its suppression. The rich peasants,
the *kulaks*, in virtue of their effective supremacy in the village,
were assuredly the principal gainers by the agrarian revolution.
Socialism would thus have a new and powerful category of
enemies in the countryside. The future socialisation of the land,

and therefore of production in general, would involve in the future a sharp conflict between the town proletariat and the peasant masses. The course of events was to confirm this reasoning; its final endorsement came ten years later.

Lenin did not deny the opportunist tendency, if not the opportunism, of his agrarian policy. He had changed his tactics many times on the question. Before 1905 his programme was the most modest among all the Russian socialist programmes. The first revolution convinced him of his error. "Having exactly foreseen the direction of the movement," he said, "we were in error as to the degree of its development." At that time he advocated the confiscation of the great estates for the benefit of the smaller peasants. In his pamphlet, *To the Poor Peasants*, he wrote: "The Social-Democrats desire to expropriate only the large estate-owners, only those who live on the labour of others. *They will never dispossess the small and the 'middle peasant.'*" Later on he adopted nationalisation of the land, that is to say general expropriation, even of small properties. Finally, in 1917 he took over the programme of the Social Revolutionaries, his traditional enemies, translating it into action by his famous Decree. This Decree confiscated large landed property, to be placed at the disposal of local agrarian committees and regional peasants' soviets; the final solution was left to the Constituent Assembly; the "peasant memorial" of the Social Revolutionaries, a résumé of agrarian claims, served meanwhile as a guide.

In reply to those who reproached him with his change of front, Lenin said of this "memorial": "What does it matter who drew it up? As a democratic government we cannot evade the decision of the masses, even if it is not in accordance with our views." He was frankly to admit a few days later: "*We shall not realise the Bolshevik programme: our agrarian policy is drawn from the peasants' memorials.*" Three years later he explained this change of programme.

At the time of the October Revolution [he said], we had concluded with the *petty-bourgeois* peasant class a political alliance which, if not formal, was at least quite serious and effective, by accepting *en bloc* with one modification only, the agrarian programme of the Social Revolutionaries, *that is to say by concluding a compromise to prove to the peasants that we in no way desire to impose a regime on them, but on the contrary to come to an understanding with them,*

and indeed he was only recognising an accomplished fact, for the peasants were dividing the land without consulting anyone.

In spite of his intention to "prepare the ground in such fashion that no bourgeoisie can ever raise its head again," he had created the conditions for a capitalist renaissance in Russia, in the expectation of a European revolution which would solve the paradoxes of this backward country. He afterwards made the admission: *"The peasants have incontestably gained more from the revolution than the working classes. . . . That proves certainly that, up to a point, our revolution was a bourgeois revolution."* But in 1917 he subordinated all considerations of principle to the seizure of power, which required the purchase of the sympathy or at least the neutrality of rural Russia. In Trotsky's arresting phrase, "the young Russian proletariat was only able to accomplish its task at that time by dragging with it the heavy mass of the peasantry, just as one drags out a lump of earth with the roots of a tree."

Lenin was evidently preoccupied with other considerations in decreeing his earliest governmental measures. Without any illusions as to achieving socialism along the path into which circumstances had led him, he expected to be able to diverge from that path when the progress of the socialist revolution was assured in the west. He said repeatedly that the extension of the international revolution would put Russia in the position of a backward Soviet country. And he set himself to hold on as best he could until the fall of capitalism in Europe, which seemed to him to be assured in the immediate future. This conviction accounts for all the actions contradictory to his programme; where others saw hasty change of front in cynical repudiation, he conceived himself as faithful to his aim while temporarily changing his methods. To his mind tactics were infinitely variable, and this "doctrinaire," often accused of dogmatism, liked to quote a phrase from Goethe's *Faust*: "Theory, my friend, is grey, but the tree of life is eternally green."

The most violent surprise reserved for his opponents and for many of his followers was his domestic policy. For him dictatorship was no empty phrase; he was determined to exercise it through his Party as the mandatory of the poorer classes who had followed his teaching, and to prolong it even when he no longer had their confidence. "The dictatorship of the proletariat presupposes violence against the exploiting classes," he said, but, refusing to be bound by any law, he soon came to use violence against any opposition, even peaceful or legal opposition, against any non-Bolshevik party, whether of workmen or peasants, even against the Social-Democrats whose programme was still accepted by the opposing sections. After having demanded liberty from the socialists when they were in power, on the ground of their principles, he now refused it to them for tactical reasons. The dissolution of the Constituent "may be said to have been the turning-point of this policy," said Rosa Luxemburg, disturbed as to the fate of a revolution which she praised without losing her critical sense.

Under Kerensky, the Constituent Assembly, constantly deferred, became a myth, and the Bolsheviks angrily demanded that it should be summoned. At first sight their demand appeared to be in flagrant contradiction with the demand for power for the soviets. Lenin never made the point clear, but he appears to have envisaged a "composite State" harmonising the Constituent and the soviets, the national and the municipal power; Zinoviev and Kamenev have reported some remarks in this sense. On the morrow of the October Revolution, fidelity to the Constituent was immovable. The principal Soviet Decrees were provisional pending ratification by the Assembly. Lenin declared: "We shall submit all the peace proposals to the decision of the Constituent." Trotsky wrote: "The country can only be saved by a Constituent Assembly representing the exploited working classes." Statements of this kind abound.

The elections yielded unexpected results at Petrograd; more

than half the votes went to the supposed "usurpers." The Bolsheviks cherished for the moment the chimerical hope of similar
success in the provinces; the support of the Social Revolutionaries
of the Left, represented on the Council of Commissars, and the
stern action against the Kadets were expected to secure a majority for the Soviet regime. But the results as they came in dis-
pelled the illusion; the peasantry followed tradition in voting
for the Social Revolutionaries without making any distinction
between Left and Right. Lenin saw the danger, and desired to
parry it by the preventive measure of another postponement and
a modification of the electoral law. The Central Committee
thought otherwise. Bukharin spoke of excluding the Right from
the future Assembly and convening the Rump as a Convention.
Stalin urged the necessity of getting rid of the Kadets, already
outlawed by Decree. Amid the anxiety and hesitancy of the
ruling organizations, the idea of dissolving the Constituent made
headway.

The Bolsheviks obtained in all a quarter of the votes, but in
the two capitals, in the industrial towns, in the army on the principal Fronts and in the fleet they had a majority. As Lenin had
foreseen, the distribution of forces assured their preponderance
in the decisive quarters. The Social Revolutionaries, with more
than half the votes, but scattered over the countryside, remained
impotent before the real governing body. The Kadets were
numerically the second urban party. The Mensheviks paid dis-
astrously for their errors and compromises, except in the Caucasus, where Georgian Social-Democracy remained invulnerable.

The Constituent Assembly, the dream of many generations
of revolutionaries, was adjourned on the day it met, on the demand of a sailor, without having ventured to oppose the Soviet
Government's policy on peace and land. The decree of dissolution, signed by Lenin, was received next day. The objections
raised by the Bolshevik Right met with no response, and the
Third Congress of Soviets automatically sanctioned the operation. Russia remained indifferent, though there were a few mild
protests in socialist and liberal circles. Parliamentarism on the
western model could not be acclimatised in this enormous and

backward country, where the active minority imposed itself without a parliament on a passive majority incapable of insisting on its parliament, under historical conditions in which democracy no longer existed anywhere. The bourgeoisie had postponed the Constituent when the Bolsheviks demanded it, and began to demand it when the Bolsheviks suppressed it—a reversal of rôles which emphasises the anachronism of an institution inherited from bourgeois revolutionary tradition in other lands and defenceless against the accomplished fact of a new "specifically Russian" system at home.

The supporters of the Constituent expected salvation from a spontaneous break-down of Bolshevism, from an outburst of popular feeling, from some unknown remedy arising from the seriousness of the disease, or, most of them, from help from outside. Gorky justly remarked: "Even now that the people are masters of their fate, they continue to expect a *barin;* for some of them this *barin* is the European proletariat; for others, the Germans, the creators of an iron discipline; others think that Japan will save them; no one trusts to his own right arm." The Bolsheviks had the advantage of relying upon themselves, pending the world revolution.

After the event, Trotsky condemned the Constituent as a "belated echo of an epoch outdated by the revolution." The elections had followed too close on the insurrection, the rural districts were ill-informed of the events in the towns, the lumbering machine of democracy did not correctly represent the rapid development of the political situation in a country so vast and so ill-organised. To which Rosa Luxemburg replied, in the name of the principles of Bolshevism, that *it was necessary to break the antiquated Constituent and to convoke instead an Assembly derived from a renovated Russia.* According to Trotsky, she said, "the body elected by the democracy would always reflect the image of the masses at the date of the elections, just as, according to Herschel, the starry heavens represent the celestial bodies, not as they are when we look at them, but as they were at the moment when they sent their rays from an immensurable distance, to our earth." This negation of any living bond between the elected and the electors is contradicted by historical experience, showing that the "living wave of the people's opinion constantly bathes, inspires and directs their representatives." The friendly criticism received no response; the disagreement implied insuperable opposition, not only on the particular issue, but between two conceptions of the revolutionary dictatorship.

In reality, Lenin and Trotsky, equally sincere in summoning and in denouncing the Constituent, had not foreseen the realities corresponding to their abstract formulas, and, by revising the formulas on the basis of actual circumstances, they found justification in the complexity of the facts for the most unpremeditated solutions. Doubtless they did not recollect Plekhanov's forecast at the Social-Democratic Congress of 1903, justifying a future blow at universal suffrage, until they found themselves faced with inevitable civil war. But, again, the conclusion of peace came about quite differently from the way in which they had intended. Another proof of the truth of a pre-Marxist prophetic remark by J. de Maistre: "Men do not so much lead revolutions; revolution leads them."

4

LENIN had often propounded the dilemma: an honourable, democratic peace or revolutionary war. The Bolsheviks, unanimously convinced that they had to defend their country under a socialist regime, understood such a peace as the end of hostilities without annexations or indemnities and with the right of self-determination for the peoples. German imperialism, in virtue of this right, proposed to support the counter-revolution in Finland, Poland and Ukraine. The theses of Lenin and his disciple Stalin on the national question might be interpreted in an opposite sense. The refusal of the Allies to agree to an armistice preliminary to a peace in which there should be neither victors nor vanquished, drove Russia to choose between a hopeless revolutionary war and the separate peace scorned by intransigent Bolshevism.

The impossibility of reconciling revolution and imperialism was evident at the first meeting at Brest-Litovsk. Clinging to the hope of an imminent social revolution in the west, especially in Germany, the Bolsheviks desired to gain time; they multiplied their appeals to the international proletariat, manifestoes sent out by wireless, which were intercepted and everywhere censored. The German ultimatum cut short these manœuvres; they had to capitulate to obtain a respite, or to expose themselves to invasion with the certainty of disastrous defeat.

Lenin was the first to grasp the alternative of life and death. On the morrow of the *coup d'état* he had sounded a warning against unreasoning optimism. "Our party," he said, "never promised to secure an immediate peace. We said we would immediately make peace proposals and would publish the secret treaties. That has been done; the struggle for peace is beginning." On the approach of danger he had no hesitation in making a frontal attack on the bellicose romanticism of the Party, and resolutely proposed acceptance of a "shameful peace"; for, he said, the socialist Republic required a truce, and revolution in Germany might be delayed.

But his own words on a war of revolution were remembered by the Party, which was disposed to translate them into action. Once more, Lenin was in a minority. Against him were ranged the Left Communists, advocates of breaking off negotiations and of perishing in a life and death struggle rather than compromise with the enemy; among these were the most energetic and able of the militants: Bukharin, Pyatakov, Preobrazhensky, Radek, Joffe, Krestinsky, Dzerzhinsky, Pokrovsky, Ossinsky, Sapronov, Kollontai, and many others, supported in the Soviets by the active section of the Left Social Revolutionaries. Unconsciously the neo-Jacobins were falling into the same political error as the Girondins, denounced first by Marat, and then by Robespierre. In the Central Committee of the Party, Lenin could only rely with certainty on Sverdlov, Stalin, Sokolnikov and Smilga, not counting Zinoviev and Kamenev, who, as "October-deserters," were rather compromising associates. Trotsky, without identifying himself with the Left, took

a "centrist" standpoint, which consisted in renouncing battle
but without signing peace, and, for the moment, in a prolongation of the Brest negotiations with the idea of publicly demonstrating the incompatibility of the policies of the parties and of
encouraging revolutionary activity in the Central Empires.

Stalin prudently followed Lenin. But how? According to
Trotsky, he had no settled convictions, but temporised, manœuvred, and intrigued; he supported both Lenin and Trotsky,
trying to keep in with both of them while the result was uncertain. "Stalin," he says, "took no active part. No one took much
notice of his hesitation. Certainly my main preoccupation, to
make our conduct on the peace question as comprehensible as
possible to the world proletariat, was a secondary consideration
for Stalin. He was interested in *peace for one country only*, just
as later on he was interested in *socialism for one country only*.
In the decisive vote he was with Lenin."

Though Stalin took no public part in the discussion, he shared
in the secret deliberations of the Central Committee of the Party,
which was already the real Government of the Republic. The
minutes of this "secret group of leaders" show that he was more
decided than Trotsky admits, though he did not necessarily rise
to the level of Lenin's motives. His first speech on the question
is thus summarised by the Secretary, Helen Stassova:

Comrade Stalin thinks that in adopting the slogan of a war of
revolution we are playing the imperialists' game. Comrade Trotsky's
position is no position at all. There is no revolutionary movement
in the west, there is no action, only potential action, and on that we
cannot rely. If the Germans begin the offensive, our counter-
revolution will be strengthened. Germany can attack, for she has
Kornilov's troops and the Guards. In October we spoke of a holy
war, because we were told that the mere word peace would be the
signal for revolution in the west. But that was a mistake. The introduction by us of socialist reforms will rouse revolution in the west,
but we need time for that. By adopting Comrade Trotsky's policy,
we should create the worst conditions for the movement in the west,
and therefore he [Stalin] proposes the adoption of Comrade Lenin's
motion.

Thus Stalin came round to Lenin's conclusions, but for national reasons, while Lenin had arrived at them just because of "potential" international revolutions. Revolution has not begun in the west, said Lenin in reply to Stalin, but *"nevertheless, if we altered our tactics for that reason, we should be traitors to international socialism."* He only proposed to sign peace in the belief that it would be annulled by the "general socialist revolution." Stalin, on the contrary, only conceived of a revolutionary movement in the west under the influence of socialist reforms in Russia.

Trotsky's compromise of *"cessation of the war, non-signature of the peace, and demobilisation of the army,"* was adopted by the Central Committee by 9 votes to 7, a provisional solution which had at least the advantage of preserving the Party from a mortal breach. Stalin recognized this at the next meeting, when he said: *"The intermediate position of Trotsky's has provided us with a way out from a difficult situation."* It was the same position which Stalin had recently described as no position at all.

Lenin wore down his opponents with obstinacy and skill. Internal dissension was unusually sharp. More than two hundred soviets which were consulted on the subject pronounced for rupture of the Brest negotiations, and only two important soviets were for peace. The Left disclosed several shades of opinion. By 7 votes to 6 the Central Committee once more supported Trotsky's proposal to refuse the resumption of negotiations. But on that very day another meeting was hastily summoned, on the news of the German offensive. The Kiev Rada came to terms with the Central Empires, in the name of self-determination, and Ukrainian nationalism became the handmaid of the invaders. In the north Dvinsk was captured and Petrograd threatened; the old Russian army declared itself incapable of fighting, and the new one did not yet exist. Lenin's thesis was hourly strengthened.

Every possible error had been made, and Trotsky wavered, beginning to come over to Lenin's view. Stalin cut the matter short: "We must speak plainly. The Germans are attacking, we are defenceless. It is time to say bluntly that negotiations must be renewed." Lenin, with more assurance than ever, reiterated his argument in short, cutting phrases. "It is no use jesting with war. We are losing rolling-stock and making our transport worse. We cannot wait, for the situation is plain. The people will not understand that if there were to be a war we ought not to have demobilised. Now the Germans will take everything. The game has come to such a pass that the downfall of the revolution is inevitable if we persist in a middle policy." Trotsky wavered, but insisted on first asking the Central Powers for their terms. Stalin replied: "After five minutes' hurricane firing we shan't have a single soldier in the line. This confusion must be ended. I don't agree with Trotsky. A question like that is merely paper talk. We must now consider the whole situation and say that we are for resumption of negotiations." On the vote, Lenin won by 7 to 5, with one abstention. Trotsky, unconvinced, nevertheless voted with Lenin, fearing an irremediable split.

The internal crisis in the Party was at its worst; discord amounted to paroxysm. Trotsky resigned from the Council of Commissars, and Lenin threatened resignation from the Central Committee. "We are turning the Party into a dung-heap," cried Bukharin, sobbing in Trotsky's arms. The Left began to publish papers in opposition to the official press. They treated Lenin as "phrase-maker and opportunist," capable of "the same faults as Kautsky" and they denounced the "profound mistake which will ruin the Russian and the international revolutions." At the next sitting of the Central Committee, Stalin sought to conciliate the extremists. "It is possible," he said, "not to sign, but to begin negotiations." Lenin would yield nothing. He said: "Stalin is wrong in saying it is possible not to sign. We must sign the terms laid down. If you do not sign, you sign the death sentence of the Soviet power in three weeks. These conditions do not affect the Soviet power. I have not a shadow of hesitation. I do not lay down an ultimatum and then run away. I want no more revolutionary phrase-making. The German revolution is not ripe. It will take months. The conditions must be accepted." By 7 votes to 4 and with four abstentions, including Trotsky's, Lenin obtained a relative majority for submission to the imperialist conditions of peace. The Central Committee pronounced unanimously for a future war of revolution.

Four members of the Left, including Bukharin and Bubnov, immediately resigned their "responsible positions." With Lenin's assent they reserved the right to agitate in the Party against the resolution adopted by the Central Committee. A breach seemed inevitable. Six People's Commissars, including Pyatakov and Uritsky, followed Trotsky in resigning. Stalin, who was evidently uneasy over the lack of leaders, made deserving efforts to conciliate them in terms unusually friendly for him. Trotsky, once more in disagreement with Lenin, nevertheless did his best to safeguard unity.

The Seventh Bolshevik Congress was summoned to vote on the ratification of the "shameful peace"; the various soviet bodies had in the end to conform to the decision of the sovereign Party.

This special Congress was held in March in the dramatic atmosphere of the first rumblings of civil war, with only 29 duly elected delegates. Stalin was not there. He was no orator, and he rarely appeared on great occasions in the assemblies. Without even appearing in the forefront or inscribing his name in the revolutionary annals, a self-effacing but capable executor of Lenin's instructions, he was useful as an administrator in a small group which was in fact, if not formally, gathering into its hands all the political prerogatives of the State. At that time Sverdlov calculated the Party membership at 300,000; one-fourth must have been lost in less than six months, under the fear of the coming fall of the new regime.

The majority of the Congress rallied to Lenin, repudiating retrospectively the formula "neither peace nor war," and exhibiting little anxiety to do justice to the imposing part played by Trotsky at Brest, or to his disinterested mediation between the rival sections in the Central Committee. Trotsky, bitterly offended, resigned all his offices and functions in the Party and in the Soviets. Lenin had severely criticised his "revolutionary

phrase-making" which, by concealing the enormous danger in
which the revolution stood, aggravated it. Riazanov, although a
Right Communist, left the Party, and was soon followed by
Kollontai. The Left section continued its violent opposition. But
civil war was soon to rally all revolutionaries to the defence of
the "socialist fatherland in danger." Before separating, the Congress decided to modify the old Social-Democratic programme,
at last obeying Lenin's wishes and adopting the name Communist.

Lenin had resumed the ascendancy which was henceforward
to be unquestioned. The incarnation of the political and tactical
intelligence of Bolshevism, strengthened by inflexible determination turned unceasingly on a single aim, he imposed his authority
by plain common sense, of which most of his comrades and followers showed themselves destitute in great emergencies. Because he had outlined a policy whose logic was elementary, *"not
to fight when you were assured of defeat,"* he was to pass for a
genius in a party which owed him everything—its origin,
organisation, doctrine and programme, its strategy, and its
tactics, its theory and practice, and the conquest and maintenance of power, a party which nearly lost everything by
losing confidence in its leader and inspirer. His distinctive supremacy really lay, apart from his personal qualities, in the essential faculty of discerning "the grain of reality in the straw of
words." In this he showed himself genuinely deserving of the
only praise he desired, that of being a Marxist. In this respect
Trotsky's political weakness was evident, in spite of his brilliant
outward gifts. The Brest episode shows up the idealism of the
one and the realism of the other.

Under the circumstances, Lenin thought it wrong to risk the
fate of the revolution begun in Russia on the single card of a
coming revolution in Germany, and wished, as Radek puts it,
"to gain time." When his own words on a war of revolution
were recalled he replied: "We were speaking of the need of
preparation and of carrying on revolutionary war. . . . But we
never promised to embark on such a war without considering
the possibilities and chances of success." The socialist revolution
is ripening in all countries, but it will come *"at the end of the*

end, and not at the beginning of the beginning." We must learn to retreat. The man who can't adapt himself to the worst situation "is only a talker, not a revolutionary." The Left Communists "take the nobleman's, not the peasant's point of view." The Treaty of Brest will have the same fate as the Peace of Tilsit. Peace is only a means of reconstituting one's forces. . . . Peace is a truce between wars; war the means of securing a better peace. It must not be possible to say with truth that "revolutionary phrase-making about the revolutionary war ruined the revolution."

Hardly had the Communist Government obtained respite on the new western frontier when they had to face manifold and constantly increasing dangers at home. A new "Time of Troubles" opened for Russia. During the year 1919 the situation took a sinister turn in the country given up to fire and blood.

5

WHILE the Germans occupied, in addition to Finland and Poland, first Estonia, Latvia and Lithuania in Russian territory, and then the Ukraine and the Crimea, and, lastly, Georgia, where they were summoned by the Menshevik Government in aid against a Turkish invasion—civil war broke out under many forms. Plots, treason and mutiny followed. There was sabotage in the public services and a strike of officials and technicians. After the repressions of the risings of Kaledin on the Don, and of Dutov in the Urals, the mobile "Cossack Vendée" was constantly in revolt. In the north the Finnish counter-revolution, supported by German troops, threatened Petrograd. Presently, English and French forces were to occupy Archangel and the Murmansk coast. On the middle Volga detachments of Czechoslovak prisoners of war on their way home raised armed revolt. On the lower Volga, Krasnov's Cossacks were approaching Tsaritsyn. In the Kuban the first volunteers of Denikin's future army were assembling to the south of the Caspian; Whites with some English officers from Persia threatened the Baku Commune, then in the hands of the Reds. On the Roumanian frontier Bessarabia was invaded. In the Far East the Japanese were landing at Vladivostok, and, but for the opposition of the United States, would have advanced along the Trans-Siberian railway, and re-established "order" in Asiatic Russia, which was ravaged by bandits, by "great companies," and "infernal columns," so called. Finally, after the blockade, military intervention on the part of the Allies was to be expected, and their agents, missions, embassies, fictitious consulates, fomented and supported sedition and political crime.

In rural Russia groups of "partisans" of all colours were operating. The peasants hid their grain, refused worthless coinage, and returned to a system of barter. Inflation reached astronomical figures. The local soviets, at the end of their resources, levied extraordinary contributions, decreed requisitions, and carried out arbitrary confiscations. In the starving towns industrial production fell almost to zero, commerce was dying, and scarcity compelled increasingly drastic rationing. Instead of "workers' control" of industrial undertakings, the Communists decided on their gradual nationalisation by force, in order to keep them going, at the request sometimes of the workers, sometimes of the owners. The Mensheviks incited strikes, the Social Revolutionaries revived terrorism, the Anarchists formed their Black Guard filled with Whites, the counter-revolution organised itself in "Liberating" and "Patriotic" leagues. In this indescribable chaos the "building-up of socialism" hoped for by the Bolsheviks was pushed into the background by the necessities of the defence of the revolution.

In vain Lenin had sketched out in April 1918 a constructive programme of the "successive tasks of the Soviet power," emphasising the following essential measures: economic reconstruction by rigid calculation and control of production and distribution, the organisation of positive and creative work by one-man direction in industry, the employment of highly-paid specialists, the adoption of the Taylor system, piece work, the incentives of emulation and of force—while he denounced the hysteria of the Left, "Communists of disaster." Repression was a more urgent task than administration. Trotsky, now Commissar for War, had summarised the same programme in his formula, *"Work, discipline and order will save the Republic of Soviets."* But first of all, the implacable enemy had to be crushed, as the event proved, if they themselves were not to be exterminated. Jaurès was not a false prophet when he wrote at the end of the last century: "In the present condition of Europe, and in so far as the course of events can be foreseen, it is no longer possible to hope, unless one is blind, or to assert, unless one is a traitor, that socialism will be achieved in the advanced nations by peaceful means. The nation which first achieves socialism will see all the frenzied powers of reaction hurled against it at the same time. It will be lost if it is not itself prepared to seize a sword, to answer bullet with bullet, so that the working class of other countries may have time to organise and rise in its turn."

In May, the hostile newspapers, which demanded armed foreign intervention, were suppressed; the brief period of a free press was at an end. In June, "anti-soviet" parties were excluded from the soviets; the soviet monopoly of politics had begun. Volodarsky was assassinated in Petrograd by Right Social Revolutionaries. The Cheka seized hostages; its repressive measures were still moderate, while the Whites, by their mass shootings and hangings, were sowing the seeds of inexpiable hatred and ensuring severe reprisals for themselves. The Red Terror was hardly yet equal to the White Terror. But a merciless struggle was beginning in the villages; expeditions of workmen went there ostensibly to seize bread from the kulaks, but really to take it from all peasant farmers, and they provoked sanguinary rural warfare. The industrial centres had to be fed at all costs. Committees of "Poor Peasants" were formed, on Lenin's initiative, to break the resistance of those who refused to supply cereals, to requisition cattle, and to confiscate surpluses. Necessity knows no law. The essential was not "a socialist experiment," but the mitigation of famine.

Stalin set out for Tsaritsyn, where Voroshilov was then in command, in charge of a detachment of Red soldiers, provided with two armoured cars, to direct operations for the collection of food in the south. The national question might wait, and for that matter, would wait for a long time. Most of the energetic militants were mobilised on the "Food Front," if they were not commissars with the armies. In any case all fronts tended to become one, and, instead of differentiation of functions, a mass of work and responsibilities of all kinds had to be undertaken. Dzerzhinsky, Pyatakov, Smilga, Sokolnikov, Ivan and Vladimir Smirnov, former workmen such as Serebriakov, Shliapnikov and Voroshilov went into the army, some as commissars, some as improvised generals. Stalin also began his military career haphazard; he found Tsaritsyn in inextricable disorder which made his task impossible without exerting pressure on the command, the headquarters of the Tenth Army.

There is nothing about Stalin in the military works, or the historical memoirs and studies on the Russian Civil War. For ten years no communist author thought it worth while to give him any notice. Trotsky's name is associated throughout the world, by friends or enemies, with the victories of the revolution; Stalin's share was not discovered until 1929. There were violent domestic rivalries before Voroshilov suddenly thought of filling up the gap, and before Trotsky made the necessary documentary corrections to his belated tribute. Stalin's reputation as a soldier does not emerge enhanced, but there is further evidence of his organising capacity, his dictatorial method, and his faculty for intrigue; here also are the beginnings of a personal antagonism which was soon to weigh heavily on the destiny of the Republic.

The history of the Red Army is bound up with the life of Trotsky, as the history of the Bolshevik Party is bound up with Lenin's. To these two men, who complemented one another, the revolution owed its salvation in its critical hours. This may be said without injustice to the achievements and the heroism of the Party and of the picked few among the workers and peasants. Marx and Engels, who did not exaggerate the historical rôle of individuals, said, *"For the realisation of ideas you must have men with practical ability."*

Trotsky recognised the pre-eminence of Lenin, and the latter in turn appreciated Trotsky's value. Gorky has reported some remarks made by Lenin about Trotsky in private conversation. "Show me any other man," he said, "capable of organising an almost model army in one year and moreover of winning the sympathy of professional soldiers. We have that man. We have everything. You will see miracles." That did not prevent differences of opinion, for the very simple reasons which led Bonaparte to say somewhat paradoxically, *"rather one bad general than two good ones."* But in those terrible years the profound agreement and reciprocal esteem between the two principal leaders, reinforced by a Sverdlov in administrative affairs, a Dzerzhinsky at the police, a Rakovsky for war and diplomacy in the Ukraine, and many other able and distinguished militants, gave the revolutionary Government an authority unparalleled except, *mutatis mutandis*, in the case of Robespierre and Saint-Just. Other times, other men, other circumstances, other historical stages, and other social conditions—but the analogies are sufficient to justify the parallel.

Stalin was not yet an outstanding personage, and was still unknown in the country and in the Party, but nevertheless he must be counted among those hardened revolutionaries who were always available for the most unexpected tasks. Theoretically under the orders of Trotsky, who was Commissar for War and President of the Revolutionary Council of War, he nevertheless had direct access to Lenin as a member of the Central Committee of the Party, an extra-constitutional body which was already the supreme authority. Moreover the Council of Commissars was to cease to exist as the nominal Government when the Left Social Revolutionaries broke with the Bolsheviks, whose peasant policy and peace tactics they violently opposed.

At the beginning of July 1918, these "hysterical maniacs of the Left" attacked the Communist Party during the Fifth Congress of Soviets, tried to revive war with Germany by assassinating the ambassador, Mirbach, and attempted to overthrow the Council of Commissars by bombarding the Kremlin. The revolt was stifled in twenty-four hours, and was the beginning of the end for the Left Social Revolutionaries; some were shot, others imprisoned, and their party was shattered. (The anarchists, al-

ready roughly handled in April, soon suffered a like fate.)
Thenceforward the communists monopolised the Council of
Commissars, and almost had a monopoly of the Executive of the
Soviets. The Bolshevik Central Committee did not need to take
any formal steps to be able to exercise the dictatorship through
their Political Bureau. At the same period, and at the instigation
of French diplomatic agents, the extreme Right of the Social
Revolutionaries and the Whites, led by Savinkov, provoked, by
the Yaroslavl revolt, the first great massacre of the civil population and the destruction of one of the finest cities of old Russia.
The episode recalls the Lyons incident of 1793. Terror breeds
terror. Under the shadow of this tragedy, the Congress of
Soviets, interrupted by bombing and cannonade, passed, on
Sverdlov's motion, the Constitution of the Socialist Federal Republic of Soviets, an idealised codification of the existing order,
preceded by the Declaration of Rights of the Toiling Masses. In
this solemn charter nothing was said of the dictatorship of a
single Party or of the communist monopoly of power. But force
of circumstances in fact concentrated the public power in the
hands of the victorious Party for the time being.

Meanwhile news from the Front was not reassuring. On the
Volga the commander-in-chief, Muraviev, committed treason
and then killed himself. Below Tsaritsyn, where Voroshilov was
unequal to his task, the Cossacks pierced the Red Line. The
Soviet army, occupying an immense Front, was ill-nourished, ill-
equipped and badly officered, and was everywhere in retreat.
The Communist Party mobilised all their fit men and their last
resources. Stalin hastened to the Front.

A few minutes before starting, he wrote to Lenin: "I harry
and abuse all those who deserve it, and hope for early improvement. Be sure we shall spare no one, neither ourselves nor others,
and we shall send grain. If our military specialists (the fools!)
did not sleep and dawdle, the line would not have been broken;
if it is repaired, it will be in spite of them."

In reply to Lenin's expressed anxiety about the Left Social
Revolutionaries at Tsaritsyn, where the anarchists had attempted
a rising in May, Stalin replied: "As for the hysterical maniacs,

be sure that our hand will not falter; with enemies we shall
act as enemies." Indeed it was abundantly clear at this time that
Stalin was a man whose hand did not falter.

There is a significant phrase in his short note about "military
specialists," that is, professional soldiers. Stalin had no use for
them. His aversion is expressed in a telegram in which he says:
"Our specialists are psychologically unfit for decisive war against
the counter-revolution." A whole section of the Party shared
this prejudice. The "military opposition," recruited especially
among communists of the Left, advocated guerilla war, independent guerilla bands, the election of officers by their men, federalism and improvisation in military affairs. Just as the remnants
of the Left opposition accused Lenin of blindness, of opportunism and of compromise with capitalism because of his practice of using specialists in industry, so the military opposition
reproached Trotsky with his centralised methods, strict discipline and employment of specialists in the army. The nucleus of
this opposition was at Voroshilov's headquarters at Tsaritsyn.
Stalin secretly encouraged it.

Now, if Trotsky was able to put the Red Army on a con-
scripted instead of voluntary basis, raise its effectives from
100,000 to one, and then to two or three millions, to form sixteen armies in a Front of 8,000 kilometres, it was by incorporating, as Dubois-Crancé did, the sound elements of the old
army in the new, by using professional soldiers under the surveillance of revolutionary commissars, by abolishing the election
of officers and the soldiers' council and by instituting rigid discipline under a single command. The resistance of Tsaritsyn to
the orders of the Revolutionary Council of War only made defeat certain. As Trotsky explains in *My Life*, the opposition
could not do without specialists, but they chose mediocre ones.

Though he was not a Left Communist, Stalin supported
this opposition in a new way. Trotsky says that this intrigue
was directed against him. Why? Trotsky does not say. Probably, even before the October Revolution, Stalin had been
jealous of the popularity of an opponent outside the secret
circle of professional revolutionaries who thought the direc-

tion of the revolution a preserve of their own. For Stalin and
his like, Trotsky was, if not an intruder, at least a convert, and
if no one now ventured to contest the pre-eminence of Lenin,
the stronger men necessarily competed for preponderance of
influence with the master. Stalin and Trotsky, so different in
their birth, education, intellect and culture, both had a passion
for domination.

Voroshilov, an unconscious witness against himself, says that
the centre of the Tenth Army presented a lamentable picture
of confusion and impotence when Stalin arrived. His presence
rapidly made itself felt in the rear and at the Front. Stalin
showed "colossal energy," and purged the commissariat, the
administration, and the staff. The tone of his letters to Lenin
shows the spirit by which he was animated. "I shall make good,"
he said, "the local deficiencies and many others. I am taking
and shall take measures to deprive unsuccessful officers and generals of their command in spite of rules, which I shall break if
necessary. For this I naturally assume full responsibility before
the superior courts."

Stalin was especially successful in the town. He organised a
local Cheka, and instituted inexorable repression. On this matter,
Voroshilov quoted with satisfaction a White witness, the turn-
coat Nossovich, who wrote of Stalin: "It is only just to say that
his energy may be envied by every former administrator and
that his capacity for adapting himself to his task and its circumstances might be an example to many others." The atmosphere
of Tsaritsyn changed. "The Cheka is working at full speed";
every day new plots were discovered, and all the prisons were
overflowing. An engineer and his two sons, who had come from
Moscow, were arrested for conspiracy. "Stalin's decision was
brief: 'Shoot!' The engineer Alexeyev, his two sons, and several
officers with them, some belonging to the organisation, others
only suspected, were seized by the Cheka and immediately shot
without trial." Stalin's hand did not falter.

There are no statistics of the victims under his proconsul-
ship. The same initiative and the same firmness were shown

everywhere on all occasions. In this memorable month of July, when the days of the Soviets appeared to be numbered, the Ural communists under Byeloborodov executed the fallen Emperor and his family on the approach of the victorious Czechoslovaks. A Left Communist, the workman Myasnikov, killed the Grand-Duke Michael. In August, after the loss of Simbirsk and Kazan, Trotsky started in person to the middle Volga where the fate of the revolution was in the balance, and formed the legendary armoured train in which for more than two years he hastened from the most dangerous point of one Front to another.

At the end of the same month, the Civil War entered on its acutest phase. Simultaneously an attempt was made to kill Lenin, and Uritsky was assassinated at Petrograd; the secret organisation of the Right Social Revolutionaries was at work. Trotsky, on the way to Moscow, had the luck to escape the bombs and bullets of the terrorists. This time the Cheka replied with lightning swiftness. The Red Terror was openly endorsed and martial law imposed. Five hundred counter-revolutionaries were executed at Petrograd, as many at Kronstadt, perhaps a hundred at Moscow, and an unknown number in the provinces. The Russian Revolution had its September massacres. Atrocities on one side were made good on the other. The press published lists of hostages, and announced mass arrests. There are no exact statistics of the number of victims. All trace of democracy vanished in the fury of suppression. At the Front panic-stricken communists were shot. Some days later the Fifth Army of Ivan Smirnov took Kazan, Tukhachevsky re-entered Simbirsk with the First Army, the Red guerillas of the Urals under the workman Blücher effected a junction at Perm with the Third Army after marching 1,500 kilometres and after fifty days of murderous fighting.

Trotsky had other cares besides the struggle for Kazan. Tsaritsyn headquarters caused him anxiety because of its obstinate opposition, its flagrant lack of discipline, and the obstruction of Army Headquarters' plans. Voroshilov, still quoting Nossovich, admits the pernicious rôle played by Stalin:

A characteristic peculiarity of this drive was the attitude of Stalin to instructions wired from the centre. When Trotsky, worried because of the destruction of the command administrations formed by him with such difficulty, sent a telegram concerning the necessity of leaving the staff and the war commissariat on the previous footing and giving them a chance to work, Stalin wrote a categorical, most significant inscription on the telegram—"To be ignored!" . . . . The entire artillery and a section of the staff personnel continued to wait on barges at Tsaritsyn.

Lenin could not have been aware of this very significant incident, but he interested himself in this conflict. Knowing something about Stalin he suspected him of improper conduct, but sought to reduce friction so as to get the full value from all his personnel. At the beginning of October, Trotsky telegraphed to him:

I insist categorically on Stalin's recall. Things are going badly on the Tsaritsyn Front in spite of superabundant forces. Voroshilov can command a regiment, but not an army of 50,000 men. Nevertheless I will leave him in command of the Tenth Tsaritsyn Army on condition that he reports to the Commander of the Army of the South, Sytin. Up till now Tsaritsyn has not even sent reports of operations to Kozlov. I have demanded that reports of reconnaissances and operations should be sent twice daily. If that is not done to-morrow I shall send Voroshilov and Minin for trial and shall publish the fact in an Army Order. So long as Stalin and Minin remain at Tsaritsyn, their rights, in conformity with the Statutes of the Revolutionary Council of War, are limited to those of members of the Revolutionary Council of War of the Tenth Army. We have only a brief interval to take the offensive before the autumn mud, when roads here are not practicable either for horse or foot. Without co-ordination with Tsaritsyn no serious action is possible. There is no time to lose in diplomatic pourparlers. Tsaritsyn must either submit or get under. We have a colossal superiority of forces, but complete anarchy at the top. I can put a stop to it in twenty-four hours provided I have your firm and definite support. At all events that is the only course I can see.

Next day Trotsky communicated with Lenin by direct wire: "I have received the following telegram: 'The execution of Stalin's fighting instruction No. 10 must be suspended. I have given full instructions to the Commander on the Southern Front, Sytin. Stalin's activities destroy all my plans. . . . VATZETIS, Commander-in-Chief. DANISHEVSKY, member of the Revolutionary Council of War.' "

Stalin was immediately recalled to Moscow. By way of special consideration, Lenin sent Sverdlov to fetch him in a special train, and Trotsky, on his way to Tsaritsyn, met them en route. A conversation took place between Trotsky and Stalin. "Is it true that you want to turn out the lot?" asked the latter resignedly, speaking of the "opposition" at Tsaritsyn. Submission was only apparent. Stalin harboured resentment and bided his time.

At Tsaritsyn, when Trotsky sought an explanation with Voroshilov, this peculiar soldier admitted frankly that he did not mean to carry out instructions unless he thought them right. Whereupon Trotsky indicated unconditional obedience to superior orders on pain of immediate dispatch to Moscow under escort for trial. Voroshilov had to give way, but Trotsky had one personal enemy the more. And when the Commissar for War turned his back on Tsaritsyn opposition continued, secretly supported by Stalin. This at any rate is Trotsky's version, in the preceding as in the following pages; but he bases it on irrefutable documents and no one has ever been able to query them.

Voroshilov also had to be recalled after another telegram from Trotsky to Lenin: "It is impossible to leave Voroshilov at his post after he has nullified all attempts at compromise. There must be a new Revolutionary Military Council with a new Commander at Tsaritsyn, and Voroshilov must be transferred to the Ukraine." This was another indirect hit at Stalin. After this the defensive and offensive capacity of the Tenth Army was stimulated under Trotsky's influence. The workman Shliapnikov entered the new Revolutionary Council of War on the Tsaritsyn Front.

In the Ukraine Voroshilov played the same game, still with secret support from Stalin. Trotsky was obliged to telegraph to Sverdlov: "I must categorically state that the Tsaritsyn policy, which led to the complete disintegration of the Tsaritsyn army, cannot be tolerated in the Ukraine. . . . The line pursued by Voroshilov and Rukhimovich means the ruin of the entire enterprise." Stalin intrigued in the shadow, but Trotsky saw through his game.

In reply to Lenin and Sverdlov, who sought to smooth things over, Trotsky replied: "A compromise is of course necessary, but not one that is rotten. . . . I consider Stalin's patronage of the Tsaritsyn policy a most dangerous ulcer, worse than any treason or betrayal by military specialists. . . . Read carefully once more Okulov's report on the demoralisation of the Tsaritsyn army by Voroshilov with the help of Stalin." The prospect of Anglo-French military intervention in the Ukraine did not permit tergiversation on Trotsky's part; nevertheless he did not insist on extreme measures.

After temporising for some months, Lenin finally telegraphed to Voroshilov: "It is absolutely imperative that all agitation be stopped immediately, and that all work be placed on a military basis; that no more time be wasted on all the fine projects about separate groups and similar attempts at restoring the Ukrainian Front. Discipline must be military. . . ." He asks him to put an end to "chaos, palaver, and disputes about precedence." On the same day, he summoned the Political Bureau of the Central Committee which took Trotsky's side and called on Voroshilov to carry out his duty, "otherwise Trotsky will summon you to Izium the day after tomorrow and will make detailed arrangements." Next day the Central Committee empowered Rakovsky and Trotsky to take energetic measures to recover from Voroshilov the munitions which he had secured illegally. Lenin wrote by direct wire to Trotsky: "Dybenko and Voroshilov making free with military property. Complete chaos, no serious help given the Donetz base." By dint of tenacity, Trotsky had defeated Stalin's influence and had liquidated "Tsaritsynism."

But at what price? In his *My Life*, a source even more essential for Stalin's biography than his own, Trotsky admits that he hustled and offended many people during the disturbed period of his supreme command. "But in the great struggle that we were carrying on," he said, "the stakes were too big to

permit me to consider side-issues." There is no doubt whatever
that he was inspired by the interest of the common cause. But in
the difficult period of internal dissensions he came into contact
with all those who were discontented or annoyed. When
Lenin had offended comrades by his fierce polemic, he always
sought once he had won his victory, to bind up the wounds
and to conciliate the vanquished. Trotsky did not take the
trouble, and scornfully accumulated enemies. It was a weakness
in a politician.

Stalin, he says, "carefully picked up people with grievances.
He had leisure for it and it was to his personal interest"—an
allusion to his reputation for idleness, which Bukharin confirmed.
The latter says: "Stalin's first quality is laziness and his second is
implacable jealousy of anyone who knows more or does things
better than himself. He even tried to dig under Ilyich." In speaking of the recriminations heaped on Lenin with every failure at
the Front, Trotsky says that Stalin secretly directed the machinations. The Assistant Commissar for War, Skliansky, who was
highly valued by Lenin, and compared by Trotsky to Carnot as
a distinguished organiser, suffered from Stalin's underhand
attacks. Stalin gathered round him a group of disappointed and
ambitious careerists. Trotsky reports a characteristic story revealed by Menzhinsky. The latter learned that Stalin had suggested to Lenin that Trotsky was forming a cabal against him.
An invention of this kind recalls the old accusations made at
Tiflis, the suspicions felt at Baku, and many other incidents.
Trotsky ends this passage in *My Life* by saying: "But Stalin was
obviously sowing trouble. Not until much later did I realise how
systematically he had been doing that—almost nothing but
that. For Stalin never did any serious work."

With due allowance for controversy, Trotsky no doubt had
in mind intellectual work and high politics. For Stalin was not
only lazy and intriguing as Bukharin and many others thought;
his faults were allied with compensating qualities, but on a
limited scale. His brutal energy in police repression, and his calculating intrigue in personal relationships, together with a certain
flair for day to day politics, gave him in the narrow Party circle

an important place in the shadow of men who were indispensable. These minor qualities, given a favourable time and place,
were to assist his elevation.

A letter from Lenin to Trotsky shows well how Stalin succeeded in circumventing others without exposing himself to
attack. After his recall from Tsaritsyn, Stalin pretended to seek
an understanding, to advise Voroshilov to submit, and he asked
to be allowed to show what he could do on another sector of
the Front. Lenin wrote:

Stalin is anxious to work on the Southern Front. . . . He hopes
that in actual work he will be able to demonstrate the correctness
of his view. . . . In informing you, Leon Davidovich, of all these
statements of Stalin's, I request that you consider them and reply
first as to your willingness to talk the matter over with Stalin personally—for this he agrees to visit you—and second, if you think it
possible to remove the friction by certain concrete terms and to
arrange for the joint work which Stalin so much desires. As for me,
I consider it indispensable to make every effort for such an arrangement with Stalin.

Trotsky, less intransigent in his actions than in the bitterness of
his memoirs, replied favourably, and Stalin was appointed to the
Revolutionary War Council of the Southern Front. There, he
unsuccessfully continued his machinations, but with greater
prudence and caution.

6

STALIN's new appointment coincided with great historic events.
On the first anniversary of the October Revolution, the military
and political map of Europe had greatly changed. The Central
Empires had suffered disastrous defeats on the Western Front
and in the Balkans; there was mutiny in the German fleet, revolution in Bulgaria, in Austria-Hungary and in Germany, and
there were preparations for a general peace. The economic and
military intervention of the United States had enabled the Allies
to keep going in the last lap. Moreover, the end was hastened by
the so-called Bolshevik poison in the Austro-German armies,

assisted in the rear by Joffe, the ambassador of the Soviets in Berlin.

These disturbances were not yet the world socialist revolution counted on by Lenin, but he thought he saw in them the first steps towards an "October" with two continents for its stage. The delay in the realisation of his expectations had made him wary without quite depriving him of the hope of a universal social conflagration. "The world proletariat is with us, and marches at our heels," he said, at the least sign of revolt in the belligerent countries. "There is no issue from this war except in revolution," he repeated on another occasion, and later on he said more emphatically, "Only the workers and peasants of all countries will make peace." The first rumblings of the German Revolution led him to declare that "the crisis in Germany is beginning; it will inevitably end in the seizure of power by the proletariat." He was so obsessed by the course of the Russian Revolution that it seemed to his mind the only immediate prospect open to the whole world. "World history in these days is hastening more and more towards a world workers' revolution."

Nevertheless he was disquieted by the victory of the Allies, a vague menace of armed intervention in favour of the Whites in the Russian Civil War. "We have never been nearer a world-wide proletarian revolution, but neither have we ever been in such danger ourselves." But there were stronger grounds for hope than for fear. In November, at the Sixth Congress of Soviets he declared: "A whole series of countries are invaded by the flames of the workers' revolution. Our expectations are being accomplished, all our sacrifices are justified."

Trotsky expressed himself in similar terms: "History is developing, perhaps against our will, but on the lines we have marked out. . . . The end will be as we have foreseen . . . the fall of the gods of capitalism and imperialism. . . . Soviet Russia is only the vanguard of the German and the European revolution. . . ." Stalin did not at that time venture public expression on these matters. The Left Communists were retracting or were silent in face of the tangible results of Lenin's tactics.

The leaders of revolutionary Russia thought the German Revolution more important than their own for the future of humanity. In the name of the interests of socialism, they declared themselves ready to sacrifice the revolution of the most backward country to that of the most advanced. In theory Lenin thought it "obligatory to risk defeat and even the Soviet power," if necessary, to save the German Revolution. In practice no such eventuality presented itself. Germany only accomplished a superficial political revolution, and the Soviet Republic had all it could do to save itself.

For the Civil War took on greater proportions with the end of the war of nations. Thanks to the retreat of the German armies, the Reds hastened to occupy the Baltic and Lithuanian provinces, which were immediately converted into little Soviet States. In the Ukraine, where fifteen governments or so succeeded one another in less than four years, they disputed the ground with the reactionary troops of the Hetman Skoropadsky, the nationalist insurgents under Petlura, the anarchist peasants of Makhno, guerilla bands of all sorts and the *haidamaks* of the highways and byways. In the east they penetrated into the Urals, after having dislodged the Committee of the Constituent Assembly from Samara and the Directory of the Social Revolutionaries from Ufa, but they had to retreat before Kolchak's White Army under the orders of the Omsk dictatorship protected by the Allies. In Siberia their isolated guerilla bands fought desperately against the generals and atamans who exercised an unbridled tyranny over vast areas.

By decree of the Executive of the Soviets, the Republic had been proclaimed in a state of siege. To unify the commissariat for the Red Army there was created in November a Council of Workers' and Peasants' Defence, presided over by Lenin, with the inevitable Bureau under Trotsky. The various organs of the State and the Party were ill-suited to the exigencies of the situation, and it was sought to remedy the defect by supplementary organisations. In fact the same men were to be found in all the superior courts, and the Political Bureau of the Bolshevik Central Committee took over more and more of the responsi-

bilities of the dictatorship. Stalin was one of the six members of
the new Council, a proof that Lenin and Trotsky relied on
his energy in military organisation.

On the last day of the year, Lenin telegraphed to Trotsky:
"From below Perm there are a series of messages from the Party
on the catastrophic condition of the army and its drunkenness.
I send them on to you. They ask for you to go down there.
I thought of sending Stalin, fearing that Smilga might be too
gentle towards X..., who is said to be drinking and unable to
restore order. *Telegraph your views.*" In fact the Third Army
in retreat had evacuated Perm and was in danger of leaving
Vyatka exposed to the enemy. Trotsky replied, confirming
Lenin's information and said in conclusion: "I agree to the dispatch of Stalin empowered by the Party and by the Revolutionary Council of War." Perhaps he was not sorry to be rid
of Stalin in a northern region. It certainly was wise to send
Stalin where a firm hand was required. The Central Committee,
that is, its all-powerful Political Bureau, chose Dzerzhinsky and
Stalin to inquire into the capitulation of Perm and the defeats on
the Eastern Front, charging them to "restore at the earliest possible moment Party and Soviet activity in the zone of the Third
and Second Armies."

This meant a journey of inspection on the Vyatka Front and
a mission for the political and administrative reorganisation of
the rear. "Party and Soviet activity," in other words the functioning of the official institutions, was to be re-established by the
two special envoys. This shows to what an extent the Soviet
State was separated from the people, and how "superior"
initiative was substituted for the conscience of the masses.
Lenin's thesis on the State without bureaucrats, police or
professional army had been forgotten. But the exceptional
situation seemed to justify exceptional measures.

In publishing not long ago Lenin's dispatch on the defeat
at Perm, Voroshilov thought it necessary to falsify it by the
suppression of the words: "I send them on to you. They ask
for you to go down there. .... Telegraph your views." There is
evident intention to conceal Lenin's constant references of

difficult situations to Trotsky, and the confidence between the two. Voroshilov pushes complaisance so far as to impute the journey of Dzerzhinsky and Stalin to Vyatka to the fall of Uralsk, nearly 1,000 kilometres to the south. The reports of Stalin and Dzerzhinsky justify no such suppositions. All they do is to demand three regiments to reinforce the morale of the Third Army.

According to Voroshilov, who cites no documents on the subject, Stalin denounced "the inadmissible criminal proceedings of the Revolutionary Council of War in the direction of the Front," an obscure allusion aimed at Trotsky. If the statement is true, it shows how little notice Lenin took of Stalin's denunciations. Trotsky remained in supreme command throughout the Civil War and after it.

Stalin's last report briefly indicates the principal object of his activity. "The district Cheka has been purged, and its numbers filled by other militants of the Party." As at Tsaritsyn he was especially preoccupied with the police coercion. Evidently his experiences convinced him of the possibility of a weak government maintaining itself by force, by the physical destruction of opponents and the intimidation of waverers. His close collaboration with Dzerzhinsky, President of the Cheka, was not fortuitous. Their Vyatka mission appears to have lasted two or three weeks.

Stalin did not again appear at the Front until five months later, the interval being devoted to organising activity. He was not one of the theorists of the Party, but considered himself no less useful, to use his own expression, as a "practitioner." He wrote little for the press, and had no part in elaborating communist policy at this period, when the Third International was founded. Taking little interest in theoretical questions, or in international problems, he took no part in the inaugural session.

The disaster of the Spartacus League in Germany, then the assassination of Liebknecht and of Rosa Luxemburg, had darkened the prospects of revolution. But Lenin renounced neither his hopes nor his plans, and he had at heart the creation of a Communist International. No one in his Party raised any

objections when he proposed to summon to Moscow the Conference, to which, in addition to Bolsheviks of the various
nationalities inside Russia, there was only one single delegate
representing a Party, the German Communist Party. The
other participants, recruited from refugees, émigrés, exiles,
represented no one but themselves. The Spartacus delegate
brought with him the posthumous view of Rosa Luxemburg,
definitely hostile to the premature formation of a new International. This was also the definite opinion of the Central Committee of his Party. After much hesitation, Lenin ignored it;
the Communist International was born of his will. He was not
disturbed by a modest beginning. The political fortune of his
own original group, of which he had been the only fully conscious member, seemed to him to promise the future victory
of the Communist embryo organisation on a world scale. A few
days after the conference had transformed itself into a congress
the proclamation of a Soviet Republic in Hungary and then in
Bavaria, where no Communist Party even existed, fortified him
in his illusions.

But peace was not secured at home. On the contrary, the
Civil War was to be intensified in the course of 1919, with
the concentric advance of the armies of Kolchak and Denikin
on Moscow, and the march of Yudenich on Petrograd. The
Soviet Republic, cut off from its natural resources, was for a
moment reduced, in the current expression, almost to the old
grand duchy of Moscow. A *levée en masse* and superhuman
tension of the physical and moral strength of the Party were
required for the restoration of the frontiers.

Nevertheless, the mortal menace of serious military intervention by the Allies began to be dissipated. On this question
Lenin said: "If we have been able to exist for a year after the
October Revolution, we owe it to the fact that international
imperialism is divided into two groups of wild beasts. . . .
Neither of these groups can dispatch any considerable forces
against us." And later: "*They could have crushed us in a few
weeks.*" Replying to the boasts of his associates he said: "A few
hundred thousands of the army of millions of the Entente . . .

could have crushed us by military force." In fact foreign intervention was extraordinarily capricious and incoherent, and was
limited to aimless landings. The Czechoslovak anabasis, for want
of men and guns, was not an expedition but a retreat in good
order. Clemenceau's bellicose intentions were foiled by the
opposition of President Wilson and Lloyd George; the abortive
project of a conference of the various Russian Governments at
Prinkipo was symbolic of the contradictory currents. Moreover,
war weariness in Army and Navy, shown especially on the
French ships in the Black Sea, were factors against the dispatch
of an expedition.

The Civil War remained "Russian versus Russian" and the
mirage of armed intervention only played into the hands of
the Reds, who were placed in the classic pose of defending the
frontiers, and stimulated in their favour what was left of Russian patriotism. Marx's remark on the Revolution of 1848—
"there were none of those great foreign complications which
might have excited the energy and precipitated the course of
the revolution, stimulated the Provisional Government or
destroyed it"—explains why the Russian Revolution benefited
in the end by danger from outside. The Allies grasped the truth
later. The Mensheviks were the first to realise it, then the Social
Revolutionaries, both of whom repudiated any connection with
foreign intervention. The Georgian Social-Democrats only, disavowed by their Russian comrades, persisted in reckoning on
armed help from the Allies. Lenin was able to state that "in all
countries, the bourgeois intelligentsia, the Social Revolutionaries
and the Mensheviks—that race unfortunately exists everywhere
—condemned intervention in Russian affairs."

At the Eighth Congress of the Communist Party, henceforward the single political body in the country, the military
opposition was disarmed without appeal, after secret deliberations of which minutes have not been published. Stalin dared
not openly defend them and, as usual, did not appear on the
tribune. But he succeeded in being appointed to the drafting
Committee of the resolution as representing the majority, that
is to say by simulating an opinion he did not share. His

special kind of cleverness is seen in these tactics. In the absence of Trotsky, detained at the Front, his army proposals, put forward for him by Sokolnikov, were unanimously voted, with Lenin's support.

The adoption of the new programme led to an academic controversy between Lenin and Bukharin on imperialism and to a new discussion of the national question, but without any new arguments. Against Lenin and Riazanov, advocates of the righ of self-determination, Bukharin and Pyatakov maintained the exclusive rights of the working classes. According to the report of the debate, Stalin sided with the Left section, but aware of the inconvenience of open difference from Lenin, took no public part. Once more Lenin won the declaration on the principle of self-determination, which the Bolsheviks violated in practice.

The Congress decided on a volte-face with regard to the peasants, robbed and persecuted by all parties in the Civil War, and exhausted by the pillage practised by the "commissarocracy." For Lenin, as reported by Sosnovsky, to have spoken of stopping the " 'abominable Bashi-Bazouk' policy" towards the "middle" peasant, the Reds must have exceeded all bounds. A series of outrageous abuses of power by the Soviet village authorities were denounced and condemned. The peasants were reducing their sowings, and hiding their reserves, and were on the verge of revolt. They had to be treated with consideration, and concessions had to be made if agricultural production was to be restored. Recalling the question of Engels—"might it not be necessary to repress the rich peasants by force"—Lenin declared: *"We shall not permit any violence against the 'middle' peasant; we do not insist, as resolutely as in the case of the bourgeoisie, on complete expropriation."* The Committee of Poor Peasants had done its work. The decision represented paper concessions, problematical in its application.

Ossinsky and Sapronov had already criticised the rapid degeneration of the Party and the Soviets into a parasitic bureaucratic system. In practice, in spite of the Constitution promulgated the year before, the Communist Central Committee was

supplanting both the Council of Commissars and the Bureau of
the Executive of the Soviets. This same Central Committee, moreover, no longer itself existed, as a whole. Its meetings became
steadily rarer. "One man always had the threads in hand," Lenin
in policy, and Sverdlov in administration. Contrary to Lenin's
thesis before October, officials were not elected, nor responsible
to the people, but formed a privileged social class. The local
committees of the Party substituted their authority for that of
the Soviet Executive Committees; the military and police organisations had no respect for any legal institution. In vain Ossinsky
proposed to amalgamate the Council of Commissars and the
Executive Bureau of the Soviets, to introduce into the new body
the principal members of the Communist Central Committee
to assure unity and continuity of direction, and to rationalise
the administrative machine. The resolution adopted promised
reforms which the Civil War and an uneducated people rendered
impossible of realisation.

The election of the new Central Committee produced six
names *on all the lists* of candidates, those of Lenin, Zinoviev,
Trotsky, Kamenev, Bukharin and Stalin. These six men were
really the secret directing group of the Party and the State, and
were accountable to no one. Sverdlov's death from typhus was
an irreparable loss to the regime of which he had been the
principal organiser. Zinoviev and Kamenev gradually effaced
their reputation as the "October deserters" by submission to
Lenin who required docile agents for minor tasks. Bukharin
had a reputation as a theorist, and was a pleasant colleague,
relatively open and friendly. Stalin, still unknown in the Party
and the country, patiently cultivated personal relations in the
ranks of higher officials; the disappearance of Sverdlov, his
former comrade in exile, left a vacant place. The position of
Lenin and Trotsky was undisputed and indisputable.

During the Congress, Zinoviev roused a storm of acclamation
by reading the message announcing the formation of a Republic
of Soviets in Hungary, adding on his own account: "Let us hope
that in Paris the radio will soon be in the insurgents' hands."
Shortly afterwards he declared, in a manifesto issued by the

Communist International for May Day: *"Before a year has passed, the whole of Europe will have gone over to the Soviet system."* Lenin's language was very much the same: "The Soviet system has conquered, not only in backward Russia but in the most highly civilised country in Europe, Germany, and in the ancient capitalist stronghold, England." Even in America, "the most powerful and the youngest of the capitalist countries, the Soviet system has the sympathies of the working masses." Lenin saw soviets everywhere, saw them in the ephemeral English Shop Steward's Committees, in the most insignificant Strike Committees, and ventured on the premature announcement that "the soviets are winning throughout the world." In hasty generalisations on passing phenomena he based his general plan on half-truths and uncertainties, sometimes on pure mistakes. "No one," he said, "will be able to pay these unheard-of debts, or make good the terrible ruin; in France the production of wheat has fallen by more than half, faminine is knocking at the door, the forces of production are destroyed." Hence he concluded optimistically: *"We are sure that we have only six really hard months to face."* The Hungarian episode led him to declare that "the bourgeoisie themselves have recognised that no other power but the soviets can survive," and from this peaceful change of regime he hopefully augured that *"other countries will attain the Soviet system by other and more humane means."*

The most critical hour had not yet struck for the Russian Revolution, abandoned to its own resources pending the realisation of these grandiose dreams. It was at hand with the almost simultaneous offensive of Kolchak in the east, Denikin in the south and Yudenich in the north.

Kolchak was the first to be repulsed, and his retreat roused dissension even among the communists. Should he be pursued into the depths of Siberia, or should forces be drawn from the Eastern Front to meet the disturbing advance of Denikin in the south? Trotsky leaned towards the second course, in error as the event proved. Stalin seized this pretext to satisfy his bitterness; he had more than once denounced Trotsky to Lenin, but in vain. Lenin stood firmly by his rival. Early in June, Stalin again found fault with the southern command with the underlying design of hitting Trotsky; he insisted on penalties in terms apparently ambiguous, but clear enough to the initiated: "The whole question is to know whether the Central Committee will be courageous enough to draw the necessary deductions. Will it have sufficient character and firmness?" Though he did not see this correspondence, Trotsky sensed intrigue, and offered his resignation.

The incident had no immediate results. But it had the double interest of making clear the Central Committee's attitude towards Trotsky and Stalin's methods. In fact the Central Committee replied by confirming Trotsky in his post, assuring him of their desire to do everything to facilitate his task on the Southern Front, *"the most difficult, dangerous and important at the moment, and selected by Trotsky himself,"* to put all possible resources at his disposal, and to endeavour to hasten on the Party Congress, being *"firmly persuaded that Trotsky's resignation at this moment is absolutely impossible and would be the greatest disaster to the Republic."* This resolution is signed by— Stalin.

Fresh divergence of view arose over the operations against Denikin. In substance, Trotsky's plan was for an offensive across the working-class regions of Kharkov and the Donetz Basin, socially favourable to the Reds. The plan of the general staff on this Front, on the other hand, the plan supported by Stalin, was to cross the Cossack peasant country, which was socially favourable to the Whites. At first the Central Committee approved the second plan, but the event showed that Trotsky had been right. The ill-timed attack on the Cossacks drove them into the arms of Denikin, helped the enemy, and soon wore itself out. Meanwhile the Whites advanced into Great Russia, captured Kursk, then Orel, and were marching on Tula, the principal arsenal of the Republic and only 200 miles from Moscow. The error of the Staff, of the Central Committee, and of Stalin— of Lenin in the last resort—cost dear in life and war material. Also it led to an alarming situation in the South at the very moment of extreme danger in the North.

The Seventh Red Army, weakened by many desertions and demoralised by long inaction, was retreating on Petrograd. Stalin had spent three weeks on this Front in June-July, at the time of the surrender of the Krasnaya Gorka fort, easily retaken four days later. The whole affair resolved itself into a plot quickly repressed. In this matter Voroshilov attributes to Stalin "immense creative work," and the liquidation of "a dangerous situation in front of Red Petrograd." In reality there is no evidence of this in any published document of that date or for ten years afterwards, or in any memoirs; on the contrary the position of Petrograd grew steadily worse until October, when Lenin thought it lost and resigned himself to its evacuation.

The abandonment of Petrograd would have been a major disaster. Trotsky hurried to Moscow to oppose it energetically, with the help of Krestinsky, Zinoviev, and, this time, Stalin. He wanted to defend the city at any cost, even if it involved street fighting. Lenin submitted to his arguments, Trotsky's plan was adopted and the Commissar for War went to the North-West Front.

If ever situation was remedied by one man, it was in this amazing case, as was admitted in both camps. Petrograd was panic-stricken, its fall was announced throughout Europe, the Whites were, so to speak, at the gates. Trotsky was the soul of the resistance. His attitude revived the confidence of the disheartened population, aroused day by day the initiative and confidence of the defence, and galvanised the working classes in their adhesion to the only revolutionary Party. He was to be seen on horseback literally under machine-gun fire, bringing back stragglers to the front line. In a fortnight, at the cost of heavy sacrifices, Yudenich's army was definitely defeated.

"The saving of Red Petrograd was an invaluable service to the world-proletariat, and consequently to the Communist International. The first place in this struggle of course belongs to you, dear Comrade Trotsky . . ." said Zinoviev emphatically, in a message from the Executive of the new International. This was the general tenor of the resolutions of thanks and of the unanimous congratulations sent to Trotsky. In this case Lenin had all but committed an irreparable mistake in observing to excess the retreat tactics consciously employed a year earlier. His collaboration with Trotsky balanced the disadvantages arising from unlimited personal authority. Happily for the regime, its founder did not pretend to omniscience or omnipotence, and tried to secure collective rule.

The Political Bureau bestowed on Trotsky the Order of the Red Flag. The revival of decorations in the army, so contrary to communist ideology, could be explained, if necessary, as a temporary stimulus for the soldiers, most of them uninstructed peasants; but the practice was extended and consolidated by bestowing orders on the leaders. Originally there was no idea of creating a Civil Order, but the first step was to lead to a second, then a third. Trotsky had neither the rigid sense of principle nor the political intuition to limit the evil by his own example. Thus the rapid resumption of past customs day by day belied the scarlet colours of the Revolution.

On the same occasion, Kamenev proposed to decorate Stalin, to the great amazement of Kalinin, Sverdlov's nominal successor, who asked: "For what? I can't understand why it should be awarded to Stalin." Bukharin's reply was instructive. "Can't you understand? This is Lenin's idea. Stalin can't live unless he has what someone else has. He will never forgive it." Lenin had discerned Stalin's jealousy and sought to avoid anything which might excite his enmity to Trotsky. When the decorations were given, Stalin had the sense not to appear and no one understood why his name was mentioned.

The Republic of Soviets celebrated its second anniversary. Contrary to all expectations it had survived, and might last— if it denied its own programme. But peril persisted, and the Southern Front was too near Moscow. Trotsky's plan, tardily approved by Stalin on his own account, had to be adopted. In a letter full of insinuations, the date of which Voroshilov carefully omits to give, Stalin proposed a new plan, in agreement with that proposed by Trotsky, and in his turn threatened resignation, "otherwise my work at the Front would be absurd, criminal, and futile; this gives me the right, or rather the duty to go anywhere else, to the devil if need be, but not to remain on the Southern Front." A severe reply from the Political Bureau called him to order. "The Political Bureau regards the framing of your demands in the shape of ultimatums and resignations as inadmissible." Notifications of this nature fed his repressed hatred, the virulence and effectiveness of which were underrated by Trotsky.

Stalin's military historiographer, his close collaborator and subordinate, Voroshilov, declares—after ten years' reflection—that before starting for the Southern Front, Stalin had secured a ruling forbidding Trotsky to interfere in the business of his sector. If this were the case, the Commissar for War, President of the Revolutionary Council of War, member of the Central Committee and of the Political Bureau, would have been excluded from the main Front. It would have been easy to extract the confirmatory document from the archives. Voroshilov carefully abstains from all reference to it. On the other hand the collection *How the Revolution Armed*, vol. ii, book 1, contains no less than 80 documents relative to Trotsky's activities on the Southern Front. Not everything that Trotsky has to say in his later writings with regard to his quarrel with Stalin is invulnerable, but the documents cannot be refuted; Voroshilov has not taken the risk of attempting contradiction. Indeed the actual state of affairs can be deduced from this polemical literature without going into details.

Early in the following year, after Denikin's defeat, Stalin was nominated to the Caucasian Front, but evaded the task on the ground of the malevolent interpretation which would be placed on his frequent changes from one post to another. In reply to Lenin, ordering the dispatch of two divisions to the Caucasus, he said: "I do not see why the care of the Caucasus Front should rest especially on me. Responsibility for reinforcing the Caucasus Front rests normally with the Revolutionary Council of War of the Republic, whose members to my knowledge are in perfectly good health, and not with Stalin who is overloaded with work." In answer to this discourteous telegram, Lenin insists, with an implied reproof: "It is your business to hasten the dispatch of reinforcements from the South-West Front to the Caucasus Front. You must help in all ways and not dispute as to whose business it is." The interchange is characteristic of the two men.

Stalin was again engaged in military affairs in 1920 during the Polish campaign. During the summer, the former leader of the *bojowci* expropriators, Pilsudski, forced the exhausted Reds into another war by advancing with the Polish army into the Ukraine as far as Kiev. By an ironic chance, Stalin, the virtuoso of the *boyeviki* expropriations, was at the headquarters of the retreating army. The reverses roused a burst of fighting energy in Russia. The Red Army of the Southwest, having been reinforced, pulled itself together, and the Poles had to evacuate Kiev and retreat faster than they had advanced—more than 600 kilometres in five weeks. These suddenly altered circumstances occasioned a sharp strategic and political difference among the communist leaders. Trotsky and Radek argued resolutely for the conclusion of peace. But the majority, including Lenin and Stalin, wanted to exploit the success to the full, to develop the offensive, to take Warsaw, and to realise after their own fashion self-determination in Poland by helping Polish communists to establish a Soviet Republic.

They were falling into the bellicose error of the "Girondism" of the Left Communists, and forgetting Robespierre's clear statement: "The wildest idea that can enter the head of any politician is to think that it is sufficient for a nation to carry their arms among another nation to make them adopt their own laws and constitutions. No one loves armed missionaries." The result was to stimulate Polish national unity under pressure of a foreign enemy, instead of stimulating the class struggle. The Central Committee had agreed with Lenin, but events proved him to be wrong. The advance of the Reds began as an adventure, and ended in severe defeat.

One of the causes of the catstrophe, says Trotsky, was the action of the Southern Front headquarters, where Stalin was the leading political personage. This can be proved without going into all the details. When the army group commanded by Smilga and Tukhachevsky on the north had dangerously thinned its front towards Warsaw by too rapid a march, Stalin proposed to lead the Southern Army towards Lemberg, contrary to his instructions to help the Northern Army group by attacking the Poles in the flank. Stalin endangered the main action in the desire to inscribe on his banner the capture of a great city. "Only after repeated orders and threats did the south-western command change the direction of its advance. But the few days of delay had already had their fatal effect." Voroshilov passes over this feat of arms in silence.

Lenin was not the last to understand the significance of his defeat. He referred to it frankly on several occasions. Amongst his other commanding qualities he possessed that of often acknowledging his errors and of learning from them. "We were wrong," is a frequent phrase in his writings and his speeches. With regard to the Warsaw mistake, Clara Zetkin relates in her *Reminiscences of Lenin* that he said: "Radek predicted how it would turn out. . . . I was very angry with him, and accused him of 'defeatism.' But he was right in his main contention. He knew the situation outside Russia, especially in the west, better than we did." Neither was he grudging in his praise of Trotsky. More than anyone else, he was conscious of the lack of capable men in his Party, and he did justice to the best of them. "Good staff officers are just the element lacking in all revolutions," wrote Engels to Marx, half a century earlier. Lenin knew something about it by experience.

Stalin also took part with Frunze in the operations against the last of the great White armies, levied in the south by Wrangel; but sickness shortened his military career. Voroshilov does not attribute to him any exploit of any particular merit on this Front. Had he any responsibility for the cruel massacre of unarmed prisoners ordered by Bela Kun in the Crimea after the final victory of the Reds? It must not be assumed, in view of the uncertainty of the dates of his presence at the Front.

With this last battle, which cost the Whites a hecatomb of victims, the Civil War drew to a close, after two years of struggle comparable only, in modern times, by the size of the forces

involved and the bitterness of the fighting, to the War of
Independence. The Russian struggle was shorter than the American, but the technique of armaments made it more intense and
the extent of country covered by its operations made it more
costly in life. More than a year elapsed before the remnants of
the insurgent troops were dispersed in Ukraine, Siberia, Turkestan, and before the conquest of the Caucasus was achieved.
Nevertheless, the year 1920 opened for the Soviet Republic a
new era, that of peaceful work.

7

STALIN emerged from the war matured and tempered. He had
won no notoriety, but under Lenin he had acquired the technique of government, a modicum of empirical political science
and confidence in himself. At the Front he learned to hold life
and human suffering cheap. And this "hard" man among the
"hards" had become still more hardened to repression in the
rear.

Around him there were many gaps. Sverdlov, the master-
organiser of the dictatorship, Uritsky, Volodarsky, Chudnovsky, and many others, were gone; his comrades and rivals in the
Caucasus, S. Shaumian, called "the Lenin of the Caucasus,"
and P. Djaparidze had been killed by the English among the
twenty-six commissars executed after the fall of the Baku Commune. The decimated cadres of Bolshevism had a new world to
create. Infinite possibilities seemed to lie open to the bold survivors. What ambitions came to birth in Stalin? From some lines
which he wrote later in memory of Sverdlov, it is clear that he
felt himself misunderstood and unjustly kept in the background
of events: "There are men, leaders of the proletariat, who are
not talked about in the press, perhaps because they are not fond
of talking about themselves, but who are, nevertheless, the vital
sap and the authentic leaders of the revolutionary movement."
He is certainly speaking awkwardly about himself, in honouring Sverdlov.

He was probably voicing long harboured bitterness, but also

a certain truth. In Soviet Russia, as elsewhere, writers and orators attract public attention without always deserving it. Usually
silent in great assemblies and unnoticed in the press, Stalin remained unknown outside the limited circle of official politics,
although he shared the effective power wielded behind the
closed doors of the Political Bureau and the Central Committee.
But unresigned to his position in the background and unsuspect-
ing of the future in reserve for him, he was biding his hour with
the patience and typical prudence of the peasant.

During the revolutionary days of 1917, Lenin, envisaging the
possibility of assassination, asked Trotsky: "If the Whites kill
us both, do you think that Sverdlov and Bukharin will be able
to carry on?" He did not think of Stalin as an eventual successor,
nor, of course of the "October deserters." A careful observer
of men, he was incapable of error in assessing the intellectual
and moral level of his comrades and followers, however close
their relations. He told Trotsky that Zinoviev was bold when
the danger was past, an opinion confirmed by Sverdlov: "Zinoviev is panic personified." Of certain Left Bolsheviks he had
written: "Lunacharsky, Manuilsky and Co. have no brains."
His estimate of the others of his following was not more flattering. On the other hand he valued at their true worth his serious
collaborators, supporting and encouraging them in every
difficulty.

By the tragic light of the Civil War, he no doubt discerned
that Stalin and Dzerzhinsky were the strongest characters, with
the exception of Sverdlov and Trotsky. In 1919, between two
campaigns against the Whites, he secured Stalin's nomination
as Commissar for Workers' and Peasants' Inspection, the new
control organisation which was neither more nor less "workman
and peasant" in character than the other Soviet institutions, and
which only added one bureaucratic complication the more to
the machine. The utility of this Commissariat, as in the case of
the Commissariat for Nationalities, was sufficiently expressed by
the fact that the Commissar who presided over both of them
spent his time at the Front. But the choice of Stalin at that time
is significant.

There is no ground for Trotsky's hypothesis that Lenin, who had only just met Stalin from time to time before he returned to Russia, formed an unfavourable opinion of him after seeing him actually at work. That appears to be an anachronism. Lenin respected Stalin not for his brain but for his fist. It was several years before he changed his opinion of the "wonderful Georgian."

Substantially different was his appreciation of Trotsky, whose rhetorical and romantic quality he did not like, but whose intelligence, culture, initiative and energy he understood how to use in the interests of the revolution. With him he shared the direction of affairs and its responsibilities, and with him he maintained a permanent friendship, implicit or explicit, except in case of an open difference of opinion in which controversy was admissible. On the Bolshevik attitude towards the peasant question he wrote in *Pravda:* "I entirely support Trotsky's statement. There is not the smallest disagreement between us. . . . I subscribe with both hands to what Comrade Trotsky has said." On another occasion he defended Trotsky when he was charged with excessive severity. "If we have defeated Kolchak and Denikin," he said, "it is because discipline is stronger with us than in all the capitalist countries of the world. Trotsky has established the death penalty, and I approve of this." He even gave him a signed blank paper agreeing beforehand to his most disputed acts: "Knowing the strict character of Comrade Trotsky's orders, I am so convinced, so absolutely convinced, of the correctness, expediency and necessity for the success of the cause of the order given by Comrade Trotsky that I unreservedly endorse this order." Their fundamental agreement was not one of the least factors in the stability of the regime.

In the division of work, dictatorial power was divided between the Political Bureau, the Revolutionary Military Council and the Extraordinary Commission (Cheka)—all three extra-Constitutional authorities. Lenin directed the first, Trotsky the second, and Dzerzhinsky the third. In the last resort decision rested with the Political Bureau, but, practically, Trotsky and Dzerzhinsky, each assisted by colleagues, exercised almost unlimited authority in their respective domains. At one time *Pravda* was able to state that the formula "All power to the Soviets" had been replaced by "All power to the Chekas." The country was covered with a close network of Chekas, superior, local, departmental, provincial and regional, without taking into account the special Chekas for transport and other departments. At the top of this police pyramid, the Central Cheka was responsible in theory to the Council of Commissars, in reality to the Political Bureau. In fact it had means of securing automatic confirmation for its actions, except for the very rare interventions of Lenin or Trotsky acting on direct information. The end of armed hostilities reduced military control to the camps and garrisons, but left a ramified Cheka which perfected itself by simplification of its operation. The Political Bureau and the Cheka, each the instrument of the other, held the prerogatives of government in their hands, much as in France the Committee of Public Safety and the Committee of General Security did under Jacobin rule. The circumstances were parallel, but not identical; the same causes had produced analogous results.

But in Russia the machinery for coercion forged in the Civil War period survived the circumstances which had made it necessary and historically justifiable. Peace was not immediately attained, the professional revolutionaries, increased in number, remained on the alert, and the state of war, theoretically abolished, persisted under new forms, by force of inertia and as being the easiest governmental method.

Before the Constitution was in being, the Republic of Soviets enjoyed a semblance of constitutionalism, complex and ill-defined. Local soviets had some power. Social-Democrats, Social Revolutionaries and Anarchists had representatives of precarious standing in the Soviet executive. The harried Opposition, in spite of repressive measures, issued journals with frequent changes of name. The Communist Party as yet only exercised a relative dictatorship; its committees and sections shared authority within limits under a domestic regime which tolerated controversy. The outburst of terrorism and the counter-terror was soon to change this state of affairs.

Lenin had not been caught napping. In this matter he had never changed his opinion, for he had written in *Iskra* in 1901: "In principle we have never renounced, and cannot renounce terrorism. It is an act of war . . . indispensable at a certain point in the struggle," though he agreed that terrorism "was not in itself sufficient." He had never envisaged the terror as a permanent instrument of his "democratic dictatorship." At first events were stronger than he, and he afterwards found it expedient to prolong the use of means intended for exceptional circumstances. The word "shoot" recurred like a sinister *leitmotiv*, often simply as a threat, but the violent language was in itself a sign of weakness.

In so far as Lenin and Trotsky adopted the terrorist theory they travestied Marxist doctrine, of which they professed themselves faithful interpreters. They had no reply ready when confronted with Engels's statement that terror meant *"the domination of men who were themselves terrorised,"* that it consisted of *"useless cruelties committed to give self-confidence to men who are themselves afraid."* A considered opinion confirmed by Marx, who praised the Paris Commune for having *"remained innocent of the violence common in revolutions and especially in the counter-revolutions of the upper classes."* Twenty-five years earlier Marx had written: *"Revolution will show less bloodshed, less vengeance and fury, in exact proportion to the degree in which the proletariat is reinforced by socialist and communist elements."* Regarded from this aspect the Russian Revolution showed singular poverty in those elements.

Whites and Reds accused one another of beginning reprisals in the Civil War and of the worst exactions and persecutions. Both sides produced many doubtful documents and many wild assertions. But pending examination of these, there is enough truth in them to make it unnecessary to undertake a minute study of the truth of any individual instance; given a certain degree of horror, the variants are unimportant. The essentials are already known before the archives have yielded their secrets and before all the witnesses are free to speak. Hostages shot, prisoners exterminated, the innocent massacred, villages burnt, rape, pillage, reprisals, hangings and torture—the whole is too generally true for it to be worth while to verify the details.

History proves that there is nothing specifically Russian about these abominations. There is evidence of them in all wars and revolutions. Jaurès justly observed: "Revolutions are a barbarous means of progress. However noble, fruitful or necessary a revolution may be, it always belongs to an inferior and semi-bestial epoch of humanity." And might not Lenin be said to admit this in giving the advice *"not to shrink from barbarous methods to combat barbarism"?* Also Trotsky, in speaking of revolution "with its heroism and cruelty, its struggle for and scorn of the individual."

In justification of the Bolsheviks, it is fitting to quote some other reflections of the *Histoire Socialiste de la Révolution Française:*

When a great country in revolution struggles at the same time against interior factions which are armed, and against the world, when the least hesitation or the least fault can affect the future of the new order, perhaps for centuries, those who direct this immense enterprise have not the time to rally the dissidents, or to convince their adversaries. They cannot pay much attention to discussion or combination. They must fight, they must act, and to guard intact their full capacity for action, in order not to dissipate their strength, they use death to create around them that immediate unanimity which they need.

There is nothing specifically Russian, and certainly no connection with "experiments in socialism," in the outburst of peasant savagery caused by centuries of despotism and ignorance, in the awakening of atavistic brutality roused by war between so-called civilised nations. These are phenomena natural in the backward state of Russia, the country of which Gorky wrote in his *Revolt of the Slaves:*

A people brought up in a school which dwells vulgarly on the terrors of hell, tutored with blows of the fists, with rods and whips, cannot have a tender heart. A people who have been trampled down by the police will be capable in their turn of trampling on the bodies of others. In a country where iniquity has been triumphant for so long it is hard for the people to realise in a day the power of justice. You cannot expect justice from those who have never known it.

Bolshevism could not escape the psychosis of systematised murder. At the end of the Civil War it was soaked in it. Its principles, practice, institutions and customs had been turned into new channels by the weight of the calamities it had endured. It was its misfortune rather than its fault. There is a remarkable disparity between Bolshevism conservative and Bolshevism triumphant. But in passing from "War Communism" to communism in peace, the chosen few owed it to their doctrine, their culture, their socialist past and their revolutionary present to move into the "more humane path" of which Lenin spoke. To renounce that path by adopting the dictatorship in opposition to democracy, instead of raising themselves to the height of a synthesis, was to compromise the future irremediably and to make the boldest effort abortive. But by following out their own programme the Bolsheviks, with the aid of the workers of other countries, could have made a reality of this Socialist Federal Republic of Soviets, which was neither republican, nor socialist, nor federal, and could have revived the soviets which had virtually ceased to exist. Their impotence to attune speech and action, theory and practice, confirmed the truth of a prophetic saying of Rosa Luxemburg's: "In Russia the problem may be posed: it cannot be resolved."

Chapter VII

THE SOVIET REPUBLIC

WHAT remained of the Bolshevism of yesteryear at the end of the Civil War? A changed theory with the old vocabulary adapted to changed circumstances. A veteran Party with a tried and tested hierarchy, but whose ranks were gradually debolshevised by the army of recruits attracted by the magnet of power. At the Eighth Congress in 1919, 313,000 Party members were represented; in March of the next year 611,000 members.

Though the Bolsheviks were victorious, the fundamental basis of traditional Bolshevism was outlived. Nothing of it was left except the organisation of professional revolutionaries—a military conception. It is true that the original phalanx, their ranks decimated, admitted no change, convinced that they were faithful to their original tenets in spite of concessions to expediency. But within a very few years the impossibility of reversing the changes made became clear.

One by one Lenin's fundamental October theses were abandoned—soviet democracy, the suppression of privileges, equality of remuneration, the abolition of the professional police, army and bureaucracy, peasant usufruct of the land, the right of self-determination. Gradually faith in the immediacy of a socialist world revolution, the imminence of the end of the capitalist regime, and the Messianic belief in the universal spread of the Russian example faded from the minds of Leninists. Doubt began to assail the minds of the leaders, and conquered the mental passivity of the led. As for the non-political masses, over-whelmed with privation and poverty, they thought of nothing but day to day existence; they fled from the famished towns, and bitterly disputed with the rural authorities for their black bread.

"*The dictatorship of the proletariat means that never yet has the proletariat of the capitals and the industrial centres been placed in so terrible a position as to-day*," declared Lenin roundly; "the industrial proletariat, in attaining its dictatorship, is enduring unprecedented sufferings from famine." He added that the hunger in Moscow was abominable. Later on, insisting on the same truth, he said: "*The dictatorship of the proletariat has imposed upon the ruling class, the proletariat, sacrifices, suffering and poverty, unprecedented in history.*" Again in 1921 he wrote: "The situation of the working class is very hard; they suffer frightfully." And a year later: "The people think remedies must be found for famine and terrible poverty." At that time relative sincerity in Government declarations was the rule.

Under these tragic conditions, the requirements of food supply and defence took precedence of everything else, to the detriment of theory and programmes. "We have committed many faults, but we had to act as quickly as possible, to reorganise our army supply at all costs. . . ." In these words Lenin sought to excuse his divergences from his political theory, and to warn his followers against making the divergences the rule. But he was referring rather to economic expedients than to the dictatorial measures taken at first against his opponents, then against all classes of malcontents, whether workmen or peasants, revolutionaries or socialists. In publicly admitting his mistakes he did not include in them the abandonment of soviet democracy during the terror. On this point practice contradicted theory without eliciting any retractions from him.

He maintained that the dictatorship was exercised "by the proletariat organised in the soviets directed by the Bolshevik Communist Party." In practice nothing and nobody could withstand or mitigate this monopoly of direction, which came to mean exclusive power.

Rival parties were outlawed, in violation of the Constitution, and the remaining Social-Democrats, who had formerly been invited to sit on the Soviet Executive, were to pass into exile. But Martov and his comrades formed a "legal" opposition, having accepted the October Revolution as historically necessary, abandoned the Constituent Assembly, and even mobilised their members in defence of the Republic. "We will give you legal status, but will reserve power for ourselves only," said Lenin, who, however, kept power in his own hands, but did not legalise the position of his peaceful opponents. The Left Social Revolutionaries, like the anarchists, were ranked as counter-revolutionary. Afterwards the same fate befell the trade unionists, the Zionists and the most inoffensive Tolstoyans.

Liberty of the press and the right of assembly existed only in memory. Lenin's decree promising "complete freedom of the press" had no value except as a museum-piece. Not only the soviets, but the trade unions and the shop committees, were transformed into docile tools of the ruling party. To quote Lenin again: "All the committees of the great majority of the trade unions are composed of communists and merely carry out the Party instructions;" and the party was under the complete control of "a Central Committee of 19, permanent work at Moscow being carried on by two still smaller committees, the Orgbureau (Organisation Bureau) and the Politbureau (Political Bureau), of five members each elected in plenary session; a real oligarchy." Lenin did not shrink from the word "oligarchy" in spite of its implication, and he went on frankly to declare: "Not even the simplest question . . . is settled by any of our republican institutions without instructions from the Central Committee of our Party," that is to say from one of the two all-powerful bureaux, from this "real oligarchy."

These words, written in 1921, expressed a profound change in the communists, who were determined to maintain in peace time the system and the so-called provisional methods suggested by civil and foreign wars. Trotsky, defending terrorism in special cases, had declared: "Our task will be easier, every citizen will have more freedom, and the pressure of the proletarian State will be lightened with every step of our advance." The contrary happened. Lenin also promised an early relaxation of the dictatorship, increasing mildness of the political system. But the "oligarchy" established summary methods of government under the state of siege and under martial law, which imperceptibly became second nature to the new Bolshevism.

The death penalty, abolished after the Red victory in agreement with their original intention, was restored three months later and maintained permanently after fighting had ceased at home and on the frontiers. At one time the Bolsheviks, in common with other Social-Democrats in Europe and America, joined with the International in demanding the abolition of the death penalty. Plekhanov's statement in 1903, which they quoted as their authority, only referred to a few exceptional cases. Lenin, referring to the defence of Hyndman, the English socialist, of the death penalty, criticised him for his "bourgeois and Philistine ideas." And when he had recourse to this extreme measure at the beginning of the Civil War, there were numerous protests from the Party—Dybenko went so far as to resign. But after years of practice and custom the only communist voice raised in 1922 against the inclusion of the death penalty in the Civil Code, the corner-stone of the dictatorship, was that of Riazanov.

Between 1917 and 1920 Lenin had successively declared for the democratic dictatorship of the workers and peasants, then for the dictatorship of the workers and the poor peasants, and then for the dictatorship of the workers. After October he did not hesitate to declare: "Yes, dictatorship of a single party, and we will not yield an inch." He came to the dictatorship of the Communist Party, the only one qualified in his view to interpret the history of the revolution, and finally to the dictatorship of its Central Committee, of its Political Bureau, of an "oligarchy." Such was Stalin's political education.

"At the bitter end, everything will revolve around one

man who will, *ex providentia*, unite all power in himself."
Plekhanov's prophecy was not yet accomplished but, in the
opinion of many communists, it was on its way to fulfilment.
"Dictatorship *over* the proletariat"—Trotsky's former criticism
of Lenin—was the formula adopted by all the opponents of
the new regime. The "Old Bolsheviks" of the Right recalled in
secret their warnings in October against the "maintenance by
political terrorism of a purely Bolshevik Government." Nevertheless Lenin personally was not inclined to personal power or
to violence; he yielded to the force of circumstances and the
development of a system.

It was the embodiment on the scale of an immense State of
the military idea of the close organisation of professional
revolutionaries under the orders of the "secret circle of leaders."
But during the prolonged anxiety of years in which none dared
to hope for lasting security, in economic distress and political
and social peril, the democratic habit of the Party inherited from
Social-Democracy gave place more and more to an increasingly
autocratic centralism. The consequences of six years of civil
and foreign war were not easily effaced. The Tenth Congress
of the Party had to recognise "the militarisation of the organisation" and took measures to put an end to it, but with what
success? Dictatorship and military discipline were essential in
the "conditions of the struggle and the positive action demanded
by historical facts," Bukharin was to write. *"But if our Party
. . . has a military organisation, it must naturally construct Soviet
institutions in its own image."*

Military exigencies were not the only cause of this evolution.
Now, as in the past, economic disorder and peasant anarchy
engendered counteracting military methods of organisation,
subordination, and command, applied in earlier times by Peter,
Alexander I and Nicholas I. Demobilisation might increase the
trouble, and consequently an empirical solution was sought in
"armies of workers," the utilisation of military units for urgent
and elementary civil tasks.

Trotsky based great hopes on this partial application of the
principle of compulsory labour, though the Mensheviks had

declared that it must be uneconomic and parasitic and doomed to failure; one of them, Abramovich, compared the attempt to the methods employed by the Pharaohs for building the Pyramids, and, in Russian history, to the military colonies of Arakcheyev, who, under Alexander I, sought to mould the peasants to garrison life on the Prussian model, out of admiration for Frederick the Great. But Trotsky maintained that "labour armies had demonstrated their vitality," that "this almost scientific experiment lighted up our path." He rebutted the Menshevik argument by declaring: "The militarisation of labour is only an Arakcheyev method when it is carried out against the wishes of the workers themselves." This was practically an assertion of the identity of the proposal by the "oligarchy" with the workers' wishes, and the statement was liable to be disproved by the event. Trotsky's statement might be paraphrased as "the same methods with other aims." Replying to the Egyptian allusion he put the rhetorical question: "Who are the rulers? The working class or the nobility, the Pharaohs or the peasants? . . ." But this simplification of the problem did not automatically simplify the solution, and the labour armies had to be dissolved and their failure admitted. Stalin was president of the Council of the labour army in the Ukraine; but left no trace or recollection of his activity.

"Who are the rulers?" No one could have answered Trotsky with certainty at this transitional period of upheaval of the economic and social structure. The Political Bureau certainly ruled behind the façade of the Council of Commissars and the Executive of the Soviets, in the name of a particular conception of the interest of the working-class majority and of historical progress, but how clearly was that conception interpreted and how far could it reckon on the tacit assent of the people in the absence of conscious approval? To form any opinion on these matters some expression, however imperfect, was necessary of the wishes and sentiments of those workers and peasants whose sole representatives the Bolsheviks claimed to be.

Before the October Revolution Lenin had written: "The struggle of parties for power might develop peacefully within the soviets on condition that the latter *renounce distortions of democratic principles* such as allotting one representative for 500 soldiers and one for 1,000 workmen. *In a democratic republic attacks on principle of this kind cannot be tolerated.*" He developed the thesis in his own fashion: *"One workman's vote is worth those of many peasants."* Contradictions grew: "We admit neither liberty, nor equality, nor workers' democracy if they are contrary to the theory of the liberation of labour." Who was to be the judge of whether they were contrary? The Party alone, that is to say its officials from the lowest to the highest, its super-imposed committees, its responsible militants constituting what Anglo-Saxons call the "machine" and Germans the "apparatus," and, in the last resort, the Central Committee, its two bureaux, in short a sovereign oligarchy whose members were co-opted.

Ever since the terror, the soviets, originally elected by the workers, then by the active minority, had been nominated directly or indirectly by the Party Committees, except in insignificant villages where there were no communists. But local power did not extend beyond minor municipal business. On instructions from the administration, the preponderance of the Party was ensured by the mechanical control of the machine over all the wheels of the State. Congresses of Soviets developed into meetings strictly regulated by paid officials, and were compelled to obey instructions from above and to vote resolutions automatically and unanimously. This metamorphosis of the regime was realised step by step, unconsciously, without premeditated calculation or preconceived plan; it was the result of the general lack of culture, of the apathy of the exhausted masses and the efforts of the Bolsheviks to overcome anarchy.

Lenin soon realised the facts, but he could not devise any other way of preventing counter-revolution in Russia, pending the spread of revolution in Europe. His well-known slogan, *"We shall only attain final victory in association with the massed workers of other countries,"* is reiterated in his important speeches and reports. "The Russian proletariat single-handed cannot bring the socialist revolution to a victorious conclusion," he had written in 1917 in his farewell letter to the Swiss workers. "The complete victory of the socialist revolution is impossible in a single country; it demands as a minimum the active co-operation of several advanced countries, of which Russia is not one," he said at the Congress of Soviets in 1918. "It is obvious that only the proletariat of all the advanced countries taken together can win the final victory," he repeated in 1919. "Victory in Russia alone will not accomplish the revolution, without its extension to other countries," he reiterated in 1920. "Revolution will break out in other countries, or we shall perish," he was to say in 1921 in summing up frankly the ideas of the Bolsheviks in October. "We have always pronounced and repeated this elementary Marxist truth that, for the socialist victory, the joint efforts of the workers of several advanced countries are necessary," he wrote in 1922. Trotsky always held the same opinion. The *A.B.C. of Communism*, by Bukharin and Preobrazhensky, a text-book circulated by the million, said: "The workers' communist movement can conquer only as an international communist movement." The isolation of the Soviet Republic justified, in Lenin's eyes, every kind of coercion for maintaining the "dictatorship of a single party."

That did not prevent him from asserting, "we stand . . . for a proletarian State based on the proletariat, whose administrative organs are elected by the proletariat. Our State grants the proletariat all political rights and attracts the peasants to it through the proletariat." In spite of these confused and contradictory statements, the Constitution became an ideal removed more and more from reality. And indeed the privileges "granted" to the proletarians by themselves, by their own State—as against communist principle, which by definition aimed at the extinction of all privileges—could not have been anything else but fictitious in the "terrible situation," the "unprecedented sufferings of the famine," "poverty unequalled in history," inflicted on this same proletariat, as Lenin admits.

Among other reasons this last turn of events had drawn from him the admission: *"The peasants have certainly gained more from the revolution than the working class . . . which proves, indeed, that our revolution was, up to a point, a bourgeois revolution.*" Had he not in 1906 warmly approved Kautsky for having demonstrated that the Russian Revolution would be neither bourgeois, nor socialist? Not bourgeois, "because the bourgeoisie is not one of the motive forces of the present revolutionary movement in that country," nor socialist, because the revolution "could not *in any way* enable the proletariat to assume *alone* the hegemony or the dictatorship." The only Russian Social-Democrat, therefore, to foretell the approaching socialist revolution and the dictatorship of the proletariat was Trotsky, violently opposed by Lenin and the Leninists. Now Lenin no longer admitted the contradiction when he spoke almost in the same breath of a bourgeois revolution and the proletarian State, of peasants gaining economic advantages and of the political privileges of the proletariat. He generalised by defining the task of revolutionary dictatorship to be the building of "socialism". . . .

It was a singular reversal of rôles: before the revolution the Social Revolutionaries, carrying on the Populist tradition, attributed a socialist character to the future revolution, while the Social-Democrats, both Right and Left (except Trotsky), were preparing for a bourgeois revolution; during and after the revolution both were to perform the exact opposite of what they had promised, except the Mensheviks, who had not gone back on this point, but were to ruin themselves by abdicating on behalf of the liberal bourgeoisie. Chernov and the Social Revolutionaries defended capitalism; Lenin and the Bolsheviks undertook, despite their theory, to impose socialism by force.

The latter were aware, nevertheless, that the great majority of the nation had followed them in October, not for their programme in its entirety, but to secure peace and land. They had no answer to Rosa Luxemburg when she wrote: "*Socialism, by its nature, cannot be imposed, cannot be established by* ukase." Their inconsistency was to justify her penetrating remark that "the greatest valour and the most sublime sacrifices of the proletariat *in a single country* are inevitably caught up in a whirlpool of contradictions and mistakes."

But while Lenin justified the "dictatorship of a single party," and eventually an "oligarchy," in the name of the socialism which he was trying to establish in a country of whose immaturity he was aware, he replied to Kautsky's complaints by saying that "the soviet power is a thousand times more democratic than the most democratic of the bourgeois republics." He based his remarks on the text of the Constitution, which reserved for the exploited *on paper* many of the liberties refused to exploiters and parasites. But apart from the fact that the letter of the Constitution remained dead, Rosa Luxemburg had refuted the sophistry in advance, by showing that a franchise limited to workers would only be useful in a society able to assure all its members of useful work, and "a decent life worthy of civilisation." She admitted the impossibility in Soviet Russia of satisfying this primary demand of the toiling masses, who were thus deprived of all rights, and she concluded by citing the Marxian axiom that "it is the mission of the proletariat on attaining power to substitute for bourgeois democracy a socialist democracy, not to destroy all democracy."

But in order to understand Lenin, driven to expedients by the necessity of self-preservation of the Bolshevik State, and compelled to contradict himself by the cruel paradox inherent in the situation of a revolutionary vanguard in power isolated in the midst of a backward country, account must be taken of his absolute disinterestedness in the service of socialism and of his unyielding frankness to the working people whose cause he espoused. So far from idealising either his own acts or those of the helpers sheltered by his prestige, he looked the bitterest reality in the face and called a spade a spade—defeat, retreat, compromise, error, bore their true names. If the policy of the Party sometimes was guilty of demagogy, it was against his will; he waged incessant war on self-satisfaction, and continually encouraged healthy honest self-criticism among his followers, by precept and by example. Less self-deceived than any of his comrades, he was always the first to admit "we have made a mistake." In this connection his words at the beginning of the new regime must be quoted: "We are only beginning our task in Russia and at the moment we are making a bad beginning," and his advice to European workers that they should say to themselves: "What the Russians are doing badly, we shall do better." This was not the first time that he told his followers bitter truths, and it was not to be the last.

2

THE Political Bureau, the supreme organ of the dictatorship, whose very existence remained unsuspected not only in Russia at large but for a long time among the communist rank and file, was originally a secret insurrectionary Directorate elected by the Central Committee at the instance of Dzerzhinsky, a few days before the *coup d'état*. It consisted of seven members: Lenin, Trotsky, Stalin, Zinoviev, Kamenev, Sokolnikov, and Bubnov. The rules of the Party did not provide for it, but experience in action showed it to be indispensable. The difficulty of calling urgent plenary meetings of the scattered Central Committee had given rise before this to a "small Central Committee" of eleven members who shared current responsibilities among themselves.

The seizure of power restored its function to the Central Committee, but the course of events and the exigencies of intensive and varied activity were soon to necessitate the creation of a new Political Bureau composed this time of four members (*chetvyorka*): Lenin, Trotsky, Sverdlov and Stalin, bound, before coming to any decision, to consult members of the Central Committee who might be in the Smolny Institute at the time. During the Civil War, Trotsky and Stalin were generally, like most of their colleagues, at the Front; Lenin and Sverdlov carried on the work of the Politbureau or of the Central Committee by themselves, seconded by Krestinsky, and at times by Kamenev, Bukharin, Preobrazhensky or Serebriakov. On important occasions, one body or other was specially summoned. There was no conflict of powers; it was necessary to act quickly and as effectively as possible, to shorten preliminaries and to economise strength by sharing responsibility.

Alongside the Politbureau, there was the secretariat of the Central Committee, conducted at first with the assistance of an energetic fellow-worker, Helen Stassova. This modest task had gained no special position in the hierarchy such as was afterwards confided to an equipage of five persons under the control of Sverdlov. When Sverdlov died, no successor of his calibre was found. Kalinin succeeded him as President of the Executive of the Soviets, while Stalin gradually absorbed his administrative functions at the Central Committee. Stassova continued to act as secretary, assuming an increasingly dictatorial manner which presently led to her being shelved.

As the Party grew in numbers and the dictatorship became stricter, it became necessary to strengthen the permanent administration and to define separate functions. With a membership of five—Lenin, Trotsky, Stalin, Zinoviev and Kamenev—the Politbureau handed over some of its administrative function to the Orgbureau (created in 1919) with the same number of members. The two bureaux had a common secretariat consisting of Krestinsky, Preobrazhensky and Serebriakov. This was the summit of the edifice.

Under this system, the Central Committee properly so-called sat in plenary session at long intervals, and could do no more than ratify the reports and resolutions of its leaders and officials. In reality the Politbureau was gradually to reach almost absolute power, qualified only in decreasing measure by what public opinion was left within the Party ranks, instructed, disciplined and directed by a monopoly press. The Council of Commissars, the Executive of the Soviets, the Council of Work and Defence, the Supreme Economic Council, the Revolutionary Council of War, the Cheka—all the administrative organs of the State, were subject to it in fact, if not by Soviet law, and the Party was the main bulwark of the bureaucracy under which "sympathisers" and "non-party" men filled minor posts.

Trotsky alone of the Five of the Politbureau has published memoirs throwing some light on the personal relations of its members. "When I disagreed with Lenin," he says, "I mentioned it aloud, and, when I thought it necessary, even appealed to the Party." But Stalin, Zinoviev and Kamenev, if they disagreed with Lenin, "which happened much more often than in my case, usually kept silent about it, or, like Stalin, sulked and hid away for a few days in the country somewhere near Moscow." Trotsky declares that differences between Lenin and himself were rare; they understood one another with few words; spontaneously and independently they reached the same conclusions. "Many a time," he says, "Stalin, Zinoviev, or Kamenev disagreed with me on some question of great importance, but as soon as they learned that Lenin shared my opinion, they lapsed into silence." We may regard the readiness of the "disciples" to renounce their own ideas in favour of Lenin's in any way we choose, but this readiness clearly contained no guarantee that without Lenin they were capable of arriving at the same conclusions.

The question arises of the value of Trotsky's testimony, necessarily laid under heavy contribution in any study of the men and the events of this period. Credence can obviously be given to irrefutable documents and to facts well-known and verifiable in Russia and in the international revolutionary movement. It is equally certain to anyone knowing anything of the man and his character that remarks repeated from memory have in no case been invented and may be accepted as genuine except for the exact words. But caution must be exercised in using passages dealing with internal dissensions in which Trotsky, sometimes unconsciously, modifies statements to suit himself and changes the facts, for example, by errors in date. His wilful temper leads him to distort his recollections on lines to which everything is made to conform in a more or less arbitrary fashion. Though he is exact in his memory of ideas, he seems to suffer from amnesia with regard to his manifest errors and contradictions and his conflicts with Lenin, the importance of which he tends to minimise. Moreover, he remembers only the failings and misdeeds of personages who have broken with him, and only the virtues and services rendered of the very few who have remained faithful to him; he is more impartial if they disappeared too early to have had the opportunity of disavowing him. He is malevolent towards Stalin from a fundamental contempt which does not exclude the truth but which calls for prudence and discretion in using his material.

Trotsky admits that his relations with Lenin were shadowed on the occasion of a discussion on trade unions in 1920. Stalin and Zinoviev obtained, so to speak, legal means of transferring their conflict from the wings to the stage itself. They did their utmost to make use of the situation. It is proved that Stalin cherished jealous and tenacious enmity, dating from friction in the Civil War, against the most brilliant of the revolutionary leaders. But even the reading of Trotsky does not explain Zinoviev's motives. Trotsky does not explain why Lenin's closest auxiliaries showed hostility to him on every favourable occasion. Probably the old rivalries of the émigré period were revived as soon as the counter-revolution was mastered. And Trotsky, rather haughty and distant, convinced of his superiority, could not cause them to be forgotten.

The Party, quite unaware of the dissensions at the top, was surprised by the discussion on trade unions. The weariness caused by the years of civil war and the iron discipline imposed induced a certain intellectual and political torpor, shaken only on the occasion of the annual deliberative assemblies. This time outspokenness in the ranks produced a violent shock.

In 1920, at the Ninth Congress, there were signs of opposition against the dictatorial methods of the Central Committee, and energetic attacks upon the bureaucratic "degeneration" of the "oligarchy." According to Yurenev, the high officials of the Party stifled the right of criticism by getting rid of the protestors by measures amounting to administrative exile. "One is sent to Christiania, another to the Urals, a third to Siberia." Maximovsky denounced the despotism of the ruling bureaucracy and declared: *"Fish are said to begin to putrefy from the head downwards. The Party is beginning to suffer at the top from the influence of bureaucratic centralism."* Sapronov, becoming more and more the mouthpiece of these views, declared that no notice was taken of the decisions of the Congress of Soviets; commissars took upon themselves the illegal arrest of "whole provincial executive committees." He said from the tribune: "It's all very well to talk of electoral rights, of the dictatorship of the proletariat, of the tendency of the Central Committee to the dictatorship of the Party; in fact, this leads to the dicatorship of the bureaucracy of the Party." And he asked Lenin *whether he believed that the salvation of the revolution lay in mechanical obedience.* A workman, Lutovinov, said: "The Central Committee, and especially its Orgbureau, has been transformed from a supreme directing organisation into an executive dealing with the most minute and unimportant matters"; it interfered arbitrarily in the smallest details, and nominated even the most obscure officials. Yakovlev declared that the Ukraine had become a place of exile. *"Comrades unwanted for one reason or another at Moscow are deported there."*

The Opposition chose solid ground in demanding *democratic centralism* in accordance with traditional Party theory. But they put themselves at a disadvantage by insistence on parliamentary forms and by the inconsistency of their principal demand—the collective or *"collegium"* administration of businesses, in spite of the costly lessons of experience which induced Lenin to restore personal technical management. The Central Committee was unanimous in turning down this proposal.

At the end of that.year the inextricable difficulties of productive enterprises, of the exchange, and of food supply led Trotsky to raise boldly and fully the question of the place of trade unions in economic life. He had saved the transport industry for the time being by applying to it crude army methods, with a perseverance recognised by Lenin and the whole Party. Inspired by these first results of the system, he thought it opportune to extend it generally by incorporating the trade unions in the State and transforming them into governmental institutions for industrial purposes. This idea of a "democracy of producers" meant obligatory trade unionism for the workers, and for the trade unions subjection to the political and economic administration of the State, that is, to the Communist Party. Under Trotsky's plan the trade unions would have had no functions, other than participation in production, in the workers' State.

Lenin did not agree. The War Commissar's methods had already caused bitter conflict in the transport workers' union, and threatened the destruction of the whole trade union movement. The failure of the experiments in militarisation was conclusive. The hour had come to alleviate the pressure exercised on the working classes, not to make the yoke heavier. To make the trade unions State organisations would be premature. Lenin summoned to his side his regular co-workers, Stalin, Zinoviev, Kamenev, Kalinin, with trade union leaders such as Tomsky and Rudzutak, and prevented Trotsky from carrying out his plan.

The State of which Trotsky spoke was an abstraction, he said in a heated debate. *"Our State is not one of workers, but of workers and peasants"*; moreover, *"one with many bureaucratic deformities."* The trade unions had to defend the workers' interests against a State of this kind. *"Such is the sad reality."* The notion of a producers' democracy is inconsistent, a syndicalist error. *"Production is a continuous, democracy an occasional, necessity."* And after referring to the thousands of communist mistakes, he reiterated: *"We have committed many mistakes, certainly. Prehaps most of our decrees require modification. I agree absolutely."* But that, he thought, was no reason for plunging into Trotsky's infinitely more serious error.

Trotsky was supported by Dzerzhinsky, Rakovsky, Bukharin, Sokolnikov, Pyatakov, Andreyev, and by the three Party secretaries—Krestinsky, Preobrazhensky and Serebriakov. For a moment Lenin was in a minority on the Central Committee. Once more he had to manœuvre, to temporise, to wear down the solid bloc of his opponents. Keeping in the background as much as possible, he used every possible means of checkmating them, including Zinoviev's demagogy and Stalin's astuteness. The discussion soon took a bad turn, and degenerated into venomous polemics. Trotsky was very successful with large audiences, but Stalin and Zinoviev, under the aegis of Lenin, easily counteracted him among officials who were former militants, by lavish promises and by exploiting the various resentments and grievances left by the Civil War.

The Party decided rather by intuitive and personal reasons than by defined principles. The two "platforms" advocated at meetings held by the two sides were not strikingly differentiated; indeed both used many common formulas, democratic truisms, and pedantic and obscure terms. Both sides talked of the great historic mission of the trade unions. But had the time come to incorporate them in the State? The last Party Congress had said so, and Trotsky might make use of it. Lenin did not deny the fact but begged for no hurry in applying the decision. Trotsky maintained that incorporation was already being accomplished. Zinoviev accepted the principle and contented himself with discussing methods. The trade unions are a school of communism, Lenin maintained, and Trotsky did not assert the contrary. This Byzantine controversy, regarded by Lenin as an "inadmissible luxury" and a threat of schism, lasted for several months, rousing passion and even hatred. *The Party is sick, the Party is feverish,*" said Lenin anxiously.

The Tenth Congress was summoned to effect a composition between the two opposed groups. But more groups appeared in support of the great ones' quarrels. The almost recognised Opposition for Democratic Centralism, represented especially by Bubnov, Boguslavsky, Ossinsky and Sapronov, regarded the two principal groups as representing two tendencies of "one and the same group of former advocates of the militarisation of economic life"; for their part they merely proposed practical measures of reorganisation of the administrative centres of industry and of the trade unions. The Workers' Opposition, with Shliapnikov, Alexandra Kollontai, Lutovinov and others, advocated investing the trade unions not only with the administration as well as with the work of production, they desired also the "syndicalisation" of the State. Riazanov, almost alone in his opinion, denied the trade unions any part in economic life; their sole function was the defence of corporate interests. Nogin foresaw the disappearance of the trade unions through their fusion with the State economic administration. But attention was concentrated on the propositions advanced by Lenin and Trotsky.

Stalin's visible share in this crisis was limited to one article,

Our Differences, in which he paraphrased in simple phraseology, didactically and with many repetitions, Lenin's arguments against the application of bureaucratic, military methods in the trade unions.

After repeating that "our differences are not differences of principle," Stalin goes on to say:

There are two methods: the method of force (the military method) and the method of persuasion (the trade union method). The first by no means excludes all persuasion, but such persuasion is subject to the exigencies of the method of force, which it is intended to supplement. The second method also does not exclude some degree of force, but this force is subject to the exigencies of the method of persuasion, which it is intended to supplement. It is as inadmissible to confuse these two methods as it is to put the army and the working classes into the same bag.

This stylistic example is very characteristic of his writings.

The army, Stalin continues in effect, is made up mainly of peasants; that is why methods of force are necessary, as otherwise the peasants would not fight for socialism. But the workers, "a homogeneous social class, organise themselves voluntarily into trade unions, and are 'the salt of the Soviet State.'" He summarises his argument as follows: "Comrade Trotsky's mistake is to underestimate the difference between the army and the working class, to put military organisations and trade unions on the same level, to try by inertia to transfer the military methods of the army to the trade unions, to the working classes." The article reproaches Trotsky with "following out the same old semi-bureaucratic, semi-military line," and, in a calm and judicial tone giving no idea of the bitterness of the conflict, it argues for the necessity of the "normal methods of proletarian democracy in the trade unions" and for the use of "methods of persuasion."

In March 1921, the Tenth Congress put an end to the interminable argument by supporting Lenin with 336 votes against 50 for Trotsky and 18 for the Workers' Opposition. The resolution adopted was modified a year later, and the disputants agreed that the fevered discussion had no real relation to the problem. Peremptory assurance on one side, categorical certainty on the other—without considering the injury inflicted on the common task.

How came Trotsky and his friends to make the tactical mistake of provoking a pitched battle in which defeat was a foregone conclusion? At the time a struggle for supremacy in the Party meant raising the question of power. Lenin did not so much criticise the principles of the propositions themselves as the method of creating conflicting communist groups, at the risk of schism. The rally of strong personalities round Trotsky alarmed him as a symptom of future danger, and led him to lay a tighter hand on the Party administration and to use only the most docile instruments for the purpose. Instead of strengthening confidence in him, Trotsky had awakened the distrust of former opponents, who now sought to isolate him. All his supporters, except four, were driven from the Central Committee —limited to 25 members and 15 deputy-members, and among the victims were the three too independent secretaries—Krestinsky, Preobrazhensky and Serebriakov. They were succeeded by the passively obedient Molotov, with two assistants. Stalin was a member both of the Orgbureau and Politbureau and worked for his future in silence.

The Congress carried on its deliberations in an atmosphere of suspicion and vigilance; the session coincided with an outburst of popular discontent. The Petrograd workers showed signs of revolt, the Kronstadt sailors threatened violence, the Red Army grumbled, there were definite peasant revolts in several districts, notably in the Tambov government. It was not a matter of "growing pains" in the trade unions, but of a real crisis in the revolution. It was no longer a matter of minor defects in the machinery such as were daily noted in the official press, but of a serious disease in the Soviet body politic. Bread, fuel, essential foodstuffs were lacking in town and country. Production, transport and trade were paralysed. In vain the terrorist dictatorship hoped to meet the crisis by requisition and repression; without a rapid change of tack the Soviet Republic would be on the rocks.

The Party had no foresight, but the first flicker of revolt sufficed to show Lenin the mistakes in his policy. While the Congress, knowing that the army could not be relied upon, was mobilising its members to crush rebellion, Lenin prepared his New Economic Policy, substituting taxes in kind for requisitions and restoring a limited freedom of internal trade. A hundred and forty members of the Congress departed for Kronstadt, a dangerous point because of its proximity to Petrograd and the possibility of foreign assistance. Trotsky took charge of the sanguinary business. Three hundred delegates were mobilised at a sitting. Before the vote on the trade unions was taken, the delegates from the peasant districts began to hurry home. "The Congress is fading away," said the President, Kamenev. Stalin delivered his customary discourse on the national question to a distracted audience, a discourse "with no relation to time or space," said Zatonsky. The Democratic Centralist Opposition did not push their argument. The Workers' Opposition, accused of Syndicalist heresy, alone persisted against the majority. The Congress, concerned with Kronstadt and guns, cut short its sittings.

3

THE economic situation steadily deteriorated from the first days of the revolution onwards. Contrary to their programme, the Bolsheviks had undertaken to introduce socialism—that is communism—without any transition, in a country whose unpreparedness they were the first to admit, at a time when stocks of food in the depopulated towns and the village reserves were exhausted. Driven by the desperate necessities of civil war and by the mystical-romantic strain inherited from anarchism, they destroyed all private enterprise, though they could not replace it by popular initiative; they confiscated the product of individual labour before they had created collectivist production.

The "privileged" classes, workers and soldiers, maintained a bare existence on a wretched ration, while the peasants, many of them half starved and all of them infuriated, defended themselves by concealing supplies, by refusing to sow, and now and then by arms. The "abominations of the Bashi-Bazouks," referred to by Lenin at a Communist Congress, still went on. Official resolutions promising considerate treatment of the peasants proved to be mere empty phrases, as were so many decrees, laws, instructions and circulars, like the Constitution itself. The 1920 harvest could not be other than disastrous. With an industry twenty per cent less effective than before the War, finances wrecked by the unlimited issue of paper-money, and foreign trade reduced to illicit and secret barter, the Soviet economy was evidently insolvent.

Later on Lenin called this War Communism, a formula designed to justify his policy after the event by the extraordinary circumstances of the time. But he contradicted himself once more by admitting the responsibility of the communists for the policy of blind and cruel spoliation. *"We have made many mistakes,"* he said, *"and it would be most criminal not to recognise that we went too far."* He admitted their failure in this matter. *"We have been defeated on the economic front, heavily defeated,"* he said, and added more precisely: "Our attempt to *attain communism straightaway* has cost us a more serious defeat than all those inflicted on us by Kolchak, Denikin and Pilsudski." Insisting on past errors, he continued: *"Generally we thought it possible . . . to begin without transition to build up socialism."* In fact, at one time his utterances were propagandist and encouraging to prevent despair, at another critical and truthful to destroy illusions or over-optimism.

War Communism was in fact at first a partly unconscious effort, then a conscious and determined one, towards establishing socialism "by assault." The authorised theorists of a party which claimed to follow Marxism had forgotten its least controvertible economic postulates in the madness of political success, as is abundantly proved by their conviction in 1920 that they could dispense with money. At that time Trotsky wrote in a manifesto: "Money wages tend more and more to be replaced by payment in kind; the continual issue of paper-money and its rapid fall in value merely attest the disappearance of the old financial and commercial system." At the end of that year the communist press announced free food for workmen and employees as "a further step towards the abolition of one of the capitalist survivals under the Soviet regime—the monetary system," as the end of the "fetish of money," since the public services—transport, housing, lighting, amusements—were all to be free. (*The A.B.C. of Communism* provided for the use of money in a socialist society before communism was attained.) Less than a year later Lenin, in a metaphor perhaps inspired by Thomas More, was advising strict care of gold in Russia until the time should come, "when we have conquered the whole world," to build in the public squares lavatories of gold.

Neither the socialisation of banks and of capital, nor the nationalisation of industry, nor the collectivisation of agriculture satisfied the plans of the October victors. Before the *coup d'état*, Lenin, replying to the allegations of the bourgeois press that nationalisation and confiscation were equivalent, declared his real intentions with perfect frankness; he said the Bolsheviks on attaining power would nationalise the banks *"without taking a kopeck from any owner of property*," because for the Bolsheviks nationalisation simply meant effective control. Similarly the syndicalisation of industry or obligatory cartellisation *"would make no change as regards property and would not take a kopeck from anybody*." Lenin repeated "not a kopeck" several times. The suggestion of the expropriation of the peasants was a malicious invention, "for even in case of a real socialist revolution, socialists would not and could not expropriate the small peasant." These various promises ended in the complete socialisation of banking, industry and agricultural production. In the passion aroused by attacks on the revolution, they went on from "the expropriation of the expropriators" to the expropriation of the expropriated.

The seizure by the State of works and factories was no more a part of the Bolshevist than of the western socialist programme. Combating "the infantilism of the Left" in 1918, that is the utopists hoping for immediate, outright socialism, Lenin wrote: "We have already confiscated, nationalised, broken and destroyed more than we can do with." But the hostility of the owners and the technical staffs, the hopeless failure of workers' control, the incapacity of the trade unions in technique and management, the Brest Treaty with clauses protecting German property, pillage and the abandonment of industrial undertakings following on civil disturbance—all were incentives to the adoption of a radical solution. (The State monopoly of cereals was adopted under Kerensky in similar conditions, because no other course was open to him.) Nevertheless, instead of seizing the earliest occasion of demobilising the industrial army, the Bolsheviks were to end by idealising a makeshift, and under pretext of "seizing stolen goods," were to exist by seizing goods that no one had stolen. This negation of their principles, aggravated by misreading their own social theory, led to the terrible miscalculations of which the Kronstadt insurrection was the culminating episode.

The protest of the workers and sailors, originally absolutely pacific, was reflected by the discontent of the Petrograd proletariat, worn out by privation, disappointment and the brutal behaviour of the "Commissarocracy." At the end of February there were a great many strikes in the northern capital, and workers' meetings to demand bread and liberty, reform of the Soviets and the restoration of trade. Socialists of various shades seized the opportunity of shaping the agitation in conformity with their views. The communists replied by arrests, the closing down of factories where there was agitation, the suppression of demonstrations. Zinoviev, President of the Petrograd Soviet, simply used police methods.

But cold and hunger, lack of coal and the reduction of rations —due partly to the stagnation of the railways—roused the people. The crews of the ships and the garrison at Kronstadt held an important meeting at which Kalinin himself was received with all the honours, with music and bunting. They passed a resolution demanding, in accordance with the Soviet Constitution and the Bolshevik October Programme, free elections for the Soviets; liberty of speech and liberty of the press for workers and peasants, Left Socialists, anarchists, trade unions; the liberation of workers and peasants who were political prisoners; the abolition of the privileges of the Communist Party; equal rations for workers; the right of non-profiteering peasants and artisans to sell their products. A deputation sent to Petrograd was imprisoned. Zinoviev had no other argument.

Thereupon a provisional revolutionary Committee was elected at Kronstadt, where most of the communists had joined the movement. They merely issued proclamations, but that was enough to alarm Zinoviev, who infected Moscow almost with panic. The Council of Labour and Defence replied by decreeing a state of siege and denouncing the counter-revolution, Social Revolutionaries, the White Guards, the Black Hundreds, French espionage, Russian Generals. . . . This was conflict, not concilia-tion. Bloodshed became inevitable. After a fruitless summons to surrender, Trotsky ordered the bombardment of those he had once called "the pride of the revolution."

If the sailors and workmen of Kronstadt had meditated a plot or prepared a plan, they would have waited for the thaw which would make their fortress impregnable and expose Petrograd to the guns of the fleet. But they hoped to win simply by the justice of their claim, and the solidarity of the Russian labouring classes. The sons of poor peasants, most of them destitute, they knew they were the interpreters of the people's grievances. Their political sincerity and their fidelity to the revolution were both beyond doubt. But the heavy "machine" of the Bolshevik Party was no longer sensitive to the purity of the best intentions. Attacked on the ice by the *Kursanti* (selected cadets), the mutineers defended themselves, becoming rebels in spite of them-selves. The Red Army, when ordered to attack the forts, refused to march. It had to be purged, reorganised and strengthened with communists arriving from the Tenth Congress. By a sinister and ironical chance the Kronstadt Commune perished on March 18th, the fiftieth anniversary of the Paris Commune.

Some victories do not inspire boasting. Trotsky devotes just two lines in *My Life* to the Kronstadt affair, drawing atten-tion to it as a "last warning" to his Party. Too much importance must not be attached to the vulgar diatribes of Bolsheviks anxious to discredit the defeated party, but it is probable that the counter-revolutionaries sought to share in the rising in order to turn its course to their advantage. But who was mainly responsible? Trotsky made it clear enough when he wrote: "The system of famine rations was associated with increasing disturbances culminating in the Kronstadt insurrection." And famine rations were the consequence of the so-called War Communism, tardily abandoned by Lenin after this "last warning."

But the legitimate character of the rebels' claims was implicitly confirmed by the change in policy, proposed by Lenin at the Tenth Congress, the adoption of the New Economic Policy, the N.E.P., which was to correct disastrous utopian measures. The essential requirements of the exhausted population were satisfied by putting a stop to rationing and arbitrary confiscation, by permission to small producers to sell their goods, by reopening the markets—in short by the restoration of limited and controlled capitalism. Even if political aspirations were still brutally crushed, economic relief appeared to mark the first step towards better times.

The N.E.P. brought solace to the country, but caused stupefaction in the Party. The distracted militants obeyed, without understanding. Riazanov was almost alone in daring to protest against Lenin's unusual procedure in brusquely imposing a volte-face of this kind without preliminary consultation or any chance of consideration. The Workers' Opposition echoed him, but raised no serious objection to the accomplished fact. The gravity of the situation prevailed over formalism. *"If we had not transformed our economic policy, we should not have lasted many months longer,"* Lenin told the next Congress.

The Party followed with docility, but somewhat unwillingly, before expressing its astonishment once more at the clear vision of its leader. But Lenin, in fact, acted late, and was by no means a pioneer. Had not Trotsky, two years earlier, invited the Central Committee, through Stalin, to wipe out the abuses which were overwhelming the "middle" peasants on the Volga and to punish the Soviet officials responsible? Did he not propose, next year, to replace requisitions by a graduated tax in kind, to establish a fair exchange of manufactured goods for agricultural products in order to stop the decay of rural life? Lenin thought to refute him by accusing him of being a "free trader," and the Central Committee rejected his proposal by eleven votes to four. Stalin, as usual, figured among the majority. Two months before Kronstadt, at the Congress of Soviets, the Menshevik Dalin advocated the tax in kind and the right of the peasant to dispose of his surplus. Lenin was not the first to make the proposal, and in this case showed none of the genius claimed for him by his disciples—genius which he really did display in October; what he did show was a supple intelligence quick to recover after a brief divergence into error.

With the N.E.P. Lenin yielded ground on the economic front in order to maintain the political privileges of the Party. He returned to some extent to his true programme and applied the tactic of compromise to relations between classes at home which he had used with success in relations with capitalist countries. In this matter his ideas were clear enough. On the morrow of the Great War he dictated to Chicherin a note to the Allies offering to recognise loans and debts, to give economic and even territorial concessions. In 1921 he advised German Communists to accept the Versailles Treaty as the Bolsheviks had accepted the Peace of Brest-Litovsk. His belief in an inevitable world revolution enabled him to reconcile rigid theory with the devices of concession and compromise. He instinctively conformed to Napoleon's law of war, "the art of which is merely to gain time when one has inferior forces," and who considered principles as the ranges dominating the surrounding valleys.

The complex problems to be solved at home did not lend themselves to the relatively simple solutions adopted in foreign relations. Lenin felt justified in tacking to meet the wind, in circumventing obstacles, in zigzagging back and forth. More than once he emphasised the fact that there were no books teaching how to make a successful revolution, and that, as Marx had not settled all doubtful points, they must learn to help themselves with his help. The N.E.P. was not a sudden idea, but a change of orientation, followed by gropings and discoveries, by a series of decrees successively rectified or completed. It implied the restitution of houses on conditions, the leasing of small and medium-sized enterprises to their former proprietors, the letting of factories, concessions to foreigners, the re-establishment of wages, the rehabilitation of money, the restoration of private trade, and the suppression of free public services. Nobody knew quite how much ground must be abandoned. *"We have been defeated in our attempt to attain socialism 'by assault',"* explained Lenin, to encourage the shaken morale of the Party, but "not defeat itself, but the fear of recognising it is the greatest danger." Six months later he announced a "further retreat," and within a year the "end of the retreat."

His many scattered and fragmentary definitions of the N.E.P. emphasise now one aspect, now another, as occasion demands. One of the least satisfactory is that which affirms the necessity *"of abandoning the immediate building of socialism to revert in many economic matters towards State capitalism."* On the subject of State capitalism he directed attention to a pamphlet of 1918 in which he had written: "If revolution is delayed in Germany, we shall have to study German State capitalism, to imitate it as best we can, not to be afraid of dictatorial measures to hasten the assimilation by barbaric Russia of western civilisation, and not to shrink from barbarous methods to fight barbarism"—a rescript more deeply engraved in the memory of his successors, and especially of Stalin, than any other.

It is not easy to find a brief textual statement of his general argument, so important, in the later development of the Bolshevik regime. Quotations from various writings, reports, speeches, and commentaries, give a general idea of it.

First we notice a revision of his view as to the immediacy of an international revolution: "Confident expectation of the world revolution does not imply expecting it at a fixed date . . . its development which grows with increasing rapidity may bring revolution in the spring, but it may not." In 1919 he still thought that "the disintegration of German imperialism is leading Germany not only to republicanism but to the socialist revolution." In 1920 he prophesied with conviction that "the day is not far distant when we shall march hand in hand with the German Soviet Government." In 1921 his embarrassment is shown by statements contradictory in themselves, such as: "International revolution is growing. But it would be simple folly to suppose that we are going to receive immediate help in the shape of a lasting proletarian revolution."

On State capitalism, which he considers a great step forward for Soviet Russia, Lenin writes: "It is a capitalism which we can and should admit, because it is indispensable for the peasant masses." He recalls the well-known theory that "capitalism is an evil by comparison with socialism; it is a good thing in comparison with the feudal system, or with small scale production." Concessions—"alliance or economic marriages with capitalism" —are necessary in the most backward of great European countries: "concessions are perhaps the simplest, the cleanest, the most exactly defined form adopted by State capitalism in the Soviet economy. Co-operation is also a sort of State capitalism, but less simple, less clearly defined, more complex." Illusions in this matter should disappear. "The rights and liberties of co-operation, in the present state of Russia, mean rights and liberties for capitalism. To hide one's head in the sand, to avoid having evidence of this, would be either foolish or criminal."

Finally he constantly insists on economic alliance with the peasants, indispensable after the military alliance; the only way of accomplishing it is to give freedom of trade, and freedom of trade means a return to capitalism. To refuse this freedom would be "folly and real suicide." For agreement with the peasants "alone can maintain the socialist revolution in Russia, unless there is revolution in other countries." The peasants must be convinced that the communists are "really coming to the help of the small peasant, ruined, destitute, and dying of hunger, in his present horrible situation. Either you must convince him of this or he will send us to the devil. . . . This is the meaning of the New Economic Policy."

But the Bolsheviks were far from agreement on the historic significance on the N.E.P., which was greeted by their opponents as a Russia repetition of Thermidor. They were disposed to regard it as a Thermidor, carried out by themselves and salutary for the revolution. Lenin said nothing on this point; evidently he had nothing to say to Trotsky's remarks:

The Mensheviks all over the world talk of the Thermidor of the Russian Revolution. But it is not they, but we ourselves who have made this diagnosis. What is still more important is that the Communist Party itself has made concessions to Thermidorian aspirations, to the desires of the small bourgeoisie, the concessions which were necessary for the maintenance of the power of the proletariat without breaking up the system or leaving the helm.

Later on the spectre of Thermidor was to be evoked with less serenity in new circumstances of internal struggle.

It is a common temptation to seek precedents in other revolutions for the better understanding of the stages of a great contemporary political and social upheaval. Parallels occur to the mind in many situations even when they are not strictly alike, for instance between certain personages. Real resemblances are indicated between Nicholas Romanov, Louis Capet and Charles Stuart, between Alexandra Feodorovna, Marie Antoinette and Henrietta Maria. Comparisons, if not drawn too exactly, may well be made between Lenin and Robespierre or Cromwell as the central figure of great revolutions. Circumstances sometimes suggest a parallel with George Washington, and more often with figures in Russian history. But men who "live in the future" are less given to identifying themselves with the shades of past heroes. The Petrograd Soviet in its time played a part somewhat similar to that of the Paris Commune; the Bolshevik Party to that of the Jacobin Club. Yet neither was to suffer the fate of its forerunner. The Russian Civil War recalls in more than one respect the American Civil War. The "Social-Democratic *Gironde*" and the "Cossack *Vendée*" are not meaningless phrases. The destruction of the Levellers and the "enragés" finds parallels in the Soviet Republic. Every revolution has its Moderates and its Extremists. The Terror, a "dictatorship of distress," as the younger Carnot called it, was not a Russian discovery. Other examples are forthcoming. But all comparisons of this kind are only useful in exemplifying the differences and the real characteristics of interesting events in the lives of individuals or groups. But, with all these superficial similarities, history does not repeat, but moves onward. The most striking analogies do not provide material for understanding, much less foretelling, events, unless economic circumstances and historical conditions are taken into account. In this respect differences of social significance are more important than surface resemblances. Therefore the over-eager prophets of a Thermidor, still more of a Brumaire, have now plenty of leisure to meditate on the unique character, which they mistook, of the Russian Revolution.

Lenin was wiser when he faced the dilemma of the liberals who supported the new regime. He stated it correctly: Was the N.E.P. an evolutionary or a tactical measure? To this "class truth propounded by a class enemy" he replied frankly. "*A development such as that expected by Ustryalov is possible. History has seen all sorts of metamorphoses. . . . Great historical issues are decided by the masses.*" And pending the great conflagrations which are to set the multitudes in motion, the selection of communists and the quality of their work may prevent, he thinks, a temporary expedient from degenerating into an irremediable development, and may pave the way for a future which will be decisive in favour of the revolutionary point of view. The N.E.P., said Lenin, is settled "definitely and for a long time." Therefore the choice of agents was of the first importance. "We must not shrink from recognising that in ninety-nine cases out of a hundred, responsible communists are not at their posts, do not understand their job and need to learn." Every man in his place. The opportunity for Stalin to take his was at hand.

4

PERSONAL conflict between revolutionaries has often precipitated the decline of their movement, pre-determined by more deep-seated causes. The Russian Revolution seemed to be an exception in this respect during Lenin's lifetime; neither discords nor reverses were allowed to break the fundamental solidarity of the leaders. The new fact which emerged was the organisation of the founders and leaders of the revolution into a coherent and disciplined party, whose unity was to be the essential element of stability in the regime.

But behind this smooth façade obscure rivalries were undermining the edifice. The discussion on trade unions had disclosed acute enmities, which were not terminated by the N.E.P. In Trotsky's case there was no longer any trace of disagreement with Lenin, who, for his part, was anxious to secure co-operation between former opponents. With Lenin's entourage it was otherwise. Trotsky, though he stood alone in the Politbureau and almost alone in the Central Committee, still seemed formidable to the fraternity of Old Bolsheviks, who were determined to restrict him to certain departments and to lessen his influence by scattering his supporters, so that they might keep their own hands on the key positions in the Party and in the State. Zinoviev, Kamenev and Stalin secretly winked at each other over this plan. To assure its success they sought an effective instrument in the Secretariat of the Central Committee, a position supposed to be limited to technical and executive functions, though in fact its importance was growing imperceptibly because it controlled appointments.

In 1922 they succeeded. After the Eleventh Party Congress, Stalin became General Secretary in succession to Molotov, who was relegated to the post of assistant. The operation passed almost unnoticed, so modest had the duties appeared to be. Nobody objected, except according to Trotsky, Lenin. But Trotsky's memoirs are at fault in the date, which is a year too early, and his statement appears to be contradicted by Lenin's praise of Stalin during the session of the Congress. It is true that contradictions are a constant feature in the words and acts of the Bolshevik leaders. *"This cook will prepare only peppery dishes,"* said Lenin of the new secretary, but no doubt later and among friends.

At that time Stalin was still unknown outside a small circle of militants and officials, but those who had to do with him in

their daily work were disturbed by his rise to the top. Krestinsky's remark that he was "an ugly creature with his yellow
eyes" expresses an antipathy fairly widespread. Perhaps Lenin
under-estimated the ultimate rôle of a subordinate official of
the Politbureau, when he raised no objection to Stalin's nomination. However that may be, his failure to do so left the field
open for the moment to the small clique which occupied the
strategic points in the administration.

Thus an important event in the revolution was accomplished
silently, and its promoters neither understood its importance nor
foresaw its consequences.

At the height of his power, Lenin exercised almost judicial
functions of arbitration in disputes between his colleagues, while
he was mainly responsible for the direction of the Soviet State
and of international revolutionary activity. His bold policy in
introducing the N.E.P., following on the success of the Brest-
Litovsk tactics, strengthened his reputation for infallibility in
communist circles. Thanks to him, the Soviet Republic could
celebrate its Fifth Anniversary in peace. No one dared to criticise
him openly, though he maintained his habitual modesty of
demeanour. If his tone was at times imperative in discussion, it
was the expression not of pontifical certainty but of conscious
superiority in political experience over his opponents. If he
censured his own errors, he did not spare other people's. He
might have adopted as his own the well-known saying: "My
esteem for myself is small when I examine myself . . . but when
I compare myself with others it is considerable." Hence the
contrast between his intellectual reservations towards great
problems and his assurance in controversy. To drive home his
points he said sharp things either in the interests of simplification
or with the intention of waking up his audience. Nevertheless
he showed constant kindliness to less gifted colleagues, endeavouring to keep them up to the mark and to give them their
share in the common task. His moral ascendancy in the Party
was associated with an anxious solicitude for one and all; he
husbanded their strength, sought for mutual understanding and

helped them by advice and support. He was prodigal of his own strength.

The qualities which first attracted Lenin to Stalin, says Trotsky, were his "firmness and his practical mind, which is three-quarters cunning." But in the end he had to admit Stalin's "ignorance . . . his very narrow political horizon, and his exceptional moral coarseness and unscrupulousness." He says that Lenin sought out Stalin, Zinoviev and Kamenev for the execution of current business and minor tasks on his instructions and under his control. In the Central Committee, as elsewhere, he needed docile auxiliaries of the type of Rykov and Tsiurupa, who with Kamenev acted as his deputies at the Council of Commissars when he was obliged to save his own strength. This statement is correct but summary, and further explanations are necessary to understand a situation already pregnant with crisis.

The whole system of government depended on the personality of Lenin, whose greatness, under given historical conditions, had created a state of affairs strangely different from that laid down in the Soviet Constitution.

Political, economic and administrative institutions were subject to a parallel series of strictly communist organs at each stage. The Party was superimposed on the State like a lid of the same shape on a pyramid. At the top, the Politbureau held in its hands the threads of all the powers delegated to inferior bodies. As President of the Council of Commissars, Lenin merely put into effect decisions made in the Politbureau under his direction, allotting the work to the departments concerned. Latterly he abandoned this formal task, and Trotsky also ceased to waste time at the Council, now transformed into an executive committee of high officials. A "Small Council" was added, for drafting laws.

The Executive Committee of the Soviets, deprived of the prerogative assigned to it by the Constitution, was a sort of parliament, an occasional assembly of secondary officials committed beforehand to vote automatically for the Bills submitted to it by its Permanent Bureau, but free to discuss minor details. Under the Politbureau there was also the Council of Labour and Defence, whose powers were indefinite, and which tended to handle all subjects; the Supreme Economic Council, intended to deal with production and trade, but absorbed in industry; the Gosplan, charged with estimating national resources, and preparing plans and devising means. All these organisations, with the Commissariats of Finance, Transport, Agriculture, Foreign Trade, Workers' and Peasants' Inspection, the Soviets of the two capitals, and the central committees of the co-operatives and the trade unions, etc., were incessantly competing for bureaucratic authority, since they had no power of initiative, and were for ever in conflict. Lenin was not exaggerating when he declared they had a chaos of authorities of all sorts.

In the chaos he alone had the authority to mediate between the contending bureaux and to ensure the dominance of a clear idea of the general interest. But this rôle involved the employment by him of agents less and less capable of acting except on his instructions. Stalin in the Party Secretariat, Zinoviev at the Petrograd Soviet, Kamenev at the Moscow Soviet, Bukharin at the Press Bureau, Kalinin at the Executive Committee of Soviets, Kamenev at the Council of Labour and Defence, Rykov at the Supreme Economic Council and later at the Council of Commissars, Zinoviev, Radek and Bukharin at the executive of the Communist International—this placing of the pieces on the chess board was not ineffectual while a Lenin was there to direct it. Left to themselves, as they had been on several earlier occasions rather unfortunate for their reputation as communists, where would these epigones be?

Two of the principal departments of State—the police and the army—had acquired a measure of autonomy, by reason of the confidence reposed by Lenin in their respective heads.

The powers of the Cheka, theoretically reduced in 1920 and again in 1922 when the Extraordinary Commission was merged in the "State Political Direction" (sic) or G.P.U., were not, in theory, unlimited. The *Collegium*, presided over by Dzerzhinsky, had to submit its proposals to the Commissariat of Justice. In fact, an official of the Commissariat was ex-officio attached to the *Collegium*. This was subject only to surveillance in principle by the Politbureau, which deputed one of its members to represent it in exceptional cases. Thus Stalin, as representative of the Politbureau on the G.P.U., continued the police activity he had begun during the Civil War. Of course, neither Lenin nor any of his immediate colleagues could verify, except in rare cases, the statements made by Dzerzhinsky and Stalin, while the *Collegium* had extensive opportunities of shaping opinion in the Politbureau on questions of repression. Like all political police, the G.P.U. tended to ensure its indispensability by exaggerating dangers, real and supposed. Dzerzhinsky had recourse repeatedly to the classic means of securing sanction for his severity—resignation, because of the impossibility of being responsible for public order and the security of the regime without sufficient powers. Eventually the G.P.U. recovered the omnipotence of the Cheka, contrary to the earlier intention of the Party and to the spirit of the 1922 reforms; it took on monstrous proportions in the Soviet Republic, which Lenin had prematurely defined as a "new type of State, with neither bureaucracy, nor police, nor permanent army."

Trotsky held a place apart. In the Politbureau his agreement with Lenin was decisive. The Party felt itself incarnate in these two men. Their names seemed indissolubly connected in the popular mind, and their persons permanently associated with the supreme responsibility. By comparison with the bureaucratic chaos described by Lenin, the Commissariat for War was a model institution, consulted by the Politbureau on many matters other than military. Trotsky had got together a personnel adapted to his rational, orderly, exact and effective methods of work, and he used them for the successful execution of the most varied missions. Wherever disorder or carelessness demanded salutary intervention, as in the Education Commissariat, fallen into discredit under Lunacharsky, Trotsky was appealed to, in the hope of results similar to those obtained for the war services, the Ural industries and transport. He was esteemed for his intellectual fertility, his active contribution to the press and to the world of thought, as much as for his qualities as a statesman and an organiser. He dominated without effort the congresses of the Third International. And yet he exercised no authority in the governing sphere of the new State, in the "machine" of the dictatorship, corresponding with his many-sided prestige.

The machine, more and more differentiated from the Party as the Party was more and more isolated politically from the State, represented the whole of the varied parts of the bureau-cratic Soviet regime built up on the ruins of the former Imperial administration, the product of persisting social conditions. A quarter of a century of industrial progress, still negligible in spite of the modern equipment of the great enterprises financed by foreign capital, had left Russia far behind the civilised coun-tries and had not created either a middle class or proletariat to counterbalance peasant barbarism, "the semi-barbarism and the very real barbarism" which Lenin had described as the greatest obstacle to socialism. The presumptuous intelligentsia had been swept away by the revolution, driven to emigrate or scattered over the country; the working class were repeatedly decimated in the Civil War, and partly driven back to the rural districts by famine, partly absorbed in the new bureaucracy. There re-mained the immense rural population whom Gorky had de-scribed as "a great flaccid body, destitute of political education, almost inaccessible to ideas capable of ennobling action," and "brutalised by the conditions of their life, patient to an almost revolting degree, and with a cunning of their own." Unless this human material could be regenerated by vigorous democratic methods which would encourage the development of its best elements, the new regime, in the opinion of sincere, clear-sighted revolutionaries, would be condemned to develop in the bureau-cratic and police tradition of the Imperial regime, until the time came for a supplementary revolution. It was the task of the Party, that is to say of its "machine," to give this great inert mass the direction and the impulse to that democratic progress inscribed on its programme. But the democracy promised by primitive Bolshevism was disappearing in the priviliged Party as it had disappeared in the enfeebled country. The "machine" was already living its own life, with its interests distinct from the aspirations of the people whose sole interpreter it claimed to be. The concealed opposition which Trotsky encountered in this machine was not fortuitous. If it was not yet openly declared, this was owing above all to Lenin.

To what extent did individual antagonisms vitiate the relations among the "summits" of the machine? Gorky saw fit six years afterwards to add to his report of Lenin's eulogy of Trotsky, some alleged remarks by Lenin: "Still, he is not one of us. With us, but not of us. Ambitious. There is something wrong about him, something of a Lassalle." If Gorky did not invent this doubtful addition, the date is enough to reduce its significance. In any case, it is clear that to old Bolsheviks like Gorky he was not "one of us" in the sense that he did not fit into any given category. In the same way the men who directly handled the "machine," Zinoviev, Kamenev, and especially Stalin, felt ill at ease with a man who had none of their familiar and sometimes vulgar preoccupations.

In a healthy, normal party acting in accordance with democratic ideas, questions of precedence would not have assumed such alarming proportions. But the Bolshevik Party, as it developed physically, was transformed still more profoundly in the moral and political sense. Arrogating to itself the monopoly of revolutionary conscience, it denied all liberty to the workers alleged to be non-class-conscious, that is, to the whole of the working population not enrolled in its books, and eventually forbade it to its own members for fear that, under popular pressure, they might become the interpreters of grievances of all kinds. As the number of their adherents increased after the victory, the circle of privileged persons enjoying civic rights was more closely drawn together, so as to form a sort of Masonic hierarchy, thus translating into fact Trotsky's old prophecy: *"The Party Organisation is being substituted for the Party, the Central Committee for the Organisation, and finally the Dictatorship for the Central Committee."* There was not yet any single dictator, because Lenin refused a personal dictatorship and shared power with the Politbureau. But would the equilibrium of the oligarchy be stable without its founder?

At the Eleventh Communist Congress the Party numbered about 515,000 members, instead of the 730,000 at the preceding Congress. A party purge had eliminated about 150,000 on various charges of corruption, bribery, ambition, drunkenness, chauvinism, anti-semitism and abuse of confidence. Many militants resigned in disgust at the passive obedience imposed on the rank and file communists. Most of the new members were inspired by narrow and interested motives. Protests against the internal organisation of the Party were again made at this Congress, which defeated a proposal to exclude the Workers' Opposition; permitted by Lenin, this was the last manifestation of independence against the leading officials.

"The English Parliament can do anything except change a man into a woman. Our Central Committee is more powerful—it has already changed more than one extremely revolutionary man into a woman, and the number of these women has increased incredibly," said Riazanov, reproaching the oligarchy with "violating the most elementary rules of democracy." Stukov criticised the "original privilege," thanks to which Lenin alone was free to do as he liked. "We must," he said, "give other comrades the possibility of speaking freely within the Party without threatening them with damnation for saying to-day what Lenin said yesterday." Shliapnikov cited in his defence Frunze, who "promised to convince me with a machine-gun," a figurative, but significant, remark. V. Kossior commented on the diminution in numbers. "Many workmen," he said, "are leaving the Party. . . . The reason is the rule of force, which has nothing in common with real discipline and which is practised among us. Our Party carries wood and sweeps the streets, votes but decides nothing. The not over-healthy proletariat cannot stand this atmosphere."

But the severest accusation of all brought against the Politbureau was by Lenin, *à propos* of a purchase of jam which exhibited the pusillanimity, the red tape and fear of responsibility of the high Soviet bureaucracy. "How is it," he asked, "that in the capital of the Soviet Republic two inquiries, the intervention of Kamenev and Krassin, and an order from the

Politbureau have been necessary for a purchase of jam?" Lenin put it down to lack of education among communists, the necessity of taking action against incapable officials, etc., but omitted the real cause of the evil—the undemocratic Soviet regime. He persisted in justifying in vague terms the exorbitant powers of the Politbureau: "All serious affairs of State should be brought before the Politbureau," forgetting that civic inequality, the lack of guarantee of legal security for most citizens, make every jam contract an affair of State, because the avoidance of responsibility, shifted from lower authorities to higher authorities up to the Politbureau, is the only way of securing impunity. He gives excellent platonic advice. "We must," he says, "learn to tackle the simplest business in a civilised way," but turns a blind eye on an essential cause of the backwardness of civilisation: the suppression of all liberty. He evades the difficulty by using a metaphor: "Our apparatus is bad perhaps, but the first steam engine is said to have been a bad one. Our State machine may be execrable, but it exists, the greatest of all inventions is accomplished, the Proletarian State has been created."

The confusion of the functions of the Party and the State, leading to an accumulation of duties, was strongly criticised, and Preobrazhensky cited Stalin as a case in point: "Take, for instance, Comrade Stalin, a member of the Politbureau and in charge of two Commissariats. Is it conceivable that one individual is equal to the work of two Commissariats, besides that of the Politbureau, the Orgbureau, and a dozen committees of the Central Committee?" To which Lenin replied in general terms that "there were no men available," and with regard to Stalin, silent in the Congress, that "we must have someone to whom any national representative can appeal and tell his story. Where is he to be found? I don't think Preobrazhensky can point to anyone but Stalin. It is the same for the Workers' and Peasants' Inspection. The work is stupendous. But to cope with it there must be a man with authority at the head; otherwise we shall be disgraced and ruined by petty intrigues." These remarks were made a few days before Stalin was nominated to the Secretaryship of the Party. If Lenin really held at that time the bad opinion of Stalin which Trotsky attributes to him, he hid it very well.

The truth apparently is that Lenin's opinion was altered by experience in this as in other matters. He did not always weigh his words, nor attribute such importance to them as not to contradict them on occasion. His intellectual honesty enabled him frankly to revise opinions proved to be erroneous. After the Congress, relations between Lenin and Stalin were modified as relations between Stalin and Trotsky had been at an earlier date. The Commissariat of Nationalities was soon to be abolished. Lenin made an inquiry into the Workers' and Peasants' Inspection which proved devastating to the Commissar. And, as Secretary of the Central Committee, Stalin was soon to be irretrievably discredited in Lenin's eyes.

But, meanwhile, an unexpected event happened, upsetting the personal aspects of the dictatorship. At the beginning of May 1922 Lenin succumbed to his toil; the brain of the revolution showed signs of paralysis. It was merely a first attack of arteriosclerosis, but a definite malady. The Party could not believe that Lenin was lost to them, and Trotsky shared the irrational optimism. Others, devoid of sentiment, had a clearer vision, and calculated coldly on the eventual repercussions of the inevitable loss; they were the three members of the Politbureau, who felt themselves, as a group and as units, inferior to the fourth.

5

STALIN had begun a secret and unprecedented task in the secretariat of the Party. One by one he rearranged the personnel of the machine, on mysterious considerations known to himself alone.

Only a pretext was needed and often even this could be dispensed with. As a rule, discipline was sufficient reason for nominations and transfers. In the heroic period, the Party preserved its equalitarian principles, the maximum wage, solidarity, and devotion to the cause. But in so vast a country as Russia, with

few means of communication, and a dull provincial life, disgrace
or advancement was a matter of a few kilometres. Removal
from one institution to another might involve moral and material
advantages. Then, at various stages in the hierarchy, the particular employment might offer more or less advantages in the
present and prospects for the future. "Anybody being good
enough for anything, anybody can be moved at any time to
any place"—this ironical dictum of a French politician was very
applicable to Soviet Russia. At the last Congress, Lenin had said
that *the choice of men was the crucial point*, but without laying
down the criteria of choice. Stalin had his reasons.

He never formulated them in so many words, but they may
be deduced from a number of circumstances.

The main idea of his Party was crystallised in the simple and
almost mystical belief that the interests of humanity should be
represented exclusively by an ideal proletariat, this proletariat
in its turn by a transcendant Central Committee, and that Committee by its Politbureau. In his capacity of Secretary Stalin
might, then, regard himself as the pivot of the Soviet system, a
miniature Russian model of the future universal socialist republic, the Party being identified with the State and the
immanent dictatorship being incarnate in an irremovable "oligarchy," recruited by co-optation.

This tier upon tier of abstractions of which the topmost only
was a tangible reality, the immeasurable power of the Politbureau over 130,000,000 people, had nothing in common with
the Marxism which the Bolsheviks religiously invoked as their
model. "We took the Marxist doctrine all ready made from
western Europe," said Lenin. A conception of this kind "taken"
from outside, a synthesis of German philosophy, English economics and French socialism, could not be assimilated in a generation by so backward a people, not even by its vanguard.

Like all ordinary Bolsheviks—of whom he was typical—Stalin
hardly knew anything about Marx except through Lenin, and
he adopted the letter of Marxism without comprehending its
living spirit. Having accepted as dogma once for all the mixture
of conditional truths and proved errors which constituted Bol-

shevism, the Russian approximation to Marxism, he displayed his inflexible determination in the service of this faith by incorporating himself in the machine to such a degree that for a long time Stalin, the instrument of the machine, and the machine, the instrument of Stalin, were indistinguishable.

He did not invent the passive obedience which he exacted by all sorts of means from his subordinates. He only accentuated to excess the military notion of discipline inherited from War Communism, and erected into a theory by Lenin and Trotsky against their own principles. *"The remedy invented by Lenin and Trotsky, the general suppression of democracy, is worse than the evil it was supposed to cure,"* wrote Rosa Luxemburg as early as 1918. *"At a time when political life is being stifled everywhere,"* she added, *"it is a calamity that life should be more and more paralysed even in the Soviets."* This was equally true of the Party itself, reduced in a few years to a state of lethargy. The evolution of Bolshevism in this respect is worth exhibiting at both ends of the curve.

In 1917, at the Executive of the Soviets, the Bolshevik Chudnovsky "ventured" to criticise Lenin, Stalin and Krylenko for their "unparalleled tactlessness and frivolity" in the address to the army enjoining negotiation with the enemy. Lenin replied that "there can be no question of 'venturing' or 'not venturing' the most violent criticism; *such criticism was a revolutionary duty*, and the People's Commissars did not claim infallibility."

In 1921 at the Trade Unions Congress, at which there were 3,500 delegates of whom only eight were Social-Democrats, a committee nominated by the Central Committee of the Party to "direct the Congress" dictated the resolution to be passed by the "Communist fraction," which nevertheless adopted a resolution of Riazanov's. The Committee instructed Tomsky to defend its resolution, but he faltered, confronted by the strong conviction of his comrades. The Central Committee then decided to disallow the resolution passed, dismissed the bureau of the Congress, sent Tomsky to Turkestan and Riazanov abroad, and intimidated the fraction which was compelled to retract under threat of reprisals. Another special committee in which

Stalin and Dzerzhinsky, experts in repression, took part, inflicted a "severe censure" on the exiled Tomsky. On his return, the impenitent Riazanov was forbidden to speak at any meeting or to lecture at the University; he was only permitted to speak at the annual congress of the Party where the congress members are carefully selected, and where conformity is assured.

This one case out of a thousand indicates how roughly humble militants may be called to order, and one may guess how ordinary mortals, outside the privileged communist circle, are likely to be treated. Bearing in mind Lenin's remark that "the vote of a single workman was worth several peasants' votes," and the consideration accorded to the rights of trade unions, there can hardly be any illusions as to the effectiveness of public opinion in the Soviet Republic at the beginning of the N.E.P.

In resigning himself to concessions and compromises in the economic sphere, Lenin thought it necessary to reinforce the dictatorship in the political sphere. "We need the iron hand," he said. Alluding to the abuses perpetrated by "pseudo-communists" in the rural districts, he wrote in 1921: "Clean all that up by terror—summary procedure, the death penalty with no appeal." Presently judicial procedure would appear to be superfluous; the death penalty alone would remain. "Mensheviks and Social Revolutionaries, openly confessed as such or disguised as non-Party men, we will keep in prison," he continued. A year later the tone is worse: "It's a case of machine-guns for the people called Mensheviks and Social Revolutionaries." The weight of the iron hand was soon felt by all citizens, including trade unionists and communists. In the Party there was henceforward only one valid dogma, that of the Politbureau, an orthodoxy of which Trotsky had once said: "Anyone who denies it should be expelled. Doubt is almost denial. Questioning is almost doubt." But Trotsky had forgotten his youthful polemics, and Stalin had no notion of salvation outside the official and ever-changing ideology of his Party, settled from time to time by its accredited leaders.

Recourse to the "iron hand" did not displease Stalin, who was naturally disposed to this method of government. Lenin had not foreseen all the effects of the method carried to extremes and without his instructions. When he returned to work after several months of illness and convalescence he seemed to scent the danger of a misuse of the dictatorship by his disciples.

Lenin saw with uneasiness the evil development of the bureaucracy of which the Party machine was the spinal cord. At first he thought the degeneration of the communists into irresponsible and despotic bureaucrats could be cured by placing them under the supervision of a new Control Commission independent of the Central Committee and the Inspection Commissariat. He thought of a special commission to "fight bureaucracy" to be directed by Trotsky and himself in order to purge and regroup the personnel of the Party. Anxious to secure more initiative and freedom of action for the People's Commissars, he wanted to make Trotsky his deputy and his eventual successor at the Council of Commissars, and to reorganise the governing personnel with this end in view.

In this series of reforms at the top, the political consciousness of communists was not taken into consideration, and the system of the Bolshevik Central Committee remained intact, with its Politbureau, its Orgbureau, and its Secretariat. There was no idea of reviving the life of the Party or of giving back their rights to the workers.

Trotsky seemed to Lenin the safest of his successors, most capable of ruling in the spirit of socialism. All that was needed was to incorporate him in the small body of traditional Leninists, but there the difficulty began. It was unanimously agreed that Trotsky was the most eminent person in the Central Committee both in intellectual eminence and in strength of character. But that did not make him Lenin's natural successor; what he lacked was a special political sense without which no man can claim to be a party leader. Had not his past shown him to be incapable of forming a permanent group or of attaching himself to any section of Social-Democracy? Even in the Communist Party his personality seemed to be autonomous. During the revolution he was able to measure himself with Lenin. But what would he do in the Politbureau without Lenin, and could

he associate himself with those Leninists, who thought six of
themselves not too many to act as counterpoise to him? Stalin,
Zinoviev and Kamenev, the secret triumvirate at the top, were
supported by their deputies at the Politbureau, Bukharin,
Kalinin and Molotov. With his knowledge of men and his
psychological instinct, Lenin soon saw that the obstacle to this
future arrangement would be Stalin.

Stalin was the most obscure member of the Politbureau, but
the only one who was a match for Trotsky in temperament and
in will-power. He easily surpassed his colleagues in ordinary political action by his dexterity in intrigue, his suppleness as a
tactician, and the use he made of small means. Too wary to enter
into doctrinal controversy, he gained his ends by his chosen
methods of "practical work," seizing every opportunity to withstand either Lenin or Trotsky, and to get his way on details.
On his favourite subject of nationalities he thought he could
escape from Lenin's guidance, and on this point came the definite evidence of incompatibility between the recognised theorist
and the misunderstood practical man.

The origin of the rift appears in secret correspondence of
1922. Revision of the Constitution was under consideration, with
the idea of transforming the Socialist Federative Soviet Russian
Republic into the Union of Socialist Soviet Republics, in which
the various component nationalities were to have equal rights.
On paper Russian hegemony would be done away with, Moscow
would become the seat of two Executive Committees of Soviets,
that of the Russian Republic and that of the Federated Republics. Stalin opposed the scheme by criticisms correct enough in
form. "The co-existence of two Central Executive Committees
at Moscow," he said, "of which one would doubtless be an
Upper and the other a Lower Chamber, will give rise to friction
and conflict." (Strangely enough, he still took constitutional
fictions seriously.) Touched on the raw by an allusion of Lenin
to his excessive haste, he returned the compliment by reproaching him with dangerous "national liberalism"; according to
Stalin, acceptance of Lenin's "liberal" views would give too
much importance to minor nationalities and would encourage

nationalism in the States. Lenin on the other hand suspected Stalin of the crude pan-Slav chauvinism of a Russian whose nationality was newly acquired. All the theses, dissertations and resolutions they had drawn up in common led only to irreconcilable divergence when confronted with facts.

Among the contradictions of Bolshevism there is none more violent than that between theory and practice in regard to nationalities, and Stalin emphasised it with characteristic roughness.

Harsh historical necessity had substituted for the right of self-determination the right of Bolshevism to dispose of the small neighbouring peoples faced with imperialism and revolution. What the Red Army could not accomplish in Finland and Poland it did accomplish first in the Ukraine, then in the Caucasus, by methods similar to those adopted by the United States in the annexation of Texas. The Georgian Socialists' dream of creating a new Switzerland between Europe and Asia was nothing but a dream in the circumstances. In the elections for the Constituent Assembly in Georgia the Mensheviks scored 640,000 votes, the Bolsheviks 24,000. In spite of this imposing demonstration of popular sentiment expressed with approximate freedom, the Red Army had the last word three years later by helping the 24,000 to dispose of the 640,000 by armed force. All the rest was pure talk.

"The relative stability of the Menshevik regime," wrote Trotsky, "was due to the political impotence of the scattered peasantry," but that argument was still more applicable to the Bolshevik regime in "All the Russias." In 1920 a European socialist delegation visited Georgia, and on his return E. Vandervelde described the enthusiastic throngs of peasant converts to socialism. He recalled a day, at Gori, Stalin's native place, "when a whole village came to meet us, bearing the red banners of the International." A few months later foreign communist delegates visited the same spot and found the red flags honouring another International.

The course of events confirmed Rosa Luxemburg's prophecies and dissipated the sophism of the right of self-determination.

When it came to deeds the Bolsheviks trod their principles underfoot by invading Georgia, as the Mensheviks—conscious, in Tseretelli's words, "of the community of interest binding together all the peoples of Russia" under the autocracy—defied the Bolshevik programme by separation from the Soviet Republic.

Lenin's apprehension was not solely due to Stalin's expression of Russian chauvinism, but still more to his increasingly dangerous activities. After the sovietisation of the Caucasus by armed force, the bureaucracy and the police of the victors followed the army. And, just as in Russia and the Ukraine, so in Georgia, the "iron hand" fell heavily on communists, workmen and poor peasants, after having first struck at socialist opponents of all shades. Stalin went to the spot in 1921 to organise the administration after his own fashion.

The Berlin *Sozialisticheski Vestnik* reported on this mission substantially as follows: Stalin, armed with large powers, arrived in Tiflis, dismissed Makharadze for inadequate firmness and replaced him by Mdivani; similarly Tsintsadze was replaced by Atabekov. (The former was President of the Council of Commissars, the latter President of the Cheka.) Makharadze apparently refused to imprison respected socialists like Djibladze, and was roughly handled by Stalin. All this was done in the name of the Georgian Communist Central Committee, but really on his own initiative. After summoning a workers' assembly, Stalin delivered a speech outlining a programme, received in hostile silence, and the meeting was followed by arrests. The People's Commissars of the little "Sister Republics" were unceremoniously dismissed by the General Secretary of the Party, but this was only a foretaste. At that time Lenin agreed, often without knowing the truth. Within less than a year, Stalin was in open conflict with Mdivani, a comrade of his youth, as he had been earlier with Makharadze and with Tsintsadze, the famous *boyevik*, Kamo's comrade in ambushes and expropriations. For the Georgian communists subjected to Stalin's caprice, there was only one resource, first and last—to appeal from Lenin ill-informed to Lenin better-informed. Five years after the October Revolution the rights of the nations of the former Empire were reduced to a vague hope of the providential intervention of one man. And it was the rights of communists of the first rank that were in question.

The progress realised at this stage must be stated: the Soviet nations of Russia, Asia, the Ukraine, and the Caucasus were on an equal footing in their common deprivation of liberty. In complete contrast to the circumstances of the French Revolution, the number of "passive citizens" steadily increased until the category of really "active citizens" was reduced to the equivalent of an Upper Ten Thousand, though on a lower economic level. The masses, levelled downwards, suffered the unwritten law of a new kind of patriciate, divided into several ranks under the Politbureau and its Secretariat. The final corrective to all abuses—Lenin's relative wisdom.

6

"We are living in a sea of illegality," was one of Lenin's first remarks on his recovery, in a letter from the Politbureau addressed to Stalin. He had recovered his speech, if not the use of all his faculties, and had resumed a limited intellectual activity permitted by his physicians. In the summer of 1922 he followed more important affairs, gave advice and dictated notes from a retreat near Moscow. He was no longer the indefatigable and encyclopaedic Lenin of former times, but he was perfectly clear on controversial matters.

In September he attacked Stalin on the national question after hearing from Mdivani about the Georgian situation. He discussed the matter with both sides and prepared for a formal debate. In October he resumed effective work at the Politbureau and took cognisance of the enhancement of the evils he had noted before his illness: everywhere carelessness, parasitism, the impotence of the "machine."

He had already bluntly commented on the ignorance of communist officials, their boastings (com-boasts), and their lies (com-lies). "Every day," he said, "we hear, I especially on account of my position, so many glib communist lies, so many com-lies, that it's enough to make me sick, violently so, sometimes." The quaint expression "com-boasts" had a great success, so well did it fit the facts. "The communist kernel," he continued, "lacks general culture. If we take Moscow with its 4,700 responsible communists, and the whole bureaucratic machine, which is the directing spirit? I doubt very much whether it is the communists. They do not lead, they are led." The general culture of the middle classes in Russia was "inconsiderable, wretched, but in any case greater than that of our responsible communists."

Signs of degeneration were now obvious not only in the machine but at the top. Military decorations were followed by the Order of the Red Flag of Labour, a pseudo-revolutionary imitation of the honours of a despised society. In Lenin's absence, to the general surprise, Stalin had arranged for the name of Tsaritsyn to be changed to Stalingrad. Not for nothing had the Secretary of the Party placed, removed and replaced many militants. Soon Elisavetgrad was to become Zinovievsk. The same personages gave their names to schools, factories and ships. Plenty of officials were ready to flatter those in power. Others showed a mistaken zeal in the wrong quarters—thus Gachina became Trotsk. It is significant that no one dared to flatter Lenin in this way; he would not have tolerated it. At Petrograd, the State printing press had printed a pamphlet by Zinoviev with the profile of the author vignetted like a Roman consul, and Lenin was weak enough to pass it over. Trotsky had not the political sense to object. Riazanov alone protested. The decadent Jacobins of the proletariat were heedless of the famous warning of a bourgeois Jacobin, Anacharsis Clootz: "France, beware of individuals." Barras gave his name to a ship launched at Toulon, but that was under the Directory.

In November of the same year, Lenin intervened by letter against a decision of the Central Committee on the State monopoly of foreign trade, a monopoly establishing socialist protectionism in the shelter of which nationalised industry was beginning to recover. Krassin, Commissar of Foreign Trade, explained clearly one of the advantages of the system: "The interests of the capitalist countries—and of individual capitalists in each country—are conflicting, and, thanks to the unity and concentration of our commercial system, it will not be difficult to arrange matters so as to interest any capitalist group or firm, with which agreement on certain conditions is possible." But Stalin and his colleagues shortsightedly adopted a resolution against the trade monopoly, under the influence of Sokolnikov and in the absence of Lenin and Trotsky. Without its unquestioned advisers, the Central Committee showed itself incapable of taking any step without going wrong. Pressure from Lenin, Trotsky and Krassin was necessary to make them reverse their decision.

At the Fourth Congress of the Communist International, the two leaders of the revolution shared between them the main topic: *Five years of the Russian Revolution and the prospects of World Revolution.* As at former Congresses, they gave the young international organisation the best of their ideas, ripened by experience and adjusted to the hard lessons of historical fact. Once more Lenin reminded them that "we have committed many follies, and shall commit many more," giving as the reason Russian ignorance and isolation, and the inefficiency of the "machine." "At the top," he said, "we have perhaps ten thousand—I don't know how many—of our own people; in the lower ranks hundreds of thousands of former Tsarist officials." He concluded by strongly insisting on the necessity of study: "We must first learn to read and write, and to understand what we have read." Study—he recurred to this recommendation, his constant theme, under various aspects, until he died.

In November he delivered a last address to the Moscow Soviet, emphasising one aspect of the N.E.P., the offer to capitalists of advantages which would compel any State whatever to conclude an arrangement with them. He advised communists to learn the arts of reckoning and of trade, he condemned the "machine," and demanded its reconstruction—"the old machine persists, and our immediate task is to rebuild it otherwise." More than ever, he concluded, the N.E.P. is our watchword, and the "Russia of the N.E.P. will develop into socialist Russia."

In December, he dictated letter after letter on the foreign trade monopoly, and entrusted Trotsky with the task of defending their common idea at communist meetings. Simultaneously he was anxiously occupied with the question of nationalities, which took an unexpectedly serious turn in the conflict provoked by Stalin in Georgia, and with the problem of renewing and reorganising the "machine." He saw in Stalin's personality the incarnation of the deviations, the development of which threatened the future of the revolution. The most urgent task seemed to him to be to prevent Party schism, the cause of which he discerned, and for that purpose to maintain the stability of the directing group in the Central Committee. On December 25th he wrote a confidential note, every word being carefully considered, for the next Party Congress, in which he feared he might not be able to take part:

I think that the fundamental factor in the matter of stability—from this point of view—is such members of the Central Committee as Stalin and Trotsky. The relation between them constitutes, in my opinion, a big half of the danger of that split, which might be avoided, and the avoidance of which might be promoted, in my opinion, by raising the number of members of the Central Committee to fifty or one hundred.

Comrade Stalin, having become General Secretary, has concentrated an enormous power in his hands; and I am not sure that he always knows how to use that power with sufficient caution. On the other hand Comrade Trotsky, as was proved by his struggle against the Central Committee in connection with the question of the People's Commissariat of Ways and Communications, is distinguished not only by his exceptional abilities—personally he is, to be sure, the most able man in the present Central Committee; but also by his too far-reaching self-confidence and a disposition to be too much attracted by the purely administrative side of affairs.

These two qualities of the two most able leaders of the present Central Committee might, quite innocently, lead to a split; if our Party does not take measures to prevent it, a split might arise unexpectedly.

Thus Lenin hoped to prevent the disastrous consequences of the open feud between Stalin and Trotsky simply by increasing the membership of the Central Committee. At the last Party Congress, the Eleventh, membership of that committee had been increased to 27 members and 19 deputy members. The Control Commission had five members and two deputy-members. This was not enough as counterpoise to the "two most able leaders," one of whom was isolated from the machine, and the other unknown outside it. But the influence of the Central Committee decreased as its numbers grew. Its increased dimensions compelled it to delegate its powers to the Politbureau, which had all the means at its disposal for the creation of a clientele of its own in the ancient acceptation of the term. Lenin, looking at political phenomena from the angle of power, was blind to this; he no longer conceived of reform except as emanating from the top. This note, long kept secret, but gradually becoming partially known in the upper circles under the name of Lenin's *Testament* before it was divulged abroad, goes on briefly to characterise four other personalities.

"The October episode of Zinoviev and Kamenev was not, of course, accidental," says Lenin, advising that it ought as little to be used against them as the earlier non-Bolshevism of Trotsky. He gives an apparently self-contradictory opinion on Bukharin, "the most valuable and biggest theoretician of the Party"; but his "theoretical views can only with the very greatest doubt be regarded as fully Marxist, for there is something scholastic in him (he has never learned, and I think never fully understood, the dialectic)." Finally, Pyatakov is distinguished "in will and ability, but is too much given over to the administrative side of things to be relied on in a serious political question." Here "administrative" means "bureaucratic," in Pyatakov's as in Trotsky's case.

In this remarkable document Lenin gives careful appreciations, and expresses himself in subtle nuances. But his intention is clear enough; it is to induce modesty in his near colleagues by indicating their weaknesses, so that they may not continue the old grievances; at the same time he describes Trotsky as the most capable; as regards Stalin, he contents himself with a warning against the tendency of the Secretary of the Party to abuse his powers. But, a little later, he thought it necessary to emphasise the warning, and to give it categorical expression. On January 4th he added a few lines, this time without any diplomacy:

Stalin is too rude (grub), *and this fault, entirely supportable in relations among us communists, becomes insupportable in the office of General Secretary. Therefore, I propose to the comrades to find a way to remove Stalin from that position and appoint to it another man who in all respects differs from Stalin only in superiority— namely, more patient, more loyal, more polite and more attentive to comrades, less capricious, etc. This circumstance may seem an insignificant trifle, but I think that from the point of view of preventing a split and from the point of view of the relation between Stalin and Trotsky which I discussed above, it is not a trifle, or it is such a trifle as may acquire a decisive significance.*

Between December 25th and January 4th, fresh information on the Georgian business had roused Lenin's indignation and made him regret not having attacked Stalin more energetically and actively. Stalin had made use of Dzerzhinsky and Ordjonikidze to maintain his oppressive policy in the Caucasus which Lenin considered a disgrace to the regime, Ordjonikidze having gone so far as to use violence on a Georgian comrade. Lenin, outraged, wanted to exclude him from the Party and to make Stalin responsible for his subordinate.

On December 30th he writes in one of his confidential notes that "if Ordjonikidze so far lost control as to use physical force, as Dzerzhinsky has told me, that shows into what a morass we have sunk." He describes the Russian State machine as "*borrowed from Tsarism and barely touched by the Soviet world.*" It is a "bourgeois and Tsarist mechanism." Under these conditions the liberty of the nationalities to "leave the Union," provided by the Constitution will be a "*scrap of paper,* impotent to defend the races of Russia against these true Russians, chauvinist Great Russians, essentially cowardly and cruel like the typical Russian bureaucrat." Have we taken, he asks, the necessary measures to protect the persecuted races from their tyrants? To ask the question was to answer it. And after these transparent allusions to Stalin, he mentions him by name: "*In this matter Stalin's hastiness and bureaucratic enthusiasm, and his spite against the notorious 'social chauvinism' played a fatal part: generally speaking spite is a most evil factor in politics.*" He accuses Dzerzhinsky and Stalin, both of them Russians by adoption, of "true-Russian" nationalism, observing that Russians by adoption are worse than native Russians when they become chauvinist.

The next day Lenin supplemented this note, insisting on the necessity of distinguishing between the intolerable nationalism of the oppressor country and the excusable nationalism of the oppressed country. "*He who has not understood that distinction certainly knows nothing about the attitude of the proletariat on the national question.*" After this direct hit at Stalin, he explains the urgency of giving the smaller races not only formal equality, but compensation for the outrages they have suffered during centuries. "The Georgian who neglects this aspect of the matter and accuses others of 'social chauvinism' (when he himself is not only a real 'social chauvinist' but an uncivilised rascal in the service of a Great Power), is really attacking the solidarity of the proletarian class. . . ." Thus were Stalin and Ordjonikidze definitely judged by their master.

On that same day, December 31, Lenin wrote a third note drawing practical inferences from the general considerations just stated. Among others—"Ordjonikidze must receive exemplary punishment"; and "the enormous mass of unjust and prejudiced verdicts of Dzerzhinsky must be revised"; finally, "Stalin and Dzerzhinsky must be held politically responsible for this nationalist Great Russian campaign."

Lenin did not stop there. He dictated another article against Stalin's policy on the national question. "He was very much worried about it and was preparing to intervene on this question at the Party Congress," wrote his secretary to Kamenev. "Just before his last relapse he told me that he would publish this article, but later on. After that he fell ill without having given definite instructions." The article was shown to Trotsky, on whom Lenin relied for the defence at the Congress of their common point of view.

Meanwhile the "chaos of all kinds of authorities" and its disastrous effects on economic life made Lenin extremely anxious, and he wrote to the Politbureau in support of a proposal of Trotsky's. The latter attributed the disorder and wastefulness to the want of planning. As early as 1920, generalising his experience with transport, he had advocated a unified economic plan to correlate, control and stimulate the activities of the various offices responsible. He would have liked to amalgamate the commissariats dealing with economic questions, and to assure unity of direction by the Council of Labour and Defence—the Supreme Economic Council having become virtually the Commissariat of Industry. But this project involved the use of "labour armies," the failure of which had its repercussions on the notion of any general plan. The Gosplan, a State planning institution, created to co-ordinate partial plans, had no influence. Trotsky proposed to extend its competence and strengthen its powers, to make it an economic general staff under the Council of Labour and Defence. The electrification scheme, drawn up at the end of the Civil War, did no more than meet immediate needs within narrow limits. The Gosplan would draw up and keep up to date a methodical scheme for the direction of production, distribution and trade. Lenin now approved Trotsky's "sensible idea" with some reservations on detail. The very Lenin who at the beginning of the revolution had said "There is not and there cannot be any concrete plan for the organisation of economic life. Nobody can produce one. The masses alone can do it, thanks to their experience. . . ." It remained to realise it in the face of rival institutions.

Lenin knew he was so ill that he had to think of the revolution in the future without himself, but he did not sufficiently realise the gravity of his position to use his last reserves of strength to the best advantage. He hoped to take a personal part in the Twelfth Congress of the Party and himself to secure the adoption of the salutary measures he had in mind. His thoughts evidently revolved round a main point, the reform of the bureaucratic machinery of the State, and dwelt insistently on two or three questions the importance of which was insufficiently grasped by the Party—general education, the relations between nationalities, co-operation.

He published *Leaves of a Journal* on the stagnation in public education, that is, "public ignorance" in the Soviet Republic, censuring empty phrases about "proletarian culture" and urging efforts first of all to reach the "ordinary level of a civilised State in western Europe." On January 25th, *Pravda* published his article, "How to reorganise the Workers' and Peasants' Inspection." There was no mention in it of Stalin, for the Bolsheviks avoided discussing their private affairs in public, but the criticism of the Inspection was directed against him personally and injured him among the initiated. Improvement was necessary in the State machine, "*a survival to a large extent of the former bureaucracy*," and "*with only a superficial new coat of paint*." Lenin proposed to elect from 75 to 100 new members to the Control Commission, which should meet the Central Committee in periodical Party conferences and should be amalgamated with the reorganised Inspection. Unconsciously he was accelerating the movement towards a complete confusion of authorities, the annulment of all effective control and the autocratic omnipotence of the Politbureau.

In February he dotted the "i's" in an article entitled "Better less, but better," overwhelming for Stalin. "Our condition is *so sad*, not to say *so repugnant*, as regards the State machine," that reorganisation from top to bottom is essential. The lack of elementary education is the most serious matter for Russia. "To renew our State machine, we must set ourselves—first, to learn; secondly, to learn; thirdly, to learn." The Inspection ought to be the instrument of this renewal. But in what condition had Stalin left his Commissariat? "Let us speak plainly. The Inspection has now no authority at all. Everybody knows that there is no worse institution that our Inspection. . . . I ask any present leading official of the Inspection or anybody in touch with it to tell me honestly what use such a Commission is to us." Then follows a minutely detailed scheme of reorganisation, covering some years of work.

Discredited both as Commissar of Nationalities and at the Inspection, Stalin did not think he was directly threatened in his position as Secretary of the Party. But he instinctively prepared to resist. At his suggestion the Politbureau not only opposed Lenin's scheme, but objected to the publication of the article. The "machine" understood the allusion to the Party bureaucracy and stood on its defence. Lenin grew impatient; Krupskaya telegraphed; Trotsky intervened. A certain Kuibyshev, a colleague of Stalin's, suggested printing the article in a single copy of *Pravda*, to quiet "the old man." In the end the Politbureau gave way, and the article appeared in the ordinary way, on March 4th.

Next day Lenin addressed himself to Trotsky: "I beg of you to look after the Georgian affair at the Party Congress. The 'persecutions' carried out by Stalin and Dzerzhinsky must be considered, and I do not trust their impartiality. On the contrary. If you agree to undertake the defence, my mind will be at rest." On the following day he wrote to Mdivani, Makharadze and others: "I am following your business with all my heart. Disgusted with Ordjonikidze's brutality and the connivance of Stalin and Dzerzhinsky, I am preparing notes and a speech on your behalf."

Fresh machinations by Stalin in Georgia decided him to have done with it. "*Vladimir Ilyich is preparing a bomb for Stalin at the Congress,*" said his secretary on that same day, March 6th, repeating Lenin's own words. Feeling that his health was worse, he sent Trotsky the material for his "bomb," an article and notes on the national question. Trotsky wanted to inform Kamenev. Lenin sent word: "Under no circumstances." Why? "Kamenev will immediately show everything to Stalin, and Stalin will make a rotten compromise and then deceive us." But a few minutes later, finding speech already difficult, Lenin feared he would be able to do nothing, and, on second thoughts, sent Kamenev a copy of his letter to Mdivani. "Vladimir Ilyich is worse, and hastens to do all he can," explained the secretary. The sick man put all his strength of will into a last mental effort, but sclerosis of the arteries increased rapidly. There was an interview between Trotsky and Kamenev. The latter was coming away from Lenin's house, where Krupskaya had told him: "Vladimir has just dictated to the stenographer a letter to Stalin breaking off all relations with him." It was Lenin's last letter.

7

AT THE moment when its founder was losing consciousness, on the eve of the Twelfth Communist Congress, the Soviet Republic, more firmly established, was recognised *de facto* by six and *de jure* by twelve States. In the ranks of the Powers it took a place implicitly granted the year before at the Genoa Conference, and then renewed commercial relations, concluded treaties, and sent missions and ambassadors to foreign Powers. It was even able to contract the semblance of an alliance with Turkey and an *entente* with Germany. Thanks to the antagonism between the United States and Japan, the vast areas conquered under Tsarism in Asia up to the Pacific coast were returned. There was no longer any immediate threat on the frontiers. The Red Army passed to a peace footing.

At home the last rebel bands were broken up in the Ukraine and in the Near East; Soviet rule was everywhere established and consolidated. Two years of the N.E.P. were already reviving the forces of production, in spite of the great famine of 1921 which surpassed in horror the similar calamity of 1891, and struck down from 15 to 20 million human beings, half of them children, and even gave rise to cases of cannibalism. The population, decimated by war, revolution, counter-revolution and famine, resumed the vigorous increase common to backward countries, and numbered more than 133 millions at the census of March 1923.

But the economic thermometer fell sensibly in spite of the first good effects of the N.E.P. Public revenue, or rather the total value of production, had fallen from 11 milliard roubles in

1913 to 5.3 milliards in 1922; agricultural production from 6.7 to 4 milliards, industrial production from 4.4 to 1.3 milliards. (Other statistics give rather higher figures, but in identical proportions.) The relative share of small artisans in industrial production had greatly increased; it represented more than one-half in 1922, whereas in 1913 it was less than one-fifth. The explanation is to be found in the larger fall in large and medium industrial undertakings.

In the country 51 million *dessiatins* were sown in 1922 as against 82 million in 1916 and more than 100 in 1913. The gross grain harvest was 2.8 milliard *poods* in 1922 as against 3.8 milliards in 1914 (and about 6 milliards in 1913). The reduction was still greater for industrial crops, hemp and flax, sugar-beet and cotton. There was a corresponding fall in livestock: 124 million head of cattle in 1923 as against 183 million in 1916. Export had ceased. The peasantry as a whole were still in want, in spite of the division of the expropriated land and the abolition of the former dues.

More than three-quarters of the arable land and pasturage were cut up into small holdings, lessening in proportion to the increase of "souls," the multiplication of "hearths"; the scattered strips did not permit of intensive cultivation. Generally speaking the routine of the *mir* continued to exist side by side with the fictitious soviet, together with the periodical redistribution of strips and the triennial survey. In many villages, individual holdings had diminished, for lack of any State or landowners' estates to be nationalised. In theory there were no longer landless peasants. But in fact there were such, and millions had no horse to draw their mediaeval wooden plough.

Social equalisation to a "medium" level between the *kulak*, supposed to be rich, and the *bedniak*, undoubtedly poor—such was the result of the revolution for the peasant at this time. There were no even approximate statistics for the *kulaks*, whose relative prosperity was dissimulated in various ways.

Enterprises of a socialist character were said to cover about two per cent of the cultivated land, divided between 4,000 *sovkhoz* (Soviet domains, State farms), and 13,000 *kolkhoz* (collective undertakings—artels, co-operative farms, agricultural communes).

In the towns, where works, factories and workshops employed only about half the labour employed before the War, the average wage had fallen from 32 roubles a month to 7 roubles in 1922, rising in 1923 to 16 roubles. But most of the workers, divided into 17 categories according to their skill, received less than the medium wage. Serious unemployment, which could not be computed, was aggravated by the competition of masses of the lower middle class and by the influx of surplus peasants. Relief of unemployment was practically non-existent.

Industry and transport were working at a loss, with exorbitant costs of production. The consumer paid three times as much as in former times for manufactured goods, absolutely necessary and of the poorest quality. Lack of goods produced uncontrollable speculation in which even the Co-operative and State shops shared. There appeared the greedy and crafty N.E.P. man, the incarnation of a new trading class formed to meet every risk and danger. Very soon retail trade was mainly in private hands.

But the State, controlling heavy industry, transport, foreign and wholesale trade, had nothing to fear from this limited revival of capitalism. The monopoly of political power in the hands of the Communist Party enabled it to regulate legislation and finance in favour of socialised enterprise in the competition opened up by the N.E.P. Concessions granted to foreign capitalists were few and might remain very small. Lenin was not wrong in justifying retreat, "difficult especially for revolutionaries accustomed to advance," by saying "having conquered so vast a territory, we had space to retreat without the loss of essentials."

The October Revolution had not only destroyed the material survivals from the Middle Ages, slavery and feudalism, as Lenin said modestly in 1921. There remained a great positive inheritance as a basis for the creation of the most democratic republic in history and for taking the first steps towards a socialist regime. The internecine differences of a hostile world gave Soviet Russia more than one respite, and offered great possibilities for taking advantage of international division of labour and for safeguarding her subversive independence by exploiting the rivalries inherent in a society based on competition. The future then would depend largely on the heirs, on the ability of their victorious party to become a constructive party, and, as Lenin wished, to associate in their grandiose effort, the whole of the working people.

Clandestine pre-revolutionary activity and the Civil War were a bad preparation for the Bolsheviks' future task. Former conspirators, agitators and destructive agents had to turn into the omniscient technical experts of a new economic and social order in an undeveloped country, described by Bukharin as a "gigantic laboratory," in which a willing personnel had to be improvised at the same time as the instruments of production. They had to learn by experience. Lenin did not leave behind him infallible recipes, but only general directions and advice which might be useful to his followers when left to themselves.

"*Above all don't let us be afraid of constant self-criticism, of correcting our mistakes and frankly avowing them.*" This open sincerity towards himself and the workers and peasants should have survived as a cardinal principle of his theory and practice. "We are not afraid of mistakes. Men have not become saints because the revolution has begun," he wrote in his *Letter to the American Workers.* This is no rhetorical phrase. He often quoted a sentence of Marx on the "part played by stupidity in revolutions," knowing no other antidote to this poison than self-criticism, of which he gave examples in the fight against "com-lies" and "com-boasting." In the costly apprenticeship stage "we must not be afraid to admit and to study our mistakes in order the better to repair them."

He was as conscious as anyone of the gap between his schemes and their realisation. "Up till now, we have been drawing up programmes and making promises. The world revolution could not be started without programmes and promises. The essential thing is cool consideration of where and when mistakes have been made, and the knowledge of how to begin over again." He did not confess his errors either to encourage them or to wash his hands of them. "We have certainly committed errors and suffered failures, many of them. But was it possible to realise a type of State new in history without mistakes and failures? We shall not cease to correct our errors and to seek a better application of Soviet principles—by trying to correct ourselves."

Nevertheless Lenin seems to have been blind to one most important phenomenon—the organic transformation of the Party on which his hopes and his optimism were founded, a Party which he thought was the "real vanguard of the vanguard class."

At the beginning of 1923 the Party had 485,000 members, nearly all of whom were members of the bureaucracy. A never-ending purge eliminated the bad elements. "No profound and powerful popular movemnt in all history has taken place without its share of mud, without adventurers and rogues, without swaggering and noisy elements," said Lenin, before admitting, at the time of the N.E.P., that "a ruling party inevitably attracts careerists and industrial speculators who deserve to be shot." But the purge was apt to hit the best brains, those least docile and most refractory to the passive obedience which was gradu-ally substituted for discipline by consent. Subjected to a hier-archical system aggravated by the force of inertia and by eco-nomic distress, the Party lost the habit of thinking for itself and acting of its own accord. The Politbureau's methods of govern-ment and the administration of the Secretariat intensified the torpor consequent on the tension of revolution and war. As in France in 1793, where sections and districts were bureaucratised by the division of functions and the lassitude of the sectionaries, so the average Bolshevik militant became enslaved to the Soviet State for the sake of a job. In this period of unemployment and privation, the Party membership card was as good as social insurance. Selection on the ground of fidelity and ability gave way to advancement for the careerist.

In this new caste with its petty privileges there were subdivi-sions: at the bottom a plebs to be mobilised on occasion for the

worst and most thankless tasks; at the top intellectual work
and the little perquisites of power fell to the aristocracy of the
so-called "responsible officials"; for the intermediate classes, the
main anxiety was to avoid disgrace, to get a foot on the ladder.
Civic rights were reserved to registered communists; they enjoyed relative security and had easier access to the seventh rank
in wages, better lodging, a less uncertain future.

"It is useless to deny that many militants are mortally weary.
They have to attend 'Saturdays' twice or four times a month,
out of working hours; excessive mental strain is demanded; their
families live in difficult conditions; they are sent here to-day and
there to-morrow by the Party or by chance; the result is inevitably psychological exhaustion." These words of Zinoviev, true
in 1920, were not less true in 1923, but only of a decreasing
number of the lower ranks. As the regime acquired greater
stability, the others had increasing advantages, intrinsically
small but valuable by contrast with the surrounding poverty.
The "Saturdays" in question disappeared. The "great initiative"
hailed by Lenin, voluntary Saturday work, rapidly degenerated
into compulsory work, and was admitted to be an illusion. In
the same speech Zinoviev, repeating Lenin's words, demanded,
*criticism, great freedom of criticism within the Party. We have
always asserted it in theory; now is the time to put it into practice.*" But at each Congress, at each Conference, the same
phrases, never translated into fact, were used to calm the same
discontent.

The remnants of the earlier freedom of criticism fell to the
Upper Ten Thousand, to the new political patriciate. "With
what human cargo did the Communist Party enter the revolution?" asked the exiled Menshevik, Dalin. "Not more than
five or ten thousand, a third of whom were intellectuals. That
is the original capital producing so large a dividend." This
ten thousand constituted the upper stratum of the amorphous
society grown up in penury. The symptoms of decadence had
not obscured their revolutionary mentality, and a chosen few
kept intact the spirit of traditional Bolshevism, maintained a
communion of ideas with communists of no rank, with obscure

units scattered among the labouring masses. How many were to persevere in the original path? Only experience would show.

The Party, then, is a complex which escapes summary definition, in which old forms exist side by side with new types, where habits are met by innovations. Discussion between the various ranks of the organisation becomes more and more rare. At the top, a few men give orders which the machine executes as it pleases. The regular offices transmit the instructions. All initiative, all driving power comes from above. Official institutions, which but yesterday were consultative assemblies, now merely register decisions from above. The Party Statutes are treated in the same way as the Constitution. Many Congress decisions never get farther than the paper they are written on, especially if their tendency is towards the restoration of liberty. Committees of all sorts abound, there are ramifications of the Party in towns, cantons, districts, provinces, federated countries. The committees become more numerous, jostle one another and build up a many-storied machine which retards the movement of the heavy State machine. The executive institutions of the Soviets, on an analogous but even more complicated model, are each under the orders of the corresponding Party institution. Generally the directing element is identical in the two. In factories, State institutions, dwelling-houses, schools, trade unions, consumers' co-operative societies, the army, the militia, the police —communists are grouped into cells and sections which delegate their authority. The Union of Communist Youth, the Comsomol, with its 400,000 members, has its own cells everywhere. Where communists are not numerous enough, "sympathisers" act as auxiliaries. This extraordinary network extends irresistibly. A system of administration and government altogether unforeseen, but explicable by Gorky's remark that "we live in the midst of a mass of persons destitute of any political or social education."

"The Party will endeavour to guide the activity of the soviets, but not to supplant them"—a vain resolution passed in 1919, but, like many others, never applied, and confirmed many times since, without thereby becoming any more applicable. The decisions adopted at the last Congress under Lenin's inspiration —to restore a certain amount of power to the People's Commissars, to reduce the machine to the minimum—these had the same fate. The Party had guided the revolution, had won the Civil War, had mastered anarchy, forged the mechanism of power, and breathed life into an embryonic economy. Its driving power was to carry it beyond the objectives originally fixed. Time was needed to assimilate the new conditions. Six months after Kronstadt did not Russia suffer the ravages of a terrible famine which could not be made good all at once the next year? Only in 1923 did the N.E.P. create circumstances propitious for a return to normal constitutional methods. But Lenin was no longer there to direct the operation implied in his latest writings. Some hoped that he would once more surmount his physical disability. Meanwhile it was for the Politbureau to put into force the popular democracy formulated in the theory and the programme of Bolshevism.

Now if the Party was "entirely apart from and above everything," according to Bukharin's tremendous admission, the Politbureau in its turn, in relation to the Party, was "entirely apart from and above everything." The interest of the cause, popular aspirations, revolutionary progress, became for it so many abstractions divorced from reality. By its isolation it lost all sense of the situation and any power of interpreting it in the light of principles. Its opinions were based on reading official reports and police dossiers. As early as 1922, when Lenin and Trotsky sanctioned the theatrical trial of the Social Revolutionary Party, their only knowledge of the terrorist deeds to be condemned was derived from the biased information of the Cheka. In the Communist International, bloody deeds were and are fomented without the knowledge of the regular Executive Committee. For one affair such as that of Georgia in which Stalin almost succeeded in deceiving the Central Committee, how many others were prepared and decided on the word of officials. With Lenin laid aside—and even if his last counsels had been followed—if Stalin had been removed from the Secretariat and the Central Committee enlarged to a hundred members as the unknown *Testament* suggested, there would have been no fundamental change without giving back to the Party, the trade unions and the soviets the right to make their voices heard. But that does not seem to have entered the minds of the people at the top, and the voices from below were stifled.

At the beginning of the revolution Gorky had said opportunely, "The old order of things is materially destroyed, but it lives on morally among us and in us. The hundred-headed hydra of ignorance, barbarism, stupidity, treason and villainy is not slain." The warning remained necessary when the N.E.P. was introduced. Bolshevik theorists, it is true, were expected to abolish in five years the spiritual inheritance of the past, the centuries-old atavism of oppression and servitude. Driven by extraordinary conditions to extraordinary measures, they only proposed action in the direction of their ultimate aim, and for that purpose to harmonise sooner or later the means and the end. But they had to take care, while there was yet time, to avoid the tendency to follow the line of least resistance in making a virtue of necessity, in perpetuating a dictatorship of distress, and in losing their *raison d'être* in order to keep themselves in power.

Chapter VIII

THE HERITAGE

ISUNDERSTANDING within the Political Bureau grew steadily more acute during the second phase of Lenin's illness in 1923. Stalin, Zinoviev and Kamenev coalesced to form the dominant triumvirate—the *troïka*—and organised in secret a section to oppose Trotsky, to lessen his influence and to isolate him in the machine. Faced with the prospect of the definite disappearance of their master, they already began to reckon on the vacancy and to take the necessary steps to assure the succession, which was virtually theirs. Trotsky might easily have thwarted their plans and cut short their intrigues by a public revelation of the matters in dispute. But he hesitated to move because of the uncertainty about Lenin's health. This is his explanation, made, however, afterwards. He feared a wrong interpretation of the part he would be called upon to play—a vulgar parallel with a historic precedent. Their obsession with the French Revolution sometimes misled the Russian revolutionary leaders. For instance, the accusation of Bonapartism had been brought by Lenin against Kerensky, by Martov against Lenin; and Trotsky temporised in order to avoid the same comparison.

The Party knew nothing of these underlying discords, and for a long time Trotsky did nothing to enlighten them. By his silence he played into the hands of the *troïka*, who alone stood to gain by concealment. Lenin's notes on the national question were kept secret, and only communicated to a few initiated persons. Only Krupskaya knew of Lenin's *Testament*. No one

had any ground for suspecting a breach between Lenin and
Stalin. The immediate cause of this last complication was Stalin's
rudeness to Krupskaya, who, by keeping her husband informed,
hindered the General Secretary's operations. That Lenin should
act on such a pretext proved that his mind was made up finally
with regard to Stalin. The latter extricated himself by sending
to Krupskaya, at Trotsky's suggestion, a letter of apology which
arrived too late for Lenin to read. By a tacit consent, which was
natural, all the principal antagonists admitted the necessity of
maintaining secrecy on the real nature of internal discussions
tending to discredit the Party. Under cover of this general
silence Stalin was able to intrigue unhindered.

At the Congress of Soviets in December 1922 he had reported
in favour of a closer union between the various Federated Republics, his reports being based on a pretended initiative of the
Transcaucasian delegations. The scheme required a session of
the First Congress of the Soviet Union, to sanction the "treaty"
concluded between the principal nationalities for the political
and economic centralisation of the regime, with a simultaneous
assertion of the theoretical right of the contracting parties as
free agents, and of their administrative and cultural freedom.
In reality everything was regulated, prescribed and ordered by
the Political Bureau; neither nations nor parties were consulted
at all; the delegates were elected by regional committees nominated from above by other committees in Moscow. As for the
Treaty of Union, it was to be, as Lenin had foreseen, merely
another "scrap of paper" in the archives dealing with the Constitution; so true is it that the Bolshevist theories on the national
question had no relation to facts under the conditions of a terrorist dictatorship indefinitely prolonged.

Stalin deferred his defence of his Caucasian policy for the
Twelfth Congress of the Party. It was incontestably a clever
one. Trotsky made his task easier by moving an agreed amendment to the resolution. For the first time the deliberations of the
Party took place without the participation, direct or indirect, of
its founder. Krupskaya abstained from transmitting to the Congress the *Testament* that Lenin had prepared for them under the

modest title of "Notes" *(zapiski);* she still hoped for his recovery, and for his return to the work of government. The National programme was not divulged either, and Lenin's notes on that subject, communicated in committee, had only a limited and unauthorised circulation among bored officials. Stalin spoke from the tribune as *rapporteur* for the Political Bureau and the Central Committee combined. He denounced the nationalism of those Georgians who were hostile to Transcaucasian federation from dislike of Armenians and Tartars, a hostility manifested in Mdivani's decree expelling recent immigrants from Tiflis. Thus instructed, the Congress registered approval of the general policy adopted in Georgia by the Party Secretariat, with a mild reproof of the excesses of Ordjonikidze and his friends. In any case the delegates were chosen by the machine, and therefore prepared to vote *en bloc* for the proposals put forward by the directing organisations. Agreement in the Political Bureau carried with it automatically unanimity in the Congress, led and dominated by a *praesidium,* just as the Party was by its Central Committee—always under the same triumvirate.

But in 1923 the increasing gravity of the economic situation drove the national question into the background. The country passed through successive crises: scarcity of commodities, industrial products at prices below cost, lack of raw materials, prolonged delays in wage payments, increasing unemployment, currency depreciation, fall in agricultural prices, paralysis of trade, etc. Under the incitement to production provided by the N.E.P., industry fell behind agricultural production, State production below individual and family production. Resources were insufficient to subsidise industry up to the standard of its requirements, to reconstitute working capital and enlarge the basis of operation. Foreign loans were impossible, and the yield of domestic loans inconsiderable. Concessions were negligible, export was hardly beginning to recover. The Party was anxiously seeking a policy. In these troubles and uncertainties Trotsky alone expressed any clear ideas. The Political Bureau had instructed him to present to Congress an official report on industry, and Stalin had even pretended that he would like to see him

entrusted with the report on general policy, formerly assigned
to Lenin.

Trotsky found the principal cause of this permanent crisis in
Soviet economy in the disparity between the prices of industrial
and agricultural products. "The peasant, paying for manufactured goods, coal, petrol, etc., in terms of wheat, is buying two
and three-quarter times as dear as in 1913." Graphically expressed, the disproportion was shown by an acute angle like
that formed by the blades of a pair of scissors. If the phenomenon
is aggravated or persists, the scissors would sever all exchange
between town and country. By this metaphor Trotsky clearly
indicated the danger, and stressed the urgency of price adjust-
ment.

A rise in the price of cereals was primarily dependent on
export; a fall in the price of manufactured articles depended
on a more rational utilisation of machinery, materials and
labour. It was therefore necessary to reduce overhead costs, to
suspend the operation of non-essential undertakings, to concentrate scattered industries, to suppress waste, to establish
rigorous calculations and strict accountancy—an enormous task
to look forward to, and a prosaic one for romantically-minded
revolutionaries. "To put it mildly, there is absolute chaos," said
Nogin, describing the State economic organisations; and he was
confirmed by Trotsky, who said: "There is information in the
Workers' and Peasants' Inspection showing that about eighty
per cent of our calculations are unfounded." According to him,
the other twenty per cent were not much better. For example,
a certain State Trust declared a profit of four trillions of paper
roubles, when the Inspection was able to prove a real loss of
750,000 gold roubles, and this was no exceptional case. With a
view to the institution of a new economic order in line with the
communist programme, the progressive development of production and the rationalisation of its methods, Trotsky insistently
urged the elaboration and application of a general plan, under
the direction of a competent "great General Staff," in the shape
of the Council of Labour and Defence assisted by the Gosplan
(State-Planning Department). He recalled simply a primary

truth of socialist theory, one of its fundamental criticisms of capitalist society, providing for the substitution of planned production, distribution and exchange for a free market, competitive rivalry and unregulated supply and demand. But, though by no means new and though approved in principle, his idea was not accepted without scepticism by the bureaucracy, who pretended to applaud it while opposing the force of inertia against its realisation in practice; it was interpreted as a cloak to a secret intention by Trotsky of making himself dictator in economic matters by assuming the direction of the departments concerned.

Where were the indispensable new resources for industry to be found? Some thought by increasing the taxes on agriculture; according to them two years of the N.E.P., one of which was a famine year, would have increased sufficiently the taxable capacity of the peasantry. Against this "Left" point of view, Trotsky recommended that taxation should not exceed limits permitting "*peasant economy to be brought to a higher level and greater future wealth for the peasant.*" This declaration of the necessity of enriching the cultivators was by no means a chance expression on his part, for before the Congress he had already said to the Ukrainian Communist Congress:

Those comrades who, like Larin, maintain that we are not demanding enough from the peasant masses are certainly mistaken. We ought not to exact from the peasant anything more than he can really give. *We ought to act so that he will be richer this year than last year.* He will understand this formula if we put it as the foundation of our internal policy; it is profoundly different from War Communism. Then we demanded from the peasant the whole surplus of his production over his immediate needs; but with no surplus, an enterprise totters and falls. To-day we say to him: a surplus is indispensable to advancement of your business, keep it. *For, unless there is advancement in agriculture, we shall have no industry.*

In conclusion Trotsky proposed simplification of taxation, that it should be made intelligible to the peasant and easy of payment, and that a money equivalent for the tax in kind should be fixed to improve the peasant's lot. This proposal was adopted at the Moscow Congress as it had been at the Kharkov Congress.

A member of the Political Bureau certainly did not take a step of this kind without the preliminary assent of his colleagues. Their intimate co-operation assured a minimum unanimity in action, if not in opinion. The Bolshevik idea of discipline, reinforced by the administrative methods and organisation of the ruling bureaucracy, presupposed the obligation of unanimity in deliberative assemblies, after debate sometimes impassioned but always reticent; there was also the anxiety not to furnish arguments to the watchful enemy. The average Bolshevik had to reckon with the probable unpleasantnesses consequent on too crude frankness. What militant from Moscow, Petrograd or Kiev would expose himself with a light heart to transfer to Archangel, Irkutsk or Vladivostok, real exile in accordance with Tsarist tradition, even though the pretext were the necessities of the service? After so many sacrifices, heroism was no longer the fashion, and those who were incapable of adapting themselves fell back on the old practice of subterranean propaganda. At the Party Congress Ossinsky might still throw doubt on the infallibility of Lenin; the very same reflexion uttered outside the Congress would expose an ordinary mortal to the suspicion of counter-revolutionary tendencies. If Kossior permitted himself to allude to the attitude of the triumvirate towards Trotsky, this was only possible within closed doors and then not without risk. So all the decisions of the Twelfth Congress were accepted without subsequent opposition.

Nevertheless the discussion revealed many differences. The open tribune of *Pravda*, an intermittent survival of democracy reserved for privileged members of the Party, had permitted beforehand the expression of very various opinions following Lenin's articles on the Workers' and Peasants' Inspection. The opposed solutions were the subject of polite and prudent controversy at the Congress, but only among delegates with a consultative status, none of whom could modify any vote by their speeches.

Krassin and Ossinsky criticised Lenin's suggestions, the former raising objections to the "hypertrophy of control" by the inspecting organisations of the Party or the State, the second combating the confusion of functions between the State and the Party. "Our weakness lies in incapacity to organise production, not in insufficient control," said Krassin. "Our aim should be the maximum of production with the minimum of control." Contrary to Lenin, who advised the union of the Soviet Inspection with the Communist Control Commission, Ossinsky desired to separate the functions of the Party from those of the State and to reform the various superior organisations with their overlapping prerogatives and functions. His sensible idea of putting order into the chaos of superior authorities of all sorts, denounced by Lenin, was bound up, however, with a juridical pedantry compromising its scope. On the other hand the importance attached to "bourgeois specialists" seemed to him excessive, while Krassin thought it inadequate. The latter also considered that increase of capital investment in industry inevitably demanded larger concessions to foreign capital. Opposition was raised this time by isolated individuals rather than by groups or sections. There was no looking to the Left or to the Right, as was pretended by Larin, an ex-Menshevik who had gone "Left" and constituted himself the unseasonable defender of the working class against a hypothetical "swamp of the Right" or an indefinable pro-peasant tendency. Larin demanded an increase in wages and the maintenance of unprofitable undertakings at the cost of the rural districts. The *Praesidium* called on Preobrazhensky, the recognised mouthpiece of the traditional Left, to refute him. This Congress was inspired by optimism to order, in spite of the atmosphere of uncertainty caused by Lenin's absence, and a subtle malaise due to "the Trotsky question" which was in the air.

In accordance with Lenin's last public suggestions the membership of the Central Committee was increased to 40 members, and that of the Control Commission to 50. The central organisations were henceforward to meet in joint session. Lenin had not foreseen, and no one realised, that this would mean a lessening of their authority in their respective statutory functions, since a governing body of a hundred persons could only meet rarely, and then only to register accomplished facts and to invest with full powers the two supreme Bureaux, consisting now of seven members each with four deputy-members. In practice the triumvirate, surrounded by trusted partisans, maintained the authority they had achieved. Stalin, confirmed in his functions, emerged unscathed from a Congress at which Lenin had intended to turn him out of the Secretariat. Krupskaya had informed no one, and Trotsky, waiting on events, allowed the proceedings to go on without saying anything to clear the atmosphere or prepare for the future.

2

UNANIMITY was only apparent, at the bottom as at the top of the Party. Various clandestine opposition groups were persecuted by "the machine" and tracked by the G.P.U. Anonymous pamphlets were secretly circulated. Communists expelled for disobedience and militants acting with them, immune for the time being because of their obscurity, used conspiratorial devices to counter the Government's police measures, operating now within the only legal political organisation after they had secured the suppression of all opposing parties.

The *troïka* had easily got rid of their first critics by sending them on missions far away from Moscow, in the supposed overriding interests of communism; if the Party was the permanent incarnation of the revolution, if the Political Bureau was the sole qualified interpreter without appeal of the opinion of the Central Committee, no Bolshevik worthy of the name could raise any objection if he received from the Secretariat marching orders and a new post. In this respect the principal personalities to be removed owed it to discipline to resign themselves, the more so since the Soviet Union, in creating diplomatic relations with various European and Asiatic States, had embassies to fill. Exile under these conditions was endurable, sometimes even attractive, and in some cases corrupting. Thus Krestinsky, Ossinsky, Yurenev, Lutovinov, Kollontai, Rakovsky and others were to go abroad, where they had been preceded on valid pretexts by Krassin and Joffe. Less prominent objectors were unceremoniously dispatched to Siberia, Mongolia and the Far East.

To isolate Trotsky and make him impotent was the unavowed plan of Stalin and his partners. After sending Krestinsky to Berlin, the change in Rakovsky's position, on the ground of the necessity of having an imposing ambassador in London, tended to deprive Trotsky of his best supporter and to separate him from his closest friend, the President of the Ukrainian Council of Commissars, guilty of the further crime of disapproving Stalin's national policy. The change entailed a complete upheaval of the bureaucracy at Kharkov and Kiev. All the secretaries of the Ukrainian provincial Communist Committees were scattered to the four points of the compass for having demanded the maintenance of Rakovsky at his post in the interest of the common cause.

As for the attempts at resistance against the official policy among the workers by less notorious militants, the triumvirate did not shrink from any method of coercion to break them.

Only small local groups of the old, broken-up Workers' Opposition survived. But a more active section, the Workers' Truth, issued some proclamations from the end of 1922 onwards. It attacked as a "new bourgeoisie" the higher and middle officials of the Party, of the trade unions and of the State, denounced the political and material advantages they enjoyed, and refused to acknowledge as a dictatorship of the proletariat a regime of "tyranny and exploitation." "*The gulf between the Party and the workers is steadily deepened*," they wrote in their appeals. The workers, subjected to "implacable exploitation," housed in "frightful tenements," were, moreover, "deprived under threat of repression and of unemployment of all possibility of using their votes." The Labour Code was no more effective than other illusory charters. "*The dictator class is in fact deprived of the most elementary political rights*." This dissident section demanded freedom of the press and freedom of association for "the revolutionary elements of the proletariat."

In 1923 another opposition was secretly organised, the Workers' Group, which expressed similar grievances, undertook the defence of proletarians "absolutely without rights," declared the trade union organisation to be "a blind instrument in the hands of the bureaucracy and a bureaucratic appendage of the Political Bureau," and accused the Party of having established *"not the dictatorship of the proletariat, but the dictatorship of the triumvirate."* This group took part in increasingly frequent strikes with the intention of giving them a democratic-revolutionary direction, demanded unrestricted freedom of the press, and made preparations for a general strike by way of protest against the abuse of power.

Outside these two secret communist groups of small numerical importance, smaller ones were created here and there without knowledge of one another. All these expressed the same criticisms, but with many differences in theoretical matters, confusion arising on those points in which Bolshevism is tinged with liberal or anarchist ideas. These groups did not produce a single leader capable of guiding them in a tangled situation. But the significance of the movement, parallel with effervescence among the workers themselves, is undoubted. The Party must already have become divorced from its social origins not to be aware of it.

In the course of that year, especially from July onwards, strikes of increasing dimensions broke out, revealing the reality too long unrecognised by the Kremlin—the proletariat, struggling for its morsel of bread, in unconscious rebellion, against the "dictatorship of the triumvirate." Compensation for the intolerable privations inflicted on the workers was not provided by Congress voting one thesis after another, formally satisfactory, but inoperative and rapidly forgotten. There were continuous economic crises, and famine wages, paid after long delays in depreciated currency, did not cover the elementary requirements of the wage-earners. Extended unemployment, reduced production, the high price of commodities beyond the means of working people—all testified to the blindness of the rulers and explained the exasperation of the ruled. The salutary decisions on economic matters adopted by the last Communist

Congress—for the concentration of industry, rationalisation in technical and administrative matters—were not enforced any more than other resolutions, laws and decrees impossible of application; all the evils of the regime grew steadily worse until September 1923, when the workers' demonstrations became so serious as to compel the Political Bureau to carry out the most pressing reforms.

It was not difficult to take penal measures against the so-called fomenters of disturbance, to arrest the leaders, to exclude their followers from the Party, and to deprive the heretics of work and the means of existence. The causes still had to be remedied if a repetition of the trouble was to be avoided.

Although they were consenting parties at the rigorous measures adopted against their comrades, Trotsky at the Political Bureau and his supporters in the Central Committee were not, nevertheless, quite satisfied with this purely repressive policy. A committee of inquiry, presided over by Dzerzhinsky, demanded from communists the immediate denunciation, either to the Control Commission or to the G.P.U., of illegal groups within the Party. Another special committee of the Central Committee, with powers superior to those of the ordinary economic organisations and the regular State Commissariats, took extraordinary measures to stop the crisis, to mitigate it, and to lessen the angle between the blades of the "scissors." Having no illusions as to the efficiency of these various expedients, Trotsky determined to break silence.

In a letter, dated October 8th, to the Central Committee and the Control Commission, he recapitulated his accumulated complaints, his criticisms, and his defence.

Substantially, he blamed the Political Bureau for the "alarming symptoms" which had shaken the Party from its torpor. "The best militants," he wrote, "felt anxiety about the methods employed in the arrangements for the Twelfth Congress, and since that time everything had gone from bad to worse." This was a clear allusion to Stalin and to his astute methods of handling and placing obedient officials, and removing the refractory to other posts. The unhealthy internal condition of the

Party and the discontent of the workers and peasants provoked
by the mistakes made in economic policy were the two essential
causes of the new difficulties to be faced. The alliance (*smychka*)
between town and country, insisted on by Lenin, was becoming
an empty phrase, instead of a practical effort to reduce costs of
State production. Far from assuming increased importance, the
Gosplan was neglected and the main economic problems were
settled by the Political Bureau without preliminary study or
serious method. Thus "chaos began at the top." The disparity
between industrial and agricultural prices tended to liquidate
the N.E.P., for the peasant could no longer buy when he found
that a pood of wheat was worth two boxes of matches. Industry
was loaded with unproductive financial charges, as, for example,
the useless advertisements imposed by the local committees of
the Party to meet the deficit on their publications.

In developing these accusations, Trotsky attacked Stalin without mentioning his name. After the Twelfth Congress the Party
Secretariat had nominated officials in economic affairs, on the
grounds not of their competence, but of their subservience to
the Party. The General Secretary himself selected the secretaries
of the provincial committees who, in turn, chose the secretaries
of subordinate committees, and so on, down to the smallest
"cells." Thus there was a hierarchy of secretaries, a machine of
secretaries, a psychology of secretaries. Elections ceased. The
workers' democracy talked of in official literature was pure
fiction; the dictatorship of the bureaucracy was further from it
than War Communism had been. At the worst moments of the
Civil War the Party had been able to discuss openly the interests
of the revolution; now any exchange of opinion was impossible.
A large class of communists no longer took the trouble to think;
the masses only learned the decisions that had been taken by
the decrees issued, and discontent, deprived of expression, produced internal abscesses, in the form of secret groups.

The Political Bureau, continued Trotsky, had come to the
point of balancing the Budget by restoring *vodka* (spirit made
from grain, forbidden under Tsarism in 1914) as a State
monopoly. The legislation on alcohol and alcoholism involved,

among other things, the danger of making the Soviet revenue independent of the progress of national prosperity, and the bureaucratic hierarchy independent of the Party. The prohibition of any discussion even of this unfortunate scheme was an indication of danger, corroborated by the dismissal of an editor of *Pravda* for the sole crime of having demanded free examination of the project.

In another connection, the Political Bureau had arranged to make Stalin a member of the Revolutionary Council of War, for considerations other than military. Voroshilov and Lashevich were appointed to it for reasons openly avowed by Kuibyshev, who said to Trotsky: "We think it necessary to combat you, but cannot openly treat you as an enemy; that is why we must have recourse to these methods." Identical measures had been employed against Rakovsky in the Ukraine.

In conclusion, Trotsky demanded an end to the bureaucratic rule of the secretaries, and the restoration of the Party democracy within proper limits, to prevent irremediable degeneration. For a year and a half, he said, he had abstained, vainly, from carrying the struggle outside the Central Committee. "I now think it not only my right, but my duty, to tell those members of the Party, who are sufficiently prepared, experienced, politically conscious, and therefore able to help the Party to emerge from the impasse without convulsion or shock."

The Political Bureau felt compelled to reply to this indictment. In a document, a secret one like Trotsky's own, they charged Trotsky with the ambition of an "economic and military dictatorship," reproached him with having declined Lenin's invitation to act as his deputy on the Council of Commissars, of failing to attend either the sittings of that organisation or the Council of Labour and Defence, of taking no initiative in economic, financial or budgetary questions, of acting on the formula of "all or nothing," and of refusing to work in economic matters, contenting himself with constant criticism of the Central Committee. Evading their antagonist's indictment, the Political Bureau recalled earlier disagreements between Lenin and Trotsky, and proceeded to accuse him of repeated imprudences in foreign policy, of rash acts which might have precipitated armed conflicts now with Poland, now with England.

Trotsky replied on October 24th. He referred to the differences which had arisen in the course of a single year between Lenin and those desirous of exploiting the prestige of his name, especially in regard to the monopoly of foreign trade, the national question, and the Workers' and Peasants' Inspection. He emphasised his agreement with Lenin on these various questions as well as on the fundamental question of economic planning. He referred to Lenin's devastating criticism of the Inspection, that is of Stalin, following on the Georgian affair which had been equally awkward for the General Secretary; he revealed the hostility of the Political Bureau to the publication and to the tenor of the last article written by Lenin. Kuibyshev, who had proposed to print a single issue of *Pravda* containing the article, to deceive Lenin while concealing his ideas from the country, had been placed at the head of the Control Commission, which had been perverted from its proper function and subordinated to the Secretariat, to that bureaucracy which it was its business to supervise. . . .

The Party knew nothing of all this, and, even later, was never to know much about this epistolary controversy, the cautious style of which ill concealed a cold violence restrained with difficulty. Neither side was anxious to shatter popular illusions about the men in power.

Meantime the Central Committee received on October 15th a letter signed by forty-six well-known personages, who expressed themselves in the same sense as Trotsky, some of them with reservations on points of detail. The greater part were former "Left" communists, with some representatives of "Democratic Centralism": Pyatakov, Preobrazhensky, Serebriakov, I. Smirnov, Antonov, Ossinsky, Bubnov, Sapronov, V. Smirnov, Boguslavsky, Stukov, Yakovleva, V. Kossior, Rafail, Maximovsky, and other well-known militants: Byeloborodov, Alsky, Muralov, Rosengoltz, Sosnovsky, Voronsky, Eugenia Bosch, Drobnis, Eltsin, etc. Rakovsky and Krestinsky, on mission abroad, had not been able to sign. Radek, in a separate letter, declared agreement with Trotsky to be indispensable.

The forty-six called for the convocation of a special conference to take the measures dictated by the circumstances, pending a Congress. Radek, on the other hand, urged the settlement of the difference within the Politbureau itself. He was just about to start for Germany, where the economic and political situation indicated the approach of a revolutionary upheaval, in consequence of the French occupation of the Ruhr, passive resistance and a currency catastrophe. He invoked the gravity of these events in support of his opinions.

But the prospects of revolution in Germany, confidently reckoned on by communists in all countries, provided a new motive of discord among Bolsheviks. The German Communist Party, subordinate in principle, like all national Communist sections, to the Executive Committee of the Communist International, was to follow in practice the instructions of the Russian Political Bureau, which exercised the predominant influence in the international Executive, and which alone disposed of the various resources essential to the revolutionary movement. Now there were contradictory opinions in the Political Bureau. Zinoviev, President of the Executive of the International, undecided without Lenin, hesitated and manœuvred, consulted Radek, who had the reputation of an expert, and sought a mean between premature action and sterile delay. Trotsky advocated offensive tactics, advised preparations for insurrection, and even the fixing of a date. Stalin, on the contrary, walked warily in his first essay in world politics. In August, he had written to Zinoviev and Bukharin as follows:

Should Communists strive, at the present stage, to seize power without the Social Democrats? Are they ripe for that? That is the question, in my opinion. In seizing power we had in Russia certain reserve resources: (a) peace; (b) the land for the peasants; (c) the support of the immense majority of the working class; and (d) the sympathy of the peasants. German Communists have nothing like that. They have, indeed, a Soviet country as neighbour, which we had not, but what can we give them at the present moment? If the

Government in Germany falls now, so to say, and the communists seize it, they will end in a smash. That, at the best. At the worst, they will be hewn in pieces. . . . The fascists are certainly not sleeping, but it is to our advantage for them to attack first; that will attract the whole working class to the communists. . . . Moreover, all our information indicates that fascism is weak in Germany. In my opinion we should restrain and not incite the Germans.

At this time the acute turn of events weakened Stalin's point of view. Secret information from Berlin convinced the Political Bureau of the imminence of social revolution. At the end of September preparations were hurried on for an expected "new October." German communists asked for a leader from Moscow, naming Trotsky. Consternation and annoyance on the part of Zinoviev, who offered himself! The Political Bureau refused both, choosing Radek and Pyatakov, who started in mid-October, when the internal crisis of Bolshevism was acute.

It was not the moment for a war on theories. This had been adjourned by common accord in order to concentrate attention on the new revolution on the march. The truce was short; it ended with the disappointed hopes of communist victory in Germany. On November 7th, on the occasion of the sixth anniversary of the Soviet Republic, *Pravda* published an article by Zinoviev, who in the name of the leaders and under pressure by Trotsky and the forty-six, announced "workers' democracy" within the Party, and opened a public discussion. Communists were free to speak.

After such a long period of silence the Party felt the need of self-expression, but dare not open their mouths for fear of reprisals. The "workers' democracy" of which Zinoviev spoke, prescribed in its statutes and its programme, and in the decisions of all the Congresses, notably of the Tenth, had for long been an empty phrase. There was no reason to expect a real change.

Outside the communist ranks, nobody was interested in a democracy reserved for privileged persons, for a tiny minority. At that time the Party only numbered 351,000 members, all officials with the exception of 54,000 workers who were favoured in the workshops. In addition there were 93,000 aspirants on probation, and the Young Communists. The discussion started dully. It was hard to overcome inertia and mistrust, hard to obtain the first articles, the sense of which was contained in the formula, "better late than never." The intervention of Preobrazhensky and Sapronov gave the polemic a start; an opposition of the Left on undetermined lines began to develop against the dictatorship of the triumvirate.

Simultaneously the Political Bureau sought to establish agreement among the leaders, and, on December 5th, they adopted a resolution giving satisfaction to Trotsky—on paper. In this document they praised the N.E.P., together with Trotsky's propositions at the Twelfth Congress in regard to the Gosplan, the general staff of the Socialist State, concentration of industry, and general rationalisation. They condemned "excessive material inequality" among communists, the "luxury" of some, the "bureaucratic narrowness" of others, the "demoralisation" of militants with a bourgeois tendency, and the "bureaucratisation" of the Party machine. Communists were promised workers' democracy, the right of criticism, liberty of investigation, appointment by election of their officials, representatives and committees. This was the "new course" demanded by a Bolshevist *élite*, by Trotsky and the forty-six, with the intention of applying it to their Party, to the trade unions, and to the Soviets, to the advantage of the whole working population.

There was still time to orient the revolution in the direction of a Soviet democracy, relative only, it is true, but real as far as it went. If the bureaucratic and militaristic tendency of the regime, the product of bitter civil war in an immense undeveloped country, had lasted beyond the conditions which gave it birth, it is certain that no human force would have been capable of bringing it to a full stop. The circumstances, historical and social, incontestably lessened individual responsibility in this matter. Nevertheless, three years of peace with other nations, and two years of comparative calm at home made it possible to embark upon a new stage. The democratic opposition understood this and worked for it. The triumvirate pretended to understand, but their mental reservations soon hardened. The

ill-informed majority gave their approval to both without clearly
understanding the divergencies. Clearly the "new course" could
only be realised by the collective intelligence and energy of the
Party; a handful of well-meaning men would be powerless
against the conservatism inherent in the machine. Failing this
unanimous effort, the specific characteristics of the former
Russia would reappear sooner or later under new forms, for they
were inevitable in any autocratic system established in the same
barbarous environment.

Evidently the "new course" could not be accomplished in a
day. The Party had to be prepared to resume the responsibility
for its own fate, together with the future of the revolution, and
to effect a fundamental transformation which would affect other
Soviet institutions. The prime movers in this matter must themselves be the active and vigilant agents for carrying into effect
the promises of the Political Bureau, and for re-educating the
members of the bureaucratised system to carry out the common
work. But instead of adopting this point of view, the new opposition decided to demand there and then a radical change in the
equipment of the Party, and the immediate election or re-election
of all its officials. Fearing that the prospect of democracy would
prove as evanescent as former hopes they wanted to secure the
destruction of the machine.

The opposition led by Preobrazhensky and Sapronov was
doomed in advance by this initial blunder in tactics. The threatened bloc felt it had a good case, and struck unsparingly. The
discussion opened quietly, but a storm developed, rousing the
50,000 "cells," the innumerable groups, the many committees
and the various higher organs of the Party. As many as thirty
columns of *Pravda* were filled daily with an arbitrary selection
of articles, resolutions and reports, misrepresenting the views
of the Left, perverting their plans, and spreading inaccurate or
tendencious information without giving an opportunity for
denial, refutation or explanation. There could be no doubt as
to the issue of the unequal struggle between the masters of the
machine for the formation of opinion, and a few unarmed militants. At the moment when their ideas were in the ascendant,

the impatient "oppositionists" courted the fate of their predecessors by their lack of political tact and their clumsy strategy.

Trotsky, who had been ill since the beginning of November, took no direct part in the debates. Outside a small circle of initiates, he was thought to be a supporter of the Political Bureau and the Central Committee. After one very cautious article, "Ideas on the Party," on the occasion of an anniversary, he only published two essays, "On Officialdom in the Army and Elsewhere" and "On the Connection between Town and Country," in the same sense as his earlier interventions in the Central Committee; but the underlying implications were not intelligible to the general public. Suddenly he thought it necessary to define his position with more frankness, and, without abandoning his diplomatic reserve or openly approving the Opposition, he addressed, on December 8th, a letter to the meeting of militants in Moscow, which was published two days later in *Pravda*.

Under the title of *The New Course* he commented on the resolution adopted with his support on December 5th, explaining his view of the dangers of bureaucracy and the possible degeneration of the "Old Guard" of Bolshevism. Against those who hoped once more to bury the workers' democracy, he demanded the dismissal of "mummified bureaucrats," and summoned the younger generation to emancipate themselves from passive obedience, servility, and careerism. "The new course should, as its first result, bring home to all that henceforward no one should dare to terrorise the Party."

This gave a sharp turn to the discussion. Attention was directed to Trotsky, whose attitude seemed to be different from what was commonly supposed; in spite of careful drafting, the letter confirmed the thesis of the malcontents. The triumvirate took fright at the implicit support given to the Opposition of the Left, and, interpreting it as a threat to themselves, resolved to seize the opportunity to discredit the principal adversary. Stalin gave the unexpected signal for personal attacks on Trotsky. The latter was faced with what he would have liked at all costs to avoid—an open struggle for the succession to Lenin.

3

ON DECEMBER 2nd, in the course of the public controversy, Stalin had delivered before the "enlarged assembly of group committees, group organisers, members of discussion clubs and bureaux of cells of the group of Krasnaya Presnia" (the lesser Party officials or candidates for permanent office), an address in his elementary schoolmaster style suited to a childlike audience. For the sake of greater clearness and simplicity, and so that nothing might be omitted, he proceeded by way of enumeration of ideas and arguments borrowed from Right and Left, not avoiding detailed repetitions and incontestable truisms. He listed five causes of the "defects in the internal economy of the Party," describing them imperturbably, first, second, third and so on. He then enunciated a series of eight remedies, developing them without haste, first, second, third and so on, down to the eighth. As usual he took pains to stand midway between the extremes, and carefully delivered his well-conned theme which his subordinates were carefully to recite to *their* subordinates. At the close of his discourse he referred politely, even deferentially, to Trotsky, whose name had been invoked in the press by an opponent. His discourse was only a paraphrase in anticipation of the general ideas embodied in the Resolution adopted by the Political Bureau three days later.

But after Trotsky's letter, there was a change of tone. On December 15th *Pravda* published an article by Stalin in which the leaders of the Left were taken to task, by insinuation and obscure allusions rather than by direct attack. "Among the Opposition, we see comrades such as Byeloborodov, whose *democratism* cannot be forgotten by the Rostov workers; Rosengoltz, whose *democratism* has long excited emotion in the Donetz Basin; Alsky, whose *democratism* is universally recognised," Etcetera. To sum up, he accused the new champions of workers' democracy of being no more democratic than himself in their current activities. As for Trotsky, he evokes his unorthodox past with an undercurrent of would-be irony.

As is apparent from his letter, Comrade Trotsky counts himself
as one of the Bolshevik Old Guard, declaring his readiness to share
in the responsibility arising from this fact, if charges of later
heresies were brought against the Old Bolsheviks. In expressing his
willingness for self-sacrifice, Comrade Trotsky no doubt displays
nobility of sentiment. Agreed. But I must undertake the defence
of Trotsky against himself, because, for reasons which will be
readily understood, he cannot and should not hold himself responsible for any later heresies of the original group of Old Bolsheviks.
His offer of sacrifice is no doubt a very noble thing, but do the Old
Bolsheviks need it? I do not think so.

This reference to the past had no particular inherent interest
and does not seem, *a posteriori*, especially aggressive. But, in the
atmosphere of that time, it was understood by "the machine"
as indicating a target and as an authorisation to strike; henceforward Trotsky was no longer to be immune from attack as
Lenin had been, and ambitious officials would know what was
expected of them. Behind the scenes the great leader of yesterday could be secretly disparaged and whispers of Bonapartism
were permissible.

The *troïka* did not yet feel strong enough to attack Trotsky
openly. It was to be enlarged for the conduct of the campaign
into a *semiorka*, a secret committee of seven members, by the
addition of Kalinin, Tomsky and Rykov of the Political Bureau,
also of Kuibyshev. They had their agents, emissaries, auxiliaries,
their cypher for correspondence, their own sectional discipline.
They disposed of considerable State resources, of all sorts of
means of persuasion, pressure, intimidation and corruption.
Lacking the intellectual resources of their adversaries, they enjoyed the compensating advantage of long experience of internal
strife and were not embarrassed by any scruple in attaining their
ends. Stalin held the threads of the conspiracy in his hand.

As compared with so formidable a coterie, determined to
maintain themselves in power at any cost, the opposition were
indefinite, and lacked cohesion and continuity of effort. Far
from constituting a fraction, as they had been accused of doing,
they acted intermittently, often as occasion offered and with
sharp changes of front, and were incapable of pursuing a steady

policy. Their spokesmen relied on individual initiative, without unanimity and sometimes in direct contradiction of one another. Instead of confining themselves to the actual question of democracy, a claim in harmony with the interests of the workers and the principles of communism, and the only battlecry which would keep awake the critical consciousness of the Party— Pyatakov, Preobrazhensky and I. Smirnov decided to create a diversion by discussing the most difficult problems of finance and industry. Ossinsky defended other ideas on similar subjects. Radek improvised more or less able spoken journalism. Sapronov and his friends fought ardently and rashly for "democratic centralism." Shliapnikov came forward once more, in disagreement with them all, in the cause of the old Workers' Opposition. Trotsky, confined to his bed, committed the irreparable mistake of laying himself open to blows he could not return, and had to endure all the inconvenience of the struggle without being able to hope for the smallest advantage to the cause to be defended.

The *troïka* easily got the better of such opponents. They were able to bribe the least determined, like Bubnov, and to punish the clumsiest, like Antonov, by nominating the one to the other's post as head of the political education department of the army. Others were neutralised by skilful nominations and punishments, some by promises and threats. The remainder were submerged in the sheep-like loyalty of the interested bureaucracy. In the complicated network of the meetings of the bureaux of the cells, enlarged group committees, conferences of responsible militants, etc., the officials, under the authority of the Secretariat, enjoyed an automatic preponderance. Working-class opinion, already misrepresented by open voting, because of the danger of victimisation, hardly penetrated through the six stages of Party organisation—cell, group, locality, province, republic, Soviet Union—the stages below the Central Committee, the seventh rung of the system.

In the last resort the triumvirate only had to diminish the importance of the man who towered above them in prestige, to disparage him sufficiently to destroy too flagrant a disproportion between the members of the Political Bureau. For that purpose Trotsky offered an adequate pretext by his cautious letter on *The New Course*, which said either too much or not enough. Too much, for a leader accepting responsibility for the regime; too little, for an opponent determined to reinstate forgotten truths and to reanimate a supine movement.

Nevertheless, Stalin's polemic created a very disagreeable impression on Soviet public opinion. No serious revolutionary admitted the suspicion cast on the most eminent personage of the revolution now that Lenin was gone. The triumvirate sensed the breath of general disapproval, and promptly manœuvred to appease anxiety.

On December 18th *Pravda* published a reassuring statement from the Political Bureau, briefly defending Stalin and roundly asserting that:

The Political Bureau denounce as malevolent invention the suggestion that there is in the Central Committee of the Party or in its Political Bureau any single comrade who can conceive of the work of the Political Bureau, of the Central Committee or its executive organs without the most active participation of Comrade Trotsky. . . . Believing friendly co-operation with Comrade Trotsky to be absolutely indispensable in all the executive organs of the Party and the State, the Political Bureau hold themselves bound to do all in their power to assure this friendly co-operation in the future.

As if by chance a *Letter from the Petrograd Organisation*, remarkably similar in terms, appeared on the same day:

Without concurring in the errors of Comrade Trotsky, the Petrograd organisation declare that, in agreement with the Central Committee of the Party, they naturally consider friendly co-operation with Comrade Trotsky in all the governing institutions of the Party to be indispensable. There has been, and probably will be again, more than one disagreement in the Central Committee. But certainly no comrade conceives of the governing institutions of the Party without the active participation of Comrade Trotsky.

The simultaneous appearance of formulas so closely in agreement leaves no doubt of the origin of these "spontaneous" utterances. Similarly, a flood of resolutions adopted in the most remote provinces and reproducing word for word the Moscow text, condemning the "sectionalism of the Opposition" and the "errors of Comrade Trotsky." The hierarchy of secretaries carried out their functions. Exceptions were not yet impossible, but nothing could alter the rule; when *Pravda* received from Kiev a resolution favourable to the minority, a certain Nazaretian, Stalin's secretary, falsified it by a stroke of the pen. Trotsky, Pyatakov and Radek, armed with the original document showing the falsification as irrefutable evidence, appealed to the Control Commission, which, in obedience to the all-powerful Secretariat, censured the plaintiffs, not the forger. The machine presented a united front, and the Opposition were much mistaken if they thought it vulnerable.

The triumvirate had no intention of losing Trotsky's collaboration in the Government. They were content with diminishing the prestige of the "organiser of victory" sufficiently to remove him from the plenary succession to Lenin, which they proposed to divide amongst themselves. They were no longer willing to serve in the second rank, and, indeed, they denied Trotsky's possession of the qualities which gave Lenin, the founder of the Party, his unique importance. Trotsky's supremacy would have meant, for them, at an early date, the advent of a new ruling group and the gradual elimination of the Old Guard of which they professed to be the nucleus. Faced with this eventuality they would shrink from no means to wear down Trotsky's influence and to strengthen their own dominance.

In spite of unlimited administrative pressure, the Opposition obtained half the votes in Moscow, because the "new course" expressed the democratic desires of the lower stratum of the Party. The young people in the communist universities, among others, rallied to their side. The revolutionary tradition was still maintained, beneath the cloak of bureaucratic obedience. But the hierarchy of secretaries, though still not perfectly organised, was already strong enough to break any attempt to threaten its existence. Sympathisers with the Left, charged with "deviation from the Right," with semi-Menshevism, with opportunism, and, finally, with "Trotskyism," were prevented, in the interests of the dictatorial demagogy, from sending delegates to the regional conferences supposed to reflect party opinion. Clearly, the course of the central conference arranged for January 1924, at which the Opposition would be reduced, by various artifices, to a minimum, was fixed in advance on the lines laid down in the offices of the Secretariat.

If circumstances as a whole favoured the machine, the Opposition nevertheless owed its defeat primarily to the illusions of its leaders. They need not have provoked a premature shock without counting the consequences, without fixing practicable objectives, or assuring themselves of sufficient chances before running the risk. At the start, they had undertaken the impossible in a frontal assault—without any preparation and at a moment of declining revolutionary enthusiasm—against a position impregnable to all but indirect attack. In no case would the quality of their theories have compensated their strategical blunders in method. At the best, this Party of 351,000 members, including some 300,000 officials, could not support an imprudent declaration of war against the bureaucracy. The timid action actually taken bore little resemblance to the high-sounding and aggressive phraseology used, which was empty and dangerous if it was not to be translated into effective attack.

But their mistakes in these circumstances were due to the deep-seated cause of their final defeat: the Bolshevist mystical theory of the Party "entirely apart from and above everything else," an abstract identity, essentially invulnerable. The Opposition were lost by their idealisation of the very evil they proposed to attack under another name, and it was in vain that they differentiated between the Party on the one hand and its organisation and leaders on the other, without in fact driving a wedge between them. Since the bureaucratic State and the bureaucratic Party were inextricably bound together and the communist monopoly was declared inviolable, the reform of the regime was only possible by the slow process of evolution or the rapid method of revolution; the Opposition could make up their minds neither for one nor for the other. Alone in complying with the constitutional fiction of the Party, openly mocked by the majority, they wanted to act rapidly without recourse to force, that is to say, with due respect to the forms of the Constitution, which were to be used for their destruction.

Trotsky, their responsible head, could not be ignorant of what his opponents, once aroused, might do. He had had to do with them in similar circumstances when Lenin was there to intervene and to prevent the worst. He had had experience of Stalin from the time of the Civil War onwards, in constant personal contact with him at the Political Bureau; he had known the other two even longer, since the bitter disputes in the emigration. Before the War of 1914 he had clearly seen in the Bolsheviks certain "negative aspects," which he defined as "theoretical formalism, legalist rigidity, a police-officer's distrust of historical evolution, egoism, and conservatism in organisation"— faults stereotyped after their accession to power and after the transformation of the Party into the framework of the State. He knew that, with Lenin's disappearance, Bolshevism would lose its great capacity for self-criticism, a source of life-giving energy which attenuated and to some extent compensated the original flaws.

Then, at what he thought the decisive moment, he took action to reinvigorate the Party, without taking into account the circumstances and the state of opinion, as if the Party conformed strictly to its statutes and principles, and its leaders to the laws of fair play. He repeated, in an exaggerated form, the tactical mistake he made in the trade unions discussion of 1921, by raising, indirectly, the question of the supreme power without any chance of settling it, thus arousing the hostility of his rivals without gaining anything by so doing. After having supported unanimity "at the top" and the roughest means of imposing it on the rank and file, he suddenly gave the impression of infringing that unanimity when he was not in a position to undertake the struggle. It is not certain whether he opposed the arbitrary arrest of Bogdanov (who had stood outside the Party since his rupture with Lenin and had devoted himself to scientific studies), who was imprisoned after the 1923 strikes on the bare suspicion of connivance with the Worker's Truth. However that may be, he associated himself with the severe repression of the intrigues of this dissident section and of the Workers' Group. Yet now he condemned police methods and demanded democratic reform in the Party. After the Political Bureau had met his demands, at any rate in theory, he appeared to be taking the offensive against his colleagues, perhaps so as not to leave to its own devices the Opposition, whom he had inspired but had failed to guide and restrain. But, if his published letter provided his supporters with arguments, it also provided the triumvirate with weapons against him and an admirable pretext. The inevitable retort put him on his defence. In the name of the interest of the Party he declined to reply to the campaign of defamation fomented by Stalin. Nevertheless he wrote three articles defining the grounds of his intervention, and, on the eve of the January conference, he collected them under the title of *The New Course*, with some additional chapters. By this hesitating procedure, he lost the advantages of silence. On the other hand, the lofty ideas, the subtle allusions, and the discreet polemic of the book were comprehensible only to a picked few, who did not weigh heavily in the bureaucratic scale; moreover the little pamphlet, published in a small edition, was very soon unobtainable, owing to precautions taken by Stalin. After this, on medical advice, he left for the Caucasus. . . .

On this disconcerting line of action, his own memoirs provide valuable comment drawn from the unpublished journal of his wife, N. Sedova.

Trotsky [she writes], was alone and ill, and had to fight them all. Owing to his illness, the meetings [of the Politbureau] were held in our apartment; I was in the adjoining bedroom and heard his speeches. He spoke with his whole being; it seemed as if, with every such speech, he lost some of his strength—he spoke with so much "blood." And in reply I heard frigid and indifferent replies. Everything had been settled beforehand. Why should they get excited? After each meeting of this kind, Leon Davidovich ran up a temperature; he emerged from the room drenched to the bone. . . .

Trotsky exhausted himself utterly in eloquent speeches to an audience of six, from whom he had nothing to expect but implacable hostility. In the meanwhile he was being busily discredited in Party circles. There could be no better proof that intelligence, culture, many-sided talent, powerful temperament and high character are not enough to make a great politician. Outstanding as was his personality, the Trotsky of the October Revolution and the Civil War had only reached his full stature as a man of action owing to his contact with Lenin.

Stalin, "endowed with all the astuteness that Trotsky lacked" —notes Max Eastman, the American communist writer and the scrupulously accurate annalist of this crisis—was then entering on the decisive phase of his arid career. The capture of the heritage of October did not demand the qualities of a Lenin and a Trotsky necessary for its achievement. There was no question at all of filling the place of a man who was irreplaceable, for Lenin's eminence arose from his brain, not from his functions. What was required was to have the last word in the Political Bureau, to have practical control of the Central Committee, which could arrange the composition of the Party Congress as it pleased. Stalin was to succeed in this by ranging against Trotsky a sort of syndicate of mediocre Old Bolsheviks, of whose moderate opinions he made himself the spokesman and whose faithful agent he pretended to be. The Political Bureau ordinarily sat once a week, and left the Secretariat, which met daily, a certain margin of initiative and interpretation. For the moment Stalin asked no more.

The Opposition did not have the elementary good sense to absent themselves from the Conference of January 1924, and found themselves reduced to three delegates with voting powers. Stalin played an important part. In his report on the "construction of the Party," he reproached the absent Trotsky with "six serious errors," commenting on these at great length. "First error": the publication of his letter on the "New Course" after the adoption of the official resolution. "Second error": the adoption of an ambiguous standpoint. "Third error": differentiating the Party and its machine. "Fourth error": ranging the younger generation against the older ranks and imputing degeneration to the latter. "Fifth error": describing the students as the most accurate barometer of the Party. "Sixth error": the demand for freedom of grouping within the Party. To the Oppositionists who had invoked an explicit decision on democracy from the Tenth Congress he replied by quoting a secret clause of this decision providing for the exclusion of the recalcitrants in certain cases of indiscipline.

In any case he showed some respect to "Comrade Trotsky, whom I should certainly not put for one moment on the same plane as the Mensheviks," but he consistently decried him. In his concluding speech he said: "We have taken all the necessary measures to ensure friendly co-operation with Trotsky, although I must say that it has not been at all easy to do so."

The *troïka* felt obliged to respect in Trotsky the famous name, which, together with Lenin's, personified the revolution among the Russian people and in international opinion. Zinoviev had declared in a report at Petrograd in December: "Comrade Trotsky's authority is recognised as completely as his merits. Amongst ourselves, there is no need to say more. But error is still error." On the other hand, it was necessary to reckon with the possibility, more and more remote indeed, of Lenin's restoration to health and return to business, and to do nothing irreparable in view of such an eventuality. In concluding the conference Kamenev announced: "Vladimir Ilyich is better," and he spoke of "the moment when Lenin will return to his post." The Opposition based great hopes on this vague prospect.

On his way to the Caucasian Riviera, Trotsky received a telegram at Tiflis station, on January 21, 1924. Stalin informed him of Lenin's death.

4

THE event was not unexpected; for more than a year Party members had been growing accustomed to the idea of the master's final disappearance. But the grief of his disciples was none the less poignant, especially after the disappointments of the immediate past. If the people as a whole, weighed down by poverty and weariness, received the news without apparent emotion, it was a hard blow to the communists, the only politically active section of Soviet citizens, and painful even to the most hardened.

Even though Lenin had no longer taken any part in the administration of the Party or of the State, his very existence nevertheless compelled some respect for a certain formal Marxist tradition in Bolshevism; it exercised some restraint over his heirs, too ready to sacrifice principles to the immediate interests of the Government, and over the ambitions centred on the inheritance of the revolution. After his death his successors, liberated from all doctrinal scruples, gave free course to their initiative, and gradually revealed the true nature of their domination.

The first measures taken by the Political Bureau imposed mourning in various forms on the whole population, with the intention of exploiting it for their own ends. At Moscow, the militia ordered flags to be hoisted and draped with crape, under pain of a fine, before any reason was given. Under the pretext of honouring the dead, the machine used the grossest artifices of fetichist religions, modernised by the most trivial advertisement. The press undertook to awaken a fictitious mysticism, to elaborate special ceremonies for the ignorant masses whom it was their mission to enlighten. Embalmed like that of a Pharaoh, the body of the great materialist revolutionary provided interminable spectacular ceremonies, was permanently exposed to the public curiosity, awakened, stimulated and encouraged by all possible means, captured and canalised in a quasi-perpetual file passing beside the corpse. A sanctuary erected outside the wall of the Kremlin commemorated the unconscious outrage of the Leninists on Lenin's memory. The crowd were attracted to it, the workers marched past under orders, children were brought there, until there began the endless procession of superstitious peasants mixed with incredulous tourists.

The tomb of Karl Marx in Highgate Cemetery is marked by a simple slab of stone. The ashes of Engels were scattered from an urn into the North Sea. But in the twentieth century, in the only country whose Government professed to be inspired by the *Communist Manifesto*, the corpse of an illustrious man was to be exhibited in great pomp in a funeral monument inspired by the mausoleum of Tamerlane. A contrast significant indeed, and that not only in externals; for the embalming of Lenin's remains found its counterpart in the Communist International in the mummification of its founder's work, the petrifaction of his thought, misunderstood by those who pretended to be its natural inheritors and its qualified interpreters, though they were even incapable of understanding the ancient saying that "Great men have the world for their sepulchre."

It was not enough for Lenin to have been a hero, a superman, a genius; the triumvirs of the *troïka* made him a kind of deity, whose prophets they aspired to be. In deifying him they were preparing their own future beatification. If they were to be believed, Lenin had known, seen, foreseen everything, had said and predicted everything. His portrait—full or half-length, full-face and profile, was modelled in statuettes, struck on medals, painted on signs, woven into handkerchiefs, printed, engraved, embossed, embroidered, reproduced in millions of copies—took the place of the icons, by way of rivalry between creeds. The same effigy was repeated on walls, in stations, on grocers' shops, on plate, ash-trays, cigarette-cases and ordinary household utensils. Pious, unaesthetic pictures illustrated in black and white and in colours a raw mass of pretentious literature in prose and verse. *Izvestia* published a requiem, between two ecstatic articles, above a drawing in bad taste. Some photographed Lenin's armchair, others collected relics. On all sides his name was given to towns, streets, institutions, factories, clubs, sports-grounds, and to innumerable places and things. Petrograd became Leningrad, and there were Lenino, Leninsk, Leninskaya, Leninakan, Leninsk-Kuznietsky, Ulianovsk, Ulianovka. Feverish zeal inspired the crassest commemorative plans. Under the thin varnish, already disappearing, of imported Marxist theory, there reappeared the familiar face of ancient, barbaric Russia.

In the midst of these noisy manifestations of collective delirium, in which Pharisaism was mixed with natural enthusiasm,

Stalin more than anyone else struck the note. On the eve of the funeral, at the Second Congress of the Soviets of the Union, he delivered a strange speech, perhaps the most typical among all his writings, for he left nothing to improvisation, and the text was carefully prepared in advance. Among paragraphs consisting of elementary statements, of well-worn truisms, of tiresome repetitions delivered with the note of absolute certainty which betrays ignorance—are intercalated litanies with Slavonic assonances, in which the former pupil of the Tiflis Seminary addresses the deified Lenin as "thou," and reveals his clerical mentality unabashed. At the end he assembles a series of fervent invocations, detached from their context, to make a sort of creed for the use of aspirants to the Leninist religion. The result is worth quoting:

In leaving us, Comrade Lenin commanded us to hold high and to keep pure the great name of Member of the Party. We swear to thee, Comrade Lenin, to honour thy command.

In leaving us, Comrade Lenin ordered us to conserve the unity of our Party as the apple of our eye. We swear to thee, Comrade Lenin, to honour thy command.

In leaving us, Comrade Lenin ordered us to maintain and strengthen the dictatorship of the proletariat. We swear to thee, Comrade Lenin, to exert our full strength to honour thy command.

In leaving us, Comrade Lenin ordered us to strengthen with all our might the union of workers and peasants. We swear to thee, Comrade Lenin, to honour thy command.

In leaving us, Comrade Lenin ordered us to strengthen and enlarge the Union of the Republics. We swear to thee, Comrade Lenin, to honour thy command.

In leaving us, Comrade Lenin enjoined on us fidelity to the Communist International. We swear to thee, Comrade Lenin, to devote our lives to the enlargement and strengthening of the union of the workers of the whole world, the Communist International.

A unique document, but only incomprehensible if one forgets one essential truth, expressed by Lenin: "We took Marxist doctrine ready-made from western Europe." With few exceptions, Bolsheviks in general had not assimilated modern revolutionary thought, whose terminology they had borrowed without being able to modify their inborn mentality as "people of a country doubly backward from the point of view of economy and of culture, people more tortured than any others by the past," as Gorky describes them. Thus, even before he was laid in his monumental grave, Lenin had been denied in theological terms, and through him Marxism, even down to the religious homage and solemn oaths of the adepts of State Bolshevism, the ideology of revolutionary decadence.

The six Commandments of the new church, formulated by Stalin in this speech, are prefaced by an *exordium*—in which the orator exalts the *esprit de corps* of his comrades in arms. No other document displays so completely what Lenin had denounced under the names of "com-lies" and "com-boasting." We may quote as an example the following passage:

> We communists are people of a special type. We are carved out of special matter. We are those who form the army of the great revolutionary strategist, the army of Comrade Lenin. There is no higher honour than to belong to this army. There is no loftier title than member of the Party of which Comrade Lenin was the founder and director. It is not given to everyone to be a member of such a Party. It is not given to everyone to endure the misfortunes and the storms involved in belonging to such a party. The sons of the working classes, sons of poverty and struggle, sons of incredible privations and heroic efforts—they are the men to be members of such a party. That is why the Leninist Party, the Communist Party calls itself the party of the working classes.

The intellectual level of language of this kind makes it unnecessary to report similar remarks of the same tenor by lesser personages. Under the French Revolution, after the assassination of Marat, similar extravagances are recorded. A petition was brought to the bar of the Commune proposing "that the body of Marat should be embalmed and borne through all the departments of France . . . so that the whole world might gaze on the remains of the great man"; an orator at the Cordeliers Club recited a canticle, "Heart of Jesus, heart of Marat"; some apologists desired to call Montmartre Montmarat to commemorate the *Ami du Peuple*. It was the naïve expression of a spontaneous outburst of popular emotion, not a cynical calculation of the leaders. Moreover the Sansculottes had no pretensions to historical materialism and did not quote *Das Kapital*. And at that time Robespierre was there to express regret that men were busied with "excessive hyperbole, ridiculous and vain images, instead of thinking of the remedies required by the state of the country," and to oppose the elevation to the Pantheon of Marat, who had consistently protested beforehand against this "violent insult," and had taken the precaution to write: "I would rather a hundred times never die than have to fear such a cruel outrage." There was a David to declare to the Convention: "His burial should be of the simplicity suitable to an incorruptible Republican who died in honourable poverty." There was an Hébert to say at the Jacobin Club: "There are men who would like us to believe that we should substitute one religion for another. They arrange processions and funeral ceremonies for Marat as was done for the saints. We have prevented that profanation; let us maintain our active vigilance. . . ."

In Soviet Russia, Krupskaya alone had enough conscience and enough true fidelity to Lenin's mind to urge restraint on the sectarists of the Leninist cult:

Do not let your sorrow for Ilyich find expression in outward veneration of his personality. Do not raise monuments to him, or palaces to his name, do not organise pompous ceremonies in his memory. . . . In his lifetime, he took so little account of that kind of thing, which distressed him. Remember how much poverty and disorder there still is in our country. If you wish to honour the name of Vladimir Ilyich, create creches, children's playgrounds, houses, schools, libraries, ambulances, hospitals, houses of refuge, etc., and, above all, realise his teachings in your lives.

But her honest and timid voice found no hearers in the tumult of official adoration. The Congress of Soviets decided to erect six monuments as a beginning. Riazanov, once scornful of "those who would like to transform the Red Square in Moscow into a cemetery, with funeral monuments into the bargain," would not thenceforward venture on such an allusion. The Society of Old Bolsheviks later on expressed its disapproval of funeral ceremonies with a great orchestra and idolatrous images, demanding for the dead the equality which society refuses to the living, but—with exceptions for such cases as Lenin's, thus admitting opportunist derogations from the principle. Trotsky objected, he says in his *My Life*, to the erection of the scandalous mausoleum, but not in public, and no one knew anything about it.

Lenin had unconsciously foretold his own fate in writing of the great revolutionaries persecuted during their lifetime:

After their death, an attempt is made to convert them into inoffensive icons, to canonise them, so to speak, to surround their name with an aureole of glory for the consolation and the deception of the oppressed classes, while the real substance of their revolutionary teaching is emasculated, its incisiveness dulled, and the doctrine debased.

His inheritors very soon fulfilled this clear-sighted judgment. They had good reason to seek a new name for the creed they substituted for the now decadent traditional Bolshevism.

Leninism was now declared to be the legalised and exclusive theoretical basis of the Soviet State. Formerly the term Leninists had been applied to the partisans of Lenin, himself a strict Marxist in theory, who would not have tolerated any other doctrine in his party. Henceforward Leninism was to be the strict retrospective and formal observance of the printed works of Lenin, irrespective of their relative value, their obscurities and contradictions. Lenin's *Works* became a new Bible, cut up into verses as if they contained definitive answers to all the problems of history.

According to the ideas of Stalin, communists throughout the whole world, in the present and in the future, would only have to repeat immutable, axiomatic phrases learned by heart (more or less correctly interpreted by accredited commentators) to save themselves the trouble of thinking, studying and understanding; they must also beware of any "deviation." The most innocent remark, the smallest chance word uttered by the great man became gospel for quotation outside the context. A special

Institute of Leninology received the task of deciphering the most insignificant scraps of Lenin's writing, and, if any had been thrown in the fire, to collect and scrutinise the tiniest fragments. Instinctively the Leninites respected the letter the better to stifle the spirit.

How many times had not Lenin courageously declared "We have been mistaken," and publicly acknowledged his mistakes, in order to discourage "com-boastfulness" and to encourage healthy self-criticism, at least within the Party ranks. At the last Communist Congress, Ossinsky had been able to observe, without incurring the charge of sacrilege, that even Lenin had at times been mistaken—a reflection indicating the usefulness of a reaction against sterile mimicry. "We do not desire to exclude the possibility of error in Lenin," Zinoviev had said in his report of the month before. Nevertheless the myth of Lenin's infallibility was created, less out of reverence for Lenin than as an *a priori* justification of the dangerous policy of his successors. In a quotation, rarely to the point, Stalin and the machine were always to find an effective silencer. And as a decisive argument in reserve for unbelievers, the G.P.U.

Between the old Bolshevism and the new Leninism there was properly speaking no breach of continuity. Lenin's death hastened an evolution already commenced, developing phenomena of which the beginnings were evident during the Civil War. In the tactics and organisation of the Party many Russian elements which had nothing to do with Marxism had for a long time been tending to push into the background ideas acquired in the school of western socialism. The Muscovite past developed into the Soviet present, often under unexpected aspects, in ordinary life. Six years of revolution had not inculcated in a convulsed society either respect for the person, the sense of individual responsibility or consciousness of the rights and duties of the citizen. On the contrary, many Bolsheviks who had been in contact with European mentality before October were to find themselves "Russified" after the Kronstadt mutiny, impregnated with the special psychology of the country in which, formerly, according to Gorky's summary, there flourished "absolute rule,

the enslavement of man, cynical falsehood and bestial cruelty."
A primitive and ill-digested sociology, gradually reduced to
naïve schemata, offered no resistance to the inveterate habits of
a society more than a century behind the evolution of the
civilised world, in which rapid industrial advance here and there
contrasted with mediaeval conditions still surviving.

Even in Lenin's lifetime, the combination of imported Marxian
and local ideas had yielded strange results: for example, the
kind of social alchemy by which the Party expected to raise the
general level by fixing the proportions of workers, peasants, and
intellectuals; the Leninist prejudice of a new kind of original
sin, imputing to individuals as a crime their non-plebeian birth;
the habit of leading out the workers in street demonstrations
without telling them the reason, of treating them as flocks
hemmed in by drivers with the threat of punishment in case of
evasion, and of dictating to them regularly, as slogans, stereotyped formulas of approval or blame in the columns of a newspaper. These examples show persisting peasant ignorance beneath the heavy phraseology of so-called determinism.

Bolshevism was a Russian simplification of Marxism, appropriate to the conditions of a vast rural country with clearly
divisible classes; it met the necessities of the time and the place
for the revolutionary conquest of power. After the victory
Lenin had gradually to purge it of its initial programme, under
pressure of circumstances, and to abandon for the time being the
democratic ideology borrowed from Marx. Excessive schematis-
ing, due mainly to the limitations and ignorance of his followers,
deformed it to the verge of caricature. Leninism was to embody
an even narrower version of impoverished post-revolutionary
Bolshevism, a fresh step away from authentic Marxism, of which
it retained the "straw of words" while losing the "grain of
reality"; it was in the end to develop into a complicated theology,
with its dogma, its mysticism, and its scholasticism.

Stalin constituted himself its first classical author with his
pamphlet, *Foundations of Leninism*, a collection of lectures
delivered to the "red students" of the Communist Sverdlov University at the beginning of April 1924. This laborious compila-

tion, in which plagiarisms alternate with quotations, displays nothing of Lenin's critical faculty. All that is living, apposite, conditional, and dialectical in the work drawn upon becomes passive, absolute, affirmative, imperative and categorical in this manual for use as a catechism, which, moreover, contains misinterpretations. Signed by anyone else the dull little book would have passed unnoticed among many others. But as the Secretary of the Party, Stalin could make its perusal obligatory on candidates for admission, who were subject to periodical weedings out and were compelled to take elementary lessons in theory at which they learned by heart abstract aphorisms. More than two hundred thousand workmen, most of them politically uneducated, were admitted all at once, at the time of national mourning, into the Communist Party to "improve its social composition," and Stalin's lectures were to be used in their education. "A combination of Russian revolutionary inspiration and the practical spirit by the American," was, according to the professor of Leninism, Lenin's "style of work," and should form the "perfect type" of Leninist.

In his final chapter, Stalin could not forego a hit at Trotsky, whom he had already disparaged on the weak pretext of the "permanent revolution." In derision of Trotsky's schemes of state-planning, he said: "Who does not know that disease of 'revolutionary' construction, whose cause is a blind faith in the power of schemes, in the decree that is to create and arrange everything." Perhaps he had forgotten the letter in which Lenin approved Trotsky's "sensible idea" of the State Planning Commission, perhaps he pretended ignorance of it in the interest of his campaign of insinuation. However that may be, vigilant hostility towards Trotsky can be read between the lines, revealing the implacability of the writer.

5

ON HIS return from the Caucasus, Trotsky had lost none of his prestige outside the Party. On the contrary, the conflict among the leaders rather brought him additional consideration dictated

by very various sentiments. The expectation of an indefinable
lessening of pressure, aspirations towards greater well-being,
desire for change, need of liberty—all these were condensed in a
vague hope of which he became the incarnation in spite of himself. The applause with which he was everywhere received,
which could not be mistaken for the ovations prescribed for
officials, took on the significance of a spontaneous plebiscite.
Advanced youth, apparently impermeable to the intrigues of
power, hailed him simply as the best man, in spite of the artificial
fog created to deceive them.

But, in Party circles, the *troïka* had taken the opportunity
in his absence further to undermine his position and to continue their disparagement of a non-existent "Trotskyism." A
new publication, the *Bolshevik*, produced especially to fight
Trotsky and his supporters, ostensibly for scientific principles,
in enormous solid articles, made it its task to preserve "the
purity of Leninist principles," evidently threatened by any
thinking brain, and proclaimed, in a first combative editorial:
"We were, are, and shall be, hard as a rock." Official instructions, whispered from the highest to the lowest in the hierarchy
of secretaries, suggested ways of showing zeal at the expense
of the Opposition. Omission of Trotsky's name from a list of
the honorary presidents of a meeting, the removal of his portrait from an office, denunciation on all occasions of his "errors"
or "bourgeois heresies," might serve to strengthen a man's position or advance his career. To be suspected of so-called
"Trotskyism" was to run the risk of losing livelihood, employment, lodging and daily bread, at a moment of extensive unemployment and a housing crisis, in a State in which the employee
is, more than anywhere else, in every respect at the mercy of
authority.

After Lenin's death, the reactionary selection of officials
undertaken by Stalin after his advent to the Secretariat took a
rougher turn. The Forty-Six, reduced to silence by administrative measures, more or less scattered and intimidated, had submitted or repented, thanks to the working of the nominations
system. The quite recent resolutions on workers' democracy

were so many "scraps of paper" to be buried in dusty files. The promised "new course" was a dangerous chimera, soon to become treason against Bolshevism. At the Revolutionary Military Council, on which Unschlicht and Frunze had taken the places of Voroshilov, Lashevich and others, Stalin in person made open preparations for the eviction of Trotsky. The latter did not even attempt to defend himself to safeguard a principle, he neither defended his colleagues nor attempted to state clearly in public the principles at stake. His army colleague, Skliansky, unexpectedly relieved of his post, was replaced by Frunze. In the name of party discipline, Trotsky was silent, and Pyatakov, the principal representative of the Opposition beside him, was the docile instrument of Stalin's manœuvres.

The Thirteenth Congress of the Party was to realise to the full the ideal of the triumvirate, a hundred per cent unanimity, at least in appearance, of an organisation seriously described as "monolithic." Trotsky himself was not among the delegates. With some other non-conformers, he only had consultative powers in his capacity of member of a central organisation. Nevertheless that did not decide him to stand apart from these machinations. At the opening session, the Assembly transported itself to Lenin's mausoleum to gaze on the corpse, after a march past of young pioneers (children belonging to communist associations), ready to swear fidelity to "Lenin's will." The customary addresses, congratulations, and the handing-over of flags and presents by so-called workers' delegations, received exaggerated importance, contributing not a little to deprive the Congress of any deliberate character. Last of all a "non-party" worker, sent as if by chance from the "Trotsky factory," urged protection for the Old Guard of Bolshevism. Although not a single spectator was misled by these proceedings, Party loyalty forbade making fun of the spectacle, and even the Opposition treated with respect the new ritual, fully developed for the first time. Four months earlier, it had been possible for Riazanov at the preceding conference to refer to the "Old Bolsheviks, called by Lenin old imbeciles"; such irreverence was henceforward out of the question. In order to combat a ridiculous proposal for the transfer of the remains of Karl Marx from London to Moscow, the old *frondeur* prudently made some flattering allusions to Stalin.

Interest was concentrated on Trotsky, whose silence was more disquieting than words. To speak before a regimented audience of this kind would have been not only to waste time, but to imply recognition of the sham debate as real and to sanction a huge bureaucratic imposture. After long hesitation, Trotsky was weak enough to yield to the entreaties of his friends and to walk into the snare set for him.

"Received with a storm of applause," according to the official press, he stood on the defensive and, with extreme caution, he cited the excellent but derisory resolution of December 5th, with quotations from his enemies to corroborate his own statements. Bukharin, especially, had described the internal state of the Party in accurate terms, without suspecting the importance of his statements: "In most cases, elections have become pure formalities; not only are votes taken without preliminary discussion, but on the single question of 'Who is against?' And, as a vote against authority puts the delegate in an awkward position, the matter is settled." Bukharin's whole statement corroborated the current accusations of *a dictatorship over the Party*, following the dictatorship over the proletariat. After quoting from it at length, Trotsky then referred to Kamenev in support of his opinions on state-planning: "We may make many mistakes if we do not set before us the aim of co-ordinating a plan for the whole of our national economy." By this rhetorical method, the triumvirate was refuted by one of its members, especially Stalin by Kamenev, and Trotsky maintained his views intact though with many formal precautions.

But to speak without incurring violent contradiction in the atmosphere of distrust, assurances of loyalty must be given. Trotsky proposed to provide these in two ways. First, by praise of the excellence of Soviet democracy in the recent affiliation of 240,000 workers to the Party, "Lenin's levy." This levy, he thought, brought the Party nearer towards being an elected party. Had he not just shown, with Bukharin's words in support, the inanity of elections within this privileged party, and still more on its circumference? Could he fail to recognise the real motives of this collective enthusiasm under the regime of which he was beginning to know the disadvantages in his own person? The new adherents joined the Party, not by elective affinity, but as a legitimate measure of defence, on account of a natural anxiety to secure work, some semblance of civic rights, and other moral and material advantages. They were not free to choose or to take a different course. They were far from representing the pick of the working class, and were, for the most part, illiterate; their adhesion did not presage any regeneration of the degenerate Party. Their recent conversion gave them no authority to criticise, still less to oppose. These neo-Bolsheviks had been instructed by the hierarchy of secretaries in catch-words of the worst type of religious Leninism, and could have nothing in common with the communism of Marx and Lenin. In any case, in Russia the word communist does not mean an adept in communism, but a member of the Party, the party in power and the only legal party. That is why the miraculous "push" only took place after the decision to open the doors of this exclusive party, and to close them again after the desired number of recruits had been admitted. In his report on the organisation, Stalin had stated to the Congress that in certain provinces seventy per cent of members were politically illiterate, on a general average fifty-seven per cent, and "Lenin's levy" were drawn from a still lower stratum. (Some days after he admitted to sixty per cent of political illiterates *before* "Lenin's levy" and eighty per cent *afterwards*.) Nevertheless, Trotsky entirely concurred in the aberration of the Party, going so far as to put a false interpretation on the accession of members, and thus subscribing in advance to the most reactionary decisions of the "elected Party," the instrument of the dictatorship of the triumvirate.

He added a profession of faith completing his implicit retraction of any critical conception of the Party:

None of us desires or is able to dispute the will of the Party. Clearly, the Party is always right. . . . We can only be right with and by the Party, for history has provided no other way of being in the right. The English have a saying, "My country, right or wrong," whether it is in the right or in the wrong, it is my country. We have much better historical justification in saying whether it is right or wrong in certain individual concrete cases, it is my party.... And if the Party adopts a decision which one or other of us thinks unjust, he will say, just or unjust, it is my party, and I shall support the consequences of the decision to the end.

This abstract reasoning amounted to giving a free hand to Stalin, master of the Party through the machine, master of the State through the Party.

About a dozen suitably chosen speakers undertook to refute Trotsky. With one accord they accused him of parliamentarism and diplomacy, reproached him with lack of frankness and many other things. The 1,164 delegates would perhaps have taken their turn at the tribune in repeating the same lesson, if Krupskaya had not interrupted the tale. Without agreeing with the Opposition, she expressed disapproval of the disloyal attacks of the triumvirate, fearing the consequences for the revolution of a war to the knife between communists. Immediately after Lenin's death, she had written to Trotsky to assure him of "Vladimir Ilyich's" warm regard for him and of her own affection. She spoke at the Congress on the side of the majority, but in order to make it clear that the comedy had lasted too long. With a bad grace, Stalin and Zinoviev decided to end it, though they deplored the "Christian Socialism" of Lenin's widow.

In his concluding speech, Stalin reiterated all that had been said in the course of the exhaustive discussion. He enumerated four points on which the Opposition were in error, and three errors in principle of Trotsky's. Incidentally, he gave a twist to Trotsky's thesis of the final infallibility of the Party: "The Party, says Comrade Trotsky, makes no mistakes. That is not true. The Party often makes mistakes. Ilyich taught us to instruct the Party to learn from its own mistakes." Stalin went on to say: "Our Party has become the elected organ of the working classes. Show me any other party of this kind. You cannot, for there is none in the world. But it is strange that even so powerful a party does not please the Opposition. Where in this world will they find a better? I fear that they will have to look for one in the planet Mars." The rest of the speech is on the same argumentative level. One is tempted not to quote from an author of this kind, whose works provide the reverse of an "embarrassment of choice." Conscious that in his party votes no longer depended on the views expressed, Stalin sought neither to demonstrate nor to convince; he merely affirmed. And behind each affirmation could be felt the threat.

In conformity with the careful arrangements made by the Secretariat, the Congress declared what Zinoviev called a hundred per cent Bolshevist unanimity. Stalin's bureaucratic system was nearing perfection. All that remained to be done was to foresee and to prohibit misunderstandings such as the inopportune storm of applause which had greeted Trotsky's appearance, though this could have no possible effect on the course of events. The new Central Committee had eighty-seven members, including deputy-members, and the Control Commission more than 150. But instead of enlarging the governing oligarchy, as Lenin had mistakenly supposed, this numerical increase reduced still more the importance of the two committees, to the advantage of their small bureaux and, in the last resort, of the General Secretary.

From this new test Stalin emerged with a great advantage. By a decision of the former Central Committee, adopted at his instigation, he had succeeded in avoiding the reading of Lenin's *Testament* to the Congress, in spite of Krupskaya's belated insistence. It was communicated only to certain selected delegates, at a separate meeting, with explanatory comments to diminish its importance. The "old man" was sick, not *au courant*, and ill-informed by those around him. . . . At the first session of the Central Committee Stalin proffered his resignation, which was of course refused under the circumstances; most of the members owed their posts to him, or were afraid to lose them by incurring his hostility. Any opposition would have been useless at the time and would have provoked reprisals; Trotsky dare no more disturb unanimity than anyone else.

"Hundred per cent Bolshevist unanimity" had still to be affirmed by the Communist International. The majority of the International Executive would have taken the side of the Opposition, if the question had been raised. That was clear from the individual opinions of the members. In theory their decision outweighed any contrary opinion of a national section or "fraction." In fact, the Third International, created by the Bolshevik Party, remained subordinate to it. Intellectually it was relatively, and morally, absolutely dependent, and its recent formation on the sole initiative of Lenin made it impossible for it to withdraw itself from the discipline of Moscow, until it attained maturity. Zinoviev took care not to consult the Executive, which had no other channel for expressing its opinion. The Fifth World Congress of Communism was arranged for June 1924. The preliminary work was carried out according to the rules and practices current in the Soviet Union, so as to create a world organisation in the image of the mother section. It was accomplished in less than six months under Zinoviev's direction, simultaneously with operations of the same kind conducted by Stalin in all the Russias in the name of "bolshevisation."

With rare exceptions, the Communist parties of Europe, America and Asia stood in need of subsidies from the Executive, that is to say from the Bolshevik Party. This irresistible pressure induced a kind of solidarity. In the more independent sections, where some resistance was attempted, there were plenty of opportunities of restoring order, if necessary, by surgical operations. If there were neither good nor bad pretexts, they could be invented. The International knew nothing about the realities of the Soviet system, and Trotsky did not feel he had the right or the strength to enlighten it. Nevertheless Zinoviev's emissaries spread treacherous statements about the "new Danton," even the "new Bonaparte." There was even talk of a plot amongst the *Kursanti* of the Kremlin. A severe crisis in Germany, following on the abortive revolutionary movement, and the general depression, fanned the plans of the triumvirate. Long experience in manipulating internal quarrels and sectional intrigue, in handling money contributed by the liberal bourgeoisie or secured from profitable expropriations before they had had a State Budget at their disposal, and the habit of treating their own militants as mercenaries and of exploiting human credulity, had enabled the inventors of Leninism to secure their own ends— deceiving the simple, neutralising waverers, inspiring mediocre minds with fanaticism, corrupting politicians, and isolating the more honest and thinking men.

The "Congress of Bolshevisation" endorsed the results they had accomplished, enabling them to transfer Leninist methods to the international arena, to generalise throughout the revolutionary movement the topsy-turvy method of selection adopted by Stalin in the Soviet Union. The Soviet method of ceremonies, parades, and endless functions was adopted for the edification of the sceptical and for strengthening the morale of the delegations. The day after the pompous opening at the Grand Theatre, the Congress marched solemnly to music to hold a session in the Red Square around the Lenin mausoleum, to hear and discuss in the open air the report on the first motion in the proceedings, in the presence of hundreds of thousands of workers, also provided with bands, after the inevitable inspiring defile past the corpse. The whole thing had a magic spontaneity, and took place during factory working-hours. The usual "non-party" man and the other inevitable personages to be seen at all the Moscow congresses of that time, appeared to recite their congratulations and to distribute banners in the course of the session to stimulate the fervour of those present. A wave of tense fanaticism prevented any cool or reasoned statement on the Russian question.

On this occasion, Trotsky was wise enough not to be provoked into controversy. He had understood at last. But, to complete the comedy, the assembly which had just disavowed him invited him to draw up its concluding manifesto. It proved to be the last of the great messages, annual events since the foundation of the International, from Trotsky's hand. A year earlier, Clara Zetkin had written of Lenin and Trotsky: "The Congress paid its tribute of gratitude and admiration to the personal, imperishable work of these two illustrious leaders of

the Russian Revolution and of the world proletariat." But now
the idea of such homage entered nobody's head, though the
hurrahs of the crowd for Trotsky are still noted at this date in
the Communist Press.

Stalin, present but unobtrusive, took part for the first time
in the proceedings of the International. Whether because of
ignorance of foreign languages, or unpreparedness on foreign
affairs, or for both reasons, and from native caution, he did not
ascend the tribune. He was only heard in the Polish Committee, in which Russian was spoken by the delegation directly
concerned. Of his speech in committee we must note the retrospective justification of the treacherous attacks on Trotsky and
the Opposition during the recent conflict. "First," he said,
"history knows no struggle without its victims. Secondly, opposition cannot be defeated without shaking the authority of its
leaders. Thirdly, complete victory over opposition is the sole
guarantee against schism." He was more concerned with discrediting an opponent than with refuting him. It is not ideas,
but individuals, that count. Criticism is a crime against the security of absolute power; it must be stifled, to prevent any ultimate
fissure in the dictatorship party.

6

THE heresy hunt was indeed resumed with greater zest after the
"Bolshevisation" Congress of 1924. Taking the utmost advantage of the attitude of obedience and patience imposed on the
opposition parties in all countries by Trotsky's tactics, the ruling
section gradually but thoroughly deprived the International of
its *élite*. First in Paris and Berlin, and then from New York to
Shanghai, all communists who persisted in distinguishing between discipline and servility, all men capable and guilty of
independent or original thinking were henceforth to be treated
as suspect, denounced as opportunists, classed with counter-
revolutionaries, and expelled, first singly and then in groups.
Thus a continuous series of expulsions and splits eliminated, in
turn and by differing methods, the initiators of the contemporary

communist movement in the two hemispheres. It soon became
clear how right Rosa Luxemburg had been in maintaining, in
opposition to Lenin, that the foundation of the new International was premature, that it could not live by itself or survive
its founder. The Communist parties were transformed into
ramifications of the Soviet State, under a common autocracy,
with identical structural faults and defects in detail. The *troïka*,
determined to deprive Trotsky of all outside support, might
have chosen to sacrifice an organisation which was parasitic and
had no future; in fact they abandoned the principle, while
maintaining the instrument.

In the Soviet Union, to have abstained from denouncing
Trotsky was sufficient reason for disgrace, for removal from
any political position, and often for the deprivation of work
and livelihood. But neither annoyances nor persecution put a
stop to the increasing popularity of the hero of October and of
the Civil War among the small active portion of the urban
population, and especially among revolutionary youth. Special
pamphlets, in which hired scribblers sought to revive former
controversies and to mystify the reader by overwhelming the
living Trotsky with dead quotations from Lenin, were scattered
broadcast, but to no effect, for no one took any notice of the
spiteful attacks. Neither the *History of a Deviation* by S. Kanachikov, and its still more insignificant imitations, nor the articles
of the numerous writers in the entourage of the *troïka* carried
weight against Trotsky's important speeches and memoranda
on the principal questions of the day: the hegemony of the
United States of America, the decadence of England, the crisis
of the German Revolution, the multiple problems of the Far
East. Party study-circles had no other new materials for study
except these great panoramic dissertations, intellectually far
superior to the combined production of all the brains of the
"Leninist" Central Committee. People queued up to hear them,
and the verbatim reports in the press were eagerly sought after.

All this exasperated the uneasy inheritors of Lenin's power,
on the watch for the slightest blunder on the part of their
adversary. But Trotsky took care to avoid occasion for fresh

discords, avoiding thorny questions and personal friction. He spoke of all sorts of things except Soviet Russia. Nevertheless, his indomitable verve as a polemist did in some of his writings find expression in allusions in which subtle scorn and implicit irony, too recondite to be understood by his ill-informed hearers, were intelligible enough to the parties concerned. His valuable collection of biographical material, *Lenin*, conveyed the impression that the peace re-established in the Party was nothing more than a truce, an impression confirmed by the malevolent reviews. For the initiated it was clear that the defeated Opposition did not admit defeat and hoped to reverse it, though they had no very clear idea how; they seemed to hope for a revival of the thought and conscience of the Party, forgetting that the Party, bureaucratised as it was, and hampered now by 240,000 ill-informed neophytes, bore little resemblance to the ideal. In spite of his notorious incompetence on the subject, Stalin in September contributed to the "literary campaign" (sic) against Trotsky a long article "On the International Situation"—his first essay on this theme. Refuting the thesis of Trotsky and Radek on the delay of world revolution, he affirmed confidently that "the workers are moving towards revolution and demand revolutionary leaders." The proof lay in the "decisive victory of the revolutionary wing of the Communist parties in Germany, in France and in Russia, and in the increasing activity of the left wing of the English workers' movement. . . ." The pacifism of the democratic governments of Europe "may be expected to lead not to the strengthening but to the weakening of the bourgeois power, not to the adjournment of the revolution to an indefinite period, but to its acceleration." Pacifists and democrats alike were seeking to "deceive the masses by sonorous phrases about peace under cover of which they were preparing for a new war." As for Social-Democracy, it was, objectively considered, "the moderate wing of fascism." Similar statements, more vigorously expressed, adorn Zinoviev's prose at this period.

Thus, once more in 1924, Stalin continued to announce the imminence of revolution in Europe and to confound dawn

with sunset, in spite of the evidence and of the lessons to be
learned from the many years of persistent refutation by events
of the over-hasty prophecies of Bolshevism. His Leninism consisted in repeating in and out of season what Lenin had said
with more or less justification in other circumstances when
error was not without excuse. He was under no necessity to
reconsider his theses or to give them more profound study, for,
in fact if not in Soviet law, no one was permitted to question
his assertions, evidently agreed upon in the *semiorka*. Kamenev,
Kalinin, and others besides Zinoviev took them up in their own
way, though they were quite ready to say the opposite if the
signal were given to do so.

But four months later (January 27, 1925), with the remarkable facility for contradiction which the Bolsheviks regard as
transcendental politics, Stalin was to think better of the relative stability of capitalism and the ebb of the revolutionary
tide. And at the end of March in the same year, he refuted
himself, without ceasing to maintain his own infallibility.
"Capitalism has succeeded in recovering from the post-War
shock"; the international economic position evidenced the success of capitalistic reconstruction, and, finally, "there is no
doubt that in Central Europe, in Germany, the period of the
revolutionary tide has closed." The chorus of Leninists followed
him as one man in his retractation, maintaining that they had
never changed their minds. Eventually the representatives of
the so-called revolutionary wing of which Stalin boasted, the
"revolutionary leaders" of 1924 in Germany, in France and
elsewhere were almost all of them expelled from the International as being unworthy, opportunist or traitors.

Meanwhile, many alarming signs of a new crisis appeared in
the "Soviet Fatherland." Absorbed in their pedantic and meaningless controversies, the dictators had neglected the economic
situation of the country and the condition of the working classes.
Superficial optimism and propaganda, which failed to conceal
a policy dictated from day to day, were useless for the solution
of the difficult problems confronting the revolution.

The stagnation of industry at a level below the meagre pre-

War standard deprived the State of material resources, workmen of the necessaries of life, and peasants of manufactured goods. The monetary reform of 1924, which substituted the gold-chervonetz for the depreciated rouble, was carried out at the cost of the proletariat. Semi-starvation wages were often paid months behind-hand, sometimes in unsaleable goods, sometimes in coupons on almost empty co-operative stores. The *troïka* found no other expedient except the restoration of the State monopoly of alcohol, which had been carried through the Central Committee against the opposition of Trotsky and Krupskaya, the latter invoking in vain Lenin's opinion on the national poison. The only method of covering further deficits was to put further pressure on the workers in town and country.

The wretched wages were reduced in various indirect ways: obligatory deductions under pretext of "voluntary" subscriptions, the extension of the piecework system, lowering of the rates of payment simultaneously with increase of the standards of individual production under a complicated system of co-efficients and categories. Increasingly severe police repression, together with the fear of unemployment, imposed silence on the working classes, who had no organisation for self-defence, since the trade unions were annexes of the bureaucratic State. Stalin had confessed in 1923 that the number of trade unionists had decreased from 6,000,000 to 4,800,000, "a smaller but more serious number" which, however, had been "recently swollen by an almost nominal membership." This admission was still relevant to the actual circumstances, for the fictitious character of membership continued with an external increase in membership due to compulsory registration. In 1924, Stalin rectified the statistics, bringing down the figure to 4,300,000, a figure less than the "more serious" one of the year before, without more real significance. On paper the trade unions advanced from 5,000,000 "members" in 1924 to more than 10,000,000 in a few years, the number of trade unionists exceeding at one time those qualified for membership, for the trade unions, like the soviets, had ceased to be realities. The workers looked neither for protection nor for help to the wasteful administration in the hands of a machine of 27,000 officials, strictly subordinate to the Party bureaux. They could hope for nothing better from the privileged communist caste. The result was disaffection directed against the regime.

Discontent was no less serious in the countryside, lacking industrial products, robbed of the fruits of individual labour by low fixed prices for grain, and loaded with taxation collected under inexorable pressure. The official communist documents mention, among other causes of distress, the consequences of the last famine, the insufficient harvest of 1924, agricultural unemployment (Preobrazhensky calculated the surplus agricultural labour at twenty million). To these causes were added abuse of power and denial of justice on the part of the village authorities, illegal action of all kinds by the local pseudo-soviets; requisitions, confiscations, impositions, arbitrary arrests, all these aggravated by mass deception and malversation to the prejudice of the State. In his *History of the Communist Party*, compounded as it is of the most barefaced falsifications, E. Yaroslavsky, one of Stalin's officials, is compelled to admit the "abstention of the peasants from the elections" in the autumn, and says that "the majority of the population did not take part in them." In fact the minority ceased to vote, for the whole system was reduced to a sham. The peasants, robbed and ill-treated, lost patience and began to meet bureaucratic tyranny by crimes against communists, the assassination of the "rural correspondents" of the press, whom they hated as spies. The Party condemned the action of the *kulaks* accordingly, but it was too easy to confound under this term anybody and everybody. "We are too apt to call any peasant who has enough to eat a *kulak*," confessed Zinoviev in June 1924. There was a minor civil war, of which the most acute manifestation was in Georgia (August to September 1924), a real armed insurrection.

If there were any doubt in Moscow of the significance of the phenomenon, Stalin dissipated hesitation by the one word: "Kronstadt." And, just as in 1921, there was an inglorious episode in the history of Bolshevism. Georgian Social-Democracy, profoundly divided in opinion on this question, certainly had something to do with this unhappy attempt at insurrection.

But there are many indications that police provocation was the decisive factor, that is to say, that the Tiflis Cheka, well informed of the popular dissatisfaction, and employing secret agents in local socialist circles, urged on the rising at a convenient moment in order to stifle it successfully.

In a fortnight, prompt and brutal repression "liquidated" the bloody insurrection, which had gone further than the police had intended and revealed the full gravity of the situation in the provinces. Action unprecedented even in the most tragic moments of the revolution was taken. Five members of the Social-Democratic Central Committee, among them N. Khomeriki and V. Djugeli (who had nothing to do with the insurrection, for they were imprisoned before it took place), were executed without trial, with some dozens of other persons neither more nor less responsible.

Stalin, at the centre of things, and his accomplice Ordjonikidze on the spot, had coldly designed and carried out the cruel manœuvre, perhaps taking advantage of the circumstances to avenge personal scores with their former rivals in the Caucasus. Recalling Lenin's indignation against the action of the *"Dierjimordes"* against their communist comrades at Tiflis, it is easy to see who was responsible for the bloodshed in this affair, without the assistance of the explanations of the vanquished. Moreover, Stalin did not hesitate to make the admission in his own way when he said: "What has happened in Georgia may happen throughout Russia, unless we make a complete change in our attitude to the peasantry." Molotov for his part declared: "Georgia provides a startling example of the breach between the Party and the mass of the peasantry in the country." On another occasion Stalin, in a speech in which he declared the necessity of criticism in words borrowed from Lenin, placed the onus of the errors committed on subordinate officials:

Either non-party peasants and workers must be able to criticise us, or we shall be subjected to criticism in the form of insurrection. The Georgian insurrection was such a criticism. So was the Tambov affair. Kronstadt no less. Of two things one: either we give up our optimism and bureaucratic methods and allow the right of criticism to non-party workers and peasants who suffer from our mistakes, or discontent will accumulate, and we shall have criticism in the form of insurrection.

It is difficult to believe that the same man could use language like this after having ruthlessly ordered directly contrary proceedings. But the Kremlin talked in one way and acted quite otherwise. With a new vocabulary and in spite of the different historical stages of development, the degenerate Bolsheviks were unconsciously renewing the Tsarist Russian tradition in matters of governmental action. "The terrible Russian hypocrisy is no man's doing," wrote Michelet, to whom "the insoluble problem of the Empire" seemed to consist in keeping under a common rule peoples differing as widely as possible in degree of civilisation. Apart from its meaningless verbalism, Stalin's whole policy consisted in imitating absolutist predecessors in the maintenance of power, by a combination of cunning and violence, with opportunist alternations of severity and concession. Neither the privileged Party, nor the Opposition represented by Trotsky thought of complaining so long as the blows were not directed against themselves. But when once the dictatorial machine of the new oligarchy was set in motion and perfected, it stopped at nothing, acted according to its own lights in a society in which the habit of subservience had become second nature in the course of centuries.

In the sinister light of the Georgian alarm, Stalin's methods became clear enough; under his instruction the rôle of the police was continuously extended. If the Cheka was nominally only maintained in the Caucasus, where a war regime was permanent, the G.P.U. was just as powerful in the rest of the Union. Already more numerous, active and powerful than the Okhrana, it was the essential tool of the Political Bureau for the settlement of all problems. It is no fortuitous coincidence that the remodelling of the Supreme Economic Council in 1924 began with the nomination of Dzerzhinsky to its head, and went on to the introduction of certain former "Chekists" as heads of departments. At the Revolutionary Military Council, Unschlicht, another member of the G.P.U. Council, supervised the military personnel suspected of "Trotskyism," and prepared bitter draughts for the unorthodox. For Stalin government meant penalties and terrorism. As for the presidency of the Council of Commissars, it was all very well to appoint a mere Rykov after Lenin's death, but only because little influence was attached to the Ministry; the real power lay elsewhere.

In the Party, police interference became more and more oppressive, creating a painful atmosphere of distrust, espionage and treachery. Inspired by the Central Control Commission, directed by Kuibyshev and a kind of specialised annex to the G.P.U., innumerable committees of local control reinforced by still more numerous temporary disciplinary committees, tracked "deviations" and hunted out all sorts of recalcitrants. The friends, colleagues or supporters of Trotsky, or those supposed to be such, were specially aimed at and gradually eliminated from universities, political institutions and army establishments. These measures facilitated the promotion in the hierarchy of the zealous partisans of the Political Bureau. The ignorant "Lenin recruits" were available to fill gaps at the bottom. Even faithful tools of the caprices of the Secretariat no longer felt safe; as in the Society of Jesus, obedience to the will of superiors was not enough; their wishes had to be anticipated. One of the secretaries of the Moscow Committee, an experienced bureaucrat, made responsible for an ovation given to Trotsky, was dispatched to Turkestan, where he had leisure to consider the art of distributing tickets for a suitably packed audience.

In the course of this "first year without Lenin" the recoil of the spirit of October was shown in disturbing symptoms for the suspect Communist Left. Widespread apathy, weariness and fear everywhere indicated an advanced stage in the process of turning "professional revolutionaries" into regular bureaucrats. In the irremediable confusion after Lenin's disappearance, self-interest caused substantial reductions in the phalanx of dissenters from Leninism. The anxiety of the individual to maintain the minimum of relative well-being reserved for privileged workers generally carried the day over secret conviction. There were exceptions. Some militants, incapable of compromising with their consciences, were driven to misery, sometimes to despair. A series of suicides marked the track of this unexampled moral depression. Among these unfortunate persons, most of them obscure, are the names of Eugenia Bosch, heroine of the Ukrainian Revolution; of Lutovinov, the intractable leader of the Workers' Opposition, on his return from his "mission" of exile in Berlin; of Glazman, Trotsky's secretary, expelled from the Party. In high places the nervous state of the victims was alleged in explanation, but, in order to stop the epidemic, it was deemed expedient to invalidate a number of expulsions likely to cause scandal. For in most of the cases the suicides were the results of so-called party purges.

"In Russia, the final word of reproof is equivalent to-day to the papal excommunication in the middle ages." This observation of Custine's in his remarkable letters *On Russia in 1839*, is accurate nearly a century later. No salvation outside the Party— this tacit axiom of Leninist dogma reveals a singular slowness of development of civilisation through three revolutions in this country where, according to this discerning author, "the great distances, isolation, marshes, forests and the severe winters serve as conscience in the rulers and patience in the ruled." The basic causes of despotism, still intact under the forms of Sovietism, entail the same consequences as of yore under not very different aspects.

On learning of the death of his close collaborator, Trotsky wrote an obituary article for *Pravda*. Publication was refused. A member of the Political Bureau and of the Council of Commissars, that is to say, of the sham and of the real Government, could not honour the memory of a dead comrade without giving offence to the machine. Stalin wove his plot with perseverance, with a watchful eye on the movements and the reactions of his opponent. The hostile ring was gradually drawn closer around Trotsky. To all appearance, the *troïka* was ready to enter the arena on the earliest occasion to shake the popularity which they feared. Trotsky was well enough informed of these manœuvres and preparatory discussions to be on his guard. Nevertheless, under circumstances which his detractors could not have hoped for, he was imprudent enough to give them the desired opportunity.

In October 1924, he published without consulting anyone two volumes under the title *1917*, a collection of his writings of the great year of revolution, together with an essay on *The Lessons of October* by way of introduction. In it he established a parallel between the Bolshevist victory of 1917 in Russia and the communist defeat of 1923 in Germany, preceded by a revolutionary failure in Bulgaria, in order to draw from these examples an historical explanation and strategical lessons. He demonstrated especially the necessity of never letting slip any propitious moment for revolt under penalty of a long period of waiting for another favourable moment, and emphasised the useful lesson to be drawn from Russian experience for the international communist movement. After a sketch of his personal interpretation of the facts of October, he ended by a disparaging summing up of the past of Zinoviev and Kamenev, defining bolshevisation in terms of the education and selection of leaders to preserve them from flinching at the decisive moment. Stalin's name is not mentioned in the text, but the reference to the "defensist" position of *Pravda* in 1917 up to the time of Lenin's arrival at Leningrad clearly aimed at the General Secretary.

All that Trotsky did was to synthesise ideas collected from here and there from his earlier essays, articles and speeches. But at this juncture and in this aggressive form, publication meant opening a conflict, the issue of which lay entirely with the machine. It meant also consolidating the union against himself of men who, under the dictates of common sense, should have been left to be set at variance among themselves. In June 1924, Stalin had given to Kamenev a lesson in elementary Leninism in the course of a speech to the district secretaries, and had taken the liberty of making some rude remarks about Zinoviev— very clear indications of a future conflict. Moreover Trotsky was ill once more, a prey to fever, and unable to fight. Again he exposed himself uselessly to blows which he could not return. The *troïka*, furious, had no scruples on this head; on the contrary, they exploited Trotsky's physical weakness, and replied to *The Lessons of October* by a declaration of war on Trotskyism, as a pernicious doctrine unknown in Lenin's day and suddenly revealed to the profane. An extraordinary discussion was opened by an anonymous feuilleton in *Pravda* entitled "How not to describe the October Revolution." It was a unilateral discussion, in which anyone could take part except Trotsky, who was perforce silent. Leninism was in danger. Meetings of officials, of secretaries, and of militants were summoned to hear long "reports" on the new misfortune threatening the revolution. Lenin's *Complete Works*, cut up into fragments, were drawn upon to prove the case, and if necessary the contrary. Trotsky was put on trial before the tribunal of a dumbfounded Soviet opinion. Russia and the Communist International were haunted by a spectre—the spectre of Trotskyism.

In reply to Trotsky's sixty pages, which, be it said, were not to be had at the booksellers, as the edition had been cut down at the astute direction of the Secretariat, the Party and the country were submerged by a flood of diatribes. The note of indignation and the leading ideas were provided by Stalin, Zinoviev and Kamenev, followed by other members of the Political Bureau and of the Central Committee, then by lesser personages. In this atmosphere of over-excitement Krupskaya herself felt compelled to contribute to the argument—with courtesy and moderation it is true. Among the most eager assailants were those who had an old grievance against the former head of the Red Army; Yaroslavsky, Lunacharsky, Manuilsky, Raskolnikov, Gusev. All the professed Leninists more or less capable of holding a pen hastened to catalogue Trotsky's "errors" past and present, to refute his "semi-Menshevism," to denounce his indiscipline and his pessimism. Thousands of resolutions demanding severe measures were adopted "spontaneously" from the White Sea to the Black Sea by people who had never read a word of the incriminated text, for good reason, and demanded severe penalties, as in the days of Custine "the immense extent of territory is no barrier to everything being carried out with magical punctuality and co-ordination, from one end of Russia to the other." The press reproduced columns of defamatory harangues delivered from every platform; these were afterwards printed in pamphlet form and distributed by the million. (Money was lacking for schools, for orphanages, for hospitals, paper for school books, but neither money nor paper was spared in the enterprise.) The printing presses were working night and day to combat Trotskyism.

The main object was to disguise the reasons for the discord, the real stakes in the game. Hence the invention of an imaginary heresy to be placed in antithesis to an unreal Leninism. Who in such circumstances dare speak of rival clans or of individuals? The titles of the polemics: *Trotskyism or Leninism* (Stalin), *Leninism or Trotskyism* (Kamenev), *Bolshevism or Trotskyism* (Zinoviev)—were chosen by the *troïka* to represent the eternal antimony between Good and Evil, and the theme was amplified by every variation of their common stock of ideas and by every imaginative device.

Lenin's successors were sufficiently skilled in petty politics to attribute the origins of the conflict to Trotsky alone. Rykov declared on their behalf that the Party was engaged in a new discussion. "Once more it concerns Comrade Trotsky. This is the fourth time since October." In fact the principal theme of the *Introduction* was rarely mentioned. The essential task of the ruling clique of the moment was to maintain silence on what Trotsky had really written, to impute to him statements he had never made, to recall pre-War dissensions, to revive old forgotten tales, to dig up old quarrels in out-of-date letters. Later on Zinoviev confessed as much. "It was a struggle for power," he said, "the whole art of which consisted in linking old dissensions with new problems."

The Party were somewhat stupefied to hear Trotsky accused of "deviation towards the Right" in his theoretical exposition of the "permanent revolution." Stalin and his auxiliaries maintained that this capital error had as its implication a premature dictatorship of the proletariat, and therefore an "under-estimate of the peasantry." This lucky hit, repeated to satiety, became the main indictment. At a sign from Stalin thousands of Philistines began to conjugate the verb to "under-estimate." The accused was also taxed with individualism and anti-Bolshevism, after being reproved for depreciating the Party by implication. Trotsky neither knew nor understood, had never known nor understood, the Bolshevik Party, according to the defenders of "the machine." This was repeated with variations by the champions of the "machine," among others by Yaroslavsky, who, only a year before, had said that Trotsky "had made clear better than anyone else the rôle of the Communist Party among the working class." Stalin, who, ever since the Tsaritsyn affair, had harboured obstinate resentment, undertook in collaboration with Gusev a reestimate of Trotsky's military ability.

To this flood of insinuation, reproach and insolence, there was no reply from any quarter. The "discussion" was limited to the ruling clique, amidst the mute consternation of the communist rank and file, the unhealthy curiosity of a public greedy for scandal, and the satisfaction of the counter-revolutionaries. The Opposition, caught unawares and under violent provocation, could do nothing but sit still and allow the storm to pass. Trotsky had been so inconsiderate as to place them in an untenable position by his impolitic initiative. His less firm supporters seized the opportunity to abandon a lost cause and abjure their errors. For, as all the ambitious knew, there were rewards to be had for apostasy and ingratitude.

"*The Lessons of October* was only a pretext," admitted Zinoviev. But Trotsky had gratuitously supplied a pretext, starting the quarrel with a learned thesis on strategy, very provocative both to friends and rivals, and of no interest to the unhappy people. By his own fault he incurred the danger of ostracism and familiarised public opinion with the idea of his own disfavour. Rumours of his arrest were already current, and were believed even in Party circles. His book was believed to be confiscated and forbidden, and the inculpated *Introduction* was secretly copied. Panic rumours had to be denied officially: "No member of the Central Committee has raised or will raise the question of any sanctions against Trotsky. Measures of suppression or expulsion would not aid a settlement," said Kamenev at Moscow, and Zinoviev used similar language at Petrograd.

Stalin agreed: "I am a declared enemy of sanctions. We do not want sanctions, but a theoretical polemic against the revival of Trotskyism."

But though apparently unfounded, the general suspicions were not without foundation. Resounding accusations of "semi-Menshevism" sometimes, in improvised speeches, of plain "Menshevism" could have no other logical sequel than early expulsion from the Party, and then police measures against the dissidents, whether they were socialists or communists. Two of the three members of the *troïka* did secretly propose the expulsion of Trotsky from the Party, that is, his outlawry. Zinoviev and Kamenev indeed did not shrink from the idea of immediate imprisonment for their adversary. They would probably have attained their object but for Stalin's veto. Now that Trotsky was defeated and reduced to silence, his enemies lost the principal reason for their alliance—the fear of being deprived of the Lenin inheritance.

The artificial and superficial excitement of 1924 ended in January 1925 with the joint session of the Central Committee and the Control Commission. As usual every question was settled in advance. Deprived of his functions at the Revolutionary Military Council, under the form of resignation, Trotsky remained a member of the Political Bureau, in spite of a "categorical admonition" calculated to diminish his prestige. "I yielded up the military post without a fight, with even a sense of relief," he wrote. The decision taken in his case ended in a way that sheds light on a certain aspect of Leninism, both in essence and in form—a crude Russo-Asiatic duplicity expressed in a self-styled Marxian terminology.

4. Consider the discussion as ended.

5. Continue and develop the work of the Party so as to explain from beginning to end the anti-Bolshevist character of Trotskyism, from 1903 down to *The Lessons of October*, and charge the Political Bureau to furnish all the propaganda organisations (Party schools and others) with the necessary explanations on the subjects; insert in the curricula of political instruction explanations of the *petty-bourgeois* nature of Trotskyism, etc.

6. In addition to explanatory propaganda in the Party, the Young

Communists, etc., a broad popular explanation of the deviations of Trotskyism is indispensable for the worker and the peasant masses.

Disparagement of Trotsky thus took a permanent place at the moment when the rulers were pretending to suspend it. Any objection or contradiction, which might be ascribed to Trotskyism by those who monopolised the power of public expression, incurred henceforth the most rigorous Party measures. Like the Russia observed by Custine, the Soviet Union became "a country in which the Government says what it likes, because it alone has the right of speech." In offices, clubs and shops, everywhere, indeed, portraits of Trotsky were hunted out by the machine. Ambitious officials, or the best informed of them, showed their zeal by displaying the portrait of Stalin. Reduced to clandestine communication, the Opposition could only distribute in secret and in small numbers copies of the proscribed writings of Lenin: letters on the desertion of Zinoviev and Kamenev in October, notes on the question of nationalities, and finally the unpublished *Testament*. The diffusion of this subversive literature, hindered and repressed by the G.P.U., cost those who were found taking part in it exclusion from the Party, that is, the loss of wages and house-room. Denunciations and abjurations decimated the ranks of the demoralised Left. Although the younger supporters gave evidence sometimes of cowardice, sometimes of ambition, Trotsky had founded his hopes on them.

"The Party was condemned to silence. A regime of pure dictatorship was established in the Party machine. In other words, the Party ceased to be a Party." This retrospective remark of Trotsky's may be supplemented by the statement that the ex-Communist Party, formerly the Social-Democratic Party, emerged from the "discussion" profoundly disunited, much weakened in morale, and politically discredited. No further credence was accorded to the fallacious assertions of the priests of the Leninist cult, whose vocabulary—republic, democracy, election, party, trade unions, Soviet, discussion—corresponded to nothing generally understood by those terms. Under a superficial "monolithic unity," there was discernible irreducible antagonism and actual schism. The year 1924, beginning with the death of Lenin and ending with the fall of Trotsky, revealed irreparable dissension. Already there were whispers in Moscow —behind the scenes of the Central Committee—of a broken triumvirate, of Kamenev and Zinoviev in conflict with Stalin.

7

THE conflict of the triumvirs, arising out of differences on the course to be pursued against Trotsky, was soon transformed into a struggle for precedence which became more envenomed in the course of 1925.

Stalin, as against the more rabid Leninists, evidently represented average opinion in the ranks of the higher officials in opposing too violent reprisals. In his own clumsy, rough way, and within the limits of the upper ranks of the Party, he desired no doubt to imitate Lenin, so skilful in conciliating opponents after having put them in the wrong. Anxious to humble Trotsky, while at the same time facilitating the necessary changes and reserving the possibility of future collaboration, he prudently put considerations for and against in his speech in November 1924 on *The Lessons of October*. "I am far from denying the undoubtedly important rôle of Comrade Trotsky in the uprising. But I must state that Comrade Trotsky did not and could not have played any special rôle in the October uprising; that being the president of the Petrograd Soviet, he only carried into effect the will of the respective Party authorities which guided every step of Comrade Trotsky." And a little later in the speech: ". . . Trotsky, who was a relative newcomer in our Party in the period of October, did not and could not have played any *special* rôle either in the Party or in the October uprising. Like all the responsible functionaries, he was only executing the will of the Central Committee and its organs."

Nevertheless it was Stalin who had deliberately written in 1918: "The whole work of the practical organisation of the insurrection was carried out under Trotsky's immediate instructions. . . . It may be definitely asserted that in the matter of the rapid passage over of the garrison to the side of the Soviet and the skilful organisation of the work of the Military Revolutionary Committee, the Party is primarily indebted to Comrade Trotsky." But respect for the truth, like self-respect, were "middle-class prejudices" in the eyes of the degenerate Leninists. Examination of the documents would have been punished as treason against the revolution; no one dare venture on it.

Stalin did justice in his own way to Trotsky's fighting qualities: "Yes, that is true, Comrade Trotsky really fought well during October. But Comrade Trotsky was not the only one who fought well during the period of October; even such people as the Left Social Revolutionaries, who then stood shoulder to shoulder with the Bolsheviks, did not fight badly, etc." Finally, of the chief of the Red Army he said: "I am far from denying the important rôle Comrade Trotsky played in the Civil War. But I must declare with the utmost emphasis that the high honour of organising our victories belongs not to any individual person but to the great collective of front-rank workers of our country—the Russian Communist Party." He then cited a surprising version, according to which Kolchak and Denikin had been put to flight "in spite of the plans of Comrade Trotsky," and defied him to contest it, thanks to the privilege which authorised him to say what he pleased under the shelter of the G.P.U.

When all is said, Stalin had the advantage over his fellow Bolsheviks of knowing in his heart his own shortcomings, a silent modesty which is not incompatible with the self-confidence which he displayed in his actions as dictator. He still attached a certain importance to the benefit to be derived from the ideas, talents and activity of the man he disparaged. Why should it be impossible for him to capture the force which Lenin had been able to employ in the best interests of the Party? All the internal dissensions emphasised Trotsky's incapacity to form a group capable of supplanting the actual people in power. The General Secretary became the more aware of his strong position at the centre of the machine, as it revealed to him the impatience and the powerlessness of his adversaries. This sense of security was confirmed in Stalin by his natural empiricism, a propensity for living from day to day, leaving to their own devices those whose services he might employ.

Zinoviev and Kamenev on the contrary had sufficient faculty for superficial generalisation to fear the consequences of their too easy success. In declaring their hostility to the repressions, they sought to dissimulate their own real intentions. Inferior to Stalin in many respects in character and temperament, but fortified by a certain amount of western culture and educated under the shadow of Lenin, they were too wary to be satisfied with the result obtained without at any rate seeking for some long-range policy.

Earlier than anyone else except Lenin, Zinoviev had seen the complexity of the problem of the Secretariat as early as 1923, and had hoped to solve it, whether by reducing the powers of the Secretary, or by enlarging them in the hands of a bureau of three members—Stalin, Trotsky and Zinoviev or Kamenev. Having himself reason to complain of Stalin's high-handed procedure, he thought the time was ripe to reform the organisation of government. With a little patience and tact, Trotsky would easily have disarmed his most redoubtable rival, and then assured without any great effort his predominance among the others; it was his lack of foresight, his impulsiveness and reticence that consolidated the bloc of the Political Bureau against him. A new phase opened with the disintegration of the so-called Leninist Old Guard, which Stalin had once likened to a "compact wall" without a breach.

Trotsky, even as an object of universal scorn, seemed more dangerous than ever to the "deserters of October," haunted apparently by the Bonapartist danger they had conjured up in imagination, and in a hurry to have done with the man who was irreconcilable in defeat, from whom they feared a fresh offensive. After vainly demanding his expulsion from the Party, and then, in default of this, from the Central Committee, or at least from the Political Bureau, they manœuvred under cover of various committees to wear out Stalin's resistance, the only serious obstacle to their scheme. The Leningrad "machine" under Zinoviev, part of the Moscow officials under Kamenev, and some provincial militants served them more or less consciously. Reduced to minor tactics, they worked for the removal of Stalin from the Secretariat to the post of Commissar of War and for his replacement by a person named Rudzutak. This manœuvre only served to unmask their secret intentions, without preventing the nomination of Frunze, which had long been prearranged by Stalin.

Before the meeting of the Central Committee in January, at which the resolution condemning Trotsky was debated, the governing clique had concerted in private a unanimous line of action. Violent differences emerged. Stalin, sure of his majority, stood firm. Zinoviev, despairing of success, offered his resignation, knowing it could not be accepted. In the end a sham compromise was reached, Stalin agreeing to stiffen the resolution and Zinoviev renouncing the demand for Trotsky's expulsion. But the coalition of the Old Bolsheviks was broken for ever; a merciless struggle for Lenin's heritage had begun.

In fact Stalin had won once more. By his instructions the attacks on Trotsky were sensibly attenuated. He himself set the example by suddenly discovering that Trotskyism, denounced only yesterday as a form of Menshevism, was in reality the "right wing of Communism." Master of the situation at Moscow, he laid a restraining hand on the extreme bolshevisation initiated by Zinoviev in the International, and prevented in advance the purging operations contemplated.

In an interview in February with the German Communist writer, Wilhelm Herzog, implicitly repudiating the supposed "Left" demagogy of Zinoviev, he was lavish in promises of prudence and caution, contrasting it with practice within the Soviet Union, and he constituted himself the protector of the Opposition of the "Right," threatened with exclusion in Germany under the pretext of Trotskyism. This unforeseen interference in Zinoviev's domain constituted a discreet warning to him. Three weeks later, he wrote to the spokesman of the Communist Left in Berlin to reassure him by extolling the "new types" of leader of whom he aspired to be regarded as the model. In his confidential letter he referred to the history of the Bolshevik Party: "With us in Russia, there has always been this process of the waning of the old leaders, generally of the literary type," and went on to mention Lunacharsky, Bogdanov, and Krassin among the decrepit, though having others in mind. He condemned on paper the policy "which creates within the Party a regime of intimidation, of fear, a regime which develops neither self-criticism nor initiative," as if he really had no use for such methods. He formulated an opinion worth noting on these leaders: "It is a bad thing for the leaders of the Party to be feared without being respected. The leaders of a party cannot be real leaders if they and their judgment are not respected as well as feared."

Simultaneously he toned down the prolonged polemic from the January meeting onwards. One of the co-directors of the *Bolshevik*, Vardin, a converted ex-Menshevik, was dismissed for extreme anti-Trotskyism and then sent to the Caucasus. The blow was indirectly aimed at Zinoviev who persisted secretly in his obstructive tactics. In *Pravda*, Raskolnikov denounced in unusual terms the pamphlet of a certain Zalutsky on Trotsky as "sickening." It had been inspired by Zinoviev. Through intermediaries, the Leningrad dictator was already accusing Stalin of opportunism and of "semi-Trotskyism"; at his instigation the ruling committees in the northern capital were demanding a more intransigent policy in Moscow. He also made arrangements for a new publication, the *Leninist*, as a rival to the *Bolshevik*, tainted with Trotskyism. The Political Bureau forbade it. Thus gradually enmity within the omnipotent bureaucracy itself was growing up in the name of the "monolithic" front.

With characteristic firmness, Stalin called the bluff. He kept a tight hand on the instrument which his former friends now wished to wrest from him—the Secretariat, gradually transformed from the executive organ into the effective organ of power. In Party circles in touch with the "top," no more was said of the dictatorship of the *troïka* but of the dictatorship of

the Secretariat; the dictatorship of the proletariat had long fallen
out of the reckoning. The Political Bureau became a consultative
committee dominated by a sort of camarilla constituted around
Stalin. In this way the formal presence of Trotsky was not in
absolute contradiction with the official policy. Of the seven
members—not counting deputy members and leaving aside
Trotsky—Bukharin, Rykov and Tomsky gave Stalin an automatic majority of four votes against Zinoviev and Kamenev. In
the absence of Trotsky or anyone else, three deputies were on
his side, Kalinin, Molotov and Dzerzhinsky; there was nothing
to fear from the fourth, Sokolnikov, a friend of Kamenev's.
This balance of forces ensured the stability of the government
until the next Party Congress, when the machine, instructed
beforehand, would easily re-establish the "hundred per cent monolithism." But an unprecedented thing happened. The annual
Congress, punctually assembled in even the worst days of the
Civil War, was put off from March to September, then to
December, the necessity for consultation of the Party becoming
less and less felt. Meanwhile, Stalin did not require much imagination to counteract the manœuvres of his new opponents. As he
had acted with their complicity when it was desired to isolate
Trotsky, so now he placed, displaced and replaced officials.
Playing alone on a gigantic chessboard, he could move the
pieces as he wished without hindrance. This time it was the
supporters of Zinoviev and Kamenev who suffered—Safarov,
Zorin, Kharitonov, Kviring and many others, following Vardin.
Under the supreme Secretariat, the principal regional committees
would soon be provided with secretaries completely trustworthy
—Uglanov at Moscow, Kaganovich in the Ukraine, other subalterns in the Urals and at Ivanovo-Vosnessensk. The Caucasus
Committee was entirely subservient since the events which had
moved Lenin's indignation. All the essential strategical positions
were thus occupied in due course by Stalin's fraction except
Leningrad, where Zinoviev was surrounded by his bureaucratic
tools, but was powerless against the machine as a whole.

In April 1925, a conference of the Party unanimously voted
the various resolutions dictated by the Political Bureau, i.e.,

in the last resort by Stalin. It confirmed and accentuated the policy of conciliation adopted towards the peasants since the Georgian insurrection, and proclaimed in an order repeated a thousand times: "Look to the countryside." Reduction and simplification of the land-tax, the redistribution of land, re-establishment of the wages system, various concessions to cultivators of all kinds, extension of rights of buying and selling, measures "to encourage and guarantee the process of healthy saving," in the rural economy, were calculated to assist a recovery of agriculture. Once more "Bashi-Bazouk outrages," condemned six years earlier by Lenin, were repudiated. A "new rural policy," declared Stalin in his *Replies* to the *Questions* enunciated by the students of the Sverdlov University. There appeared to be no divergence of view in the Government. The fractions kept a wary eye on each other and waited patiently. If secret, silent preparations were being made on one side or the other, the Party could not suspect the fact.

In a long report made in May, Stalin strongly emphasised the principal lines of this new policy towards the peasants, regardless of providing arguments for his enemies: "Any party which hides the truth from the people, which fears light and criticism, is not a party, but a clique of imposters doomed to ruin. . . . We must," he said in a jargon more and more confused, "follow the line of liquidating old administrative and governmental methods, the line of giving life to the soviets, the line of transformation of the soviets into real elective organs, the line of implanting in the countryside bases of soviet democracy." It is essential that "Communists in the rural districts should abandon monstrous forms of administration." In fact the manifold errors of the recent past must be abandoned, and more seriousness and competence must be brought to the work. Platonic assurances for the future corresponded to the revealing admissions on the recent past and the immediate present.

According to Bukharin, the accredited theorist of the fraction of which Stalin styled himself the executant, the intention was really to extend the New Economic Policy to the country districts where it had not yet been possible to apply it. "We must tell the peasants, all the peasants, to enrich themselves, to develop their business and not to fear spoliation," cried the former leader of Left Communism, anxious to stimulate "increase of farms belonging to the more prosperous peasants and *kulaks*." This was only an emphatic statement of unanimous opinion general in the Central Committee.

In 1924 Chicherin, not without instructions from above, had declared in an interview with foreign concessionaires: "*Enrich yourselves!* let us say in the words of Guizot. *Enrich yourselves!*—for in this way we enrich ourselves." Beginning from 1925, there was no more talk of the class struggle in the villages, except to forbid any stimulation of it; as for the iniquitous *kulaks*, they received the less disparaging name of "the more prosperous peasants," in current speech. Zinoviev and Kamenev did not dissent from Stalin and Bukharin, from Molotov and Kalinin on this subject. Far from under-estimating the peasantry, Trotsky himself had two years before anticipated his colleagues in saying of the peasant in general: "*We must so act that he will be richer next year than he is this*," and, advising against any increase of taxation, "*so that peasant prosperity may increase and the peasant grow richer in the future.*" As early as September 1925, Trotsky proposed to enlarge "the scope of capitalist traders in rural districts," and to reinforce capitalist farming so as to encourage progress in production even with the help of capitalist methods. At the end of November, at Kislovodsk, he was heard to declare: "There is no direct danger in the economic system in the country districts," and to deprecate the "dekulakisation of the *kulak*." Guizot's famous phrase, transformed by Bukharin, reflected with some exaggeration a collective evolution in the direction of a return to the October programme, which had been changed by War Communism.

Stalin goes still further. Being ready "to change from top to bottom our attitude towards the peasants," he envisages as unavoidable the restoration of the small proprietor, and in consequence the denationalisation of the soil. To prepare public opinion he summons the Soviet journalists and gets this question put to him: "Would it not be necessary in the interests of agriculture, to guarantee to the peasant for ten years the land which he cultivates?" To this Stalin replies: *"Even for forty years."* At his suggestion the Commissar for Agriculture in Georgia drew up the basis of an ordinance along these lines. The peasant insurrection of the preceding year had therefore not been in vain. But Zinoviev and his supporters, determined to take up a Left position against the Right tendency of the Stalin fraction, guilty of "semi-Trotskyism," found an excellent pretext in a flagrant doctrinal flaw. The "kulakophile" tendency was undeniable, and that was more than enough to afford a decent excuse for personal rivalries. Moreover, Bukharin had some rather extremist disciples, young "Red" professors who in their writings paraphrased the master and compromised him more deeply. Excellent opportunity for denouncing heresy. The fire, latent beneath the cinders of official optimism, was revived in a controversy behind the scenes, Zinoviev having incited Krupskaya to write an article against Bukharin aimed at Stalin through his adviser. Would they dare to impose silence on Lenin's widow? Warned in time, Bukharin refuted the refutation, and this was sufficient to permit of the refusal of the *imprimatur* to both texts with pretended impartiality. Stalin met the attack skilfully. Foreseeing an incident at the approaching Congress, he anticipated matters and suggested the retraction of the inopportune formula. Bukharin acted accordingly, and admitted his mistake, reserving freedom to justify himself later.

Of this passage of arms the public knew nothing. The little which had been publicly expressed was lost in insipid and unintelligible documents which few had the courage to read, and the underlying meaning of which was impenetrable to ordinary mortals. No more enlightening was the long, mysterious article by Zinoviev in September entitled *Philosophy of the Time*, with its ambitious and misleading title and its veiled insinuations. Only three months later and thanks to a violent open conflict, the Party learned that Stalin had only consented to the insertion of this article after substantial modifications. All this was made more obscure by the fact that the various writers cited Lenin interminably, were for ever boasting of their Leninism, and, from sheer force of habit, repeated from time to time the same allusions to the shade of Trotskyism.

Stalin, however, no longer limited his activities to the modest rôle of an executant. His victory over Trotsky and the mathematical certainty of check-mating Zinoviev opened up to him new horizons. He now aspired to be Lenin's spiritual successor, as he was his temporal successor. Even in its degenerate state, the Bolshevist tradition demanded a leader capable of theorising practice, if not of giving effect to theory. Beyond criticism as General Secretary, whose actions were assured of automatic sanction by the Political Bureau, his weak point was exposed when he began to argue doctrinal points. Here Zinoviev thought him vulnerable, and here he sought to get in his blow.

In his polemic against Trotsky and against the theory of "permanent revolution," Stalin could no longer restrain his natural inclination for a national form of socialism, repressed during Lenin's lifetime, but apparent as early as 1917 in his reply to Preobrazhensky: "The possibility is not excluded that Russia may be the country destined to prepare the way for socialism." In his 1924 essay on *October and the Theory of the Permanent Revolution* Stalin wrote: "The victory of socialism is possible even in a country relatively undeveloped from the capitalist point of view," and he championed "the Leninist theory of revolution and of the victory of socialism in a single country." After the conference of 1925 he said in his report: "Can we construct socialism unaided. . . ? Leninism answers this question in the affirmative." In reality, this meant for communists of this particular brand a breach with Lenin's fundamental internationalism; and the renunciation of Marxism.

Without going back to Marx and Engels, whose thesis, whether valid or not, requires no interpretation as to the international character of the socialist revolution, it is sufficient to refer to the principal writings and speeches of Lenin to establish an insoluble antithesis with the Leninism of Stalin.

As far back as 1906 Lenin looked forward to "the socialist revolution in the west as the sole guarantee against a restoration," laying it down that "the Russian Revolution can conquer by its own strength, but can in no case maintain and consolidate its conquests unaided." Afterwards he consistently affirmed as "an elementary truth of Marxism" the impossibility of establishing "socialism in a single country," down to his last article *Better Less, but Better*, in which (1923) he recognised that *"we are not civilised enough to pass directly to socialism, although we have the political premises for it."* His strategy and tactics were invariably supported by considerations connected with the world revolution at every decisive step he had to take. The intellectual and economic backwardness of the Soviet Republic is not the only argument. In 1918 Lenin declared that socialism was inconceivable in a single country, "even in one much less backward than Russia," and, always counting on outside help, he calculated in prudent terms the necessary delays: "It is very doubtful whether the next generation . . . can realise socialism in every department." Next year he said: ". . . We know that we cannot establish a socialist system now—God grant that it may be established in our children's time or perhaps in our grandchildren's time." His opinion in this matter was consistent and incontestable.

But by ransacking his *Complete Works* some phrases, more or less explicit, susceptible, when torn from their context, of a different interpretation, may be found. Sometimes he improvised summary formulas, useful at the moment for the point he had to prove, though there was no pretence of incorporating in them the whole of his doctrine. For example, definitions in which words are given a restricted or relative meaning, according to the question under discussion, sometimes expressions intended to cheer up his audience. Just as Napoleon attributed military success, now to artillery, now to the bayonet, now to the commissariat, to morale, to good administration, to the mobility of the army, to the commander-in-chief, to the health of the troops, to discipline—so Lenin emphasised what was important for his argument at the moment. To attribute to his expressions for a particular occasion an absolute interpretation would be to mutilate or to minimise his ideas, often to misunderstand them. But this is what Stalin did with regard to

"Socialism in a single country," a statement of the problem as inadequate as the answer to it.

Before the revolution, in 1915, Lenin enunciated in a few lines the mere hypothesis of a socialist victory "first in a few capitalist countries, or even in one alone," but in a very restricted sense and without reference to Russia. Stalin took this hypothesis literally, and transformed it into a dogma. He quotes it again and again, eked out with fragments derived from the imposing text of the *Complete Works*, which Zinoviev was also to invoke to prove the contrary proposition. In an article on co-operation, appearing after *Better Less, but Better*, during his illness, Lenin enumerated "the conditions necessary to build up the integral fabric of the socialist society—by means of co-operation and co-operation alone." Stalin confused the abstract with the concrete, and deduced from it a confirmation of his own view. He forgot that at the Thirteenth Congress, in announcing the number of seven million co-operators, he had himself to correct it by saying in euphemistic terms: "I do not believe in these figures, because adhesion to the Consumers' Co-operative Societies is not yet entirely voluntary, and it is certain that it includes 'dead souls.' " In fact the co-operatives, like the trade unions and the soviets, tended to disappear with the principle that co-operative trading became state trading. Lenin was speaking of free and conscious co-operation, not of the deceptive label. In Stalin's language, "not yet completely voluntary" meant obligatory and consequently, in accordance with the authority which he had arrogated, resulting in an imitation completely sterile.

But Lenin also said: "The success of socialism in Russia demands a certain lapse of time, at least several months," and no one thought of repeating that. Again he said: "Socialism is a matter of accounting," which did not prevent Stalin from rightly recognising at the previous Congress: "Our statistics are one-legged." Lenin said further: "Communism means the power of the soviets, plus electrification" . . . which neither proves the existence of real soviets, nor of the economic and technical level corresponding to the general use of electricity. He set down the equation: "Soviets + proletarian democracy = dictatorship of the proletariat—the elements of which were still to be created in Soviet life. He even enunciated the aphorism: "Every cook ought to learn to govern the State"; an aphorism easy enough to push to absurdity, but one which was not to prevent him from one day proposing to remove the "head cook," for whose "peppery dishes" he had no taste. Examples might be multiplied.

Suppose for a moment that Stalin was right to interpret strictly and literally hasty phrases of this kind, closing his eyes to anything which explained, modified, or decreased the importance of their tenor, this would merely have increased the list of the contradictory statements to be found in Lenin's writings. If that was what the pundits of Leninism wanted, that was the way to do it. This, indeed, is the impression left by the laborious compilations of Stalin and Zinoviev, rivals in orthodoxy. The latter, in his book on *Leninism*, revised by Krupskaya, sets out half a hundred quotations drawn from the *Complete Works* to embarrass his ex-colleague, who replied with half a dozen extracts. But for those who are able to discern what I. Babel calls the "mysterious curve of Lenin's straight line," Stalin's aberration in time seems obvious; it is due to a reversion to the utopian conceptions of the first half of the nineteenth century, to a method of reasoning outside time and space, the negation of the dialectic only too much insisted on by the Leninists of the decadence. To approve it, in the interests of a fraction, Bukharin would have had to retract his *A.B.C. of Communism*.

Stalin was not personally able to defend the reactionary idea of "Socialism in a single country" except by retracting his own assertions, copied from Lenin less than a year before. In fact, in *The Foundations of Leninism* he wrote: "Can we succeed and secure the definitive victory of socialism in one country without the combined efforts of the proletarians of several advanced countries? Most certainly not . . . For the definitive triumph of socialism, the organisation of socialist production, the efforts of one country alone are not enough, particularly of an essentially rural country like Russia; the efforts of the proletarians of several advanced countries are needed." Under any government with a minimum of democracy, Stalin would have been compelled to have respect for the theory he had recently advanced or to retract plainly. The dictatorship of the Secretariat permitted him to modify the awkward passage of his pamphlet, cut out in new editions, and to get out of the dilemma by an explanation imposed by the G.P.U.: "Socialism realisable in a single country, except in case of aggressive capitalist intervention."

Of the hundred and forty millions of Soviet subjects bowed beneath Stalin's yoke, still anonymous in 1925, there were indeed some who understood the need and the urgency, before proclaiming socialism in words, of accomplishing in fact the first steps in the way of material and moral progress, of giving bread to the legions of abandoned children, work to the millions of unemployed, healthy habitations to the innumerable working-class families crowded in hovels, a human level of existence to the mass of wage-earners, and elementary instruction to the illiterate population. Rightly or wrongly, Marxists thought that there were no "Utopias to be introduced ready-made for the workers," and that what was required was not "to realise an ideal but to release the elements of the new society existent in the old bourgeois society itself." Each generation had its own task, determined in the last resort by economic conditions and limited by historical circumstances, on the world scale. Advance in the direction of socialism meant more than indefinite promises of the integral communist programme to the people plunged in ignorance and poverty, subject to inequality and injustice, deprived of rights and liberty, and under a regime which engendered and perpetuated privilege. But in substituting Leninism for Marxism, Stalin's fraction tried more or less consciously to suppress every vestige of imported theory. Only to the members of the Political Bureau was some right of criticism and liberty of opinion permitted, and of that Trotsky prudently did not avail himself, and Zinoviev and Kamenev were not to exercise it for long.

8

THE Fourteenth Congress of the Party met in December 1925, after being twice deferred. No preparatory discussion preceded it. The traditional "free tribune" of *Pravda* was not open. Everywhere the plethoric "theses" of the Political Bureau were voted unanimously, under the constant threat of administrative and police repression. Trotsky's fate sufficiently indicated what less highly-placed opponents would have to face. With ordinary men the Government showed little ceremony, having both the power to condemn without appeal to civil death by expulsion from the Party, the means of depriving the "undisciplined" and their families of the means of livelihood by deprivation of work, and finally the resource of turning them out of their homes at any moment by their all-powerful caprice.

There were worse fates. In addition to the communist workers imprisoned and deported by secret procedure for wrong opinions, many modest militants of the minority were incarcerated, accused, condemned without proof, without witnesses, without defence. Every individual guilty of any independence of mind, even if he were a convinced communist, thus risked ruin under an unverifiable pretext, sometimes expiating ostensibly a youthful peccadillo or the venal fault of a distant relative. "In Russia to talk was equivalent to conspiracy, thinking was revolt; alas! thought is not only a crime, it is a calamity," noted Custine under the Iron Tsar—a saying true to-day. As in former days, Siberia was peopled by exiles of all shades of politics. It is unnecessary to modify the words of F. Lacroix, another contemporary of Nicholas I, who was distressed to observe that "the most innocent might, on the slanderous denunciation of some wretch, be arrested and dispatched, without trial, to that terrible country for the rest of his life." ... With such means of pressure and intimidation, there was no difficulty in securing "hundred per cent unanimity."

Accordingly, great was the surprise at the explosion of a new discord. The Party had had no reason to suspect it. At Leningrad as elsewhere there was complete unanimity on the Government propositions. It was the same everywhere, without knowledge of the case or any liberty of judgment; the proof was to be found in the insuperable antagonism of the fractions which had "voted" the same resolutions. The struggle begun in the high regions at the "summit" was not visible from the plain. After the death of Frunze, the nomination of a Commissar for War gave rise to competition between Voroshilov, Stalin's candidate, and Lashevich, a supporter of Zinoviev. The Central Committee elected them both, the first as chief, the second as deputy. Stalin did not care to force a decision. The public was unaware of the significance of the double choice and of the circumstances of Frunze's death. In the Moscow literary review, *Krasnaya Nov*, under the mysterious title: *History of the Unextinguished Moon*, and the more explicit sub-title: *The Assassination of the Commandant*—the Soviet writer, B. Pilnyak, published an equivocal tale where the allusions to Stalin are precise enough. In it there are two chief characters, a military leader of high rank suffering from an ulcer, which is well on the way to being cured, and an all-powerful politician member of a *troïka* which governs the country; the second has secretly decided on a surgical operation for which the first has no need and which is thought necessary by none of the great doctors called into consultation. The soldier has gloomy forebodings but does not dare to resist the orders of his political superior and dies under chloroform. Stalin had the number of the review confiscated and took sanctions against the editor and the author. But the question remained where it was.

People knew nothing of what underlay certain controversies academic in appearance. "Socialism in a single country" was not the only subject in dispute. Without naming one another, Stalin and Zinoviev were at loggerheads on the question of whether the dictatorship was to be that of their Party or of the proletariat, each of them citing Lenin profusely. But both under different formulas had the same unavowed intention—the dictatorship of a coterie. For his part, without mentioning names,

Kamenev began to explain the difficulties in the way of the advance of the Soviet Republic. These were the formation of a rural bourgeoisie disposing of a third of the crops and of two-thirds of the surplus for sale; the poverty of the mujiks lacking horses and implements; active speculation in goods, and the rapid accumulation of private capital. According to the Central Bureau of Statistics, State property was valued at 11½ milliard roubles, private property at 7½ milliards, not including houses. Thus, said Kamenev, co-operation representing only half a milliard "supports especially the most settled classes"; capitalism is developing under the impulse of the majority of the peasants, State production is not yet socialist, since it provides goods partly for the processes of purchase and sale. Confronted with the capitalist danger, concluded the Vice-President of the Council of Commissars, the new regime could only reckon on a working class whose wages were still below the pre-War level and were retarding the progress of industry; a remedy had to be found for this disturbing situation, perhaps by establishing for the workers a sort of collective participation in the returns. This thesis was directed fundamentally against the "kulako-phile" tendency of Bukharin, Kalinin and others, including Stalin.

In the course of this year, the latter had several times proposed a "new course in the rural districts," denouncing the "absence of control, the arbitrary procedure of the leaders" in his replies to students and letters to young communists. "A succession of presidents, of district executive committees and members of cells have gone to prison for this reason," wrote Stalin, with regard to administrative abuses. As for concessions to be made to the peasants, they "will certainly be increased as our economic position improves." Later on, "the Constitution will be enlarged to include the whole population, including the bourgeoisie," he affirmed, quoting Lenin (*Questions and Answers*). The dictatorship of the proletariat is "violence within legal limits towards capitalists and owners of land," not towards the working people. And as if to confirm the veracity of the protests raised in all quarters, he recommended "more attention to the aspirations and needs of the working class . . . more sensibility and respect for the dignity of the working class." But formal assurances lavished on the disillusioned proletariat had not the same interest as the new promises with regard to the better-off peasants and the bourgeoisie.

The reaction of Zinoviev's fraction to this remarkable development was shown in the theses of the Political Bureau drawn up by Kamenev and passed unanimously, stating the theoretical consequences, three weeks before the Fourteenth Congress. The general trend of this document is to rectify the "Right" orientation with which Stalin was reproached, prescribing the support of "the poor and middle classes of the peasantry," emphasising the importance of the trade unions in production, and of co-operation in socialist competition with the *kulaks*, insisting, in agreement with Trotsky, on the necessity of developing industry according to a fixed plan. Stalin had no hesitation in countersigning it, well knowing that the future did not depend on platonic statements of this kind. A few theses more or less cost him little, provided that his machine was not affected. Every useful precaution had been taken against this. That was clear at the regional congresses preceding the Moscow Congress—at Kharkov, at Leningrad, where the new Opposition was subjected to the first shots of the bureaucratic offensive.

Stalin at first abstained from overt intervention. The signal was given to say nothing about Kamenev and Zinoviev, but to attack their supporters, so as to reserve the chance of an opportune compromise between the principal figures. In the same way, when there was conflict among the great boyars, the "small men" had to bear the brunt of the battle, sacrificed to the authority of the supreme oligarchy. But Stalin's new opponents were not yet aware of the transformation of the Party into a social class interested in the preservation of the *status quo* and passively solid for the leaders, nor of the degeneration of the regime into the dictatorship of the Bolshevik caste over the working classes. They thought they could amend official policy without attacking the principle of power, by securing internal reforms at the top. In this illusion, shared by the whole Opposition, they

advanced to throw themselves against the "steel wall of Leninism," an expression used without irony by the "wall" itself, just
as if they had learnt nothing from the experience of the Left
Opposition. Incited in the Political Bureau by Bukharin's theses
"on the work of Communist Youth," studded with transparent
allusions to their critical attitude, Zinoviev and Kamenev voted
against them and placed themselves in the position of an intransigent minority. This led to a public discussion, the issue of
which was not in doubt.

In a speech aimed at the new Opposition, Bukharin accused
his opponents of pessimism, of defeatism, of anti-Leninism for
having described State Soviet industry as a form of State capitalism, that is as a system of exploitation of the workers, and
accused them of "bringing grist to the Menshevik mill." Kamenev defended himself by extracts from Lenin in exact agreement with his views, and quoted Bukharin, who had admitted
in 1925 his consistent disagreement with Lenin on the two questions of "proletarian culture and State capitalism." Molotov
riposted with other quotations from the *Complete Works*, enabling him to condemn without rhyme or reason "every kind of
incredulity, and defeatism." On the same note, an address from
the Kharkov assembly censured "the panic mentality of certain
comrades." Having attributed to the Central Committee "un-
derestimation of the *kulak*," the Opposition in their turn were
confronted with the accusation of "underestimating" the middle
peasant. . . . Moreover, as President of the Council of Labour
and Defence, Kamenev saw himself made responsible for all the
economic miscalculations of the moment: a wrong estimate of
the harvest, the rise in the price of cereals, the fall in the chervonetz. In vain he defended himself by sheltering behind the approval secured from the Political Bureau—the procedure once
used against Trotskyism was applied to his Leninism. In addition he laid himself open to easy refutation by proposing the
participation of the workers in the returns in a country in which
industry was working at a loss. He was accused of demagogy,
not without foundation, and not only under this head, for "certain Leningrad comrades" had suggested the augmentation of

the membership of the Party by several million units in one year, to bring the number up to 90 per cent of the proletariat. The most differing themes were therefore mixed in an inextricable confusion, well fitted to mislead opinion for the benefit of the dominant fraction and to facilitate the specific task of the machine.

As was expected, and just as in Trotsky's case in 1924, Kamenev found himself isolated at Moscow, although he was a member of the Political Bureau, President of the Council of Labour and Defence and Vice-President of the Council of Commissars, President of the Moscow Soviet and Director of the Lenin Institute—to mention only his principal titles. Krupskaya was the only one to take his part, without the least chance of influencing a vote. Too late a comer to the Opposition, she had lost the moment for any useful intervention. Stalin did not hesitate to disparage her secretly, having no fear of disagreeable revelations. The zealous hierarchy of secretaries would do the rest, expert in the isolation of awkward personalities.

Among the notorious illusions prevalent in the polemic of that time, one is particularly worth notice, as throwing light on ulterior events. Kamenev based his argument about the "*kulak* danger" on the figures provided by the Central Statistical Bureau, an institution p litically neutral and objective in its methods, if not in its results. Stalin had no difficulty in cutting the knot; under his instructions the Control Commission, an organ of repression whose praesidium, together with the College of the G.P.U., constituted a sort of Star Chamber, annulled the relatively scientific information, and substituted its own statistics faked to suit governmental considerations. The result was a substantial diminution on paper of social antagonisms in the countryside, and harvest returns more favourable to the poor peasants and less abundant for the *kulaks*. "Access to figures is a privilege of the Russian police," as Custine had already observed under the Iron Tsar.

The paradox was more apparent than real. The Communist organisation of Leningrad had unanimously approved its leaders, exactly as the Party as a whole had done, and thanks to methods very similar, thinking it was sharing the general unanimity and without suspecting any discordant note. Its delegates formed the only opposition at the Congress in which majority and minority were rivals in Leninomania and "monolithism." Suddenly Stalin opened fire, and Zinoviev, at last mentioned by name, was seen to be in a desperate position. President of the Communist International, member of the Central Committee and of the Political Bureau, President of the Leningrad Soviet, he was accused in his turn of all imaginable offences against Leninism in the special jargon of the hour: revisionism, sectionalism, schism, pessimism, defeatism, Menshevism, liquidationism, and panic and hysteria. He had lost all right of reply, all means of defence, except the Leningrad *Pravda* which he was accused of abusing. At the beginning of the Congress his fate was irrretrievably fixed.

After the report of the Central Committee, which Stalin, now in the forefront, presented, Zinoviev was so imprudent as to ask to speak as joint *rapporteur*, in order to justify himself, to explain his position—an unheard-of "scandal" as the exasperated majority declared. A hundred and fifty speakers put down their names in a feverish atmosphere. Only half of them could be heard, alternating with the handful of those "in error," Kamenev, Sokolnikov, Krupskaya, Lashevich, Yevdokimov and some others. Thousands of quotations from Lenin were exchanged without any conclusion being reached. The Congress addressed an appeal in grandiloquent terms to the communist workers of Leningrad, over the head of their delegation, to stigmatise the crime of an opponent who had suspected the Central Committee of "degeneration and Thermidorism"; to beware of the error of Zinoviev and Kamenev. "The pronouncements of Zalutsky on the degeneration of the Central Committee and on our Thermidorism reveal, on examination, the whole gamut of the ideology of liquidation." Both sides accused one another, with justice, of stifling working-class opinion and violating democracy; with equal bad faith, they blamed the other party for over-estimating this or under-estimating that, for "Right" heresies or "Left" errors. Zinoviev's *Leninism* and his

History of the Party, works circulated by authority in millions of copies, and only recently obligatory for students, were now denounced as contrary to authentic Bolshevism and held up to ridicule and were declared no longer worthy of the official *imprimatur*. An ironic comment on "monolithism" was provided by the spectacle of Lashevich and Voroshilov, the two principal army commanders, speaking from the tribune as declared enemies. Zalutsky had already "acknowledged his error" on Thermidor; all the leaders of the new Opposition were summoned to follow his example, under threat of reprisals.

With a speech from Kamenev, the controversy took an extraordinarily virulent turn; for the first time the question of which everyone was thinking but of which no one spoke was plainly stated, the question of Stalin's position. This was the culminating point of the Congress. In a hostile and excited audience, before which the Leningrad fraction put up a hopeless fight, Kamenev explained his grievances in the tumult. The stenographic report is attenuated but revealing:

Kamenev. . . . We object to the creation of a headship theory; to the setting up of a "head." We object to the Secretariat, uniting policy and organisation in itself, being placed above the political organism. We stand for an internal organisation of the supreme power so as to assure full power to the Political Bureau, which contains all the political brains of our Party, and subordinate the Secretariat to it as the technical executant of its decisions. . . . (Uproar.) We cannot consider normal, and think harmful to the Party, the prolongation of a situation in which the Secretariat unites policy and organisation, and, in fact, predetermines policy. (Uproar.) . . . . I have become convinced that Comrade Stalin cannot play the part of co-ordinator of the Bolshevik general staff (*Various speakers:* "A lie! Humbug! That's it, is it? The cards are on the table!" Clamour and cheers from the Leningrad deputation. "We won't give you the commanding positions! Stalin! Stalin!" The delegates rise and cheer Comrade Stalin. Thunders of applause. "That is how to unite the Party! The Bolshevik general staff should be unified!")

Yevdokimov, from his place:—Long live the Russian Communist Party! Hurrah! Hurrah! (Delegates rise and shout Hurrah. Clamour. Long and loud applause.) Long live the Central Committee of our Party! Hurrah! (Delegates shout Hurrah.) The Party above all! Yes, indeed! (Applause and hurrahs.)

Various voices. Long live Comrade Stalin! (Loud and prolonged cheers. Cries of hurrah. Clamour.)

The situation was thus made clear, but too late to influence the course of events. The force of inertia exerted its irresistible pressure to the advantage of the existing system. Except in the Leningrad fraction, members had been chosen and instructed by the apparatus devoted to Stalin. Special measures were to be taken to bring the new Opposition to their knees; protesting delegates hurried "spontaneously" from Leningrad to the Kremlin, and disavowed the official delegation. Floods of telegrams dictated by Moscow came in as "spontaneously" from the most distant provinces censuring the dissenters and demanding their submission. It was wasted effort for Zinoviev to address the "steel wall" of fanatical Leninists, to demand "internal democracy" in the Party, "real liberty of discussion," collaboration of "all the former groups" (that is of earlier defeated oppositions) in the administration, "election of all committees," and, finally, "limitation of powers" of the bureaux of the Central Committee and especially of the Secretariat. He was reminded of his conduct during the October Revolution. Krupskaya protested in vain against the remarks addressed to a member of the Political Bureau availing himself of his right to speak, an intolerance in contrast to the licence accorded to the "Bukharin school." Other members of the new Opposition succeeded no better, with good reason; when Stalin replied to his critics it was to give the final blow to the vanquished.

He began by revealing Zinoviev's subterranean manœuvres in the last few months, and complained of the "calumnies" of the minority. Had they not unjustly attributed to him "sympathy with the idea of re-establishing private property in land"? He made a brusque attack on the impotent opposition, described the view of Sokolnikov and Krupskaya on State capitalism as "nonsense," and demonstrated Zinoviev's ignorance of Leninism and of Bolshevisation. As for Kamenev, he was not a Leninist at all but a liberal. Point by point, with the help of quotations from Lenin's *Complete Works*, he distorted his opponents' theories, before coming to his real subject. "Yes, comrades, I am a frank, rough man. That is true; I don't deny it." He related the efforts of the new Opposition to exclude Trotsky. "We did not agree with Zinoviev and Kamenev, being fully aware that an amputation policy is full of dangers to the Party, that the amputation method, the method of bleeding—they demanded blood—is dangerous and infectious; to-day, one is amputated, another to-morrow, a third the day after. What will be left of the Party in the end?" Then, a series of differences, ending with the incidents of which Bukharin was the hero. "Now, what do they want to do with Bukharin? They want his blood. That is what Zinoviev demands, in his embittered concluding speech. You demand Bukharin's blood? We will not let you have it; be sure of that." He admitted a difference of views in the Opposition, except on the very problem to be solved:

. . . Despite this diversity of opinion, they are all united on one point. What is it on which they are all united? What is their platform? Their platform is that there ought to be a reform of the Secretariat of the Central Committee. That is the only point upon which they are fully united. The statement may seem strange, even ludicrous, but it is a fact.

There is a history behind all this. In the year 1923 after the Twelfth Party Congress, these people, assembling in a "cellar" (laughter), elaborated a platform in accordance with which the Political Bureau was to be abolished and the Secretariat was to become the leading political and organisational body. It was to consist of Zinoviev, Trotsky and Stalin. What was the meaning of this platform? It meant that the party was to be led without Rykov, without Kalinin, without Tomsky, without Molotov, without Bukharin. The platform came to nothing, not only because it did not represent any principles, but also because the Party cannot be led without the aid of those comrades I have just named. When a written question was addressed to me from the depths at Kislovodsk, I refused to have anything to do with the scheme and said that if the comrades wished it, I was ready to give up my own position—quite quietly without either open or hidden discussion and without formulating demands for the protection of the rights of minorities. (Laughter.) Now it seems a new stage is beginning, opposed to the first. Now they are demanding not the politicalisation of the

Secretariat, but its technicalisation, not the suppression of the Polit-bureau, but its omnipotence. . . . My only fear is that the Party will not agree. (*A voice:* Excellent!)

Stalin's game in all its simple astuteness is exposed in this speech. Master of the mechanism of government by the hold of the Party over the State and the absolute prerogative at each stage of each Communist organ over the one below it—the supremacy of the Secretariat crowning the edifice—the General Secretary affected to share power with his colleagues on the Political Bureau and the Central Committee, whom he was always able to confront with the *fait accompli* and, in case of resistance, to eject. He flattered the vanity of secondary personages by affirming the impossibility of directing the Party without them—the same Party which it was possible to conduct without Lenin—and he granted them nominal authority in consideration of his own omnipotence. In other matters he sought a provisional middle course between opposed radical solutions both in the political and practical, economic domains —a policy dictated by innate prudence, by his desire for stability, and by way of precaution against any eventuality. The only difficulty in sight was that of paralysing any future attempt at opposition before it obtained a footing in the Central Committee or the Political Bureau. In this Stalin succeeded easily as far as Trotsky was concerned, and now carried out the same operation against Zinoviev, with the assurance that he could repeat the measures if necessary.

He concluded his final speech by promises expressed in his monotonous, trivial style. "We are opposed to amputation. That does not mean that leaders may strut about lording it over their comrades. No, not that. We are not going to bow down before our leaders. (Shouts of 'Good!' Cheers.) We stand for unity, we are against amputation. The policy of amputation is hateful to us. The Party desires unity and will accomplish it, with Kamenev and Zinoviev if they so desire, without them if they refuse. (Shouts of 'Good!' Applause.)"

Thereupon the Congress was practically over by its eleventh session, though it went on sitting, without even discussing economic questions—the most important of all—for the sole purpose of suppressing Kamenev's statement in the Order Paper. The real work was done behind the scenes, where the Opposition wasted their efforts in vain palavers to obtain a last-moment compromise and save their faces. Meanwhile the emissaries of the majority, dispatched to Leningrad, took possession of the local press, and, in one workshop and one quarter after the other, diverted the unanimity of the flock to a course diametrically opposed to what they had voted for before. "Thoroughly perverted by political servility," as Lenin had once said, the rank and file were unaware of the direction in which they were being led. On December 30th, the Leningrad *Pravda* proclaimed the exact opposite of its recent emphatic statements, under identical headlines evoking "iron unity," the "Leninist line" and other sacramental rubrics. "Hundred per cent monolithism" would soon be restored, at the price of displacing some three thousand communist officials suspected of "deviation." Ordjonikidze was on the spot, intent on reestablishing discipline.

Thus Stalin, having repudiated a "policy of amputation," proceeded from words to action; by a characteristic mental reservation, he preferred to inflict unemployment and hunger on his opponents, an almost infallible procedure, under Soviet conditions, for demoralising the refractory and bringing them back to the paths of wisdom. Even at the Congress he had allowed himself a joke, with a threat behind it, at Riazanov's expense—"Riazanov is homesick for Turkestan"—because of an irreverent remark of the learned director of the Marx-Engels Institute. A phrase of Glebov-Avilov's, frequently cited in the controversy, threw light on the meaning of the hint: "No one will care to vote against the motion and for that reason find himself sent to Murmansk or Turkestan." The ice of the Arctic Ocean and the burning sands of Central Asia, the scurvy and malaria awaiting dissidents were considerable factors in the calculations of both sides. The hardiest hesitated to expose their relatives and their children to the persecutions of the G.P.U. by persisting in opposition to the point of heroism. "It was current practice in Moscow," wrote the historian, S. Platonov, "in cases of political offences, to prosecute not only the offender, but his whole family." Ivan the Terrible, Boris Godunov and their successors governed by these means, and Stalin inclined to the same methods.

Stalin's preponderance was more and more obvious from the date of this Congress onwards. Reports in the press laid stress on the violent incidents in which he took part, passing over in silence dangerous revelations. The Party was only just beginning to learn the name already feared in the higher stages of the machine, and the masses, knowing nothing of these Byzantine disputes, were still in ignorance in spite of the multiplication of portraits issued from the State printing-press. But the very fact of his having delivered the political report of the Central Committee brought Stalin notoriety, enhanced by the unexpected disgrace of Zinoviev and Kamenev.

Stalin's clear-sightedness is not revealed in a first reading of this interminable speech, the triviality of which is ill-concealed by its pompous form. He supplements the poverty of its substance by verbiage. It is a succession of analytical résumés of the documents supplied by the Bureaux and Commissariats concerned, with the addition of comments representing average opinion in the ruling clique on current affairs. In foreign policy Stalin predicts definitely that "if the Dawes Plan is pregnant with revolution for Germany, the Locarno Pact is pregnant with a great European war." On internal policy he expresses an optimism reflecting the security of the bureaucratic regime delivered free of all the known oppositions, and now armed to discover and crush any new ones. The only passage in the report which had particular interest at the time referred to the dangers of over-rapid industrialisation in the Soviet State, which might result in irreparable economic disturbance and "certain famine artificially brought about," but observations of this kind were regarded as commonplaces and received hardly any notice.

Sokolnikov had said at the Congress: "Lenin was neither president of the Political Bureau, nor General Secretary, but, nevertheless, he had the last word in politics. . . . If Stalin

wants to win the same confidence, let him win it." Stalin secured supremacy by other means, of which none as yet knew
the secret. All that was known was that he had been able to
secure for himself a majority of five against Trotsky in the
Political Bureau, then three against the Zinoviev-Kamenev combination, and thus to control the enormous "machine." This gave
him control over millions of persons subordinate in different
ways to his dictatorship. By a singular inversion, he controlled
the composition of the assemblies whose mandatory he was supposed to be. They all, in the last resort, were dependent on him,
and did their best to serve him to ensure their own security or
for advancement. The numerous malcontents abstained from
protest, because the construction of the Party made it possible
to intercept communications from top to bottom, to preclude
communication between groups, and to suppress it, if desired,
right and left.

"From the ordinary bourgeois point of view," wrote Lenin
before and during the revolution, "the notions of democracy
and dictatorship are mutually exclusive." Stalin thought them
incompatible. The tendency under his rule was to efface the
remnant of democracy remaining in decadent Bolshevism. It
may be said of the Leninists, as their master wrote of the Social-
Democrats, that they had denied their own principles, "just as
Christians, when once theirs had become a State religion, forgot
the simplicities of primitive Christianity and its revolutionary
democratic spirit." Under cover of an obsolete vocabulary, the
protection of a series of bureaucratic screens, and the aegis of a
numerous and varied police, Stalin seized regal prerogatives one
by one. In the stern severity of the stage during the terrible years
of danger, the General Secretary appeared simply to be the first
among the Bolsheviks. But the hour was coming which Plekhanov with his acute vision had foreseen: "In the long run, the
whole will revolve around one man who, *ex providentia*, will
hold in his hands all the threads of power."

Under pretext of a considerable numerical increase in the
Party, from 735,000 members and probationers to 1,088,000 in
the interval between two Congresses, the new Central Commit-

tee was to have 106 members, the Control Commission 163, actual members and deputy-members. Most of the Opposition had been expelled, the rest counted for nothing. Chronic hypertrophy of all the higher organisations, at sessions becoming steadily less frequent, reduced their statutory authority to nil as against the permanent executive organs, which could not be prevented from legislating by decree and ruling the country by despotism. Membership of the Political Bureau was increased to nine. Trotsky and Zinoviev remained, as hostages or figureheads. Stalin strengthened his section by adding Kalinin, Molotov and Voroshilov to Bukharin, Rykov and Tomsky, whose automatic acquiescence was not guaranteed for ever. Kamenev returned to the rank of deputy-members, from which Sokolnikov disappeared; Dzerzhinsky, Uglanov, Petrovsky and Rudzutak were to constitute the reserve. Thus members, afraid of moving a step down, and deputies hoping for a step up, offered many possibilities of intrigue and manœuvre to a supple and consummate intriguer. The General Secretary would henceforward have a majority of seven members stable enough to give him time to envisage a coming crisis and make his arrangements accordingly. Except in the event of an unlikely simultaneous attack from five hostile colleagues, Stalin held the equivalent of consulship for life, the permanent Secretaryship. In five years Stalin realised by inches his *coup d'état*. He, the cleverest if not the best of all the aspirants, held Lenin's inheritance.

Chapter IX

THE INHERITOR

W HO is Stalin?" After the 1925 Congress everyone was asking himself this question which Skliansky had put to Trotsky earlier in the year. "The most eminent mediocrity in our party," Trotsky replied, although in earlier days he had described Stalin to Max Eastman as "a brave man and a sincere revolutionary." These descriptions are not entirely contradictory, since revolutionary sincerity, physical courage and intellectual mediocrity may all go together. In fact the description adequately fits the average Bolshevik under Lenin, but the change in Trotsky's tone, after an interval of less than a year, was unmistakable.

Trotsky, therefore, took a long time to form the more unfavourable opinion which later he was to express in so many ways in his writings. No one knew what the General Secretary was capable of; and Stalin himself, before he had so easily got the better of his clumsy and impatient rivals, probably had no idea of the prospects that would one day be open to him. As usually happens in such cases, his horizon broadened as his responsibilities increased. The heads of the Party looked on him above all as an "organiser," a vague expression which later became more precise as the astonishing results of his particular talents made themselves felt. Those who were close to him knew that his chief superiority over his over-eloquent colleagues was his precious gift of dumbness, a natural tendency not to waste words, in addition to the gifts of order, punctuality, devotion to the Party and capacity for hard work, which Lenin had admired. But these gifts do not explain his final domination. Although, in his fraction, Dzerzhinsky was morally and Bukharin culturally his superior, no one was his equal in shrewdness, manœuvring, administrative ability or in the continuity of his drive towards power. Yet at that time no one saw him as a future figure in history nor as the typical representative of a growing social class.

Trotsky explains his unfavourable opinion by saying: "The victorious counter-revolution may have its great men. But its first stage, Thermidor, has need of mediocrities who cannot see beyond the end of their noses." According to this view, expressed after long reflection, a Thermidorian reaction had already begun in Russia, of which Stalin was the unconscious instrument. "For the first time I attacked squarely, one might almost say, with physical conviction, the problem of Thermidor," Trotsky goes on, forgetting his own thesis of 1921 on the N.E.P. as a Thermidor accomplished in good time, and within the necessary limits, by the Jacobins of the proletariat. The incident of Zalutsky shows that he was not alone in reasoning thus. Although this shabby accuser rapidly retracted, the accusation of "Thermidorianism" gained ground. Thus, on this point, Trotsky and his worst enemies thought alike; and soon the latter in their turn were borrowing his arguments in favour of planned production, industrialisation, and the democracy of the Party.

Nevertheless, Trotsky still hesitated to declare himself between the two fractions at odds with one another. In 1925 he was made President of the Committee of Concessions and director of technico-scientific services. After a diplomatic holiday in the Caucasus, he took up his new duties with "that praiseworthy ambition which urges a man to excel at whatever he puts his hand to," as Washington said, and abstained from becoming involved in the quarrels of the triumvirate. Both in speeches and writings he urged the necessity of improving the quality of industrial products, and also studied projects for electrification, preparing notes on the great Dnieprostroy scheme. Feeling that it was politic to make a show of official optimism, he published a series of articles: "Towards Socialism or Capitalism?" in which he refuted those socialist theoreticians who saw in the economic restoration of Russia a retreat from the revolution. In these he quoted, with child-like confidence, the doubtful statistics of the Gosplan, from which was to come "the magnificent music of developing socialism." Collective economy was gaining the ascendency over private initiative, according to the "statistics," and he endeavoured to show that the rate of progress forecast must lead to its success. He took no account of the uneconomic means of coercion used by the State to repress capitalist tendencies and to secure an artificial control. As regards external events, he considered the social revolution in Europe in the near future as the most likely hypothesis.

But Stalin was in no way grateful to him for this attitude. He put increasing difficulties in his way, rendered his work impossible and persecuted his collaborators. Trotsky gave further proof of submission by disavowing those rare foreign communists who defended him. He even went so far as to condemn Max Eastman, whose book, *Since Lenin Died*, exposed all the facts of the crisis in the Bolshevik Party as far as was possible with the documents and information then available. He even denied the existence and the suppression of Lenin's *Testament*, by quibbling with words. Krupskaya followed his example. For the sake of the good of the Party, which perhaps they misunderstood, and which they certainly interpreted very narrowly, and confused with reasons of state, Bolsheviks of all colours put their solidarity as a caste above the truth and laughed at all honesty as a limited prejudice. Trotsky himself hoped to buy a political truce by sacrificing the comrades who had been his allies in ideas and in the struggle. Vainly, for by so doing he encouraged Stalin and discouraged the Opposition. At this point the conflicts of the integral Leninists provided the respite he needed; Trotskyism was no longer a burning question, but was discussed only in an academic manner. Stalin and Zinoviev, in their controversy over socialism in one country, quoted their old adversary without passion. Kamenev charged him with excessive optimism, which was almost equivalent to a compliment, and took on himself the reproaches of pessimism which were once reserved for the metaphysician of the "permanent revolution."

At the Fourteenth Congress Trotsky remained silent. He hesitated to take sides, although tempted to give the demagogues of the new Opposition who dared to talk of democracy a piece of his mind. His ex-lieutenant, Antonov-Ovseënko wrote to him, "I know that you were ready to intervene at the Congress against Zinoviev-Kamenev. I bitterly regret and deplore that the impatience and blindness of the comrades in our fraction should have caused you, against your own judgment, to abandon this intervention which was already decided upon." The rank and file militants in the two opposition groups, all equally ill-used, tended to fraternise and wished to bring their leaders together. After the Congress, Trotsky was obliged, at the Central Committee, to disapprove on principle of any repression against those who were defeated. Both sides then made advances to him and a more hopeful prospect began to open out for him.

Despite their common lot and the desire of their partisans to come together, an alliance between the old Opposition and the new appeared, in 1926, to be impossible. Trotsky was supposed to represent the Left of the Party, while Zinoviev, Kamenev, Sokolnikov and others were the Right incarnate. According to his own theory, the two currents reflected irreconcilable class antagonism, proletarian and bourgeois. At a pinch, the Left might support a centre bloc, of which Stalin was the typical expression, against the danger from the Right, but a coalition of the two wings would mean that both were compromised. It was no accident that Zinoviev and Kamenev should have "flinched" in October, and quite recently demanded Trotsky's exclusion, or that Sokolnikov should be the most hostile to the economic and industrial plans of the Left. If the new Opposition rallied itself around the limited democratic programme of the old, it was by an egotistic instinct of self-preservation. But Zinoviev could not do otherwise than confirm Trotsky's point of view on the utopianism of establishing socialism in Russia alone. Next Kamenev was found defending the ideas of the Left on planning and industry; his views on the disquieting progress made by peasant capitalism agreed with those of economists of similar tendencies. Ideas also coincided on Thermidor, but this was as yet unadmitted. All this caused great distress of mind among the leaders of the minorities and in the ranks, in which there was a strong conviction of the necessity for unity of all the oppositions without distinction of origin.

While the adversaries of the dominant fraction were getting together, Stalin was not losing any time. Control Commissions and "packed" local Committees executed his orders with precision. The cadres of the Party, the trade unions and the State were purged by police measures. In Leningrad and elsewhere, thousands of Oppositionists were dismissed from their places and rendered destitute. In the Communist International and its sections a similar fate overtook the misguided followers of the ex-President. Everywhere places were open for those who were willing to stake their fortune on the new master. This gave food for thought to any who might have been recalcitrant. Zinoviev and Kamenev were faced with the loss of all their posts of influence, being left only with titles which the stranglehold of the machine rendered valueless. The rest of the old guard were to be still more roughly handled. Stalin's creatures and minions waited for the spoils, taking possession of all offices and prospects of advancement. The bureaucratic rampart grew and strengthened around the Secretary of the secretaries.

Stalin managed with caution the changes necessary for his slow and prudent advance towards absolute power. He disarmed his critics in the Party, but made use of some of the more capable of them in subordinate positions where they were allowed to find refuge. By this means he disguised to some extent the inadequacy of those who had recently been promoted and also gave prominent members of the minority a chance to amend their attitude at leisure, to make their choice between their costly convictions and their immediate personal interest. The embassies and commercial missions swarmed with Oppositionists, rendered impotent by their isolation from one another and the necessity of making a show of orthodoxy before foreigners. Many were also to be found in the Departments of Economics and of scientific research, where ex-Mensheviks were also employed, and among specialists of all categories. Most hard hit were the rank and file working-class supporters, who had great difficulty in finding work. Together with the dismissed functionaries, these unemployed maintained an undertone of discontent, which those leaders who were not reconciled to retreat and were looking for a way out were glad to claim as the first symptoms of a "turn." The new Opposition, less adept at the theoretical researches beloved of the old, built up a clandestine organisation according to the standard pattern and lulled itself with hopes of working for revenge. In other directions, the good offices of mutual friends and of reconciled enemies gradually softened the more marked discordances between the various dissatisfied groups. At a session of the Central Committee in April 1926, the only two minorities represented both submitted similar amendments and made parallel reservations, and on the following day a pact was concluded: the impossible was achieved under the banner of "the Opposition bloc." Zinoviev and his partners rendered homage to the clairvoyance of the Left whose political and economic programme they adopted. Trotsky retracted his severe condemnation of the October defaulters. "A reciprocal amnesty," commented Stalin.

Into this "unprincipled bloc," as the reigning oligarchy at once named it, Zinoviev by ingenious arguments succeeded in luring the remnants of the Workers' Opposition which had been hostile to Trotsky. The Georgian communists, whom Stalin had turned out, also joined. The classic plank of democratic centralism was already part of the programme of the section of the Left known as Trotskyist, and all the other already defeated sections now came to add their weakness to the common fund. Since the leaders were now agreed, most of their partisans followed, although disliking the idea of victory under the banner of Trotsky. The divergent opinions which still existed were felt to be of less importance than the essential points of the common programme: industrialisation of the country and democratisation of the Party. In reality, the main object was to attack the monopoly of power, not in order to abolish it, but in order to turn out those who held it and divide it among themselves.

Already Trotsky had more or less handed Stalin the dictatorship by his lack of foresight, his tactic of patient waiting broken by sudden and inconsequent reactions, and his mistaken calculations, yet up to that time all was not entirely lost, the last word had not been said. But with the formation of the "bloc," Trotsky achieved his final ruin as a political leader, by this association with men devoid of character or credit who had nothing concrete to offer to offset the disrepute they brought with them. Whatever he may say after the event, he did not understand the nature of the evolution of Bolshevism nor the root of the problem which had to be solved. His most brilliant gifts were a handicap in a struggle in which Stalin's minor talents were just what was needed. He imagined that he had gained the adherence of the "Leningrad workers" whom Zinoviev had deceived and could not now undeceive. In reality he introduced the germs of panic and decomposition into the "bloc." He had the illusion of gaining, if not a majority of the Party, at least a sufficient section to make Stalin pause, but he had forgotten that the genuine Party no longer existed. (He had himself written many times, "The Party will cease to be a party.") He hoped to dispose of the legend of Trotskyism by allying himself with the originators of this falsehood; but what he did in reality was to range himself with the Leninism of the epigones, whose degeneracy he himself had pointed out. By contradictions and complications which the masses could not follow, he threw away all chance of getting a genuine following, or of dissociating himself from the opposing fraction. The working class, whose highest hopes he bragged of representing, was by now so profoundly disappointed by the course of the revolution that it had no longer any faith in any section of a Party whose promises had proved to be such lies. For years had gone by, already the tenth anniversary of October was drawing near, yet the conditions of the masses were getting steadily worse.

2

THE standard of life in the industrial centres in 1926, taking all salaries into consideration, was definitely lower than under the old regime. The averages, which the statistics recorded with fussy precision, were arrived at by totally unscientific subterfuges, but odd fragments of information demonstrated the fallaciousness of the official figures. All those with inside knowledge are aware how much store Stalin sets by statistics and how he causes them to be falsified at need. In any case, only a very small portion of the proletariat received as much as or more than the "average" wage, and a comparison with 1914 indicates a state of misery. As Riazanov truly said on this point, "There are certain categories of workers who have a wage 110 per cent higher than before the War, but in fact they live 100 per cent below the level of a human existence."

That was not all: various illegal reductions in wages under the form of deductions for obligatory contributions and forced subscriptions, long delays in payment, sometimes even of several months, which meant a corresponding depreciation in value, the shameful and crying inequality at the factory between specialised and unskilled workers and between men and women doing the same work, an inequality greater than in any capitalist country, the disregard of the laws and decrees in relation to protection, safety and assistance of the workers, the shameful exploitation of women and children, general disregard of the eight-hour day and the constant violation of the collective contracts by the State as employer, these were the real facts of the situation as stated in the documents of the Soviet, side by side with hollow propaganda phrases. The Central Committee recognised that the housing shortage was a "catastrophic state of affairs"; the average space occupied per worker in Moscow was less than three square metres. The press described in horrible detail the worm-eaten and insanitary barracks where each inhabitant occupied "the dimensions of a coffin."

And these were the privileged wage-earners. The lot of the

disinherited was even worse. From a mass of incoherent figures given by various organisations, which admitted to more than a million unemployed, for the most part without any relief, it is possible to arrive at the truth by multiplying four or five times the number disclosed. Kalinin calculated that the unemployed agricultural labourers amounted to 15 million; the Assistant-Commissar of Works later admitted to 25 million. The population was increasing by 3 million a year and unemployment and misery were in proportion.

Homeless children were another directly connected phenomenon, which the People's Commissars described as "our greatest evil" and Semashko as "a living reproach to our conscience." Official figures admitted to 7, 8 and 9 millions of abandoned children, living by begging, stealing, prostitution and crime. "The roots of this evil are not only in the past but in the present" noted Krupskaya, distressed to find that the trouble was "three-quarters due, not to the misery and carelessness of the old days, but to conditions to-day, to unemployment and to the extreme poverty of the peasants." Anyone outside the Bolshevik aristocracy who had used similar language would soon have lost the last remnants of his liberty.

Dzerzhinsky, one of the few people in responsible positions who preferred plain speaking to the satisfaction of commanding a lot of terrified functionaries, explained the under-consumption to which the Soviet population was condemned by the shortage of manufactured goods and the consequent increase in agricultural prices: all the basic industries (coal, steel, etc.) had decreased since 1914, productivity of labour was less in spite of payment by piece work, costs of manufacture were up and imports were stopped. Consumption had fallen on an average by more than half, per head of the population, by two-thirds for certain basic necessities. Nevertheless, the Government announced that in the tenth year of the revolution, production was equal to before the War. "In Russia, the classic country of lies and charlatanism, figures have a purely relative value and lend themselves with remarkable elasticity to all sorts of metamorphoses," says F. Lacroix in his book *Mysteries of Russia* from which we have already quoted.

The unified Opposition could not shut its eyes to the uncomfortable picture of the "total costs" of the revolution. Stimulated by those elements which were closest to the working class, companions of Sapronov or Shliapnikov, and filled with a natural desire for popularity, they put the elementary demands of the workers in the forefront of their programme. But they put forward nothing which the majority could not accept and the solution was no nearer since they had no means of realising it. Fearful of incurring the reproach of Menshevism or pessimism, they dared not broach the question of bringing the N.E.P. to an end, which Lenin had hinted at, nor face up squarely to the need for reform of the system of government. Their economic policy, which was still vague, did nothing to alter the "general line." It did not lay down any practicable and rapid scheme for overcoming the deficit on industry and transport, replacing outworn equipment, reducing the net costs, stopping speculation by middlemen and stabilising the collapsing chervonetz. Owing to this, all their plans for raising real wages and their respect for the eight-hour day were no more than the abstract solicitude of Bolsheviks for the proletariat, since all these identical plans had existed on paper for ten years. Their abuse of the bureaucracy was no more forceful than that of some of the actual leaders. Dzerzhinsky at the Central Committee declared: "When I look at our apparatus, at our system of organisation, our incredible bureaucracy and our utter disorder combined with every conceivable sort of red-tape, I am literally horrified." Bukharin, speaking at a Communist Youth Congress, recognised the danger of a "hardening of caste distinctions" and admitted the "incontestable degeneration" due to the "complete immunity" of Communist Party members. The Opposition did not, therefore, have a monopoly of platonic reformist criticism nor of ineffective goodwill. On the question of democracy, Sokolnikov caused a scandal by suggesting that other parties should be allowed. Ossinsky alone agreed with this, thinking that if the Mensheviks and Social Revolutionaries were legalised, then all communists would be obliged to unite against the common enemy.

The two fractions were more completely divided on the question of planned economy. The traditional Left attributed all misfortunes to the fact that industry lagged behind agriculure, and offered as a cure the speeding up of industry as part of the complete economic plan, in order to weld together the town and country and to equalise the supply and demand of goods. In opposition to this "industrial deviation" the majority alleged the lack of funds which the State had at its disposal. Stalin had predicted at a recent Congress: "*Since, however, there is a great lack of capital in this country, we have good reason to expect that in the future the growth of our industry will not proceed so rapidly as it has in the past.*" The passage in his report in which he makes this remarkable prediction also replies to the proposals of the Left which he purposely exaggerated:

We might devote double the present sum to the development of industry. *But this would bring about an unduly rapid tempo in the development of industry, so that, owing to the lack of a sufficiency of free capital, we should not be able to keep step with that development, and there would certainly be a fiasco*—to say nothing of the fact that if we were to spend so much upon industry, there would be nothing left over for agricultural credits.

We might increase our imports twofold, especially the import of machinery, in order to hasten the growth of industry; but this, by making our imports greatly exceed our exports, would lead to an unfavourable balance of trade, and would disturb our exchange. This would mean an undermining of the foundation *on which alone a carefully planned guidance and development of manufacturing industry is possible.*

We might greatly increase exports, without paying heed to any other of the main constituents of our economic life. We might do this regardless of the condition of the home market. *The consequences of such a policy would inevitably be to produce great complications in the towns, owing to an enormous increase in the price of agricultural produce, this meaning a decline in real wages and a sort of artificially organised famine* with all its disastrous consequences.

The "industrialists" considered it unnecessary to set aside further credits for agriculture; in fact, they hoped to get from the countryside funds to subsidise industry. In his studies for the Communist Academy and in his much-discussed work *The New Economy*, Preobrazhensky attempted to demonstrate this theoretically. According to his thesis, the stage of primitive capitalist accumulation such as Marx analyses in *Capital*, must inevitably be gone through by all socialist societies without colonies, in order to set up an "accumulated fund" at the expense of the peasant producer. In 1925, Kamenev's unexpected views on the prosperity of the *kulaks* gave unforeseen confirmation to the economic algebra of the Left, since, failing any financial co-operation from abroad, it disclosed a valuable source of revenues and subsidies in the interior. The "bloc" wavered between different methods of laying hands on the capital of the peasants and merchants: forced loans, re-assessment of taxation, readjustment of prices. Thus were the *kulak* and the N.E.P. man to become sleeping partners in State industry in spite of themselves.

In April 1926, the Central Committee, following the Leninist principle of appropriating ideas from the Opposition in order to render them unworkable, had admitted that industrialisation was "the principal task" and that "a disciplined plan" was the only way out of the disorder. Rykov, in his official report on the economic situation and the budget, attributed the scarcity of goods and the agricultural stagnation from which the Soviet Union was suffering to the backwardness of industry. But during the debate Stalin poured ridicule on the idea of vast plans quite disproportionate to the resources of Russia, and in particular on the project of an immense power station on the Dnieper, which he compared to the purchase of a costly and useless gramophone by a mujik whose cart was in need of repair. Later, in summing-up at Leningrad, he made frequent allusions to the "industrial deviation," but in an impersonal manner, since the evasions and shiftings of the Opposition still left him somewhat in the dark. While reiterating "the slogan of industrialisation proclaimed at the Fourteenth Congress" and declaring that "our country has entered upon a new period of the N.E.P., a period of bold industrialisation," he polemicises thus: "It is impossible to develop industry in the void, if there are no raw materials in the country, if there is no food for the workers, if there is no agriculture, however undeveloped, since this is the prime market for industry." Even more than in America, according to him, industry must depend on the internal market, and particularly on the peasant market. Exports must be developed but not by depriving the population, "since the workers and peasants wish to feed themselves like men." No exaggerations of the Dnieprostroy type. "We are too fond of building fantastic plans for industry without reckoning up our resources. People seem to forget that it is impossible to make plans, or to embark on any enterprise, more or less grandiose, without a certain minimum of resources and a certain minimum of reserves." Finally, Stalin, with obvious implications, rebuked "those persons who look on the mass of labouring peasants as a foreign body, an object to be exploited for the benefit of industry, a sort of colony." As against the industrialist Left, Stalin set himself up as the defender of the peasants.

In 1923 Trotsky had objected to any additional taxation of the farmers in order that "the peasant might become richer"— an incontestable precedent for Bukharin's "Enrich yourselves!" "We are fond of describing any peasant who has enough to eat as a *kulak*," said Zinoviev in 1924. In 1925 Trotsky still spoke of enlarging "the scale of profits of the capitalist-merchants in agriculture," of strengthening "the capitalist economy of the farmer." But in the same year Kamenev suddenly discovered the *kulak* danger and reproached the Central Committee with under-estimating it. In 1926 the "bloc" was insisting that the better-off peasants had considerable reserves: it was there that the State should look for the resources necessary to develop industry and so come to the rescue of the proletariat. This volte-face had two good harvests in a ruined country as its only justification.

On July 20, 1926, Dzerzhinsky replied to the full Assembly of the Central Committee: "The mujiks have hoarded up 400 million roubles, perhaps 4 each. . . ." The disconnected and passionate speech which contained this pertinent remark, as well as the few lines quoted on bureaucracy, was his last political act. The founder of the Cheka died after leaving the tribune from which he had violently apostrophised his opponents Kamenev and Pyatakov and threatened the Opposition with "fresh gunpowder" in the autumn. Although this threat was omitted from the printed text, it made a great impression on the audience. The atmosphere of tension and nervousness throughout this session of the "Bolshevik Parliament" was intense, not so much owing to the economic questions under debate as to the particular political circumstances at that time. Dzerzhinsky's death, following immediately on his menacing words, which the press did not reproduce, brought to a head the emotions born of other events. The Opposition "bloc" openly declared itself, "seriously and for a long time to come," as Zinoviev said, and the struggle for power entered on a new phase.

3

As soon as he learned of the result of the negotiations between his adversaries, Stalin set himself to break up the alliance. He attempted first to discredit Zinoviev and Kamenev by printing the unpublished letter of Lenin, in which he stigmatised the "deserters" of October. This letter had been suppressed in the *Complete Works*, but had already been circulated illegally in the Party by the Trotskyists. The two friends replied by demanding the publication of the *Testament*, which they had themselves helped to suppress, and the existence of which Trotsky and Krupskaya had only recently been forced to deny. This Stalin refused, at the same time redoubling police precautions for the suppression of clandestine factional activity; the increase in secret meetings, the passing of prohibited documents from hand to hand, and the alarming increase in spontaneous strikes, might give the Left their opportunity. Zinoviev's followers actually held a conspiratorial meeting in a wood at which Lashevich, the Assistant-Commissar for War, spoke; the inevi-

table spy having reported this to Stalin, he seized the pretext to
strike his blow. For this he made use of a private letter seized at
Baku, two years earlier, written by Medvediev, an old member
of the Workers' Opposition which was now part of the "bloc."
Stalin always utilised to the utmost any weapon that came into
his hands. He hoped now by attacking the subordinates to
strike at the leaders, perhaps to overcome them.

Pravda opened a campaign against a new "danger from the
Right," with the idea of compromising the Left. The confiscated
letter, mangled and falsified, formed the basis for this. Medvediev had, in a private letter, dared to envisage the desirability
of a broad policy of concessions, in imitation of Krassin, just
as Lenin before him had envisaged an extension of the N.E.P.
This was sufficient to bring down on him the accusation of
being "100 per cent Menshevik." He had written in confidence
what many, even among those close to Stalin, were saying under
their breath, that the Communist sections in different countries
were artificial growths and the so-called representatives of the
international revolution in Moscow were "lackeys" supported
by "Russian gold." This condemned him as a blasphemer and
a liquidator. Medvediev and his comrades had no means of
clearing themselves publicly. Neither had Lashevich and the
others. The Politbureau alone controlled all newspapers, pamphlets and meetings. Agents of the Secretariat began to spread the
suggestion that the Opposition had not only set itself up against
the Party but also against the State. Voices clamoured for violent
measures, expulsions. Stalin likes to set going exaggerated demands in order that he may appear in the rôle of mediator,
proposing a compromise, which can then easily be put over.

When the July session opened, in an atmosphere heavy with
alarming rumours, in which the word "Thermidor" continually
recurred, nothing remained but to ratify the measures which
Stalin and his friends had already discussed. The Control Commission had prepared all their weapons for intimidating the new
Opposition, which was not expected to show fight. Stalin had
boasted privately of "bringing Zinoviev and Kamenev to their
knees." But these two declared their solidarity with the other

militants convicted of "fractionalism" and "defeatism." They declared their allegiance to the theses of the Left which they had recently violently abused for imaginary "Trotskyism." Later, they worked themselves into a state of indignation over the permanent state of siege then existing in the Party, but it did not occur to them to demand the restitution of consitutional liberty for everyone else in the State at the same time. Their opponents reminded them in vain of their own violent attacks on Trotsky, their demands for his expulsion, even his imprisonment, with quotations from their own articles and oratorical diatribes. They replied by lifting the veil from the machinations of the "anti-Trotskyists," in which they themselves had played a large part, the activities of the *semiorka*, and the rest. Zinoviev admitted that he had made a worse mistake in 1923 than in 1917. "Yes, on the question of bureaucratic repression, Trotsky was right, and I was wrong." He demanded the reading of the famous *Testament*, which everyone spoke of by hearsay and yet which was not supposed to exist. Stalin felt impelled to make known Lenin's secret letters on the national question and on the State plan; for the curiosity aroused relaxed momentarily the discipline of the fraction without breaking it. Trotsky alone benefited by this glimpse into the past, but the audience remained unshaken. The minority had eighteen votes at the beginning of the session and eighteen at the end. Of these, five, among whom were Smilga, Rakovsky, and Ossinsky, constituted a "buffer-group," intended to deaden shocks, a tactical ruse which had no effect; Stalin always sees through these little games, although his enemies rarely see through his.

A fresh quarrel broke out over international policy. The Opposition criticised Stalin for sending an untimely ultimatum to China about the Manchurian railway, a move which might have led to armed conflict, without consulting the Politbureau. They held him responsible for the action of the Polish Communist Party in supporting Pilsudski in his military *coup d'état*. They challenged him on the sterility of the collaboration between the Russian and British trade unions, and on Tomsky's rôle in the British General Strike. He was blamed for all this because no internal or external action was ever taken in the name of "Moscow," except with Stalin's initiative and consent.

The last question raised let loose an interminable polemic in which the "Anglo-Russian Committee" figured largely and helped to confuse an already complex question still further. In 1925 Trotsky had written a book on the future of England in which he predicted the imminence of a revolution in that country and the final victory of communism. The Politbureau, which had to conduct simultaneously both the foreign policy of the Soviet Union, which was necessarily opportunist, and the Communist International, which was, by definition, revolutionary, had embarked on a queer diplomatic adventure with the General Council of the Trade Union Congress using the bureaucratic Russian trade unions as intermediaries. An Anglo-Russian Committee, drawn from high officials of both organisations, was set up to secure mutual understanding and co-operation, based on highly ambiguous principles from which both parties hoped to further their own ends. The English hoped that by affecting sympathy for communism they would increase the commercial relations between the two countries, thus benefiting both their own capitalists and the unemployed, while the Russians, by professing an insincere devotion to trade unionism, hoped to make use of the trade unions for their own ends. When the General Strike began in 1926, Trotsky felt that his prophecies were about to be confirmed, and that its sudden collapse could only be due to the treason of the leaders; from this he concluded that the Anglo-Russian Committee must be dissolved and the "traitors" unmasked. Neither his friends, Rakovsky and Radek, nor his new ally Zinoviev, shared this simple-minded view. Tomsky, head of the Russian trade unions, had endorsed the decision to end the strike, and Stalin's fraction felt that the Committee could still be put to further use.

The Opposition, which was brought round to Trotsky's point of view, made yet one more mistake in attempting to use the "English question" as a stick to beat Stalin, since it was a question in which the distressed Russian masses had no direct interest. They wasted time on it at the Central Committee and wore themselves out making speeches behind closed doors which the press would never publish. They bared the flank of the Opposition to reprisals without any tactical necessity for so doing, and thus allowed themselves to be forced out of their last remaining Government positions without being able either to defend or demonstratively to retire from them. The result was that the majority, instead of being split, were driven closer together.

The balance-sheet of the July encounter was strongly in Stalin's favour. Little he cared about the magnificent doctrinal theses of his critics, or the brilliance of their literature. His policy was based on more immediate human realities. Lashevich, caught out in flagrant insubordination, had been relieved of his military posts, excluded from the Central Committee and allotted a post of secondary importance in Siberia; Zinoviev, suspected of connivance, had been eliminated from the Politbureau, where Rudzutak took his place; Kamenev had been forced to resign from the Moscow Soviet and dismissed from the Commissariat of Commerce, which was taken over by Mikoyan; Kuibyshev had been chosen as Dzerzhinsky's successor on the Economic Council; Ordjonikidze, Mikoyan, Kirov, Andreyev, and Kaganovich had been chosen as alternates for the Politbureau—these were the "organisational conclusions" announced by Stalin and ratified with mechanical precision by the Central Committee. Against these minutely worked-out arrangements, the finest thesis in the world was not worth the snap of a finger.

Following on the thinning-out at the top, came a purge of the lower ranks; thousands were recalled, particularly in Leningrad, which still swarmed with refractory persons, despite the apparent unanimity on the surface; the usual method being an "administrative change" to that part of the country where the thermometer falls to below forty-five degrees in winter. "We have triumphed but not convinced," admitted Kalinin on his return from a punitive expedition to Leningrad. For example, Ossovsky, someone quite unknown, was expelled from the Party with a terrific outcry; let those who would not take this warning beware! With a remarkable unanimity of thought and expression, all the telegrams received from the provinces expressed their "entire and complete approval" of the severity of the Central Committee, even demanding that it be increased. By a curious bureaucratic irony, "Zinovievsk" called for greater severity against Zinoviev. The machine was so perfected as to obtain similar telegraphic resolutions from Berlin, New York, Paris, London, Prague and Stockholm, where emissaries of the Secretariat had fulfilled their task as prompters to the "bolshevised" sections of the Communist International.

By increasing the number of alternates in the Politbureau, Stalin was strongly defending his rear, since the newly promoted members, owing their improvised careers to him, would certainly support him if necessary against the titular members who might desert him. Ordjonikidze had always been a crony of his, Mikoyan was another of his Caucasian followers, Kirov, who had fallen heir to Zinoviev's position in Leningrad, had never expected to climb so high, Andreyev and Kaganovich both had a temporary "Trotskyist" aberration to do penance for, and Stalin is enough of a psychologist to know that deserters make the humblest followers. After all that had happened since Lenin's death, there were plenty of mediocrities who coveted a seat on the Central Committee or the Control Commission, plenty of third-rate officials who aspired towards the Politbureau. The expert use which Stalin made of these ambitions was devastating for his antagonists, who were all infected with intellectual superiority.

But he was not content merely to manipulate men. He was haunted by the Leninist tradition which urged him also to meddle with ideas. In any case, men and ideas appear to him inseparable and he can only understand the latter through the former. At the Executive of the International, where Zinoviev, the so-called President, no longer had the right to open his mouth, Stalin attacked the "deviations of the Right and the extreme Left," by which he meant anyone who opposed any of the dogmatic commonplaces of the majority; he accused one opponent who attempted to carry on an "ideological struggle" without "discrediting the leaders of the Opposition," of having the "morals of a vicar." He repeated his well-known assertion: "I say that such a struggle cannot exist in nature. I say that whoever agrees to the struggle on condition that the leaders are not attacked, is denying the possibility of any ideological struggle within the Party." At least his opponents were duly warned, but instead of acting on the warnings they stuck to their profitless abstractions.

While implacably abusing other people in order to discredit their ideas and limit their influence, Stalin was careful to put himself in a good light in order to strengthen his policy. But he took care always to say the opposite of what he did, and to do the opposite of what he said. In making the partly autobiographical speech at Tiflis, from which we have already quoted, he snubbed the flatterers who described him as the "hero of October," "leader of the International," etc. "This is all nonsense, comrades, nothing but foolish exaggeration." At the same time he wasted no opportunity of commercial self-advertisement in order to acquire that notoriety which neither his actions nor his work had yet brought him. All the illustrated papers were ordered to reproduce his portrait, which still did not become popular, and the walls of all offices were adorned with a photograph, of which innumerable copies were printed, in which he figured at Lenin's side . . . before the rupture, of which everyone was ignorant (at the Gosizdat, already several times purged, flourished a "Stalinist" functionary, as his followers were now beginning to be called). He wished to give his name to other towns as well as Stalingrad; Iuzovo became Stalino, and Iuzovka Stalin. One day there were to be Stalinabad, Stalinsk and even Stalin-Aoul, in the Caucasus. Many servile functionaries thought to do themselves good by christening streets, establishments and enterprises in this way; Stalin never disavowed them since they furthered his own wishes. Bureaucratic conformism began to consist more and more in a hypocritical admiration, demonstrated by external signs, of the arid personality of the General Secretary.

The same brutal contrast between theory and practice was shown when Stalin, in his April report in Leningrad, exhorted his hearers to democracy. They knew how much of that to believe. He blamed the conduct of the "police brigade" established under Zinoviev, while making use himself of the same methods, doubled and tripled, throughout the whole of Russia. "The Party ought to embark resolutely on the path of internal democracy," he declared without a smile to his subordinates, not one of whom had been elected or was controlled from below, and who had his mandate to efface all vestiges of liberty and crush out any slight desire for independence. "The method of persuasion is our principal method of work," but he was speaking to a circle where it was already customary, on the pretext of discipline, to suppress the slightest conscientious objection or the least individuality of ideas as an attack on morality or the crime of *lèse-révolution*.

The would-be objective historian of the future, who refers only to the official documents will have difficulty in separating truth from falsehood in Stalin's written and spoken discourses. He is not the first statesman who has made use of the spoken and written word sometimes to conceal his intentions, sometimes to cover up the deficiencies in his knowledge. But the material and spiritual conditions of Russia and the resources of modern technique for propaganda and intimidation have enabled him to achieve heights in this direction which were quite unknown before the Soviet "experiment." The same applies to his henchmen. The more the monopoly of the Party developed into the omnipotence of the Secretariat, the more often one heard autocrats praising democracy, bureaucrats denouncing bureaucracy, wasters preaching economy, ignoramuses extolling science, and everywhere a complete contradiction between the real and the ideal.

After the lively altercation in July, Stalin sought to deprive his opponents of their favourite weapon by sending out a call "to all Party organisations and Soviets" to put an end to bureaucracy, waste, and inertia. "Our economic and administrative apparatus consumes approximately two milliards of roubles a year. It should be possible to reduce these expenses to three or four hundred million, to the benefit of our industry." This was exactly the thesis of the Left, to within a hundred million anyway. A further unprecedented anomaly: The message was signed by Rykov, President of the Council of Commissars, by Stalin as Secretary of the Central Committee of the Party, by Kuibyshev, as President of the Party Control Commission. These titles and signatures implied for the first time a public usurpation of attributes and prerogatives, an open violation of the Constitution, no article of which allowed for the unwarrantable interference of the functionaries of any Party whatever in the affairs of the State. But Stalin, by reason of the powers which the G.P.U. gave him, codified the situation in his own person. If, on paper, he still allowed a little authority to the Council of Commissars, it was only for the benefit of the gallery and to soften the transition.

In his speech at Tiflis he mentioned in particular the General Strike in England and the happenings in Poland. But anyone unversed in the casuistry of decadent Bolshevism, unaccustomed to the examination of this sort of thing, would have had difficulty in distinguishing his views from those of the Left. Besides which he never hesitated to quote from Trotsky or Zinoviev without indicating the authors, contenting himself with arriving at different conclusions or with omitting the conclusions altogether. When by any chance he produced an original idea, such as: "The British Communist Party is one of the best sections of the Communist International," when speaking of a group whose influence on social life in Britain was nil, he gave a sample of his ability, but the complete atrophy of all critical spirit among the governed, as well as the firm hand of the governors, saved him from any unpleasant contradictions. Except within the walls of the Politbureau and the supreme Economic Council, where Trotsky and Pyatakov fought side by side a battle which was never heard of outside, the Opposition kept quiet and bided its time.

Would it have the wisdom to await the ripening of the disagreements which were already beginning in the majority fraction? This would not have suited Stalin, whose aim was to hasten the expulsion of the irreconcilables. A Party Conference was due to be held in October 1926, the Congress having been adjourned until the following year. It was essential to confront the assembly with an accomplished fact, and since the Opposition seemed in no hurry to attack, Stalin set himself to provoke them.

He was an expert at this sort of task. In September he launched a "campaign of explanation," that is to say defamation, against the gagged minority. Trotsky and Pyatakov were eliminated from the Department of Economics; Kamenev refused to go to Japan. The Oppositionists, slandered, abused and subjected to threats, had nothing but secretly duplicated pamphlets and clandestine conversations to defend themselves with. The majority of the Party never heard anything of their declarations or their "theses." Krupskaya decided at last to part with a copy of the famous *Testament,* which was immediately sent abroad, where it was published by Trotsky's friends. But in Russia its underground circulation was very small, and in any case, came too late to be effective. Under these conditions any attack was hopeless for the present and without value for the future. Nevertheless, the defiant Opposition was unable to resign itself to keep silent and "wait and see," which was the only possible tactic in the circumstances. They did not then understand the need to take a long view, "to re-educate the new generation and look ahead" and also, as Trotsky wrote later, but too late, "not to be impatient, not to fret oneself or others, but to learn and to wait." The Opposition persisted in visualising the Party as an unalterable entity, from which it was only separated by a temporary misunderstanding. After a prolonged internal debate, in which the prudence of some members continually clashed with the impatience of others, it was decided to take the decisive step. At the beginning of October 1926, the foremost militants forced their way into the Communist cells in the factories, with the intention of replying to the attacks of Stalin's agents. Stalin asked for nothing better.

4

THE annals of Bolshevism contain plenty of bitter fights, barbed polemics and noisy and passionate episodes. But in this Party, where Lenin practically never used the familiar "thou" to anyone, the strictest courtesy was always the rule, even in the midst of the Civil War, and exceptions strike a jarring note. The era of Stalin inaugurated new usages.

The Oppositionists were made aware of this by their reception at the workers' meetings: shouts and insults, volleys of whistles, a systematic uproar. Flying squads of interrupters were dispatched by lorry to any point where the members of the Left were speaking, with orders to drown their voices by various methods imitated from fascism, to assault them if need be and throw them out by physical force. It was not necessary for Stalin to give exact instructions for this procedure; his lieutenants were quick to see what was expected of them and to make it known that the hooligans would not be punished. In general, the Opposition did not succeed in making itself heard. Even if it had, the result would have been the same, since the proletariat would not have followed their overlearned and theoretical viewpoint, being frightened of prolonged unemployment above all things. Radek was able to speak for three minutes—and Trotsky, who had once received an ovation in that same factory, was forced to leave the platform after an equally short time, without being able to explain his programme. "The Party does not want arguments," *Pravda* constantly stated. An artificial outbreak of collective hysteria whipped the bureaucracy to a fury. The press devoted entire pages to vituperation against the renegades, fractionaries and counter-revolutionaries in prose; Demian Biedny, the official versifier, abused and mocked at them in verse. Molotov, under the direct inspiration of Stalin, did not blush to upbraid them for having gone into emigration under the Tsar, as if Lenin and the entire staff of *Iskra* had not done likewise, following the example of Herzen and Bakunin. Even anti-Semitism was used against the leaders of the Opposition. One ironic detail was that the Zinoviev University anathematised the "criminal attempts at schism" of its namesake. And Kirov announced without a smile: "If we are speaking of democracy, there has never been greater democracy in the history of our Party than we have to-day."

After a few days of this unparalleled democracy, the Opposition, faced with the dilemma of submission or insurrection, chose to retreat. On October 4th it offered to make peace with the Politbureau, which imposed its own conditions, and on October 16th it submitted. In a declaration signed by Zinoviev, Trotsky, Kamenev, Pyatakov, Sokolnikov, and Yevdokimov, it recognised its offences against discipline, condemned its own fractional activity, disowned Krupskaya for an innocent allusion in her speech at the last Congress, repudiated its followers abroad, and finally abandoned its members of the old Workers' Opposition. While it is true that they did not abjure their intimate convictions, they promised to remain in a state of political catalepsy, and to submit themselves without reserve to the Central Committee, which Stalin had called in plenary session for the express purpose of receiving this capitulation and confirming its sanctions: that Trotsky and Kamenev be removed from the Politbureau and replaced by Kuibyshev and S. Kossior; that V. Smirnov, author of *Democratic Centralism*, be expelled from the Party for having spoken without permission; that a whole series of rank-and-file militants be accused, dismissed, recalled. As for Zinoviev, he was invited to resign from the Presidency of the International, which he did soon after. Towards the end of the month, all the essentials being already decided upon, the Conference was allowed to begin. . . .

Stalin had prepared a thesis on the "Opposition bloc" to which he imputed lack of principles, a defeatist ideology, opportunism, Menshevism, Trotskyism, and which he accused of destroying the unity of the Party and weakening the dictatorship of the proletariat. He dragged up again Zinoviev's and Kamenev's celebrated back-sliding in October, repeated all that had already been said a hundred times on the various questions in dispute and refuted the industrial deviation afresh: "*The industrialisa-*

tion of the country can only be achieved by relying on the progressive amelioration of the material situation of the peasant majority."

During the sitting he gave a long report on the subject. After his biased history of recent events, he reopened the hackneyed argument over socialism in one country, then dug up all the old controversies, such as that on the "permanent revolution," in order to show Lenin and Trotsky in opposition. He insulted Zinoviev, to whom he attributed a "limited nationalist spirit," and Radek, who had ridiculed him at the Communist Academy with his allusions to Shchedrin's satires, coining such phrases as "socialism in a single district" or even "socialism in a single street." He quoted Trotsky's unfortunate phrase "the magnificent historic music of developing socialism," the unflattering appreciations which Trotsky and Zinoviev had written about one another, their later retractions, and frequently quoted Lenin, whom the Oppositionists had constantly used against him. To the industrialists he said yet again: "One cannot further the progress of industry by neglecting the interests of agriculture, or by brutally violating those interests." Finally, Trotsky having predicted the ultimate exclusion of all Opposition, he made a vehement denial: "This assertion of Comrade Trotsky's is absolutely without foundation; it is completely false."

The representatives of the minority, present by right at the Conference as members of the Central Committee, were authorised to reply to the bureaucracy, which had already decided to hear nothing and to interpret everything in the worst possible light. They wasted their time and strength in speaking before this hostile audience as though they recognised in it the authentic representatives of the Party, and confined themselves to prudent generalities, couched in an amicable tone, which corresponded neither to the acuteness of the conflict nor to the gravity of the occasion. Reduced to a defensive position, enmeshed in their own unfruitful strategy, they abandoned their most telling arguments, glossed over differences and blunted their criticisms. The need to manœuvre took precedence over their slogans to the point of rendering them unrecognisable. In order to prove that Trotskyism was no more, Kamenev read Trotsky's retraction on the "permanent revolution": "Experience has invariably shown that wherever any of us disagreed with Lenin on any fundamental point, Lenin was always correct." In his pamphlet the *New Course*, Trotsky had once written: "With regard to the theory of the permanent revolution, I can find absolutely no reason for retracting what I wrote on this subject in 1904, 1905, 1906 and later."

It is quite obvious that these subtleties, incomprehensible to the lay mind, disillusioned the few remaining workers who were faithful to communism, disgusting them alike with the Opposition and the bureaucracy. They had the further unfortunate result of obscuring urgent and immediate questions under a veil of incomprehensible chicanery. Although the two fractions agreed on the necessity of safeguarding the monopoly of their Party, and called vainly on the name of Lenin to arbitrate between them, the Right still reproached the Left with every sort of opportunism dressed up in revolutionary phrases, with petit-bourgeois and Social-Democratic deviations, while the Left accused the Right of idealising the N.E.P., under-estimating the economic power of the *kulaks*, etc. As a practical measure, the Opposition proposed the exemption of the poor from taxation, the raising of workers' wages, and the increase of subsidies to industry; all this by means of a milliard roubles to be obtained, half by cutting down the expenses of the bureaucracy, and half by increased taxation of the bourgeoisie in the towns and on the countryside. Already labouring under the accusation of demagogy, and unsure of its historic parallels, the Opposition did not dare to speak openly of Thermidor, nor to call Stalin the "grave-digger" of the revolution, or the Tsar of the *kulaks*, as he was called in whispers, nor openly to compare Voroshilov to General Cavaignac.

At the end of his oration, Stalin triumphantly announced that "Comrade Krupskaya has forsaken the Opposition bloc." Two days before, a letter from Shliapnikov and Medvediev, extracted by threats, had been made known, in which the signatories confessed their errors, judged and humiliated themselves and repented. The moral forces of several Oppositionists were weakening by reason of the impasse into which Trotsky and Zinoviev had strayed; new discords on tactical questions broke out among the shattered ranks. Sapronov and his followers felt ill at ease among the "big guns" of the industrialists. Stalin was fully informed of all this and intrigued to his utmost to increase the differences, while at the same time the machine increased its external pressure: cells, sections, committees, all manifested a fantastic and unanimous loyalty, which deceived no one.

During the Conference, the "ideological struggle" continued unabated outside. Zinoviev complained of a verse quoted from Alexander Blok by a Saratov newspaper: "Is it our fault if your skeleton is crushed by the grip of our soft and heavy paws?" In *Pravda* Larin stated the alternatives: "Either the Opposition must be excluded and legally suppressed, or the question will be settled with machine-guns in the streets, as the Left Social Revolutionaries did in Moscow in 1918." In an editorial Bukharin swore deliriously to defend, in the name of the Party, "the Leninist purity of his ideology like the apple of his eye" and proclaimed Lenin's disputed "heritage" to be sacrosanct.

In December the dispute was carried on at the Executive of the International, in front of those whom Medvediev had called paid "lackeys." Stalin could have avoided another sham debate, but he preferred to save his face by posing as a believer in universal communism, as continuing the work of Lenin, when he was merely his temporary heir or at most his imitator. Tirelessly he recited the statement which all his hearers had already heard or read to satiety, that litany from the *Complete Works* which he had already composed for his earlier interventions. Trotsky and Zinoviev gave everlastingly the same answers, which to-morrow would be denounced by *Pravda* as "lack of discipline." Clara Zetkin, converted to Leninism, mocked at their "bag full of quotations," and the chorus of international followers reviled the heterodox.

But the leaders of the Opposition, urged on by their followers who were weary of diplomacy, began to raise their voices in order to demonstrate the constancy of their ideas. Stalin became more violent, more aggressive, in fact more scurrilous. He exhumed all the ancient errors, real or imagined, of his opponents, and revealed the incident of the telegram of congratulations which Kamenev had sent to the Grand-Duke Michael at the time of the February Revolution. Kamenev invoked a denial, signed by Lenin, in his defence, but Stalin challenged this, stating that Lenin had, in the interests of the Party, knowingly written the opposite of the truth. Thus did personal animosity and a spirit of cliquishness now take precedence over "ideology," so much stressed in official political literature; and this between persons who had once prided themselves as much on the correctness of their relations as on their doctrinal rigour. Trotsky, always anxious to discover a struggle of classes behind the struggles of the cliques, would nevertheless not admit the truth of Jaurès's just observation: "History is a strange battle, where the men who fight against one another often serve the same cause." Later he was to attempt to explain his defeats, without explaining anything, by the dumb pressure of the prosperous peasants and the influence of world capitalism, reflected through the laborious empiricism of Stalin.

The Party, therefore, began the tenth year of the revolution, more disunited than ever before. The split which Lenin had foreseen was gradually taking place in fact. Both camps prepared themselves for fresh clashes after the end of 1926, putting no faith either in the promises of democracy from the Right or of discipline from the Left. Stalin arranged his pieces on the chess-board, where the so-called Trotskyists were mere pawns: Ordjonikidze as President of the Control Commission; Chubar to fill the vacancy as alternate of the Politbureau; Bukharin at the helm of the International, without the title of President; lesser personages everywhere where the machine did not appear to be secure. The Opposition, on its side, completed its organisation as a clandestine Party within the only Party, with its own hierarchy in miniature, its Politbureau, its Central Committee, its regional and local agents, its foundation groups, its subscriptions, its circulars, its code for letters. Nevertheless, Zinoviev became discouraged and hesitated whether to persevere. The Sapronovists considered blazing their own trail. Among Trotsky's supporters, many began to doubt their previous convictions. But a fresh problem arose to reawaken the antagonism of the two fractions: civil war in China, which *Pravda* hailed yet again as "the thunder of the world revolution."

Since the death of Yuan Shih-kai, in the absence of any stable and recognised power beyond certain provincial frontiers, the Chinese Republic had beeen passing through troubled times, delivered over to military bandits and feudal war lords. The generals, in the pay of the rival Great Powers, divided between them an ephemeral authority over the immense territory, broken by alternate advances and retreats, alliances and ruptures. Finally two poles of attraction emerged: in the North, the militarist reaction, headed by Chang Tso-lin and centred around Mukden; in the South, the democratic revolution, directed by Sun Yat-sen from Canton. The nominal Government at Peking, which was in the hands of Wu Pei-fu, really only had jurisdiction within the ancient capital, despite the support of the British. Various generals, among whom was Feng Yu-hsiang, converted to Christianity, and thereafter looked on as a pawn of the United States, sold, lent or withdrew their co-operation in accordance with a thousand vicissitudes. Thanks to Lenin's policy of placing China on a footing of equality, without regard to the "unequal treaties," Bolshevism exercised a considerable influence on the national revolutionary movement. Joffe, as Ambassador from the U.S.S.R., had negotiated and begun an intelligent Russo-Chinese co-operation, of which Karakhan, his successor, saw the first fruits. On his death-bed, Sun Yat-sen dictated two messages: one to the Kuomintang, his party, and the other to the Executive of the Soviets, expressing the wish for a permanent bond between the two revolutions and a lasting alliance of solidarity between the two countries. With his base in Manchuria and aided by the Japanese, Chang Tso-lin succeeded in extending his operations towards the south, preaching the traditional morality of Confucius as against Sun Yat-sen's semi-socialism. He succeeded in taking Peking, and even Shanghai for a short while. But the Kuomintang was supported inside the country by the bourgeois nationalists, the liberal students, the workers and the peasants, and by the Soviet Union from outside. It had succeeded, despite the violence with which the revolting proletariat was treated by the professional soldiers, in raising and training troops with a new mentality who were capable of defeating mercenaries not fighting for an ideal. The Chinese University in Moscow, directed by Radek, the officer-instructors, sent from Russia to the Military School in Canton, among whom was Blücher, under the name of Galen, finally the Russian advisers to the Communist Party, now incorporated in the Kuomintang, such as Bubnov and Borodin, who dispensed large subsidies—all these played no small part in the victorious march of the Southerners towards the North and the valley of the Yangtse, under the command of Chiang Kai-shek. In 1926 the balance of forces was in favour of the Reds. Wu Pei-fu, beaten by Chang, by Feng, by Chiang and others, gradually faded from the scene, as did also Sun Chuan-fang, another venal general of merely temporary importance. Feng rallied decisively to the Kuomintang. The so-called "popular" armies had occupied Hankow and were advancing on Nanking and Shanghai. This, broadly and simply outlined, was the situation in China at the time when Stalin began to take an active part in the leadership of the International.

The young Chinese Communist Party had not renounced its independent press, its political physiognomy and its freedom of action of its own free will, to become the powerless Left wing of the bourgeois Kuomintang. This course of conduct was forced upon it by Moscow. Stalin and Bukharin, his inspirer and ideologue, claimed to be encouraging a socialist evolution in China by means of penetration into the Kuomintang, where the "bloc of four classes," the revolutionaries of the country and the epoch, was to be sealed. The weakness of the Chinese bourgeoisie, Stalin told the Executive of the International in November 1926, justified this tactic, and even authorised communist participation in the capitalist government. He expected that the victory of the Cantonese would bring about democratic liberties "for all revolutionary elements in general and for the workers in particular." In order not to alarm this insignificant bourgeoisie, to reassure Chiang Kai-shek, with whom he had once exchanged signed photographs in Moscow, and to gain the confidence of the civil and military chiefs of Canton, he ordered his emissaries to shut their eyes to the bloody repressions of strikes in the south. He forbade the arming of the workers, the creation of soviets and the encouragement of peasant revolts, even ordering the suppression of these. Already in March 1926, when Chiang Kai-shek had staged a *coup d'état* in Canton in order to curb the communists, the Soviet press had had orders to suppress the truth, while simultaneously Bubnov was urging his Chinese subordinates to submit. According to Borodin, the latter were to fulfil the rôle of political "coolies" in the Kuomintang, which was now admitted to the International as a "sympathetic" section.

Trotsky, on the other hand, while disagreeing with Radek and Zinoviev on several points, demanded a separate policy and organisation in order to rescue the communists from the guardianship of the Kuomintang. Both sides searched the pages of the *Complete Works,* looking there for a solution which could not be found. It is true that Lenin had always recommended the support of all revolutionary movements, whether bourgeois or nationalist, and advantageous compromises with democratic and liberal parties, but only on the condition that the Communist Party did not give up its liberty nor lose sight of its socialist programme, did not lose itself in or become confused with such parties. Trotsky could make use of this to the fullest extent. But Stalin compared the Kuomintang to the British Labour Party, into which Lenin himself advised the Communist Party to try to enter. Without doubt this was a complete misunderstanding of the different social nature of the two parties, and the disparity between their historical circumstances. In addition, since the death of Sun Yat-sen, the Kuomintang had been transformed in very much the same manner as the Bolshevik Party since Lenin's death. . . .

In March 1927, following Chiang Kai-shek's entry into Shanghai, where he formed a "popular" Government, two communist ministers participated in the national Government at Hankow. In April, the President of the Kuomintang, Wang Ching-wei, and the Secretary of the Communist Party, Chen Tu-hsiu, proclaimed a permanent collaboration, and the subordination of the military authorities to the civil power. In Moscow, Stalin, irritated by the criticisms of the Opposition, himself guaranteed Chiang Kai-shek's fidelity to Sun Yat-sen's *Testament* and the Soviet alliance, before a large audience of "active" militants. Radek, on the contrary, predicted a fatal breakdown in the Communist-Nationalist coalition, and gave warning that the workers were in grave danger from Chiang's machine-guns. A few days later came the news of a military *coup d'état* in Shanghai: of hundreds, presently of thousands of workers massacred, the Red Government dissolved by the "popular" army, the Russian agents in flight and the members of the Communist Party hunted down. The same thing, preceded by a search of the Soviet Embassy in Peking, took place in Nanking, Canton and elsewhere. The Soviet press exploded into imprecations, fulminating with rage and impotence. Chiang Kai-shek was now a deserter, a traitor, a counter-revolutionary, a feudalist, a dictator, an executioner, a Cavaignac, a Gallifet. Stalin was just in time to prevent *Pravda* from publishing his lamentable discourse. But the disaster on the Pacific stained him with the blood of the workers. The indignant Opposition came to the fore again; an address presented to the Central Committee by eighty-three Oppositionists was covered with signatures. The fractional struggle broke out with renewed vigour around the Chinese question, about the middle of 1927.

5

UNSCATHED, Stalin survived an upheaval which must have overthrown him under any régime which was in the smallest degree democratic. There was an excellent reason for this: he enjoyed a complete monopoly of all the means of information and comment, both in print and on the platform. The entire press belonged to him and praised his foresight unblushingly. Not only the immense economic and political administrative apparatus, but also the police and the army were under his orders, through intermediaries. He was free to do whatever he liked except against the members of the Central Committee and the Polit-bureau, unless he had a majority there. No despot in any age or in any country, has ever enjoyed such powers of deceiving public opinion, or, if that failed, of suppressing it. The Oppo-sition, by word of mouth and by duplicated pamphlets, were able at the end of several months to influence twenty or thirty thousand people at most. The "Declaration of the Eighty-three" collected about three thousand signatures, but most of those sympathisers who were not already marked down, ab-stained, not wishing to subject themselves to reprisals to no good end. A certain number of workers' circles existed in secret, holding no communication with one another for fear of the spies, both professional and amateur, which swarmed every-where. Collective apathy and individual instincts of self-preserva-tion between them gave Stalin a free hand, provided always that he continued to safeguard the privileges of the "oligarchy."

At the beginning of the nineteenth century, Griboyedov's masterpiece *The Misfortune of Having Wit*, which was forbid-den by the censor, was circulated to the extent of some 40,000 copies, according to some authorities. In the tenth year of Bol-shevism, Trotsky's writings were in the same position. This is not the only instance of regression to an earlier century, a reaction which makes the parallel between the Iron Tsar and the "Steel" Secretary even more striking.

When Stalin slakes his vindictiveness by omitting Trotsky from the official history of the revolution, when he denies facts and falsifies texts, and removes from the libraries all books and documents which, though authentic, are contrary to his views, when, in order to deny that his principal adversary played any part in 1917 or in the Civil War, he expurgates the life-stories and memoirs of his contemporaries, witnesses and participants, even Lenin's own unpublished papers, when he causes the anniversaries of the Red Army to be celebrated without mentioning the most important name, and orders that the film *October* be made as though Trotsky had never existed, how can one help being reminded of Custine's description of the sovereign autocrat, who "adjusts the history of his country to suit his good pleasure, and dispenses each day to his people those historic verities which coincide with the fiction of the moment"? Whether it be a Tsarist Empire or a Soviet Republic, "in that country, historic truth is no more respected than the sacredness of an oath." The printing of certain pages of a *Soviet Encyclopedia* was held up so that the biography of various persons who had ceased to be in favour while it was in the press could be re-written.

The general public was no better informed about the present than the past, on the defeats in China than on the earlier victories in Russia. Stalin scourged the Opposition even in their graves. When the ashes of Skliansky, who was killed in an accident in the United States, were returned, he refused to allow the urn to be placed in the sepulchre in the Red Square, as though wishing again to illustrate Custine: "In Russia, the dead themselves are subjected to the caprices of the man who rules over the living."

After the sinister miscalculations of Shanghai and Canton, the dark story continued with the arrest at Peking of twenty Chinese communists, condemned to the horrible torture of strangulation by garrotting. Among them were a founder of the Party, Professor Li Ta-chao, and a young girl, Chen Pai-ming. But Stalin continued to demonstrate in theses and in imperturbable speeches the correctness of his line, and to re-prove the leaders of the Opposition for urging a break with the Kuomintang and the creation of soviets in southern China. At that time he staked his hopes on Feng Yu-hsiang, the Christian General who claimed to be a follower of Sun Yat-sen, and who like so many other mercenaries, and like all the brotherhood of enemies of Bolshevism, called himself a spiritual son of Lenin.

In any case, the affairs of the Far East only interested Stalin in relation to his position in the Party. His friends did not conceal his project of beheading the Opposition by "liquidating" the most important leaders; once expelled from the Party, these intractables could be handed over to the G.P.U. But for this it was necessary to have the consent of the Politbureau. At this period, it was whispered in the corridors of the Kremlin, by those in the know, that since the Politbureau had lost its Left wing, it was divided into Right and Centre factions, four votes against four. Rykov, Bukharin, Tomsky and Kalinin were named as Rightists, without anyone knowing exactly what the division was about. Thus one half of the Politbureau paralysed the other. (The position of Kuibyshev, the ninth member, was still in dispute, since it was illegal by statute to be a member of both the Central Committee and the Control Commission.) Stalin found himself thus in temporary difficulties at the top.

The manner in which he extricated himself from this embarrassment clearly demonstrates his superiority on the low level where he manœuvres with such skill. Foreseeing all eventualities, he had already enlarged the Politbureau and the Central Committee in order to surround himself as far as possible with docile followers. But his fraction was still not entirely homogeneous since he had to take into account those old Bolsheviks, whose intellectual ability Lenin had not thought much of, but who had helped to defeat first Trotsky, then Zinoviev. Until the whole process was complete, until the genuine Stalinist camarilla formed the majority in the Politbureau, Stalin was forced to make terms, to manœuvre, to temporise. For this reason he did nothing in haste, but continued his silent work of modifying the numerical proportions to his advantage, even to the extent of only one vote.

On various occasions Trotsky had believed it possible to launch a frontal attack against the stable kernel of the Central Committee. Zinoviev had also made two separate minor attempts, once against Trotsky in concert with Stalin, and once against Stalin with his own forces. Stalin himself never left anything to chance, and never risked an open conflict without accurately measuring his forces and reckoning up his votes. It is therefore necessary to follow carefully the tiresome bureaucratic mutations, the "general post" of the functionaries, since the vital and palpable secret of the Secretary's dictatorship lies in just these colourless combinations, which force us to explore what Carlyle called "the obscure and indescribable regions of history."

Stalin had against him a body of more or less respectable traditions, static tendencies consecrated by time, and reputations which were long established, even overvalued. In order to accustom the Party, or rather the leading cadres, to a revision of customs and a fresh standard of values, it was necessary to proceed slowly and by insensible gradations. After cleaning up the Politbureau, he prepared people's minds for a purge of the Central Committee. There was no hurry about going further: people accepted a downfall more readily than an expulsion. Having already postponed the Party Congress, first for some months, then for a year, he adjourned the Congress of the Soviets for the same period, and put off the Congress of the International to an unspecified date. Little by little it became a habit to allow the Central Committee, or its organs, or, in the last resort, the General Secretary, to act on their own. When the Right in the Politbureau began to be irksome, Stalin exercised patience and compromised, sure of the Central Committee and reckoning, with undeniable perspicacity, on his adversaries' stupidity and the poltroonery of his accomplices. And in fact, one after another, they later came to his aid at the right moment. The period was fertile in occasions and pretexts.

Diplomatic relations between the Soviet Union and Conservative Britain, already very strained by Russia's part in the General Strike, became acute in 1927, after the Chinese affair. Stalin took advantage of an atmosphere favourable to patriotic exaltation, to take the Opposition at their word when, before the Central Committee in April and in the recent "Declaration of the Eighty-three," they imprudently affirmed: "The threat of war grows greater every day." Exploiting this justification for a state of siege, he set the ignorant population on the alert and proclaimed that the revolution was in peril, only too glad to put the Left in the position of supporting the enemy. Bukharin's and Voroshilov's speeches having already provoked the beginnings of a panic, a run on the shops, Stalin had to calm people's fears by declaring: "We shall not have a war this spring, nor even in the autumn, because our enemies are not yet ready for it." The bogy of war, first raised by the Opposition, could only favour the bureaucracy; the closer the danger, the more severe the dictatorship. At the end of May, Trotsky made an unusually violent and useless speech before the phantoms who composed the Executive of the International, in which he mixed the Anglo-Russian Committee, the Kuomintang, the Soviet bureaucracy and the coming war. Stalin, replying, refused to consider what he had said, "the more so since he reminds one more of an actor than a hero," but continued, nevertheless, to argue step by step the undesirability of forcing the pace of the Chinese Revolution, the need to maintain the understanding with the Kuomintang and to oppose the creation of Chinese soviets. He concluded: "I have just received news that the British Conservative Government has broken off relations with the U.S.S.R. . . . The Party is threatened with war from some directions, with splits from others. Thus there is a sort of united front from Chamberlain to Trotsky. . . . Have no doubts that we shall know how to break this new front." The tone then became more venomous with mutual accusations of Menshevism and treason.

The Opposition continued to strengthen Stalin's position by its thoughtless tactics which resulted in bringing together persons who were previously disaffected. It attacked Tomsky without measure over the Anglo-Russian Committee, and Bukharin over China, which caused them to draw closer to their protector. Stalin seized this propitious moment to summon the Politbureau and propose Trotsky's and Zinoviev's exclusion from the Central Committee, under threat of resignation. Not realising the full gravity of their action, which opened an unlimited field of action for Stalin, the Right gave way. The Control Commission followed suit, despite the unexpected resistance of Ordjonikidze. A tragic external event lent its aid to Stalin's manœuvre. The assassination of Voykov, Soviet Ambassador to Warsaw, produced a devastating terrorist repercussion in Moscow. Twenty former capitalists and aristocrats, among whom was a Prince

Dolgorukov, none of whom had anything to do with the attack, were seized without preliminary warning as hostages, and executed by the G.P.U. Stalin's hand did not waver, and at such a time, when the Kremlin was talking of a new Sarajevo, the Politbureau could not resist.

The Control Commission justified its resolution on "Trotsky's and Zinoviev's lack of discipline," by the fractional activity of the guilty ones. The Opposition had broken its promises, distributed its forbidden literature, held a demonstration by accompanying Smilga (who had been banished to Siberia under cover of a "mission"), to the station (a lapse which was made especially marked by reason of a similar demonstration the day of Kamenev's departure for Rome). In addition, Zinoviev had allowed himself to make certain criticisms at a commemoration ceremony, and Trotsky had done the same at the Executive of the International. Previously he had "libellously accused the Party of Thermidorianism" before the Control Commission, which therefore submitted to the Plenary Session of the Central Organs a demand that "Trotsky's and Zinoviev's names be erased from the list of members of the Central Committee." There had been no instance up to that time of anything unexpected happening in such a case. It seemed as though nothing now remained to impede the bureaucratic Nemesis.

Stalin, however, met with misfortune in China, where Feng Yu-hsiang, following in Chiang Kai-shek's footsteps, severely discomfited him by turning on the communists. *Pravda* covered the new "traitor" with insults, which, however, in no way prevented the various Chinese generals from hanging and shooting Reds of all shades of opinion, decimating the workers' trade unions and drowning the peasants' revolts in blood. "More than ten thousand proletarians and revolutionary intellectuals have already fallen beneath the murderous blows of the united counter-revolution. Hundreds of the finest sons of China are being slaughtered daily. Prisoners are submitted to indescribable tortures," so people read in a manifesto in Moscow. It only remained for Stalin to pick on Wang Ching-wei, representative of the Kuomintang Left, in order to bring about a fresh disaster, the debacle of the social revolution in China, the collapse of his last illusions, and an exposure of the scandalous bankruptcy of his adventurist strategy. This final turn took place in July 1927, when the session opened in an unbelievable state of disorder.

In order to divert attention from his own heavy responsibility, Stalin made use of an audacious diversion, which deceived no well-informed militant, but might affect the morale of their followers. He sought for a scapegoat, finally throwing on to the shoulders of his Chinese subordinates, his instruments and victims—those who survived the butcheries—the responsibility for the whole series of mistakes committed, thereby stirring up an opportune crisis within the Chinese Communist Party. He had already ordered them to leave the nationalist coalition government, if not the Kuomintang, and he now, at last, took over the Opposition slogan, "Form Soviets." Now that the game was lost, he considered this appropriate. But his chief manœuvre consisted in threatening the Bolshevik assembly with the menace of war.

"The foremost problem at the present moment is the danger of a fresh outbreak of war . . . directed particularly against the Soviet Union," he wrote, without believing it, since in private conversations he was cynical enough to comment ironically on this fairy-story. The Left walked into the trap, the more readily in that they had been the first to sound the alarm. The war question became the centre of all the debates. "The Soviet Union is menaced by armed aggression, and in these conditions . . . it is essential that our Party be a united whole, and that the masses which surround it also close their ranks," said Krupskaya, who found it natural to read her one-time fraction a lesson. Chicherin and Ossinsky alone stood out against the panic thesis, and the future was to confirm their sensible and courageous words. Trotsky affirmed the willingness of the Left to fight for the "socialist fatherland," without subscribing to any *union sacrée*, but considered Stalin incapable of achieving the victory, and posed the alternatives: "Thermidor or the Opposition." When accused of defeatism he quoted the example of Clemenceau, who opposed the Government of his country and his class, not in order to hinder its defence but to help in the conduct of the war. When he was interrupted with reminders that the Party existed, he replied: "You have strangled the Party," yet he continued to express his irrational belief in that Party, which Sapronov had called a "corpse." Stalin jeered at the "comic-opera Clemenceau" and his "little group which has more leaders than soldiers." What did the signatures at the bottom of the "Declaration of the Eighty-three" signify when compared to the immense majority which he professed to represent? And his tone changed for a final warning. *"In order to conquer this majority it would be necessary to start a civil war in the Party."* This was clear. Stalin would not abandon power without resorting to armed force. As for the Opposition, it never made use of anything stronger than words.

Apart from the artificial bogy of war which dominated the assembly, almost all the old disputes which had been argued and re-argued since Lenin's death, were brought up once again. Differences over October, divergencies during the Civil War, the antecedents of Trotskyism, the Anglo-Russian Committee, the Chinese affair. The two fractions fenced indefatigably with quotations, contradictions and threats. But, as usual, the decisive struggle took place in the wings, where the monolithic character of the bureaucratic machine was, as everyone knew, beginning to show serious fissures.

Stalin worked hard to separate Trotsky from Zinoviev, to expel the first and to bring the second to his knees. This calculation was sound, but a little premature. As a result of their frantic cries that war was imminent, the deceivers had finished by half-convincing themselves, and had certainly terrified the majority of the deceived. If the Soviet Union was perhaps on the eve of general mobilisation, how could they afford to dispense with the services of such tried combatants as Trotsky, Smilga, Muralov, Mrachkovsky and so many others? Ordjonikidze could not resign himself to it and sought for a compromise. The provincial delegates were also uneasy and argued that people's minds were not yet prepared. Nevertheless, the exclusion was unanimously voted, following the usual rule, but amid a feeling of great uneasiness, and by an irregularity of procedure, in the absence of Ordjonikidze, who did not concur.

Meanwhile Stalin could content himself with the results achieved, in order, later, to press his advantage further. There was no urgent question for him in the Party at that time and from then on no one in the State could oppose him. The Congress fixed for December 1927, would be chosen so as to ensure the election of a truly harmonious Central Committee. The preliminary discussions in November would coincide with the Tenth Anniversary celebrations, whose well-organised atmosphere of overpowering enthusiasm, would facilitate the task of the omnipotent apparatus. Stalin therefore came to an agreement with Ordjonikidze, who, in turn, invited the Left to take up a more conciliatory attitude in order that they might be saved. Trotsky and Zinoviev agreed and after various hidden manœuvres and laborious bargainings, the exclusion was annulled, the Opposition once more promised to dissolve, and escaped with "a severe reproof and a warning." Twelve days spent in settling accounts and in exasperated altercations terminated with a soothing remonstrance. But Stalin had trimmed his sails only in the absolute certainty of finally achieving his aim. If he was unable to find a pretext, he would know how to invent one.

"Never before has the Opposition been so unshakably convinced of its position, nor held to it with such unanimity," said Trotsky. In fact, however, his disorientated fraction had already lost or was about to lose, in addition to Krupskaya, many prominent people originally in Zinoviev's circle, notably Sokolnikov, Zalutsy, Shelavin, and Zoff who had made a full apology. Each week other less prominent Oppositionists recognised their errors, sometimes stooping to denounce their comrades as proof of their servile submission. Conversely, Sapronov's group detached itself in order to take up a franker and more radical position. His "Platform of the Fifteen" pointed out the pressing danger of a Thermidor, demanded the re-establishment of the soviets, defended Lenin's democratic principles formulated in *State and Revolution*, criticised the G.P.U. for "suppressing the legitimate discontent of the workers," and the Red Army "which threatens to become an instrument of Bonapartist adventurism." The disintegration which was beginning could not be checked so long as Trotsky persisted in regarding the symptoms merely as growing pains.

Nevertheless, the weakness of the Opposition was due far less to lack of numbers than to its intrinsic inability to reason concretely, to its insoluble internal contradictions and to the impenetrable obscurity of its perspective.

Although the Party was no longer a party, although the Party had been strangled, yet for Trotsky the Party still remained sacred, untouchable and taboo. In his eyes, the State, the proletariat, the *kulak*, the N.E.P. man, the bureaucrat, were so many definite abstractions like the Party. At first he based his hopes on the new generation, which as a whole displayed all the defects of the preceding one, together with a few of its own, and with certain good qualities lacking. Common sense and experience told him to spend time on educating an *élite*, but, himself a prisoner in an unfortunate "bloc," surrounded by vulgar politicians, he acted as though he shared their absurd impatience and incurable aberrations. When aiming at the oligarchy, he attacked only individuals, not principles, failing utterly to engage the attention of the working masses, the importance of whose active adherence he discounted.

The members of the Opposition vied with one another in mystic and dogmatic Leninism, burying beneath an avalanche of captious quotations from the Scriptures, or unintelligible pamphlets on China, a people who lacked everything and no longer had any rights but only duties. In the new religion of the State, its best elements represented, as against the Jesuitism of the bureaucratic caste, not Free Thought or Rationalism, but a sort of Protestantism or Jansenism, respectful towards a common Scripture. Certainly it can be said of them that, members of a privileged Party and yet despising these privileges, the original core of their group contained "the only characters who never succumbed to the universal fascination of power," as Renan wrote of Port-Royal; but such little public opinion as still

existed was unable to distinguish shades of Left and Right in the
degenerate Bolshevik Party and therefore unable to tell the good
from the bad in it. Such sympathy as the Oppositionists did succeed in arousing or conserving, was, generally, less for their doctrines than for the men who were sufficiently courageous to
defy the dictatorship and thus give to the one-time citizens,
now become passive subjects, an onerous example in revolutionary citizenship.

Trotsky feared that if he were defeated there was bound to
be a Thermidor, followed by the inescapable Brumaire, yet he
declared to the Americans in August 1927, speaking of the
opposing sides in the struggle, *"What separates us is incomparably less than what unites us."* He saw himself in the position
of Babeuf under the Directory, and would have liked to bring
about an upsurge of proletarian Jacobinism; but far from conceiving of a supplementary revolution in order to suppress the
regime of oppression and Bolshevik-Soviet exploitation, he
planned long-term reforms which would only perpetuate it.

His views on external politics were equally unconvincing.
He was over-anxious to load on to Stalin's shoulders what was
really a collective responsibility, in which Lenin had a large
share, and in which all the chief Leninists have had a part according to their importance. He was careful not to criticise that
political dualism which had been shown for example by the
Party's verbal solidarity with the Turkish Communists, at a time
when the State was in fact allied with Mustapha Kemal who
was dispatching them to the scaffold; but he waxed indignant
over the collusion with Mussolini, to whom Rykov had telegraphed astonishing congratulations. He is not convincing when
he holds Stalin responsible for all the reverses and misfortunes
in the international arena, where communism under Lenin had
already met with defeat in Germany, in Hungary, in Finland
and in Italy, and under Zinoviev in Germany again, in Bulgaria
and in Esthonia, long before the checks in Britain and the
Chinese catastrophe.

Inconsequent tactics complemented the theoretical contradictions and the illogical policy of the Opposition. It did not know

the correct time to throw its full influence and weight into the scale, nor when to be patient and allow favourable circumstances to ripen, while still working for its revenge. By aiming its blows at the wrong time and place it rallied the maximum of bureaucratic unity against itself, and lined up all the conservative interests, whether conscious or unconscious, behind Stalin, instead of disarming some and neutralising others. Passing from sterile waiting to a hopeless offensive, it struck blindly at the "wall" of the Party, and set against itself those whom in other directions it sought to convert to its ideals. It dissipated its energies on doctrinal exegesis and problems of revolutionary strategy when it should have concentrated on the root question of the regime, on which all the rest depended. . . .

6

BETWEEN two sessions of the Central Committee, Stalin speeded up the preliminaries for a major surgical operation which he had been planning for a long time. One may well believe that the rupture with the Anglo-Russian Committee (finally accomplished in September 1927—but by the Trade Union Congress), and the final doom of the Chinese communists, had aroused his deepest rancour against his too clear-sighted adversaries. His spokesmen therefore took advantage of their monopoly of the press and platform to deal a moral blow at the Opposition, already physically fettered, and to prepare people's minds for the "dry guillotine," at the very moment when *Pravda* was boasting of "the unprecedented extension of democracy under the Soviet regime." Stalin's spies strained every nerve to ferret out indiscipline, or, if possible, to provoke it in order to suppress it. Expulsions multiplied throughout September, and towards the end of the month the Executive of the International eliminated Trotsky, in defiance of the statutes. A new "crime" was discovered by the G.P.U. in the shape of a "clandestine printing plant"; twelve persons, guilty, or said to be so, were expelled from the Party. Preobrazhensky and Serebriakov attempted to shield them and met the same fate; so did thirty of their comrades in Leningrad, on other charges. Mrachkovsky and various others were thrown into prison. Obviously the long-awaited denouement was at hand.

In October, Trotsky and Zinoviev were finally expelled from the Central Committee, before whom they made yet one more superfluous speech, amid an unprecedented uproar, drowned by interruptions and insults. For the last time they seized the chance to lend themselves to a scene which Stalin had adroitly prepared. The latter no longer thought it necessary to preserve any decorum. His discreet and valued agent, Menzhinsky, nominal chief of the police, presented a report on the Opposition which consisted of an absurd and incoherent story about a military plot, intended to implicate them in counter-revolutionary activity with one of Wrangel's officers, who was, in reality, an agent of the G.P.U. This was an obvious provocative machination—"Thermidorian" Trotsky called it—in which the uneasy but submissive audience clearly perceived Stalin's expert hand.

One cannot even compare the Soviet G.P.U. to the Tsarist Okhrana. It is necessary to go back to the time of Nicholas I in order to have some idea of this formidable institution, a cross between the famous Third Section of the Chancellery and the terrible Corps of Gendarmes, but with an up-to-date technique. The parallel is rendered more exact by the fact that the veritable head of the police was the "Steel" Secretary, as the Iron Tsar had been in his time. Everyone felt himself to be under Stalin's surveillance, direct or indirect, and no member of the Bolshevik Parliament, outside the Left, dared to contradict or to oppose him. Corrupt persons and fanatics set the tone and the rest resigned themselves to voting anything. Amid an inconceivable uproar, in which the efforts of the cabal were clearly evident, Trotsky, the finest orator of the Party, was forced to *read* his speech word for word in order not to lose the thread, and to cut it short before he had finished. None of those who expressed their disgust confidentially in the corridors had the courage to declare it in the hall. Amid a chorus of outcries, only the more moderate of which were recorded by the stenographer, "renegade . . . traitor . . . scum . . . chatter-box . . . boaster . . . liar . . . Menshevik," Trotsky succeeded in making himself heard above the racket: "Stalin's present organisational victory is the prelude to his political collapse." Whistles and cat-calls prevented him from going further.

Stalin, certain of an attentive silence, replied first by a personal defence, delivered in his repetitive style: "That the principal attacks are directed against Stalin is perhaps explained by the fact that he has a greater knowledge than certain comrades of the knaveries of the Opposition, and that he is less easily deceived. That is why Stalin is particularly attacked. Who is Stalin? Stalin is an unimportant individual. Take Lenin. . . ." And he quoted yet again the old polemics from the days of emigration, when Trotsky harshly castigated "Maximilian Lenin."

On the question of the *Testament*, which the Opposition always raised, he denied having suppressed it, took refuge behind the unanimous decision not to publish it, and finally quoted Trotsky's denials of its existence to Max Eastman. "It is said that in this *Testament* Lenin proposed that the Congress should examine the question of replacing Stalin in the post of General Secretary. This is quite true. Let us read this passage, although you have already heard it several times . . ." And he read aloud Lenin's well-known lines:

Stalin is too rude, and this fault, entirely supportable in relations among us communists, becomes insupportable in the office of General Secretary. Therefore, I propose to the comrades to find a way to remove Stalin from that position and appoint to it another man who in all respects differs from Stalin only in superiority—namely, more patient, more loyal, more polite and more attentive to comrades, less capricious, etc. . . .

He went on to vindicate himself, secure in the mathematical conviction that the votes were already his, but strengthened also by the errors of his opponents.

Yes, comrades, I am rude towards those who rudely and traitorously break their word, who split and destroy the Party. I have never concealed it and I do not conceal it now. Right from the first session of the Central Committee, after the Thirteenth Congress, I asked to be released from the obligations of the General Secretary-ship. The Congress itself examined the question. Each delegation examined the question, and every delegation, including Trotsky, Kamenev and Zinoviev, voted unanimously in favour of Stalin remaining at his post. What could I do then? Abandon my post? Such a thing is not in my character. . . . At the end of one year I again asked to be set free and I was again forced to remain at my post. What could I do then?

After this self-justification came the speech for the prosecution:

They complain of our arresting wreckers, men who have been expelled from the Party and are carrying on anti-Soviet intrigues. Yes, we have arrested them and we shall arrest them so long as they undermine the Party and the Soviet power. . . . They say that such things are unknown in the history of the Party. This is not true. What about the Myasnikov group? And the Workers Truth group? Does not everyone know that Comrades Trotsky, Zinoviev and Kamenev themselves supported the arrest of the members of these groups?

He turned derisively to Zinoviev who had predicted war in the spring of 1927, then in the autumn: "Now it is winter and still the war has not come." He observed that before his "chatter" about Thermidor, Trotsky had in the *New Course* denied "those historical analogies with the great French Revolution (the downfall of the Jacobins) with which the superficial and incon-sequent liberals and Mensheviks seek to console themselves." He accused the Opposition of wishing to form a rival party, which they denied. The intransigence of the Bolshevik caste on this point is well known. "Under the dictatorship of the proletariat, two, three, even four parties may exist, but on con-dition that one is in power and all the rest in prison," as Tomsky and Bukharin, the Rightists, were soon to say, paraphrasing one another. What a regression in the ten years since Lenin promised "a peaceful competition between parties inside the Soviets!"

The assembly arranged the programme for the next Congress. By an impudent paradox they rendered involuntary homage to the industrialist Left at the very moment when they condemned it to death, by adopting "Directives for the elaboration of an economic Five Year Plan," thus breathing life into the project that Trotsky had cherished since 1920. But there was a great difference in the tone of the two projects, and the proposed tempo of future industrial progress. The Opposition hastened to prepare "counter-theses" of a more ambitious nature, destined for the Congress. The Governmental fraction, safe in its control of the means of persuasion and coercion, finally allowed, with democratic generosity, one month and a special page of *Pravda* for preliminary discussions. The Left asked for three months, since several weeks at least were necessary to get replies to certain correspondence. As to the freedom to speak one's mind, no one was deceived on that score, knowing very well what it cost those who were courageous enough to make their views known.

The officials of the Party, according to Stalin, numbered 100,000 persons in 1927, out of a total of 1,200,000 members and candidates. In addition, approximately half the effective total, say nearly half a million, consisted of State functionaries, trade union or Co-operative administrators, or those of other institutions connected with the Party. The other half, employed on production, enjoyed appreciably greater material security than non-party members and asked only to be allowed to consolidate this. In these conditions, the rank-and-file communist was faced with a choice between comfortable orthodoxy and hopeless unemployment. Those heroes who were prepared to sacrifice their minimum of comfort, sometimes their children's bread, for their principles, were still unable to make their voices heard at the Congress through the six successive stages, which filtered opinions from below, deadening them from stage to stage and finally suffocating them altogether.

At the end of October, Rakovsky and Kamenev took the risk of holding an open meeting in Moscow, but they were greeted with howls and were unable to speak. In other places similar attempts met with the same result. Nevertheless, the Opposition decided to continue with its combative tactics and to risk a street demonstration on the day of the great anniversary. Encouraged by the modest but fortuitous success of a demonstration in Leningrad, it hoped to make an impression on the bureaucracy by the evidence of its popularity.

That Zinoviev should show such presumption is not surprising. But Trotsky might have remembered Cromwell who, when he returned triumphantly from his campaign in Ireland, wisely remarked that "the crowd would have been still larger if they had come to see me hanged," or Washington, meditating, as he listened to the acclamations after his elections to the Presidency, "on the quite different scenes which perhaps I shall one day witness, in spite of all my efforts to do right." But, relying on their hypothetical and dogmatic social science, Bolsheviks of the Left, as well as those of the Right and Centre, are disposed to mistake their desires for the reality, their fears for a certainty, and to generalise from every occurrence, no matter how accidental. The Opposition was intoxicated by contact with its partisans in small illegal meetings, particularly when it unexpectedly succeeded in filling the amphitheatre of the Higher Technical School. On November 7, 1927, aliens amid the joyous mood of the celebration, carrying enigmatic slogans inscribed on placards, they launched themselves into the unheeding crowd which filed past singing revolutionary songs—a crowd like that of any other country but at the same time a Soviet Russian crowd, trained to march in line, collectively credulous but sceptical in its component elements, worried and passive, animated by a vague sentiment of revolutionary patriotism tempered with lassitude.

This time Stalin was not caught unprepared. The Opposition, submerged in the indifferent multitude, found itself face to face with well-trained bands, which, according to an official communiqué "pelted them with rotten potatoes and galoshes," which proved that these henchmen were there on purpose, since no one habitually sets out to celebrate the anniversary of a revolution supplied with rotten potatoes, and galoshes are far too expensive for anyone to throw away, especially at the beginning of the winter. The placards of the Opposition were torn down, the carriers molested, pushed, battered and sworn at by the crowd. A pistol shot—the bullet glanced off Trotsky's car. In Leningrad a brisk skirmish of the same kind resulted in Zinoviev's arrest for several hours. These were all the outstanding incidents of the day. Two small but fierce minorities alone were opposed to each other, the masses remained neutral and inert. On this point Trotsky notes in his *My Life:* "Those who could see, understood that a rehearsal for Thermidor took place in the streets of Moscow on November 7, 1927."

7

THE over-emphatic and banal manifesto issued by the Soviet Executive in honour of the anniversary contained a "surprise" among its hackneyed pronouncements and sacramental exclamations: the seven-hour working day was proclaimed, but in the form of a promise to bring this into operation a year later, by successive stages determined by the progress of the rationalisation of industry. In a country where it was officially admitted that the eight-hour day was not enforced, and where the workers, most of whom earned famine wages, were compelled to devote long hours each day to buying poor quality necessities such as bread for themselves and milk for their children, this future reform had not the importance that it was given in the official statement. The Opposition, infuriated by the demagogic unreality of this "gift," never ceased to point this out, a fact which did not endear it further to its opponents. But this new quarrel was only accessory to a wider disagreement over economic policy. The manifesto said nothing about the Five Year Plan, already agreed to in principle by the Central Committee; the leaders still refused to give it a position of more than secondary interest. The counter-theses of the Opposition soon made it a centre of conflict.

A vast mass of apparently documented literature, filled with figures and illustrated by diagrams, purported to show that materially Russia, after ten years of the revolution, had been restored to the low level of before the War. But the whole thing was based on false premises and conditional assumptions. It did not take into account the movements of population, the loss of huge productive territories, the depreciation of the currency, the collapse of external trade, the destruction and depredations caused by the Civil War. On the other hand the Gosplan admitted that the average level of consumption per head still remained well below the wretched pre-War level, and according to the economic plan under discussion, it would not equal it until 1932, which would be the fifteenth anniversary of October. These authoritative calculations showed up the statistical fictions published for propaganda purposes, and stimulated the Left, whose counter-theses criticised such an "insufficient and utterly pessimistic plan."

The Five Year Plan produced by the Right did not, according to these theses, resolve a single difficulty, neither unemployment, nor low wages, nor the housing crisis, nor the inflation of the currency, nor the famine of goods. Indirect taxes, which increased with each budget, were crushing the working class. The production of spirits alone would have tripled in five years, while the development in general consumption goods would be trifling. What was necessary, according to the theses of the Left, was an increased investment of capital in industry. There were a milliard poods of grain in reserve on the countryside; by means of a forced loan of 150 million poods, the State could give a vigorous impulse to the whole economic system, find work for the thousands of unemployed and put fresh goods on the market in considerable quantities. The subsidies allowed to industrial production should be raised, first to 500 million roubles a year, and then increased progressively up to a milliard roubles during the next Five-Year period. It went without saying that this plan could not be realised without the collaboration of its Left promoters, still less against their opposition, and it therefore implied a more democratic "regime within the Party."

But the Opposition had by that time scarcely any means of making known its views, which were ironically dubbed "super-industrialist." By the time *Pravda* published the counter-theses, the delegates to the local, regional, provincial and national conferences which preceded the Congress, had already been chosen almost everywhere. Further, a merciless repression choked the voices of all minorities. The few discussion journals, a parody of democracy, only served to encourage one-sided polemics. Finally, the Central Committee openly encouraged the breaking up by force of the private meetings of the Opposition. During an arranged interview with foreign visitors Stalin replied to a well-timed question: "You will not find a State anywhere else in the world where the proletariat enjoy so great a liberty of the press as in the U.S.S.R."

On the same occasion he expressed himself on the subject of *vodka*, the returns on which were more than 500 million roubles, a proportion more or less equal to the "budget of drunkenness" under Tsarism. "I believe that we shall very soon succeed in abolishing the *vodka* monopoly, and reducing the production of alcohol to the minimum required for technical needs, and later in liquidating the sale of spirits altogether." But his most interesting remark this time was on socialism in the countryside. *"We hope to realise collectivisation with reference to the peasants, little by little, by means of orderly economic, financial, cultural and political measures."* This is the traditional Bolshevik thesis, in which there is no question of using force. "Collectivisation will be complete when all peasant enterprises have been transformed on a new technical basis of electrification and mechanisation, when the majority of working peasants have been organised in co-operatives, and the majority of villages contain agricultural associations of a collective character."

The interview ended with some grandiloquent words about the G.P.U., which Stalin was not afraid to compare to the Committee of Public Safety of the French Revolution, despite the fact that the Soviet Union had not been at war for seven years and that more exact comparisons could be found in the history of Russia under the Tsars: "We do not wish to repeat the mistakes of the Paris Communards. The G.P.U. is necessary to the revolution and the G.P.U. will continue to exist for the confounding of the enemies of the proletariat." No allusion here to the hunting down of proletarians, socialists, libertarians, syndicalists, Tolstoyans, communists, revolutionaries of all schools, of which the various opposition tendencies were the victims.

On November 15th the Control Commission decided to expel Trotsky and Zinoviev from the Party. Everyone knew that this meant prison or deportation almost at once if the Congress approved of it. The other Left leaders were expelled from the Central Committee and deprived of their offices in the Party and the State. In Moscow people said that Stalin was determined to "strike the Opposition in the belly," to deprive it of work and hence of food and lodging. On the 16th, Joffe, one of the principal inactive Oppositionists, committed suicide. He had been ill for a long time and exposed to the hostility of the Politbureau, but above all, depressed by the persecutions of his fraction, he wished to register a protest against the expulsion of his friends: "This infamy . . . means inevitably the beginning of a Thermidorian period" in Russia. In his spiritual testament, a poignant letter to Trotsky, he adjured him to stand firm as Lenin had done and refuse to compromise. The G.P.U. searched the dead man's home and attempted to forbid the funeral cortège entrance to the cemetery. They were still afraid of using physical violence and creating a scandal, without direct instructions from above, but the hour when they would repay their opponents was soon coming.

One week after the first Soviet Ambassador to Europe and Asia had made his tragic gesture, Stalin announced the discomfiture of the Opposition, which, for very good reasons, had not obtained one per cent, and would not have a delegate at the Congress. "A declaration of unity signed by thirty-one Trotskyists has been sent to the Politbureau," he declared, "but what answer can one make to this hypocritical declaration by thirty-one Trotskyists, when the lying promises of the Opposition have again and again been contradicted by their splitting activities?" On December 2nd the Fifteenth Congress opened, a real conclave of functionaries, where "100 per cent unanimity" was guaranteed by every conceivable means.

It was a real masterpiece of its kind. In the whole solid mob of 1,669 delegates, the Left did not possess a single vote. One or two of its representatives, candidates for expulsion, were present according to their incorrigible custom, with consultative rights. What the right to speak consisted in, they were again to learn to their sorrow when they attempted to exercise it. Ceremonies of congratulation took up an enormous proportion of the time. The Congress received nearly 1,500 addresses, motions, telegrams of greetings and congratulations, dispatched under instructions from the centre, and the delegates applauded a vast number of so-called workers' and other delegations, as was expected of them. The less the time allowed for debate, the heavier and longer grew the reports: a vast tome of 1,400 pages enshrined these oratorical excursions, which stretched over thirty sittings. Stalin held forth throughout an entire day, showing his powers of endurance at least, and the other rapporteurs did their utmost to hold the floor for the longest possible time, making up in quantity what they so completely lacked in quality. On a "proposal" from the leaders, which was equivalent to a command, the obedient assembly "decided," that is to say accepted, a modification of the statutes which, in effect, legalised its arbitrary adjournment. Thereafter the Congress would not meet more often than once every two years. But there was no guarantee that this new stipulation would be respected, any more than all the other protective clauses, legal or constitutional. Finally, in accordance with Stalin's secret desire, the membership of the Central Committee was increased to 121, including alternate members, and that of the Control Commission to 195, in order to enlarge "the basis of the apex" for the benefit of the Secretariat.

The long Political Report given by the General Secretary, a document typical of bureaucratic optimism, concluded with a flattering enumeration of ten Bolshevik victories on diverse fields, both internal and external. Everything was for the best under the best possible dictatorship. . . . Surrounded by serried ranks of interested henchmen and docile followers, Stalin was secure in spinning out a string of statistical material, which had been furnished by prudent functionaries, far too cautious to risk allowing a personal idea to creep in. If he light-heartedly affirmed that: "We live on the eve of a new revolutionary upsurge, both in the colonies and the older countries," and was later proved wrong by facts, he could always fall back on Lenin's similar prediction, made at quite a different time. Having stolen from the Left his plans for industrialisation, at least on paper, he boasted of "the unprecedented rhythm of our socialist industry," and borrowed from Lenin a vague phrase on the need to "catch up with and surpass the most advanced countries on the economic field," which he transformed into an urgent slogan.

It goes without saying that the more backward a great country is, the more rapidly it will advance in certain circumstances, under the pressure of external competition and the application of the technical knowledge of its rivals, in order to raise itself to the level of a modern state. But this very rapidity demonstrates its backwardness, and is not a cause for boasting, for that "com-boasting" which Lenin so disliked. Tsarist Russia knew periods of feverish industrialisation, before the Soviets. And although one cannot conceive of democratic socialism without mechanical production, it is easy enough to speed up the production and forget the socialism.

Stalin was less satisfied with the state of agriculture, which was too widely spread, in too small strips, and insufficiently productive. Following the Opposition, he awoke, in his turn, to the *kulak* danger. According to the evidence, the well-to-do peasants were forced to hoard their grain since they were unable to exchange it for stable currency or for manufactured goods, while the poor peasants vegetated on infinitely subdivided patches of ground, without the necessary manure or tools. "What is at issue is the change from small individual peasant enterprises to large-scale cultivation, on the basis of collective cultivation of the soil . . . using a new and improved technique," but always going slowly, without compulsion, using the forces of persuasion and example: "Those comrades who think of disposing of the *kulak* by administrative measures, by the G.P.U., are wrong. This is an easy but not an effective way. The *kulak* must be dealt with by economic measures on a basis of revolutionary legality. And revolutionary legality is no empty phrase. It does not, however, exclude the use of certain administrative measures against the *kulaks*. . . ."

No administrative measures, therefore—but administrative measures all the same. And by this euphemism Stalin meant what Lenin termed "the abominations of Bashi-Bazouks," confiscations of wheat from the more provident cultivators, pillage which was at the same time official and illegal, and which could not be carried out without clashes and cruelty. "Administrative" meant the police and the military, since such administration is only practicable by armed men. This prospect meant war against the peasants who held back their grain, or a policy of spoliation such as the majority had reproached the minority with advocating, but which they had annexed, like industrialisation, to their own programme.

On the Opposition, which was the principal theme of the Congress, Stalin was content to repeat all the old stories. He drew up a brief "balance-sheet of the discussion": approximately 4,000 votes were cast for the Opposition, he said, but without explaining that more than a thousand expulsions had intimidated the Party members. A year later Stalin was to speak retrospectively of 10,000 votes against the Central Committee, plus twice as many who did not vote, say 30,000 Oppositionists under the bureaucratic terror, "under the knout of the administration" as Trotsky and his followers named it later. Here is another example of the truth of statistics: Stalin mentions 10,346,000 as the round total of paid workers in all categories both in the towns and country, and S. Kossior gives the number of trade unionists as 10,000,000. The entire total of wage-earners would thus be enrolled in the trade unions, including children, day labourers, domestics, wet-nurses and the millions of illiterates in remote places, far from towns and communications, where occupational unions could not possibly exist. . . . The other calculations, coefficients and percentages with which the various secretaries and reporters juggled are as little to be trusted.

"The Opposition must disarm, utterly and completely, both in the ideological and the organisational spheres," Stalin concluded. The audience, excited by a series of venomous speeches, knew what its masters expected of it and demonstrated without stint. Trotsky and Zinoviev, already expelled, were not there to reply. Rakovsky, only recently Ambassador in Paris and re-called by the Government as the result of a hostile campaign waged against him by the reactionary French press, was abused like an intruder, covered with insults and sarcasms, interrupted and mocked at every phrase, then at every word, finally chased off the platform, where he had had the useless courage to expose himself as in a pillory. Other comrades of the same tendency were not much better treated. Kamenev alone succeeded more or less in making himself heard, for his conciliatory manner, full of implications, seemed to indicate new possibilities. . . . Nevertheless, the Opposition renewed its desperate efforts to avoid the inevitable.

In a declaration signed by 121 names and countersigned by another 52, the Opposition protested its loyalty and admitted responsibility for the lack of discipline: "We have no disagree-ment of principle with the Party." It denied having accused the Central Committee of Thermidorian deviations, promised to cease the fractional struggle, to dissolve its organisation, to be completely obedient in future and to propagate its opinions only within the limits laid down by statute. By this means it hoped to obtain the reinstatement of those who had been expelled and the release of the prisoners.

But everyone at the Congress was aware of a latent split in the fragile "Opposition bloc"; the G.P.U. had spies every-where and was well informed through its censorship of corre-spondence. According to Trotsky, Zinoviev had already been considering "capitulation" for a year. Further, Stalin insisted on a complete surrender and the abjuration of all heresy, with-out reserve. On December 10th Ordjonikidze received two separate declarations of submission, one from Kamenev and others who renounced even their right to propagate their ideas legally, and one from Rakovsky and others who were not pre-pared to do this. On the 18th the expulsion of the 75 leading members of the Trotsky-Zinoviev group and of 23 members of the Sapronov group was voted unanimously. Immediately after, Rakovsky and his friends drew up a fresh declaration of their fidelity to Bolshevism: "Having been expelled from the Party we shall make every effort to return to it."

The Opposition "bloc" was at an end. Zinoviev and Kamenev who had formed it "seriously and for a long time to come," also made a fresh declaration in which they retracted their most intimate convictions, confessed imaginary sins, endorsed the accusations made against them and disavowed their foreign comrades. "Deserters" in 1917 and "capitulators" in 1927, they crawled on their knees before Stalin, exactly as he had calculated that they would. Nevertheless, this *mea culpa* did not save them; the Congress postponed taking a definite decision on their fate for six months in order that they might give proofs of their conversion.

The Opposition having been put outside the law, if one can so express oneself with reference to a regime so completely illegal, the Congress had fulfilled the main task which Stalin had laid down for it. On all other points on the agenda it adopted resolutions put forward by persons in the Secretary's confidence, Rykov's and Krizhanovsky's "directives" on the Five Year economic plan among them. Neither the directors nor the directed understood as yet exactly how and when the plan could be realised, as seven variations of it were being examined. Unless it drew on those sources of revenue indicated by the despised Left, which would bring it into violent conflict with the peasant producers, or took steps to suppress private trade, which was going against the fundamental principles of the N.E.P., the Soviet State would be unable to find the means to finance industrialisation on the grand scale. At the same time, various technical and cultural problems, which could not be solved in five years, presented themselves. But no one wasted time on these considerations, since some had no voice in the proceedings and the rest relied on the conclusions of the experts.

The Congress automatically ratified along with everything else the double-faced foreign policy of the Politbureau, which was pacific, accommodating and compliant on the diplomatic side, and subversive, arrogant and disastrous on the side of the enslaved ex-International. Recent happenings had revived interest in China in a most sinister way: during the night of the 10th to the 11th of December—(its coincidence with the Congress clearly demonstrated its lack of spontaneity)—a local rising broke out in Canton. Stalin's agents fomented this action in order to provide their chief with news of a victory to use as an argument against the "pessimism of the Opposition." It was a revolutionary rearguard action, isolated, artificial and doomed to failure. The Canton Commune, surrounded by the military forces of the Kuomintang, only lasted forty-eight hours, and its downfall let loose an appalling carnage. More than 2,000 communists, or those who were supposed to be such, were massacred on the spot, or tortured. One of Stalin's emissaries to China, Lominadze, had reported to the Congress that approximately 30,000 Chinese workers had been put to death in the five months from April to August 1927. After the crazy uprising in Canton and the bloody repressions which resulted during the next few weeks, the most reliable estimates put at 100,000 the total of victims of the catastrophic policy pursued under orders from "Moscow." With Chinese communism practically annihilated, a handful of survivors, among whom was Chen Tu-hsiu, the ex-secretary, went over to the Opposition and were expelled. Thus ended a whole cycle of aberrations and adventures from which Stalin emerged utterly discredited as a theoretician and strategist of revolution, at the price of a hundred thousand human lives.

But no one in Russia understood the cause of the disaster, and those who knew, or who wished to know, were paralysed. Having defeated the Opposition, Stalin hastened to finish it off. He was only waiting for a pretext to apply Article 58 of the Code which dealt with counter-revolutionary crimes and misdemeanours. He was very soon to find this in two letters intercepted by the G.P.U., inoffensive documents in which the anonymous authors stigmatised the "treason" of the "capitulators" considered as a "fact of history"—large words for a beggarly recantation which was not difficult to predict.

On January 19, 1928, the press announced in veiled terms
"the banishment from Moscow of the thirty most active members" of the Opposition, with Trotsky at their head. On the list
of the proscribed were Radek, Preobrazhensky, Smilga, Serebriakov, I. Smirnov, Byeloborodov, Sosnovsky, Muralov, Sapronov, and V. Smirnov. Various others, such as Rakovsky,
Boguslavsky and Drobnis, were "requested to leave Moscow."
It was the deportation of the irreconcilables under a hypocritical guise. Hundreds, then thousands of arrests and dismissals followed in an effort to exhaust physically or to break the morale
of those "traitors" who dared to take the name of Bolshevik-
Leninists. One typical characteristic of post-Leninist Bolshevism: Zinoviev and Kamenev seized the same pretext as Stalin
for denouncing the comrades of yesterday and begging indulgence from their masters by shamelessly treading the defeated underfoot. In their individual as in their international
relations, Lenin's epigones passed with the utmost ease and with
no intermediate stage from extreme humility before the strong
to extreme arrogance towards the weak. *Pravda* let it be understood that these capitulators who had taken "the decisive step"
would soon be restored to grace. As a contrast, the tribune and
leader of the October Revolution, the organiser of the Red
Army, took the road to exile, as he had done under Tsarism.

8

THE Opposition was defeated more by its own faults than anything else. The simple fact that Stalin took four years to bring
it to its knees, shows how badly it made use of the resources
it had acquired from the past, while remaining incapable of
reserving anything for the future. Even if one believes, like
Trotsky, that the outcome of the conflict was inevitable owing
to the irresistible reflux of the revolutionary wave, an unsatis-
factory and metaphorical explanation, yet a more conscious and
better directed minority might have gained time and strength
in order to intervene effectively. The original positions held
by the Left in the Politbureau, the Central Committee, the Coun-

cil of Commissars, the economic sphere, the army and diplomacy were by no means negligible, so long as they did not persist in attacking with their eyes shut the largest possible number of adversaries at one time, or in competing with the majority in orthodox Leninism. At least these positions provided an opportunity for some serious work of consolidation, to be undertaken without hope of immediate success, but while patiently awaiting the inevitable regroupment of forces. Instead of this, the Opposition sacrificed everything and threw everything away, only to finish by proclaiming its principled agreement with its persecutors.

This fundamental identity prevented them from making a bid for the active sympathy of the masses, "deceived in the hopes which the first days of the revolution had given them," as Buonarotti wrote of the French masses at the time when Babouvist ideology and the Conspiracy of Equals were being elaborated. In Russia under the Secretary, as in France under the Directory, the masses were "starving, without work, spending each day in a struggle to live till the next, languishing in a profound indifference: some of them even blamed the revolution for the countless evils that oppressed them." Trotsky, pushing the parallel with the French Revolution to its limit, compared himself in 1927 to a Babeuf who had not lost his head; by this honoured but out-of-date authority he sought to conceal his suicidal tactic. This historical example was not to his advantage, since his precursor had excuses for his equalitarian utopianism, inspired by antiquity, which a realistic disciple living a century and a quarter later, could not lay claim to. As an additional contradiction, Trotsky confirms the neo-Bolshevik doctrine of the unity of the Party, while the whole logic of his attitude drives him to ask for help from outside it—an unconscious justification for the persecutions under which his fraction disintegrated, denied their principles or went astray.

It seems as though the Opposition were unaware of one essential phenomenon: that the best men of the revolution had been absorbed into the minor, intellectual offices of the State, by reason of their capabilities, while the most mediocre, those who were useless in the domain of production, exchange, finance, teaching, etc., had become the buttresses of the Party, the "top layer" of Soviet society, by reason of their political prerogatives. Lenin had already been alarmed by these facts when he commented on "the lack of culture in the leading cadres of communists," who were not even aware of their own ignorance. Every Bolshevik who showed himself unfit for responsibility in one of the vital spheres of work, finished up by finding a place in the hierarchy of the secretaries. Thus a process of natural selection was already taking place, even before Stalin took control of it for his own ends, and this became more and more accentuated as the needs of the national economy became more pressing. A division of function very quickly produces a social differentiation as a result of material favours being added to civic privileges. Trotsky did not show clear-sightedness in respecting the new dominant caste of parasites as if it constituted a permanent *élite*.

There is some resemblance between this formalistic respect for the Party and Robespierre's deference towards the Convention in Thermidor. Trotsky even repeated his French predecessor's mistake in unnecessarily alienating, by vague and hidden threats, those whom he should have reassured, won over or rendered neutral. In both cases the actual power of empirical politicians, by a cynical combination of force and astuteness, won a victory over doctrinaires, ill-provided with common sense. Trotsky, although always prompt to refer to the Thermidorian precedent, preferred not to dwell on this aspect of things. Neither did he realise how closely the Bolshevik Left were related to the Jacobins who, in the year II, succumbed to a coalition which included the Maratists, the "enragés" and the future Equalitarians, together with a mixed pack of demagogues, moderates, speculators and terrorists. On the other hand, he, who was unable to learn from the teachings of history, nevertheless drew exaggerated, superficial or contradictory parallels with Thermidor, in order to construct a rigid scheme which finally misled the Oppositionists.

In 1921 he visualised the N.E.P. as a sort of auto-Thermidorianism, salutary if kept within bounds. In 1923 he denounced as inconsistent the implicit hypothesis of a Thermidor among the other historical analogies with the French Revolution. From 1926 onwards he became disquieted by the menacing Thermidorian perspectives, and the 7th November 1927, seemed to him a repetition of Thermidor. In exile his views became more dubious and conditional. But in October 1928 he deduced that unless the Opposition had a place in the Government, the Right would enter directly, and Stalin circuitously, "on the Thermidorian-Bonapartist road." In December of the same year he accused the Politbureau of "preparing a Thermidor, the more dangerous because unconscious," and declared: "For six years we have lived in the U.S.S.R. under conditions of a growing reaction against October, and in this way are clearing the way for Thermidor." In his *My Life*, written in exile in 1930, he wrote without equivocation: "With us, Thermidor has been very long drawn out. At least for a little while, intrigue has taken the place of the guillotine." Finally, to complete the muddle, he denies all his previous reiterations, in order to teach a lesson to the Leftists of the "Democratic Centralism" Group who were too inclined to follow them to the letter, and asserts that the Soviet Thermidor is not an affair of the past or the present, but a question of the future. He thus avoids giving a clear answer to a question which he himself boldly posed before he shrouded it in obscurity.

Without going further into the large number of variations, which it is not necessary to describe in detail, nor into the undoubted similarities between the two post-revolutionary situations, it is, however, essential to bring their vital differences into relief, in order that the subject may be fully understood. As Marx noted in another connection: "Happenings which are strikingly analogous but which occur in different historic milieux, often produce totally different results." In France, the direct economic consequences of Thermidor were the end of requisitioning, of the taxation and rationing of prime necessities, the annulling of the *maximum* and of the law allowing suspects to be dispossessed, the decrees of Ventôse. In Russia exactly the opposite effects began to be felt, following on the deportation of the "ungovernables." On the political plane, Thermidor meant the abolition of the Committee of Public Safety, the dilution and dispersion of the power in favour of the Consulate, and, after the recall of the Girondins and the partial return of the émigrés, it led to the White terror. In Russia, on the contrary, the power became more concentrated, the Dictatorship of the Secretariat was reinforced, and the regime could only maintain itself by a fresh outbreak of Red terror.

In truth, the year 1928 shows a marked recrudescence of police oppression both in the Party and the State. Stalin struck unceasingly both at the Left and the Right whenever the least objection was raised. As Fouché suppressed the "remains of Robespierre," so he attacked the remnants of Trotskyism first. The G.P.U., no longer held in check, discovered traitors in all directions, and when it could find none it invented them. The demoralised Opposition disintegrated, and the majority of its supporters in Leningrad capitulated in small groups. Yaroslavsky's statistics calculated that by February 1st, 5,755 had been accused of deviations, 3,258 had been expelled and 3,381 had capitulated individually. There is no record of the numbers imprisoned and deported. Trotsky noted in his recollections: "Krupskaya once said in 1927 that if Lenin were alive he would probably be in a Stalinist prison. I think she was right." On the last day of February, Pyatakov, the best known of the Opposition leaders after Trotsky, recanted in his turn. "One of the pillars of Trotskyism," as the communist press said, had collapsed. One month later, Krestinsky and Antonov-Ovseënko also abandoned their comrades in misfortune and did penance. The decomposition of the traditional Left had begun.

Ever since Brest-Litovsk in 1918, the moment when the majority of the Central Committee were for him, Trotsky had been gradually losing his supporters through a long series of internal crises. At the time of the Kronstadt affair in 1921 he still had nearly half the leading circle at his side. During Lenin's illness in 1923, an imposing fraction remained faithful to him despite the earlier defection of Bukharin, Dzerzhinsky, Andreyev and others. After the Fifteenth Congress, Zinoviev and Kamenev abandoned him, together with their followers. During the interval he had broken with old rebels such as Bubnov and Rosengoltz, as well as with recent ones, such as Krupskaya and Sokolnikov. He had lost his support from the army and his followers among the youth. Sapronov's group broke away from the main fraction for other reasons. The defection of Pyatakov, Krestinsky and Antonov at the beginning of 1928 was a split in the fundamental nucleus.

After each of these incidents, Trotsky attempted to console himself by saying that revolution is a great destroyer of men. He heaped praises on his comrades in arms before their defection, and spared them no reproach after, but he never paused to assess his own responsibility. The truth was that if the turncoats were able to change from one camp to another with such ease, it was because only a short distance lay between them. Many Bolshevik-Leninists were unable to see anything fundamental enough in their divergencies with the Leninist-Bolsheviks, to make suffering and adversity worth enduring. The special psychology of Bolshevism also helps to explain these sudden turns which at first sight seem so disconcerting. One knows that for Lenin's disciples, the end justifies the means. The ethical notions to which all revolutionary schools subscribe, were not current in the higher ranks of this Party, except in the form of literature. Thomas More beheaded, Giordano Bruno burnt alive, Campanella tortured—these are examples of heroic constancy which might be praised but should not be followed. The plain fear of being rejected by the patrician caste of Bolsheviks, of sinking among the plebeians of the Soviet, was sufficient to shake the weaker ones. The risk of uselessly exposing their innocent families to cruel reprisals sometimes broke the resolution of the strongest. But the Opposition only became indignant against this monstrous abuse of the "police knout" in those cases when its own members were the victims.

For Stalin allowed to no one the exclusive rôle of martyr. He treated difficulties of all kinds by the same methods. In an effort to cauterise the sores of industry, he attacked the tech-

nicians and the functionaries, whom the G.P.U. accused of
"economic counter-revolution," misconduct, sabotage, spying,
and high treason by preparing for a military intervention on the
part of France and Poland, champions of the expropriated Russian bourgeoisie. According to these accusations it would appear
that a widespread conspiracy, lasting five or six years, had been
able, with impunity, to ravage the Donetz coalfield, flooding the
pits, destroying machinery, embezzling the funds, ill-treating
the personnel, even beating up the workers, unknown to any of
the Soviet institutions, trade union or governmental, economic
or political, administrative or police. The worst enemies of Bolshevism never levelled a severer accusation against the regime.
The idea was to stage a trial amid terrific publicity, which, by
its resounding death sentences, would terrify all the intellectuals
in the State service, and exculpate the apparatus, which was
responsible for the catastrophe. In the "Shakhty affair" the
people were presented, for the first time, with the astonishing
spectacle of fifty accused who seemed more anxious to convince
the judges of the gravity of their crimes than to extenuate them.
By what methods of interrogation and procedure did the G.P.U.
obtain these astonishing and all too impressive results? No one
was to know exactly until later, but already it was possible to
form an approximate idea.

This dismal parody of justice, carried through in the supposed
interests of an ailing industry, was matched by fresh troubles
in the domain of agriculture, where Stalin also made use of harsh
measures of constraint. During the winter, foodstuffs were scarce
in the towns because the peasants stored their harvests rather
than sell them to the State at the low price offered. The shops,
co-operatives and warehouses were denuded of their stocks in
order to provide food, but still supply and demand remained
unequal, and an extreme scarcity resulted. Extraordinary measures were necessary to feed the Red Army and the centres of
production: communists were mobilised for expeditions and
requisitions in the villages, cereals were requisitioned by violence
and peasants arbitrarily arrested. The number of assassinations
corresponded to the crimes and misdeeds of the tax and food

collectors. The Congress of the Soviets was adjourned to the following year. Stocks of rye were purchased from Canada. In the spring, when the famine danger had receded, but only as a result of brutal measures, a fresh menace appeared: the peasants, despoiled, molested and discouraged, cut down their sowing so as not to produce any excess over their own needs. War to the knife was declared between the bureaucratic State and the rural population, for although the Party only denounced the malignity of the *kulaks*, the entire peasant population stood together against the enemy. Stalin who had quite failed to foresee this critical situation attacked it with his usual energy. Most unwillingly, and only at the eleventh hour, he began to apply some scraps of the programme of the Left which he had rejected. "The machine sometimes gets out of control. . . . The machine does not work exactly, and often not at all, as the man at the wheel expects," as Lenin once said.

In April 1928, Stalin announced the naked truth before an audience of functionaries: decrease in the wheat harvest, scarcity of goods, inadequate industry, and technical backwardness of agriculture, which was on too small a scale and too primitive. In place of the 18 millions of peasant enterprises existing before the revolution, ten years after it there were 25 millions, and the process of subdivision was still going on. Conclusion: the development of large-scale rural enterprises must be pushed to its limit, *sovkhoz* (Soviet State farms) and *kolkhoz* (collective farms) must be developed into "grain factories," a perspective which implied a more resolute class struggle against the *kulaks* and speculators, pioneers of capitalist economy.

From the depths of Siberia, Turkestan and Kazakstan, the Oppositionists applauded this "turn to the left" as a confirmation of their theories. Animated discussions were carried on, verbally and by letter, as to the attitude to be taken up to the new position. Stalin purposely allowed those in deportation a relative freedom of expression in order to keep himself informed on their state of mind and to make use of their disagreements. He learned thus that Radek, Preobrazhensky, Smilga, Serebriakov and various others thought of giving in and asking to be reinstated in the bosom of the Party which had now turned towards their ideas. While still carrying on repression everywhere, he did his utmost to stir up discord among the exiles by means of intermediaries. But a fresh crisis was developing in the Politbureau, which threatened his personal dictatorship. The harsh emergency measures during the winter, which had violated the agricultural Code, and resulted in renewed War Communism, had alarmed the Right, who wished to preserve the N.E.P. and fought against the turn to the Left. Bukharin, Rykov, and Tomsky were no negligible opponents since Voroshilov and Kalinin supported them. Against this new majority Stalin could count for certain only on Molotov. The two unclassified members, Rudzutak and Kuibyshev, were generally supposed to be waiting on events, before throwing their weight on the stronger side, but the truth was that certain bureaucratic complications at that time kept them temporarily out of the discussions. The Party, the International, and the public both within and without, were ignorant of all this, since nothing leaked out from the Central Committee, which, in its session of April 1928, had been unanimous in its decisions. Lenin's inheritor was face to face with his final test.

His tactics consisted, as they always did in such circumstances, in marking time, avoiding any open conflict until such time as he had a majority in the Politbureau, even in satisfying the new Opposition by words, which he did willingly so long as he retained freedom to act as he wished. In his aforementioned speech, he soothed the Right on the N.E.P. question: "It would be foolish to speak of . . . suppressing the N.E.P., of a return of food requisitioning, etc. Only enemies of the Soviet power could think of this. No one draws greater advantages from the N.E.P. than the Soviet power." At the Fifteenth Congress Molotov had also declared: "On what road must we continue to advance towards socialism? No one can have any doubts on this question. It must be on the road of the N.E.P. and unity with the peasants." An editorial in *Pravda* on April 12, 1928, demonstrated the perfect accord in the Government. "Only counterrevolutionary liars could talk of suppressing the N.E.P."

But in other directions Stalin prescribed in his circulars "the building of socialism" on the countryside, and the more rapid fusion of small family or individual holdings into large holdings cultivated in common, despite the fact that Molotov had said at a recent Congress: "We must certainly not forget that in the coming years our agriculture will develop principally in the form of small peasant enterprise." Secretaries of parties cannot control evolution, although they have authority over men. "The machine gets out of control. . . ." One contradiction more or less mattered little to Stalin, whose great gift was for hanging on.

This man, who was reputed to be taciturn, let himself go at that time in frequent and prolix speeches. In May, at the Communist Youth Congress, he returned again to one of the main themes of his April report, "self-criticism," the special liberty to censure oneself and make periodic confessions, thus encouraging mutual revelations everywhere but among "the tops," which meant that the dictators became invulnerable. In June he again spoke about agriculture to an audience of students: the "normal" sowing of pre-War days had been reached in 1928, he affirmed, in fact in cereals it had been exceeded by 5 milliards of poods, approximately 81 million tons. (The following year Rykov established that the said harvest had in fact fallen from 96 million to 73 million tons, for a population which had increased from 138 millions to 154 millions, a considerable drop in the relative average, and that the sown corn-lands had diminished by sixteen per cent per head.) In a letter published on June 12th, he appears to attack abuses of his instructions committed by subordinates who were in too great a hurry to confiscate all the belongings of the *kulaks:* "Dekulakisation under our conditions is lunacy."

In July, after an ordinary session of the Central Committee which passed a resolution tending to encourage individual agricultural enterprises, "which will be the basis of wheat production for a long time to come," he admitted in a report to Leningrad "administrative despotism, violation of revolutionary legality, searching of homes, illegal perquisitions, etc., which have worsened the political situation in the country," and promised "the immediate liquidation of any renewal of food requisitioning or of attempts to close the markets," which meant a continuation of the N.E.P. After these intentional concessions to the Right, he made a mysterious reference to "certain comrades" who wished to favour light industry at the expense of heavy industry, and to "those who do not understand" the official policy. In Party circles these veiled references were understood to convey a warning. Only the best-informed understood to what and whom Stalin referred. But information was secretly whispered and soon became well known.

On July 11, 1928, Bukharin and Kamenev had a secret interview arranged by Sokolnikov. The same evening Kamenev dispatched an account of the conversations, completed by some of his own reflections, to Zinoviev, doing penance at Voronezh. Six months later the Trotskyists secretly published these revealing documents. Thus Bukharin, in spite of himself, makes a truthful and sincere contribution to Stalin's biography, the most noteworthy after Trotsky's evidence. His words, recorded by Kamenev often literally, throw a brilliant light on diverse obscure points.

9

Sokolnikov was the first to tell Kamenev of "the final rupture between Bukharin and Stalin." In addition, Voroshilov and Kalinin had "betrayed" the Right, which was rendered powerless in the Politbureau. The two chief figures, searching for reinforcements for the future, would doubtless turn to Zinoviev and Kamenev, whom Stalin boasted of "having in his pocket." "In this tragic situation," Bukharin asked for an interview.

An hour later, at Kamenev's house, the foremost theoretician of the Party gave the impression of being "at bay"; his lips "trembled with emotion"; he was terrified of carrying on him anything "in writing." Why? "Do not let anyone know of our meeting. Do not telephone; it is overheard. The G.P.U. is following me and watching you also." He expects the Stalinists to make advances to the Left, including the Trotskyists, and wishes to keep his interlocutor informed. His disconnected and feverish story would hardly be comprehensible outside a very close circle of initiates; it is sometimes necessary to reverse the order so as to give it some kind of coherence, quoting actual topical allusions and making a résumé of the rest.

"We consider Stalin's line fatal to the revolution. This line is leading us to the abyss. Our disagreements with Stalin are far, far more serious than those we have with you." He regrets that Zinoviev and Kamenev are no longer in the Politbureau.

"For several weeks I have refused to speak to Stalin. *He is an unprincipled intriguer who subordinates everything to his appetite for power*. At any given moment he will change his theories in order to get rid of someone." Relations have become bitter to the point of insults. If Stalin pretends to retreat, it is only so that he may the better grip his opponents by the throat. "He manœuvres so that *we* appear as splitters." A significant fact: when Bukharin had to read a declaration to the Politbureau, he had to take great care not to let the manuscript leave his hands, because "you cannot trust *him* with the smallest document."

The Right theoretician attempts to define Stalin's "line." "Capitalism has developed through its colonies, through loans, and by exploiting the workers. We have no colonies and no loans, so our basis must be tribute paid by the peasants." This is equivalent to Preobrazhensky's thesis, he says indignantly. According to Stalin, "the more socialism grows, the stronger will grow the resistance" (which Bukharin describes as "idiotic illiterarcy") and as a result "a firm leadership is necessary." Self-criticism must not approach the leaders but compromise the Opposition. *"This results in a police regime."*

In foreign affairs Stalin's policy is further to the Right than the Right itself. "He has succeeded in expelling the Communist International from the Kremlin." At the time of the Donetz trial (in which German engineers were implicated) *"he* did not demand any capital punishments." In discussions with foreign powers, Stalin always gives way. "This line is disastrous but *he* allows no opportunity for discussing it." The *leitmotiv* throughout is: "*He* will suffocate us."

"Us" means Bukharin, Rykov and Tomsky, supported by Uglanov, Secretary of the Moscow Committee. The higher functionaries in Leningrad "are mainly with us, but they are terrified when we speak of removing Stalin," so they oscillate without being able to make up their minds. "Andreyev is with us, but he is being removed from the Urals. Stalin bought the Ukrainians by withdrawing Kaganovich from Ukraine . . . Yagoda and Trilisser are with us. There have been 150 small rebellions. Voroshilov and Kalinin funked at the last minute. . . . Stalin has some special hold on them that I do not know of. . . . The Orgbureau is with us." Nevertheless the majority of the Central Committee do not yet realise how grave the peril is. And Stalin is working to replace Uglanov by Kaganovich and to regain control of the Moscow and Leningrad *Pravdas* which are edited by Rightists. Bukharin has already discounted Ordjonikidze's co-operation. "Sergo is without courage. He came to me abusing Stalin in the most violent fashion, but at the decisive moment he betrayed us."

The conversation touches at intervals on the food problem. The Politbureau would again have to take extraordinary measures to procure cereals in October: "*It means War Communism and shipwreck.*" With Stalin and his "obtuse" supporter, Molotov, "nothing can be done." But what does the Right suggest? "The *kulaks* can be hunted down at will, but we must conciliate the middle peasants."

At the forthcoming Congress of the International, Bukharin was to present and comment on a projected theoretical programme: "Stalin has messed up the programme for me in dozens of places. *He* wanted to read a report on this subject to the Central Committee himself. I had great difficulty in preventing him. *He* is eaten up with the vain desire to become a well-known theoretician. *He* feels that it is the only thing he lacks."

In despairing tones the narrator asks himself whether all is not already hopelessly lost. "What can be done?" he asks several times. He compares Stalin to Genghiz Khan, and says that whether the Right intervene or whether they refrain, he fears they will be "strangled." Faced by this gloomy perspective, a last-minute lucidity inspires him: *"The Party and the State have become one: this is the misfortune."* Stalin, who is leading the country "to famine and ruin," will accuse the Right of defending the *kulaks* and speculators. "Stalin is only interested in power. While giving way *he* has kept hold of the leadership, and later *he* will strangle us. What is to be done? Psychological conditions in the Central Committee for dismissing Stalin are ripening but they are not yet ripe. . . . Stalin knows only vengeance . . . the dagger in the back. We must remember *his theory of sweet revenge."* (One summer night in 1923, opening his heart to Dzerzhinsky and Kamenev, Stalin is supposed to have said, "To choose one's victim, to prepare one's plans minutely, to slake an implacable vengeance, and then to go to bed. . . . There is nothing sweeter in the world.")

After this discomforting reminiscence, Bukharin relates the most recent happenings. He had demanded that a resolution to be submitted to the Central Commitee should be examined collectively. Stalin refused and then tried to coax him: "Bukharin, old fellow, you would really unnerve an elephant." Nevertheless, neither would give in. Bukharin insisted and Stalin invited him to talk it over, flattering him: "You and I are the Himalayas, the rest are unimportant." But later, in the Politbureau, a "savage scene" took place. Stalin sharted to "shout," Bukharin repeated the "Himalaya" metaphor and Stalin cried: "You lie! You invented that in order to rouse the members of the Politbureau against me." After this the decisions which were unanimously adopted favoured the "anti-Leninist" Right, but as always, were only on paper. Stalin believes that he is indispensable and attacks Bukharin, but he is leading the revolution to ruin. Industrialisation will inevitably lead to famine. *"Stalin's policy is leading us to civil war. He will be forced to drown the rebellions in blood. . . ."*

Through these disjointed confidences, shot through with occasional well-known truths, one can discern nothing of the old Party of Lenin. The degeneration which had been taking place for a long time had now become complete degradation. The faults which always existed in the Bolshevik Party in embryo, and which were so repugnant to Plekhanov, Martov and Trotsky, had now developed to the point of crushing any respect for the individual, any ethical or scientific scruple, and all sentiment of human and social dignity.

Stalin had now reached the point of having his closest colleagues spied on, though the latter nevertheless made use of Yagoda and Trilisser, Menzhinsky's two assistants at the G.P.U., who had come over to the Right as the result of 150 peasant insurrections in six months. (Similarly, a collision in Moscow in June 1928 between unemployed and militiamen, following the pillaging of several shops, had given the Chekists food for thought.) In the Politbureau, arguments had been replaced by sordid trickery and coarse offensiveness. On both sides the adversaries lent themselves to unprincipled combinations with those whom they had tried to discredit, for at the same time that Bukharin was sounding out the capitulators, Stalin was intriguing with the banished fraction, bargaining, tricking and finally withdrawing. Both sides had appropriated some portion of the dismembered Opposition's programme, the Right the democratic demands, and Stalin the economic plans. The Politbureau dictated to the G.P.U. and the courts the sentences they were to pass in important cases. If Stalin had been relatively restrained over the Donetz affair, it was not from mildness but from diplomatic fear of Germany, who would protect her nationals. Although the Right had a majority, the General Secretary could freely disregard decisions which had been taken in opposition to his wishes. "Do not think that the Politbureau is merely a consultative organ to the General Secretary," Bukharin said to him one day, but without making any difference to the state of affairs.

What was the "special hold" that Stalin had over Voroshilov and Kalinin? Certainly he had access to all the police records and dossiers through Menzhinsky; he knew some people's pasts and the present history of others, but even this does not explain all his exploits. The explanation is to be found in the incredible anecdote of "the Himalayas." Stalin flattered or slandered grossly in private conversations, stirred up hatred among his satellites, caused the best friends to quarrel, put words into people's mouths that they had never used, and won over the uncertain by insinuations, lies, provocations and threats. We know this through Bukharin, and other sources confirm it: anecdotes on this theme were rife everywhere. All the suspicions of his criminality, aroused in his youth at Tiflis and Baku, both when he was in prison and at liberty, by the curious coincidences which occurred and by his underhand manœuvres, were confirmed by time and experience. However low and vulgar his oriental method of dividing in order to rule, it produced some astonishing results in the Politbureau, where a majority vote at the decisive hour gave him freedom of action for a long time.

He made use of the same weapons against the new Opposition as he had against the old: recalls, displacements, nominations—the "bureaucratic knout" until the time came for the "police knout." At the "Congress" of the servile International, which sat for forty-five days in July and August, he did not deign to put in an appearance, but allowed Bukharin to discourse to his heart's content. There did not appear to be any difference between the two policies.

Particularly on foreign policy, Stalin expressed the same views as both the Right and the Left. In July 1928 he said that "the essential problem . . . is the struggle between Britain and America for world domination," a plagiarism from Trotsky, and predicted a breakdown of the unstable equilibrium between "the Soviet and the capitalist worlds." He always kept up the fiction that Europe and America thought of nothing but attacking Russia. In August, his mouth-pieces vigorously denounced the 1928 Pact "renouncing war" as being a war-like manœuvre against the U.S.S.R. "The Kellogg Pact is an integral part of the war preparations against the Soviet Union," declared Chicherin among others. Shortly afterwards, the Council of Commissars, at the command of the Politbureau, ratified the "imperialist" document.

From September onwards, the Party press began to hint
vaguely at a danger from the Right. But Bukharin was still
allowed to publish in October his *Observations of an Economist*,
urging the need to form reserves, not to force the pace of industrialisation too rapidly, nor to invest excessively in heavy industry, to take the material resources into consideration when
making plans for construction, etc. Stalin affirmed in a speech:
"There is neither a Left nor a Right in the Politbureau. I can
say that here in all frankness" (sic). But in a circular letter to
the Central Committee he spoke of opportunist deviations in the
Moscow Committee, and sanctions swiftly followed. Various
functionaries were dismissed from their posts, including a certain
Riutin, noted in the past for his violent persecution of the
Left. The following month Uglanov was forced to resign. The
Right took these blows without flinching, following the example
of previous oppositions as though resigned to suffering the
same fate.

Nevertheless, its leaders conceived a curious and misguided
tactic to clear themselves of all suspicion of heresy and to defeat
Stalin's manœuvres. They produced theses and resolutions
against their own tendency, for submission to the Central Committee, called for November. Another account by Bukharin
is in place here, transcribed and published like the other by
the diligent efforts of the Trotskyists.

While on a visit in the Caucasus, the unhappy author of
The A.B.C. of Communism became alarmed by the "stupidi-
ties" of Uglanov, who was already preparing to recognise his
errors, and by Rykov's isolation in Moscow:

Not being able to arrive in time for the next session of the
Politbureau, I took an aeroplane. At Rostov we were stopped. The
local authorities received me queerly, implying that flying was not
good for me, etc. I wished them in hell, and we went on. At
Artemovsk we landed again. I was hardly out of the cabin when I
was handed a sealed letter from the Politbureau with a categoric
order to put an end to the flight on the pretext of the state of my
heart. Before I had time to pull myself together, G.P.U. agents had
led my pilot away and I was faced by a workers' delegation demanding a conference. I inquired the times of trains; nothing

before the next day. There was nothing for it but to have the conference.

Arrived in Moscow after this tragi-comic Odyssey, Bukharin and his supporters formulated a list of demands, which Stalin feigned to accept at once. A commission was set up to put them into action, but the wily Secretary did not call it together, and by this means he gained three days. Under the veil of unanimity in the Central Committee then in session, the Right presented him with an ultimatum. Violent disputes broke out behind the scenes and the three leaders of the Right resigned. According to Rykov, Stalin received their statement "with trembling hands. He was pale and said he was prepared to give in." This was merely pretence, let it be understood. These trifles shed more light on the state of men and things than all the literature, solid, pretentious and indigestible, which is turned out by the yard to deceive public opinion.

Other conversations, reproduced by the same sources, show the opinions of outstanding people on Stalin and his entourage. Pyatakov, who advised the Right not to do battle, observed: "Stalin is the only man we must obey, for fear of getting worse. Bukharin and Rykov deceive themselves in thinking that they would govern in Stalin's place. Kaganovich and such would succeed him, and I cannot and will not obey a Kaganovich." Kalinin, a shame-faced Rightist, used these actual words when speaking of Stalin: "He chatters about veering to the Left, but in a short space of time he will have to apply my policy threefold; that is why I support him. . . ." Amid inextricable conspiracies, consultations, comings and goings and minor intrigues, Zinoviev and Kamenev abased themselves by importunate prayers, in the hopes of improving their rank in the bureaucracy. Ordjonikidze listened to them, offered to intervene, made constant promises, but never obtained anything. What equivocal game was this other sly Georgian playing, with his sympathy for all splitters and condolences for all unfortunates? "Ordjonikidze told me in 1925 to write against Stalin," Zinoviev stated before his expulsion. Bukharin considered him a coward. Krupskaya explicitly warned against him. The most plausible hypothesis seems that he was the conscious instrument of Stalin's Machiavellism.

This was the atmosphere, these the realities behind the austere façade. At the Plenary Session of the Central Committee in November, Stalin pronounced yet one more discourse on the "industrialisation of the country and the Rightist deviation." Repeating Lenin, he went back to Peter the Great and paraphrased a classic passage from a pamphlet published on the eve of October: "We must catch up and surpass the most advanced countries, or perish. Full steam ahead or we perish." Thus he justified the tense financial effort shown by the increase of the subsidies to industry to 1,650 million roubles for the current financial year. (The Left, accused of industrial demagogy, had not asked for half that.) On the burning question of cereals he said nothing new, merely wrangling for a long time with Frumkin, a Rightist, who said that agriculture in the U.S.S.R. was in jeopardy. He demanded that collective enterprises be developed and individual cultivation stimulated, both at the same time; an insoluble contradiction arising out of the compromise adopted at the Politbureau. Finally, while denying the existence of a deviation to the Right in the Party, he devoted half his comments to it, and concluded: "On the Politbureau we are, and shall remain, united to the end."

This gratuitous assertion resolved none of the outstanding problems, neither that of wheat nor any of the others. The year 1928 finished as badly as it had begun, if not worse. In December the famine made itself felt even in Moscow, which nevertheless occupied a favoured position. Soviet economy had reached a fresh impasse. The interdependence of stunted industry and backward agriculture brought corroboration to the theories of any opposition, whether of the Left or the Right.

On the countryside, forced "bargaining," a recent introduction, State buying of the harvest on the spot at a non-remunerative price, and a fresh agricultural tax on the *kulaks*, had not made good the deficit in the winter stores. The obstinate peasants buried the grain, or refused to sow it. Others took up technical cultivation which was more lucrative. An unnatural and unforeseen phenomenon was that a number of mujiks, hounded by the militia, went to the towns to buy their rye flour, in order to profit by the fixed scale of prices, which was often five times less than the market price. Avid speculators exploited the differences in prices. Local famines caused an outbreak of brigandage. The stubborn peasant resistance flamed into revolt against the insatiable police State, and the "Red Cock," secular symbol of the Jacquerie, sprang to life everywhere on the communal *ishas*, the village soviets and the barns of the *sovkhoz* and *kolkhoz*. A ferocious guerilla war was waged against rural journalist-informers, hated functionaries, and honest communists whose zeal carried them too far. Statistics of attacks, murders and burnings increased from day to day.

In the towns, rationing, bread cards, endless queues outside shops, privation and insecurity, growing unemployment and the fall in real wages, the constant decline of the rouble and the constant rise in the cost of living, all gave the lie to Stalin's optimism. Industry produced bad goods at exorbitant cost price, and always ran at a loss. The seven-hour day was still nothing but a fraud, like most of the legislation for the workers. Everything was lacking except *vodka*, which ravaged the working class. Against this background of material and physical misery, a sharp moral crisis was corrupting the youth and undermining Soviet society, prostrate beneath the knout. The press pointed to an alarming increase in prostitution, and the growth of anti-Semitism. The depravity and criminality engendered by poverty, drunkenness and bureaucratic oppression had grown to such proportions in 1927 and 1928 that the official records could no longer suppress them, since a "flood of scandals" had tarnished the reputation of the Party. "Thefts, lies, violence, cheating, unheard-of abuse of power, unlimited arbitrariness, drunkenness, debauchery, everyone speaks of these as facts that have been admitted for months and years, tolerated, no one knows why." Thus wrote Rakovsky on the liabilities of this retrograde regime, which announced its ambition of building socialism in a single country in order to set up there a civilisation without parallel.

10

BUT as the granaries emptied the prisons filled. Stalin began the year 1929 with a round-up of approximately 300 communists suspected of "illegal Trotskyist organisation," and charged with "anti-Soviet actions." Only half of these were mentioned in the press. Nothing restrained him any more, now that he had collected five votes in the Politbureau. Before dislodging the Right he intended to sweep out the remains of the Left. The dismembered Opposition reckoned that at that time, between 2,000 and 3,000 of its members were in captivity, but this approximate figure was later raised to 5,000. Among those detained were Stalin's old Caucasian comrades: Mdivani, Kavtaradze, Okudjava, and even Koté Tsintsadze, once the hero of the expropriations. If Kamo had not been the victim of an ordinary street accident in Tiflis in 1922, he would no doubt have shared the same fate as so many of the original revolutionaries who had rebelled against servile bureaucratism. Police operations were crowned in February by Trotsky's exile to Turkey, the only country which would agree to harbour him. The Right, behind the closed doors of the Politbureau, voted against Stalin's "sweet revenge," but this platonic gesture from the minority had no concrete value. It had let its hour go by.

Freed from the "super-industrialists," Stalin hastened on with super-industrialisation. He no longer had any choice: pressure from the peasants forced him to radical action. There was shortage of bread, and in order to obtain a sufficiency for the future, the State had to set up its own "grain factories." In a circular published on January 1st, the Central Committee urged its thousands of subordinate committees "to reinforce the socialist sector of mass economy . . . to develop the *kolkhoz* and the *sovkhoz* . . . to take the offensive against capitalist elements." Collectivisation of agriculture, an unexpected but inevitable corollary of increased industrialisation, called for appropriate machinery, tractors, steel, petrol. Enlarged industrial production called for factories, equipment, modern constructions. Everything hung together, wood, oil, iron, cement, naphtha, electricity, transport. To obtain the indispensable aid from abroad, it was necessary to export raw materials to pay for technicians and tools. It was therefore essential to co-ordinate all the elements of economic activity into a general plan to suit the circumstances. Stalin, who had despised Trotsky's "plan-making," now found himself forced, in self-defence, to put the Five Year Plan, still in the exploratory stage, into execution. Arguing against the Left, he had predicted in 1925 that "the future development of our industry, will probably not be so rapid as up to the present," and he fought against the "industrialist deviation" by demonstrating that too rapid progress *will certainly ruin us . . . undermine our currency . . . inevitably lead to . . . a great increase in the price of agricultural produce, a fall in real salaries and an artificially-produced famine.*" Nevertheless he went forward amid all these perils.

In February 1929, following the "brilliant success of the second industrial loan," the press announced the irresistible desire of the proletariat to subscribe to a third issue. By a miracle, each of these efforts corresponded exactly to the calculations already made by the Gosplan and the Finance Commission. From March onwards, still with the same remarkable spontaneity, workers began to form themselves into "shock brigades," issuing "challenges" to one another to speed up production in the name of "socialist competition." The newspapers were full of figures, percentages, coefficients, diagrams and comparative tables. Platforms and loud-speakers rang with slogans and appeals. Assemblies, conferences and congresses of all kinds echoed and amplified them. It was essential to "catch up with and surpass" Europe and America, and even to bring about complete socialism, a classless society, almost immediately.

To these methods of persuasion, which aroused the sporting spirit of a part of the naïve and ignorant youth, who were captivated by the scope of the task and the grandeur of the ultimate aim, Stalin added the pressure of his ultimate argument: in May, three of the most eminent Russian technicians, von Mekk, Velichko and Palchinsky, were tried without witnesses, condemned without proofs and executed without comment. The G.P.U. accused old men of seventy and seventy-five of all kinds of counter-revolutionary activity in the railways, and gold and platinum mines, with the aim of overthrowing the Soviet power and aiding foreign military intervention. How an engineer in the auriferous district of Siberia could foment counter-revolution and encourage a non-existent invasion, it is difficult to understand. But the G.P.U. had power of life and death over the subjects of the "socialist fatherland" without being called on to submit proofs. And Stalin felt that it was necessary to use these exemplary punishments in order to inspire the leading personnel of industry with salutary terror. For him also, the famous epigram, "bloodletting is a necessary part of political doctoring," was true.

"The Government has not yet approved any Five Year Plan," Molotov had declared in February, commenting on a suggestion for estimating future progress and comparing it with the present rate: "Cast-iron and steel have not yet reached the pre-War level. . . . With a few exceptions (coal and sugar), the Soviet Union's share in world production is still below what it was." The imposture of the Tenth Anniversary announcements on the economic restoration of Russia, having thus been admitted by one of the imposters, he goes on to praise the "general line" of the Party and to attack again the already prostrate body of Trotskyism and, finally, the deviation of the Right. In April, the Central Committee adopted further theses from the Politbureau on the Plan. In May, the Council of Commissars ratified the "optimum version," the Sixteenth Congress accepted it, and finally, the Fifth Soviet Congress consecrated it. The Five Year Plan, already more or less in application before surmounting all these bureaucratic hazards, then ceased to be a means and became an immediate end and the ruling idea of the regime.

Following the adoption of this "historic" resolution, of "world importance," as the Soviet press was fond of saying on any and every occasion, the bureaucracy evolved fresh innovations and novelties with the aim of "speeding-up the rhythm" in order to realise the grandiose *piatiletka* in four years instead of five. After "work without pauses," devised in order to get the most out of the material, came the five-day week, which meant a reform of the calendar, the suppression of Sundays and religious holidays. There followed a flood of decrees of "capital" importance, according to their promoters. "Shock brigades" went to the villages to lead the "socialist offensive" against private property. Stalin presently decided to "suppress the *kulaks* as a class," he who, six months earlier, had expressly encouraged individual enterprises and had written the year before, "Dekulak-isation under our conditions is lunacy." Military language cor-responded to the methods of the time; frequent "mobilisations" of "shock troops," "attacks" on all "fronts," "conquests" of "strong-points" by "detachments and brigades"; all that this vocabulary meant was that workers, galvanised by frenzied propaganda, threatened with penalties, and stimulated by bonuses, had hewed coal, melted steel or cultivated the land. *"Russian government consists in barrack discipline in place of the normal order of a city, a state of siege has become the normal state of society,"* stated Custine once, probably not realising how long this would remain the case, and that a century later it would still be true.

The banished Opposition could have disavowed any responsi-bility for this return to War Communism. But, on the contrary, it hailed the first signs as a "step to the Left," and the final ar-rangements fixed in 1929, as a true march to socialism, inspired by its own ideas. In this state of mind, those Oppositionists who had already been tempted to "turn towards the Party," now thought only of getting back there at any price. In July, Radek, Preobrazhensky, Smilga, Serebriakov and Drobnis broke with Trotsky and capitulated to Stalin, out of love for the Five Year Plan, and a few weeks later I. Smirnov, Byeloborodov and hun-dreds of others followed them. Even the last four intractable ones, Rakovsky, Sosnovsky, Muralov and V. Kossior, and their friends, raised no objections to the official policy except the injustices done to the original "industrialists," and the danger of a future "zigzag to the Right." "The Left Wing, from whose platform all the essential ideas of the Five Year Plan have been copied, still suffers under repressions and calumnies," Trotsky complained in November 1929, but, he wrote, "the greatest successes are combined with the most formidable difficulties." He admitted that already "prodigious conquests" had been made in industry, paralleled by a slow but real progress in agriculture.

Stalin rapidly disillusioned them over the expected "zigzag to the Right." Certainly he did not relax his rigorous treatment of the impenitent Trotskyists. The *Bulletin of the Opposition* published in Paris described the appalling conditions of imprisonment in the Siberian "isolators," and called for aid for those in deportation who suffered from privations, illness and police surveillance. The defeated fraction already mourned several of its members; in October 1928, Gregory Butov, one of Trotsky's secretaries, died in prison from a hunger strike; in November 1929, another of Trotsky's collaborators and secret agent of the intelligence service, J. Blumkin, was executed by the G.P.U. on his return from a mission abroad: he had had an interview at Stamboul with his old chief and agreed to convey an innocent message to Russia. V. Smirnov, the theoretician of Democratic Centralism, was to perish in Siberia. Others, less well known, suffered or were to suffer similar fates. But without relaxing the struggle against the Left, Stalin began to take more and more brutal measures against the Right, whose revealing silence and secret obstruction threatened to interfere with his policy.

Throughout 1929 he repressed the "opportunists" by the methods which had already been proved effective in earlier conflicts. After humbling the smaller fry, of the calibre of Uglanov, he turned his attention to the more important sinners. It was in vain that Bukharin quoted, a little later, one of Lenin's letters in which he wrote, "If you get rid of all those who are intelligent, but not strictly obedient, and only keep the docile idiots, you will certainly ruin the Party"—he in his turn was able bitterly to estimate how short was the distance between the Capitol and the Tarpeian Rock, as he passed rapidly along the road to disgrace on which Trotsky, Zinoviev and their followers had already preceded him. The revelation of his interview with

Kamenev and Pyatakov had irreparably damaged him. But this time history repeated itself in a totally uninteresting manner: it would have been possible to predict all the main stages in advance. Furthermore, the Right never had the courage to stand up for its opinions, it allowed itself to be defeated over details, and never used any other manœuvre than flight. There was no need to deport it in order to make it bow the knee.

In July, Bukharin was expelled from the Bureau of the International. In August, *Pravda* opened fire against its own editor, who "lacked faith" like Trotsky, "over-estimated difficulties" like Zinoviev, and had never ceased, all his life, to be wrong, and even to contradict Lenin. . . . All his present and past, genuine or imaginary, faults were listed. The Lenin Institute searched through old papers, deciphering notes and scribbles of the Master, in an effort to find critical and derogatory remarks about Bukharin, and even printed intimate marginal annotations in order to discredit him. A special pamphlet was devoted to his old differences with Lenin. Papers and reviews published in a slightly altered form so as to turn them against him, those diatribes from which the Opposition had had to suffer at his hands. His works, which millions of young people had been taught to regard as classics, were suddenly discovered to be full of heresies and were put on the Index. *The A.B.C. of Communism*, which had already had Preobrazhensky's section cut out, was now withdrawn from circulation. In November, after the usual threats and attacks, Bukharin was thrown out of the Politbureau. Rykov and Tomsky, accomplices whom Stalin wanted to segregate from him, escaped with a severe warning. At the same moment, Uglanov and three others capitulated. The indifferent public were told only that the "bankrupt" Rightists, who had once been model and irreproachable Leninists, had accused "the Party"—for which read Stalin and his acolytes— of bureaucracy, Trotskyism, military-feudal exploitation of the peasants, and had condemned the "offensive against the *kulak*." A few days later, Bukharin, Rykov and Tomsky, branded as criminals and filled with panic, recognised their errors. . . .

It is scarcely worth while describing how these so easily

terrorised terrorists were supplanted by greater mediocrities, eager to inherit the places around Stalin which they had been promised in exchange for their support. The majority of the newcomers are not worth naming, nor are their bureaucratic achievements worth a mention. More significant is the sudden collapse of this timid and calculating opposition, made more marked by other simultaneous manifestations of the same kind: the repeated confessions of Zinoviev and Kamenev, in astonishingly platitudinous terms, the fresh recantation of Shliapnikov, at a time when all these men were out of political activity and had neither said nor done anything worth repenting—finally the shameful recantations of the "red Professors" of Bukharin's school. The Bolshevik mentality, which had evolved from implicit amoralism to declared cynicism, no doubt explains many things, but not such a complete and rapid triumph for Stalin. The main reason must be sought in the "police regime" which Bukharin once lamented in despair, and which made Chernishevsky's words, repeated by Lenin, so true: "Unhappy nation, nation of slaves; high and low, all are slaves."

Russia under the Soviets was not so much reminiscent of pre-revolutionary Tsarism, which was a worm-eaten autocracy, a despotism tempered by corruption and lightened by certain tolerances and relatively liberal customs. It was more like Russia in a more barbarous age, notwithstanding the modern technique. One notices more and more analogies with the observations made by the first travellers or ambassadors to Muscovy: Guillebert de Lennoy, the Fleming; Barbaro and Contarini, the Venetians; Chancellor and Fletcher, the Englishmen; Possevino, the Italian; Margeret, the Frenchman; Olearius, the German; and their successors, Carlisle, Collins, Jean Struys, without going back as far as Marco Polo. "The revolution has overthrown the monarchy. . . . But perhaps it has only forced the external malady deeper into the organism," wrote Gorky in 1917, a poor theoretician but an intuitive essayist and, for once, a good prophet. The G.P.U. which at first was reminiscent of the Okhrana, then of the Third Section of the Chancellery, and finally of Ivan the Terrible's *Oprichnina*, revived the grim ancestral tradition of the knout. S. Platonov in his *History of Russia* says: "The banishments, deportations and executions of suspects, the violence with which the *oprichniks* treated traitors . . . all this made Moscow tremble and inspired in everyone an attitude of passive and resigned submission." Under Stalin, as under Ivan the Terrible, the Opposition was broken by the same measures, and it is no accident that S. Platonov himself died in exile. Under Stalin as under Godunov, informing was turned into a system of government; finally, as under Peter the Great, into a State institution. No one trusted his fellows any longer or dared to express his thoughts to neighbours, friends, or relations. The G.P.U. had approximately 20,000 functionaries, 30,000 secret agents, 60,000 chosen spies, without counting those in the *Chon* (detachments for special purposes), at the disposal of the Party; but these figures give a feeble idea of its power: as auxiliaries it had not only the militia and the army, in case of need, but the millions of Party members and the Young Communists, all pledged to denounce their comrades, and, in addition, the thousands in the so-called voluntary associations subject to the State power, the offices of the Soviets and trade unions, the house committees, and all the multitude of secretaries and employees which made up the structure of the State. Reversing the old axiom which Peter the First introduced into military law, and to which Catherine II gave lip-service, namely, that it is better to pardon ten criminals than to condemn one innocent man, the G.P.U. sacrificed a hundred innocents rather than miss one "traitor." Spying in all forms, paid, voluntary or obligatory, and sometimes provocation, furnished ample material for its amazing technique of inquisition and punishment. The knout, which had been abolished by Tsarism in the preceding century, under Stalin became once more "the favourite instrument of the State Nemesis" as Shchedrin once put it. Between the hammer and sickle, emblems of primitive manual labour and an unproductive economy, the subjects of the Soviet caught a glimpse of the invisible but terrible threat. The mystery which surrounded all the proceedings of the G.P.U. aggravated further the idea which the population had formed of the physical and moral tortures inflicted in the Lubianka prison and its fellows in the provinces. But a modern all-powerful police has more refined instruments of torture for extracting confessions than actual knouts, racks and thumbscrews. The Bolsheviks condemn themselves by quoting the famous example of Peter, the reformer Tsar, with whip and gallows, who "civilised with a knout in his hand and knout in hand persecuted the light" as Herzen described him, and of whom Puškin said that his ukases were "as though written with a knout." Although their favourite historian, Pokrovsky, had condemned Peter for "believing in the knout as an instrument of economic progress," Stalin fell into the same error. "Civilisation and science were offered us at the end of a knout," Herzen once wrote. Stalin did not conceal that the Five Year Plan, and socialism in a single country, could not be achieved in any other way. Under his empirical but resolute leadership, the knouto-Soviet State, if one may thus revive one of Bakunin's forgotten formulas, blindly tackled a more profound social and economic upheaval than that of October, a revolution decreed from above against the feelings and interests of those below—the widespread collectivisation of agriculture, by force if necessary, in complete violation of the elementary principles of socialism, and even the calculations of the controlling plan itself.

Lenin had always conformed strictly to Marx's and Engels's ideas on agricultural theory. "Engels underlined the fact that socialists do not dream of expropriating the small peasants, who will come to understand the advantages of mechanised socialist agriculture only by force of example." He had emphasised this on many occasions, and under War Communism he stated: "We will not permit any violence towards the middle peasant. Even in the case of the rich peasant we do not say 'complete expropriation' as firmly as for the bourgeoisie. . . ." He introduced this explicit thesis into the fundamental resolutions of the Communist International: "*As a general rule the proletarian power should leave the rich or comfortably off peasants their lands, only taking them over in the case of direct opposition.*" For him, the peasants expressed "the will of the immense majority of the working population." And in one of his last speeches he recommended that the peasant masses be moved "immeasurably, infinitely more slowly than we have dreamed, but in such a fashion that the whole mass comes with us." Stalin, who was familiar, at least at second hand, with Marxist thought on this point, and had plagiarised from Lenin on more than one occasion, boasted of being able to solve the agricultural question in a socialist sense and with great rapidity, by using terror.

Strengthened by the apparent rallying of both Left and Right around the Five Year Plan, free of any open opposition, and undisputed master of the machine, the "genial secretary," as he was ironically called, could, in future, do as he liked. Of the Bolshevik Old Guard, some of whom were dead, some politically moribund, shackled and discredited, he alone remained amid the "nonentities" that he had jeered at in front of Bukharin. He did not fail to take advantage of an opportunity which presented itself to strengthen his authority over the G.P.U., which had become contaminated by opportunism at the top. Terrified of returning to Russia, the Soviet functionaries abroad preferred emigration, and a scandal broke out in Paris when the First Counsellor at the Embassy, terrified by a superintendent from Moscow, climbed over a wall in order to get away. Stalin profited by this to accuse the G.P.U. of lack of vigilance; he replaced Trilisser, a Rightist, by Messing, and reorganised the board of control. As first assistant alongside Menzhinsky, the irremovable President, he retained Yagoda, whose sympathies with the Right had not been lasting. Feeling this instrument to be reliable for the future, he accelerated industrialisation in the towns and collectivisation in the country, he spurred on the Party and, in particular, the Young Communists, which speeded up the inexorable wheels of the bureaucratic and police machine. Everything for the Plan and by the Plan: the entire life of the Russian people could thus be summed up from 1929, "the year of the great turn."

Adopting this proud title, Stalin waited only five months after the adoption of the *piatiletka* before announcing victory. In an economico-military speech of untranslatable bombast, in which the ritual refrain "Lenin said" frequently occurred, he announced "a great turn on all fronts of socialist construction . . . under the banner of a stern socialist offensive against all capitalist elements." In a paroxysm of "com-lies" and "com-boasts" he announced that all levels set by the plan had been reached and passed, except perhaps the formation of cadres of "red technicians," but that the Party only had to make up its mind, in order to "attack the problem of cadres and carry this fortress at whatever cost." . . . He stated that investments in industry had increased in one year from 1,600 million roubles to 3,400, without revealing how this had been done, or why the Left had once been guilty of an unforgivable crime in proposing an annual subsidy of from 500 to 1,000 millions. He enumerated a list of extraordinary successes and final conquests, of "formidable progress" and "increased rhythm," and mocked at the bankrupt Right, to whom he had recently publicly sworn "solidarity to the end." But for "unprecedented success" there was nothing to equal agricultural collectivisation, despite "the desperate resistance of all the forces of darkness, from *kulaks* and priests, to Philistines and opportunists of the Right." Entire villages, cantons, districts, even regions had joined the *kolkhoz*, it appeared, but Stalin made no mention of the implacable pressure on them, beyond a brief reference to the "workers' brigades, disseminated by tens and hundreds throughout the principal districts of our country," and whose task, not yet fully understood, was already beginning to resemble the "dragonnades" of the Camisard war. He expatiated on the collectivisation of millions of hectares and the number of quintals harvested, emphasising the importance of tractors . . . in the future. "We are going full steam ahead towards socialism through industrialisation, leaving our century-old 'racial' backwardness behind. We are becoming a land of metals, a land of automobiles, a land of tractors, and when we set the U.S.S.R. on an automobile and the mujik on a tractor, let the noble capitalists, so proud of their 'civilisation,' attempt to catch us up. We shall see then which countries can be 'labelled' as backward, and which as advanced."

These elephantine boastings, in which ignorance and presumption, complicated by nationalism, were mingled, merit comparison with the vain words of Peter the Great: "Let us hope that in a few years we can humiliate the neighbouring countries." . . . One trait which persists through the centuries is the disdain which Russia, Tsarist or Soviet, affects for the west, whose civilisation she copies, paying the teachers highly, without ever succeeding in catching up with or outstripping anyone. Peter is said to have made the impudent assertion: "We need Europe for a few dozen years, after that we will turn our backs on her." Stalin was content to reduce the period to five years, then to four, and his courtiers exaggerated even further. General Brussilov was thinking less of this aspect of things than of parallels with important personages, when he wrote in his *Memoirs*: "Many of these historical characters who are thought of as great men were Bolshevik in their methods of government and action: Ivan the Terrible, Peter the Great, Pugachev." It is worth noting that Lenin had anticipated Gorky, Brussilov and many others, in drawing a somewhat damaging parallel between Peter and himself. "If the revolution in Germany does not come quickly, we must apprentice ourselves to the school of German State capitalism, imitate as closely as we can, not sparing dictatorial action to make this imitation even more rapid *than Peter's forcing the imitation of the west on barbarous Russia*, not shrinking from barbarous methods to fight barbarism." But Lenin thought it necessary to cut out the phrase referring to the cruel, torturing Tsar, who assassinated his own son, when he quoted his own remark three years later. Stalin, devoid of any socialist humanity, seems to have followed particularly the advice to make use of barbarous methods, one of those imprudent phrases which "the old man" must have regretted leaving for his narrow-minded disciples, who were unable to understand the spirit of it. No doubt the aphorism comes from a reminiscence of Engels, from whom Lenin borrowed so much: "Humanity, descended from animality, has needed to use barbarous, almost animal, methods in order to escape from barbarism"— a retrospective view in which one finds not the slightest suggestion for future conduct.

Stalin's article on the "great turn" written in cold blood for the Twelfth Anniversary of the Revolution, hardly represents the tone of delirium demanded from the press. "Prodigious," "colossal," "unforgettable," "marvellous," every sort of superlative was dragged in to describe achievements which would have seemed ordinary and everyday anywhere else—achievements such as digging a hole, laying bricks, sowing rye, or particularly those magnificent plans, still merely sketched, or in the blueprint stage, whose fulfillment was said to mean "catching up with and surpassing" Europe and America. Ten years before, when the first electrification scheme was proposed, Bukharin had produced a lyrical invocation to Bogdanov's *Red Star*, a utopian romance in which an earthdweller finds himself on a socialist Mars during a period of "great works," the transition from capitalism to communism. After treating the author as a counter-revolutionary (he was one of the pioneers of the movement, remarkable both for his knowledge and character, and he died in 1928, following a medical experiment which resembled suicide), the Bolsheviks drew inspiration from his romance, characteristically exaggerating it and indulging their passion for the gigantic, their cult of machines, their mysticism over tractors and their novel form of "delusions of greatness." Lacking any sense of reality, Stalin and his apparatus satisfied themselves with dreams, and by a curious auto-suggestion perhaps even persuaded themselves that their vague hypotheses were well founded, since their subjects appeared to be deceived by them. One has only to read Custine to find this tradition already well rooted: "The best way to give the lie to the most patent facts and to deceive everyone's conscience most completely, is to begin with one's own."

Starting with the astronomer, the Abbé Chappe d'Auteroche, in the eighteenth century, all serious observers have noticed that Russians have a "particular gift for imitation." In this direction, Stalin, by imitating the external aspects of American industrialisation, was no more an innovator than Peter before him, since from the time of Godunov, Russia has mimicked the Poles, the Swedes, the Dutch, the Prussians, the English and the French in succession. Herzen truly said "We have been a thousand years on earth and two centuries at school, learning imitation." All backward countries must go through a stage of scientific and technical instruction, during which they must borrow from other civilisations, but the knouto-Soviet State, following its own line of national despotism, cut itself off from real progress by concealing a genuine inferiority under a mask of arrogance. Lenin's bitter remark about Zinoviev, "He copies my faults," applies even more strongly to his heir, who, in addition, copied all the defects of his capitalist models. And just as the Bolsheviks were unable to assimilate Marxism, a synthesis of various western cultures, but took over a simplified form decked out with learned terminology, so they could not take the shortest road to rational production, but ruined their natural economy in order to erect vain-glorious "giants" of electricity, metallurgy and machinery, "the greatest in the world," or said to be so.

It would be difficult to distinguish in Stalin's professions of socialist faith at that time the varying proportions of hypocrisy and ignorance. But as one watches the sacrifice of the individual worker to the parasite State, and that of the revolutionary generations to the myth of the too-fascinating Plan, one cannot doubt one primary fact: five years after Lenin's death, Leninist notions of socialism had no longer anything whatever in common with the doctrines put forward under the same label. Stalin's industrialisation was based on an intensive over-exploitation of the workers, and his collectivisation on the absolute servitude of the peasants. Since there were no large loans from abroad, nor rich classes to be taxed, the workers in the factories and the semi-proletariat in the fields had, in Russia, to bear the cost of "building socialism" in a single country. In order to finance the Plan, which had been transplanted from the planet Mars to a sixth part of the terrestrial globe, and which was out of all proportion to the normal resources of the Soviet Union, there was no other method than to increase the many schemes of extortion and coercion which were already in operation under various pretexts, heavy taxes, unlimited inflation, continual rise of prices, forced-voluntary loans, raised by a levy on wages.

As even this was not enough, there was nothing left but to expropriate the few remaining possessors of goods or means of production, the *kulaks* first, "those who have enough to eat," and then the small shop-keepers, the artisans, the middle peasants. This road meant the end of the N.E.P., of concessions and private trade. Before the end of 1929 Stalin was to declare: "Lenin said that the N.E.P. was introduced thoroughly and for a long time. But he never said for ever." The inconsequent Secretary had already promised several times during the year to maintain the N.E.P. as a working principle. Judging from the evidence, he no longer knew himself where his empiricism was going to lead. "The machine gets out of control." Less than a month after Stalin had pronounced a funeral oration over the N.E.P. in ambiguous terms, Krizhanovsky, the chief engineer of the Plan, quoted with remarkable appropriateness some other words of Lenin's: "How can we approach socialism? Only through the N.E.P."—a last echo of a policy in its death-throes.

A marked revival of War Communism and terrorism accompanied this new effort to bring about socialism by "assault," this time without the excuse there had been in October 1917. While sparing the skilled workers who were recognised as indispensable, and even given certain material privileges at the expense of the disinherited classes, Stalin redoubled his demands on, and severities towards, the harassed, overburdened and undernourished proletariat. He wished to raise the level of production by means of decrees and disciplinary regulations, and to compensate for technical deficiency, bureaucratic fraud and governmental incompetence by the sheer physical effort of the workers, who had the alternative of consenting or running away to wander in thousands from shop to shop and factory to factory, seeking bearable conditions of life. But the misery of life in the towns was "caught up and surpassed" by the horrors of the collectivisation. In spite of the "victory on the wheat front" proclaimed by Mikoyan, the communist brigades, which scoured the countryside in order to convert the recalcitrant mujiks, committed excesses before which the earlier "abominations of Bashi-Bazouks," and even the historic exploits of the *Oprich-*

nina, paled. Entire trainloads headed north, transporting the de-kulakised *kulaks,* who were nothing but uprooted peasants with their families, deprived of everything, torn from the *isba* and their native land in mid-winter. By ruinous taxes, sales by auction, total confiscations followed by series of arrests, sometimes by summary executions, murders of revenge and ferocious reprisals, by the use of every method of pressure and constraint, the machine, under Stalin's orders, produced a panic rush towards the refuge of the *kolkhoz.* The majority of the peasants, after this education, preferred to kill their stock and destroy their belongings rather than hand them over to the despoiling State; the poorest alone, having nothing to lose, and hoping to benefit from the loans, seed, and tractors promised in the Plan, allowed themselves to be rounded up. Complete migrations depopulated regions which had been made fruitful by the labour of many generations: for example the departure en masse of the German colonists on the Volga, the exodus of the woodcutters from Karelia, the shepherds from Kazakstan, the escape of the inhabitants of the frontier zones under the fire of the frontier guards. "The whole of peasant Russia at this moment is screaming with pain and despair," stated a correspondent of the Paris *Communist Bulletin.* Innumerable suicides which found no place in the statistics, even collective suicides among the Chermisses in Siberia, darkened the tragedy still further. This is how the miracle of the increase in *kolkhoz,* which made Stalin dizzy, was brought about.

While struggling against the workers and the peasants, the technicians and the intellectuals, the Left and the Right within his Party, Stalin was also waging a pitiless war against the Church and the believers, thus betraying once more, by his methods, the Bolshevik tradition to whose heritage he laid claim. Lenin had subscribed unreservedly to Engels's views when he reproved the Blanquist Communards for attempting to "suppress God by decrees," and later reproached E. Dühring with "surpassing Bismarck" by his methods of combating religion. His definite conclusions in this domain were the complete opposite of the aggressive and brutal egoism of his epigones. Ever since the days of *Iskra*, he had maintained that "even the Jesuits had a right to freedom of propaganda," with the stipulation that the proletariat should be protected from it by persuasion. "To declare that war against religion is one of the political objects of a workers' party, is merely an anarchist phrase," he affirmed, and even said that "If a priest comes to us wishing to join in our political work, if he carries out conscientiously the tasks which the Party gives him, without interfering with its programme, we can accept him into the ranks." The Soviet Constitution "allows to every citizen the right to put forward religious or anti-religious propaganda" (an article which was modified with a stroke of the pen in 1929), and the Bolshevik programme prescribes "careful avoidance of any offence to the sentiments of believers." For ten years the separated Church and State had managed to live in relative peace, occasionally broken by bloody conflicts as when, during the great famine, precious metals were requisitioned from the sanctuaries for the alleged benefit of the sufferers. The Government limited itself to encouraging schisms, supporting the dissident sects, while at the same time stimulating anti-clerical propaganda. But a fresh phase began when Stalin reopened hostilities against the peasants. The alliance between priests and *kulaks* served to justify all the misdeeds of the Party in the countryside. Official irreligion was transformed into systematic de-Christianisation by violence: churches of the various faiths were closed and demolished or taken over, as were chapels and monasteries, sacred books were seized, and proselytism forbidden, icons were burnt and priests deported or condemned to death. Under pretext of a militant materialism, by methods which were a caricature, adults suspected of "idealism" were forcibly inculcuated with atheism, which was already obligatory in the schools. Peter the Great took a quarter of the bells from the churches and melted them down for artillery, Stalin confiscated the whole lot to make carburettors. With two centuries between them, the savage Tsar and the police Secretary made use of the same blasphemous buffoonery, educative carnivals, burlesque processions and profane parodies, but the second, like the first, succeeded only in wounding the faithful by his persecution of the clergy, and outraging their forms of worship, without uprooting any of their beliefs and superstitions, which took refuge in clandestine prayers and were hidden deep in their consciences. The degenerate Bolsheviks appealed to Marx's words about religion being "the opium of the people," but their "victories on the religious front" were obtained by the same barbarous methods as those of the greatest of the Romanovs, the most arbitrary of despots, and they had themselves made use of Leninist dogma as a narcotic, and then indulged in the fetichist worship of a mummy.

On December 21, 1929, Stalin's fiftieth birthday, the entire Soviet press came out with immense headlines, immense portraits and immense articles. The praises of the Dictator were also immense. The finest human qualities and many super-human virtues belonged to Stalin, the man of steel, according to the censer-bearers of his train. His modesty, his courage and his devotion to the cause were only equalled by his wisdom and foresight. It was he who had organised the Bolshevik Party, led the October Revolution, commanded the Red Army, and been victor of the Civil War and the wars outside Russia. Added to all this, he was the leader of the world proletariat. His practical ability was on a level with his theoretical gifts and both were infallible: no one had ever seen him make a mistake. And the *leitmotiv* which recurred through all these dithyrambs was: the man of iron, the soldier of steel, with variations on the metallic theme: Leninist of brass, Bolshevik of granite. The same formulas, the same hyperboles, the same exaggerated expressions of admiration and submission, all conforming strictly to the model as issued from Moscow, were to be found in the thousands of addresses, messages and telegrams received from all parts of Russia, which filled entire pages of the newspapers and continued to occupy several columns for weeks to come. The State publishers issued millions of copies of selections, in which the panegyrics stretched to more than 250 pages, without counting the innumerable greetings which were simply listed under their place of origin. An official bust was mass-produced and distributed by order, Stalin's name, which had already been given to several towns, was now bestowed on factories, power stations, agricultural ventures, barracks and schools. . . .

Ten years earlier, on April 23, 1920, the fiftieth birthday of Lenin had been celebrated in Moscow—Lenin, who was the true originator of Bolshevism, the founder of the Communist Party, the authentic victor of October and the real creator of the Soviet State. It was an intimate gathering of the Moscow Party Committee. A modest pamphlet of thirty pages remains as a souvenir of this gathering of old friends. Between 1920 and 1930 a profound change had taken place in Moscow, and the contrast between these two celebrations illustrates its original national aspect. Lenin, who was loved and admired by his Party and honoured by his adversaries, would never have put up with anything resembling these fawning eulogies, still less with an adulation inspired by self-seeking and fear. Stalin, who was detested even by his dependents, but who was addressed like a Tsar or a God, rewarded his self-seeking apologists, bought or extorted insincere compliments and unloosed a torrent of immemorial servility. He himself had changed greatly since his speech at Tiflis when he reproved his flatterers. The historic atavism of ancient Muscovy, held in check for a long time by a slow capitalist evolution and by western influences, revealed its tenacious vitality both in Stalin's omnipotent person and in the transitory regime, which was struggling to lift the Soviet empire to the level of the highly-industrialised countries, "not shrinking from the use of barbarous methods," in order to arm it for the universal conflict and prepare it for future conflagrations. But there was not the smallest trace of socialism, either in fact or in tendency, at this moment when the new privileged caste was elevating its chief to such a pinnacle.

In the unlimited homage rendered to Stalin by servitors who were anxious to attribute to him merits which he had not got, and talents which he undoubtedly lacked, while not yet daring to make him out a genius, one is struck, amid a thousand declarations of the same value, by those which couple "a rhythm of industrialisation such as the history of humanity has never known," or "the great process of socialist industrialisation," with the name of Stalin, the persecutor of the industrialist communists. Propaganda blazoned abroad the balance-sheet for 1929, which was insignificant compared with the expenditure of workers' energy and the amount of capital invested, and which made use of tons of metal which were still to come from furnaces not yet completed. It seemed as though the peasant from the Caucasus, who had resisted so obstinately the industrial projects of the Opposition, before deporting them, was now especially anxious to demonstrate his priority in this sphere. Nevertheless, the material conditions of existence went from bad to worse in Russia, which was "going full steam ahead towards socialism." After bread, the other foodstuffs were rationed, then manufactured goods. The number of mouths to be fed increased, but goods of primary necessity became more scarce as the prices rose. At the beginning of 1930, the level of consumption per head was below the wretched pre-War level both in quantity and quality, for even the President of the Gosplan had admitted at the last Party Conference "that in two fields, that of iron and that of wheat, we are considerably behind 1913." The birth-rate (2.3 per cent) showed that the population was growing annually by 3½ millions and was approaching a total of 160 millions. And with still greater reason than Custine in the preceding century, "one trembled to think that for such a multitude of arms and legs there should be only one head."

Chapter X

STALIN

EFORE the Five Year Plan the "totalitarian" Soviet State was already acquiring its distinctive features, and the same may be said of the personality of Stalin who was its incarnation. Both were fully developed during the course of the memorable five years of industrialisation and collectivisation. Even the memory of the socialist or communist programme disappeared, except for the prisons; and the initials "U.S.S.R." took on their enduring if not definitive meaning.

The fulfillment of the Plan was to triple or almost triple the industrial production of pre-revolutionary days, and to increase agricultural production by half in absolute figures, without taking into account the development of the population. To succeed it was necessary to invest the maximum amount of the national resources in the planned economy, eighty-six thousand million roubles according to financial calculations, whence the necessity of taking, for this purpose, a growing share of the general revenue, by the employment of various unavowable means—indirect taxes, forced loans, low wages and high prices, unlimited fiduciary inflation, the seizure of crops and livestock; that is to say, by robbing the working masses, restraining their purchasing power to the extreme limit, and inflicting unspeakable privations and suffering. It was necessary to acquire the technical equipment of foreign capitalism at great expense and, in order to do this, to export at a loss, challenging world competition by a species of dumping and emptying the country of a large part of its economic substance in spite of the dearth of manufactured commodities and foodstuffs in the interior. (Ordjonikidze stated in 1929: "On the twelfth anniversary of the Soviet Power, we are lacking almost all the products of agriculture.")

On the other hand, a theoretical rise in salaries would follow, estimated at seventy-one per cent, but on the impossible condition of doubling the output of work, noticeably reducing the cost of production and retail prices, increasing the quality of merchandise, enlarging the areas of cultivated land, and increasing the productivity of the soil. This was to augment the rouble's value by one-fifth.

The Plan, therefore, in practice, exacted the sacrifice of the contemporary generation, which was bled and oppressed in the name of a slender material progress, doubtful for future generations, and with very problematical perspectives for economic progress in the present; this apart from political, social, intellectual and moral problems. The bureaucracy, under the pretext of reinforcing the "socialist sector," in reality a new sort of State capitalism, was postponing the human conditions of socialism to the Greek Kalends.

It is true that the *piatiletka* prophesied and the Government promised to raise the cultural level of the population. Industry could not hope to catch up with any country, much less to outstrip it, without a certain degree of public instruction and the necessary staff. In four years a new personnel of 80,000 engineers, 150,000 technicians, and 800,000 qualified workmen was to augment the old. Collectivised agriculture needed specialised workmen, agriculturists and mechanics by the million. But to educate the population and to form an *élite* needed time, experience, material means and above all other spiritual conditions. The failure of Bolshevism in the matter of primary education and general culture did not encourage hope for the miraculous change, notwithstanding many noisy but sterile scholastic reforms. Within their own Party the Leninists replaced scientific doubt and the critical spirit by the *magister dixit* of the worst mediaeval scholasticism, borrowed from the decadent Pythagoreans. Thus they have instinctively fallen into their own specific type of obscurantism with a forbidding terminology, and have brought even lower into the depths the people whom they claimed to have freed from the powers of darkness.

"Ignorance," said Clara Zetkin, "has surely, in a measure, facilitated the revolution, by preserving minds from the contamination of bourgeois ideas." Lenin agreed with this, but only during "a certain period of our struggle," that is, during the period of destruction, for "illiteracy is difficult to reconcile, cannot in fact be reconciled, with constructive activity." He had to remind his obtuse disciples several times of the impossibility of installing socialism without universal elementary education. His latest writings advocated "putting education and culture in the centre of our activity," and reproved vain tirades on proletarian art in order to insist on reading and writing before anything else. He recommended also "giving the teacher a higher place amongst us than in any other country." But after his death, the lamentable state of public education and the privations of the teaching body contradicted the grandiloquent and lying assertions of official propaganda.

In 1923 the Party had proclaimed its intention of "liquidating illiteracy" amongst adults for the tenth anniversary of October, an "historic decision" according to Bubnov and others. But in 1924 at the Communist Congress, Krupskaya stated: "In November the teacher got four roubles, now he gets 10-12 a month, and he is starving . . . the price of bread has risen and for 10-12 roubles he can buy less bread than he could previously for four. But the teacher draws this miserable salary only after a delay of two or three months, and at times never receives it at all." At this Congress the teachers' delegate admitted to about seventy per cent of illiterates, a figure which Zinoviev confirmed. Shortly afterwards Zinoviev revealed a "shocking situation" in the country schools, and depicted the school-mistress as being in rags and without fires in winter-time, and the master "who has no means of living because we have paid him nothing."

That same year Lunacharsky spoke plainly in this connection of a "catastrophe": there were less than 50,000 primary schools in place of the 62,000 under the old regime, and that for an increased population. The average salary of a rural instructor, drawn often after a delay of six months, was at times lower than 10 roubles per month. There was a whole series of provinces where the teacher was starving in the full sense of the word. Not until 1925 did the teachers hold their first semblance of a conference, convened, in fact, by the authorities; they were then admitted to the rank of citizens and electors and became eligible for non-existent soviets. They were no longer treated as intellectuals without a place in the sun. Their way of life was improving little by little, that is to say, hunger, illness and mortality were growing less amongst them, and prostitution and mendicancy were tending to disappear. But salaries, premises and scholastic supplies remained far below a decent minimum.

In 1927, after the tenth anniversary, there was no longer any question of liquidating illiteracy, in spite of all the "historic decisions." The programme of the Party: free and obligatory, equal and polytechnic education; free food, clothing and scholastic material for all students; pre-school and post-school institutions, crèches, clubs, libraries, popular universities, etc., showed itself on all points a mockery like the other promises of Bolshevism. In 1928, *Pravda* (2nd September) recorded the "stabilisation of illiteracy." In 1929, *Izvestia* (11th July) calculated the proportion of absolute illiterates to be sixty per cent, without counting the aged or incurably ignorant who had forgotten their alphabet; nothing then had changed since Tsarism. It was the first year of the industrial Five Year Plan, and it was no longer a matter of lectures or of literature, but of coal, of iron, of tractors and turbines. Stalin aimed at doing for the advancement of technique what he would not do for socialism: Lunacharsky, dilettante, prattler and muddler, nominally the principal cause of the careless handling of the Commissariat of Instruction, was abruptly relieved of his functions and replaced by Bubnov, who introduced the discipline of the army into educational methods. In 1930, the Central Committee decreed compulsory education, of course without being able to carry it out, and beginning with the following year all the so-called revolutionary innovations were one by one annulled. The former classical system was reestablished, including the one

man management of schools, a university hierarchy, uniformity
of curriculum, discipline, text-books, examinations and diplomas.
Even the brigades of students which had formed part of Bubnov's
plan for taking "the offensive on the cultural front" did not
survive the experiment.

Stalin believed that he could solve every problem simply by
means of his machine. From some 800,000 in 1913, according to
N. Rubakin, the number of functionaries had increased to more
than 7,365,000 before the N.E.P., to decline later and establish
itself at about 3,722,000 in 1927, excluding those belonging to
the Party with its multiple affiliates and those in the trade unions
and co-operatives. Even more than in Custine's time, there was
"a whole crowd of people whose interest lay in perpetuating
and concealing abuses." The incomplete statistics do not permit
an exact estimate of the total, which perhaps exceeded 5,000,000
in 1930. "We are unable to master this enormous machine created by the extraordinarily backward state of civilisation in our
country," sighed Bukharin in the days when he was permitted
free speech; but Stalin did not intend to lessen the instrument
of domination which he had inherited and which he has since
learned to perfect. On the contrary, by suppressing the N.E.P.
he added still more force to the bureaucracy, which, by means
of the *kolkhoz*, began to penetrate even into the practical management of agriculture, as well as to achieve control of commerce, the co-operatives and the body of artisans. Step by step
with the industrialisation of the country, an unprecedented
bureaucracy increased and solidified. Varied in its forms, it was
fundamentally unalterable, the curse of a country lorded over
by "too large a number of all too petty functionaries." It would
require a special work to describe the mischief done by red-
tape, the insatiable parasitism, certain monstrous effects of which
are occasionally pointed out in the leading Bolshevik organs
which, however, carefully avoid speaking of the real causes of
the evil. "Take our immense Soviet administration. You will
find there a colossal number of good-for-nothings who do not
want socialism to succeed," declared Ordjonikidze in 1929, already with no illusions; and he added: "People nobody knows

what to do with and whom nobody has any use for are placed in the Control Commission." The fatal consequences reveal themselves in every economic and political balance-sheet of the regime.

At the top of the bureaucratic pyramid, the Party machinery, purged of all heterogeneous elements, gave Stalin perfect security after the pitiful collapse of the Right. The occurrence of new insubordination, individual or on the part of small groups, seemed not unlikely in the immediate future, but this would be a mere game which "the master" could put an end to at once.

It becomes useless to follow in detail the operations styled "organisational," revocations, nominations and mutations whereby Stalin exercised a limitless sovereignty, the secret efficacy of which may be explained in three letters—G.P.U. After Lunacharsky, other People's Commissars who had served their turn—Semashko, Unschlicht, Briukhanov—were sacked peremptorily, without even the usual formalities observed in the dismissal of domestic servants. Beyond the bureaucratic corps whom these matters closely concerned, nobody gave any attention to the paltry four or five lines in which the newspapers mentioned the degradations, without any explanation. Public opinion was annihilated and experienced Bolsheviks thought in slogans learnt by heart. The only apparent reason for the sudden ascent of a Syrtsov, promoted to the presidency of the Council of Commissars for Russia in place of the deposed Rykov, was that Stalin had to nominate somebody of whom he could be sure, right or wrong. Nobody could otherwise explain the appointment of Molotov to be head of the Council of Commissars for the Soviet Union—another post withdrawn from Rykov—unless one assumed also that Stalin wanted to get rid of the Secretariat. The endless succession of interchangeable personages in the reigning oligarchy ceased to impress—whether Ordjonikidze returned to the Politbureau, or Kaganovich succeeded Molotov as First Under-Secretary of the Party, or the endless mutations of the Kuibyshevs, Andreyevs and Rudzutaks. In the bureaucratic constellation, whence the Yaroslavskys, the Skrypniks and even the Kirovs were shining with a somewhat tarnished brilliance, new and obscure stars appeared, from Akulov to Posty-shev, without anyone knowing why or how. Voroshilov and Kalinin, shamefaced Right-wingers who had deserted at the right moment, vied with each other in orthodoxy and submission for the sake of keeping their places.

It was no longer sufficient for Stalin to be feared and obeyed —the defeated victims must further his career and honour his person in order not to disappear altogether. Fallen to the rank of subordinate functionaries, Pyatakov and Radek multiplied their pledges of servility in the hope of inspiring some confidence in "the boss." Zinoviev and Kamenev, crazy with terror after the revelations of their relations with Bukharin, bought their pardon by denouncing the latter. Bukharin managed to save himself by denials and fresh reiterations of repentance, apart from the threat of suicide.

By preference, Stalin avoided surrounding himself with corpses; not that human life seemed precious, or worthy of respect, but because he found greater advantages in dishonouring an adversary than in causing his death. He could crush oppositions without physically suppressing their leaders who in any case would not take up arms. Experience taught him to despise men, consciously to exploit their weaknesses, to adjust suppression proportionately to the resistance offered. A new procedure made its appearance in *Pravda*, that of declarations of apostasy and letters of denunciation, worthy products of post-Lenin Bolshevism.

Before calling the Sixteenth Party Congress in 1930, Stalin reorganised the staff of the Secretariat, rearranged the functions of the Central Committee, renewed bureaux, sections, commissions, and the myriad committees which form the close network of his administration. The Party dealt with, there was a clean up of the trade unions, the libraries, the universities, and theatres. In one case it was the friends of Bukharin, Rykov and Tomsky, the former supporters of the Right, who suffered; in another, the victims were now Dostoievsky, now Schiller, now Dickens, then Lohengrin and Werther, according to the initiative or influence of ridiculous but powerful ignoramuses. The Academy of Sciences was not spared. By means of various arbitrary sanctions, a number of Bolsheviks was forced upon it, under the threat of cutting off its income and on the pretext of strengthening the social sciences. Thus the ruling power forbade all impulse to intellectual independence and in practice subordinated the Academy to the needs of its own propaganda. Custine had already seen in the Russia of old that "here, even men's souls are led by a rope." When the Central Statistical Department annoyed Stalin, he suppressed it, because according to his press "statistics cannot be neutral" and "class statistics" are necessary. Accordingly, the professors of Soviet journalism maintain that "information does not consist in the dissemination of news, but in the education of the masses," "information is an instrument in the class struggle—not a mirror to reflect events objectively." Thus every lie is justified in advance in the name of the more or less misunderstood interests of the revolution. To make use of another century-old observation of Custine: "Here to lie is to protect society, to tell the truth is to upset the State."

The Sixteenth Congress, held two and a half years after the fifteenth, in total disregard of the statutes, at last realised Stalin's ideal, long accomplished in the congresses of the Soviets: a meeting where chosen orators discourse to order, where the chorus applauds to order, carries motions to order and sings the International to order. Henceforward, in the Party sessions, as formerly in the deliberative State Assemblies, the delegates confined themselves, like good little children, to hearing the lesson they would subsequently have to recite to their inferiors, in their capacity of pretentious school-masters. Many previous Congresses had shown the same tendency; but the process was more marked the further one went from the October Revolution. "Russia, this infant nation, is only a school on a huge scale. Everything goes on there as in a military college, except that the students don't come out of it until death." Thus wrote Custine; but if the present resembles the past, history has left no memory of a spectacle as degrading as that of these Bolsheviks. The Right-wing cowards were dragged onto the platform to beat their breasts and confess their errors before an audience of fanatic or venal delegates, which thundered its hatred according to instructions with the one and only motive of pleasing the despot. Rakovsky, from his exile, could well comment on "this savage picture of bureaucrats let loose. It is difficult to say who has most lost the feeling of dignity, those who bend humbly beneath the jeers and hoots, submitting to the outrages in the hope of a better future, or those who, in the same hope, are responsible for these outrages, knowing beforehand that the adversary must yield." Hideous scenes these, but on the morrow, insulters and insulted will sit side by side as colleagues on the Central Committee.

Stalin's report to the Congress expounded once more the platitudes of Leninism in regard to international politics: the whole world was undermined with antagonisms, the bitterest of which ranged in opposite camps the United States and England; the League of Nations was a moribund institution; Social-Democracy was losing all influence while the Communist Parties were marching from victory to victory; capitalist stabilisation was ending and everywhere the revolution rumbled; the bourgeoisie, especially in France, "the most aggressive and militaristic country in the world," was seeking a way out in war against the U.S.S.R.; etc., etc. The rest of his speech was devoted to the internal situation and summed up in the stereotyped formulas of the orthodoxy of the moment the more or less bogus statistics prepared by frightened experts without convictions, terrorised by politicians without knowledge. The same assertions reproduced in all the official literature of this period only assume their full significance when placed in the framework of the ill-matched facts and contradictory proceedings which trace from day to day the tortuous graph of the "general line."

2

STALIN scarcely counted on the good will, still less on the spontaneous enthusiasm, of the workers in order to arrive at the remote aims formulated in the Plan. He had opposed himself too much to the industrialist tendency to have any illusions in this respect. His optimistic public statements might deceive a large part of the youth, but not the majority of the working class, jaded by promises, and still less the peasant masses, defiant by nature and hostile by experience. He foresaw a certain "artificially organised famine" in consequence of a too rapidly organised industrialisation, but did not change his policy until forced to do so by the circumstances or, more precisely, by the growing difficulty of stocking the cereals indispensable to the food supplies of the towns. Through lack of industrial merchandise to exchange for agricultural products, he had to use force to tear the crops from the peasants. Thus necessity compelled him to take the road which foresight had prompted Trotsky to urge upon him. Passing from one extreme to the other, from caution to rashness, he remembered a phrase of Lenin as justification and cover for the wildest extravagances: "We must excite the enthusiasm of conscientious workers and peasants by a great ten or twenty years programme, by a clean-cut and lively perspective, absolutely scientific in its foundations." But the joy in labour demanded or stimulated by vulgar artifices won over neither the exhausted proletariat nor the sceptical peasantry, and the strenuous efforts of the "shock-brigades" with all their badly-paid rivalry did not compensate for material unpreparedness, technical backwardness and professional incompetence. Stalin as much through natural inclination as through the logic of the system was led to break through obstacles by draconian measures.

The cruellest "offensive" made itself felt first in the country districts. Collectivisation, like every other obligation imposed upon the people of the Soviet Union, was styled voluntary, in flagrant contradiction of the Plan which had established beforehand the percentages to be realised. "It would be the greatest absurdity to try to introduce communal agricultural work into such backward villages, where a long education would be necessary before the preliminary attempt." Lenin had said this repeatedly. He had been resolute on the necessity of "getting into the good graces" of the small producers, to transform them by "a very long, very slow and very prudent work of organisation." He could only conceive of harmony between a socialised industry and an individualistic agriculture in a free and pacific co-operation, without the least constraint, direct or indirect. Stalin appeared to understand him, to judge by the speeches which preceded his pitiless mobilisation of the "shock-brigades" against the peasantry. But in complete contradiction to his reassuring declarations, and without taking any account of the Plan, which contemplated collectivising and mechanising in five years one-fifth of the agricultural establishments, he carried through by blood and iron in one year three times the expectations of the Five Year Plan. In a single month the number of farms grouped in the *kolkhoz* exceeded that brought about by twelve years of revolution—on paper, that is, for tractors and machines, not to mention organisation and the consent of the victims, were still sadly lacking. This result was obtained by arbitrary expropriation and illegal pillage, and only at the price of an unexampled repression. This Stalin entitled "liquidation of the *kulak* as a class," but thousands of poor and middle peasants themselves succumbed. No contemporary records have been able to keep up with all the mass arrests and executions, the suicides and the assassinations which collectivisation dragged in its wake. Statistics abound in empty figures and trifling coefficients, but do not register these numerous victims, any more than the G.P.U. yields its secrets of the barbarous deportations of millions of human beings, transplanted to arctic regions and beyond the Urals. Whole villages, cantons and districts were depopulated and their inhabitants dispersed and decimated, as happened in ancient times in Assyria and Chaldaea. An American correspondent extremely favourable to Stalin's interests estimated at 2,000,000 the approximate number banished and exiled in 1929-1930 (*New York Times*, 3rd February, 1931). But the truth would appear still more atrocious in its full extent if it were known that the "dekulakisation" was pursued without respite in the course of the following years, and that the official figures vary between five and ten million for the number of *kulaks*, not including the unfortunate mujiks presumed to possess a little more than the average. (Shortly after the first Five Year Plan, in 1933, the Rostov press, accidentally disobeying the command of silence, announced the deportation *en bloc* of three *stanitsy* of Cossacks from Kouban—about 50,000 persons; but more than 100,000 inhabitants of the same region had preceded them on the northern road to misery.) It can be considered then that 5,000,000 villagers *at least*, regardless of sex and age, have been chased from their hearths and doomed to a life of iniquitous misery, many to death. Mr. H. Walpole, who has attentively scrutinised the data of the Commissariat of Works, arrives also at the total of 4 to 5,000,000 for 1931, a figure which the succeeding years easily surpass. He has noted it in his introduction to *Out of the Deep, Letters from Soviet Timber Camps*, a collection of heartbreaking letters from deported Mennonites, the authenticity of which is guaranteed by the editor of the *Slavonic Review*. A qualified and informed eyewitness, I. Solonevich, one of the few who have escaped from the Soviet prison where he worked in the departments of planning and assessment, confirmed these estimates in 1935 with new data. It is impossible to know how many have perished of hunger and cold in the northern forests, in the building of great public works and in concentration camps. But partial information gives us some idea, not precise though none the less terrible—especially of the appalling number of child victims expelled with their mothers, sometimes in the dead of night, and transported from the temperate climate of the south to glacial regions where many of these little innocents have found premature deaths through lack of shelter, of proper care and of the barest necessities. What, in the face of such facts, were the famous proscriptions of Sulla and the two triumvirates, so often evoked by the socialists after the Commune? The historians of the Asiatic empires of antiquity or the middle ages could alone produce anything comparable.

But Stalin, though deaf to the misfortunes caused by his blind policy, could not remain indifferent to its disastrous results on economy. If human life were of little account to him, he at least had to grapple seriously with the problem of livestock and crops. The outraged peasants killed their animals and ate their seeds, either to avoid confiscation, or to protest in their own way. Millions of beasts of burden were killed at a time when mechanical traction only existed on paper—and the result was an automatic restriction of ploughing and corn-sowing. Tens of millions of oxen, sheep, pigs and poultry succumbed to the same fate—there was to be a lack of milk, meat and eggs for years. Improvised legislation, too tardy and not very efficacious, punished with imprisonment the murder of an ox or calf perpetrated "through malevolence." All products were rationed, the rations grew smaller, but the greater part of the foodstuffs disappeared and the revictualling of the industrial centres was endangered for a long period. The bureaucracy blamed now the rain, now the fine weather, at times the *kulaks*, and at last bureaucratism itself. Rumours and alarms, collected by the G.P.U., spread among Stalin's associates. High functionaries in informed circles glimpsed the approach of an immense catastrophe, perhaps a change of rule, and prepared for any eventuality in their conversations, the intimacy of which did not prevent the presence of spies and *provocateurs*. The sorcerer's apprentice of the new agrarian revolution, intoxicated with his facile victory over the disarmed peasants, over women and little children, recoiled before the spectre of a famine, and decided to retreat. In an article *Dizzy with Success* (2nd March, 1930) he ceased to extol the "unheard of rhythm" of this "formidable avalanche" which had swept over the countryside, and threw the responsibility of his actions on the shoulders of the agents who carried them out. To them he imputed his own madness of a short while before; he denounced bureaucratic procedure, condemned excessive violence, the removal of the church-bells and the socialisation of the hen-houses. He discountenanced the forming of communes where production and distribution would be collectivised, and prescribed that the form should henceforth be the artel, where the house, the kitchen garden, the cow and the smaller livestock remain individual property. A circular of the Central Committee "against Leftish exaggerations" followed, reproving "the abominable, the criminal, the exceptionally brutal conduct" of certain subordinates towards the people. It denounced the division of goods, the deprivation of civic rights, the arbitrary arrests, the closing of churches, the suppression of markets, etc., seeking to limit this irresistible "voluntary" movement, and authorising the malcontents to leave the *kolkhoz*. In two weeks the number of "hearths" included in the "socialist sector" fell from 14,264,000 on the 1st of March to 5,778,000 on the 15th of the same month. The reflex continued, the "dead souls" dispersed. It was a short-lived respite, however, for the dispersal was brought to a standstill in December of the same year. Stalin then ordered the entire collectivisation of wheat districts and the partial collectivisation of other districts, with definite percentages. Under cover of the recent retreat he had had a breathing space in which to repair losses, to consolidate the positions won and to increase tenfold "police precautions." He was preparing with deliberation for "a sort of artificially-organised famine."

A veritable enslavement of industry soon rivalled the peasant servitude. A decision of the Central Committee (7th September, 1929) had instituted the "one-man leadership" of the manager in every industrial undertaking, abolishing the theoretical rights of the workmen's committees. Ensuing decrees accumulated, damaging beyond repair the sovereignty of the proletariat.

Stalin sought first to fight against the mobility of labour, for the wretched standard of living was driving the workers from one town to another, and a disorganisation of production resulted from this permanent migration. As in the eighteenth century when desertion was the last resource of the serfs if oppression became unbearable, flight seemed to the Soviet workers the only way out of their impossible situation. In October 1930, with the explicit connivance of the G.P.U. came an ordinance forbidding movements of workers engaged in rafting (wood being an essential article of foreign exchange). Another decree extended the same measure to every other industry so as to "rivet" the workers, to dispose of them regardless of their preferences, without considering bonds of parentage or friendship, and increasing the penalties for disobedience. A third measure suppressed unemployment relief and every facility for choosing abode or work. Another in November closed the Labour Exchanges and ordered that the unemployed be summarily sent where they were needed. After which the officials claimed *urbi et orbi* the disappearance of unemployment. But the following year Stalin admitted to fluctuations of labour that implied millions of workless on the roads. And the economic reviews estimated many more in the country where the non-producing surplus of the population found no employment whatever.

In January 1931, a decree requisitioned former railway workers to replace them in their previous occupation, whether they would or no. An addition to the Penal Code gave ten years' imprisonment for lack of discipline among the transport workers, and prescribed the *death penalty* in cases of premeditation. In February was instituted the obligatory "work-certificate," modelled on the soldier's certificate, which contained a summarised history of the bearer, his type of employment, punishments, fines, reasons for dismissal, etc. The object of this was to suppress indiscipline and desertions. In March there were further measures to enforce dictatorial authority in the factories, to bring pressure to bear against backward workers guilty of absence, negligence, drunkenness or laziness. In April came preferential rations for the "shock-brigades"—true blackmail of the stomach—and priority rights of lodging, heating and the most urgent necessities. In June the workers were made responsible for damages to material, thus allowing accusations of sabotage for accidents due to defective quality of tools and raw materials and to administrative chaos and governmental carelessness. The factory chiefs received full authority from the Commissariat of Works to transfer technicians and specialised workers, regardless of their consent, and to send them from one place to another like machines in contempt of every sentiment of humanity.

These were the principal links in an unending chain. The decree of the 7th August 1932 on the preservation of State property stipulated the death penalty for theft of merchandise in transport. In Novmber of the same year followed new decrees. One of them punished by dismissal a single day's unjustifiable absence from work. The other placed the former co-operatives under the direction of the factories. Thus the dismissed or defaulting worker lost his food-ticket issued by the director and, as a general rule, his lodgings. The same power of personal control was exercised in regard to production and consumption. These convicts of industry could no longer move an inch without exposing themselves and their families to death from starvation. Yet, incredible as it may seem, even with this monstrous system of repression, which is absolutely unparalleled in any capitalist legislation, Stalin was unable to control all the workers, for many preferred vagabondage to slavery. In December of this last year of the plan, he decided upon a police measure which exceeded in its scope and rigour any analogous measure under Tsarism, viz., the obligatory interior passport for the entire urban population; and for a part of the rural population living near the large towns. Nobody could move or stay twenty-four hours away from home without the visa of the G.P.U. militia and this incriminating document indicated the social origin of the bearer, his family attachments, his occupation and movements; a complete police dossier with all the elements necessary for an eventual prosecution. During the three months that "passportisation" was being intoduced, Stalin vetoed marriages, divorces, adoptions and changes of address in order to render fraud impossible. He condescended, however, to permit deaths and to tolerate births.

The peasant-proletarian was no better situated than the worker-dictator. The *death sentence* for theft applied equally to theft in the fields. A starving individual who had gleaned a few ears of wheat or stolen a few vegetables from the products of his own labour would be eligible for the capital sentence. There was subsequently a similar decree of the Central Committee against vague offences like sabotage in agricultural works and "intent to damage" in tillage and sowing. A series of contradictory decrees followed one another: piecework and payment by results were imposed in collective agriculture, everything was regulated down to its most minute details, standards of work were established, and the amount of produce expected

from labourers and tilled fields, and even from cows, was fixed
by statute. All this time a rain of circulars was pouring on the
kolkhoz where an unprecedented social phenomenon, a gigantic
agrarian bureaucracy, was being formed. In 1931, the number
of functionaries in the new "socialist sector" was reckoned at
more than 2,000,000 — administrators, managers, controllers,
brigadiers, commissioners, and divers employees. The mujiks,
also divided into brigades to regulate their daily tasks, had to
support whole legions of parasites who encroached on their own
personal share, and to bear the enormous general expenses which
burdened net costs and were responsible for budget deficits.
Arakcheyev, the Minister of Alexander I, famous for his military
peasant colonies, would not have dreamed of calling a shepherd
a "commander of the flock" nor dared to have envisaged a
bureaucratic militarisation on such a scale.

In proportion as collectivisation extended, famine became
rapidly accentuated. Tractors transformed after a short while
into scrap iron, mechanical instruments left to rust in the open,
did not balance a diminution in the flock or the abandonment
or destruction of old implements. All the orders, counter-orders
and decrees from Moscow could not save wheat from rotting,
potatoes from frost-bite, or weeds from springing up, where
there was a lack of elementary precautions and of any stimulus
to work. Losses and waste took on extravagant proportions.
Neither the mobilisation of workmen and students and of school-
children for the sowings and harvestings, nor the mobilisation
of young communists for wood felling, of doctors, scientists
and artists—each in turn organised into shock-brigades—could
take the place of the good will or the interest of the cultivators,
any more than the mobilisation of the peasants for heavy industry could answer the needs of modern mechanisation. Stalin
tried in 1932 to ward off the crisis caused by the break up of
the agricultural system by means of new decrees, such as the
right to individual possession of a cow and of small domestic
animals granted to members of the *kolkhoz* (March), reduction
of stocks and of State levies (May), conditional semi-freedom
of trade granted to *kolkhoz* after payment of rents and taxes

(May), guarantees to the communal groups of the boundaries of their domains (September), obligation of the last free peasants to lend their horses to the *kolkhoz* that needed them (September). All these palliative measures brought some not very palpable relief, but it was of short duration, as Stalin is always ready to take back with one hand what he gives with the other. And as a result of his opportunism and his intransigence, the flow of blood and tears never ceases.

"Evidently killing is easier than persuasion and this very simple method is very easy for people who have been brought up amongst massacres, and educated by massacre." Gorky wrote this at the beginning of the revolution apostrophising the Bolsheviks. "All you Russians, still savages, corrupted by your former masters, you in whom they have infused their terrible defects and their insensate despotism." Babeuf made similar reflections on his contemporaries: "Tortures of all kinds—drawing and quartering, the wheel, the stake, the gibbet, the plague of executions. What evil precedents our masters have given us! Instead of keeping us in order, they have made barbarians of us, because they are barbarians themselves." There is no difficulty that Stalin does not boast of being able to solve by capital punishment or at least by prison or exile.

In 1930, when there was a currency shortage, a mere decree was sufficient to send to the firing-squad scores of Soviet subjects suspected of hoarding a few hundred roubles. Industrial miscalculations and agricultural mishaps were treated in the same way as financial difficulties. Forty-eight alleged saboteurs of food production were executed without trial after the arrest of numerous technicians, professors, scientists, statisticians and socialist or liberal co-operators who had rallied to the regime and were employed in the administration of the national economy. This helped to exculpate the chiefs, while intimidating the intelligentsia, and making a parody of justice before the credulous people. Next the existence was revealed of the so-called "Industrial Party," said to include some 2,000 members. Yet only eight of them were brought to trial, and the ringleader, to judge by the evidence, was an *agent provocateur*. The most valuable officials of the Gosplan among whom were Bazarov, Groman, Sukhanov, Kondratiev, found themselves accused of counter-revolution and wrecking (*vreditelstvo*). Terrorised by the execution of forty-eight of their colleagues, and cowed by the G.P.U. methods of intimidation, they nearly all signed the confessions that were demanded from them and admitted to crimes that they could not possibly have committed. Others were dismissed from office, like Riazanov, who remained indifferent to the threats, and Kondratiev, who took shelter behind the Communist Right with which he was in sympathy. In actual fact these criminals had in private conversations exchanged pessimistic views on exaggerated industrialisation and collectivisation, and had envisaged a possible socialist government in the event of a crash raising the question of a successor to Stalin. Two distinct and spectacular trials, conducted at an interval of three months because of the practical impossibility of contriving some connecting link, proved nothing simply because they proved too much. But ardent in the pursuit of their own destruction, the accused denounced themselves and exceeded to their very best ability the imputations of the prosecution. Their counsel always pleaded guilty, and there were never any witnesses but those for the prosecution. "It is a common practice to terrorise and even to beat up a witness to make him tell the truth," observed de Maistre when visiting Russia at the beginning of the last century. Under Stalin this method has improved: witnesses and accused are now terrorised so as to make them tell lies. The hounded engineers, cowed by the threats of their clumsy persecutors, through sheer ignorance denounced accomplices and implicated people who had died abroad several years before, and involved in their charges persons who could not possibly have been suspected of such crimes, for example, Aristide Briand, accused of "preparing for war against the U.S.S.R." The alleged Mensheviks, in reality deserters from that Party, with the exception of one of them who subsequently retracted his statements, gave evidence of secret meetings held at Moscow with Abramovich, an exiled socialist leader, who had not crossed the frontier for ten years. These were startling impostures, designed to eke out the scantiness of the charges, which were a mixture of truth and falsehood supplemented by the activities of police *agents provocateurs*. The result of this tragi-comedy of pitiless condemnations and commutations of sentences, both of them arranged beforehand, was to bring discredit on the whole affair and to confuse public opinion.

On the other hand Stalin was scoring points every day with the executions decided by the G.P.U. without any other form of trial. At this period thousands of such cases were to be found in the press, though it did not announce all of them; and the orgy of murders was to continue further. This is borne out by the execution (March 1933) of thirty-five functionaries of the Commissiariat of Agriculture accused of having "allowed weeds to grow in the fields" and other charges of the same nature. Publicity was only given in certain cases and where it might serve to set an example. It happened sometimes that the reason given to the public did not coincide with the secret one, as in the case of the thirty-five, who were shot in reality on suspicion of espionage. The G.P.U. at times deemed it useful to exploit its executions for several purposes. The mass arrests of 1930 included every type of intellectual, even the historians (Platonov, Tarlé, etc.) who could not possibly have done any harm to production or supplies, and the last peaceable socialists who had cut themselves away from politics. Finally, Stalin was not content to abuse his power of punishment—he also foresaw the need for reward: the order of "Lenin" for civilians, the order of "The Red Star" for soldiers. These two new decorations, created in 1930, carried with them a number of privileges, under the pretext of "socialist edification" but, actually, of course, in defiance of every principle of socialism.

The Party had not passed through the phase of tension of the Five Year Plan without incidents. The conflicts, however, now affected only isolated individuals, and were settled without any effect whatever on the rank and file, as in the old days at the court of Russia under Nicholas I, which F. Lacroix compared to "the movable floors in a theatre in which invisible trap-doors open to swallow up the victims consigned to the dungeon by the tyrant of the melodrama."

Syrtsov's fall in 1930, as precipitous as his sudden elevation a few months previously, was incomprehensible to the public. It was known only that the President of the Council of Commissars, worried about the consequences of "the general line," shared his confidences and vague hopes of reform, including a return to the N.E.P., with Lominadze and other lesser figures. That was all that was needed to unmask a new disaffection, almost a plot. Trotsky's informants attributed to Syrtsov a disparaging judgment on Stalin, his protector: "A stupid man who is leading the country to ruin." It all ended in the customary dismissals, exclusions, repentance and humiliations. Once more Bukharin and his fellows disavowed their comrades and . . . confessed their mistakes. That same year, Sokolnikov, compromised by his conversations with the imprisoned ex-Mensheviks, assured his safety and his embassy in London by imploring Stalin's pardon and swearing eternal obedience. Krizhanovsky lost his post in the Gosplan for unknown reasons, shortly after Rykov's disgrace. The generation of veterans, weakened by age and perverted by power, was either giving up the struggle or being swept away.

At the beginning of 1931, Riazanov was suddenly made the target for the thunderbolts of the dictator. He was reproached with keeping the documents of the Russian Social-Democracy in the archives of the Marx-Engels Institute, where they had been placed by a colleague. Accused of treason, implicated quite arbitrarily in the so-called "Menshevik affair," but excluded from the trial where he would doubtless have vindicated instead of blackening his character, the old scholar was ruined, expelled from the Party, arrested and deported; his works were pilloried, his editions of Marx and Engels prohibited, and the Institute he had created annulled by being absorbed into the Lenin Institute. The previous year the official Communist world had covered Riazanov with bouquets and compliments on his sixtieth birthday, hailing him as "the most eminent Marxologist of our time," who had devoted "more than forty years of active service to the workers' cause." But Stalin, obsessed with the idea of winning at all costs the reputation of being a theorist, was only waiting for a favourable opportunity to get rid of a scrupulous scientist who hesitated to couple without justification the name of the ignorant successor of Lenin with those of the authors of the doctrine. With him went the last refuge of social science at Moscow. Shortly after the deportation of Riazanov, hired encomiasts tried to acclimatise the formula of Marxism-Leninism-Stalinism, but they did not succeed in increasing the reputation of the man whom they thus sought to honour.

An episode which at first sight seems more obscure was the sudden fate which befell Yaroslavsky, one of the most servile agents of the government. Because of a *History of the Party* of which he was not even the author but which was published under his responsibility, this professional detractor of Trotsky and specialised tracker-down of Trotskyists fell in 1931 under the fantastic accusation of Trotskyism. The truth is that Stalin, warned of the excessive ambition of his subaltern, invented some sort of pretext to force him to a public apology so as to belittle him in the eyes of everybody. From the denunciation to the confession the operation did not last three weeks. At the same time, with a simple letter to the editorial staff of a review, Stalin revolutionised the history of Bolshevism in a hand's turn by shamelessly perverting the facts and by delivering into the hands of his functionaries and clients a whole host of very orthodox historians who had not yet learned sufficiently to depreciate Trotsky or glorify Stalin. His threatening allusion to "rotten liberalism" and "Trotskyist contraband" were too clear not to provoke an epidemic of loud denials, at once lamentable and grotesque, which revealed only too well the hopeless degradation of the revolutionary phalanx of October; Radek, Shliapnikov and many others hastened to recognise all sorts of imaginary errors in their old forgotten writings, and to recant the most innocent and least deniable truths. A certain Deborin was induced to publish abroad his philosophical deviations, whilst regretting that he had not sufficiently criticised . . . the idealism

of Hegel! The panic was designed to produce a more severe
expurgation of books and libraries and a more rigorous censorship of new publications in the spirit of Stalinist conformity.
Everyone ran the risk, through lack of zeal or mere inadvertence,
of losing his employment, lodging and breadcard and falling
into the condition of a pariah. Even the *Complete Works* of
Lenin were tainted with suspicion because of documentary
notes, the relative probity of which contradicted the legends
Stalin found useful to himself. The letter of anathema entitled
Questions Concerning the History of Bolshevism became a
"document of the greatest international significance, political
and world-historical" to quote the careerist "red professors."
For years, hack writers and party pedants appealed to its authority on every possible occasion and on every subject, continually hunting out "rotten liberalism" even on questions of
philosophy, literature and music, with which the miserable
document is no more concerned than with historic fact.

A gloomy silence spread over the Party and oppressed the
"socialist fatherland," where the critical spirit scarcely dared
venture abroad except in the stifled murmur of anecdotes and
spiteful epigrams as in Rome under the Caesars. On the surface,
unbroken unanimity reigned, and a chorus of venal eulogies of
Stalin took the place of political life in a country plunged in
toil, hardships and misery. One of the principal renegades of
the Left Opposition, Pyatakov, had led the way in identifying
the General Secretary first with the Central Committee, then
with the Party, and then with the State, giving him the personal
homage of a vassal to his lord. Falling easily into line with him,
a chorus of careerists and parvenus took care not to write or
speak anything but tributes of outward admiration for the man
on whom their futures depended. Every discourse, every article
began and terminated henceforward with a digression in Stalin's
honour, and men rivalled each other to invent new flatteries.
Mention of his name was made everywhere; it was sedition to
omit it. A jesting pun on the "genial secretary" was taken
seriously and by a slight change of meaning, the word "genius"
became inseparable from his name, which the press printed in

large characters. At the end of 1932 an obscure quarrel with a certain Riutin, allied with divers oppositionists of Left and Right, gave opportunity to exclude and deport a handful of malcontents for the crime of not having denounced anyone—among them Zinoviev and Kamenev. But the two cronies were to obtain pardon six months later when they pleaded for clemency, and not only admitted their innumerable errors but prostrated themselves before the might of Stalin. It was no longer enough to get down on your knees, you had to grovel in the dirt on your belly. The moral suicide of the survivors of the Old Guard, stubborn in claiming a political rôle against the omnipotence of their conquerors, indicated the inevitable fate of those who did not resort to physical suicide. In 1933, Skrypnik, suspected rightly or wrongly of deviating from "the general line" and of weakness or tolerance in regard to nationalism in the Ukraine, found the only solution in his revolver.

Stalin alone had the right to express an opinion, which took on the force of law, *ipso facto*, and the boyars of the bureaucracy had the privilege of repeating it, vulgarising it and commenting on it until such time as the "genius" of the land should have changed his mind or have contradicted himself. After his moderating intervention in the excesses of collectivisation, he published a *Reply to Comrades on the Collective Farms* to cover his retreat with a good score of quotations from Lenin, every one of which was a condemnation of his own practice, but from which he thought to escape unscathed by turning them against his subordinates. In a discourse pronounced in February 1931, he was not afraid to postulate the realisation of the Plan, no longer in four but in three years, "for all decisive branches of industry," and to subscribe to equally puerile blustering with the final and peremptory argument: "There exists no fortress impregnable to a Bolshevik." But his boasting could not dissipate the difficulties of industrialisation, and in another discourse in June 1931 he retreated noticeably. The low quality of labour due to the permanent evasion of the workers prior to "passportisation," which he had the audacity to explain as being caused by the prosperity of the country districts, obliged him to turn his attention to the material conditions of the proletariat. He found it necessary to modify the allocation of salaries by accentuating the inequality to the profit of qualified workers, giving them the stimulus of better food and lodgings. In euphemistic and laboured terms he declared the five-day week a fiasco. "In a series of enterprises we have continuous work, in words or on paper," he said, and commanded that "where conditions are not propitious to such an experiment we should pass temporarily to the six-day week" whilst waiting to return to the first arrangement. He canvassed the idea of "changing our policy" in respect of the decimated technical cadres: "It would be stupid and unreasonable to-day to consider every specialist and engineer of the old school as a criminal or a saboteur." He acknowledged the statistical bluffs of which he had been the first to avail himself: "In a series of enterprises and economic undertakings we have ceased for a long time to count and calculate or to establish real budgets of receipts and expenditure." But he concluded nevertheless on the habitual optimistic note.

That was his last speech before the expiration of the five-year term. The incessant lie that facts gave to his words inspired him for a time with the wise decision to keep quiet. He had given his enemies too many weapons by announcing always the contrary of what was going to happen, by dragging in the wake of the most easily predictable events, and by displaying a rare misunderstanding of international and Soviet realities, and of the economic and social theories of which he claimed to be the interpreter. On one single point he was not mistaken, but he took care not to make too much of it: he had prophesied in 1928 "a certain artificially-organised famine" in the case of a too rapid tempo of industrial development. He was saying nothing original and borrowing from the "deviation of the Right" the only idea that future events were to verify.

In fact, the famine made itself felt as early as 1931, in spite of the coupon system, the parsimonious rations, and the rigorous discipline. But this time the peasants had more to complain about than the workers, who were provided for first after the bureaucracy, the police and the army, in the order of urgency.

The State took one-half of the grain crop which had fallen to
69.5 million tons (against 96.6 in 1913) but which was again
reduced by a quarter on the average, by losses due to fraud.
But the population had increased by about 25 millions and bread
was an essential article of diet in a country where meat, milk,
cheese, indeed all provisions were almost unprocurable. The livestock which had survived the mass-slaughter of collectivisation,
deprived of proper care and fodder in the *kolkhoz*, perished in
enormous numbers. The soaring prices in the market after the
partial re-establishment of commerce revealed a precipitous devaluation of the rouble. Powerless to cope with the food-supply
of the towns, the Government wanted the workers to raise
rabbits at home and even to cultivate the land around the factories and camps. But "the offensive on the rabbit front" came
to a lamentably abrupt end, owing to the extermination of the
subjects of the experiment. The inexperienced breeders lacked
suitable premises and above all food. Stalin alone had failed
to foresee all this in the very beginning. One of the monstrosities
of the regime dated from this period: the Torgsin, an institution
of shops reserved for clients with foreign money and precious
metals, an oasis of abundance in a socialist desert. The State refused it the use of its own paper money, which it also decreed
should not cross the frontiers, and the wretched poor, indignant
but cowed with fear, dared not rummage for themselves. Even
more unbelievable was the expedient used to procure dollars.
A veritable slave-trade was inaugurated when Soviet "citizens"
were authorised to expatriate themselves, provided a ransom
were paid by their friends and relatives in foreign countries.
Although in 1932 the shortage of merchandise was becoming
more acute and famine was rapidly gaining ground, the imperturbable planomaniacs juggled with stunning masses of
figures and planned the second *piatiletka*, always promising their
mountains and marvels for the morrow. The press demonstrated
by a thousand graphic and photographic artifices the prodigious
success of national economy "on all fronts," and soothed popular
distress by stories of electric tillage, sowing by aeroplane, artificial rain produced by the bombardment of the clouds, and

other discoveries which, judging by the level of Soviet technique at that time, must be regarded in the same light as the
fantasmagoria of Fourier on the transformation of the sea into
lemonade by the action of boreal citric acid. They even proposed a grandiose plan for diverting the Gulf Stream so as to
temper the Arctic Ocean to the profit of Northern Siberia. A
frantic propaganda fed the starving masses with photographs
of Dnieprostroy and Magnitogorsk, the steel and cement "giants"
risen on the steppe for the future well-being of their posterity.
The Soviet patriotism of the young communists was warmly
praised—they were the heroes of the "working front," desperately keen to beat records. The press quoted the cubic metres
of earth excavated, of coal extracted, of metal cast. But the
temporary exploits of the shock brigades did not console empty
stomachs or lessen the nightmare of famine and its attendant horrors, scurvy and typhus. The generations which were sacrificed
to the machine-god looked in vain for a human word from the
Kremlin where Stalin, immured in silence, was turning socialism
into the ideal caricatured by Flaubert "under the double aspect
of a farm-house and a textile-mill, a sort of Americanised Sparta
where the individual would only exist in order to serve a society
more omnipotent, absolute, infallible and divine than the Great
Lamas and the Nebuchadnezzars."

3

AFTER the fifteenth anniversary of October the prosaic and
bloody industrial epic came to an end. Between the years 1932
and 1933 the Party could not dispense with a general review.
In spite of so many resolutions, orders and proclamations, each
one more full of "historic importance" or "international interest" than its predecessor, and despite immeasurable sacrifices of
every kind, the economic plans, enlarged and several times re-
cast, had still not been fulfilled from any point of view. The
U.S.S.R. had not caught up with or surpassed a single civilised
country. It threatened to eclipse neither Europe nor America
nor Switzerland nor Belgium. That did not prevent Stalin from

crying victory, when in January 1933 he at last broke the silence in order to pass under review the accumulated evidence of his bureaux and auxiliaries.

He succeeded in this only by concealing beneath his sophistries the gaping wounds of planned economy and by drowning the tragic realities in the verbiage of public meetings. He tortured statistics that had already been falsified from day to day. He played tricks with quantities, qualities, weights, and values. He himself was not sure of his starting-point, for his data comprised fragmentary and uncontrollable elements. The subordinate bodies always supplied satisfying results to the centre through their fear of unmerited punishments. "Through the habit of wanting to disguise the truth before the eyes of other people, you end by being no longer able to see it yourself, except through a veil which grows thicker every day." So wrote Custine; the same author remarked, with judicious whimsicality: "Russia is the empire of catalogues; it sounds superb when you read these lists of titles—but be careful not to go any further. If you open a book you will find nothing of what is promised; the chapter-headings are there, but the chapters have yet to be written." Trials with concealed motives, continual scandals, acute crises in every branch of activity—all are habitually accompanied by "correctives" which justly merit the title "comboasts."

In the elementary style which is so typical of him, Stalin summed up before the Central Committee the general balance-sheet of industrialisation carried out according to his methods:

> Formerly we did not have an iron and steel industry, the basis of the industrialisation of the country. Now we have such an industry.
> We did not have a tractor industry. Now we have one.
> We did not have an automobile industry. Now we have one.
> We did not have an engineering industry. Now we have one.
> We did not have an important and modern chemical industry. Now we have one.
> We did not have a real and important industry for the production of modern agricultural machinery. Now we have one.
> We did not have an aircraft industry. Now we have one.

In the production of electric power, we were last in the list. Now we are among the first in the list.

In the production of oil products and coal we were last in the list. Now we are among the first in the list.

We had only one single coal and metallurgical base, the Ukraine, which we could hardly manage. We have not only succeeded in improving this base, but we have created a new coal and metallurgical base—in the east, which is the pride of our country.

We had only one single textile industry base—in the north of our country. In the very near future we will have two new bases of the textile industry, in Central Asia and Eastern Siberia.

And we have not only created these new enormous branches of industry, but we have created them on such a scale and of such dimensions that they make the scale and dimensions of European industry pale into insignificance.

If Stalin's affirmations are taken one by one and examined individually, it will be found that all is not absolutely false in this vague and high flown statement, in which the orator avoids juxtaposing the passive with the active. It goes without saying that a people numbering 160,000,000 and submitted to a military discipline, could not possibly work in mines and on a soil of exceptional natural resources without producing anything, above all when they work under the advice and direction of 10,000 foreign technicians and specialists. But that does not answer the question whether the results are harmonious and durable and in just proportion to the exhausting effort and fantastic expenditure, as well as being in conformity with a true material and moral progress and with the final aims of socialism. And even from Stalin's point of view, nothing could justify a plan, a political system, a regime, which because of its barbaric methods ended in a return to barbarism with a superficial covering of American modernism which ill concealed its essentially Asiatic structure.

It is inexact to say that the U.S.S.R. had to start building everything from bedrock and may therefore justly boast of an unprecedented success. In the thirteenth century, Russia held the first place in the world for cast iron, for iron and copper and for the export of wood, leather and sail-canvas, a place which she subsequently lost. At the end of the nineteenth century, she surpassed the United States in the production of petrol and had in six years more than doubled her supply of cast iron and steel, and almost doubled her production of coal and naphtha. These advances and recessions point to a lesson that still holds good. Russia has always had feverish industrial booms followed by periods of torpor or depression which pulled her back. Peter the Great left about 730 factories for the most part founded by himself. The number of factories had more than tripled under Catherine II, more than doubled under Alexander I, and almost doubled under Nicholas I, but with a still greater increase of workers and an even greater sum total of trade. Under Alexander II, railway construction had increased more than twentyfold. Under Alexander III, industry had well-nigh doubled its working forces, and tripled the average scope of its enterprises. Under Nicholas II, indeed, the financial system of Witte made it possible to double the length of the railways in ten years, and in consequence to enlarge the coal and metal industries, and to inaugurate, notably at Donetz, an acceleration comparable to the burst of industry in the English mining districts at the beginning of the last century, and that of the Rhino-Westphalian districts in the 'seventies or, more recently, of the United States or Japan. In his *Development of Capitalism in Russia*, which appeared in 1899, Lenin stated: ". . . The progress in the mining industry is more rapid in Russia than in Western Europe and even in North America. . . . In the last few years (1886-1896) the production of cast metal has tripled. . . . The development of capitalism in the younger countries is accelerated by the example and aid of the older." And the industrial output of Russia was doubled between the Russo-Japanese War and the World War. The periods of stagnation do not contradict the general tendency, which is also compatible with barbarous customs. Besides, since the liberation of the serfs, economic progress had been accomplished along less abnormal lines than "mobilisation," "shock-brigades," "offensives on all fronts," mass deportations or executions. Trotsky was able to say before the N.E.P.,

"If Russian capitalism has developed not gradually but by leaps and bounds, constructing American factories in the open steppe, that is all the more reason why a similar 'forced march' should be possible to socialist economy." Without the legacy of the past in the matter of industrial concentration, with its imported machinery, technical cadres, and its influx of foreign science and capital, the Plan would not even have been conceivable.

The historic antecedents, then, must not be misunderstood. Sovetism, like Tsarism, but in an extreme measure, tends to an artificial industrialisation by the omnipresent and constant interference of the State, sheltered behind a prohibitive customs duty, and at the expense of the over-exploited working classes. And Stalin, like his predecessors of the autocracy, owes much to the lucrative participation of the "rotten West," as the Bolsheviks would say in the manner of the reactionary Slavophiles. Ivan the Terrible could not have conquered the Tartars without the help of the engineers and artisans from Germany, Hungary and Italy. Michael Romanov, the first of the dynasty, enrolled a number of Englishmen to organise his army in the European manner. Peter the Great would have been less great if he had not recruited so many instructors from Holland and elsewhere. And we know well enough the rôle played by the French and Belgians in the contemporary organisation of heavy industry. Stalin is only making use of an old tradition in appealing to the competence and experience of "moribund capitalism"; of the great firms of Europe and above all America, such as Ford, Austin, MacKee, General Electric, Westinghouse, Harvester, Cleveland Tractor, Freyn Engineering, etc., whose creative work the mouthpieces of the Party shamelessly attribute to themselves. From Tsar Peter the Great to Count Witte, all the industrialisers of Russia have wanted to make their country independent, to make it an *autarchy*, without scrupling to profit from the international division of labour. Their successor scarcely changes anything but the words when he contrasts Soviet statism and the imperialist capitalism that opens credits for him and sends him its technical experts; and when he makes comparisons between the respective curves of industry, for the short period of the Five Year Plan which ran parallel with the greatest economic crisis the modern world has experienced. It is undeniable that the high industrial coefficients of the U.S.S.R. coincided with a contrary tendency in the countries of excessive production. But here, where technique had already taken enormous strides forward, there naturally remained less to be done. Stalin unsuspectingly emphasised the backwardness of his empire when he marvelled at certain rhythms of progress and forgot the point of departure. The nearer to the zero line were the latest industries, the easier was it for him to string together imposing and deceiving percentages. He also confused economy with technique, the results of which can be bought without assimilating its processes. In the same way, he confuses industrialisation with socialism. The deception is closely reminiscent of intoxication, the more profound as the illusions were stronger.

Stalin insistently boasted of the cyclopean span of the work accomplished, which is one of the favourite themes of his literary, journalistic and photographic propaganda. In his simplicity he believes that its magnitude is sufficient to mark the superiority of an enterprise, and he copies and exaggerates the mania for "the greatest in the world" without bothering about its reasonableness, and often to the detriment of the interests in his charge. This motive of pride is not less fragile. "The bourgeoisie," says the *Communist Manifesto*, "has accomplished wonders far surpassing Egyptian pyramids, Roman aqueducts and Gothic cathedrals." A State covering one-sixth of the globe does not in any way surpass its rivals by superb, costly and infirm "giants," which are produced at a loss and contribute nothing to the satisfaction of immediate needs. The factories in which the equipment is obsolete before it is paid off put heavy charges on the budget, to the detriment of social obligations, and the gap is vast between the magnitude of the undertaking and its doubtful utility. Besides, Tsarist Russia also had to construct on the scale of its vast territory, without finding in this an historic excuse, any more than the great works of art of the two continents have spared the people economic crises, unemployment and misery. The Trans-Siberian, the longest railway in the world, and a legacy of Tsarism, could evidently not exist in Switzerland; but no Plan will ever bring the transport system of Siberia or Russia up to the level of the Confederation's railways, in the matter of regularity, frequency and hygiene. Turksib, created partly under the old regime and partly under the new, would do honour, according to Stalin's reasoning, as much to the former as to the latter. There are many, however, who would like to know the number of workmen who died from epidemics in the process of laying the Soviet sleepers over the sands that are traversed by a puffing and problematic train; the film of the enterprise is a poor compensation for all the unfruitful exploitation. The titanic dam at Dnieprostroy, the work of the American, Colonel Hugh L. Cooper, and other foreign experts in the Union, measures 770 metres long by 40 metres at the base, but the Zuyderzee dyke is 30 kilometres by 94 metres at sea level and is 134 metres wide at the bottom, yet Holland is one six-hundredth the size of the U.S.S.R., and has one twenty-third of its population, and claims no praise for this block of concrete. Each of these two works represents in one way or another an economic heresy. The American turbines at Dnieprostroy will turn uselessly for years for lack of cables to carry the current, or motors to transform the energy, or factories to use it. In France, the hydro-electric stations of Kembs and La Truyère, established without any bluff or noisy plan, are scarcely less formidable than the Dnieprostroy and have notable differences in their favour. The Colerado Central takes the prize for audacity and power, but is not worth to President Hoover, whose name it bears, the consideration that Stalin would give it. The joint use of the Magnitogorsk minerals and the Kuznetsk coal, more than 2,000 kilometres apart, produces steel at an exorbitant manufacturing cost, raised by the expense of transport and the cost of the high-pressure furnaces, forges and lead-rollers constructed by the Cleveland engineers. The Ford factories of Nizhni-Novgorod will produce motor-cars destined to founder in the quagmires, so lacking is the country in serviceable roads. The model machines from the Tractor Factory at Stalingrad, of American origin, deteriorate in a year's time in the

inept hands of an improvised working personnel. Not one of
these industrial monsters can stand up to the slightest impartial
examination nor prove what Stalin implies in the hopes of getting
away with the deception. The bridges of Newport News, of
Sydney, of the Zambezi are "the biggest in the world" and do
not solve any social problem. No more than do the Eiffel Tower,
the Empire State Building, the Suez and Panama canals, the
Saint-Gothard and the Simplon, the underground canal of the
Rove near Marseilles or the tunnels under the Scheldt at Antwerp
and so many other triumphs of engineering. The U.S.S.R. has
as yet nothing to be compared with these, and it could for a
long time to come get along much better without them than
without bread. The Rockefeller Centre was erected at an unprecedented loss. If the canal from the Baltic to the White Sea,
dug at the command of the G.P.U., by a multitude of unfortunate deported peasants (286,000 in June 1934, according to
I. Solonevich) were to justify Bolshevism, then the reclaiming
of the Pontine marshes would be an irrefutable justification of
fascism. And no language would be enough to celebrate proportionately the Great Wall of China. The idea has sprung up
spontaneously on many sides of comparing to the Pyramids,
mutatis mutandis, these palaces erected in Russia for the housing
of machines by the labour of coolies whose lodging is in
wretched hovels. Historians had already made use of the comparison in connection with Peter the Great, and the Mensheviks
had used it against the "labour armies" of Trotsky. For grandiose
as the "giants" born of the Five Year Plan may appear in this
"Empire of Façades," as Herzen would say, the waste of funds,
the squandering of energy, the losses of every description are
still more grandiose, and the sacrifices in human beings seem to
belong to another age.

Stalin has several times quoted Lenin's allusion to Peter the
Great, and many commentators have used it to suit their purpose. Though now a commonplace, it is by no means favourable
to the socialist principles of the Bolsheviks. "An apostle of civilisation with a knout in his hands, the knout in his hand being the
persecution of all enlightenment," Peter could only copy from

the West, borrowing the forms without taking the substance, seeking practical advantages without understanding the premises, and botching ill-proportioned and fictitious works that were often useless, at times harmful and always precarious. Half of his factories only existed on paper and only about twenty survived him. Of the thousand vessels, frigates and galleys of his fleet, hardly more than fifteen were sea-worthy ten years after his death. The senseless construction of Petersburg at an outlying point of the Empire, and on a swamp that became a cemetery for thousands of workmen, and the building of the port of Taganrog under almost similar conditions do not redeem the horror of his crimes. Quite the contrary. "But at last, the town exists," wrote Voltaire, pensioned by the Court of Russia and a worthy precursor of the "intellectuals" hired by Stalin to sing his praises. Sylvain Maréchal replied in his *History of Russia:* "To cement the foundations of a new city with the blood of a hundred thousand men is what Voltaire calls creating a nation. Can one play more impudently with the poor human species?" Rousseau showed his perspicacity in writing in the *Social Contract:* "Peter had imitative genius. He did not have the true genius, which creates and makes everything out of nothing. A few of the things he did were good, the greater part were misplaced." Diderot discovered the truth during his stay in Russia as is proved by his famous dictum on the "colossus with feet of clay." And Condillac was not wrong to address himself to Peter in these terms: "You have erected an immense edifice, but permit me to ask you what are its foundations. Perhaps you have neglected them so as to occupy yourself only with the exterior decoration. This magnificent grandeur, which is your creation, will perhaps disappear with you." He was not the dupe of the "profound calm—forerunner of decadence." Another question of the intelligent Abbé could also be addressed to Stalin: "What have you done to diminish this overwhelming terror which has accompanied your power and which can only create mercenaries and slaves?"

The sanguinary Tsar was not the only one to employ these methods. They show through the more seductive décor put up by his descendants. Questioned by M. de Ségur on the new buildings in Southern Russia that were shown to Catherine the Great by Potemkin, the Emperor Joseph II, who had visited them, replied: "I see in them more brilliance than reality. . . . Everything seems easy when you are lavish with money and men's lives. We could not do in Germany or in France what they risk here. The master orders, the thousands of slaves work. They are paid little or nothing, they are badly fed, they dare not let a murmur of complaint escape them and I know that in three years . . . fatigue and the unhealthiness of the swamps have been responsible for the deaths of fifty thousand men, without any complaint being made or without a word having been spoken." His opinion was corroborated in the following century in Custine's letters. "With the powers of action usurped by this prince, a true creator would have achieved many quite different miracles. But the Russian, having made an entrance on the great stage of the world after everyone else, has only the genius of imitation"; thus the French traveller speaking of Peter I. "It is only when his people submit blindly that a master can order tremendous sacrifices to produce very little" was his reflection at "the colossal childishness" of Nicholas I, who represented for him, "not the force of a great country but the uselessly wasted sweat of the wretched people." He defined Russia thus: "It is a country where the greatest things are done with the most meagre result." The commands of the master "put life into the stones, but only by killing men."

There would be novelty in the "planning," if the Plan were not in a very large measure a nebulous myth which it is impossible to take seriously, since its sponsors flatter themselves with having transgressed its fundamental principles under the pretext of speed. This means that they have accentuated the errors, the lack of balance and the disorders which they set out to remedy. A single irrefutable example demonstrates its inanity. When Stalin, in the speech already quoted, congratulated himself on a collectivisation three times that of the original Plan, without having tripled the tools, fertilisers and buildings, and without even having provided the minimum essentials originally scheduled, he clearly discredited the principle, which he could not even conceive, much less apply. Similar statements hold good for industry. With a rolling stock inferior in quantity and quality to that of 1917, with worn-out rails, rotten sleepers, and faulty signals, it was not logical to burden the transport with a triple load, unless deliberately to provoke catastrophe upon catastrophe and the ruin of the railways; which, in effect, was what did happen. The Plan aimed in principle at an economic harmony measured by indices of quantity and quality, of value and price. From this limited point of view, and if one leaves out of account the freedom of choice which had been suppressed, it was necessary to produce a certain volume of raw materials and to transform them into manufactured articles, but at the same time to reduce manufacturing costs and to raise the value of money, the salaries and the general standard of living. But the quantities aimed at were not obtained; the quality of the products deteriorated, the manufacturing costs increased, real wages fell, and the notion of comfort grew vague in the memory of the workers. No matter from what angle it is examined, the unrealisable Plan has not been carried out. The proof is easily disentangled from the muddle of statistics deliberately confused by the ever-changing standards of comparison. And without bothering to refute in detail a pseudo-scientific charlatanism, which even goes as far as to predict future crops and consequently meteorological prospects, it is only necessary to emphasise certain fundamental data to be clear on the issue.

Stalin estimated the realisation of the industrial programme at 93.7 per cent, or a production three times that of before the War, and double that of before the Plan. He did not say on what he based his calculations, letting it be thought that it was a question of quantities enumerated in weight or volume, whereas in fact his figures simply translate an arbitrary value into more or less fictitious roubles. In fact, if the key industries are examined, we have quite a different picture. In 1932, 6.2 million tons of iron were cast instead of the 10 calculated in the Plan and the 17 predicted by Stalin at the Sixteenth Congress. Forty-two million tons of coal were extracted instead of the 75 (according to the

Plan), the 90 (control figures) and the 140 fixed by the Central
Committee (decision of the 15th August 1931); 22.2 million
tons of naphtha instead of the 45 required by the Central Committee (announcement of the 15th November 1930); the capacity of the electrical power reached in theory 13.5 thousand millions of kilowatt-hours, instead of 22 (according to plan), which
says nothing of the means of using it. The results are still lower
for chemical products, for copper and other coloured metals,
for cement and building materials. Thus the percentage of
achievement in the principal branches of work is very far from
approaching Stalin's round figure, and a certain percentage must
still be deducted for faulty production. It must be clear to every
sane individual beyond the reach of the G.P.U., that the factories have only been able to make machines within the limits
of the metal and fuel supplies, to say nothing of other restrictive
conditions. The same year, 844 locomotives instead of 1,641
(Plan) were manufactured, 18,600 coaches instead of 37,000
(Plan), about 50,000 tractors instead of the promised 170,000,
and 26,700 automobiles instead of the 200,000 announced by
Stalin at the Sixteenth Congress. No better, indeed worse, is
the actual balance-sheet for the production of spare parts, minor
tools, and articles of current consumption. Thus 2,550 million
metres of cotton textiles were manufactured against the 4,700
millions of the Plan. Although this was approximately up to
pre-War level, the population had increased and the internal
market had been starved for fifteen years. In vain did Stalin try
to present a rise in price as corresponding with an increase in
production.

Almost 35 milliard roubles invested in industry and transport
have given, in quality as in quantity, nothing but deceptive
results. Beneath the whip of a deceitful emulation and an open
repression, bad workmanship ruined an enormous proportion
of the goods, sometimes a quarter, sometimes a half, according
to the particular factories—and it was no rare case when the
losses and throw-outs were three-quarters the total, or even
more. This goes to show again what trust can be put in the
varnished statistics of the Gosplan. So inferior were the products,

that in 1933 there was a decree to punish bad work—this "crime against the State"—with five years of prison. Moreover, the manufacturing costs, which should have been lowered by one-third in industry, and by one-half in building, had further increased, according to official statements, in spite of the subter-fuges of accounting used to confuse the calculations. And the output of the worker, instead of having doubled according to schedule, persisted at the original level, four or five times below the established productivity of America. It is difficult not to be reminded of a bitter reflection of Herzen's, "It must never be lost sight of that with us all change is only a change of scenery: the walls are all cardboard, the palaces painted canvas." A meta-phor, certainly, but one which covers a profound truth.

In their ignorance or their audacity, the dictators of the Soviet State made great play with the 118 milliard roubles sunk in the venture, instead of the 86 scheduled. But here the fantasy of the figures goes beyond all semblance of reality. Monetary circulation has increased by about 6 milliards in four years, instead of 1,250 millions which was set as the maximum, and this does not include the local money issued to palliate the scarcity of cash by means of notes and certificates, etc. (It increased again by two milliards in the two following years.) An adviser of Peter the Great had persuaded himself that in Russia the circulation of money depended exclusively on the will of the sovereign, and very conservative Russian financiers had condemned the gold standard long before Soviet economists. Stalin listened to experts of the same school, for whom unlimited note issues did not imply financial inflation. Nevertheless in four years the rouble had lost nine-tenths of its value instead of regaining one-fifth of it. Even at this, its purchasing power was due to administrative circulars and coercive ordinances of an inexplicable complexity. Left to the mercy of the laws of ex-change the rouble would not have been worth a kopeck. By an empirical and composite system of tariffs and reckonings, taxes and rations, which ignored all common standards of value, the relation of prices to wages varied infinitely, and money changed its value according to whose hands it was in. Hence, no figure had any precise meaning, neither the sum total of the national income, evaluated with governmental despotism, nor the individual balance-sheet, made up of so many different elements. The nominal salary did not indicate the standard of living of the recipient, who had to put up with the caprices of bureaucratic remuneration and with processes of assessment which defied all stable definition. After stopping the publication of the balance-sheets of the State Bank, the authorities had to give up establishing commercial and budgetary indices. In the chaotic state of finance was reflected the chaos of the whole planned economy, characterised in its final analysis by an absence of or a contempt for any plan.

The agricultural disaster, justly compared to the effects of a major war, caught up and surpassed the financial catastrophe which followed upon industrialisation. Contrary to the Plan, which specifically required the encouragement of individual production, 15 million peasant homes out of 25 million were forcibly collectivised into some 211,000 *kolkhoz*. But the crop of 1932 was only 7 hundredweight to the hectare and 69.9 million tons in all (against 96.6 in 1913), which was sufficient, with the abnormal losses and the normal birth-rate, to cause a famine. And that was in spite of the 10 milliard roubles expended, in spite of the use of perfected implements, in spite of the periodical mobilisation of the communists, the frantic agitation led by the press at each new season, and the "offensives on all fronts," of tillage and pasture, sowing and harvesting, housing, threshing and stock-rearing and all the work that is executed peacefully everywhere else in the world. Stalin admitted that the *kolkhoz* as a whole worked at a loss, like the great socialised industry. Other admissions revealed that the 5,383 *sovkhoz*, burdened with endowments and machines, were not yet productive of revenue. In an array of 147,000 tractors, 137,000 were in need of major repairs. In the "depôts for tractors and machines," petrol, oil and spare parts were lacking as well as professional attention. But the nightmare of collectivisation had been fatal above all to the livestock, reduced in five years to 160 millions from 276 millions. Statistical fictions only

give a feeble idea of the truth as another admission that Voroshilov allowed to escape him bore witness. "Not only the horse
but the ox, which has become a rare phenomenon in our Ukraine,
aids and will aid the tractor." From this it is easy to draw conclusions relative to meat, leather and wool. If you add to this
the fact that the productivity per hectare of technical culture
(flax, cotton, beetroot) decreased by half in a population of
165,000,000, the acute scarcity of cloth and sugar is explained
without further investigation. Thus the main reason for the
interminable shortage of merchandise, and the great famine,
which reached its culminating point in the spring of 1933, are
sufficiently clear. The *Sozialisticheski Vestnik* rated at 5,000,000
at the least the number of victims of "a sort of famine artificially-
organised" by Stalin, and all reliable information tends to confirm this figure. It is also the estimate of an extremely sagacious
observer, Mr. W. H. Chamberlin, who is well qualified to speak
on account of the length of his stay in the U.S.S.R., and his
sympathy for the Russian people.

Whilst outwardly denying the evidences of famine, as he
denied the failure of his rash plans, even though the falsified
statistics of his own bureaux pointed to it, Stalin was nevertheless
forced to take some notice and to check the presumptuous
march forward—to ruin. His shouts of triumph covered practical
instructions which became more and more modest. It was a question henceforward of concentrating effort, not on the extension
and intensity of production, but on the assimilation of the
technique so dearly paid for, on the improvement of quality,
on productivity of labour and on the lowering of manufacturing
costs. By an apparent paradox, which betrays a lot, the "Bolshevik rhythm" had to lessen its speed instead of increasing it
as mechanisation progressed. It was no longer a question of
L. Sabsovich's book, *The U.S.S.R. in Fifteen Years*, the text-
book of a perfect Bolshevik, in which the author tabulated a
great mass of absurd hypotheses on fifty per cent annual
increase in industrial production from 1933. Stalin was content
with thirteen to fifteen per cent on an average in the course
of the second Five Year Plan embarked upon. And as it is always

a long way from the programme to its realisation, the inevitable halt seems obvious enough. There was less and less talk of surpassing western capitalism. And with good cause. With a population two-thirds that of the U.S.S.R., and in a country already filled with abundance, the United States produced in 1929 about 36 million tons of iron, 546 of coal, 133 of naphtha, 120 milliard kilowatt-hours, 5,651,000 motor-cars, 229,000 tractors, and the comparison with "one-sixth of the globe" is even more conclusive for copper—1,069,814 against the U.S.S.R.'s 46,694 in the best year, 1932. Even by falsifying parallels, by the astute choice of a Soviet maximum and an American minimum, the "com-boasting" could not produce results. So much so that no one breathed another word of the second *piatiletka*, of which Molotov and Kuibyshev had sketched the main lines a year earlier at the Seventeenth Party Conference, indicating astronomical figures. The year 1933 went by without a Plan in the country of Plans.

On the other hand, modifications in the "general line" increased to the relative, but scarcely perceptible, advantage of private rural economy, by the restitution of horses and cattle to the cultivators so as to save the remainder of the stock from total loss, and by the increase of free trading among the *kolkhoz* and their members, reductions in taxes and dues, restrictions in the programme of sowing and stores, etc. The scarcity of manufactured goods even encouraged giving leases of premises to the *artels* of artisans, and providing them with tools. These precarious expedients did not prevent Stalin from introducing new coercive measures against the peasants, the chief of which was to instal near the 2,245 "tractor and machine stations," branches of Party police under the name of Political Sections. Stalin, of course, could only conceive of consolidating collectivised agriculture by increasing the police and bureaucracy.

The famine, whose black blot spread from the Ukraine and the Kouban district to the lower and middle Volga, to the Caucasus and the Crimea, over the most fertile lands of Southern Russia, and whose scope was proportional to the degree of collectivisation, still pursued its ravages until the 1933 harvest, which was exceptional both for climatic conditions and for results: 89.9 million tons, calculated on paper by multiplying the sown area by a supposed yield per hectare, and including the grain which rotted in the fields, was lost in transport or otherwise ruined. For the Plan had made provision for everything except barns to store it in, vehicles to transport it, scales to weigh it and mills to grind it. If one takes into account the losses, estimated at a quarter, and the extra mouths to feed, as well as allowing for the insignificance of exports and the excess of forage left over by the extermination of horses and cattle, the miserable pre-War level was even then not attained. Nevertheless, after the horrible period that had been endured, a certain improvement was felt in food supplies, as is the case in all backward countries where economic activity depends almost entirely on the harvest. The price of rationed bread suddenly doubled in August, which signified a general fall in real wages. But money had depreciated still more, as prices obtained in the free market proved, where wheat was sold at two hundred times the official price. Judging by the extraordinary procedure employed to preserve cereals from pillage, Stalin was not mistaken as to the real situation of supplies in the country, nor as to the conversion of the peasants to his singular form of "socialism." Precautions unheard of in the annals of agriculture were instituted: day and night watch was kept over the immense plains by sentinels and mounted guards. Watch-towers had to be erected above the sea of rye in which to place armed spies. The Communist youth were mobilised, and even the children, to spy on marauders. It was necessary to forbid access to the roads and by-paths except to those who had the password. The press congratulated urchins who had denounced their own parents, "barbers" guilty of having "shaved" a few handfuls of ears of corn, hidden them in the bottom of a pail and covered them with herbs or fruit. Will it ever be known how many starving mouths have paid for such an attempt on the "socialist property" with their liberty or even their lives?

In short, the Plan had been fulfilled only in the restricted measure predicted by those serious and prudent economists, technicians and specialists who were accused in 1930 of wanting to minimise working speeds, and were imprisoned and deported for sabotage—that is to say, for the crime of clearsightedness. Moreover, it is necessary to write off a considerable amount for spoiled production, and to add to the liabilities frozen capital, unfinished production, deteriorated machinery, wasted resources and unused new material. In a manner exactly the reverse of true economic progress, the acquirement of technique led to a destruction of wealth, to an increase in costs and to the dissipation of energy.

Without the foreign bourgeoisie, with its industrialists and bankers, its architects and engineers, its advances and credits, its patents of invention, processes of manufacture and implements of every kind, Stalin would never have obtained the minimum of what it was possible to obtain by better and more rational, cheaper and more fruitful, and more human methods. He had sacrificed consumption to production, agriculture to industry, the disinherited country to the parasitic towns, light industry to heavy industry, the working classes to the bureaucratic patriciate, and, in short, the man to the machine; only to end in anomalies, disproportions, and unco-ordinated results which were never worth the expense.

By its dictatorship over prices, the State had been able to sell very dearly what it bought very cheaply, and thus, with other too well-known methods of despoliation, it robbed the whole population to the exclusive profit of a new parasitic class. When State-controlled agriculture and industry worked at a loss, the deficiencies dragged in their wake an excess of privation and suffering, crowned by a "sort of artificially-organised famine." Certainly the collective effort has laid the costly foundations of new metallurgical and chemical industries, and created armament factories which strengthened the military power. But to offset this, there had been an accumulation of failures in finance, transport, agriculture and animal breeding, which forbade incurring an armed conflict at the risk of complete breakdown. In order to give the people of the U.S.S.R. the means of fighting, Stalin had taken from them every reason for defending themselves. Far from having freed his country from dependence on other countries, and isolating it from the world market as an *autarchy*, he had made its economy more than ever dependent on more developed and better equipped nations, as much for repairs and spare parts as for the replacement of imported implements. On the other hand, he fired the imagination of the young generation with works of imposing grandeur, awakened in them a utilitarian mysticism towards mechanisation and technique, stirred up a Soviet chauvinism, blessed with a revolutionary terminology, but directed to purely national ends. He had, besides, gone beyond the ephemeral and burdensome successes of outward display, by masterfully exploiting, in the tradition of Tsarism, the ignorance of the public, the credulity of the working class, the vanity of the intellectuals, the venality of the press and the corruption of the politicians.

Imitating Peter I, who paid the press of the day to spread throughout Europe the rumours of his imaginary victories over Charles XII long before Poltava, he went to great expense to broadcast recitals of his political triumphs and descriptions of his majestic works. But the Russians have brought their powers of persuasion to a fine art, and delight in making visitors take mole-hills for mountains and the statistical exercises of the bureaucrats for palpable realities. Vladimir Monomach, Grand Prince of Kiev, used to recommend that strangers should be cordially welcomed "because," he said, according to Rambaud, "your good or bad reputation depends on the accounts they will give in their own country." The advice has been followed by his successors. Even under Peter, one reads in Kliuchevsky, "economic enterprises produced a strong impression on superficial foreign observers. Russia appeared to them as a great factory."

Under Nicholas I, to quote again from Custine's inexhaustible collection of letters, "Moscow prides itself on the progress of its factories. . . . The Russians are proud of possessing such a great number of fine buildings to show to foreigners." Stalin has introduced nothing new in this respect either, except to exaggerate beyond the bounds of all decency. This is demonstrated by a plethora of eulogistic literature in which the inexactitude of the facts vies with the inanity of the commentaries. Tenacious adversary of industrialisation before making himself its champion in the wrong sense, he became for the New York *Business Week* the "Mussolini of Mechanics." But the prestige gained by such stratagems is of no avail in important matters where the truth demands its rights. However, the Plan has had as a result the formation of numerous bodies of mediocre technicians who are not without the capacity to improve, in the long run, and the education of millions of adolescents in the needs of industrial production, hastily inculcating in them the rudiments of general and professional culture, indispensable to the economic and technical transformation in progress. Education, restored to some of the discipline of classical pedagogy, had been made more widely available, although it must not be forgotten that the Party, in deciding anew in 1934 to introduce universal compulsory education, showed how much value could be placed on its great "historical" resolutions of "world" significance. But there again the negative elements outweigh the positive in a "totalitarian" state, where liberty of conscience and freedom of expression do not exist, where the standardised press is only permitted to express the authorised opinion of the day, where critical thought and scientific objection as well as political doubt are repressed with more severity than common crimes, and where the unlettered have a better chance of conserving their intellectual faculties and their moral health than the dishonest intellectuals depraved by official mendacity and their subjection to fear. It only remains to discover the original correlation of production relations and property forms to the social structure, after fifteen years of Bolshevik evolution, and to find out if the transitory nature of the regime tends, as the communist programme claims, to substitute the administration of things for the government of men.

4

LENIN exercised power for scarcely more than five years, during which many contradictions between his theories and his
practice had corrected the bookish concept of an intermediary
phase between capitalism and socialism. Stalin's reign had lasted
some ten years when the Party, in 1933, announced the proximity of the golden age of classless society. But a State no more
than an individual can be judged by the ideal which it glorifies.
In actuality, the case is complicated by insoluble contradictions
between the concrete and the abstract, in an extreme disorder of
ideas and values, wherein are confounded the Russian past, the
Soviet present and the immutable traits of despotism, common
to all periods and all climates. Discrimination is necessary to
see whether Stalin really justifies Spencer, who saw in socialism
"a future slavery." Liberal economy whole-heartedly denounced
as socialist all tendencies in the State direction of production,
exchange and labour. In this respect, the edicts of Diocletian on
maximum prices and minimum wages, on agricultural colonies
and on trade corporations, could justifiably find a place in an
anthology of socialist legislation—an absurd hypothesis.

Stalin has had precursors in antiquity and in the middle
ages, both in the East and West, but there can be no legitimate
authority for calling them socialists in the exact meaning of the
term. The most remarkable, Wang An-shih, lived in China
under the Sung dynasty. Assured of the Emperor's confidence,
this bold minister thought he could regenerate his mediaeval
country by so regulating economic life as to make the State
the sole owner of the soil, and the sole buyer and seller of
grain. By a series of laws, which demanded for their application
a whole host of functionaries and a new mandarinate to replace
the old, he decreed from on high a veritable agrarian revolution
(equalitarian revision of valuation and rent, loans of seed against
takings in kind, taxation of commodities, etc.). This was completed by a series of radical reforms, establishment of a salt tax
and recasting of the monetary system, the creation of a popular

militia besides the permanent army, bureaucratic conscription for the civil service and compulsory education. Of this "extraordinary experiment in 'statism'" to use the expression of G. Soulié de Morant, there remained nothing after the death of the "Chinese socialist of the year one thousand," an inexact expression of an eminent historian and orientalist, René Grousset, who is not mindful of the exact terms of sociology. Modern socialism implies, in effect, certain conditions of historic maturity, namely, the exhaustion of capitalist resources, the conscious will of the active population, the material possibilities for the workers to acquire "comfort and liberty." Between Wang and Stalin there are many similarities of conception and method, at more than ten centuries' distance, and the analogy holds good in the final results of the two attempts, i.e. famine and misery. But the differences are all to the advantage of the great Chinese reformer, too little appreciated by Abel Rémusat, Father de Mailla, the Abbé Huc and other missionaries who have studied from the same sources. In their *Empire du Milieu* the brothers Reclus have been less severe. Wang had read only Confucius and was ahead of his epoch, whilst the theorists of socialism in a single country pretend to have read Marx, and with no excuse lag behind the Utopians. If Stalin's dictatorship merits the name of socialist, the theocratic domination of the Jesuits in Paraguay would figure strikingly amongst the enterprises of the pioneers of socialism, side by side with the less famous communities of the monastic colonisers. The part, albeit subsidiary, played by the workers in the Bolshevik movement does not alter the matter. Among the African Bambaras, the blacksmiths crown their chief, but their caste is none the less despised, beneath all the ritual honours, and there has never been any attempt to cite these tribes of the Sudan and Senegal as an example of proletarian democracy.

Russian history throws a better light on the Soviet regime devoid of soviets, than the arbitrary references to Marxism, of which Stalin actually represents the antithesis. In particular, it unites the old and the new modes of mysticism. In the same way as pagan customs persisted under other forms in Christianity after the baptism of the slave tribes in the principality of Kiev, many age-old traditions have been transmitted, under other colours, to Sovietism from Tsarism, both in spirit and in custom as well as in economic, political and social organisation. T. G. Masaryk says rightly of the Bolsheviks, "children of Tsarism" like other Russians: "They have succeeded in suppressing the Tsar, but they have not suppressed Tsarism. They still wear the Tsarist uniform, albeit inside out. . . ."

In the fifteenth century, after the capture of Constantinople by the Turks, Muscovite monks saw in Moscow the third Rome, excluding for ever the eventuality of a fourth; the doctors and apologists of the Leninist religion have a similar aim in claiming Moscow as the capital of universal Communism. At the same period Joseph, "hegoumenos" of the Volokolamsk monastery, elaborated a doctrine which M. Kizevetter sums up thus: "Joseph defends a social order founded on a rigorous discipline which denies the individual the right of doing as he pleases. In the religious domain he affirms that salvation depends on the punctual observation of ritual and the literal acceptance of every word of the Holy Scriptures without any discussion whatever; he approves of the suppression by the ecclesiastical power of every manifestation of free thought in religious matters, as well as of the execution of heretics practised in Moscow. . . ." Dogmatic Bolshevism is more akin to such conceptions than to socialism, which is inseparable from the idea of free enquiry and judgment, and which has as its final aim the integral freedom of the individual. Stalin invokes Lenin on every corner of the battlefield and makes orthodox pronouncements whilst deporting to icy temperatures the little children of the so-called *kulaks*. But Ivan the Terrible was not lacking, either, in exterior signs of devotion, while he committed his appalling atrocities. And the murderous rivalry encouraged among certain young communists, exhausted by the useless task of shock-brigading, recalls at times those fanatical disciples of the Archpriest Avvakum who burned themselves alive to escape the fiery river of the last Judgment.

It is not subjection to the State which stamps knouto-Soviet

Russia with an original imprint. Under the early Romanovs, the whole population was made to submit to the State, and in various ways subjected to strict economic obligations. It had already sought to escape by flight from the Tsarist and manorial repressions, and the central control could secure it only by such rudely enforced measures as those later employed under the Five Year Plan. As early as the seventeenth century Russians were forbidden to go abroad—an undoubted precedent for the general sequestration brought about by Stalin; and books sent from Europe were not allowed to enter by virtue of a special ukase that still guides the Glavlit or Soviet censorship. The Tsar, sole owner of the country and the people, made himself the "principal merchant" and the "principal producer" in the Empire, to use the words of the English doctor, Samuel Collins. Peter the Great introduced State monopoly in the trade of articles of immediate necessity and all foreign commerce. Under his reign, a sort of State capitalism developed, and multiplied the number of officials by ten. Serfdom grew on a large scale and was introduced into industry at its inception, apart from the employment of penal labour. The institution of the internal passports adds one more resemblance to the sombre Stalin period, when the workers and peasants within a few years lost their last remaining liberties, like their predecessors, the free cultivators, who became serfs within the course of a few centuries, thus reversing the social evolution of the west. Peter's successors followed in his footsteps—trade with China became a monopoly of the Treasury, and under Elizabeth the State took charge of every possible transaction. And even when capitalism regained its rights, and re-established competition, from Catherine's time, the initiative of the Crown remained decisive for the progress of industry and transport. The military colonies of Alexander I foreshadowed future agricultural collectivisation on a small scale. The Soviet State, with more powerful material means, reproduces, condenses and generalises all these phenomena in a knot of historical conditions incompatible with intermediate solutions.

That the savage precedents of Ivan the Terrible and Peter the Great are to be recognised in Stalin's outstanding acts is not contested among observers of Russia. But in each of the principal representatives of the autocracy, gestures and acts may be found which have their parallels with contemporary Russia. Catherine used to correspond with Voltaire and Diderot, but she imprisoned Novikov and banished Radishchev. She took ideas from Montesquieu and borrowed from Beccaria, but she extended and consolidated serfdom. She avowed herself an "apostle of light," but she dared to boast of the mujik's well-being in the midst of a famine. She rewarded the self-interested praise of the encyclopaedists and employed the most despicable mercenaries. Stalin, as well, acts quite against his maxims, encouraging without what he dare not tolerate within. He supports strikes and promotes subversive acts of which he would crush the least glimmerings in the U.S.S.R. He buys the favour of well-known foreign men of letters and gags or banishes Russian writers. He keeps a whole string of hired adulators in foreign countries. Alexander I, like his father, posed as a freemason, posed as a Jacobin, quoted Rousseau, and protested against the Negro slave-trade at the Congress of the Holy Alliance, while admitting the traffic of souls in his own Empire. Stalin in the same way calls himself the defender of the workers in the capitalist countries and is himself their worst oppressor in the "socialist fatherland." Of Nicholas I, who loved to class himself as an engineer in order not to be recognised as a policeman, historians draw a portrait in which one may distinguish many of the features of Stalin's physiognomy. Between the two absolutisms, the similarities are so strong that the collection of Custine's century-old letters is worth consulting again, as one of the best works on the eternal Russia, "where you must go to see the result of this terrible combination of European science with Asiatic genius," where "the Government dominates everything and encourages nothing," where "everybody thinks what nobody says," where "the absurdities of the parvenu can exist everywhere and become the appendage of a whole nation," where "boundless evil is inflicted as a remedy," where the "force of despotism lies solely in the mask of the despot," where "the reciprocal mistrust of the Government and the subjects banishes all joy in life," where "the inhabitants, inured to resignation, counterfeit for themselves an astonishing kind of happiness composed of privations and sacrifices." Stalin has made more true than ever the profoundly just reflections of the author whom we have so frequently quoted: *"In this country an avowed tyranny would be a mark of progress."*

Whether of divine right or popular origin, all dictators and dictatorships offer analogies in their methods and *raison d'être.* The bureaucratic absolutism incarnate in Stalin is no exception to the rule, with the ancestral Russian tradition that inspires him in spite of the Soviet novelty in which he decks himself. The combination of ruse and violence propounded by Machiavelli for the use of the Prince is practised daily by the General Secretary. But identity of means does not always presuppose similarity of aims. Bolsheviks from Lenin to Stalin at first believed that they could arrive at socialist liberty by the evil means of police constraint. This was before they had made a virtue of necessity and codified the cruel expedients of civil war for times of peace, until in the end dictatorial habit became their second nature. Without the dictators being aware of it, a metamorphosis of the regime took place, which Stalin, aided by his faults even more than by his qualities, has been able to consummate and perfect in the sense of personal power without meeting insurmountable obstacles, still preserving the revolutionary vocabulary shorn of its initial meaning. The result is a political architecture of bastard appearance, which at least two great examples will help us to understand. In Rome, the Empire "slid" into the Republic to use Seneca's phrase, while it preserved the exterior symbols. In France, the coinage struck at the beginning of the Empire bore the legend: *"République Française, Napoléon Empereur."* Caesar gave himself out as the successor of the Gracchi, and Bonaparte as the successor of the Jacobins. Stalin's Caesarism proceeds from the same causes and grows on favourable ground: in Tsarist Russia, after the October manifesto of 1905, there had been quite as bizarre a system, which the *Almanach de Gotha* called "constitutional monarchy under an autocratic Tsar." The Federation of Socialist Soviet Republics, the very name a fourfold contradiction of the reality, has long ago ceased to exist to the full knowledge of everyone; only well-meaning but very young Leninists still hope for its spontaneous resurrection at the end of the "general line"; the dominating Party has lost all illusions in this respect and forgotten its socialist programme.

So-called Soviet society rests on its own method of exploitation of man by man, of the producer by the bureaucracy, of the technician by the political power. For the individual appropriation of surplus value is substituted a collective appropriation by the State, a deduction made for the parasitic consumption of functionaries. Stalin reckoned for 1933 about 8,000,000 functionaries and employees, whose precise income it is impossible to estimate. But official documentation leaves us no doubt: the bureaucracy takes an undue part of the produce, corresponding more or less to the old capitalist profit, of the subjugated classes, which it submits to an inexorable sweating system. There has thus been formed around the Party a new social category, interested in maintaining the established order, and perpetuating the State of which Lenin predicted the extinction with the disappearance of classes. If the Bolsheviks have not the legal ownership of the instruments of production and the means of exchange, they retain the State machinery which allows them all the spoils by varied circuitous means. The mere freedom from restriction in imposing retail costs several times higher than manufacturing costs, contains the true secret of bureaucracies—technical exploitation, characterised moreover by administrative and military oppression.

It is of little importance that the small minority, thus privileged at the expense of the great majority, is not a class like the bourgeoisie, or a caste like the Brahmans. In the sixteenth century, the Cossacks also constituted a kind of class, with its economic and political prerogatives unknown in any other country except in Russia. From Siberia, Rakovsky and his deported friends wrote as early as 1930: "From a workers' State with bureaucratic deformations, as Lenin defined the form of our Government, we are developing into a bureaucratic State with proletarian-communist survivals. Under our very eyes has formed and is being formed a great class of directors, which has its internal subdivisions and which increases through calculated co-option and direct or indirect nominations (bureaucratic advancement or fictitious electoral system). The element which unites this original class is a form, also original, of private property, to wit, the State-power." And they took their stand very pertinently on a phrase of Marx, "The bureaucracy possesses the State as private property." Just as the Consulate was neither a republic nor a monarchy, the Secretariat is neither a democracy nor Tsarism, the consequence of a revolution which was neither socialist nor bourgeois.

According to Bogdanov, whose works on the subject go back to just after the first revolution, a proletariat deprived of real encyclopaedic culture, and general knowledge of organisation, will never be capable of seizing the power or keeping it in order to transform society along communist lines. And the Bolshevik regime, in spite of the intentions of its founders, engenders a dominant class of politicians, administrators, intellectuals and technicians, under which exploitation and oppression by a State of an original type persists under new forms. This last observation, *post factum*, may be found again, less strongly argued as an intuitive premonition, in one of the theses of the *Intellectual Worker*, a work published under the name of Volsky at the beginning of the century by a Polish revolutionary, Makhaisky, well known then but since forgotten. A number of communists have arrived at the same ideas by practice and not theory, but have been unable to express them in the country of official communism. Others have reconsidered, within themselves, the idealist notion of the "historic mission of the proletariat," in order to tackle the fundamental revision of doctrines which make too much of an abstraction of the real man, whether bourgeois or proletarian. It remains to be seen whether such conceptions, whatever they are worth, will regain force, wide currency and vitality for the generations destined to take their lesson from the revolution, above all, from the phase which we may call, in Herzen's word, *retrovolution*.

This revolution has passed through three principal stages, each one of some five years' duration. After War Communism, the vain attempt at a complete economic nationalisation, Lenin's N.E.P. was an attempt to control a composite economy, tolerating a sane competition between the State sector and capitalist initiative so as to realise by degrees a national socialisation. But Stalin, incapable of following this political heritage of harmonising industry and agriculture, and balancing production and consumption, preferred the security of an integral statism to the risks of a special test which the N.E.P. implied. His "great turn" was only possible at the price of mass slaughter at its inception and of absolute mass servitude in the present and future. To take this course, a great contempt for human life and dignity was necessary and also an entire misunderstanding of the spiritual postulates of socialism. Stalin had the singular courage of taking upon himself the most atrocious responsibilities, whilst still continuing to make use of a worn-out language. But the edifice built in fifteen years of Bolshevism will endure only under an unlimited pretorian dictatorship, and could not resist an upheaval of any importance. The Russian people have always benefited by wars which shook the ruling power—unveiled its weaknesses and excited general discontent. The Crimean War hastened the liberation of the serfs, the Russo-Japanese War unleashed the first revolution, the World War precipitated the fall of Tsarism. There is every evidence that Stalin's regime, if it had to rely on its own strength, could not withstand the supreme test any better.

It is easy for a State which monopolises armaments, along with everything else, to break strikes and to crush peasant revolts, distributed over an immense area. The hesitant military intervention of the Allies after Brest-Litovsk was only a mockery, as Lenin recognised without any pretence. But a war of long duration would demand other national and moral resources than interior repression or the first campaign of the Red Army. Neither industry nor agriculture, and still less transport, is ready in the U.S.S.R. to endure the high tension of a modern war. A report of Kaganovich admits 62,000 railway accidents for the year 1934 alone, 7,000 locomotives put out of action, 4,500 trucks destroyed and more than 60,000 damaged. These figures increased in the first months of 1935, and there were "hundreds of dead, thousands of wounded." After, just as before, the Five Year Plan, the inhabitants had to undergo hours and hours of waiting and interminable formalities to get a needle in Moscow, or a nail in the provinces, or a little salt practically anywhere, a railway ticket, a box of matches, a gramme of quinine. Stalin allows himself the frequent spectacle of imposing parades with defiles of tanks and aeroplanes, but he does not realise that in war-time his engines will lack oil or petrol, his artillery will lack munitions, and he will be unable to repair them as soon as they are put out of commission. He may condemn to death for culpable negligence the mechanics and drivers who have escaped from accidents, but that cannot improve the railways or the rolling stock. Whether in regard to equipment, re-stocking, "management," or sanitary services, nothing encourages the rulers to optimism regarding organisation and technique.

The reports of the G.P.U., on the state of mind of the population, gives them no more assurance. The peasants hope for any sort of change, and are only waiting for arms to settle their arrears of accounts with their oppressors. The workers feel scarcely less aversion to the hierarchy of secretaries, in spite of all the propaganda employed to convince them of their advantageous position. The youth alone, which knows nothing of the recent past or of life in foreign countries, accepts with elation the ideology of Soviet chauvinism and would defend the frontiers without reservation if not with enthusiasm. But its warlike impulses, so vigorous in expeditions without peril and without glory against the unarmed peasants, will lose vigour under cannon and machine-gun fire. The Red Army, reinforced by a partial mobilisation, would suffice for the protection of the U.S.S.R. in a conflict limited to neighbouring countries, but not in a conflagration world-wide in scope, entailing general mobilisation. Stalin is aware of this, as is proved by the pliant manœuvres of his diplomacy whose flexibility borders on resignation and betrays a significant anxiety.

For fifteen years, and above all since Lenin's death, the Bolsheviks have vociferously announced an approaching and even imminent general conflict. They have denounced the aggressive intentions of every country against themselves and accused specifically France, England and the United States of fomenting a new armed intervention in Russia. According to them, the League of Nations was only a "League of Brigands," a war machine erected against their socialist fatherland, and every European and international agreement, from the Locarno Treaty to the Kellogg Pact, concealed "a sword directed against the Soviet Union." Under the most futile pretexts, they discovered menacing preparations of hostility everywhere and in every country and sounded the alarm at home and, with less reverberation, in the working-class centres of other countries. They never found enough sarcasm or insults to hurl at pacifism, wherein they detected the most treacherous enemy of the revolution. But Stalin operated a complete volte-face after the victorious exploits of Japan in Manchuria. It was in the same place where the Red Army under Blücher had three years previously inflicted a military "lesson" on the Chinese to safeguard Russian "rights" in a railway, that the love of peace now counselled a retreat before the Japanese. From 1932 onwards, the U.S.S.R. concluded a series of non-aggression pacts or friendly *ententes*, first with Roumania and Poland and later with France and the United States, those very States whose anti-Soviet machinations and "war-like designs" the rulers of Russia were incessantly unmasking and branding.

Already Litvinov, at Stalin's orders, had proposed universal disarmament with striking insistency, but in the tradition of the famous rescript of Nicholas II, which was the forerunner of the Hague Conference. In 1933, the advent of Hitler in Germany accentuated the pacific tendencies of Bolshevism. Everything that had been detestable became excellent and vice-versa. Stalin and Molotov had no scruples in singing the praises of the "League of Brigands." They opposed the revision of the territorial clauses of the Versailles Treaty, which had been the objects of their incessant vituperation. They hastened to seek the support of the "imperialist diplomacy" of France, "the most aggressive and militaristic country in the world," as Stalin had said at the last Party Congress, a country which, according to Leninist orthodoxy, "had not ceased to provoke war against the U.S.S.R." In 1934, they honoured as an "eminent foreign *savant*" the very Marshal d'Espérey whom their press had always considered the "executioner" of the Hungarian Soviet Republic. They ordered their pseudo-communist stipendiaries in every country to make a rapprochement with those whom they had branded the day before as "social-traitors" and "social-fascists," meanwhile dictating a new demagogy under the form of moderation. At home they made patriotism the order of the day. Not even the cult of the "socialist fatherland," but of the "fatherland" without trimmings. However, their policy—peace at any price—was clarified by an unusual decree exempting the peasants of Eastern Siberia—from the Baikal Lake to the Maritime Province—from all or a part of the taxes and dues—the *kolkhoz* for ten years and the other farms for five. By restoring agricultural liberty in a vast region in danger of invasion, they attempted, somewhat tardily, to instil a little patriotism into farmers ready to welcome the invaders. It would be difficult to imagine an implicit confession more conclusive. But there are others, such as the new terrorist decree of June 1934, which gave warning of the death penalty for "treason to the fatherland" (the simple "flight" into other countries of a Soviet subject, civil or military, was thus classified); and the decree designated the whole adult family of a deserter as hostages to be imprisoned from five to ten years if they did not denounce their relative and for five years if they were unaware of the "crime." Such preventive measures tell a long story and show the extent of solidarity between rulers and ruled.

The defeat so longed for by an enslaved people, with the exception of the privileged Party members, the bureaucracy, the social cadres and the young loyalist generation, would be, for the Stalin of legend, the beginning of the end. The dictator would have no alternative but to put himself at the head of a frank social reaction and re-establish private ownership of the means of production or else fall beneath the débris of his own system. The Soviet State capitalism, formulated by Lenin and once debated by Trotsky and Bukharin, who preferred to speak of State socialism, would then evolve in a direction diametrically opposed to the inconsistent view of the few Bolsheviks who have remained faithful to their principles. There exists no bourgeoisie to seize power in the Soviet Union. The proletariat, demoralised by the secret spying and the repression exercised in its own name, bureaucratised to its core, and composed of ignorant mujiks, has for a long time been powerless to take its own destinies in hand. The disintegrated and paralysed peasant population always has an influence on events, but indirectly and indistinctly. Functionaries, intellectuals and technicians, anxious for security, will rally round the new masters in advance, being unable even to intervene as autonomous elements if the upheaval goes beyond the limits of an internal palace revolution. The police and the army are the only organic forces capable of revising the political statute in a crisis of the regime. But it is otherwise with respect to the economic basis, determined by a combination of national conditions, historic causes and general characteristics inherent in the twilight of capitalist civilisation. The greater part of nationalised industry in Russia has no individual owners nor any who could lay claim to it according to the old laws, and a return to petty agricultural exploitation seems less and less practicable. Any future order will have to face up to the burden and management of a collective property unique in the world. Whatever judgment one may make on the transformations accomplished, some of them are ineffaceable. Economic liberalism will not find a rebirth in Russia at a time when it is declining everywhere else. Nor will there arise in the predictable future any true political democracy, inconceivable on the scale of such a large State even on the hypothesis of dismemberment. The exposure of its realities can indicate far better than theoretical definitions the probable perspective and the aftermath of a political disaster, if these contradictory data are borne in mind.

All objective observations are agreed in asserting the absence of any communist orientation in the industrialised U.S.S.R. Against the grey background of common poverty, privation and want, social injustice and inequality can be easily seen. Wages vary enormously, and the advantages accorded to the most favoured aggravate contrasts that are more odious than in any capitalist country. Stalin had been an unconscious leveller until the day he became aware of the inconvenience of equalitarianism, depersonalisation and irresponsibility. In 1934 he insisted on his latest discovery. "Tastes and needs are not, and cannot be identical and equal in quality and quantity, either in a socialist period or in a communist period." To the excessive levelling of the unprivileged majority, for whom collectivisation meant a complete turning of the tables, succeeds a systematically inverse process. But there persists, as a symbol, the construction of dismal, comfortless and unattractive barracks to house the mass of the workers, considered as numbers on a register. In copying capitalism, the bureaucracy takes the worst as its model, apart from founding a few exemplary houses and institutions for the seduction of benevolent foreign tourists. Millions of women are employed in the most distasteful and strenuous work in heavy industry under the hypocritical pretext of emancipation. In addition to the so-called seven-hour day, supplementary odd jobs, obligatory attendance at the sad comedy of meetings, anxious seeking after the necessary provisions, depressing queueing at shop-entrances, etc., absorb all leisure and degrade the individual, already obsessed with the problem of feeding himself, dragging him down to a semi-animal existence. The knouto-Soviet State is the only one where the proletariat is forced, not only by means of periodic pretences of voluntary loans, to deprive itself of the meanest possible remuneration, but to put up a show of being happy about it. It is also the only place wherein the defenceless workers are shot in punishment for accidents due to worn-out material or administrative carelessness and where the poverty-stricken risk the death sentence for harmless transgressions like theft or petty pillage of crops.

Such things would be impossible without the ruthless restraint of a police and army privileged in every respect—better fed, clothed, housed and with better opportunities of recreation than the other categories of "citizens." Under Menzhinsky's nominal and Yagoda's effective presidency, the G.P.U. constitutes a veritable State within a State, with its civil and military staff, its own productive enterprises, its better supplied and better served eating places, its property, its workshops, its *sovkhoz*, with even bureaux for technical studies and labour service, well supplied with imprisoned engineers and deported workmen, whose forced labour is duly exploited. In practice its power is limited only by the will of Stalin. Protective legality for the Soviet subjects is sometimes a trap, sometimes a fiction. Not that there is any lack of texts—chancelleries and archives abound in them, as under Tsarism. "No country in the world has a greater abundance of laws than Russia," Lenin wrote at the beginning of the century. But Michelet had stressed: "There is no law in Russia. The sixty volumes of laws that the Emperor has had compiled are a vast mockery." And Custine had noted even earlier: "After a few months' stay in Russia you no longer believe in laws." Here again Sovietism does not represent any advance over the past—quite the contrary. To save the revolution, especially if nobody is threatening it, the G.P.U. arrogates to itself every possible law, from the most terrible to the most ridiculous.

Inquisitorial and penal despotism carried to this extreme kills all interest in work, all spirit of initiative, all sense of responsibility. Thus he benefits most who shirks his duties and obligations and blames his subordinates. The bureaucracy imagines it can supplement individual or collective zeal by millions of bits of paper, and draws up an abundance of futile circulars and unlimited questionnaires that nobody knows anything about, whether received or returned. Meantime, from the highest to the lowest, everybody looks to a superior command before carrying out the meanest current task. This obliges the Secretariat or the Politbureau to think of everything and to regulate everyday life in its minutest details. Almost every day the press publishes under Stalin's and Molotov's signatures,

STALIN

573

a long, solemn and circumstantial decree relative to some banal task necessitating not the slightest governmental intervention.

For example, on the 11th February 1933, the public, whether interested or otherwise, received minute instructions on the treatment of horses, bulls and camels, on the rest to be accorded to pregnant mares, the quality of hay, straw and bran to reserve for beasts of burden, the way to curry and shoe them, to harness and yoke them, arrange their stables, couple males and females, etc., the whole interlarded with menacing injunctions, and punctuated with warnings of the rigours of the law. Other orders in the same style dictate minutely the conditions of furnishing the State with sunflower oil or potatoes, or the manner in which to gather cotton, or beetroot. In place of the tutelary and simplified administration—the cheap government promised by the socialist programme—there is a complicated, expensive, vexatious and sterile regime.

Its repulsive effect may be seen in literature as well as in social life. State Bolshevism has produced neither a man nor an idea nor a book nor a great work. Nobody could think of holding the regime responsible for this, if it did not stifle original talent and creative genius, irreconcilable with narrow terrorist discipline. The renown of the best contemporary Russian writers will not enhance the greatness of the Steel Secretary, any more than the glory of Pushkin, Gogol or Lermontov gave lustre to the Iron Tsar. In arts and sciences as in philosophy and history, merit, intelligence and knowledge date from a period before Stalin, and owe nothing to this new autocracy, which tends to level character downwards, determines the duty of consciences and annihilates everything so as to have nothing to fear, contributing nothing or less than nothing to the treasury of culture. Even in the domain of cinematographic art, to which the Russian innovators have brought their splendid gifts, so well-known in the theatre, and whose purely national qualities must not be imagined as specifically Soviet, the very fine promise has been retarded, initiative choked. Rare communist writers worthy of attention among the younger group, like M. Sholokov or F. Gladkov, would have emerged and matured far better under

Tsarism, like their elders Gorky or Mayakovsky whose principal works date from before the revolution. We know that their only choice was between the official ideology and nothing.

From 1925, Stalin brought to art and literature the disciplinary methods in force in the Party and the State. He aimed only at combating the preponderant influence of Trotsky and Trotskyists like Voronsky and Polonsky, literary critics and directors of the principal reviews. In the *Federation of Soviet Writers*, the *Pan-Russian Union of Writers* group, the most important through the quality and prestige of its members, was suspected of some independence of spirit and sympathy for Trotsky's personality. To gain a point, Stalin did not hesitate to confer a fictitious authority on the *Association of Proletarian Writers*, nine-tenths composed of incompetents or simple scribblers. It was the beginning of an era of humiliations, denunciations, provocations, and persecutions which obliged true writers to take refuge in subjects with no reference to the present, childhood memoirs or historical novels, and which reduced to silence or retraction the "travelling companions" of the communists, as Trotsky called I. Babel, E. Zamiatin, B. Pilnyak, A. Tolstoy, L. Leonov, C. Fedin, V. Ivanov, V. Katayev, M. Zoshchenko, L. Seifulina, G. Oliesha, M. Bulgakov, Veressayev, and others. The sycophants of the *Association*, domesticated by the Party, were licenced to impose their unreadable productions on the public, and to censure the most eminent authors. Drawn up in shock brigades to perpetrate their extravagances, some decided to "conquer power in literature," to raise "shock-brigades in poetry," to trace "the Bolshevik line in artistic creation," to assure "a class vigilance on the edition front"; other alleged champions of the "proletarian hegemony in art" proclaimed the necessity of a "Five Year Plan for poetry" and a "Magnitogorsk of Literature." The slogan was raised to "outstrip Shakespeare and Tolstoy." A veritable carnival of folly triumphed along with the intellectual prostitution.

After Stalin's intervention regarding "Trotskyist contraband" in the historical works of the Party, the proletarian musicians declared: "In the light of Comrade Stalin's letter, new and great tasks arise on the musical front. Down with rotten liberalism with its bourgeois resonances and inimical class theories." And they undertook to "revise the scoring of the composers of the past, beginning with Beethoven and Moussorgsky." Stalin's letter was to make of "each Soviet orchestra a collective struggle for authentic Marxist-Leninism." The communist cell of the Conservatory was accused of a "right deviation" by reason of its liking for a "conductor of doubtful political opinions." After music—painting. Such and such an art critic denounced a "counter-revolutionary landscape," another obscure and ponderous nobody proscribed Rembrandt and Reubens. On the other hand, awards and medals went to the dullest reproductions, to recompense legends such as "Mauser, the War-Horse of Comrade Voroshilov" or "Grandmother of a Communist Girl." The Moscow museums were enriched with explanatory placards, according to which Renoir and Degas represent "rotten capitalism," Gustav Moreau "the art of the plutocracy," Cézanne "the epoch of heavy industry," and Gauguin "colonial policy."

To the same category of inanities belong "the struggle for the dialectic on the front of mathematics," and the "offensive on the philosophy front," whilst others extol Leninist physics, Soviet chemistry, or Marxist mathematics. To this may be added manifestations of delirium such as Krylenko's at the congress of chess players in 1932. "We must finish once and for all with the neutrality of chess. We must condemn once and for all the formula 'chess for the sake of chess,' like the formula 'art for art's sake.' We must organise shock-brigades of chess-players, and begin the immediate realisation of a Five Year Plan for chess." These clownish monstrosities extracted from the Soviet circus as typical examples of the collective insanity let loose by Stalin in an intolerable atmosphere, would have raised a burst of hilarity, were it not for the agonising presence of the G.P.U. behind the actions of the execrated *Association* and behind various communist factions of demoralised intellectuals, immoral and uncultured, and more capable of doing harm to an *élite* than producing anything themselves. Certain men of letters were able to escape the cruelty thanks to Stalin's capricious protection, others expatriated themselves with great difficulty, but the exceptions do not alter the rule. A revolutionary of the quality of Mayakovsky was not able to escape in 1930 except by suicide, as did Essenin, another great mal-adjusted poet, in 1926; likewise the proletarian poet, Kusnietzov, the symbolist poet, Vladimir Pyast, and the revolutionary writer Andrew Sobol. This gives some conception of the tragic situation of artists as well as workers and peasants. The favour accorded to B. Pasternak would have allowed him to survive under no matter what despotism and indicates even more clearly the inhuman conditions in which the majority of his confrères are stagnating. And one can well understand the conversions, prostrations, and contritions obtained from the Soviet intelligentsia, to the shame of the parvenus of the dictatorship. In 1932, with his usual abruptness and brutality to the weak, Stalin suppressed by a stroke of his pen the *Association*, producer of so much evil, which had served him as an instrument. He ordered the fusion of all writers' groups. He affects in aesthetic matters a very liberal breadth of view. But there has remained the evil of an arid conformism in Soviet art and literature, absolutely incompatible with any sort of socialism or communism.

The same contradiction finds definite confirmation in the plebiscite, contrived by every possible means of corruption and intimidation for the purpose of perching Stalin at the top of an incredible scaffolding of lies and impostures, and of forging for him the renown of a great man, of a hero, *"sans peur, et sans reproche"* of a protean and universal genius. The hagiography composed in honour of the dead Lenin is nothing besides the canonisation of the living Stalin. Followed up with a spirit of consecutiveness rare in the U.S.S.R., the enterprise reveals a continued tendency towards the crystallisation of a personal power that has the characteristics at once of Tsarism, Bonapartism and Fascism, with Oriental methods and American pretensions.

5

No INK can transcribe the systematic stimulation inaugurated on the occasion of Stalin's fiftieth birthday, and prolonged since in a crescendo of adulation, artificial veneration and adoration. Quotations can give only a very poor idea of it, since a few lines cannot sum up whole drifts of apologetic literature or reproduce typographic variations and illustrate the assorted iconography. It is incessant repetition of various processes which goes to fashion minds and which is able to determine an effective current among the crowds.

After enlivening a slightly drab biography by attributing to Stalin everything that should have been laid to the account of Lenin, Trotsky and others, the bureaucratic *camarilla*, guided by experience, soon learned to forestall the desires of its master, to anticipate his intentions and stimulate his greeds. From 1930 onwards there began a contagious outbidding among courtiers of every category, bent on outdoing the most obsequious or the cleverest. Scarcely had it passed into circulation than the word "genius" became obligatory, and he who neglected to write it for any reason, or without a reason, rendered himself liable to suspicion, and exposed himself to grievous vicissitudes. Shameless and sordid servility suggested a thousand ways of advancement in a career by glorifying the tyrant. He was painted, he was sculptured in Napoleonic attitudes. There already existed a Stalingrad, a Stalino, a Stalin, a Stalinabad, Stalinsk, and Stalin-Aoul, but ingenious functionaries continue to bestow his name on new towns in so far as appropriate geographical terminations can be found: Stalinissi and Stalinir in Georgia, Stalinogorsk in Russia. The public is wondering what is restraining Stalin from bequeathing his name to Moscow, since the highest peak of the Pamirs already bears it. You can no longer count the innumerable institutions and establishments already under the same ensign. Careerist engineers call an extra-hard steel "stalinite." The Soviet executive responded to a unanimous and unforced desire by conferring on Stalin the second order of the "Red

Flag." He later decided to recompense services rendered to industry with a medal struck with his inevitable effigy, which is scattered throughout newspapers, is pasted all over walls, and, by an involuntary but all the more admirable symbol, reigns in the empty windows of shops denuded of goods.

The men of letters, above all, vie with each other in dithyrambic servility, hoping to gain some favour, a better paid post or a more copious ration, or—a passport for foreign countries. They know that Stalin is racked by a most painful sentiment of intellectual inferiority—Bukharin had been able to discern it long since—and is particularly avid of praise for his erudition and culture which are sadly limited. Here the truth loses all semblance of fact. Stalin "has always been distinguished by his profound understanding of literature," said someone in the review, *At the Literary Post*. He ranks amongst the "profound connoisseurs and critics of Hegel," according to a contributor to *Revolution and Culture*. He is one of "the most authoritative specialists in contemporary philosophic problems," says a third. "In reality, certain pronouncements of Aristotle have only been fully deciphered and expressed by Stalin," wrote a fourth in the *Cultural Front*, its outlandish gibberish penetrated with a pungent mockery. But this presumptuous daring is no more than a very cheap compliment, and you will find presently from a fifth encomiast that Socrates and Stalin are the highest peaks of human intelligence. One pedagogue announced in the most casual manner at the Communist Academy, "the full significance of Kantian theories can be finally embodied in contemporary science only in the light of Comrade Stalin's last letter"—that same scurrilous letter on "putrid liberalism" and "Trotskyist contraband." "Every section, every line of Stalin's reasoning provides the most fertile theme for artistic works," asserts a manifesto from the *Association* in commenting on a confused and interminable speech about the Plan, and it invites all writers and critics to meditate long and seriously on the text in question. In *Soviet Land*, a prose poem magnifies "the great face, the great eyes, the great and incomparable brow" of Stalin, whose appearance produces the effect of "a ray of summer sunshine." The

Literary Gazette is not afraid to extol him as a stylist: "It is up to linguistics and criticism to study Stalin's style." This time the insult is obvious, the satire certain, and one might expect pitiless reprisals; but the eulogy is allowed to pass like the others. The editor of *Izvestia* declares in Congress: "On the threshold of the new age stand two unequalled titans of thought, Lenin and Stalin," and he concludes, "Can anyone really write on anything unless he knows his Stalin? Never! Without Stalin no one can understand anything or write anything of interest." Demian Biedny, fallen into disgrace, tries to purchase pardon by exclaiming at a meeting, "Learn to write as Stalin writes." The same poetaster has lavished praise on others in the same vein. A literary woman sees Stalin quite simply as the direct successor of Goethe. One of Kalinin's essays ends with the words, "Ask me who best understands the Russian language and I reply—Stalin." At the time of the tercentenary of Spinoza's birth, *Pravda* sees its way to insert in large letters among various philosophic extracts from Marx, Engels and Lenin, several quotations from Stalin which had nothing to do with either Spinoza or philosophy. Yet Stalin accepts this clumsy rubbish without raising an eyelid. After Aristotle, Socrates, Kant and Hegel, one Spinoza more or less is nothing to worry about. "There is no flattery too outrageous to offer this power which compares itself to the gods," wrote Juvenal in other times but in similar circumstances.

An indescribable apotheosis took place in 1934, when Stalin was pleased to call the Seventeenth Party Congress, three and a half years after the sixteenth, followed next day by a purge which lasted over a year and "cleaned up" about 300,000 unworthy members. Everything gravitated then around the celebrations of the most hated man in the Soviet Union. Elaborate preparation created the atmosphere, companies of sycophants and individual champions zealously outdoing each other in panegyric. Everyone busily collected and analysed the most banal platitudes of their idol and called them "world-historical" maxims. With the slightest pretext and on the flimsiest motives, orators and journalists vied in reiterating: "Stalin was right . . ." or "As Stalin said . . ." and everyone was at pains to invent new epithets of praise, for "shock-brigadier," "legendary figure," "beloved commander," "genial thinker," and "adored Stalin" lose their force by dint of repetition. At the opening of the Congress, the repertory swelled with new hyperboles, like that of Bukharin who styled Stalin "the field-marshal of the revolutionary army." The formula went as far as congratulating the "chief of the world proletariat," co-responsible for all the defeats of the Third International since Lenin's death, more personally responsible for the rout of 1927 in China, and directly responsible, in 1933, for the blind policy which brought communism in Germany from shameful bankruptcy to helter-skelter disorder and irreparable retreat without striking a blow. During the Congress a continuous hosanna went up from dawn to dusk on the "steel colossus," the "great engineer," the "great pilot," the "great master," the "great architect," the "great disciple of the great master," the "greatest of the theorists," the "finest of the Leninists," and finally the "greatest of the great. . . ." Stalin is genial, very genial, most genial: he is wise, very wise, most wise; he is great, very great, the greatest. . . . Superlative declension became the rule, and it was printed every day in every column and page of each newspaper, with a fawning subservience and ecstasy quite untranslatable. In the Congress, modestly styled "the Congress of conquerors," the record was beaten by one of the favourites, Kirov, who hailed "the greatest leader of all times and all nations." The speeches opened and ended with a profession of faith in the superman's glory, amid highly spontaneous ovations and irrepressible acclamations. It is impossible to describe the reception accorded to Stalin himself when he read the report of the Central Committee. After the Congress, there was an endless echo in local assemblies, press columns, resolutions and telegrams.

That is only one panel of the diptych. The other represents the inexpressible ruin of the vanquished. For at the moment of supreme exaltation, Stalin yet wished to feast himself with "sweet vengeance." He made his unfortunate adversaries lash themselves in public, confess their abjection to the tribunal, and cringe under the shouts of his minions, rabid enough to trample them underfoot. Once more capitulators of the Right and of the Left admitted their errors, and some were cowardly enough to make accusations against each other. We need not have any doubt that they exhausted the utmost resources of their vocabulary in order to pour forth a feigned enthusiasm about the victor whom they were cursing in their hearts. A dirty business this, that defies description and comment alike, in which neither cheater nor cheated was taken in by the falsity of the situation. Yet nothing could convince the Bolsheviks in their frenzy of the shame of false repentance and ignominious persecution. "Among us, it is as easy to acquit as to condemn," wrote Gorky; but in this mentality "you can see a solicitude to acquit one's self of one's own failings in advance." In making his report Stalin had stated: "At this Congress there is nothing else to expose, no one else to attack." In spite of this, blows were not spared against Trotskyism already retracted and annihilated many times, against supposed heresies rebutted and liquidated, against time-honoured opponents already rolled out flat and won over to the integral Stalinist orthodoxy. It is certain that the inflexible police and prison methods of Stalin are appropriate to the system, for they ensure him results in advance. At the close of the Congress, Sosnovsky, one of the last well-known partisans of the Opposition, sent his submission from Siberia, followed shortly by that of Rakovsky. Both disavowed their discomfited faction, renounced their impious ideas, repudiated Trotsky and paid homage to Stalin. In the prisons and isolation camps and convict settlements there remained only some courageous political opponents, devoid of influence, their names destined to oblivion. The majority of Trotskyists were disgraced by their recantations; the remainder, like Koté Tsintsadze, had died in exile. The millions of prisoners and banished, cut off from the national life, could not hope for any amnesty save by some catastrophic war. The person of Stalin was henceforth embodied in a dictatorial majesty, without equal in the world and without precedent in history.

From the course of events, the tracing of history and the unravelling of texts, there emerges in sufficiently clear relief this repulsive character whose prodigious destiny it is so difficult to explain outside of the Soviet Union. We know now the abilities and the weaknesses of Stalin, the excessive disproportion between his intellect and his will, between his knowledge and his *savoir-faire*, and the reasons for his personal success gained over the ruins of the socialist programme of his Party. We have seen him patient, meticulous, wary of illusions as of words, and strong above all in his contempt for the individual and in his lack of principles and scruples. He is a product of circumstances, he owes his political fortune to his antagonists, though one can say as much of all his dictator contemporaries. He has not succeeded in establishing himself without a certain flair, without natural faculties for intrigue and an effective alloy of coolness and energy. Clever at putting off disadvantageous solutions, at dividing his enemies and getting round obstacles, he shrinks before nothing if he can but attack, strike and crush. He had the dexterity to avoid in the Party the shedding of blood spilt so often in the country, to exhaust opposition by dilatory tactics combined with the gag, the pillory and the whole gamut of sanctions. We recognise him as cunning, crafty, treacherous, but also brutal, violent, implacable, and set always on the exclusive aim of holding the power he has confiscated by an accumulation of petty means. As Bakunin wrote of Nechayev: "Bit by bit he has come to convince himself that to establish a serious, indestructible society you must base yourself on the policy of Machiavelli and adopt completely the Jesuit system, with violence for the body and lies for the mind." In the hardest struggle between Bolsheviks and Mensheviks the latter often taxed the former with Nechayevism and Jesuitism, to the indignation of Lenin and his disciples. But a posthumous revenge was reserved for Martov with the rehabilitation of Nechayev attempted by various communist historians under Stalin, and it is not mere chance that one of them, A. Gambarov, ended his work with the statement that Nechayev's anticipations "have become embodied in full in the methods and practice of the Communist Party of Russia in the course of its twenty-five years of history."

Stalin has obviously not read Machiavelli, still less the astounding *Dialogue in Hell between Machiavelli and Montesquieu*, an anonymous book published in exile by a proscribed republican of the Second Empire, Maurice Joly. But he has followed by instinct the line of conduct traced in this ironical manual of cheating and duplicity whose precepts can be summed up in these almost literal lines:

Separate morality from politics, substitute force and astuteness for law, paralyse the individual intelligence, mislead the people with appearances, consent to liberty only under the weight of terror, pander to national prejudices, keep concealed from the country what is happening in the world and likewise from the capital what is happening in the provinces, transform the instruments of thought into instruments of power, remorselessly inflict executions without trials and administrative deportations, exact a perpetual apology for every act, teach the history of your reign yourself, employ the police as the keystone of the regime, create faithful followers by means of ribbons and baubles, build up the cult of the usurper into a kind of religion, create a void around you thus making yourself indispensable, weaken public opinion until it subsides in apathy, impress your name everywhere as drops of water hollow out granite, profit by the ease with which men turn informers, manipulate society by means of its vices, speak as little as possible, say the opposite of what you think, and change the very meaning of words. . . .

All this appears to have been written for Stalin, and resolves the oft-discussed problem of the traits common to Lenin and his heir. In the latter we can find no trace of the founder of the Soviet State. Ostensible differences apart, what was large and disinterested in Lenin, is shabby and mean in the epigone. On the other hand, there is between Stalin and Trotsky at least an essential psychological resemblance which sets them very much below Lenin: their claim to be infallible. Neither of them has ever sincerely admitted an error, whilst the first of the Bolsheviks had often set the example of an honest self-criticism in his examination of himself. Like Napoleon who said "I was the master, it is on me that all blame lies," even when his incapable lieutenants had done disservice to his plans, Lenin took the entire responsibility of his Party's actions upon himself. "The greatest chief of all times and all peoples" gives his measure by always throwing on other people—on inferiors and humble individuals—the burden of his own incidental or permanent aberrations.

Not only has he modified the meaning of words, as if under the inspiration of the apocryphal Machiavelli, but he changes the values of numbers, and accommodates them to the requirements of his personal political calculations, under cover of reasons of State. It is the same with his arithmetic as with his ethics and aesthetics—all are subordinated to the conservation of power. The fewer communists the Party contains, the more members he counts. The total bordered on three million in 1934, including candidates, and more than five million of the youth, and could double at the Secretary's fancy. Statistics string together all sorts of numbers that are without interest or reality, but not those of the suicides, capital punishments, victims of the Plan, deaths due to famine and typhus. We cannot easily find out how many imprisoned and deported keep up the maintenance expenses of the Stalinist order—a number oscillating between 5,000,000 and 10,000,000. The G.P.U. itself would be incapable of giving exact estimates.

A brochure of B. Shirvindt, director of prisons, reveals the number of condemnations pronounced by the tribunals in 1929, for the Russian Republic alone, without the Ukraine and Caucasus, etc.: 1,216,000 against 955,000 the previous year, not including the sentences inflicted by the G.P.U. The death sentences had increased in this one year by 2,000 per cent. These partial investigations throw a terrible light on the repression carried out in the whole of the U.S.S.R. by the two jurisdictions even before the peak was reached at the time of collectivisation. It is easy to understand why the pamphlet of the imprudent official was withdrawn from circulation and the information it contained prohibited. But since 1935, there has been no less conclusive information about the situation in the country as a whole, thanks to Solonevich, who was in a position to verify his calculations. He counts a minimum of 5,000,000 detained in the concentration camps, without including those in the prisons and "isolators" or the various categories of those banished or exiled; and he estimates the total number of condemned at one-tenth the number of adult male inhabitants. It would be fairly near the truth, therefore, to envisage a figure approaching 10,000,000 —to speak only of the living.

As far as ribbons and baubles are concerned, Stalin had inherited a military insignia, but he afterwards created two civil decorations, then, in 1934, the new distinction of "Hero of the Soviet Union"—apart from any recompense in money. On all points an intuitive Machiavellism guides him, often in its lowest form. The art of disguising his thoughts has no more secrets for him, his power of dissimulation equals his knowledge of provocation. For a few months in 1932 he absented himself and let rumours spread of his approaching resignation, so as to disorientate his enemies and incite them to vent their satisfaction, to keep his spies supplied with work and to chastise the prattlers on his return. He is undoubtedly the origin of the rumours from which he draws profit. In truth, none of his predecessors has dared to falsify history with so much indecency, to play tricks with the truth, attribute to himself imaginary superiorities and make himself a divine Augustus without the least title to distinction. He even stretches ambition to the point of seconding his flatterers when, as in 1934, they give him credit for—an arctic expedition with which, of course, he had no more connection than with the rhetoric of Aristotle, the "midwifery" of Socrates, the ethics of Spinoza, the metaphysics of Kant or the dialectic of Hegel. His misfortune is that tribute is always paid him by colleagues bound up with his fate, unconvinced underlings, self-interested flatterers or the conquered who are tied hand and foot; never by a man who is in the slightest degree free. He succeeds, however, in mystifying the perverted youth by the *credo quia absurdum*, taught in the name of Leninism. Brought up from a tender age to ape adults, brigaded in bands of pioneers, spoilt by a parrot-like education and the evil example of their elders, poisoned with careerism and egotism, the younger generation is to him an inexhaustible source for renewing cadres in his own way and completing the servile clientele. The greatest defeat that socialism has ever known is precisely this collective depravity which consists in inculcating into children and adolescents the very opposite of a doctrine while still preserving its vocabulary.

It was not enough for Stalin to vitiate the so-called Soviet youth in this respect. The Third International has grown beneath his hands into a despicable and sterile sect, has been transformed everywhere into an unconscious but active auxiliary of the counter-revolution. Just as the Polish communists had supported the military *coup d'état* of Pilsudski, before burning their fingers with it, so those in Germany had several times made common cause with Hitler, only to expiate soon after in concentration camps and on the scaffold the insane policy of their bad shepherds. *"The Communist International represents nothing and only exists by our support,"* Stalin said one day before witnesses, and Lominadze took note of the remark; but the cynical "chief of the world proletariat" none the less persists in maintaining the parasitic sections of his fictitious International. However, since 1925, he had decided in common accord with Tomsky to liquidate the affiliated "Red Trade Unions," and accordingly took measures to do so. It would have been but the first step in preparing for a second, according to the logic of his views, bounded as they are by national horizons; what is more it would have been, in spite of himself, in the interest of the workers' movement. The cries of the doctrinaire Left made him abandon his project, and at a later date, when he had overcome all opposition and there was no one to hold him back, he apparently no longer considered the matter urgent. He is, however, quite capable of striking from his budget a puppet International, just as he decreed in the winking of an eye the disappearance of the *Association of Proletarian Writers,* however small the advantage. He knows that the Comintern will never effect a revolution—"not even in ninety years" as he ironically remarked at the Politbureau in Trotsky's presence. But nothing decisive obliges him yet to get rid of such a tractable instrument, which he believes to be of use to his costly personal renown and to the manœuvres of his double-faced foreign policy. He will keep it as long as possible at the price of the irremediable discredit of communism in the two worlds.

Stalin has had the talent to endure, but only by disavowing his actions under a presumptuous phraseology. In 1934, the Bolshevik Congress ratified a second Five Year Plan, the relative prudence of which scarcely justified the victorious songs in honour of the first. At the preceding Party Conference, the official blusterers had calculated in advance for 1937 a production of a 100 milliard kilowatt-hours, 250 million tons of coal, 80 of naphtha, 22 of cast iron, etc., but the predictions fell to 38 for electricity, 152 for coal, 47 for naphtha and 16 for iron. Again it is only a matter of hypothesis, of which experience has proved the inanity. In other words, if by achieving the impossible, the second plan were better realised than the first, the U.S.S.R. after ten years of planification and twenty of revolution, would only produce about half the cast iron, a third the electricity and coal, and scarcely more than a third of the naphtha obtained in the U.S.A. for 1929 and that for a population more than a third greater. In respect of manufactured articles the comparison would be still more overwhelming. In 1933, at the International Economic Conference in London, Litvinov advanced the proposal of buying a milliard dollars' worth of merchandise, so acute was the lack of goods in the country of records. His country meanwhile has the effrontery to affect a complete disdain for foreign provisions. The very paper which the Bolsheviks use to deceive the public belies their fables of technical progress by its greyish dirty yellow colour and inferior quality. The conditions accepted to obtain *de jure* recognition from the United States, namely renunciation of subversive propaganda, admission of the clergy to the U.S.S.R., etc., indicated that Stalin was disposed to every type of concession to immortalise his autocracy. He made admiring speeches on President Roosevelt, kept to exclusively Russian problems in his conversations with Americans, predicted in 1933 the end of the world economic crisis, and made bantering jests about Trotsky's internationalism and the "permanent revolution." He was ready on conditions and concessions to adhere to the League of Nations, which, he had lately said, "is rotting while still alive"; and the volte-face was complete in 1934 when he dared to present as a triumph the admittance of the U.S.S.R. into the League of Brigands. But the more external agreements he concluded, the more he concentrated the power at home. Always haunted by the desire to keep a sharper watch on the details of his apparatus, he reformed the police-direction by the interposition of a "procuratorship" between the Politbureau and the G.P.U.; after that he altered the administration, by recastings and transformations, of which he alone had the secret, the Congress which decided knowing only the pretexts. In 1934, he suppressed the Workers' and Peasants' Inspection, so dear to Lenin, and replaced it by a Soviet Control Commission, modelled on that of the Party. He reshuffled the staff of the "summits," dismissing some of the People's Commissars; at the base, he multiplied the "political sections," which more directly transmitted the Secretariat's orders; and he placed over all the bureaucracies in the provinces another more authoritative bureaucracy. In the same year, he pretended to diminish the powers of the G.P.U., by transmitting them to the Commissariat of the Interior, but he effaced the name only to retain the system and the personnel, with Yagoda as chief, seconded by Agranov and Prokofiev, so that there was no definite change for the people.

His rare interviews, accorded for diplomatic ends, when he utters the most outworn truisms of elementary socialism, which exclude frankness almost by definition, contain no matter of new or useful consideration but for one exception. In an interview with a German writer, Emil Ludwig, who obtained an entrée by classing him amongst the eminent historical personalities worthy of his studies, the inevitable evocation of Peter the Great incited him to reply by a turn of phrase concealed by a metaphor: "In whatever concerns Peter the Great, he was a drop of water in the sea, and Lenin a whole ocean." He, Stalin, had no other aim than to be a worthy pupil of Lenin, that is to say, comparable to the ocean rather than the drop. He does not understand, among other things, that the worker-Tsar was in his time a leveller like himself, while forming with his "men of service" *(sluzhilye liudi)* the kernel of a future nobility. In Soviet Russia, levelling has gone on side by side with the formation of a privileged bureaucracy, whose hierarchy conceals the embryo of a class or a dominant caste. The first Emperor of China, Tsin Shih Huang Ti, a great organiser and deporter, who built the Great Wall, created an aristocracy of his own functionaries. In the same way Diocletian gave them titles that were not hereditary. It is not fatal that the Soviet bureaucracy should enlarge and consolidate its distinctive features, for its future will depend on international contingencies, not on the "clairvoyance" of its "genius." A reference by Ludwig to the three hundred years' reign of the Romanovs permitted Stalin to abuse the innocence or courtesy of his questioner, by denying all recourse to intimidation or terror, and alleging the unanimity of the worker and peasant nation. Uprisings have been as frequent under Sovietism as under Tsarism. The insurrections in the Caucasus and in Turkestan after collectivisation indicate that latent exasperation is only waiting for an opportunity to burst out. This is not the place to linger on all the conversations held by Stalin with a journalist in quest of the sensational whom he laughs at shamelessly in ineffably serious tones. Nevertheless, an incidental reflection is still worth examining: "In what concerns our conscientious workers, they remember Trotsky with resentment, even with hatred." Ludwig pretends not to know that in the Soviet Union no worker is allowed the right to a favourable opinion of Trotsky, or to the expression of it. But Stalin's tenacious animosity is an interesting revelation of his basically vindictive character, without generosity or grandeur. Even against the defeated adversary, whom he pretends to fear no longer, and to a visitor doubly strange to Bolshevism, he proffers in security his spiteful and violent words. In the zenith of his power he employs the weapons of the powerless, and at the thought of the "Man of October" he emerges from his false impassivity and in spite of himself ceases to simulate "indifference with a marble pulse."

One is always tempted to try to seize the meaning of a remote historic individuality by comparing it with others that are better known, to establish relations between the great revolutions and their protagonists. But whoever tries to find a figure approximating to Stalin in the French Revolution, where several figures have certain resemblances to Lenin and Trotsky, will not meet him there except by borrowing several types to compose a synthesis. Without losing sight of the difference of place and time, or being too carried away by analogies, one must imagine a Fouché, a man in the middle-distance of the revolution, and in the foreground of the counter-revolution, one who has a few objective characteristics of a Bonaparte without victories. Stalin has not only the principal characteristics of Fouché, virtuosity in intrigue and police methods, but there may be noticed in them both very curious psychological and temperamental concordances, apart from the common origin of their education and the striking similarities in their careers. Fouché also came from a seminary, renounced the sacerdotal calling, and later distinguished himself in "dechristianisation." Proconsul of the Convention in the provinces, he gave proof of exceptional terrorist energy which Stalin was to attain in an identical rôle—the requisitioning of supplies and the suppression of resistance. He passed through successive stages of revolutionary and counter-revolutionary evolution, and adapted himself to each of them. In the year when the Consulate became the Empire, he expurgated the archives of Nantes, his native town, of all papers concerning him. Stalin was one day to do the same, with the same arrière-pensée. If one is careful to observe due proportion, Bonaparte also can be taken as a comparison, for a reason which Jaurès indicates by pointing out that the man of Brumaire struggled against an obsolete form of counter-revolution, but at the same time introduced a new one, "the Caesarian counter-revolution, all the more to be feared because it retained on the surface some of the traits of the revolution which had been perverted." It goes without saying that no analogies can be drawn between the General Secretary and the First Consul in regard to individual qualities—it is their objective role which relates them. If Stalin had followed his inclination to favour private property, he would have become a sort of bureaucratic Bonaparte—less like the uncle than the nephew, the inheritor of a power conquered by others, and endowed with the sole genius of long patience. His schematic and limited socialism restrained him at a moment when the Left Opposition believed in the existence of Thermidor; and he turned against the rural districts after mastering the towns. But even in his war against the mujiks, he remained a peasant in his turn of mind, his manner and natural capacities; and this gives him some affinity with another dictator of a different rural extraction and a different intellectual class, but likewise a peasant—the Iron Chancellor, whose characteristics, as sketched by Engels, are typical of the Steel Secretary:

Bismarck is a man of great practical sense, great cleverness, a born and accomplished man of affairs. . . . But very often an intelligence so developed in the arena of practical life cannot be separated from a corresponding narrowness of view. . . . Bismarck has never conceived even a trace of an original political idea. But he assimilated the ideas elaborated by others. This narrowness was fortunate for him. Without it he would never have been able to consider universal history from a point of view specifically Prussian.

You need only change the last word to recognise certain traits of Stalin, who has them to a greater degree.

Soviet subjects do not have to go so far to find the complete model of their despot. They may find it in the national and classical history of their country, notably in the caricatured image of a hero of Shchedrin in the *Story of a Town*, a work unknown in the west but very much prized in Russia, which owes a renewed vogue to the antipathy which Stalin inspires. In a town, or rather an allegorical region, where each house, each social unit, has its "commander and spy," and where the inhabitants, constrained to a barrack-like discipline, have on fête-days "the freedom of making forced parades instead of working," a brute of a governor, Ugrium-Burcheyev, wields his savage rule, a symbol beyond all doubt of bureaucracy in uniform. In these pages, which cannot be condensed, Shchedrin gives an unforgettable silhouette of the "hermetically sealed personage" whose visage is stamped with "a military and tranquil certainty that all questions have long ago been solved," and who, having drawn a line, "believes he has enclosed the whole visible and invisible world within it." The contemporary Russian reader does not weary of seeing Stalin in this parodied reincarnation of the Minister Arakcheyev, only too well known by his colonies of soldier-peasants. Informed of this by the G.P.U., Stalin has taken upon himself in his turn to read the *Story of a Town* and to make the best of a bad bargain by risking a placid allusion to the author. But nobody is deceived, and the bitter Shchedrin satire is propagated to the great prejudice of the invincible "field-marshal." Stalinist functionaries have exerted their zeal in editing a Soviet fairy-tale for children in which Lenin, a prisoner on a desert island, flies away on a black swan in the company of a faithful Stalin, who proves his devotion and friendship by cutting off a finger to feed the carnivorous bird on the journey. But, Ugrium-Burcheyev also cut off his finger as a pledge of love and abnegation for his chief. . . . Whether the coincidence be voluntary or fortuitous, the effect produced is the same in ridiculousness.

Any portrait of Stalin would be premature before his fall or his death. The most necessary documentation has disappeared through the care of the party most interested. Of his former comrades of the Caucasus, some are languishing in exile, others have their mouths sealed. The coffers of the Party, the G.P.U., and the Lenin Institute will not give up their secrets until after a veritable historical upheaval—if indeed there still remain any secrets in the dossiers. The dictatorial entourage will remain silent so long as it fears the dictator or his creatures. Till then the bringing to light of new material, correspondence buried in the *cachettes*, and memoirs of contemporaries who have had the good luck to survive him, will have to be awaited. Stalin has no friend, no confidant. He loves nobody, as far as anyone knows, and nobody loves him. Among his partners he can count only acolytes whose company he avoids frequenting, so much is he bored by their intellectual mediocrity. The only man whose contact he has sought was Gorky, a captivating conversationalist as well as a great writer, and since his return to Russia Stalin's guilty conscience. Perhaps later in Gorky's papers, precious notes on his conversations with Stalin will be found. But the future Suetonius of this short-coated Caesar could only be one of his close police-auxiliaries—Yagoda for example. Biographers inclined to study his private life, his family, his customs, will be interested through professional duty in his first wife, Catherine Svanidze, sister of a third-rate Bolshevik, and in James Djugashvili, the son she left on her death. They will seek the truth of the suicide of his second wife, the only daughter of Serge Alliluyev. According to a laconic communiqué published in the press, Nadiejda Alliluyeva died suddenly in the night of the 9th of November, 1932. She left two young children, Basil and Svatlana. The next day the rumour spread in Moscow of a suicide. There are still no written proofs nor public testimony, but to appreciate the knouto-Soviet State, the incontestable truth of the fact is less important than the general immediate conviction, suicide being the only possible manifestation of a sincere opinion under Stalin.

This is not all, however, for the assassination of Kirov by a Bolshevik in December 1934, shows that the arm of despair may still serve, and for tyrannicide as well. Stalin's immunity in the classic field of terrorism, in the country of Karakozov, Zasulich, Khalturin, Jeliabov, Perovskaya, Sazonov, and Kalyayev, seemed for a long time inexplicable. Nevertheless in intimate discussions among communists, it was explained by various circumstances. Some considered as responsible the monstrous hypertrophy achieved by the police, the perfection of its preventive technique, the elaborate mass of precautions taken to guard the Supreme Secretary, the pitiless system of hostages and the terrifying zeal in reprisals. (Under Tsarism, political assassins sacrificed their own lives without the responsibility of risking that of their relatives and children.) Others maintained that individuals holding power have too little time to serve as targets— the apparent responsibility shared by dictatorial institutions preserves each dictator in particular. Moreover, they added, modern methods of deceiving opinion and spreading myths count a lot in the security of the rulers. These explanations contain some truth, but none of them demonstrates it completely. It is important not to forget that the people, although dissatisfied with the present, definitely do not desire a return to past conditions but can conceive of no better future. In this impasse, reformative goodwill loses its edge, and long years pass before a new revolutionary ideology is elaborated, susceptible of awakening pioneering abnegation in its militants. But it is not surprising that terrorism in high places awakens a terrorism below. Nothing is known of the activities of Nikolayev, Kirov's assassin, nor of the circumstances of his act, nor of the subversive group to which he belonged, nor of a so-called plot against Stalin. Stalin was able to execute fourteen communists in order to silence them, after having ordered 103 prisoners to be put to death without involving them in the least suspicion of culpability or complicity, not to speak of proof. He was able to re-arrest and cast in prison the pitiable Zinoviev and Kamenev, whose retractions, humiliations and abasements can no longer be counted. With them were condemned 17 other ultra-Leninists, such as Yevdokimov, who had gone over to the Opposition, and then many times repented, and 78 of their deported comrades including Zalutsky, Safarov and Vardin. He was able to forge an extravagant tale of preparations for assassination in order to throw mud upon gaged rebels, to overwhelm defenceless penitents, to attempt to compromise the inevitable Trotsky, in exile in a French province, and to present members of his "monolithic" and permanently purified Party as "class enemies" seeking to provoke heaven knows what "armed foreign intervention" by the murder of one Russian by another Russian, one communist by another. No sincere person gives any credence to such fables, which have no more truth in them than the alleged confessions, dragged out under pain of death, or the repentance that follows, or immediately precedes. All that we know is that Stalin, in a panic, sacrificed 117 victims, not so much to the shades of Kirov as to his personal anxiety.

Before attempting to investigate whether Nikolayev represented a superior ideal, or whether this family massacre of Bolsheviks announced any turn, we must recall to the "terrorised terrorists" who continuously quote Marx and Engels, the phrase where the one stresses the specifically Russian *modus operandi* of the *narodovoltsy*: "They can be as little moralised upon, one way or another, as the catastrophe of Chios"; and also that phrase of the other apropos of the terror, the result of "the useless cruelties committed for self-reassurance by people who are afraid themselves." Stalin's hand does not tremble to deliver innocent prisoners to the executioner, but both of them trembled, Rykov says, the day the Right sent him in a triple resignation. This man, who is supposed to be physically brave, has no moral courage whatsoever. He is not capable of looking a contradiction in the face, accepting the responsibility for his actions, hearing friendly criticism or asserting himself before an objector, and there is no meanness he will not stoop to if it is a question of conserving his power. One hundred and seventeen corpses are the ransom he exacts when a young militant, a son of the Bolshevik revolution, and brought up in the ranks of the Communist Party, resolves to translate a collective opinion in terms of revolver shots, through lack of being able to express it by legal and normal means. But he has created a state of affairs in which all serious antagonism must result sooner or later in suicide, like Skrypnik's, or assassination, like Kirov's. Between differentiated bureaucratic fractions with their Stalins of every description and their Molotovs of every calibre, between their clans and their cliques, life and death are permanently burning questions.

In the famous article, *Better less, but better*, that shone with the last brilliance of his mind, Lenin glimpsed a final clash between the East and the West—between the revolution and imperialism. "The issue of the struggle will depend in the end on the fact that Russia, India, China, etc., constitute the gigantic majority of the population. But the certainty of a definite socialist victory for all time does not guarantee our immediate perspectives. To assure our existence until the approaching armed conflagration between the counter-revolutionary and imperialist

West and the nationalist revolutionary East, that is, between the most civilised states in the world and the revolutionary States, backward as are all Oriental States, but which nevertheless constitute the majority, this majority must have the time to civilise itself." And he underlined *"We are not yet civilised enough to pass directly to socialism."* For quarter of a century, he dilated on an idea that Stalin has never been able to understand: "Socialism is impossible without democracy." And when speaking of electricity, he explicitly envisaged the whole of culture. For him, as for his masters in doctrine, civilisation, democracy, and socialism are inseparable. And if Lenin's last words have the least value, they foretell no glory for Leninists like Stalin who have too consistently misunderstood one of the essential springs of history—what the two initiators of modern communism knew in their time as "the power of expansion of democratic ideas, and humanity's innate thirst for liberty."

THE COUNTER-REVOLUTION

W E MUST distinguish a varied significance in the dates which we agree to
consider important in this history:
starting points and finishing points,
sometimes mere sign-posts in the infinite chain of cause and effect. The
counter-revolution, which had been
taking place in Russia since the illness
of Lenin—some would trace it back to the sinister episode at
Kronstadt—can be arranged in the chronological order of more
or less significant events, all of which are undeniably connected
despite their diversity.

Some of these may escape exact precision in time, but they
stand out very clear in character. The political defeats of
Trotsky in 1923, of Zinoviev in 1925, of their coalition in 1927,
of Bukharin in 1929 were landmarks in the rise of Stalin before
his "genius" was proclaimed, and strengthened his dictatorship;
but these defeats were followed by harsh penal reprisals inflicted on the most resolute opponents, and were essentially the
culmination of earlier developments. The inauguration of the
first Five Year Plan in 1928, and the universal enforcement of
the agrarian collectivisation will be judged of greater consequence from their effects than from their causes. The assassination of Kirov at Leningrad in 1934 was an event of symptomatic
significance, despite the insignificance of Kirov himself, who
had unblushingly extolled Stalin as "the greatest leader of all
times and all nations," and it acquired an increasing interest by
reason of its subsequent developments. Finally, the year 1937 will

be less held in honour as the twentieth anniversary of October
and the conclusion of the second Five Year Plan, than in dishonour as the culminating phase of an autocratic terror unprecedented in human memory.

With the lapse of time the Kirov murder has assumed the significance of an event of the greatest importance. Despite the
obscure and persistent reasons for deception by the "genial"
Stalin on this violent death, there was little doubt from the outset that the G.P.U. had contrived the crime—the murderer
served only as an instrument, and the major responsibility fell
on the all-powerful General Secretary. From all evidence, this
business was an accident in the internal struggles of high Soviet
society, a rivalry between two cliques, one of which had been
able to arm or guide the hand of a young and fanatical communist. The 117 executions ordered by the "great and beloved
leader" after the crime, the imprisonment of 97 former representatives of the old Bolshevik opposition of Leningrad—which
had been dissolved—with Zinoviev and Kamenev at their head,
the condemnation of the twelve Stalinist chiefs of the local
police, and finally the deportation to Asia of some 100,000
innocent inhabitants of Leningrad could deceive nobody. Stalin
did not have the courage to make known the exact circumstances of the murder, or the real motives of the murderer, any
more than the charges brought against the so-called instigators
or accomplices. (The verdict was only pronounced after proceedings *in camera.*) Then again, the barbaric measures taken
to reduce the population of Leningrad gave clear proof of a
determination to root out some inimical trend, to nip in the bud
some latent state of feeling after the failure to discover a real
culprit. Three years later, Stalin, "the adored," was to astonish
the world by proclaiming to all and sundry that the principal
assassin was none other than Yagoda, his closest colleague, the
Chief of the G.P.U. in person, the man whom he had promoted
to be Commissar for the Interior, the "sword-bearer" of the
regime.

But during the interval "the greatest man of our planet," as
he is pleased to hear himself called, had brought accusations

against too many of his own followers hitherto above suspicion, and had piled up indictments of too many contradictory wrongs, too many untenable imputations and demonstrably impossible crimes. His assertions were made through the agency of a prosecutor under his orders and of menial judges: they were confirmed by defendants who were at once too unanimous and too simple-minded to be honest, too eager to blacken rather than to clear their own reputations, and who could only strengthen the general incredulity towards the official version. Under such totalitarian conditions one certainly cannot trust the word of an autocrat so absolute, so lacking in moral sense, so contemptuous of the truth that a single mysterious assassination can serve him for many years as justification for the massacre of his companions in arms. For from the time of the Kirov murder, it is clear that he deliberately—in cold blood and after minute preparation—undertook the annihilation of many generations of Bolsheviks and disclosed his firm determination henceforward to leave nothing to chance. The chronology of the period is very revealing. Owing to the dull daily round of business there is often no time to assess the value of incidents, which pass unnoticed; but they are later thrown into relief, and assume, perhaps, their full significance. Stains of blood become letters of fire, and dark places are illuminated by a sinister glow.

2

STALIN, as his biography proves, has never been farseeing, except on the vulgar plane of personal relationship when the preservation of his power was at stake. In this respect the comparison of his writings and his speeches, both with one another and with his actions, is conclusive. Even when he exiled Trotsky, he did not in any way envisage his future, when, as an obsessed despot, his constant preoccupation would be to crush the indomitable adversary he himself had placed beyond the power of his clutches. Since Lenin's death he has been compelled to adopt a day-to-day policy by borrowing from right and left. He speculated on the power of a State system at the mercy of his will, by forcing fresh horrors or abrupt changes of front on the people sunk in poverty and ignorance, terror-stricken, stupefied and apathetic. A so-called soviet system was created by Lenin and Trotsky, in which, under the effective dictatorship of the Communist Party, the soviets had only a nominal existence, and which very rapidly degenerated into the omnipotence of an oligarchy. This system intercepted, destroyed, and repressed all initiative or complaints from below, through six intermediary bodies interposed between the top and the bottom, and it still permits Stalin to govern without foresight.

The following is the unimpeachable testimony of the American communist worker, Andrew Smith, after his return from Russia disillusioned in Bolshevism: "When Kirov was killed, the workers of the Electrozavod (the factory in which the witness worked in Moscow) beamed with joy. They hoped that Stalin would meet the same fate. And yet they unanimously voted for the Bolshevik resolutions . . ." With the power of life and death over Soviet subjects and, furthermore, with the monopoly of the press which he uses to deceive others when he is not deceiving himself, Stalin can easily obtain such results. But the tragedy of Smolny, the first terrorist reply to his policy of terror, gave him food for thought. He felt the warning bullet whistle past and, after burying Kirov, he prepared at one and the same time supplementary precautions, preventive measures and terrible reprisals.

He was sufficiently well informed of the state of public feeling by the *svodki* (summarised reports) of innumerable police agents, not to cherish illusions as to the sentiments he inspired, even in the most vehement of his professional apologists. He could not in any sense have been the dupe of the adulation and the extravagant praise bestowed upon him by his known enemies, with rage in their hearts, vying with treacherous friends whose fortunes were linked with his, but who were ready to betray him at the first favourable opportunity. He knew that he was hated on all sides, that his downfall was prayed for, that a thousand deaths were wished upon him and he was aware of the current stories which expressed the secret opinion of the masses. The whole terrorised population spoke aloud the opposite of what was in the minds of all, daily glorifying the "country's best son," the "master of wisdom," the "great mechanic of the locomotive of the revolution, Comrade Stalin." He could never reconcile the Bolsheviks of the "Old Guard," nor those of the younger generation, who despised and cursed him while paying him the obligatory daily homage. He had nothing to fear from the communist veterans nor their unworthy successors—the former relegated to honorary posts, the latter to ordinary jobs. His uncompromising adversaries were in prison, in isolation cells or in exile; those who had "given in"—the "capitulators"—were humiliated, outcast, discredited, or had already exhausted themselves in sterile historical exegeses and confessed themselves incapable of conscientious or energetic attack. But it was not without fear that he saw growing up a young, censorious generation, which had still to make a name for itself, but had already asserted itself by the resounding action at Leningrad, despite the numerous pitiless purges carried out by the G.P.U., in the Universities as well as in the factories.

His dictatorial prefect at Leningrad, Zhdanov, Kirov's successor, one day went so far as to let slip a significant admission: "Why should our youth learn about Jeliabov, Ryssakov, Perovskaya, any more than about the heroes who sprang from the Bolshevik Party?" In other words, Kirov's murderer, compared to the legendary *narodovoltsy*, of glorious memory in the tradition common to all socialist schools, is thus justified by those who identify themselves with oppressors. In the eyes of Stalin, however, the danger began to take concrete form. The widespread information of the police *svodki* combined to attract his attention, to awaken his uneasiness and to stimulate his vigilance. It was then, no doubt, that two complementary designs were born in his mind and began to assume shape. After careful consideration of the feelings of the country and of the circumstances, he could make use of the classical expedients of throwing out ballast and tightening the screw, thus inaugurating at one and the same time, a vast diversion and an atrocious repression.

The great diversion was to be the "genial project" of the Constitution of the "genial leader," announcing to the peoples of the U.S.S.R. all the desirable liberties—but always in the future: liberty of speech, of the press and of worship, with equal universal suffrage, direct and secret; the right of assembly, of coalition and of demonstration; the inviolability of correspondence and of the home; the security of the person. Thus Stalin discovered in 1935 what has long existed and been more or less carried into effect in Europe and America. This opening of an era of democratic felicity was indeed unique, for apparently no demand had preceded it, since Soviet society was reputed to enjoy perfect democracy and unmixed happiness in the "socialist fatherland." But after the warning of Leningrad and the executions that followed it, Stalin, ever anxious to increase the well-being of his subjects, determined to bestow out of the generosity of his soul, and in spite of everything and everyone, a new Constitution, "the most democratic in the world," which had been the exact definition of the previous Constitution. Thus, says the press under his orders, he replies to Hitler, he strikes "a blow at the heart of fascism," he shows an astonished universe the ideal regime—on paper—in contrast to fascist Italy, and above all, to national-socialist Germany.

Now was not this democracy of the future supposed to exist in its fulness and entirety at that very time? And if it was a question of replying to Hitler, would not the promised democracy owe its origin to him rather than to Stalin? Objections, which no one in the U.S.S.R. was allowed to formulate under pain of death, were of little importance to the "Father of the peoples." Thus Stalin, even before Zhdanov and in emulation of Lenin, who justified the insurrection of Kronstadt by hastening to decree the N.E.P., seemed to justify Kirov's assassination by hastening to decide on constitutional reform. (It should be noted that the sailors of Kronstadt were butchered for having demanded, among other things, respect for the Soviet Constitution.) In January 1935, immediately after the condemnation of the 97 Left Communists known as "Zinovievists," who were charged only, and *in camera*, with vague moral responsibility for the Kirov murder, Stalin secured in the Central Committee of the Party the adoption of his first draft, which Molotov unexpectedly brought to the Seventh Congress of the Soviets, then in session, to the utter stupefaction of everyone. There followed the inevitable explosion of gratitude and love addressed to "our father" Stalin. At the same Congress, Molotov proclaimed: "The Russia of the N.E.P. has become Socialist Russia." The Stalinist Constitution was to consecrate the advent of the first classless society.

The great repression was undertaken in 1935 by Stalin, the "engineer of souls," as he styles some of his fellows. It went hand in hand with democratic, or to use the fashionable word of the period, "humanist" professions of faith. It was aimed especially at all communists suspected of still taking seriously the least vestige of original Bolshevism. It also included the last survivors of the old socialist and reformist groups of parties still attached to the memory of traditional ideals. It was inaugurated directly after the Kirov murder and it formed an extension of the permanent civil war waged by the G.P.U. on the supposedly intractable population, who were, in reality, perfectly submissive, but had been provoked by insupportable conditions of life and work and tormented by an exacting, incapable and brutal bureaucracy.

The mass deportations from Leningrad corresponded to analogous measures in all the Russias. There was a "clean-up" of the so-called soviet institutions and above all of the communist organisations. In conjunction with the G.P.U., Control Commissions everywhere made ceaseless investigations, tracked down heresy and hunted down heretics. A formal purge of the Party had taken place in 1934, and another followed in 1935, under the pretext of "the verification of political identification papers." This latter purge was barely over, when it was followed by a third in 1936 "at the time of the renewal of the papers." Each one ended in some 300,000 expulsions, about a million in three years, or one third of the total effectives, estimated at almost three million in 1934 (to be precise: 1,872,000 plus 935,000 probationers). A large number of those expelled since

1935 were hounded down by virtue of Article 168 of the Code, for abuse of confidence, and severe punishments were secretly imposed; very often entire families, wholly innocent, suffered the same fate; the latest exiles to Siberia and elsewhere are counted by hundreds of thousands. Thousands of foreign communists who had come from Germany, Austria, Italy, Hungary, Czechoslovakia, Poland, to seek refuge in the "socialist fatherland" were in their turn run to earth by the G.P.U., and soon joined the others in the concentration camps and convict prisons. All this did not prevent Stalin from saying to the American journalist, Roy W. Howard: "According to our Constitution, political émigrés have the right to reside in our territory. We grant them the right of asylum, just as the United States grants it to political émigrés." An interpretation of the right of asylum which gives an idea of the prospects to be opened up by the future Constitution.

Over and above the work, great or small, carried out by his multitudinous police on general instructions, the "giant of thought," as his encomiasts call him, settles many special cases and operates himself in this, his own, sphere. Stalin has a special method, already familiar, of ensuring his preservation of power: ceaselessly he alters, one by one, the camarilla which surrounds him, by substituting for worn-out servants new men eager to get on; in order to govern, he tirelessly appoints, replaces and alters his staff. With his frequent purges, his repeated rearrangements of the staff of every rank in the various spheres of public activity, he obviously never ceases to disorganise the personnel and to paralyse work; such confusion causes incalculable loss, especially in the national economy; in the Soviet administration the result is chronic chaos through lack of continuity, responsibility and general competence. But the revolutionaries of yesterday offend the great Conservative of today, and Lenin's party is henceforth a dead weight for him, and often an intolerable obstacle. He first defeated Trotsky in the name of the "Old Guard," depository of sacred principles, of sacrosanct routine. He drew all possible profit from it to maintain himself at the summit of the bureaucratic pyramid, and won for himself a semblance of prestige from a section of the untutored youth. Now he needed men with no political past whom he could teach in his own way and who would constitute a more stable clientèle, bound to his personal destiny. As a contemporary Russian writer, who is also a good psychologist, expresses it: "He does not like men with a stainless past"; for the deficiencies of his henchmen give him a hold on their souls. The instruments of his domination over his direct auxiliaries are at once and in turn the rifle and the dossier, the prison cell and the police chit. He holds his Politbureau and his Central Committee not only by the constant threat of the death sentence and a perpetual surveillance, but by his knowledge of the misfortunes, the corruption and the short-comings of their private lives; at need, he invents them; he lays snares for the imprudent by means of his double-crossing agents; he corrupts, demoralises, incites and provokes in order to enrich his filing cabinets and his revolting arsenal. When a henchman hesitates before an impossible task, Stalin can compel him by fear of dishonour or break him without resistance. If he judges it necessary to sacrifice a gifted individual but one too tired or too unmanageable, he supplants him by pushing forward either a "man with no political past" or someone little worthy of commendation, and thereafter no consideration holds him back. It is when we know this, that we can truly appreciate his memorable words, spoken at the height of the terror: "You must reach the understanding that of all the precious assets existing in the world, the most precious and decisive are the cadres."

3

In an atmosphere of tense emotion, still heavy with the prolonged vengeance of Kirov's murder, the concert of dithyrambic praise rose to a crescendo in honour of "our sun" (sic), broken by vague threats addressed to the invisible "enemies of the people." But the enthusiasm to order concealed undecipherable political realities. In February-March 1935, after the sudden death of Kuibyshev,—to all appearance a natural one, for the

Vice-President of the Council of Commissars was addicted to drink,—Stalin proceeded to enact one of those administrative shuffles of which he alone has the secret. An official "with no political past," although already fourth secretary of the Central Committee for barely a month, Nicholas Yezhov became President of the Control Commission of the Party in place of L. Kaganovich, appointed Commissar of Transport in which post he succeeded Andreyev, the latter replacing Yezhov at the Secretariat. The rearrangement of personnel interested no one outside the Dictator's immediate circle. But Yenukidze, for 15 years the immovable secretary of the Executive Committee of the Soviets of the U.S.S.R., was liberated from his duties, since the Soviet Executive of Transcaucasia desired to have him as its president. The Attorney-General, Akulov, replaced him, and Vyshinsky, Assistant Attorney, became Attorney-General. Experienced observers were in no doubt; Yenukidze was lost, his so-called liberation preceding his disgrace; in exchanging the post of secretary at Moscow for the title of president at Tiflis, he took the path to the cemetery. In fact, three months later he was dismissed for degeneracy, laxity of morals, and frivolity; some days later he was expelled from the Party, that is to say, he was handed over to the G.P.U. But no one could flatter himself that he had grasped at the time the precise significance of the decrees relating to Yezhov and to Vyshinsky. In these appointments, however, was expressed the premeditation of the wisest of the wise.

At this time Yezhov was a "man with no political past," but not without a career. Little is known of him, except that he was the best incarnation of Stalin's bureaucratic school. A former soldier in the Red Army, promoted Military Commissar, he had climbed all the rungs of the Bolshevik hierarchy; as secretary of committees of increasing importance up to the Central Committee, he had directed for four years one of the essential services of the Party, that of the cadres. Having reached this stage, he knew the personnel, and was thoroughly conversant with his profession of "engineer of souls." Stalin must have noticed him early, inculcated in him his own methods and assured him so rapid a promotion. As president of the Control Commission, a sort of G.P.U. reserved for communists, he was soon to justify his master's confidence.

The Control Commission had ceased to be the commission of former years. In 1934, Stalin "liquidated" the old Commission, a body of 187 members consisting of old militants with a reputable past; at the same time he liquidated also the Workers' and Peasants' Inspection. For these he substituted two smaller commissions, the first of 61 members for the Party, the second of 70 for the Soviets, both for the most part composed of new members. By this reshuffle he rid himself of some 150 undesirable veterans. Not that they would have dared to permit themselves the least opposition, overt or covert; they realised too late the mistake they had made ten years earlier in supporting their future grave-digger in his struggle with an imaginary Trotskyism; but their contempt for Stalin equalled the hatred with which he repaid them. It was against them and their generation that he gave proof of his enmity, at the same time settling a personal account, when he transferred Yenukidze, in order the better to get rid of him. But he did not stop there. In May 1935, he suppressed the Society of Old Bolsheviks, pre-eminently the Old Guard, which silently irritated him. The following month he dissolved the Association of Former Political Prisoners, where a vestige of free speech still existed in the stifled tones of confidential intercourse. In February 1936, he finally liquidated the Communist Academy, also composed of veterans, and for similar reasons. No one guessed then at what goal the man, whom Radek called the great architect of socialism, was aiming.

In liquidating these institutions, considered in his circle as the most venerable, Stalin freed himself of many scruples and visibly cleared the ground for liquidating much else. In any case he renounced a heritage of which he had once asserted that he was the faithful guardian. That he wished to break with Lenin's party was implied in May 1935, in a toast to the Red Army, in which he effaced the customary distinction between the Party and the rest of the world: "To the health of all Bolsheviks, members of the Party and those outside the Party. Yes, those outside the Party. Those who belong to the Party form only a minority. Those outside the Party form the majority. But among those outside the Party, are there not real Bolsheviks?" This was the repudiation of the notion of the Party "above everything," in spite of a somewhat shabby explanation: ". . . They have not joined the Party, either because they have not had the time, or because they hold the Party in such high esteem, they see in it such a sanctuary, that they wish to prepare themselves further before entering it. . . ." Two days later he was not afraid to declare in a speech to the Military Academy: ". . . We speak too much of the merits of the leaders, of the merits of the directors. To them are attributed all, or almost all, our achievements. That, clearly, is incorrect and false." Such remarks, issuing from such a mouth, do not appear credible. They must be interpreted as a prohibition of the praising of more than one man; we shall see the proof of this later. When all the Russias, under the Stalino-Chekist knout, say the opposite of what they mean, Stalin owes it to himself to practise what he preaches. On the morrow of this invitation to lower the tone of the eulogies of the leaders, this is how Bukharin, partially restored to favour, observed instructions under pain of final disgrace, the equivalent of death: "We all wish to touch him, to feel the force of that powerful mind, of that will which radiates in every direction, of that astonishing and beloved man. Human waves carry him along. What a demonstration of unity! What an unforgettable scene of indestructible union!" But all this was about Stalin. Enough can never be said of the "genial pilot."

The Stalinist liquidation of the old Bolshevism and the old dignitaries, to which Yezhov, aided by Yagoda, the famous "sword-bearer," especially devoted his attention, did not forestall the evil, but the very relative good, which the U.S.S.R. might still expect from the twilight of a socialist tradition. It was in strict correlation with the abandonment of a cumbersome and inharmonious past, where the best of the now superannuated intentions mingled with the worst of the recent innovations.

The martyred country would not have suffered so greatly if the recrudescence of counter-revolutionary terror had not fallen on a population divorced from politics, if the reaction had seemed frank, logical, conscientious, with all its consequences, instead of being carried out by new tactical zigzags, by empirical experiments and implicit, but none the less cynical, disavowals. It would have been too much to expect Stalin openly to dispense with theories condemned by facts and by history. However, among the reforms introduced during this period under the irresistible pressure of circumstances, both in the sphere of economics and in that of social customs, there are some which register decisive failures, in the absence of spiritual and political progress. This is the revenge of natural laws, the protest of the vital forces of every society, against an inhuman and useless "experiment."

In contrast to Lenin, who called an error an error, a defeat a defeat, who always shouldered the responsibility for his actions and was able to revise invalid and worn-out notions, Stalin's system is to lay the blame upon his subordinates, whom he makes his expiatory victims in order to appear infallible. He alternates between violence and promises, in order to conceal his failures, and issues bulletins of victory at each decision to sound a retreat. Under the goad of imperative and changing necessities, and since he lacks the power of comprehensive vision as well as of generalisation, he must have recourse to palliatives, to half-measures, to empirical correctives, sometimes to a complete volte-face in order to rebuild from the ruins, where the day before he claimed he would make a clean sweep. Besides, it is his habit to take away with the left hand, on the first propitious occasion, what he is compelled to grant with the right. One can understand that the people, satisfied with the return to many normal customs, but always oppressed and exploited, are not in the least grateful to him for the slight palliatives of their misery, and regard them merely as inadequate instalments on their just due. But since the great retreat—whether provisional or definitive—is a startling reality extending all along the line, except in the matter of internal policy where the democratic concessions remain purely on the surface, it is important to follow the stages which promised immediate or future repercussions. Alexander Herzen has said of Tsarist Russia: "The most impossible things are achieved among us with incredible speed; changes, which in their importance are equivalent to revolutions, are carried out without being noticed in Europe." In addition to the terrific agrarian collectivisation which has overthrown the Russian peasantry and the ancestral mode of cultivation, Stalin's counter-revolution verifies the full significance of this reflection three quarters of a century later.

4

THE year 1935 had begun with the withdrawal of the bread cards, the first step toward the withdrawal of the other food cards in September. This implied the unification of prices and consequently the end of rationing and of unceasing regulation. An impulse was then given to the partial restoration of trade and of free markets. A year later the Torgsin, shops which sold in exchange for the precious metals or for foreign currency, were closed down, and simultaneously the rouble was stabilised, sanctioning officially a devaluation of 77.5 per cent. This marked the end of the fictitious parity of the rouble, of the boasts about "Soviet money, the most stable in the world"; it was the collapse of the theory and practice of State distribution substituted for supply and demand. The Bolsheviks have thus failed, after as before the N.E.P., in their attempts to create an economy without commodities and without money, in which the State plan would regulate the exchange of products, and money would have only a nominal value. The high rate of the new rouble at this period was still artificial, for the real depreciation appeared in the enormous divergence between domestic prices and those in the world market. But there was a clear tendency toward a more healthy fiduciary circulation of the classical type, based upon bullion reserves and better adjusted to the volume of trade. The Bolsheviks, wrote T. G. Masaryk in his *Mémoires*, "sought for and found things which had long existed and were well known"; there is hardly any sphere "in which the alphabet will not be rediscovered." This observation is particularly applicable to Stalin and his discoveries in almost every direction.

In agriculture, the new statute of the *kolkhoz* confirmed and accentuated in 1935 Stalin's previous retreat if not before the peasants at least in face of the famine. Henceforth the inhabitants of the *kolkhoz* would have the right, over and above their *isba*, to a small individual or family holding of half a hectare on an average, sometimes of one hectare, and to the personal possession of livestock: a cow, two young horned animals, two sows and their farrow, ten she-goats or ewes, rabbits, poultry, and twenty beehives. In the pasture lands, two or three cows and ten to twenty-five ewes, and even eight to ten cows and a hundred to a hundred and fifty sheep according to the locality. The reopening of the markets, the permission granted to the collective farmers to sell their surplus there, the remission of the debts owed by the *kolkhoz* to the State, the definite delimitation of their territory—these various measures, and others of fuller detail, to some extent relieved the population of the countryside. Thanks to them the threatened food-supply was ensured through private initiative. This was the flagrant defeat of the integral collectivisation predicted to the blare of trumpets at the time of Stalin's "dizziness" in 1930, and the failure of collectivisation imposed by the violence of the Party. Meantime, private cultivation developed by sheer force of circumstances.

A stronger reaction still, alternately ridiculous or dishonest, appeared in the changed attitude toward the new prejudices, the external appearance of austerity, the very style of Soviet life. Stalin authorised and decreed pell-mell one after the other, high spirits, obligatory love, family happiness, paternal duty, filial respect, feminine coquetry, masculine elegance, regulated pleasure and gaiety to order, stereotyped laughter, poetry and humanism, rouge and finery, neckties and detachable collars. After providing dear bread that was available at last without cards, he bestowed or conceded games and spectacles, song and dance, crackers and Bengal lights. Daily he "rediscovered the alphabet." After an initial Thermidor, prolonged by intermi-

nable serialisation, there followed, like an avalanche, a very banal
Directory. There were discussions about what Karl Marx wore
round his neck, hidden by his beard, but the sailor-knot of
Lenin was the dénouement of the controversy. Fashion maga-
zines, formerly forbidden as subversive, were imported or
printed; invitations were extended to Parisian dress-makers;
Comrade Molotova interested herself in perfumes, lotions and
creams. After Leninism with nitric acid, Stalinism with rose-
water and Socialism with eau de Cologne. Manicurists were
installed in the factories—the only factories in the world where
there existed prisons and guard rooms. The reform of the Civil
Code put barriers in the way of divorce, sanctioned paternity
investigations, condemned abortion, restored the family to
honour. The State encouraged the birth-rate by minute grants,
beginning with the . . . *seventh child!* Regular marriages were
encouraged, as also conjugal fidelity, love of the fatherland and
desire for offspring, thrift, and seven percent interest. Love
was no longer a bourgeois conception, nor jealousy a proprie-
tary sentiment. But the parvenu militants deserted their working-class wives, hardened in the struggle, and married young
actresses, in the absence of daughters of bourgeois or aristocrat.
The capitalists, who were anathema only shortly before, were
indiscriminately imitated; people vied with one another in
aping the "rotten West," especially its faults, which they copied
to excess. At the Kremlin—banquets, receptions and cham-
pagne. The Party organised balls, feasts, festivals, and carnivals.
They put flowers on the balconies, but they did not put them
on the tombs of the millions of victims. One fine day Stalin
visited Tiflis and spent a few minutes with his mother, forgotten for years, thus illustrating that very new truth that children must honour their parents. He had himself photographed
with his children and with other children. He was the centre of
admiration, he was extolled, he was imitated. No one might so
much as mention the millions of abandoned orphans. In the
midst of this "command performance," a decree extended the
application of the death penalty for delinquents and criminals
as from the age of twelve.

The mass of the population might stand aloof from such anachronistic and pretentious rejoicings, but a large part of the youth took delight in abandoning themselves to these novelties. The authorities sought for and found "things which had long existed and were well known": for the young who were disillusioned with the machine age, saturated with the black broth of theories, worn out with politics, theses and slogans. They provided sport in all its forms, parachutism, gliding, arctic explorations, expeditions to Central Asia. It goes without saying that everything seemed good to young and old which served as an escape, or outlet, or diversion; everything which took them further from the centres where they were in constant terror of the G.P.U., the Party and military service. The press gave first place to the heroes of the North Pole, to aeronautical exploits, to every kind of prowess. At the expense of the hard-working country, Stalin distributed dolls to some, to others watches, not to mention roubles, accordions, phonographs—here to clever children, there to deserving workmen, and most often to time-serving officials.

He hastened to register the results of this "offensive on the cultural front," to use the Bolshevik jargon, by declaring: "Life has become better, comrades. Life has become more joyful." As a result, the ten thousand newspapers of the U.S.S.R., through a hundred thousand slavish pens, daily paraphrased the profound speech of the "thrice great master" on the *happy life*. The millions of members of the Party and the Communist Youth vied with one another in repeating it, conjugating it, declining it. Some days after this pronouncement, Stalin appointed Yagoda, his closest colleague, Commissar-General for National Safety. Who knew what was being prepared? As it was, the year 1935 ended with an apparent miracle: a Christmas Tree, baptised for the occasion, the New Year Tree. Only holly and other accessories were lacking to obtain the full value of the permission, but everyone declared that they would have them ready for next year.

Pursuing his alphabetical discoveries, Stalin succeeded in conceiving an original method for increasing the output of work:

it consisted in paying the producers in proportion to their production. Piece-work wages were reintroduced: they were the object of hate under the capitalist regime, yet excellent under the emblem of the hammer and sickle. But the system of maximum payments limited the earnings of the best workmen, who lacked every inducement to apply themselves to their work. There was no personal interest, in the absence of adequate wages and available goods, and no higher, collective stimulus, since social solidarity was non-existent under the yoke of a hateful bureaucracy. Besides, the "norms" or minima of production were very low in comparison with the results obtained in every other country, because of the unskilled labour and the low level of life. In 1935, the withdrawal of the system of cards, rations and reserved shops changed the conditions of supply; remuneration in proportion to work modified the behaviour of the workers. "Norms" that remained too low had to be raised. They sought for and found "things which had long existed and were well known" elsewhere—under the names of Taylorism and the sweating system—but only too well known already in the U.S.S.R. as "socialist emulation" and "shock labour." Once more rationalisation, economy of movement, and division of labour were rediscovered. The result was *stakhanovism*, so called after the miner, Stakhanov, who first put into practice the new gospel under special conditions. The *udarniki* (shock volunteers) became stakhanovists, but were paid in proportion to their labour, with the result that wages could now vary from the normal to ten times the normal rate. To accelerate the tempo, to stimulate the champions and break records, all the honours and advantages were conferred on the foreman, thus defrauding his comrades by a strange combination of injustice and imposture. Various methods of deception and quackery were employed, in order to increase the propaganda. Stalin thought he could deceive all Russia and the whole world by trying to make it believe that the work of a gang of ten to twelve men on an average was that of a single record breaker. He has only succeeded in dividing the working class more profoundly against itself, in aggravating the social differentiation by the excessive inequality of wages, in obtaining some intensification of work and the raising of the norms. But a quantitative increase of production was only achieved to the detriment of the quality of the products, at the cost of a disastrous increase in waste, in a heavy wear and tear of machinery, and of a premature exhaustion of man-power. If by this means some thousands of future foremen and managers have sprung from the ranks to become to some degree privileged, the selection could have been accomplished more soundly and beneficially and with less ostentation. The numerous assassinations of stakhanovists by their companions in bondage, the antagonisms in the factories and workshops, which were already reported in the days of the *udarniki*, testified to a state of mind among the workers quite other than the enthusiasm prescribed by "our great beloved hero," Stalin. In short, stakhanovism served only to introduce into the so-called "socialist fatherland," in an aggravated form, methods in use in capitalist countries where the communists ceaselessly demand their abolition. To attain such an end it was more than useless to cause the shedding of so much blood and the flowing of so many tears.

5

ONE of the most remarkable phenomena of the period, the discovery of a Fatherland in the U.S.S.R., some time after the triumph of national-socialism in Germany, was the result of a great miscalculation of Stalin. He hoped at first to come to an agreement with Hitler, as he had formerly done with Mussolini, in spite of the verbal differences in doctrine, and on the basis of the similarity in method between parties of the mailed fist. Since the reception of the Duce at the Soviet Embassy in Rome, on the morrow of the murder of Matteotti, and later, under the pretext of courtesy, the dispatch of congratulations to Mussolini by Rykov after his stay at Sorrento, where Gorky spent most of his time, the relations between the U.S.S.R. and Italy became increasingly intimate and cordial. Mussolini did not conceal a discreet admiration for Lenin, and the recipro-

cal borrowings increased between the two totalitarian regimes,
hand in hand with the progress of their economic relations. In
1933, the year of Hitler's advent to power, an Italo-Soviet
commercial agreement was concluded in May, followed in
September by a pact of friendship, non-aggression and neutrality. A Soviet squadron anchored in October off Naples, and the
following year an Italian military delegation proceeded to
Moscow. Russia even placed orders for warships in Italy. Cordial
telegrams from Litvinov testify for posterity to this mutual
understanding. . . . Mussolini flattered himself that he had established a model entente with the Bolsheviks, suppressing communism at home whilst negotiating advantageously with the
so-called Soviet State. Thus Stalin thought that he would
conclude a similar pact with Hitler, on the ruins of the communist movement in Germany. The renewal of the agreement
of Rapallo confirmed him in this hope, as did the new credit
facilities granted to the U.S.S.R. by German industry. But he
had to sing a different tune when the Third Reich assumed an
attitude of determined hostility toward the Bolshevism of the
Russo-Soviet State as towards export communism. Hitler's intuition finally prevailed over the contrary view; a view fairly widespread both in the Reichswehr and in diplomatic circles, which
opposed to a new *Drang nach Oesten* the Bismarckian conception
of an alliance with Russia. In vain the Caucasian, D. Kandelaki,
appointed as commercial envoy to Berlin with a secret mission
from Stalin, multiplied advances, invitations and soundings. The
Fuehrer turned a deaf ear and persevered in his attack on Russia
through the Communist International. In the end the disappointed Stalin had no choice but to turn toward France and
England, toward the League of Nations, to play a different game,
and to awaken in the peoples of the U.S.S.R. the consciousness
of patriotic duty and of the fascist danger.

The official theme of patriotism then entered into the daily
propaganda. The mechanical insistence with which it was
emphasised indicated a rather artificial creation, conceived as a
substitute for revolutionary ideology in distress. *Pravda* even
published an editorial entitled *Sacred Love of the Fatherland*,

which bore not the slightest resemblance to the vocabulary of two days before. As usual, the Bolsheviks passed from one extreme to the other, from the most elementary internationalism to the least respectable type of patriotism. There already existed, in contempt of cherished equalitarian principles, a whole series of decorations: the Orders of Lenin, of the Red Star, of the Red Flag, of the Red Flag of Work. Stalin further devised the Order of the Heroes of the Union, and the Badge of Honour. To these were added the distinctions of Artist of Merit, National Artist, and Scholar of Merit. Promotion to honours succeeded each other in long columns in the newspapers. Those decorated benefited by material advantages in money and in kind, which increased the privileges of the new dominant class, the profiteers of the Stalinist manna. In the Army the former hierarchy of ranks and stripes was reestablished, including at the same time the rank of marshal, suppressed under Tsarism after Kutuzov. Voroshilov, Tukhachevsky, Yegorov, Budyonny, and Blücher were promoted marshals, not for their services in war, but for the political support which they brought to Stalin. All that was formerly adored, was burnt; all that was formerly burnt, was adored. Distinctive uniforms and insignia granted to the People's Commissariat of the Interior, which some persist in calling the G.P.U., rewarded leaders and agents, whom some persist in calling Chekists, and assimilated them into the military hierarchy. With the absence of restraint, which characterises them, the Bolsheviks did not fail to carry to excess the reaction against their former sobriety of dress. They flaunted shining insignia, stripes and braid. The most striking revenge of the Imperial past was perhaps the resurrection of the Cossack corps, abolished by the revolution and reestablished by Stalin in several cavalry divisions with all their traditions and their ornamental equipment, not even forgetting the *nagaïka*, so familiar to workers on strike and mujiks in revolt. It seems that in their very renunciation, the Bolsheviks of the decadence experienced a sort of morbid satisfaction which, in spite of themselves, urged them to eloquent demonstration.

This neo-Bolshevik neo-patriotism reverberated with great

noise in the educational sphere, where, perhaps more obviously than in others, the bankruptcy of the regime was already complete. All the pedagogic innovations of the revolution were annulled and old ideas restored. The statute of the "Single School of Labour" provided free school materials and a free meal; the suppression of home-work, of text books, of diplomas; the repudiation of the so-called bourgeois survivals; the administration by a "school collective" and a "school soviet"; the substitution of "combinations" (subjects for combined study) in place of classical subjects. Later there was compulsory manual labour, pseudo-polytechnic education and student-brigades. Nothing is left of all this but ruins. The nonsense of Lunacharsky, the dogmatic teachings of Pokrovsky, the laborious efforts of Krupskaya were dismissed as Trotskyism. A series of decrees reestablished the broken traditions and even the routine, the authority of directors and teachers, rules and regulations, classes and time-tables, punishments and rewards, marks and examinations, certificates and diplomas, university grades and titles. The Bolsheviks rediscovered History and Geography, as well as the Alphabet. As usual, they exaggerated the new orientation and even went so far as to bestow a uniform on the pupils of the higher institutions, then on the scholars of all the Russias; only the shortage of cloth delayed the application of this measure. Finally, revising from top to bottom the State ideology prescribed for the whole population, young and old alike, they put on the index the greater part of the historical works they had edited, refused to admit the ideas and interpretations then in force, and, revising the history of Russia as they had before revised all the histories of the Party, they strove to rehabilitate the national glories and then to inculcate in the people a nationalist mentality suited to the occasion.

With the zeal and ardour of converts, they have, since 1935, rediscovered, recognised and acclaimed, one after the other, the great men of the past, authentic or debateable, going back beyond Muscovite Russia to the period of the Teuton and Mongol invasions: Saint Alexander Nevsky, vanquisher of the Sword-Bearers; the Ataman Ermak, conqueror of Siberia; the butcher

Minin and Prince Pojorsky, gallant adversaries of the Poles; Field-Marshals Suvorov and Kutuzov. The conversion to Christianity, after baptism, of Russia in the Kiev period, becomes "a positive stage in the history of the Russian people." Not less "positive" is the role of the great Prince Ivan Kalita, who gathered together the Muscovite nation; of Ivan the Great, liberator of the Russian soil; of Ivan the Terrible, that precursor of Stalinist humanism; of Peter the Great, that worthy Bolshevik before the literature of Bolshevism. The late Pokrovsky, appointed head of the chapel of "Marxist historians," and his living disciples are discredited from one day to the next for having belittled, underestimated, and falsified the history of their mother country; not so long ago the authors who broke away so very little from the rut of that coterie were punished as heretics. The roles are reversed; exiled historians return to favour and their subservient persecutors will soon be persecuted in their turn. S. Platonov, cruelly treated, died in exile, but E. Tarlé, recalled from Turkestan, takes the rank of official historian, while the Marxist historians and other red professors are, as a beginning, thrown out of employment; and always in the name of the same idols, Marx and Lenin. This is what is called, in Bolshevik terminology, "taking the offensive on the historical front."

Once a start was made, the *Song of the Company of Igor*, an epic poem of the 12th century was loudly acclaimed; the anniversary of Lomonossov, Russian writer and universal scholar of his age, was overwhelmingly celebrated; the centenary of Pushkin, true literary ancestor of Stalin, was observed with the greatest ceremony. . . . When the prosaic bard Demian Biedny, librettist in his spare time, held up to ridicule the *bogatyrs*, the valiant knights of legend, persuaded that he would thereby enrich the orthodoxy of strict observance, his play earned for him the wrath of the Kremlin, and carried in its wake misfortune and loss of position for the producer, A. Taïrov, founder and director of the Kamerny theatre, who had previously been in high favour. This was the opportunity for the recognised critics to extol the heroes of the old *bylins*, the marvellous songs or tales of the spoken epic poetry of the Middle Ages: the peasant Ilia Murometz, the merchant Sadko, the giant Sviatogor. Nationalism became the most jingoistic patriotism, with the publication of the new "sterilised" text-books, among others the *Short Course of History* by Shestakov, drawn up by a brigade controlled by a State Commission, in which figured Bukharin, Radek, Bubnov, Zatonsky, F. Khodjayev, with Stalin as patron. In this nothing can be found save Russian victories throughout the ages.

The hasty resurrection of patriotism corresponded directly to considerations of foreign policy. Stalin then feared a military alliance between Germany and Japan, he sought alliances in Europe and in Asia, he attempted to give Russia spiritual reasons for fighting in case of war; one by one he sacrificed the principles and dogmas to which he owed his power, with the sole object of preserving it. For him everything is a question of the relation of forces. The official Bolshevik vainglory conceals an intrinsic weakness, manifest in every action taken in the international arena.

Stalin and his Party had defined pacifism as a Utopia, as imposture, deception or treason; later he proclaimed himself a pacifist. He had branded the League of Nations as a League of Brigands; he joined it without shame. He had anathematised the Versailles Treaty; he became the champion of the *status quo*. He had denounced France as the "most aggressive and most militaristic country in the world"; he concluded with France a pact of mutual assistance. He had asserted that fascists and socialists were "twin brothers"; he ordered his foreign mercenaries to come to an understanding with the socialists against the fascists at all costs, while he himself was persecuting the social-democrats in Russia. He had made war on the defenceless Chinese in order to guard the Manchurian railway; he ceded it cheaply to the Japanese as soon as they showed their teeth. When a French Minister of Foreign Affairs, following the example of his English colleague and the first United States Ambassador to the U.S.S.R., paid a visit to Stalin, thus destroying the fiction of the irresponsibility of the General Secretary of the Party for the foreign policy of the State, he hastened to make a declaration of good-will: "M. Stalin fully understands and approves the policy of national defence pursued by France, to maintain its armed forces at the level of security." This was a startling repudiation, insincere as it was, of all the activity of the Communist International since its foundation, and particularly of its French section; but to them he gave orders to suit, and soon his servitors in France, imitating their fellows in Russia, succumbed after many physical turnings and twistings. In the same way as the Chinese Communists, following much the same instructions, made a point of invoking Confucius, so the French Communists rediscovered, recognised and acclaimed Joan of Arc, Rouget de l'Isle, and Napoleon; they appropriated the *Marseillaise,* and passed straight from the most trivial anti-patriotism to the most bellicose chauvinism. For the interests of the U.S.S.R.—i.e., of Stalin—required a France which was preparing with the *union sacrée* for war with Germany.

In an interview with an American journalist, Stalin went still further: the League of Nations was no longer an instrument for imperialist war, according to the traditional Bolshevik terminology, but rather "an advantage for the friends of peace," in other words, the states opposed to Germany; "working for world revolution!" he said, "—we never had such plans and intentions"; if a "different impression" had sometimes been given, it was the "result of a misunderstanding"—and not of a tragic misunderstanding: "No. A comic misunderstanding. Or perhaps rather tragi-comic" for "the export of revolution is nonsense." After this, it remains only to tear to bits the works of Lenin, the books and the pamphlets, the collections of newspapers and reviews, all the publications of the Parties, of the International and of the Communist Youth issued before this supreme denial. Stalin is not ready to say so, but he is the man to do it.

The essentials of this literature are in fact withdrawn from circulation or relegated to the libraries. Apart from some inoffensive scholar or curious person, no one for some length of time will seek to exhume these yellowing sheets and documents, from which, be it said, there emanates a consummate boredom.

The publications of the Marx-Engels Institute were proscribed and destroyed, even before the burnings took place in Germany. The works of Lenin still figure prominently, but they are gradually pushed into the background by those of Stalin; but the public takes care not to read them, unless they are positively commanded to do so; and besides, words have lost their meaning. It would be difficult to find in the U.S.S.R. such important documents, for instance, as the decree constituting the Red Army, which is defined as "the support of the approaching socialist revolution in Europe." The only things that matter are the latest writings of Stalin, the most recent speeches of his spokesmen, the newspaper articles setting forth the perishable truth of the day, up-to-the-minute texts which render seditious and obsolete the orthodox publications of the day before, finally the current sources of information such as the Soviet Encyclopaedias, large and small, which must be thrown on the scrap-heap volume after volume, despite the many expurgations repeated by the many successive censorships, despite the many falsifications introduced in the very course of printing. Every unexpected disgrace, each "turn" implies an automatic censoring and arouses intense panic in the bookshops and libraries. No sooner has an individual high in the Kremlin's favour ceased for mysterious reason to be *persona grata*, than his unfailing loyalty appears to be the double game of a man with a double face. He is immediately denounced as a "Trotskyist" and an "enemy of the people"; the most flattering credentials are transformed into an indictment or disappear from the dictionary, and there is mortal danger in being in possession of one of his works. Who knows what will be done tomorrow, at the next discovery of another letter of the alphabet? Each thinks only of keeping out of an infernal game of which no one knows the rules, in which traps are everywhere dreaded, and chance meetings shunned. Silence itself is dangerous, for it may be interpreted as a silent censure; each must sing his part in the choir of unanimous thanksgiving daily offered to "our wise leader and master."

When Stalin, speaking of the future Constitution, declared to

Roy W. Howard: ". . . We have constructed the Socialist Society . . . not to shackle individual liberty, but that human personality may feel itself really free"; when he predicted "a very keen electoral struggle," for, as he said more precisely, "it is evident that the lists of candidates will be presented not only by the Communist Party but also by social organisations of all sorts outside the Party," everyone knew what to think, but no one knew whither the dictator was bound. The draft Constitution, adopted by the Central Committee in June 1936, provided for elections in the western fashion and a parliament called the Supreme Council; but article 126 reserved the monopoly of politics for the Communist Party alone, and rendered illusory all the promised civil liberties. It was in any case the end of the pretended power of the soviets, even on paper. Twenty years after October, it was the admission of the bankruptcy of the system which the Bolsheviks presented as a superior expression of complete democracy, as a new type of State. Moreover, the new Constitution, formally submitted for the ratification of an extraordinary Congress of the Soviets, consolidated the right of private property within the already established limits and, without limitation, the right of inheritance in direct succession. Once again Stalin has found "things which have long existed and are well known." Nor did he make any innovation when he effaced the last traces of the former soviet Federalism, when he abrogated the rights of nationalities, of which he voluntarily appointed himself protector. The constitutional change consecrated the most extreme form of centralisation, the organs of the so-called federative republics being placed in strict subordination to the central power; this, however, did no more than codify the actual situation and make it more definite. The Transcaucasian Federation, as if creating a precedent, disappeared. Soon the Cyrillic alphabet itself was to be imposed on the national minorities, contrary to the recent respect accorded, in theory, to the regional or national manners and customs. Count can no longer be kept of the recantations and contradictions; they pass almost unnoticed in the collapse of the ideals of October. Under the new Constitution, as under the old, the truth is that above the apparent and fallacious revision of the standard of values, above the expedients and improvisations which take the place of policy and principle, "when all is said and done"—to quote a prophecy even then thirty-five years old—"everything will revolve around a single man who, *ex providentia*, will unite in himself all power."

6

So LONG and impressive a series of recantations and repudiations, inflicted by the Bolsheviks upon themselves, so many insincere retractions and cynical denials, could not but arouse bitter reflections in many minds. Moreover, words remain powerless against facts, especially the facts of economics and technology in which Bolshevism has registered bankruptcy after bankruptcy. It may be presumed that in the choking atmosphere of the "happy life" under the terror, doubt among some, despair among others gave way to subtle allusions, to imperceptible implications. It goes without saying that behind the unanimity on the surface, all thinking heads are full of contradictory reservations when so many changes are taking place. But the G.P.U. exists everywhere to collect the smallest scraps, to magnify them, to falsify them, to note, when required, abstentions or absences, sighs or silences. In the offices of Yagoda and Yezhov reports abound, denunciations accumulate. Around Stalin, who exercises his tyranny from on high, and delegates powers to his favourites, the *boyars* of the bureaucracy are mutually jealous and detest each other; their respective clients lie in wait for every pretext to start unseemly quarrels. The permanent purge takes its course and the rival clans destroy each other; thousands of individuals singled out for persecution by the system of suppression, despite the pledges given by Stalin, succumb in internal intrigues and disappear with their families without leaving a trace. In the assertions of some, the denials of others, and the contradictions of all, the Bolsheviks always remain unanimous.

If one is to believe certain allusions in the Soviet press or the indiscretions of officials, many victims apparently suffer for their former relationship with some nonconformist or other. And in this respect, no one is invulnerable. In truth, the worst pretexts become excellent for the purpose of ruining a rival in the zoological struggle permanently waged for coveted posts between factions and generations, between individuals and shifting groups. Old half-forgotten "affairs" still bear mortal conquences even after a long interval. Such for example is the case of Riutin, once a bitter adversary of Trotsky, who had gone into opposition in his turn and in his own way, author of a "platform" hostile to the policy as well as to the personality of Stalin. With this we may connect, after the event, the case of Syrtsov, president of the Council of Commissars for Russia, who was abruptly dismissed and expelled and is now missing; that of Lominadze, Stalin's confidential man, his agent in China at the time of the Canton insurrection, who went into opposition and into exile, repented and was reinstated; Eismont and Tolmachev, Assistant People's Commissars, disappeared just as mysteriously. There are rumours of madness, suicide, executions. One thing only is certain: Lominadze, following the example of Skrypnik, took his life. In the middle of June 1936, it was learned that Maxim Gorky was dead; this was not unexpected, for the writer was old and ill; his death was followed by the inevitable spectacular funeral. In the middle of July, the secretary of the Party in Armenia, A. Khandjian, one of Stalin's creatures, committed suicide in his turn, and this time the news was, for some incomprehensible reason, divulged. Finally, in the middle of August, while on all sides inexplicable arrests increased in the higher ranks of the unanimous Party, the announcement was suddenly made of a public trial instituted against sixteen communists of a so-called "Trotskyite-Zinovievite Terrorist Centre." Stalin's intentions were revealed, the fruits of his long meditations and premeditations were apparent. And yet his worst enemies did not dare to anticipate the kind of surprise he was preparing.

Involved in this trial were the two closest, and also the most discredited, companions of Lenin, the unfortunate Zinoviev and Kamenev, many times routed and repenting as often, veritable political corpses dragged from the isolation-cell of Vekhnie-Uralsk to serve as puppets before the tribunal; also their followers Yevdokimov, Bakayev, Reingold; several former Trotskyists who had rallied to Stalin, the "capitulators," as Trotsky called them, Ivan Smirnov, Mrachkovsky, Dreitzer, Ter-Vaganian; finally a few confederates of rather shady character. Their record of service would normally have made them directors of the Party and the State, in which, indeed, they had lately held the highest posts. They, too, were found guilty of the murder of Kirov, and of aiming at the assassination of Stalin and his acolytes, Molotov excepted. In spite of the manifest material and psychological impossibilities involved, an attempt was even made to tax them with being under the orders of Trotsky—vanquished, exiled, disarmed, isolated, separated from them in every way. They were accused of treason, of espionage, of terrorist intrigues, of intelligence with the enemy, of collusion with the fascists, of monstrous, unintelligible and impossible crimes. They confessed everything; they accused instead of defending themselves; they denounced each other and ardently vindicated Stalin. A veritable witchcraft trial, as Friedrich Adler justly calls it. The press overwhelmed them, calling them wild beasts, singling out "dog" and "viper," and loaded them with ignominious insults before knowing anything of the facts of the case, and the party machine unloosed a thousand meetings of indignation to order, from which there rose a cheerless, artificial storm of ritual curses. The Public Prosecutor, Vyshinsky, obscured to the best of his ability questions which were meant to elucidate, and insulted in security the victims promised to the executioner. It was now clear why Stalin had ventured on this course. Without awaiting the result, Tomsky, another old companion of Lenin, committed suicide. In four days, the Sixteen were judged without proof, condemned by order, and executed. And from Stalin to Zinoviev, everyone, not forgetting Tomsky, was unanimous.

It was the Dictator who had dictated all these horrors, and it became clear that he had resolved to finish with the men of the past in order the better to finish with the things of the past, to destroy them morally and physically. He must, therefore, have decided at the time of the Kirov murder to make new human sacrifices; but he waited for the death of Gorky before beginning. And he evidently hoped to produce some effect on sceptical opinion by the insensate accumulation of charges, however untenable they were in themselves and incompatible with one another. Three months later at Novosibirsk, a trial, similar to the former but restricted to nine obscure culprits, ended in nine death sentences and six executions. In this instance, the obvious aims of the Chekist machination were to explain the failure of local industry by alleged "Trotskyist" sabotage and malevolence, to involve the Gestapo, a sort of German G.P.U., and finally to implicate various persons in the demonstrative repressions that were to follow. In fact, at the end of January 1937, the trial began of the so-called "Anti-Soviet Trotskyite Centre," or "parallel centre," both labels of police manufacture.

Among the seventeen were old Trotskyists who had long ago repented, "capitulators" who had rallied to Stalin, men like Pyatakov, Radek, Serebriakov, Drobnis, Boguslavsky, and one whose rupture with the opposition was quite recent, Muralov; with them were an old Right-Winger, Sokolnikov, opposed to Trotsky's ideas, and a few very suspicious unknowns. Again, as always, the charge was the wearisome assassination of the eternal Kirov. Once more were served up the delirious ravings about Trotskyism, fascism, terrorism, treason, espionage, backed up with charges of industrial sabotage and incredible intrigues aiming to provoke a war and the dismemberment of the U.S.S.R. Still there was no proof, no plausible presumption even, no tangible evidence, no witness for the defence, and no possible defence. Those accused of this new witchcraft admitted, as if with pleasure, the worst villainies and the least probable crimes. Their foreheads in the dust, they did not even spare their praises of the most genial Stalin. What passes for press and public opinion played their appointed parts in the funereal chant, keeping perfect time, even before the opening hearing.

The usual unanimity was maintained, including both executioners and victims. There were seventeen death sentences, thirteen executions: Radek and Sokolnikov saved their skins by disclosures obliquely aimed at the General Staff of the Red Army.

But behind the scenes, a secret and ferocious rivalry divided the oligarchs of Stalin's entourage, all the more implacable because it was limited to the closed field of the bureaucratic "summits." Whether because of disagreement between the master and his servants, or because of disputes for priority between rival cliques, Yagoda finally fell into disgrace; he was dismissed from the People's Commissariat of the Interior and from all his police functions. Yezhov succeeded him: an example of Stalin's foresight. Yagoda was relegated to the Commissariat of Posts and Telegraphs, and as in the case of Yenukidze, there could be no possible doubt: the days of the "sword bearer" were numbered, and so were those of his personal clients. Two weeks after the execution of Pyatakov, Assistant Commissar for Industry, but the real head of his department, his immediate superior, Ordjonikidze, nominal Commissar, suddenly died. This time no one believed it to be a natural death. Stalin's old Georgian accomplice had been "liquidated" by the "beloved father"; on the least risky assumption, that he could not survive the man who had been his closest colleague. Six weeks later, amid the discreet jubilation of all, Yagoda, exposed as an "enemy of the people," was thrown into prison, charged with offences against the common law: venality, debauchery, exactions, immorality. He would soon know by experience the painful fate of so many of his victims.

During the month of May 1937, the effects of Yezhov's exorbitant power began to make themselves felt in a recrudescence of terror: mass arrests and wholesale executions made the population live again through the darkest hours of the Civil War. Groups of several dozen "citizens" were shot each week, then each day, without formality, without the least guarantee of justice, or after secret trials, tantamount to pseudo-legal assassination. On the last day of May, Ian Gamarnik, Assistant Commissar for War, and Director of the Political Department of the Army, committed suicide. A heavy uneasiness weighed upon military circles, when several generals in the public eye (Levandovsky, Schmidt, Kuzmichov) were marked down by the G.P.U., imprisoned, perhaps already suppressed; enigmatic changes rearranged the higher cadres. Relentless blows shook the police and the Army, Yagoda's fall opening a new phase. In June reverberated the thunderbolt which decapitated the General Staff and struck terror into the country: under the unheard-of charge of espionage, under the ridiculous pretext of having "violated their military oath, betrayed their country, betrayed the peoples of the U.S.S.R., betrayed the Red Army," Marshal Tukhachevsky, Generals Yakir, Kork, Uborevich, Eideman, Feldman, Primakov and Putna, all well-known "heroes of the Civil War," all several times decorated with the order of the Red Flag, all classed as adversaries of Trotsky and partisans of Stalin, were tried *in camera*, condemned to death without witnesses or defence, and executed within forty-eight hours.

From all the evidence, it is obvious that the Russia which bears and suffers does not feel itself one with any of its rulers, politicians, bureaucrats, policemen, soldiers, who murder each other in secret in the name of the same ideal; without correct information, it does not understand, no one can understand, what is happening; the official "explanations"—really gross vituperations—inspire nausea even in the least indulgent adversaries of the men who perish in dishonour; the oppressed people are no doubt not sorry to see the disappearance of so many of their oppressors. But thousands of innocent people suffer on the rebound, and there are gloomy forebodings of even greater misfortunes beyond these unjust killings. In fact, the year 1937 will stand out as an indescribable nightmare in the memory of Russians, contemporary with the methodical massacre begun by Stalin under the empire of fear. It seems that Yagoda had exhausted his capacities as proscriber, slave-driver, torturer and executioner; Yezhov took his place to continue with an accelerated rhythm the sinister task prescribed by the "great humanitarian," Stalin. Although the G.P.U. was permitted to massacre without publicity, the local press began to announce capital executions, but in certain cases only, for reasons known to the authorities alone: thus the intention of spreading terror was clear.

It was then proclaimed that the so-called Soviet State was everywhere poisoned with "Trotskyism," and that in reality Trotskyism signifies fascism, espionage, sabotage, and the restoration of capitalism. Now Stalin and his auxiliaries have incessantly asserted with great advertisement, that Trotskyism was non-existent, all the while increasing the rigorous measures to extirpate it. In their accusations against their vanquished antagonists, people recognised from the start the very charges made by the Opposition against the ruling camarilla. The stronger, therefore, abuse their power to kill the weaker, not without trying to discredit them. In stigmatising them no great imagination was shown: treason, connivance with Polish or Japanese spies, with the Gestapo or the Intelligence Service became current coin (it is curious to note that the Italian Ovra has never been implicated). Thus "nests of Trotskyists," "nests of spies," "nests of fascism," were discovered in all the Russias, in towns and villages, in the countryside and on the mountains, at the head of all institutions and services. According to the revelations and denunciations of this period, the entire framework of the regime in every field, patiently selected by Stalin for ten years, consisted only of "double-faced" Trotskyists.

Since the unanimous and final vote of the "Stalinist Constitution" at the Eighth extraordinary Congress of the Soviets at the end of 1936—the last—removals, dismissals, and changes have succeeded each other in every layer of the bureaucratic hierarchy; and under such a regime they generally imply irreparable ruin for the fallen. The chief characters of the State, identified as "enemies of the people," presidents of Executive Committees and of Councils of Commissars, secretaries of the Party and People's Commissars, all unanimously elected, disappear, and with them their relations, their colleagues, their friends, and a multitude of subordinates. From Minsk to Vladivostok, from Archangel to Tiflis, the echo of daily executions alone is heard, decimating the "unanimous" Soviet staff. Intellectuals, workers, directors of factories, agronomists, officials, railwaymen, engineers, pedagogues, soldiers, militants, priests, journalists, employees, doctors, veterinary surgeons, peasants, heads of new undertakings, artists, wantonly dubbed "fascist bandits" and "Trotskyist spies," "dogs and vipers," are riddled with bullets and fall by hundreds and thousands into the common graves. No one knows whom to trust, nor in whom to confide. No one any longer dares to estimate the mass deportations. The list of suicides lengthens: Essenin and Mayakovsky, Joffe and Lutovinov set the example; after Nadiejda Alliluyeva, Stalin's own wife, after Skrypnik, Lominadze, Khandjian, Tomsky and Gamarnik, to mention only familiar names, there is Cherviakov, President of the Executive of White Russia; then I. Khodjayev, brother of two People's Commissars in Uzbekistan; then Liubchenko, President of the Council of Commissars of the Ukraine, and doubtless also Doletsky, director of the news agency, and Ustinov, Soviet Minister to Esthonia. With regard to the two latter, there is no absolute certainty; but is there any certainty either with regard to the others, concerning whom there are rumours of assassination by the Chekists? Under a terror of this kind, these are only various methods of extermination, just as the deportations often signify death after a brief interval. We shall learn later of hundreds, of thousands, more suicides, drowned by songs of "glory to the greatest man of the age."

If Stalin, his Yagodas and his Yezhovs, "engineers of souls," and experts in the art of breaking consciences, were able, by means of inquisitorial tortures, promises and threats, blackmail and bargaining, to stage several witchcraft trials in which complaisant confessions outbid each other, the majority of their victims have nevertheless refused to lend themselves to this, and it has been found necessary to put them to death without such parody of justice or under cover of various pretexts. Hundreds of persons, implicated by name as alleged accomplices, have never appeared before Stalin's "justice." Soldiers were condemned *in camera*, executed perhaps without trial. In July 1937 at Tiflis, seven former leaders of Soviet Georgia,

among them Budu Mdivani, Stalin's childhood friend, and
Okudjava, intimate friend of Trotsky, were judged *in camera*
and shot, without consenting, so far as is known, to make
lying confessions. At the end of this year of terror, there
were eight executions without trial in Moscow, of men who
never belonged to any opposition: Yenukidze, comrade of Stalin's
youth and adolescence; Karakhan, Assistant Commissar for
Foreign Affairs and ambassador; Orakhelashvili, President of the
Council of Commissars of Transcaucasia; Sheboldayev, Stalin's
creature, Secretary of the Party in northern Caucasia, and three
other less important figures. There were no deceptive confessions in this case either. The technique of extorting confessions
is painful, difficult, laborious; the results are very hard to
reconcile with the verifiable facts—indeed impossible—for after
the objective examination abroad of the two published trials
nothing whatever remains of the extravagant theses of Stalin and
his acolytes, Yagoda, Yezhov and Vyshinsky, the purveyors and
the prosecutor. It was therefore necessary patiently to await the
witchcraft trial of the so-called "Rightist-Trotskyist Bloc" in
March 1938, to hear new false confessions, not less absurd than
the former but even more incoherent, ill-conceived and badly
planned, equally unconvincing and impossible.

Of twenty-one accused in this strange amalgam, eighteen
were condemned and executed: Bukharin and Rykov, two of
the closest colleagues of Lenin, among the principal ideologists
and heads of the regime, former leaders of the Right, thanks
to whose support Stalin was able to defeat Trotsky, who had
now become Trotskyists without knowing it; Krestinsky and
Rosengoltz, People's Commissars, former Trotskyists who had
disowned their faction and rallied to Stalin at the first signs of
his strength; Yagoda, the murderer of Trotskyists, charged with
Trotskyism; People's Commissars Grinko, Chernov, Sharango-
vich, F. Khodjayev, Ivanov, all loyal Stalinists; Dr. Levin,
physician to the Kremlin, the doctor of Lenin and of Stalin;
Kriukov, agent of the G.P.U. and secretary to Gorky; and
finally a few very suspicious personages of lesser note. It is not
known why Rakovsky, considered the most guilty, benefited by

a relative clemency (twenty years imprisonment), as also the supposed poisoner Pletniev (twenty-five years); both punishments were, however, equivalent to death for men who had long passed the age of sixty. To the monstrosities of the other trials was added the novelty of "medical assassination." Yagoda, bringing pressure to bear on the doctors of the Kremlin, and having at his disposal a very special pharmaceutical laboratory, was alleged to have shortened the life of Menzhinsky, his predecessor, of Kuibyshev, of Gorky and of Gorky's son, Peshkov. With that crescendo which is indispensable to these repellent machinations in order to avoid the monotony which would make them inefficacious, the managers went so far as to accuse Bukharin of having attempted to assassinate Lenin in 1918, and to accuse Trotsky of having been in intimate contact with the Intelligence Service since 1926 and with German spies since 1921, the other accused being more or less accomplices. One part of the trial was aimed at retrospectively compromising the memory of Tukhachevsky, Gamarnik, Putna and their colleagues, dead and buried. As a matter of fact, it was a rehabilitation, for they were no longer accused of espionage, the official reason for their execution, but of toying with the idea of a *coup d'état*, that is to say, simply of secret hostility toward Stalin. Another part aimed at explaining the lamentable condition of "socialist" industry, commerce and agriculture by the conscious sabotage of "enemies of the people," with the sole aim of exonerating Stalin and his satellites, the persons really responsible. This was the most interesting and revealing part of the trial, for it disclosed irrefutable realities as devastating as the trials themselves for the regime and its rulers.

7

MUSSOLINI had taken a keen interest in this unique counter-revolution, to the point of devoting to it commentaries from his own pen in the *Popolo d'Italia*. After the sensational execution of the generals, his article entitled *Twilight* (13th June, 1937) was somewhat severe on Stalin's regime where "massacre is on the order of the day and of the night." But a month later, the *Critica Fascista* (15th July) considered, in a study of the *Fascism of Stalin*, that the latter's "fascist" reforms proved the natural force of expansion and the universality of the ideal of the Black Shirts. And during the trial of the twenty-one, Mussolini himself asked (*Popolo d'Italia* for 5th March, 1938) whether "in view of the catastrophe of Lenin's system, Stalin could secretly have become a fascist," and stated that in any case "Stalin is doing a notable service to fascism by mowing down in large armfuls his enemies who had been reduced to impotence." In large armfuls, indeed, Stalin mowed down not only his enemies, declared or secret, alleged or real, but also his "friends," his creatures, his accomplices. Between the last two pseudo-judicial exhibitions, he had mowed down not only the Old Guard of the Party and the flower of the Communist Youth, but, after the General Staff of the Red Army, all the heads of Soviet governmental, of national and local administration. (It almost goes without saying that the former oppositionists, not produced at the trials, such as Smilga, Preobrazhensky, Sosnovsky, Byeloborodov, Uglanov, etc., must have succumbed in the jails of their "socialist fatherland.")

From Stalin's circle there have disappeared in 1938 the majority of his close auxiliaries, well-known Stalinists ready for anything, members of his Politbureau, of his Central Committee, of his Control Commission, of his Council of Commissars, of his Executive Committee of the Soviets, of his Council of Labour and Defence: Rudzutak, Postyshev, Petrovsky, Chubar, Akulov, S. Kossior, Eikhe, Antipov, Bubnov, Krylenko, Unschlicht, the brothers Mezhlauk, Yakovlev, Janson, Soltz, Lomov, Sulimov, Miliutin, Kaminsky, Pashukanis, Rukhimovich, Khinchuk, Liubimov, Arbuzov, and how many others, not to mention the assassinations, the suicides, the punishments already stated. Five presidents out of seven of the Executive of the Soviets, and almost all the members or candidates; the People's Commissars in the approximate proportion of nine out of ten. And to disappear under Stalin means to perish suddenly in a cellar or to waste away slowly in an unhealthy climate. Of the directing staff of the Party formed in Lenin's lifetime, there remain, twenty years after October, only Trotsky in Mexico and, in Moscow, Stalin.

There have perished or disappeared without publicity in 1938, almost all the eighty members of the Council of War constituted in November 1934 to assist the Commissar for Defence: besides the nine leaders already inscribed on the roll of death, Generals Alksnis, Kashirin, Bielov, Dybenko, who had pronounced the death sentence on their comrades, followed by Marshals Yegorov and Blücher, Generals Savitsky, Smolin, Velikanov, Ozolin, Gorbachev, Hekker, Sukhorukov, Kuibyshev, Tkachev, Khripin, Pomerantsev, Mezis, Apse, Bokis, Admirals and Vice-Admirals Orlov, Victorov, Sivkov, Muklevich, Ludry, Kireyev, Kojanov, Dushenov, Ivanov, Smirnov-Sverdlovsky, followed and accompanied by thousands of other officers of all ranks. A man with no political past, a former secretary of Stalin who had become Assistant Commissar for War, Mekhlis, in concert with Yezhov, ceaselessly pursues the bloody purge. It is estimated in the U.S.S.R. that there have been more than thirty thousand victims in the "Red" Army and Navy— red with the blood of "his" followers shed by Stalin.

There have perished or disappeared all the chief leaders and deputy leaders of the G.P.U., following their chief: Agranov, Prokofiev, Balitsky, Messing, Pauker, Trilisser, Zakovsky, Slutsky, Deribas, Molchanov, Mironov, Leplevsky, and even former Chekists in retirement, Peters and Latsis; with them the majority of their colleagues, many of their subordinates. There have disappeared, after the two Assistant Commissars of Foreign Affairs, the ambassadors, plenipotentiaries or consuls-general Yurenev, Bogomolov, Arossiev, Davtian, Rosenberg, Antonov-Ovseënko, Tikhmeniev, Jakubovich, Bekzadian, Arens, Brodovsky, Podolsky, Ostrovsky, Asmus. Two have saved their honour with their lives by remaining abroad, A. Barmin and W. Krivitsky, the latter in the service of the Commissariat of War. Raskolnikov, proud Bolshevik who had become a humble Stalinist, must have followed their example without bothering about honour. Another, Butenko, typical example of the young Stalinist generation, openly threw in his lot with fascism.

There have disappeared, by a supreme irony of fate, the large majority of the members of the Commission of "the most democratic Constitution in the world," and those of the Commission for the revision of historical text-books, admirers of Ivan the Terrible. . . . There have disappeared almost all of those who established the Five Year Plans, theoreticians and experts, industrialisers and collectivisers, policemen and executioners, the directors of the principal industrial and agricultural "giants," and inaugurators of the greatest new undertakings, the Commissars for Industry, heavy and light, and for Collective Agriculture. There have disappeared all the statisticians, Ossinsky, Strumilin, Kraval at their head, whose faked calculations have long served as the basis for Stalin's fictions and deceits.

There have disappeared the last survivors of the Communist International, proscribers of their comrades, self-seeking flatterers of "the glorious pilot of the world October": Helen Stassova, Pyatnitsky, Bela Kun, Eberlein, Remmele, Warsky, Waletsky, Dombal, Borodin, and the majority of the mediocrities who were carving out a career in the Bureau of that corrupt and parasitic institution. They have arrested, imprisoned or deported almost all of the thousands of foreign communists, notably the Germans and the Poles, who had taken refuge in Soviet territory by virtue of Article 129 of the Stalinist Constitution: "The U.S.S.R. grants the right of asylum to foreign citizens persecuted for defending the interests of the workers, or for their scientific activity, or for struggling in favour of national liberation." Numerous among these "outlaws" are those who deplored too late the fact that they did not follow the example of their insubordinate comrades who, knowing how to appreciate the "right of asylum" and the "happy life" in the U.S.S.R., preferred to return to their own countries, there to serve heavy sentences, rather than to enjoy "liberty" under Stalin and *a fortiori* the penitentiary regime of the Soviets.

There have perished for the most part, executed after so-called

trials *in camera,* or have disappeared in the course of this interminable Saint Bartholomew of communists, the rulers of all
the pseudo-federated Republics: those of White Russia, Golo-
ded, president of the Council; Diakov, Benek, etc., People's
Commissars; in addition to Cherviakov, president of the Executive, and Generals Uborevich and Bielov; those of the Ukraine,
Bondarenko, president of the Council; Sukhomlin, vice-president; Zatonsky, Rekis, etc., People's Commissars; in addition to
Chubar, Liubchenko, Yakir already mentioned; those of Uzbekistan, Akhun-Balayev, president of the Executive; P. Khodjayev, president of the Council, and his two brothers, etc.;
those of Tadjikistan, Chotemor, president of the Executive;
Rakhimbayev, president of the Council; Imanov, Kaktyn, Shir-
inov, etc., vice-president and commissars; those of Turkmenis-
tan, Aitakov, president of the Executive; Atabayev, Sakhatov,
president and vice-president of the Council; Atayev, etc., commissars; those of Khirghiz, Isakov, president of the Council, and
his principal commissars; those of Karelia, Arkhipov, president
of the Executive; Bushuyev, president of the Council, etc.; those
of Transcaucasia and Azerbaijan, Mussabekov and Efendiev,
presidents of the Executive; Rakhmanov, president of the Council; Safarov, Sultanov, Ibrahimov, Husseinov, etc., commissars;
those of Armenia, Ter-Gabryelian, president of the Council;
Mamikonian, Kalantarian, Shakhnazarian, etc., commissars; in
addition to Khandjian who has been already mentioned.

We must make special mention of Georgia, fatherland of
Stalin, Ordjonikidze and Yenukidze, where a "man with no
political past," L. Beria, has mown "in large armfuls" for his lord
and master. After B. Mdivani, former president of the Council,
and Okudjava, Toroshelidze, Chikhladze, Kurulov, Kartsevadze
(socialist) and G. Eliava (bacteriologist), who were executed
in July of the year of terror, there were Mgalobishvili and
Agniashvili, president and vice-president of the Council; Met-
vereli, Abashidze and about ten of their colleagues, commissars;
then Gogoberidze, another former president of the Council;
Kirkvelia, Kavtaradze, commissars; S. Eliava, L. Gueguechkori,
the socialists S. Davderiani, G. Makharadze; finally Orakhelash-

vili, former president of the Council of Transcaucasia. In Adjaristan: Lorkipanidze, president of the Executive, G. Ramishvili, E. Megrelidze, G. Laguidze, and half a dozen other commissars. In Ossetia: Togoyev, president of the Executive; Maurer, secretary of the Party, etc. In Abkhazia: Nestor Lakoba, president of the Executive, and his two relations, Michael and Basil, besides a dozen commissars. Nestor Lakoba, accused of homicidal intentions with regard to Stalin, was actually the author of the pamphlet, *Stalin and Khashim*, in which he celebrates "the greatest man of a whole epoch, such as history gives to humanity only once in one or two hundred years," the "genial leader, unshakable and made of steel, our dear and beloved Stalin."

Everywhere, then, the Commissars of the People were only "enemies of the people." Everywhere the Executives are executed. Everywhere the enemies of the people who were executed had been unanimously elected, as were their successors. And Lenin had as friends, comrades, and allies, according to Stalin, only false friends, fascists, spies, saboteurs, traitors, dogs, in a word, "Trotskyists." For a dismal catalogue might be made in the same way for all the so-called responsible and directing spheres of Soviet life where the Soviets do not exist and where life precedes death by so little. The "good," the "tender," the "gentle" Stalin—expressions consecrated in the U.S.S.R. by those who have yet to receive a bullet in the neck—has spared, doubtless provisionally, only an insignificant number of individuals who have known the past: if he is to find substitutes for those in the front rank, it is not possible for him to kill everyone at the same time. Thus he has proceeded step by step, methodically, passing from the Party to the Army, from the police to the diplomatic corps, from the centre to the periphery, from industry to agriculture, from the press to the statistical bureaux, from commerce to literature.

Everyone knows that Stalin is the protector of letters and the arts, the enlightened lover of all culture: he has had Pilnyak exiled, Pasternak persecuted, and in his devotion has imprisoned even the pseudo-proletarian writers Auerbach, Kirshon, Yermilov, Libedinsky, Bruno Jasensky, Tarassov-Rodionov and their like; he has hunted down the poets Nicholas Kliuyev, Mandelstam, Selvinsky, Tretiakov; he has deported a critic like Voronsky, a philosopher like Ivanov-Razumnik, humourists like Erdman and Krotky, the historians Nevsky, Steklov, Volguin, Friedland, Zeidel, Anishev, Piontkovsky, S. Dalin; the journalists Gronsky, Rojkov, Lukianov, Lapinsky, Tal, almost the whole staff of *Pravda* and the very official *Izvestia*, together with the orthodox editorial boards of the leading reviews; the writers Ivan Katayev, P. Vassiliev, I. Makarov, A. Bezymensky, Maznin, Selivanovsky, G. Serebriakova, to mention only a few examples. As a matter of fact, no one would have been able, under a quintuple preliminary censorship, to commit the slightest crime with his pen. Stalin has sterilised the best talents of Russia, driven the real writers to moral suicide after the physical suicide of the greatest poets. He has suppressed the *Academia* publications, the only ones which did honour to contemporary book-production in the U.S.S.R., and has shot or deported the editors, critics and managers. In the realm of the theatre, he has struck down, without avowed or avowable reason, the directors and managers Liadov, Amaglobeli, Arcadin, Rafalsky, Nathalie Satz and others —even Granovsky as a posthumous insult; he has deprived Meyerhold of work and made his theatre a corpse.

How many people has Stalin butchered who did not kill Kirov? A precise enumeration is impossible when dealing with such a hecatomb. Every personality in the public eye drags in his fall sometimes dozens, sometimes hundreds of subordinates, whose wretched fate is passed over in silence. The executions are in general kept secret, except when express orders are given for publicity. We have been able to collect information from only ten to twenty Soviet newspapers which are received irregularly, according to the prevailing conditions, in the capital where, however, the press under orders abstains from reproducing the news: but there exist about ten thousand local and regional sheets which are inaccessible.

According to the testimony of Liushkov, head of the G.P.U. in Eastern Siberia, who has taken refuge in Japan to avoid the fate of his colleagues, 40,000 persons were executed on the gratuitous suspicion of plotting during the period when "the most democratic constitution in the world" was being adopted and the first "electoral campaign" was being conducted for the Supreme Council. One of his colleagues of the Trans-Siberian, Petrov, computes at five million the number of prisoners in the concentration camps alone, not including the millions of those banished or the inhabitants of the isolation camps and prisons. There has been a singular "progress" since the appearance of the work, *Russia's Iron Age*, in which W. H. Chamberlin in 1934 reported that 300,000 prisoners were cooped up in the concentration camps of Siberia alone, and that at least two million "citizens" had been deprived of liberty without the pretence of a trial during the five years of the first Five Year Plan. W. Krivitsky, a communist who has stood every test and reached the rank of general in his department, could declare to the *Bulletin of the Opposition* (December 1937) that the number of political arrests rose to 300,000 in May 1937, for the period of the trials alone, and must have reached 500,000 by the end of the year. A communist communiqué published in the Russian *Courrier Socialiste* (July 30, 1938) estimates at seven million the number of prisoners in the concentration camps alone. This figure is the nearest to the truth, if we consider the draconian measures adopted since the Leningrad purge after the Kirov murder, the surgical operations performed on the Party and followed by mass deportations of those expelled and their families, the amputations effected in all the cadres of administrative and economic activity, finally and above all if we calculate the need of penal manual labour for Stalin's public works which rival those of Pharaoh.

The Yugoslavian communist, A. Ciliga, a sincere man and an unimpeachable witness, one of the few who has escaped alive from the Soviet convict gangs, has written in his book, *Au pays du grand mensonge*: "Those who have not lived in the Soviet prisons, concentration camps and places of exile in which are shut up more than five million convicts, those who are not familiar with the greatest jail history has ever seen, where men die like flies, where they are beaten like dogs, where they are made to work like slaves, can have no idea what Soviet

Russia is, what Stalin's 'classless society' means." In the absence of scientific exactitude, impossible when such different testimony is compared, there is striking agreement as to the order of magnitude, the hallucinatory proportions. We must also take into account the frightful mortality which decimates the convicts, especially the children, the repeated arrests of the same persons, the migrations from one camp to another, and the change of work places which make the figures fluctuate.

The same author thus reveals the approximate figures collected on the spot, in the isolation-camp at Vekhnie-Uralsk: "At the end of 1932, a Trotskyist who had recently arrived told us that according to an important official of the G.P.U., condemned for a professional error, the number of arrests rose, on the authority of police statistics, to 37 millions in the course of the last five years. Even admitting that in the majority of cases the prisoners had been arrested over and over again, the figure seemed to us incredibly exaggerated. Our own estimates varied from five to fifteen millions. . . . When I was released and was in exile in Siberia, I was able to verify the correctness of many of the assertions which had seemed exaggerated and fantastic in prison. It was in this way that I was able to verify the rumours of the horrors of the famine of 1932, including cases of cannibalism. After what I saw in Siberia, I consider that the figure of five millions condemned is much too small, and that ten million is nearer to reality." Indeed in 1935, the most staid and prudent observers arrived at this average estimate. In 1937, at the time of the twentieth anniversary of October, if we bear in mind all that we have said, fifteen million condemned in the various categories would probably be the number most in accord with the facts.

At the end of the year of terror (12th December, 1937) the elections to the Supreme Council were held, to the accompaniment of rifles fitted with silencers. There was only a single candidate for each electoral district, chosen in advance, nominated beforehand by the raised hands of the electors on the recommendation of the Party and under the eye of the G.P.U.; the voting papers were printed with the name of the official candidate only who, moreover, benefited by every paper struck out or altered by a mark or stain; abstention was prohibited and was controlled by a scrutiny of passports and electoral rolls. Thus Stalin was not even able to carry into effect his project of staging a semblance of rivalry between "social organisations of all kinds outside the Party"—all of course in reality communist organisations. He had overestimated his technical means, above all his resources in men, and he had to be content with exclusive and obligatory candidatures. It was in these circumstances that his press proclaimed the dazzling triumph of the "bloc of Bolsheviks and of those without the Party," with majorities on the average exceeding 99 per cent. Hitler has in many ways copied Stalin, notably in the concentration camps; in respect for the Constitution, Stalin has had only to imitate Hitler, who took the well-known oath to the Weimar Constitution. During the electoral operations, a certain number of the carefully selected candidates disappeared through the trap-door of the G.P.U.; after the first meeting of the Supreme Council, several deputies, Vice-Presidents of the Assembly, People's Commissars, met the same fate, as if to illustrate Articles 127 and 128 of the Constitution on the inviolability of the person, of the home, and of correspondence. Virtuoso of antiphrasis, the "beloved father and friend of the people" declared in a speech on the eve of the elections: "The world has never seen elections so really free, so truly democratic. Never. History knows no other example of this nature."

8

CONFRONTED with the massacres ordered by Stalin in cold blood, and with the internecine feuds of the bolsheviks, one is led to draw a parallel with the Russia of the sixteenth century and the reign of Ivan the Terrible. It is not perhaps fortuitous that in Europe this century was that of the massacre of Saint Bartholomew and of the Inquisition, that Ivan IV was in the largest sense the contemporary of Louis XI, of Philip II, of Henry VIII, of Selim the Fierce—of cruel princes and poisoning popes. Nor is it fortuitous that our epoch of social and political change demands comparison in so many ways with the Middle Ages, or rather with the hazy idea we have of them, and that it is haunted by the related phenomena of Bolshevism and Fascism. The great social and national conflicts which have arisen as a result of the world war also suggest frequent comparisons with the wars of religion of this same sixteenth century which was that of Luther and of Loyola, of thinkers who today are curiously regaining their popularity, from Machiavelli to Paracelsus, and besides these, whether by chance or not, of the *Utopia* of Thomas More and of the true Humanism of Europe. But Ivan the Terrible did not, like Stalin, control electricity, rotary printing presses, radio, railways, tanks, airplanes, oil wells, gold and manganese mines. The combination of Russo-Asiatic mediaeval backwardness with modern technique and inexhaustible natural resources produces confusing effects as much within as outside Russia and obscures the simplest things. Much has been said about the unreliability of historical comparisons, but nothing forbids the attempt to shed a little light upon the uncertainties of the present by a knowledge of the past, if it be only to bring out the differences more clearly, to relate more exactly the known reactions of human nature to the unknown of the fugitive present and the perpetual becoming. It is not useless, therefore, to return to ancient Muscovite history in order to show certain new beginnings of history, which do not in the least exclude fresh departures and definite breaks.

Stalin, in his interview with Emil Ludwig, was pleased to distinguish himself sharply from Peter the Great, but since then, not being subject to contradiction, he has completely revised his views, as is shown among other things by the corrections made on his instruction in the historical text-books and the frequent commentaries of his controlled press. The sycophant writer, Alexis Tolstoy, whose zeal to serve the Bolsheviks is in inverse proportion to his contempt for them, carried out a "social command" transmitted from a very high place, in his novel on Peter the First and the film of the same type which aimed at suggesting constant parallels between the "worker-tsar" and the red tsar. But if these two personages are related, it is by their contempt for human life, sensibility, and dignity, and not in the way intended by Stalin.

All serious historians recognise in Ivan the Terrible the true precursor of the reforms of Peter the Great and the most finished expression of their common mentality. But no one would dream, if he were a free agent, of attributing the epithet "Great" to Stalin, although everyone would grant him that of "Terrible." The use of "barbarian methods," as Lenin said, to force industrialisation is not enough to render "great" an industrialising tsar, when civilised methods exist. The barbarity excusable in Ivan, explicable in Peter, which was characteristic of their time if we take account of the backwardness of Russia, is an enormous anachronism in Stalin, and therefore inexcusable. Moreover, it is in direct opposition to true industrial, economic and technical progress, for no modern industry could prosper under the constant threat of the knout and the revolver. As a matter of fact, very few factories, only about twenty, survived the "worker-tsar," out of the 230 which he left in theory and the hundred odd which were functioning in fact—a result of ill-omen for his imitator.

The comparison with Ivan the Terrible, on the contrary, is a great help in understanding the bloody crises of the Stalinist autocracy. Around the throne, the noble feudal families, the Shuiskys, the Belskys, the Glinskys, and later the Miloslavskys, the Naryshkins, the Dolgorukys, until the Romanovs gave the casting vote, quarrelled among themselves for places of influence, as around Stalin the secretaries and commissars, the clans and the cliques. The quarrels for precedence between the *boyars*, envenomed to the point of implacable feuds, are analogous to the antagonisms between members of the Central Committee and the Control Commission, between the system of the Party and the system of the Soviets, between the Police and the Army, between the Commissariat of Foreign Affairs and the Communist International, between Lettish coteries and Caucasian tribes. Then also, autocratic oppression paralysed the class struggle and gave free rein to the zoological struggle of castes. The workings of the G.P.U. under Stalin are comparable only to the *Oprichnina* of Ivan, an unavoidable comparison, just as the machinations of Stalin by means of the G.P.U. make one think irresistibly of the Terrible. The parallel even offers surprising similarities.

When still young, spare of words, distrustful and dissimulating, Ivan acted by surprise when he attacked the *boyars* and, as an example, threw the most important of them, Shuisky, to his dogs, who tore him to pieces; then he banished several others to distant regions. The *boyars* seized the first occasion, a fire at Moscow, to accuse the Glinsky family of wrecking and of provoking a massacre. Later, thinking that he had reason to complain of his favourites, Silvester and Adashev, the Tsar wrote: "When the treason of that dog, Alexis Adashev and his accomplices was discovered, we made our anger felt only in a merciful manner; we did not decree capital punishments against the guilty; we merely banished them to various towns. . . . At first we did not inflict the final penalty on anyone. We ordered those who belonged to the party of Silvester and Adashev to dissociate themselves from them and no longer to look upon them as their leaders; we made them confirm this promise by an oath. Not only did they not dissociate themselves from the traitors, but they aided them in every possible way, and did their best to restore to them their former power and stir up against us the most treacherous conspiracy. Then only, seeing their stubborn wickedness and their unconquerable spirit of rebellion, I inflicted on the guilty the penalty of their crime." In this passage, which relates to a period of relative clemency, one recognises—one might almost mistake it for—the future language of Stalin, though the latter is rather more vulgar. One finds again the dogs, the treason, the wrecking, the "faction," the false repentance, the insincerity of the "capitulators," the alleged conspiracy, the clemency of the despot, in short the very thesis which Stalin was to put in circulation by means of the international press in his pay.

After the departure of Kurbsky, which corresponds *mutatis*

mutandis to the exile of Trotsky, things became worse. Kurbsky addressed to Ivan a vehement message of reproach, rather in the style of the future Trotskyist *Bulletin of the Opposition*. A polemic raged; the Terrible replied in his turn, and made use of tricks to strike at the exiled Trotsky, that is Kurbsky, through his alleged accomplices: blackmail by threatening dismissal, as it were, which Stalin also was to employ on many occasions, led the *boyars* to recantation before the Tsar. The latter than carried out a profound administrative reform by creating the *Oprich-nina* whose object was to "sweep out treason," like the G.P.U. of later times. For seven years an unexampled terror decimated the "upper layers" of Muscovite society, executions succeeded tortures, the Zinovievs, Pyatakovs and Bukharins of the period perished with their followers and their families. It is said that some of the *boyars*, who were tortured to death, mingled a eulogy of Stalin, or rather of the Terrible, with their cries of pain. Every day whole groups of individuals were put to death. It is unknown even today, in spite of the controversies of specialists, what were the crimes of these victims, and perhaps it will never be known what are the secret reasons of Stalin.

When Ivan wanted to justify himself to the Poles, he wrote to them: "Many among you say that I am cruel; it is true that I am cruel and irascible, I do not deny it. But toward whom, I pray, am I cruel? I am cruel toward him who is cruel toward me." And he accuses his enemies of having poisoned his first wife. Stalin, having read the famous passage of Lenin's *Testament:* "Stalin is too rude, etc. . . . ," in the same way declared to the Central Committee in 1927: "Yes, comrades, I am rude to those who break their word rudely and treacherously, who split and demoralise the Party. I have never hidden it and I do not hide it." One could continue these instructive comparisons: the analogy is obvious in deed and in word. Stalin accuses his adversaries of having poisoned not his wife, who committed suicide, but Gorky and others: a tiny difference and, if we examine it, not to the advantage of Stalin. "We must not think that Ivan's enemies were better than he: they were as cruel toward their inferiors as Ivan could be toward them," observes A. Rambaud, and if we transfer the observation it remains valid, at least for those who head the lists of Stalin's victims.

To assure to the tyrant the maintenance of his tyranny in all its fullness both for the present and for the future: such in both cases appears to be the *raison d'être* of so many crimes, the essential reason among many secondary considerations. Of course the tyrant always claims an impersonal ideal, varying from the divine will through national interest to the safety of the revolution; but it is always a question, in prosaic terms, of the oligarchic domination imposed by violence and incarnate in an alleged superman. Amid the general dissatisfaction due to material misery, spiritual poverty and political oppression, the tyranny maintains itself only by a constant see-saw supported on the social pillars, on which its favour confers a transitory authority, and which in the long run seem dangerous to it: and from this arises the necessity of destroying them lest, in continuing too long, they assume too great an importance. Whether the privileged caste be the feudal nobility or the feudal bureaucracy, it suspects treason everywhere and constantly fears for its privileges.

We have seen how Stalin at first got rid successively of all the political factions which were capable of eliminating him, how he defeated each by a coalition with the others, dividing the spoils, namely the places, in advance. Freed of any immediate worry in the system of the pseudo-Party, he imagined he found some resistance, though it was in point of fact more the difficulties of application, in the system of the pseudo-Soviets where, in particular, the G.P.U. had ended by becoming a sort of State within the State. It is possible that in time these difficulties became a mute but conscious resistance in the Police and in the Army. Around every director of every institution, from the General Headquarters down to the least commissariat, in Moscow and in the sub-capitals, there arose a sort of clientèle which little by little accumulated certain common interests and a common *esprit de corps*. Stalin, a man of prudence, made it a principle to have each of his chiefs watched over by an associate or assistant, who in turn was surrounded by his own set and was ready to supplant the chief. These indefinable groupings among officials, formed by circumstances for the solution of urgent problems according to various criteria of docility, aptitude or chance, were not in the least homogeneous: side by side with careerists, conscientious persons well-qualified in their speciality rubbed shoulders with informers and parasites. Individual or collective purges frequently overhauled these unstable formations and modified their external features. These left as a residue carefully selected fixed groups, with their routine, their professional habits, sometimes also the last scraps of the competence necessary to the functioning of the state machine, particularly indispensable in the key positions of the economic and military administration. But the purges inspired by the narrow conservative views of the central power—safeguarding of the new privileges, fear of the least initiative, suspicious distrust of each and all—lower to a minimum the level of the men and of their work. In brief, power and knowledge contradict one another in insoluble antagonism.

Degrading struggles between the highly selected sections of the bureaucracy result from this lengthy course of action, struggles in which Stalin, in the name of his intangible preponderance, is the arbiter. There is also another result: that bestiality of the strong, that humility of the weak, the real abuses of the one, the false confessions of the other, in the absence of all normal expression of political thought and individual needs, of all respect for human personality and for any moral rule. At his ease in this *milieu*, in these surroundings, which are his natural element, Stalin incites and provokes his auxiliaries, stirs up rival passions, exploits rancour and hatred in order to guarantee in his own way the continuance of his despotism and the unique position of the supreme arbiter. He cuts short differences, separates the protagonists, and profits from the situation to impose new men. Not knowing in whom to trust and seeing traitors on all sides, he keeps changing his favourites without changing his methods, and always with identical results. From disappointment to miscalculation, from set-backs to deceptions, in the blind alley where the great, new technical and industrial enterprise marks time and often retreats, he interprets every natural weakness as ill-will, every unlucky chance as obstruction, every banal mishap as wrecking and sabotage. He must have culprits to punish in order to preserve the dogma of infallibility from on high, as well as his personal prestige.

He treats all slavish courtiers as "double-faced," or at least accuses them of lack of vigilance; he is constantly creating supplementary departments of the police bureaucracy, such as the "military councils" and the commissars in the Army following the "political sections" in the *kolkhoz*, in order to reinforce the spying system. In his eyes, all evil being treason, all good is merely a question of police and repression. The different bureaucratic sections in the various ranks of Party and State, united against their inferiors but divided before their superiors, seem to him at best as less and less apt to realise the impossible tasks assigned them by the plans, the false calculations, the badly worked out projects. They denounce and devour each other, and are sacrificed one after the other according to the necessities of a vulgar hand-to-mouth policy. At length Stalin replaces them with "men with no political past," that greedy new generation, impatient and brutal, on which he depends. In the economic blind alley in which the U.S.S.R. found itself before the twentieth anniversary of October, a mass slaughter was needed to speed things up. The Kirov murder furnished the pretext.

These "men with no political past," who have, moreover, no culture, no experience and too often no scruples, men lacking in science as in conscience, provide Stalin with sad surprises, as is shown, among other examples of the same kind, by the defection of the Soviet diplomat Th. Butenko who went straight over to fascism. It is true that the transition from Bolshevism to fascism has for a long time been easy to make. This man was not an exceptional case, his defection was merely the result of accidental causes. He was in truth a characteristic product of the neo-Bolshevism: there are many other examples. In order to be sent abroad, he must have passed through many sieves, and undergone many controls. Stalin and Yezhov answered for him still, over the signature of Litvinov, while he was en route for Rome. Nevertheless, he declared himself their enemy of long standing, and called passionately for their fall and that of their regime. Those who agree with him, and who work inside Russia, work against them in another way, by making a career; they are worth no more in the economy and the administration than in diplomacy and politics. If the renegade in question does not represent the whole of "soviet youth," which has been the theme of an abundant, but vain and deceptive literature, he belongs nevertheless to that cynical generation fashioned by the G.P.U. and formed in the school of Stalin.

At the Congress of Soviets in 1936, it was said that 43 per cent of the population had been born since the revolution, and consequently had only theoretical notions of the past. Thus Stalin draws on an inexhaustible reserve, and is visibly obsessed by this prolific increase which authorises him, as he thinks, to do as he pleases as far as human material is concerned; for it accords well with his inclination to "mow down in large arm-fuls" the old and the adult generations, as is shown, among other signs, by this phrase of his: "At the present time, there is with us each year a net increase of the population of nearly three million. This means that each year, we increase to the extent of the whole of Finland." It means in addition, to the misfortune of Russia, that Stalin estimates human life at the very lowest price; as if, apart from ethical arguments, social beings were interchangeable in work and production without regard to their culture.

If T. G. Masaryk could justly remark that "Bolshevik half-culture is worse than the absence of all culture," the suppression of this half-culture by Stalin has not brought Russia any nearer to the happiness of the ordinary people: instead of clearing the ground, it has allowed the studious youth to become imbued with schematic idiocies, primitive sophisms, notions so utterly false, and condemned by all experience, that the Bolsheviks themselves have had to repudiate them one by one and "redis-cover the alphabet" every day. The lack of rudimentary culture of the new men does not correspond to the industrial civilisation, whose carcass has been imported at great expense and implanted with many disappointments, and still less to the high moral level without which a society with socialist tendencies is inconceivable. But in the new generation it is possible to distinguish, amid the still amorphous and passive mass, two contradictory currents. The so-called "soviet" youth, conformist, poured into the mould of the Bolshevik organisation, uncultured, egotistical, devoted to sport, parrot-like, boastful, profiteering, eager for gain, grossly practical, doubtful of nothing, its head filled with orthodox pamphlets, is however sterile, in spite of its privileges. The pseudo-soviet youth, non-conformist, impossible to define in its silence, restless, enquiring, thoughtful, dissatisfied, retains its critical spirit, learns its trade, avoids politics, hides its opinions, reads the poets and philosophers, and escapes from official influence while keeping up appearances. Neither the one nor the other, for different reasons, can fulfill the hopes of Stalin.

9

THE scale of the extermination carried out between and after the trials for treason and terrorism has somewhat lessened their importance, but their significance nevertheless extends to the whole course of action. For the future history of Russia, its revolutions and counter-revolutions, it is not a matter of indifference to know whether these trials concealed some morsel of truth under the mass of obvious deceptions. Practically every one of the lies of the accusation and of the confessions, like the lies of the witnesses and of the speeches for the prosecution, collapsed under the flagrant contradictions between one trial and the next. The statements with regard to the two parts which were verifiable abroad were all shown to be false, without a single exception. The opinions foisted upon the accused were diametrically opposed to those which they were always known to have held. Their own declarations before the tribunal, about the ideas which inspired the opposition and the alleged plots, are contradicted from end to end by all the existing documents not specially prepared for the needs of the case. Finally—a proof of the "totalitarian" imposture which is really superfluous—a comparison with earlier trials, notably that of the "industrialists" and that of the "Mensheviks," establishes a remarkable identity of structure which leaves no doubt as to the technique and the police machination: the only difference is that in the earlier trials France takes the place of Germany; the only novelty is the addition of terrorism.

The general thesis of the accusation was summed up in March 1937 by Stalin in these words: ". . . From the political tendency, which it showed six or seven years earlier, Trotskyism has become a mad and unprincipled gang of saboteurs, of agents of diversion, of assassins acting on the orders of the espionage services of foreign States." The complete falseness of this need no longer be demonstrated, since it was immediately obvious on the publication of the reports of the trials and by an examination of facts, the comparison of texts, the absence of proofs, the contradictions in which the terms annul one another, the unexplained disappearance of several hundred accused and of thousands of witnesses and the material impossibilities which discredit the remainder. Moreover, certain inexplicable gaps, unjustifiable obscurities, indisputable lies, the incredible unanimity, the absolute isolation of the prisoners, the abnormal conditions of their imprisonment, the complete secrecy of the preliminary examination, the absence of any defence and of all material evidence, the obvious role of Chekists and *agents provocateurs*, the fact that similar or related trials were held *in camera*, the mechanical orgy of all too excessive insults—all this hardly adds weight to the theses. The implication as Trotskyists of men well known as mortal enemies of Trotsky refutes them; the presence of Rykov and Bukharin, and even Yagoda among the accused discredits them. Stalin himself imprudently contradicted them a year later by making Trotsky and Krestinsky belong to the German espionage service already in 1921, Rakovsky to the Intelligence Service in 1924, etc.—that is, long before the "six or seven years earlier," and at a period when the close collaboration of these persons with himself is incontestable. By the zeal of this same Stalin, Trotsky had, moreover, been abundantly accused as an agent of France, before being branded an agent of Germany—assertions more or less incompatible. In the case of the military leaders, the "espionage" of 1937 became in 1938 vague, confused and misty intentions of a political *coup d'etat*. All the charges of the indictments have the same force. There is not even the very least valid juridical presumption of guilt.

Does this mean that no doubt exists, in the nature of things, after these objective statements, which are rendered difficult of belief by the resemblance of so many accused to their accusers? Doubts still exist about too many historical enigmas, and not only in Russia, to hope that this will be fully clarified before the death of Stalin. As for terrorism—the classic reply from below to the terror from above—no definite act or concrete plan was revealed in the trials. But the assassination of Kirov by Nikolayev, the only real fact, together with various other indications, proves, in spite of the active participation of the G.P.U., the existence of an exasperated and desperate state of mind among a part of the younger communist generation: terrorism derives from this inevitably. Stalin had nothing to fear, in this connection, from his former opponents, who were astute but crushed; he has everything to fear from the simple minded, from believers, from anonymous men. Not one of the "capitulators" dreamed of killing him; each one hoped perhaps that some unknown person would do it, only to profit by his gesture and to see the tyrannicide sent to what serves as a scaffold, leaving posterity to weave him garlands. Stalin could not limit himself to sacrificing a series of Nikolayevs without reputation, in order to intimidate once again a tired, bored and hardened public opinion. He sacrificed celebrated heads, chosen for secondary reasons: old counts to settle, the thirst for vengeance to be slaked, those who were too well informed to be silenced. In addition, with the unprecedented police precautions with which he surrounds himself—an unheard of technique of protection, extending even to the minute search of his intimate friends—he never risks his life in the Kremlin except by a chance meeting with some individual very close to him and of the same type, an Ordjonikidze, for example, able for once to deceive the vigilance of the guards making the search or to seize on the wing a suddenly propitious opportunity. In public, where he appears very rarely and unexpectedly in order to avoid prepared attacks, he is surrounded by an unbelievable number of unarmed "comrades," selected with a fine-toothed comb, and by an incalculable number of janissaries. The preventive terror, and the fear of reprisals directed against their families, complete the system. The chances are thus reduced to zero in practice.

Ordjonikidze, as a matter of fact, an old accomplice of Stalin, one of those responsible for his rise, well versed in the tricks and scheming of his master and compatriot, was the sort of man to take the initiative when once he had scented his disgrace. But as it turned out, his own too opportune death was immediately suspect to the inhabitants of Moscow, a suspicion which increased after the Yagoda affair and its horrifying revelations. Stalin alone could profit by the crime. The discovery of the unusual laboratory of the G.P.U. does not allow the suggestion to be brushed aside. Since Stalin has felt the need of getting rid of the doctors of the Kremlin, the mystery of the "medical assassinations" will not be the easier to elucidate. The chapter of poisons already held a certain place in the history of Russia, next to the chapter of tortures; but in the most modern times, "socialism in a single country," the avowed end which justifies unavowable means, was required to prolong it further by some sinister pages.

Yagoda, Stalin's henchman, was quite capable of committing, under the cover of his "patron," the crimes of which he accused himself; one could not be surprised if he had also acted on his own account. It may be voiced as a conjecture that he might have got rid of Menzhinsky in order to take his place, and of Peshkov in order to take his wife. As for Kuibyshev, the affair is inexplicable, unless Stalin gave the order to "liquidate" him as a disturbing witness or a cumbersome mediocrity, in order to have at his disposal various posts to bestow. Finally, in the case of Gorky Stalin was also the only person who had both the power and the interest to hasten his death. In recent years he had refused him permission to return to Sorrento, foreseeing his departure for good and all, and for the same reason had forbidden in 1935 his participation in an international congress of "anti-fascist writers" in France. (Would not Gorky at liberty exercise abroad, in certain cases, an undesirable moral pressure on Moscow, would he not leave behind him, under new influences, writings which would damage Stalin's prestige?) After an episodic phase of friendship which was self-interested on both sides, each judging the other necessary for his glory, for different reasons and in different ways, their relations became cold on account of certain humanitarian overtures made by Gorky who intervened to limit abuses; they went from bad to worse after the secret trial of Kamenev, which scandalised and alarmed the last remaining friends of Lenin. The "genial leader" and the "genial artist" had nothing left to say to each other, nothing further to expect from each other. It may well be that the first put an end to the second to leave his hands freer for the great purge he had secretly resolved upon. But no one can honestly give credence to the police version attributing the devilish initiative to Trotsky, who morally even more than physically is as it were removed to another planet; a version charging the "terrorists" with subtle manœuvres to contaminate with influenza an old man of nearly seventy, already undermined by incurable diseases, and to administer overdoses of the remedies. On the other hand, one of Stalin's distinctive characteristics, which has been outstanding throughout his career, is systematically to throw his own misdeeds and crimes, as well as his political errors and governmental mistakes, on the shoulders of those whose discredit and ruin he is plotting.

Moreover, terrorism has no meaning or reason unless it has a personal or collective signature; by its very definition, it aims at inspiring by violence a feeling of terror of some person or thing; properly speaking, it is unthinkable for it to be anonymous or silent. Terrorism without indication of its origin fails in its object, terrorises nobody; for that reason, the death of Gorky, like that of Kuibyshev and others, spread not the slightest terror. On the other hand, any normal mind can understand that it is always Stalin who profits by the crime—if we allow for a moment the supposition of a crime. The statement of the unfortunate Dr. Levin, "Yagoda was threatening to destroy my family," as an explanation of his alleged complicity, bears out what is known of the terrorist methods of the G.P.U. under Yezhov as under Yagoda, but above all characterises the whole terrorist regime of Stalin. The mother of the "wisest man of our time," just before dying, said of him in *Izvestia:* "An exemplary son. I wish everybody one like him." The whole of Russia expresses itself in opposite terms.

A disturbing series of questions then arises, after the Yagoda trial, especially if we remember that, according to the gossip in the U.S.S.R. which is inevitable in a country without a free press, several murders of well-known people have been represented as suicides; that Budyonny could kill his wife with impunity in order to marry another, and that mysterious disappearances follow one another under the regime of the "happy life." What did Stalin's secretary, Tovstukha, die of? Why did Alliluyeva, Stalin's wife, commit suicide? Natural deaths occur in Russia, as elsewhere; that of Stalin's mother, Catherine Djugashvili, in 1937 is probably one of them; that of Lunacharsky (1933), that of Chicherin (1936), that of Anna Elizarova (1935) and of Marie Ulianova (1937), Lenin's sisters, do not appear suspicious. But was the strange laboratory of Dr. Kazakov used in only two or three cases? (And as the crowning inconsistency in the official version, the "terrorist" doctors are supposed to have restricted themselves to administering doses of digitalin and other substances which by no means require a special laboratory.) If we are to be referred back as far as the death of Menzhinsky (1934), why not cite that of Krassin, that of Dzerzhinsky, that of Lenin? Krassin, as a member together with Lenin and Bogdanov of the *troïka* which directed terrorist action in Russia after the 1905 Revolution, knew a great deal about Stalin, and did not take him for an eagle, exactly. Dzerzhinsky's name was often mentioned as a possible General Secretary of the Party, a man as firm but more loyal than Stalin. If Dzerzhinsky's successor at the G.P.U., Menzhinsky, was killed by his own successor, Yagoda, who in his turn was in effect suppressed by his successor, Yezhov, *his* sudden death can also be questioned. Moreover, there is the disturbing case of Frunze, Commissar for War, who died in 1925 of a surgical operation, carried out against the advice of the doctors but on the express orders of Stalin. The unjustified arrest and deportation of Pilnyak, the author of a short story on the drama, does nothing to dissipate suspicion in this respect.

It was inevitable that the execution of the generals should concentrate attention on the hypothesis of a military plot, even though this was not "juridically" proved; an hypothesis according to which the chief guilty parties would be those about whose confessions—assumed to bear, the biggest doubt of all, on the accusation of "espionage"—nothing whatever is known. Now, repression in the Army began with the disappearance of such generals as Levandovsky, Schmidt, Kuzmichov, etc., who were never heard of afterwards; it preceded the trial of the Sixteen, and continued with the arrest of Putna, mentioned in the trial of the Seventeen where the name of Tukhachevsky was thrown into the arena; it was marked next by the "suicide" of Gamarnik, followed by the eight most sensational executions; then came an uninterrupted series of arrests and executions in which were implicated Marshals Yegorov and Blücher, practically the whole of the General Staff, military and naval, nearly half the cadres of both the Army and Navy, and even half the Council of War which had condemned the Eight. Under the politico-police conditions in Soviet Russia, merely to pose the question of a plot involving such countless numbers and fomented in the face of such an indescribable terror, is to solve it.

Neither between officers, nor between soldiers, nor between officers and soldiers, does there exist in the U.S.S.R. the possibility of such a concerted plot, even if it involved incomparably fewer people. The plan to attack the Kremlin with the aim of a "palace revolution," revealed in the trial of the Twenty-one, could only be conceived, moreover, to break the resistance of

the garrison and, if necessary, of the special troops of the
G.P.U. But this repression has struck at the leaders of the garrison and of the G.P.U. just as much as the Army. Thus Stalin's
last version is of a plot embracing all active forces and thus
leaving nobody to attack, a plot which would never have been
put into action. Such a version is about as likely as his more
recent one which he has used as a motive for the bloody purge
in the Navy: the "young school" in the Navy, in considering
that light units (submarines, torpedo-boats, hydroplanes) were
preferable to large, costly and vulnerable cruisers and dread-
noughts, were serving the "enemies of the people" by depriving
the U.S.S.R. of a fleet of the line; but "the glorious officials of
the People's Commissariat of the Interior cut off the head of
these reptiles."

Under the Stalin regime of universal informing and systematic
preventive amputation, if any embryo of a plot ever got as far
as being uttered, Stalin alone was in a position to take the
initiative in it and to hold its strings. This is not only the opinion
of Liushkov, a specialist on the subject, but also the lesson
taught by all political experience in Soviet Russia since the death
of Lenin. The only thing that is certain in these gloomy tales
is the major responsibility, the general and particular guilt of
Stalin. Not to neglect any hypothesis, we cannot even exclude
the possibility that Stalin was not only responsible for Kirov's
assassination, as has been verified, but directly guilty of being
the secret instigator. In this case, knowing beforehand of terrorist inclinations, he would have given orders to let them
continue, perhaps to turn the murderous attempt in the direction
of Kirov, in order later to feign indignation and undertake
reprisals. The horrifying picture of carnage itself would prove
that he recognised the complicity of the whole active population, communists included, in the alleged plot. In such circumstances, a "plot" has another name in all languages. It is a
question of latent popular hatred, silent collective hostility toward Stalin, and an inexorable preventive struggle led by him,
by his personal clients, his ruling oligarchy, his pretorian guard,

all armed to the teeth, in the name of a new privileged class against an unarmed people.

Before deciding, all at once or gradually, on the vast purges in which the trials culminated, Stalin must have weighed the pros and cons, the advantages and disadvantages. The only disadvantages he could see were the loss of capable men, whom he did not believe irreplaceable, and the probable bad effect abroad, which in fact he considered negligible. As for the advantages, he saw many. He had already got rid of rivals; he now destroyed possible successors. With the same thought in the back of his mind he forbade too marked public acknowledgment of those in his immediate circle. He had once said: "To choose the victim, to prepare the blow with care, to sate an implacable vengeance, and then to go to bed. . . . There is nothing sweeter in the world!" At last he was sating his vengeance. He forces his adversaries to bestow on him diplomas of genius, under the threat of death, torture and reprisals, he compels them to dishonour themselves to deprive them of a martyr's halo, and to be sure of their future silence, sends them to their death all the same. He uses his ex-opponents for various ends, hoping to turn public execration momentarily from himself by presenting them as drunken slaves, and by attributing the economic collapse to wrecking and sabotage, thus placing on his subordinates his own complete responsibility. He lengthens the proscriptions to destroy suspects and to exile those of whom he is doubtful, and at the same time to make up the penal labour forces necessary for the huge public works. In his own way he carries out, in the interests of his personal dictatorship if not of economy and culture, the renewal of the cadres. He also gets rid of the people who know too much about him, about his past, his present, his imperfections, his crimes.

He is haunted by anxiety about his biography. His oldest comrades, Mdivani, Yenukidze, Ordjonikidze, have without a doubt paid with their lives for too long standing a friendship. Neither they, nor Gorky and Yagoda, who were nearest to him in their last years, nor Zinoviev and Kamenev, who knew him too well at the time of their close collaboration and who

were nearest also to Lenin, will write any memoirs. If there
are papers hidden anywhere, it is doubtful if those who know
of them will be able to use them for a long time to come.
Yenukidze, Krupskaya, Gorky have modified or falsified the
memoirs they had written, in the new editions, to please the
despot. Khandjian, after his suicide, was accused by his successor of having allowed works to be published in which "the
role of Comrade Stalin as creator of the Bolshevik organisations
in Transcaucasia and Armenia is ignored." Another, A. K.
Karayev, has had to answer for the crime of having "concealed,"
in a book which appeared in 1926, Stalin's part in the workers'
movement at Baku in former times. Such examples abound, and
reveal in Stalin, side by side with megalomania and a mania for
persecution, an inferiority complex which torments him. His
tamest historians are mercilessly chastised when they are unable
to attribute new merits to him, to fashion for him out of whole
cloth a past role fitting to his future stature. The "Histories of
the Party" published up to 1937, although bearing the official
stamp—even those of Bubnov and Yaroslavsky, Popov and
Knorin—are declared false or void. In 1938, a new *Short History of the Party* was published anonymously, under strict and
salutary instructions, which superseded the works of all previous
historians and became the definitive edition. Stalin requires that
in every circumstance he shall be the leading light. He destroys
the last witnesses capable of one day producing a true testimony
about him. He avenges himself now on these for not having
known how to speak, now on those for not having known how
to keep silent. And he shows the measure of his courage, as of
his "humanism," when, secure from all risk, he insults the defeated, stamps upon his prisoners, and rages over their dead
bodies.

In the same way, Stalin never has enough of grandiloquent
and artificial praise, of compliments more or less sincere. The
majority of his victims hoped in vain to disarm him by celebrat-
ing his virtues, his talents, his genius, rivalling each other in unspeakable servility. To quote, after the work of N. Lakoba, but
one extract from this anthology of fawning humility, it is

enough to dip at hazard into Bukharin: ". . . The iron hand of the workers' most remarkable guide, the commander-in-chief of millions of men, whose name is the symbol of grandiose Five Year Plans, of gigantic struggles and victories, Stalin." The editorials of *Pravda*, and of the ten thousand other papers, are in the same vein: "Millions of adoring eyes are fixed on Stalin. His name is repeated by the workers of the entire world with profound emotion. He is the hope of all the oppressed. He is the father of all who struggle for happiness and humanity." Every time the Bolshevik Fuehrer utters a few trite words, *Pravda* sees in his speech a "new stage in universal history," and loses no opportunity of declaring that "the powerful personality of Stalin epitomises all the grandeur of the coming era of humanity," or something else of the sort. The self-confessed enemies of the people, traitors, spies, Trotskyists, double-faced fascists, have all uttered or written similar dithyrambs.

Lenin was sanctified after his death; Stalin is deified while still alive. A certain delegate to a congress speaks on his mandate in these terms: ". . . At that moment I saw our beloved father, Stalin, and I lost consciousness. The 'hurrahs' resounded for a long time, and it was probably this noise which brought me to myself. . . . You will excuse me, comrades, if, finding myself in such a state of bewilderment at the sight of Comrade Stalin, I did not salute him." Zealous officials show their conformist zeal by christening localities with Stalin's name, with every imaginable ending. Other philistines organise at Batoum an exhibition of "revolutionary relics" connected with the life of the dictator. Others place his bust on Stalin Peak, the highest point of the Pamir mountains, where Lenin Peak is only second highest; others erect it on the Elburz in the Caucasus, and announce in their artificial exaltation: "On the highest crest in Europe, we have erected the bust of the greatest man of our time." As for the tsars, capital letters are compulsory when printing pronouns and adjectives referring to his redoubtable name. Eastern "poets" are paid large sums to raise the pitch of the panegyrics: "Story tellers no longer know to whom to compare Thee; poets have not enough pearls with which to describe Thee." Other verses in the same vein: "O Thou, mighty one, chief of the peoples, Who callest man to life, Who awakest the earth to fruitfulness, Who summonest the centuries to youth . . . O sun, Who art reflected by millions of human hearts." It appears also that Stalin is "more lofty than the high celestial spaces" and "clearer and purer than the clear waters of Baikal"; "his eye is more piercing than the falcon's"; finally, he is "stronger than the valiant lion," and moreover, "a magnificent garden of perfumed fruits," and further, "the most glittering diamond of the Party"; "like the sun, he darts his rays, golden springs of happiness." A hideous iconography abundantly illustrates this rhetoric.

More occidental writers also fall into line, and that without much effort. A certain Prokofiev sums up: "Everything is embraced in this immense name. Everything: the Party, the Fatherland, life, love, immortality, everything!" Another, Avdeyenko by name, with a marvellous imitation of spontaneity, recites a great heroic lay, learnt by heart, with verses in this strain: "I can fly to the moon, voyage in the Arctic, make some great discovery, invent a new machine, for my creative energy is oppressed by nobody—and all thanks to Thee, great educator, Stalin"; and the final verse: "Men of all times and of all nations will call by Thy name all that is beautiful, strong, wise, and marvellous. Thy name is and will be engraved in every factory, on every machine, on every tuft of the earth, in the hearts of all men." The prize must be given to the man who goes one better than a paroxysm. Further to the West, where the Soviet budget (largesse, author's rights, travelling invitations) maintains numerous prostitutes of the pen, there is in France a fairly well-known writer sufficiently venal to publish a biography of Stalin, studded with gross errors of history and geography and with falsifications skilfully reproduced on a groundwork of apologetics as degrading for the author as for the beneficiary. Tukhachevsky and his executed colleagues had greeted in Stalin a great master of strategy. An aviator famous in the U.S.S.R. proclaims: "Where Stalin appears, shadows melt away . . . ," which proves that it is possible to climb high and sink low, that certain types of heroism and of shamelessness are compatible.

The crew of the *Marat* wrote to Stalin: "Because they are the object of Your tenderness, animated by Your paternal love and Your solicitude, the men of our magnificent country accomplish miracles such as the world has never seen, and multiply their exploits on land, in the air, on the water and under the water." But Ivanov, the commander of this cruiser, was none the less shot as a double-faced enemy of the people. It is only too clear that these rivalries in frenzied adulation into which irony sometimes slips, mingled with derisive extravagance, betray an intense fear of not satisfying the tyrant's demands, and that the poetic and literary flatteries, works written to order and paid for dearly, have only an appearance of fervour. So many bullets in so many heads, so many convicts and so many forced labour gangs forbid any illusion on this all too revealing subject.

10

"THE soul of all poetry," it appears that Stalin is also the spirit of all prose: his hired admirers attribute to him the key role in every sphere of human activity, in industry and in agriculture, in the arts and in the sciences, pure and applied. Every result is achieved thanks to his "genial perspicacity," to his constant intervention "in all the details" of all creative work. Be it a question of oil, or cast-iron, or chemistry, or transport, or aviation, or collective farms, or architecture, or town-planning, the "great initiator" has thought of everything, foreseen everything and prescribed everything; he "settles all the chief problems personally," and moreover "looks after all the practical details himself." Even the films are due to his "daily instructions." A new Pico della Mirandola, he knows everything, and more besides; every day brings a fresh proof of that. But in 1937, on the twentieth anniversary of October, which almost coincided with the end of the second Five Year Plan, the internal situation in the U.S.S.R. was such that, well-versed as they are in presenting cooked accounts and addicted to pompous and interminable speeches, neither Stalin nor his experts dared to bring out the doctored balance-sheet of their precarious work. A deathly silence enveloped the solemn date, awaited as the most portentous of the regime.

The reason is that the second Five Year Plan, although reduced to more reasonable proportions than those elaborated beforehand in the delirious drafts, could not be better carried out than the first in any respect, and for the same reasons. "Industry is seven times more productive than before the war, and the national income has quadrupled," Stalin summed up at the Congress of the Soviets in 1936. But it is useless to quote figures which have no stable meaning; serious indices of value and quality are lacking, and for good reason. Stalin is more ignorant than anyone of the real economic situation, for he receives only false information, dictated by fear, since sincerity on the part of the commissars, secretaries, heads of trusts and enterprises is interpreted as sabotage and punished by death. The corrective activities of the police *svodki* banish illusions without correcting the figures. The reports, accounts and statistics do not reflect the real situation. Every verification or inspection reveals a lie, every analysis uncovers a snare. Comparisons in arbitrary and variable roubles teach nothing. Quantitative progress appears fallacious when one knows the corresponding investments, apart from the waste which must be deducted. Craft production, so important in former times in Russia, reached its lowest point in 1937, and does not figure in these flattering comparisons. Estimates of the national income are so much pure fantasy. The rise in cost and selling prices, preeminently negative signs, serve to swell the production figures, printed on the inferior Soviet paper. One must therefore have recourse to other criteria.

It can no longer be denied in 1937, in spite of lying propaganda, that the general balance-sheet is disastrous: the statements made at the trials to clear Stalin at the expense of his underlings prove it beyond all doubt. Railway catastrophes, mine explosions, breakdowns of machinery, waste of material, loss of live-stock, deterioration of goods, useless destruction, unpardonable sacrifices, financial deficits, commercial disorder, accidents and waste —all this chaos characterises, not the conduct of certain commissariats, but the "Soviet" totalitarian economy as a whole. Stalin knows everything, does everything, has his eye on everything, is responsible for everything, declare his apologists at every turn. In accusing Pyatakov and his colleagues, therefore, he is accusing himself in the highest degree and confessing that all is for the worst under the worst of all possible dictatorships. And here is one of the accessory reasons grafted, in the construction of the trials, onto the main considerations: the designation of people to bear the guilt of Stalin the Infallible—it being understood that the main and secondary considerations are now interchangeable, now identical, and that the economic depression and the war peril are considered by Stalin only in so far as they affect the preservation of his power.

Just as the so-called Bolshevik system has never, according to T. G. Masaryk, been anything but a complete absence of system, or in other words, a series of improvisations and an accumulation of compromises, in spite of the vaunted principles, in the same way, the so-called plans are characterised by the absence of any real plan. If there still exists in the U.S.S.R. a more or less directed economy, it is only by an infringement of the plans, by violations and transgressions which are called by the untranslatable slang name of *blatt*, which expresses the very antithesis of plan, personal combinations substituted for stable rules which make it possible to get around various obstacles. The *blatt* obviates by personal initiative the impossibilities conceived by the central authority, but it cannot solve, against the police State, all the problems. It puts off the final crisis of this pseudo-system without preventing it; it protracts with its palliatives a fraudulent bankruptcy of which arithmetical fictions, complete or partial, give no account. There are, however, true criteria which provide the key to the enigma.

One has only to compare the average wage in Soviet Russia with that of Tsarist Russia, reducing them both to a common unit of measurement (cf. Yvon, *L'U.R.S.S. telle qu'elle est*). A wage of 600 kilogrammes of bread per month in 1913 was reduced to 170 kilos in 1935, a decrease of more than two thirds. But it had risen to 800 kilos in 1927, at the time of the tenth anniversary of October, the last year of the N.E.P. In 1937 it corresponded to 260 kilos, that is, less than half the pre-war level; and here the apparent increase was due to the increased advantages of the privileged sections of the community, incorporated in the sum total. (Professor S. Prokopovich cleverly infers from partial Soviet data, which by their artifice are on the whole favourable to Stalin's regime, that the pre-war monthly wage of 24 roubles 30 had dropped to 16 roubles 50 in 1937— from which moreover obligatory deductions varying from 15 to 21 percent must be subtracted.) Expressed in the basic food commodity, black bread, a simple calculation which gets nearer to the truth than the too learned indices of the statisticians, the average working wage at the end of the second five year period is less than half the miserable wage of former times, one of the lowest in Europe, when account is taken of wages in kind (social services) and deductions (fines and subscriptions, voluntary and otherwise). The area of urban housing facilities is under five square metres per person on paper, and in fact it is less than half for the working class. Social insurances stingily redistribute with one hand a minute part of what is taken away with the other. Since the agricultural workers share the unhappy lot of the town workers as far as wages are concerned, it is the whole mass of the population which pays for this peculiarly cruel system of oppression and exploitation of man by man, ravaged by negligence and arbitrary power, venality and lies, bribery and parasitism, nepotism and tyranny, the symbolic knout and the death penalty.

From 1927 to 1937 hundreds of milliards of roubles were invested in industry and agriculture in order to give them a modern equipment—but the result has been that in fact they are operating at a loss. Even though we know what Soviet milliards are, and what Stalin's milliards are worth, the resources thus sunk in the means of production nevertheless represent a considerable drain on the national income, precisely that brutal lowering of the standard of living expressed in wages. At this exorbitant price, the technical victories appear at their true value. Not one of them was worth the expense, the sacrifice, the suffering inflicted on a great people, whom history has left without means of defence. The example of other nations, and even of Tsarist Russia, shows that it was possible to have done far better, at a lower cost and with more lasting results by more rational and more humane methods.

The industrial structure, organised without forethought under conditions of terror, is showing itself unworkable in practice, unless profound reforms are introduced—as was indeed to be expected: permanent disequilibrium, irremediable disproportions, premature depreciation of material, immobilisation of machinery, dilapidation and flaws in new buildings, frequent damages and multiplicity of accidents, forced interruptions of work, all indicate the vices of the "system" and the imperfections of the regime. The quality of production daily becomes lower and diminishes the quantity that can be used; the proportion of defective or useless articles is as much, and sometimes more than 50 per cent in certain model factories. Transport is going to rack and ruin; stakhanovism is precipitating the breakdown of indispensable and costly machine-tools. The production of consumption goods, in relation to that of capital goods, did not in 1937 come up to pre-war level, and will not do so even in 1942, at the end of the third Five Year Plan (*Pravda*, August 14, 1937). The productivity of labour in the U.S.S.R. is about one fifth that of the great industrial countries. The cost of production is five times as high, perhaps,—the official figures do not warrant a sure estimate. It is impossible to calculate the losses, the thefts, the depreciation, the deficiencies. Excessive centralisation, the number of intermediary authorities, the abuse of power, bureaucracy, formalism, suspicion and incompetence, in addition to the other wounds in Soviet society, produce sterility in industrial methods and explain to a large extent the mediocre results. It is understandable that Stalin is anxious at all costs to find treacherous saboteurs to answer for his failures, and why, in 1937, he decapitated more than half the enterprises by sending their directors to hard labour or death.

Collective agriculture suffers from the same evils as state industry, and also from evils peculiar to itself. Under the yoke of the new rural bureaucracy, with its police psychology and its red-tape, the *kolkhoz* show no profit and the giant *sovkhoz* only exist by means of subsidies, and as experience shows are bound inevitably to be parcelled out. The losses caused by the collectivisation of cattle will not be repaired for a long time, unless it be by private rearing. Cereal production fell from 96.6 million tons in 1913 to 77 million in 1936, a figure which S. Prokopovich establishes from Soviet data. But, said Stalin in December 1935: ". . . Reaping with the reaping-machine involves enormous losses of grain. . . . With this system we are losing from 20 to 25 per cent of the harvest." He thus calculated the losses at one milliard poods per year, that is, sixteen million tons, nearly a quarter of the theoretical harvest, and talked boastfully of "raising the annual grain production in the near future to seven and eight milliard poods." In 1937, a year claimed as exceptional, propaganda spoke of a gross harvest of 110 million tons, that is the seven milliard poods required by Stalin, who commands the elements as he commands men, and imposes his will on the soil, the sowings and the weather, but above all on the statistics. But this was a figure on paper, a theoretical figure proclaimed long before the harvest, a record figure from which we must subtract at least a quarter for the losses admitted by Stalin, and further losses due to ordinary administrative incompetence: a sixth of the harvest, left uncut in the fields, rotted under the snow—this in a country where gleaning is punishable by death as "injury to socialist property." Moreover, the losses sustained during transport and storage are not reckoned. The State requisitions, at ruinous prices, about 85 per cent of the produce of agriculture. The general poverty which results is pitiable; only private or family cultivation, side by side with the pseudo-socialist sector, prevents famine. In 1937 collectivisation was almost complete (18.5 million peasant families), and to bring in the last cultivators still outside the *kolkhoz* (1.4 million families), prohibitive taxes on their horses were decreed in 1938, although the year before Stalin had reminded the Central Committee of "the principle of voluntary membership." These new measures of spoliation will not be the last word, for the Bolsheviks have never finished undoing what was done and redoing what they only knew how to undo.

If industry and agriculture work at a loss and swallow up a good part of the national income, the deficit is seen in the privations inflicted on the working masses: in short, it is made up by millions of hours of unpaid labour and involves the sacrifice of millions of human lives. The test of population, which Stalin keeps concealed, speaks more eloquently than any other. On the basis of the 1926 census there were 147 million inhabitants, and assuming a birth rate of 2.3 per cent per annum, or an annual increase of roughly three million, a figure which Stalin keeps repeating, the second Five Year Plan anticipated a population of 180 millions at the end of 1937. The census taken at the beginning of that year, after a minute preparation and with an army of over a million officials, ended in the arrest of the directors of the statistical bureau and of their close collaborators, the results remaining a mystery. According to W. Krivitsky, whose excellent confidential source of information is the G.P.U.: "Instead of the 171 million inhabitants calculated for 1937, only 145 million were found; thus nearly 30 million people in the U.S.S.R. are missing." Actually, if the Plan calculated 180 million at the end of the year, that would make 177 million at the beginning, or 32 million missing. Instead of increasing each year to the extent of "a whole Finland," as Stalin said, the U.S.S.R. has lost the population equivalent of a whole Poland, or ten Finlands. Far from "reflecting the victories of socialism" as anticipated, the census reflects the defeats of Bolshevism, the disasters of industrialisation and collectivisation, which have often been compared to the effects of several devastating wars. Stalin has ordered a new census for 1939, and this time he will see to it that he obtains the total fixed in advance. But he will not bring the dead back to life, nor compensate so much physical loss and spiritual ruin.

The information, tragic in its harshness and of an inexpressible pathos, collected by W. Krivitsky, is borne out by fragmentary and approximate accounts from other sources. While a correspondent of the *Courrier Socialiste* was already able to report five million victims of the famine of 1932-33 (*Sozialisticheski Vestnik*, No. 9, for 10 May 1934), an American socialist, Harry Lang, returning utterly dismayed from a stay in the U.S.S.R., learnt from a high Soviet functionary and published in the New York *Forward* that at least six million starving people perished in the Ukraine at that period; he reports that 40 per cent of the population disappeared in certain districts of the Ukraine and White Russia; relief organisations count 104,000 dead in 1933 among German peasant colonies alone (*Forward*, 19 February 1936, etc.). A disillusioned American communist, Adam J. Tawdul, learnt from Skrypnik that at least eight million persons died of hunger in the Ukraine and northern Caucasus; Balitsky, head of the G.P.U. in the Ukraine, estimated eight to nine million victims in the Ukraine alone; Lovin, manager of the tractor works at Cheliabinsk, told him that more than a million died of starvation in the Urals, Trans-Volga and Eastern Siberia (*New York American*, 18-29 August 1935). If one thinks of the distress of the millions of exiles; of the innumerable ill-treated penal labour squads; of the concentration camps, where a frightful mortality makes huge gaps; of the overflowing isolators and prisons; of the millions of abandoned children, of whom only a minute percentage manages to survive; of the executions and punitive expeditions; in short of the multitudes "mown down in large armfuls" by Stalin, one cannot be astonished at the immense charnel-houses of this gigantic prison which with double irony is called a "socialist fatherland."

Author and abettor of waste of substance, equivalent in a modern State to several great wars lost; responsible more than anyone for a material regression and a moral decline, which drag Russia far behind in spite of her aeroplanes and tanks; Stalin finds himself caught between the fear of a limited war in which the U.S.S.R. would be face to face with a powerful adversary, and the desire for a general war in which she would benefit from powerful alliances. A war thus limited would be his certain downfall; a general war would, in his opinion, be his salvation. This alternative guides his foreign policy, which aims at bringing the U.S.S.R. into any coalition aimed against

Germany or Japan and incidentally against their allies. The Russian intervention in Spain (1936) and in China (1937) clearly illustrate his tactics of moderate intervention according to the limited means of the U.S.S.R.; he is thus able to harry and help weaken his enemies at small cost, and so to have a preponderant voice in the conduct of the war and the conclusion of the peace, while preserving intact the main part of his forces for more vital circumstances. The same perspective was willingly adopted in regard to Czechoslovakia (1938), since the principal burden of the struggle against Germany and Italy would fall on France and England. The pretence of an active, warlike patriotism, under cover of democratic or traditionalist formulae, by the Communist Parties subject to Stalin in the West and in the East, has no other motive. A parallel work of intermeddling by various methods of influence is carried out in government parties, now exploiting respectable sentiments, now inadmissible interests, and always hideous sycophancy.

Karl Marx, of whom the Bolsheviks make a use which is apt to come back on them, as long ago as 1864 denounced: ". . . the immense and unobstructed encroachments of that barbarous power whose head is at St. Petersburg and whose hand is detected in all the cabinets of Europe. . . ." Since then, Russia has only changed for the worse, and as Custine said a century ago, "the nation itself is still nothing but a notice placarded upon Europe, dupe of an imprudent diplomatic fiction." However, by his tortuous diplomacy and thanks to the bankruptcy of contemporary socialism, Stalin has without difficulty achieved partial successes, because of the deep disquiet of the old Europe, now in a state of panic before the totalitarian States, who desire to redraw the map of the world. With monstrous ambiguity he has been able to treat with the pluto-democratic States, who are blind to the antagonism between Slavs and Germans, who are not counsellors of the affinities between left and right wing totalitarianisms, who are not capable of realising the dangers in time to act quickly, and who are resigned in their shortsightedness to accept without conditions any eventual cooperation which will assure their existence in the event of war. But at the same time, by his autocratic policy and his backward economy, Stalin is sapping the power at his disposal, by depriving it of a popular basis, by suppressing the *élite*, by shaking the armed forces to their foundation, by undermining the State with internal contradictions, and by exciting centrifugal forces within his Empire. It is this which explains Moscow's glacial silence in the most critical hours of European history since the coming of national-socialism in Germany.

Eternal Russia could hold out a long time in a defensive war, but the regime would have to be transformed or to disappear in a war which threatened the country in its vital parts. This contrast between Russia itself and Stalin's regime, has inexorable consequences. A military defeat of the U.S.S.R., or an internal crisis, might be fatal to her unwary allies and turn to disaster. A final common victory won by the arms and resources of her allies, and ending in general exhaustion, would bring into force another fear expressed by Marx. If the continent of Europe persisted in capitalist excesses, the submission of man to the machine, the armaments race, the piling up of public debts, then—as the author of *Capital* wrote in 1867—"the rejuvenation of Europe by means of the knout and by a compulsory infusion of Kalmuk blood, predicted so gravely by the half-Russian and wholly Muscovite, Herzen, . . . would end by becoming inevitable."

II

BUT young Russia, bled white by Stalin, leaves the field free for Germanic dynamism, and holds itself on the defensive like the old decadent western nations, which at least postpones the apocalyptic end envisaged by Herzen and by Marx, prophets of socialism, who were often opposed in their views. Her internal regime prevents her playing in the history of our time a role in proportion to her importance, and in this respect Stalin shows himself the chief benevolent agent of Germany. This police regime is still evolving in the midst of contradictions, and will go on evolving: until, at the first serious shock, it will undergo a sudden change, announced by every sign, and prepared by invisible ferments. Before it reaches a stable stage of development, its transitory character makes it impossible to define it in a satisfactory formula; but the most striking traits of its outward appearance forbid, in any case, the flattering definitions proposed by Stalin.

Lenin, Trotsky and Bukharin, the three chief thinkers of the regime at the period when it was still permitted to think, could not agree as to its definition; the first preferred State capitalism, the others State socialism. The subsequent evolution under Stalin has both simplified and complicated the problem. The difficulty of choice is doubtless due to the identity of content in the two terms. It is significant that the same hesitation occurs in the case of the state forms of fascism. The old vocabulary is thus ill-adapted to express new historical phenomena. The new terms, Bolshevism and fascism, in themselves empty of political meaning, were necessary to describe hitherto unknown social movements and their empirical ideology. In the final analysis, these movements show so many similarities, and are open to so many mutual plagiarisms, they borrow and exchange so many things from one another, that the same word, "totalitarian," another addition to the modern vocabulary, becomes them both perfectly. Mussolini began by imitating Lenin; Hitler continued by imitating Mussolini and Stalin; the latter, in return, copies his two rivals, especially in their worst features. At long intervals the three dictators, with Stalin as leader, follow one another in the way in which they educate and discipline their subjects by bringing them into line, throwing them into prison and putting them to death. It is hardly possible that so many analogies between Bolshevism and fascism in word and deed, in means and methods, in institutions and types of men, do not reflect some historical relationship, unless one admits the possibility of a complete divorce between the essence and the form.

As for Stalin, he contends that even "the expression State socialism is incorrect." In 1936 he considered that "the complete victory of the socialist system in all spheres of the national economy is now an accomplished fact," and that "socialism, the first stage of communism, is already realised by us in the main." He went so far as to say that stakhanovism "prepares the conditions necessary for passing from socialism to communism." The facts themselves are enough to give him the lie and more than enough to condemn him. Stalin denies "State socialism" in the U.S.S.R. on the ground that the means of production are collective property. But the appropriation of profit has an unquestionably private character, and it is this which matters. Private profit is apparent in the growing social inequality, which is more revolting in its arrant injustice than in the capitalist countries where it is diminishing, more intolerable in the terminology of hypocritical equalitarianism. No society, it is true, has ever existed without a hierarchy, without authority, without natural and artificial privileges. But the socialist dream of founding one has in Russia turned into a nightmare. "The expropriation of the expropriators" has led to a sort of bureaucratic feudalism under which the proletariat and the peasantry, debased by officialdom and the mandarinate, have been reduced to a kind of serfdom. If the methods of production are not exactly capitalist, a term which in any case is indefinable, it is only because, for the majority of the Soviet pariahs, the system deserves rather the name of slavery.

Stalin analyses as follows the "governing strata" of the Party: approximately 3 to 4000 superiors, the "high command"; then 30 to 40,000 middle leaders, "our officer cadres"; lastly 100 to 150,000 subalterns, "our sub-officer cadres." These two hundred thousand individuals dominate the population politically and embrace the bureaucracy, the specialists, the intellectuals, the functionaries who occupy economically privileged positions. According to Trotsky, the most favoured social categories can be estimated at about 10 million people, that is 25 million with their families. If the population is 145 million, W. Krivitsky's figure, these privileges are at the expense of 120 million people; if it were 180 million, the figure of the Plan, they would be at the expense of 155 million. It is a regime of privilege because one of exploitation, a regime of police because one of oppression.

Herzen defined the old Tsarist Russia in a striking paradox which is still valid for the U.S.S.R.: "A mixed structure without architecture, without solidity, without roots, without principles, heterogeneous and full of contradictions. A civil camp, a military chancellery, a state of siege in time of peace, a mixture of reaction and revolution, as likely to endure a long time as to fall into ruins tomorrow."

This mixture of reaction and revolution baffles those who like classical situations, and lends itself ill to the poor resources of sociological language, which, in turn, does not lend itself to the introduction of new words and phrases. Fascism also has this disconcerting mixture; Mussolini calls it revolution, his opponents answer: preventive counter-revolution. Revolution and counter-revolution have very various interpretations, and doubtless it is no chance that in the U.S.S.R., in the quarrels over historical interpretation between the victorious Tarlé school and the Pokrovsky school condemned to silence, the revolutionary role of Bonaparte or the counter-revolutionary role of Napoleon, plays such a large part. Some saw the Russian counter-revolution in Bolshevism itself, despite the inauguration of a new juridical system of collective ownership, others recognise it only after the imposture of Stalin's Constitution. It can also be understood as the period when practice went openly against theory, when the old illusions of belief gave way to the new unbelieving cynicism, when unconscious contradiction between word and act was transformed into conscious lying. In this sense, Lenin represents the revolution in spite of its defeats, Stalin the counter-revolution in spite of its pretended victories.

We must go back a little to trace more precisely the course of this formless counter-revolution, whose effects will for long be less evident than the causes. T. G. Masaryk, more clear-sighted in sociological analysis than in his conceptions as a State builder, has best emphasised the mortal error which Lenin passed on to Stalin: "When one thinks one has reached the definitive culmination of evolution, and that one possesses an infallible knowledge of the whole organisation of society, one ceases to work for its progress and its perfection, and one's principal, and indeed sole anxiety is only to preserve one's position and power." Experience fully confirms his opinion of "this abstract regime deduced from a thesis and put into practice by violence," "the absolutistic dictatorship of a single man and his auxiliaries," a regime of rigid centralism, of inquisition and infallibility: "The Bolshevik dictatorship has its source in an infallibility devoid of all critical judgment, of all scientific spirit; a regime which is afraid of criticism and of the judgment of thinking men is, by this fact alone, impossible."

The force of things and the behaviour of men have contradicted all Lenin's optimistic forecasts, his hopes in a superior democracy as much as his semi-libertarian ideas expressed in the *State and Revolution* and other writings of the same period, at the dawn of the revolution. Nothing in the individual theses of Trotsky has stood the test any better, in particular his wordy and abstract theory of the "permanent revolution." Lenin died too soon to write the epilogue to the miscarriage of Bolshevism. Trotsky has not availed himself of the leisure afforded by exile to make a true and conscientious examination; even his memoirs do not make the contribution to history which one has the right to expect from such a protagonist; his articles and pamphlets vainly paraphrase a hackneyed argument without throwing light on a single problem. The miscarriage of Bolshevism in Russia is coupled with the irremediable failure of the International, and the lessons of experience go far beyond the sphere of civil war. Democratic socialism in its various forms, in the name of legitimate defence against fascism, is almost everywhere allowing itself to be led, circumvented and compromised by dictatorial communism. The death agony of socialist hope in the world thus opens up an immeasurable ideological crisis. It will be the part of the epigones of a powerless generation to make out the balance-sheet of national Bolshevism, of international communism and of traditional socialism, and to draw from it some useful lessons. And this should logically lead them to examine what is still alive and what is dead in the parent doctrine, Marxism.

INDEX

Abramovich, R., 260, 530
Adler, Friedrich, 626
Adler, Victor, 45
Agranov, I. S., 588, 635
Akulov, I. A., 518, 606, 634
Alexander I, Tsar, 18, 259, 260, 528, 541, 561, 562
Alexander II, Tsar, 27, 28, 541
Alexander III, Tsar, 28, 541
Alexandra Feodorovna, Tsarina, 283
Alexeyev (S.-D. worker), 51
Alexeyev (engineer), 226
Alexinsky, G., 121, 137
Alliluyev, Sergo, 16, 60, 135, 593
Alliluyeva, Nadiejda, 593, 631, 656
Alsky, 334, 340
Andreyev, A. A., 270, 429, 430, 476, 484, 517, 606
Andreyev, Leonid, 77, 104
Andreyeva, Marie, 77
Anglo-Russian Committee, 427, 428, 449, 452, 456
Antonov-Ovseënko, V., 73, 161, 334, 342, 415, 476, 477, 635
Arakcheyev, A., 260, 528, 592
Armand, Inessa, 137
Atabekov, 301
Avdeyenko, A., 662
Avvakum, Archpriest, 560
Axelrod, Pavel Borissovich, 30, 36, 38, 39, 45, 51, 55, 56, 57, 63, 90, 109, 122, 137
Azev, Evno, 136

Babel, I., 395, 574
Babeuf, Gracchus, 4, 455, 473, 529
Badayev, A., 135
Bakayev, Ivan Petrovich, 626
Bakunin, M. A., 4, 22, 23-25, 36, 90, 127, 156, 196, 435, 500, 582
Bakuradze, 3
Balitsky, V. A., 635, 670
Balmashev, S. V., 69
Barmin, Alexander, 635
Bauer, Otto, 134
Bazarov, V., 66, 121, 197, 530
Bebel, August, 84
Berdiayev, N. A., 35
Beria, Lavrenti, 637
Bernstein, Eduard, 37
Bestuyev-Riumin, 20

Bibineishvili, B., 3, 43, 44, 98
Biedny, Demian, 112, 167, 435, 579, 619
Bieletzky, S. P., 136
Bielinsky, V., 21
Bielov, General, 635, 637
Bismarck, Prince Otto von, 507, 591
Blagoyev, D. N., 102
Blanqui, Louis-Auguste, 4, 26, 41, 47
Blanquism, 91, 123, 124, 156, 157, 507
Blücher, B. K. (also called Galen), 227, 442, 568, 617, 635, 657
Blumkin, J., 496
Bocharidze, Mikha, 98
Bochorishvili, Mikha, 32
Bogdanov, Alexander, 66, 77, 132, 387, 656; member of Bolshevik Centre, 92; favours "illegal" action, 119-120; philosophical differences with Lenin, 127-128; arrest of, 346; his romance, *Red Star*, 504; on proletarian culture, 565
Boguslavsky, M. S., 271, 334, 472, 627
Bojowci, 73, 88, 93, 105, 246
Bolsheviks: split with Mensheviks, 54, 56, 58, 59, 61; hold Congress in London, 1905, 71; Conference at Tamerfors, 81-82; at Unity Congress, 1906, 85, 90, 91, 100, 105, 106, 107; definitive split with Mensheviks, 116, 129; Lenin calls congress at Prague, 1912, 129, 135, 136; demand recognition at Brussels Conference of Second International, 137, 138; and February Revolution, 145-148; April (1917) Conference, 154, 157, 158, 168; and October Revolution, 149 *seq.*; and thereafter *passim*
Bolshevik Centre, 92, 97, 109, 119, 125, 656
Bolshevik Congresses and Conferences (for earlier congresses *v.* S.-D. Party of Russia, and Bolsheviks):
—Sixth Congress (1917), 167, 168
—Seventh Congress (1918), 217, 218
—Eighth Congress (1919), 238, 239, 240, 255
—Ninth Congress (1920), 268, 271
—Tenth Congress (1921), 259, 271, 273, 278, 279, 336, 349
—Eleventh Congress (1922), 285, 292, 294, 295, 306

Bolshevik Congresses—*Continued*
—Twelfth Congress (1923), 305, 309, 311, 312, 322, 325, 326, 328, 331, 332, 337, 356, 406
—Conference of Jan. 1924, 348, 349
—Thirteenth Congress (1924), 360-364, 394, 459, 514
—Fourteenth Congress (1925), 397-409, 412, 415, 423
—Conference of Oct. 1926, 433, 434, 436-439
—Fifteenth Congress (1927), 453, 459, 460, 464-469, 470, 471, 477, 480
—Sixteenth Congress (1930), 494, 518-520, 548, 549
—Seventeenth Congress (1934), 553, 579, 580, 581, 587, 588
Bolshevik-Leninists (*v.* also Opposition, Left), 472, 477
Bolshevik Old Guard, 156, 157, 176, 191, 259, 285, 291, 339, 341, 344, 348, 354, 360, 385, 386, 447, 501, 535, 601, 604, 607, 634
Bonapartism, 63, 117, 321, 341, 385, 454, 576
Borodin, Mikhail, 442, 636
Bosch, Eugenia Bogdanova, 334, 376
Boyeviki (sharpshooters), 88, 89, 90, 91, 92, 94-106, 125, 126, 246
Brest-Litovsk, Treaty of, 213-215, 217-219, 277, 280, 286, 476, 566
Briukhanov, N. P., 517
Brussilov, General, 503
Bubnov, A. S., his *History of the C.P. S.U.*, 75, 130, 660; in October insurrection, 179; and Brest peace, 217; on Politbureau, 265; and the Opposition, 271, 334, 342; in China, 442, 443; breaks with Trotsky, 477; and Education, 514-516; on Commission on Russian History, 620; liquidated by Stalin, 634
Büchner, L., 21
Budyonny, Marshal, 617, 656
Bukharin, Nikolai I., 185, 249, 288, 315, 448, 476, 501, 646; in New York, 148; on National Question, 158, 202, 239; on Trotsky in October insurrection, 180, 183; and formation of Bolshevik Government, 191; on Constituent Assembly, 210; and Brest peace, 213, 216, 217; on Stalin, 231, 244, 483-487, 578, 580, 608, 661; member of C.C., 240, 265; on dictatorship, 259; on Trade Unions, 270; supports *troïka*, 299; Lenin on, 306; on the Party, 319, 361, 421, 459, 516; joins Stalin against Opposition bloc, 388, 391, 401, 405, 406, 411, 413, 439; on the peasants, 389-390, 399, 424; his *A.B.C.*

of Communism, 395; and the Comintern, 440, 483, 484, 487, 497; and Chinese Revolution, 442, 449; and Right Opposition, 447, 480, 482-489, 496, 497, 498, 597; confesses mistakes, 518, 532; and Five Year Plan, 504; on State socialism, 570, 673; on Commission on Russian History, 620; in Trial of "Rightist-Trotskyist Bloc," 632, **633**, **652**
Bulgakov, M., 574
Bulgakov, S. N., **35**
Bund, the, 31, 54, 66, 72, 107, 120
Butenko, T., 636, 649
Butov, Gregory V., 496
Byeloborodov, 227, 334, 340, 472, 495, 634

Catherine II, the Great, 19, 20, 499, 541, 547, 561, 562
Cavaignac, General, 166, 438, 444
Chachiashvili, Ilico, 97
Chaikovsky, N. V., 27
Chamberlin, W. H., 552, 640
Chang Tso-lin, 441, 442
Chavchavadze, I., **3**
Cheka, Extraordinary Commission (*v.* also G.P.U.), 189, 193, 221, 226, 227, 236, 250, 251, 266, 288, 289, 319, 373, 374, 425
Chen Pai-ming, 446
Chen Tu-hsiu, 444, 471
Chernishevsky. N. G., 21, 22, 127, 498
Chernomazov, M. E., 136
Chernov, M. A., 632
Chernov, V. M., 164, 166, 263
Cherviakov, A. G., 631, 637
Chiang Kai-shek, 442, 443, 444, 450
Chibriashvili, Datiko, 97, 98
Chicherin, George Vassilievich, 99, 161, 280, 390, 451, 487, 656
Chinese Revolution, 441-444, 450-452, 471
Chkheidze, George, 32
Chkheidze, Nicholas S., 15, 43, 119, 132, 135, 145, 150, 155, 204
Chkhenkeli, 135, 137
Chodrishvili, Zakro, **32**
Chorny Perediel (The General Distribution), 27, 30
Chubar, V., 440, 634, 637
Chudnietsky, Archpriest, 14
Chudnovsky, 248, 296
Ciliga, Dr. Anton, 640, 641
Civil War, 219-254, 270, 283, 289, 290, 309, 315, 319, 332, 346, 348, 356, 368, 384, 388, 435, 445, 452, 463, 509
Clausewitz, K., 146, 173
Clemenceau, Georges, 238, 451, 452
Cloots, Anacharsis, **303**

Cluseret, Gustave-Paul, 71
Cohn, Oscar, 101
Commune of Canton (December 1927), 471
Commune, the Paris (1871), 4, 71, 78, 145, 172, 198, 252, 278, 283, 464, 523
Communist International, 140, 146, 148, 154, 163, 236, 241, 243, 288, 290, 319, 351, 352, 370, 378, 386, 403, 416, 428, 430, 433, 436, 440, 442, 443, 448, 450, 471, 480, 483, 500, 580, 616, 621, 636, 676
—Executive Committee of, 335, 439, 449, 456, 497
—First Congress, 237
—Fourth Congress, 304
—Fifth Congress, 365-367
—Sixth Congress, 484, 487
Communist Party of China, 442-444, 451, 621; of France, 369, 621; of Germany, 237, 280, 335, 336, 369; of Great Britain, 433, 443; of Poland, 427, 586
Constituent Assembly, 148, 150, 152, 159, 162, 172, 174, 178, 188, 197, 207, 209, 210, 211, 257
Constitution, Stalin's, 602, 622, 623, 624, 630, 636, 675
Cromwell, 4, 5, 59, 62, 134, 283, 461
Custine, Marquis de, his On Russia in 1839 quoted, 376, 378, 382, 397, 402, 446, 495, 504, 511, 516, 519, 539, 547, 556, 562, 572, 671

Dalakishvili, Akaki, 97
Dalin, P., 280, 317
Dalin, S., 639
Dan, T., 76, 85, 119, 122, 153, 160
Danishevsky, 229
Daszynski, 105
David II, King of Georgia, 9
Davitashvili, M., 3
Deborin, A., 533
Decembrists (1825), 20, 21, 36
Degayev, 28, 136
Denikin, General, 219, 237, 241, 242, 245, 250, 275, 384
Diderot, Denis, 103, 546, 562
Djaparidze, Artshil, 110
Djaparidze, P., 71, 110, 248
Djibladze, Sylvester, 14, 15, 32, 43, 301
Djordjiashvili, Arsenius, 100
Djugashvili, Basil (Stalin's son by his second wife), 593
—Catherine (Stalin's mother), 1, 3, 5, 8, 16, 612, 656
—James (Stalin's son by his first wife), 593
—Svatlana (Stalin's daughter by his second wife), 593

—Vissarion (Stalin's father), 1
Djugeli, V., 373
Dobroliubov, N., 21
Dostoievsky, Feodor, 20, 21, 25, 518
Dreitzer, Ephim Alexandrovich, 626
Drobnis, Y. N., 334, 472, 495, 627
Dubassov, 179
Dubois-Crancé, Edmond-Louis-Alexis, 225
Duma, question of participating in elections for, 85, 118; First (Kadet), 87, 88, 108; Second (Red), 108, 117; Third (Black), 119; Fourth (War), 135, 136, 139, 144, 151
Dutov, 219
Dybenko, P. E., 192, 230, 258, 635
Dzerzhinsky, Felix Edmundovich, 222, 429, 476, 485; and National Question, 158; in October insurrection, 179; and formation of Bolshevik Government, 191; and Brest peace, 213; as head of Cheka and G.P.U., 223, 250, 288, 289, 297, 331; in Civil War, 235, 236, 249; suggests Politbureau, 265; supports Trotsky on Trade Union question, 270; his activity in Georgia, 307, 308, 311; appointed to Supreme Economic Council, 374; joins Stalin against Opposition, 388, 411, 413; on Soviet economy, 420, 424; on bureaucracy, 421; death, 425; possibly murdered by Stalin, 656-657
Dzvali, 98

Eastman, Max, 348, 412, 414, 458
Ebrialidze, Ilico, 97
Elbakidze, Arkady, 97
Elizabeth, Tsarina, 561
Eltsin, 334
Emancipation of Labour, 30, 35, 36
Engels, Friedrich, 4, 15, 35, 37, 42, 48, 49, 61, 63, 71, 78, 120, 173, 185, 193, 201, 222, 239, 247, 252, 350, 392, 500, 503, 507, 532, 579, 591, 595
Ermak, Ataman, 618
Essenin, S., 576, 631
Expropriations (v. also boyeviki), 88, 89, 92, 93, 114, 124

February (March) Revolution, 144, 146, 159, 189, 440
Fedin, C., 574
Feldman, General, 629
Feng Yu-hsiang, 441, 442, 446, 450
Figner, Vera, 27
Five Year Plan, projected, 460, 462, 463, 470, 493
—First (1928), 494-497, 500-502, 505-507, 512-513, 515, 520-529, 531, 535-

Five Year Plan—*Continued*
536, 538-540, 542-554, 557, 561, 567, 584, 597, 640
—Second (1934), 537, 538, 552, 553, 587, 598, 663-669
—Third (1938), 667
Fouché, Joseph, 476, 590
Fourier, Charles, 21, 538
French Revolution, 4, 20, 59, 65, 121, 139, 183, 251, 302, 316, 321, 353, 354, 459, 464, 473, 474, 475, 476, 590
Frumkin, M. I., 490
Frunze, M., 247, 292, 360, 386, 398, 657

Galen, *v.* Blücher
Gamarnik, Ian, 628, 631, 633, 657
Gambarov, A., 582
Gapon, Father, 70, 136
General Strike in England (1926), 427, 428, 433, 448
Georgia, description of, 6, 7, 10-13; history of, 8-9; bolshevisation of, 300-301; insurrection in (1924), 372, 373, 374
German Revolution, 213, 218, 233, 234, 281, 335, 336, 365, 368, 377, 503
Gershuni, Gregory, 69
Gironde and Girondins, 49, 63, 122, 200, 213, 246, 283, 476
Gladkov, F., 573
Glazman, 376
Glebov-Avilov, N. P., 408
Godunov, Tsar Boris, 409, 499, 504
Gogol, Nicholas, 20, 573
Goldava, Patsya, 95, 97
Goldenberg, 156
Goncharov, I., 20
Gorky, Maxim (Alexis Peshkov), 120, 503, 615, 632, 659; in Tiflis, 16; collaborates in *Novaya Zhizn*, 77; collects funds for Bolshevik Party, 92; at Capri, 128; Lenin's letter to, about Stalin, 134; hostile to Lenin and Bolsheviks after October insurrection, 176, 195, 196, 197; quoted on Russia, the Russians and the Revolution, 182, 211, 253-254, 290, 318, 320, 353, 356, 357, 498, 529, 581; on Lenin's relations with Trotsky, 222-223, 291; his literary work, 574; relations with Stalin, 593; his death, 625, 627; Yagoda accused of murder of, 633, 646; possibly murdered by Stalin, 655; falsifies his memoirs, 660
Gotz, Michael, 69
G.P.U. (State Political Direction; *v.* also Cheka), 288, 289, 328, 356, 374, 375, 382, 384, 395, 402, 408, 433, 447, 450, 453, 456, 457, 464, 465, 467, 469, 471, 476, 478, 482, 486, 488, 494, 496,

498, 499, 501, 517, 522, 524, 525, 530, 531, 545, 549, 567, 572, 575, 584, 588, 592, 598, 601, 603, 604, 606, 613, 617, 624, 629, 632, 635, 639, 641, 642, 645-647, 650, 653, 654, 656, 658, 669, 670
Griaznov, General, 100
Griboyedov, A., 445
Grinevetsky, 28
Grinko, G. F., 632
Groman, V., 530
Guchkov, A., 145
Gueguechkory, E. P., 119
Gusev, S. I., 378, 380

Hébert, Jacques, 354
Herzen, Alexander, 21-23, 25, 36, 435, 500, 505, 545, 550, 565, 610, 672, 675
Herzog, Wilhelm, 386
Hitler, 568, 586, 602, 615, 616, 642, 673
Howard, Roy W., 604, 623
Hyndman, Henry M., 68, 258

Iremashvili, I., 3
Ivan the Great, Tsar, 619
Ivan the Terrible, Tsar, 409, 498, 499, 503, 542, 560, 561, 619, 636, 642-646
Ivanov, Admiral, 635
Ivanov, People's Commissar, 632
Ivanov, V., 574
Ivanov-Razumnik, 639

Jacobins and Jacobinism, 4, 26, 63, 85, 121, 170, 183, 190, 200, 213, 251, 283, 303, 354, 413, 455, 459, 474, 562, 563
Jaurès, Jean, 189, 221, 253, 440, 590
Jeliabov, Alexander, 27, 28, 593, 601
Jitomirsky, 101, 136
Joffe, Adolf Abramovich, 79, 161, 213, 233, 329, 441, 465, 631
Joly, Maurice, 583
Jordania, Noah, 15, 42, 58, 74, 81, 87, 178, 205
"July Days," 164, 167

Kadets (Constitutional Democratic Party), 78, 87, 108, 180, 210
Kaganovich, L. M., 388, 429, 430, 484, 489, 517, 566, 606
Kakhovskoi, 20
Kaladze, R., 42
Kalandadze, Vano, 97
Kaledin, Ataman A. M., 219
Kalinin, Mikhail Ivanovich, in Tiflis, 16; opposes Lenin's *April Theses*, 156-157; President of E. C. of Soviets, 244, 266, 288; supports Lenin on Trade Union question, 270; and Kronstadt rebellion, 277; supports *troïka*, 299, 370; supports Stalin against Zinoviev and Kamenev, 388, 406, 411, 429; and peasants, 390, 399, 420; supports Right Opposition, 447,

480, 489; betrays Right Opposition, 482, 484; Stalin's hold over, 486; flatters Stalin, 518, 579

Kalyayev, Ivan P., 69, 593

Kamenev, Leon Borissovich, 166, 185, 209, 213, 274, 292, 349, 655, 659; at 1905 Congress, 71; on *Novaya Zhizn*, 77; and Duma elections, 118, 119; in Galicia with Lenin, 137
—in Revolution: his telegram to Grand-Duke Michael, 148; compromising policy, 150-153; opposes *April Theses*, 154, 156-158; imprisoned in "July Days," 165; opposes seizure of power, 173, 176; on Politbureau, 179, 265, 266; and formation of Bolshevik Government, 191, 194; his submission to Lenin, 240; proposes to decorate Stalin, 244; Trotsky on, 267, 287, 377; supports Lenin on Trade Unions, 270; Lenin on, 306; and the Georgian affair, 308, 311, 312
—in *troïka*: with Stalin and Zinoviev against Trotsky, 285, 291, 299, 321, 370; President of Moscow Soviet, 288; on State planning, 361; attacks "Trotskyism," 378, 379, 380; demands imprisonment of Trotsky, 381; Left Opposition against, 382
—in Opposition: conflict with Stalin, 383, 385, 386, 388, 396; and peasants, 390, 399, 423, 424; and Leningrad Opposition, 400-411; and Opposition bloc, 415, 425, 426, 434, 436, 438, 440, 459, 460; loses official posts, 416, 429; departure for Rome, 450; expelled from Party, 469
—capitulates to Stalin, 469, 470, 472, 477; Bukharin's interview with, 482-486, 497; his self-abasement, 489, 498; denounces Bukharin, 518; second expulsion, 535; arrested, 594, 598; in trial of "Trotskyite-Zinovievite Centre," 626

Kamo, *v.* Ter-Petrossian, Simon

Kanachikov, S. I., 368

Kandelaki, C., 44, 58

Kandelaki, D. V., 616

Karakhan, L., 161, 441, 632

Karakozov, D. V., 26, 593

Karayev, A. K., 660

Karganov, N., 133

Karpovich, P. V., 69

Kartsevadze, Ilya, 113, 637

Katayev, Ivan, 639

Katayev, V., 574

Kautsky, Karl, 37, 48, 49, 63, 64, 126, 137, 141, 163, 216, 263, 264

Kavriashvili, Theophilus, 97

Kavtaradze, Sergei, 492, 637

Kazakov, Dr., 656

Kazbek, Alexander, 42

Kemal, Mustapha, 455

Kerensky, Alexander, 145, 159, 160, 165, 166, 169, 172, 174, 176, 177, 180, 181, 182, 190, 209, 277, 321

Ketzkhoveli, L., 74

Khalturin, Stephen V., 27, 593

Khandjian, A., 625, 631, 637, 660

Kharitonov, N., 388

Khmelnitsky, Bogdan, 19

Khodjayev, F., 620, 632, 637

Khodjayev, I., 631, 637

Khodjayev, P., 637

Khomeriki, N., 373

Khrustalev-Nosar, 76, 80

Kibalchich, N., 27, 28

Kienthal Conference, 146, 155

Kirov, Sergei Mironovich, alternate on Politbureau, 429; succeeds Zinoviev at Leningrad, 430; on democracy in the Party, 436; a bureaucrat, 517; his flattery of Stalin, 580; assassination of, 593-595, 597-603, 605, 626, 627, 639, 640, 649, 653, 658

Kitskirvelli, Stepko, 97

Kizevetter, M., 560

Kliuchevsky, B., 556

Knorin, V. G., 660

Knuniantz, 58, 74, 110

Kokovtsev, Count V., 119

Kolchak, Admiral, 234, 237, 241, 250, 275, 384

Kollontai, Alexandra, 148, 161, 165, 213, 218, 271, 328

Kondratiev, 530

Kork, General, 629

Kornilov, General L., 166, 167, 178, 214

Kossior, S., 436, 468, 634

Kossior, Vladimir, 292, 326, 334, 495

Koté, *v.* Tsintsadze

Kozlov, 228

Krasnov, General, 191, 192, 219

Krassin, Leonid Borissovich, 77, 292, 426; joins Lenin in 1904, 66; at 1905 Congress, 71; at Baku, 74, 75, 110; member of Bolshevik Centre (*q.v.*), 92; and "expropriations" (*q.v.*), 92, 93, 94, 96, 97, 99, 125; and Kamo, 101; conflict with Lenin, 119, 121; Commissar for Foreign Trade, 303; on trade monopoly, 304; and reorganisation of Soviet Government, 326-327; sent on diplomatic mission, 329; Stalin on, 387; possibly murdered by Stalin, 656

Krestinsky, N., 155, 213, 243, 265, 266, 270, 273, 286, 328, 329, 334, 476, 477, 632, 652

Krichevsky, B. N., 35

Krivitsky, Walter, 635, 640, 669, 674

Krizhanovsky, G., 93, 470, 506, 532

Kronstadt Rebellion, 273, 274, 277-278, 280, 319, 356, 372, 373, 476, 597

Kropotkin, Peter, 27, 46, 90, 139, 190

Krupskaya, Nadiejda Konstantinova (Lenin's wife), on Lenin, 51, 62, 124; on 1905 Congress, 71; in Galicia with Lenin, 137; and the War, 146; and Lenin's break with Stalin, 311, 312, 322; and Lenin's *Testament*, 321, 328, 364, 414, 434; and Lenin's apotheosis, 354; censures *troïka*, 363; opposes vodka monopoly, 371; supports *troïka*, 378; supports Leningrad Opposition, 391, 395, 402, 403, 405; on education, 420, 514, 618; supports Opposition bloc, 425, 436; forsakes Opposition, 438, 453, 477; on war danger, 451; on Lenin in a Stalinist prison, 476; warns against Ordjonikidze, 489-490; falsifies memoirs, 660

Krylenko, N., 195, 296, 575, 634

Kuibyshev, General, 635

Kuibyshev, V., 311, 333, 334, 341, 374, 429, 433, 436, 447, 480, 517, 553, 605, 633, 654, 656

Kun, Bela, 247, 636

Kuomintang, 441-444, 446, 449, 450, 451, 471

Kupriashvili, Bachua, 97, 98, 102, 103

Kurnatovsky, 74

Kuzmichov, General, 629, 657

Kuznietzov, 576

Kviring, E., 388

Lacroix, F., 397, 421, 531

Lakoba, Nestor, 638, 660

Lang, Harry, 670

Lapinsky, M., 137, 639

Larin, Y., 119, 161, 325, 327, 439

Lashevich, 133, 333, 360, 398, 403, 404, 425, 426, 429

Lassalle, Ferdinand, 4, 42, 63, 140, 291

Lavrov, Peter L., 22, 23, 30, 36, 69

League of Nations, 520, 568, 588, 616, 620, 621

Lenin, Vladimir Ilyich Ulianov:
—birth, 1; work in Siberia, 16, 17; at St. Petersburg, 31; on Marxism in Russia, 35, 36, 37, 46, 47; on the Party, 39, 40, 41, 48, 49, 63, 64; and Second Congress of S.-D. P.-R., 45, 54-58; leads Bolshevik fraction, 54, 56; attacks Trotsky, 57, 123, 131-132; attitude to S.-D. split and unity, 58, 59, 62, 66, 84, 116, 138; and elections to Duma, 87, 88, 118, 119; and expropriations, 89, 91, 92, 94, 99,
102, 108, 121; at 1907 Congress, 106-108; and the reaction, 117, 118, 120; his methods, 121-122, 125-127; studies philosophy, 127-128; on awakening in Russia, 129, 130; goes to Cracow, 133; and Malinovsky, 136-137
—war and Revolution: opposes War, 139, 140, 141, 145, 146; calls for Third International, 140; and February Revolution, 147, 149, 153; arrival in Russia, 154; attitude to Revolution, 153-157, 163, 164, 167, 170; and Old Bolsheviks, 157; with Trotsky in Revolution, 161, 162, 249; in hiding, 165; changes slogans, 165-166; urges insurrection, 172, 173, 175, 176, 181, 182, 184, 189; on Zinoviev and Kamenev, 177, 306, 425, 440; and formation of Bolshevik Government, 191-195, 198; attacked by Gorky, 195-197; agrarian policy, 206-208, 239; domestic policy, 208, 209, 220, 221, 240; and Constituent Assembly, 209, 210, 212; and peace, 212, 213-219
—Civil War and after: in the Civil War, 223-225, 228-232, 235-239, 242-247; attempted assassination of, 227; relations with Stalin, 250, 285, 286, 287, 293, 294; and the Terror, 252-254; and organisation of the Soviet State, 255-258; directs Politbureau, 265-267; Trade Union discussion, 268, 270-273; and bureaucratisation of the Party, 268, 269, 288, 292, 293, 298, 327; War Communism and the N.E.P., 274-276, 279-284, 296, 314, 426; relations with Trotsky, 285, 291; his power, 286, 289; and Russian barbarism, 290
—illness, 294, 321; Stalin against, 299; and monopoly of foreign trade, 303-305; his *Testament*, 305-307; his struggle against Stalin, 306-312, 322, 328; and economic planning, 309; and dictatorship of the Party, 316, 317, 319; his death and apotheosis, 349-356; his fiftieth birthday, 510
—on China, 441-443; on collectivisation, 521-522; and Communist International, 304, 365-366, 368; on Democracy, 38, 72, 171, 172, 260, 261, 410, 453, 596; on National Question, 134, 158, 199-206, 299, 300-302, 305, 323, 427; on Russian Revolution and Soviet State, 262-264; on State capitalism, 570, 673; on World Revolution and Socialism in One Country, 163, 185-187, 233, 234, 241, 261, 262, 263, 281, 392-395
—mentioned and quoted *passim*

Leonov, L., 574
Lepeshinsky, P., 103
Lermontov, Mikhail Yurievich, 20, 573
Levandovsky, General, 629, 657
Levin, Dr., 632, 656
Liadov, 639
Liadov, M., 93, 121
Liebknecht, Karl, 141, 155, 236
Li Ta-chao, 446
Litvinov, Maxim, 66, 99, 125, 568, 587, 616, 650
Liubchenko, P. P., 631, 637
Liushkov, 639, 658
Lizogub, D. A., 27
Lobov, A. I., 136
Lomidze, Serapion, 97
Lominadze, Elisso, 97
Lominadze, V., 471, 532, 586, 625, 631
Lopatin, H. A., 28
Ludwig, Emil, 588, 589, 643
Lunacharsky, Anatole, joins Lenin's group in 1904, 66; on Trotsky in 1905 Revolution, 81; breaks with Lenin, 121; favours Trotsky at Copenhagen, 123; in "Inter-District" group, 161; in Revolution, 166; resigns from Council of Commissars, 191; Lenin on, 249; and Education, 289, 514, 515, 618; against Trotsky, 378; Stalin on, 387; sacked by Stalin, 517; death, 656
Lutovinov, L. A., 269, 271, 328, 376, 631
Luxemburg, Rosa, on Lenin's theory of the Party, 63-64; supports Trotsky's theory of Permanent Revolution, 79, 107, 156-157; on Anarchism, 90; and unity of S.-D.P.R., 128; and National Question, 135, 158, 201-204, 206, 300; and the War, 140, 141; on Constituent Assembly, 209, 211; assassination of, 236; and Communist International, 237, 368; on Russian Revolution, 254; on repression and democracy, 263-264, 296
Lvov, Prince G. J., 159

Machiavelli, 563, 582-584, 643
Maistre, Joseph de, 212, 530
Makhaisky, V. K. (A. Volsky), 565
Makharadze, G., 637
Makharadze, P., 42, 60, 74, 90, 301, 311
Makhno, N., 234
Malinovsky, R. V., 135-137, 146
Manuilsky, D. Z., 121, 148, 161, 249, 378
Marat, Jean-Paul, 59, 62, 213, 353-354
Martinov, A. S., 35
Martov, Yuri Ossipovich, 130, 135, 321, 486; and Emancipation of Labour

group, 36; relations with Lenin, 39, 62, 124; Stalin on, 51; opposes Lenin at London Congress, 54, 56, 57, 63; on Iskra, 66; and 1905 Revolution, 70, 75, 79, 81; and terrorism, 90; on Kamo, 99 seq.; and elections to Duma, 108, 119; advocates "Europeanisation," 122, 123; and Bolshevik methods, 124-127; and Malinovsky, 136; at Brussels International Conference, 137; and the War, 141-142, 147; in "sealed car" with Lenin, 153; in Revolution, 160, 170, 181; forms "legal" opposition to Bolshevik Government, 257; his posthumous revenge, 582
Marx, Karl, 4, 46, 49, 51, 63, 65, 71, 108, 113, 120, 122, 140, 176, 362, 423, 500, 532, 559, 579, 619; influence on revolutionary movement in Russia, 15, 30, 34-35, 42; on the peasants, 19; on the Russian terrorists, 28, 595; Lenin on, 48, 280; on insurrection, 86, 172, 173; on individuals in history, 184, 222; on European revolution, 185; on 1848 Revolution, 238; on staff officers, 247; on violence, 252; on stupidity in revolutions, 315; his tomb, 350, 361; on democracy, 357, 596; internationalism of, 392; on historical analogies, 475; on religion, 509; on bureaucracy, 565; his neckwear, 612; on Russia, 671, 672
Masaryk, 165, 560, 610, 650, 665, 675
Maximovsky, V. N., 268, 334
Mayakovsky, V. V., 574, 575, 631
Mdivani, Budu, 301, 302, 311, 323, 492, 631, 637, 659
Medvediev, S., 426, 438, 439
Mehring, Franz, 79, 126, 141
Mekhlis, L. Z., 635
Mekk, von, 493
Mendeleyev, Prof. D., 83
Mensheviks, 112, 113, 118, 119, 122, 129, 138, 283, 422; split with Bolsheviks at London Congress (1903), 54, 56, 58; disputes with Bolsheviks, 61-65; in 1905 Revolution, 70-81; dominant in Georgia, 74-75, 84-85; propose creation of Soviets, 76-77, 80; admit decline of Revolution, 85-86; and Duma elections, 87; oppose expropriations, 90-91, 94, 100, 105-106; demand enquiry on Tiflis expropriation, 99; at Stockholm Congress, 107-108; and the War, 139; in the Revolution, 150, 151, 155, 156, 157, 159, 160, 161, 167, 178, 181, 191, 210, 220, 263; in Georgia, 203-206, 219, 300-301; and the Civil War, 238;

Mensheviks—*Continued*
 suppressed by Bolsheviks, 297; Menshevik Internationalists, 160, 170
Menzhinsky, V. R., 121, 231, 457, 486, 501, 572, 633, 654, 656, 657
Messing, G. A., 501, 635
Michael Alexandrovich, Grand-Duke, 148, 158, 227, 440
Mikhailov, Alexander D., 27, 28
Mikhailovsky, N. K., 28, 47, 69
Mikoyan, A., 429, 430, 506
Miliukov, Prof. Paul, 145, 153, 159
Miliutin, V. P., 191, 634
Minin, Sergei K., 228, 619
Molotov, Vyacheslav M., 373, 390, 406, 481, 494, 553, 568, 572, 595, 603, 626; in Revolution, 146, 155; official appointments, 273, 285, 299, 388, 411, 517; supports Stalin, 401, 435, 480
Mrachkovsky, S. V., 452, 457, 626
Muralov, N. I., 334, 452, 472, 495, 627
Muranov, M. K., 148, 151
Muraviev-Apostol, 20
Mussolini, Benito, 455, 615, 616, 633, 634, 673, 675
Myasnikov, 227, 459

Napoleon I, 4, 134, 223, 280, 365, 393, 563, 583, 590, 591, 621, 675
Natanson, Mark, 27, 69
National Question, 133, 134, 153, 158, 199, 200-206, 239, 299-302, 322, 334, 623
Nazaretian, A. M., 344
Nechayev, 23, 25, 125, 127, 196, 582
Nekrassov, N., 20
Nevsky, V., 35, 52, 71, 75, 115, 130, 639
New Economic Policy (N.E.P.), 274, 276, 279-286, 297, 304, 305, 312, 314, 316, 319, 320, 323, 325, 332, 337, 389, 413, 421, 424, 426, 438, 470, 474, 480, 482, 506, 516, 532, 541, 566, 602, 603, 610, 666
Nicholas I, 18, 20, 259, 397, 402, 445, 457, 531, 541, 547, 556, 562, 573
Nicholas II, 35, 70, 75, 79, 144, 227, 283, 541, 568
Nikolayev, L. V., 594, 653
Nogin, V. P., 120, 129, 191, 271, 324
Nossovich, 226, 227
Novikov, N., 20, 562

October (November) Revolution, 181, 185, 190, 204, 207, 209, 225, 232, 237, 257, 260, 314, 348, 368, 383, 405, 472, 509, 519
Okhrana, Tsarist Secret Police, 28, 135, 136, 137, 138, 374, 457, 498
Okuashvili, Arakel, 31
Okudjava, Mikhail, 492, 632, 637
Olminsky, M. S., 66, 131

Opposition Bloc of Left and Leningrad Oppositions, 416-418, 421, 423-430, 433-440, 444-477
Opposition for Democratic Centralism, 271, 274, 334, 475, 496
Opposition, Left (Trotskyist), 327-329, 334, 344-349, 359, 360, 363-365, 367, 369, 374, 375, 380, 382, 386, 401, 411, 414-417, 433, 482, 483, 486, 488, 490, 492-497, 499, 501, 502, 507, 511, 534, 535, 581, 586, 591, 594, 630
Opposition, Leningrad or New (Zinovievist), 386-411, 415, 417, 598, 602
Opposition, "Platform of the Fifteen," 453
Opposition, Right, 447, 459, 480-490, 492, 494, 496, 497, 501, 502, 507, 517, 518, 530, 535, 536, 581, 595, 632
Opposition, Workers', 271, 272, 274, 279, 292, 329, 342, 376, 417, 426, 436
Opposition, Workers' Group, 330
Opposition, Workers' Truth Group, 329, 347, 459
Oprichnina, 498, 506-507, 645-646
Orakhelashvili, M. D., 632, 637
Ordjonikidze, Sergo, 99, 637, 654; in prison with Stalin, 113; Lenin's pupil at Longjumeau, 128; on C.C. of Bolshevik Party, 129; on Executive Bureau, 130; Menshevik position in Revolution, 147; Lenin attacks his Georgian policy, 307, 308, 311, 323; provokes and represses rebellion in Georgia (1924), 373; directs repression in Leningrad, 408; supports Stalin, 429, 430, 440, 517; opposes exclusion of Trotsky from C.C., 449, 452, 453; and the capitulators, 469, 489; and Right Opposition, 484; on Five Year Plan, 513; on bureaucracy, 516; murdered by Stalin, 628, 659
Ossinsky, V. V., 213, 239, 240, 271, 326-328, 334, 342, 356, 421, 427, 451, 636

Parvus, H., 64, 77, 78, 79, 156
Pasternak, B., 576, 638
"People's Will," 27, 28, 30, 34, 56
"Permanent Revolution," theory of, 77, 78, 79, 107, 156, 161, 358, 379, 392, 437, 438, 588, 676
Perovskaya, Sophia L., 27, 28, 593, 601
Peshkov, M. (Gorky's son), 633, 654
Peter I, the Great, 19, 21, 83, 259, 490, 499, 500, 503, 504, 508, 541, 542, 545-547, 550, 556, 561, 588, 619, 643, 644
Petlura, Simon, 234
Petrovsky, G. I., 147, 411, 634
Pilnyak, Boris, 398, 574, 638, 657
Pilsudski, Marshal Joseph, 70, 73, 90, 93, 105, 246, 275, 427, 586

Pissarev, D. I., 21, 47

Platonov, S., 409, 499, 531, 619

Plekhanov, George V., 108, 130, 136, 212, 258, 486; founds *Chorny Perediel*, 27; pioneer of Marxism in Russia, 30, 34, 35, 37, 38, 39, 42, 49, 51; on *Iskra*, 36, 45; supports Lenin at London Congress, 54, 56-58; breach with Lenin, 62, 63, 65, 77; and 1905 Revolution, 71, 76, 81; and Social Revolutionaries, 90; and "illegal" work, 119; on Empirio-criticism, 127-128; at Brussels International Conference, 137; and War, 139; on Bolshevism, 66, 186, 259, 410

Pobiedonostsev, C. P., 14, 28

Pokrovsky, M. N., 19, 20, 121, 213, 500, 618, 619, 675

Poletayev, 131

Polish Socialist Party, 69, 70, 90, 105

Polonsky, V., 574

Popov, A. S., 660

Populism, 21, 22, 35, 69, 181, 263

Postyshev, Pavel P., 518, 634

Potemkin, battleship, 73

Potressov, A. N., 36, 39, 56, 119

Preobrazhensky, Eugene A., 483, 497; and Socialism in One Country, 168, 262, 392; and Brest peace, 213; on C.C., 265; on secretariat of C.C., 266; supports Trotsky on Trade Unions, 270; excluded from C.C., 273; on confusion of Party and State, 293; and Left Opposition, 327, 334, 337, 338, 342; on unemployment, 372; on industrialisation, 423; expelled from Party, 456; exiled, 472; considers capitulation, 479; capitulates, 495; succumbs in jail, 634

Prokofiev, G. E., 588, 635, 662

Prokopovich, Prof. S. N., 666, 668

Proudhon, Pierre-Joseph, 4, 21, 22, 48

Provisional Government, 147, 150, 151-155, 157, 159, 177, 178, 183, 191, 204

Pugachev, E. I., 19, 23, 503

Pushkin, 20, 21, 36, 500, 573, 619

Putna, General Vitovt, 629, 633, 657

Pyatakov, George Leonidovich, on National Question, 158, 202, 239; and Brest peace, 213, 217; in Civil War, 222; supports Trotsky on Trade Unions, 270; Lenin on, 306; in Left Opposition, 334, 342, 344, 360, 425, 433, 434, 436; and German Revolution, 336; capitulates to Stalin, 476, 477; and Right Opposition, 489, 497; his self-abasement, 518; flatters Stalin, 534; in trial of "Anti-Soviet Trotskyite Centre," 627-628, 646, 665

Radek, Karl Berngardovich, and Brest peace, 213, 218; on Polish campaign, 246, 247; member of E.C.C.I., 288; in Left Opposition, 335, 342, 344, 369, 428, 435, 437; and German Revolution, 336; and Chinese Revolution, 442-444; expelled and exiled, 472; prepares to capitulate, 479; capitulates, 495; as subordinate functionary, 518; confesses his errors, 533; flatters Stalin, 607; on Commission on Russian History, 620; in trial of "Anti-Soviet Trotskyite Centre," 627-628

Rakovsky, Christian Georgievich, friendship with Trotsky, 133; and the War, 141; in the Ukraine, 223, 329; in the Civil War, 230; supports Trotsky on Trade Unions, 270; in Left Opposition, 328, 329, 333, 334, 427, 428, 460, 469, 470; as ambassador, 328, 329; expelled and exiled, 472; on depravity of bureaucracy, 491, 520, 564; and Five Year Plan, 495; submits to Stalin, 581; in trial of "Rightist-Trotskyist Bloc," 632, 652

Raskolnikov, F., 162, 378, 387, 635

Rasputin, Gregory, 144

Razin, Stenka, 19, 23

Reclus, Elisée, 6, 7, 8, 10, 205, 559

Red Army, 189, 278, 300, 312, 445, 454, 472, 478, 509, 566-568, 607, 622, 628, 634

Reed, John, 177, 184, 185

Remmele, C. A., 636

Revolution of 1848, 4, 86, 238

Revolution of 1905, 83, 149, 656; agitation preceding, 66-70; events of, 70-76, 79-80

Riazanov, D. B., pioneer of socialism in Russia, 31; at London Congress, 54, 55; outside fractions, 63, 120; at Copenhagen Congress, 123; and the War, 141; joins Bolsheviks, 161; and European revolution, 185; and formation of Bolshevik Government, 191-192, 194; and Brest peace, 218; and National Question, 239; and death penalty, 258; and Trade Unions, 271, 296, 297; and N.E.P., 279; and democracy, 292; protests against honours, 303, 354; and Old Bolsheviks, 360; "homesick for Turkestan," 408; on wages, 419; expelled and exiled, 530, 532, 533

Riutin, M. N., 488, 535, 625

Robespierre, Maximilian, 58, 59, 62, 134, 213, 223, 246, 283, 354, 474, 476

Rodzianko, M. V., 145

Romanov, A. (police agent), 136
Rosengoltz, A., 334, 340, 477, 632
Rousseau, Jean-Jacques, 4, 546, 562
Rubakin, N., 84, 516
Rudzutak, I. E., 270, 386, 411, 429, 480, 517, 634
Rykov, Alexis Ivanovich, 120, 287, 433, 517, 518, 532, 595; opposes *April Theses*, 157; and formation of Bolshevik Government, 191, 194; on Economic Council, 288; supports *troïka*, 341, 379; supports Stalin against New Opposition, 388, 406, 411; on economic situation, 423, 481; in Right Opposition, 447, 480, 484, 488, 489, 497; and Mussolini, 455, 615; on Five Year Plan, 470; in trial of "Rightist-Trotskyist Bloc," 632, 652
Ryssakov, N. I., 28, 601

Safarov, 388, 594, 637
Sakvarelidze, Niko, 111, 113
Sapronov, Timothei V., 213, 239, 268, 269, 271, 334, 337, 338, 342, 421, 439, 452, 453, 470, 472, 477
Saveliev, Maximilian A., 134
Savinkov, Boris V., 69, 224
Sazonov, Igor, 69, 593
Schmidt, Lieutenant, 73
Schmidt, Nicholas, 126
Schmidt, General V. V., 629, 657
Sedova, Natalia Ivanovna, 347
Semashko, I. A., 99, 125, 420, 517
Serebriakov, L. P., 222, 265, 266, 270, 273, 334, 456, 472, 479, 495, 627
Shaumian, 110, 112, 113, 200, 203, 248
Shchedrin, N., 21, 437, 499, 591-592
Shliapnikov, G. A., 146, 151, 154, 191, 222, 229, 271, 292, 342, 421, 438, 498, 533
Skliansky, Ephraim, 231, 360, 412, 446
Skrypnik, N., 517, 535, 595, 625, 631, 670
Smilga, Ivan T., 213, 222, 235, 247, 427, 450, 452, 472, 479, 495, 634
Smirnov, Ivan Nikitich, 133, 222, 227, 334, 342, 472, 495, 626
Smirnov, V. M., 222, 334, 436, 472, 496
Smith, Andrew, 600
Social-Democratic Party of Russia: origin and development of socialism in Russia, 15, 18, 30, 35-41, 69; First Congress of Party at Minsk (1898), 16, 31, 53; Second Congress (Brussels-London, 1903), 45-49, 53-58, 74, 90, 212; division into Bolsheviks and Mensheviks, 54, 56, 61; Third Congress (1905), Bolshevik section at London, Menshevik at Geneva, 71;

growth of Party after 1905, 84; Unity Congress (Stockholm, 1906), 84, 88, 89, 91, 100, 104, 106, 107; Congress at London (1907), 94, 106, 107, 108, 118; Conference in Finland (1906), 108; the Party and the Trade Unions, 109; Conference at Vyborg (1907), 118; definitive split, 116, 129; Central Committee transferred to Russia (1910), 123; Lenin calls Congress at Prague (1912), 129, 135, 136; Trotsky calls Congress at Vienna (1912), 131. (Thereafter *v.* Bolsheviks, Bolshevik Congresses, and Mensheviks.)
"Social-Fascism," 369, 569, 620
"Socialism in a Single Country," 392-396, 398, 414, 437, 500
Socialist International, 62, 84, 101, 113, 258; Stuttgart Congress (1907), 122, 140; Copenhagen Congress (1910), 122; Brussels Conference (1914), 137-138; and the War, 140, 146
Social Revolutionary Party of Russia, 69, 72, 81, 90, 92, 108, 112, 125, 139, 145, 151, 159, 160, 167, 181, 207, 208, 220, 221, 224, 227, 234, 238, 251, 263, 297, 319, 422; Left Social Revolutionaries, 160, 170, 174, 194, 210, 213, 223, 224, 257, 384, 439
Sokolnikov, Gregory Yakovlevich, 120, 477; on Politbureau, 179, 265; and Brest peace, 213; in Civil War, 222, 239; supports Trotsky on Trade Unions, 270; against trade monopoly, 304; in the Opposition, 388, 403, 405, 409, 411, 415, 421, 436; capitulates, 453; arranges Bukharin-Kamenev interview, 482; swears obedience to Stalin, 532; in trial of "Anti-Soviet Trotskyite Centre," 627-628
Solonevich, I., 523 545, 584
Sosnovsky, 239, 334, 472, 495, 581, 634
Soviet, Leningrad (after 1924), 403
Soviet, Moscow, 185, 288, 304, 429
Soviet, Petrograd (from 1914 to 1924), 144, 145, 147, 150, 151, 153, 160, 161, 165, 170, 180, 183, 277, 283, 288, 383
Soviet, St. Petersburg (before 1914), 76, 79, 80, 109, 117
Soviets, the, in 1905 Revolution, 76, 77, 80, 81, 86; in 1917 Revolution, 152, 156, 157, 164, 169, 170, 178; First Congress (June 1917), 160, 164; Regional Conference of Ss. of North, 180; Second Congress (Nov. 1917), 173, 175, 177, 178, 179, 181, 182, 186, 190, 197; Third Congress (Jan. 1918), 210; Fifth Congress (July 1918), 223, 224; Sixth Con-

gress (Nov. 1918), 233; 1921 Congress, 280; 1922 Congress, 322; Executive Committee of, 224, 234, 239, 257, 260, 266, 287, 288, 296, 299, 441, 606; First Congress of Soviets of the Union (1923), 322; Second Congress of S. of U. (1924), 352, 354; Fifth Congress of S. of U. (1928), 494; Seventh Congress of S. of U. (1935), 603; Eighth Congress of S. of U. (1936), 623, 630, 650, 664

Spartacus League, 236, 237

Spiridovich, General A. I., 93, 94

Stalin, Joseph Vissarionovich Djugashvili: birth and family, 1-2; at Tiflis Theological Seminary, 2, 13, 15; his mother on, 3, 5; Yenukidze on, 4; racial characteristics, 8
—early political activity: converted to socialism, 16; joins S.-D.P.R., 17; early years in Party, 31-33; as "professional revolutionary," 39, 41; and strikes at Tiflis, 42; expelled from Tiflis S.-D. Party, 43; Batoum and Siberia, 44; alleged correspondence with Lenin, 50-52; possibly originally a Menshevik, 58, 59; escapes from Siberia and returns to Tiflis, 60-61; and 1905 Revolution, 73-75
—from 1905 to 1917: participates at Bolshevik Congresses, 81-82, 84-85, 87, 106, 109; and elections to Duma, 88, 118; directs expropriations and terrorist acts, 94 *seq.*; in Tiflis, Baku, and prison, 109-114; denounces comrades to police, 110, 112, 114; second exile and escape, 115-116; becomes member of Bolshevik C.C., 116, 129-130; during period of reaction, 120; on émigré dissensions, 128-129; connection with *Pravda*, 130-131; with Lenin at Cracow, 133; on National Question, 133-134, 152-153, 158, 199-206, 239, 274, 299-301, 322, 323; St. Petersburg and exile, 135, 137, 138, 142, 143; and the War, 141
—in the Revolution: on E.C. of Petrograd Soviet, 148, 150-151; takes over *Pravda*, 151-153; position before Lenin's return, 154-155; rôle in Revolution, 156, 158, 167, 168, 169, 173, 177, 183, 184; early opposition to Trotsky, 162; member of Politbureau, 179; on Lenin, 182; on Trotsky, 183; on world revolution, 186; and formation of Bolshevik Government, 191, 194; Commissar for Nationalities, 199, 202, 203, 311; and agrarian question, 206; and Constituent Assembly, 210; and peace negotiations, 212-214
—in the Civil War and after: his part in the Civil War, 221-224, 235, 236, 243, 244; and the Military Opposition, 225-232, 241, 242, 245; confirmed on C.C., 240; his position after Civil War, 248-250; Commissar for Workers' and Peasants' Inspection, 249; his political education, 258, 281; on Politbureau, 265, 266, 273; disagreement with Lenin, 267; and Trade Union discussion, 268, 270-272; intrigues for power, 285, 287-289, 291; activity as General Secretary, 285, 293, 295, 296, 299; urges abolition of trade monopoly, 304; activity in Georgia, 301, 302, 307; Lenin's struggle against, 305-312, 319, 322
—struggle against the Oppositions: in the *troïka* against Trotsky and Left Opposition, 321, 328, 329, 331, 332, 334, 339-343, 346-348, 356, 358, 360-365, 369, 375-377, 385; and the German Revolution, 335-336; on Lenin's death, 352, 353, 355; on Leninism, 357; at Thirteenth Party Congress, 360-364; and replacement of cadres, 366; and the Comintern, 367; on Trade Unions, 371; and the Georgian insurrection of 1924, 372-374; campaign against "Trotskyism," 378-382; on Trotsky's rôle in the Revolution, 383-384; split in the *troïka*, 383-385; against Leningrad or New Opposition, 386-388, 403-411; policy toward peasants, 389-391; "Socialism in a Single Country," 392-396; at Fourteenth Congress, 398-399; and economic planning, 400; disparages Krupskaya, 402; Stalin's rôle, 412-413; against Opposition Bloc, 414, 416-418, 425, 427, 429, 430, 434-440, 445, 449, 452-453; and statistics, 419; opposes industrialisation, 422-424, 436-437; and Anglo-Russian Committee, 428; names towns after himself, 431, 577; and bureaucracy, 432-433, 460, 474, 517-519, 564; and Chinese Revolution, 442-444, 446, 450-451, 471; and Right Opposition, 447, 456-459, 461, 465, 468-470, 472, 476-477, 480-490, 492; opposes rapid collectivisation, 464, 467-468, 479, 481; at Fifteenth Congress, 466-469; and the Shakhty affair, 478; and the famine, 490-491; and the capitulators, 497-498; his fiftieth birthday, 509-511, 577-579

Stalin—*Continued*
—the First Five Year Plan, 493-497,
501-507, 515-516, 520-529, 535-556,
561, 587; the repression, 499-500,
530-531, 534-535; and international
politics, 520, 586-588; mutations of
personnel, 532-533; and socialism,
558-563; and war, 566-569, 571; and
the Soviet State, 572; and Literature
and Art, 573-576, 619; at the Seventeenth Congress, 579-581; and the
Comintern, 586
—the Kirov murder, 593-595, 597-601,
603; his new Constitution, 602, 604,
622-623, 630; liquidates various organisations, 607-608; his counter-
revolution, 610, 617; and Soviet
economy, 610-615; and foreign affairs, 616, 620-621; mutations of personnel, 624-625; the Moscow trials,
625-630, 652-660; the repression, 631-
642, 647-651; Mussolini on, 633-634;
compared to figures in Russian History, 643-646; adulation of, 660-663;
and Second Five Year Plan, 663-672;
imitates Hitler and Mussolini, 673;
and the Soviet State, 673-675
—his character and methods, 33-34,
115, 431-432, 448, 512, 581-585, 589-
593, 596, 605-609
—mentioned and quoted *passim*
Stassova, Helen D., 214, 266, 636
Steklov, G., 150, 155, 161, 639
Stepanov, I. I., 66
Stepniak (Kravchinsky), 27, 30
Stolypin, P., 93, 117, 136, 196
Struve, Peter, 31, 35, 66
Stukov, I. N., 292, 334
Sukhanov, N., 150, 160, 530
Sun Yat-sen, 441, 443, 444, 446
Svanidze, Catherine (first wife of
Stalin), 593
Sverdlov, Jacob Mikhailovich, 223,
224, 244; in Siberian exile with
Stalin, 133, 137, 142, 143; at Sixth
Party Congress, 167; in October Rev-
olution, 179; and formation of Bol-
shevik Government, 191; and Brest
peace, 213; as administrator, 217,
240; in Civil War, 229, 230; death,
248; Lenin on, 249; on Politbureau,
265; Secretary of Party, 266
Syrtsov, S. M., 517, 532, 625
Sytin, P. P., 228, 229

Taratuta (Victor), 125, 126, 127
Tarlé, E., 531, 619, 675
Ter-Petrossian (called Kamo), 43, 93,
95-104, 121, 125, 203, 301, 492
Ter-Petrossian, S. Medvedyeva, 97-98

Ter-Vaganian, V. A., 626
Testament of Lenin, 305-307, 320, 321,
322, 364, 382, 414, 425, 427, 434, 458
Thermidor, 282-284, 403, 404, 413, 416,
426, 438, 450, 451, 453, 455, 457, 459,
462, 465, 469, 474-476, 591, 611
Tikhomirov, L., 28, 136
Tkachev, Peter N., 26, 36, 41
Tolstoy, Alexis, 574, 643
Tolstoy, Leo N., 20, 68, 129, 574
Tomsky, M., opposes *April Theses*,
157; supports Lenin on Trade Un-
ions, 270; at Trade Union Congress
(1921), 296, 297; supports *troïka*,
341; supports Stalin against New
Opposition, 388, 406, 411; and Anglo-
Russian Committee, 427, 428, 449;
in Right Opposition, 447, 459, 480,
484, 497, 518; advocates liquidation
of Red Trade Unions, 586; suicide,
626, 631
Trade Unions, discussion on, 268-273;
Congress (1921), 296; Committee of
Russian and British T. Us., 327-328;
Red T. U. International, 586
Trial (1922) of the Social Revolution-
aries, 319
Trial (June 1928), the "Shakhty Af-
fair," 478
Trial (May 1929), of von Mekk, Ve-
lichko and Palchinsky, 493-494
Trial (Nov.-Dec. 1930) of the Indus-
trialists, 529, 530, 652
Trial (March 1931) of the Menshe-
viks, 530-532, 652
Trial (Aug. 1936) of the "Trotskyite-
Zinovievite Terrorist Centre," 625-
627, 657
Trial (Nov. 1936) at Novosibirsk, 627
Trial (Jan. 1937) of the "Anti-Soviet
Trotskyite Centre," 627, 628, 657
Trial (June 1937) of the Eight Gen-
erals, 629, 657
Trial (March 1938) of the "Rightist-
Trotskyist Bloc," 632, 633, 657
Trilisser, M. A., 484, 486, 501, 635
Troïka of Stalin, Zinoviev and Kamenev, 299, 321, 328, 329, 330, 337,
339, 341-344, 347, 349, 351, 359, 361,
362, 363, 365, 368, 371, 376, 377, 379,
381, 383, 387, 398, 413
Trotsky, Leon Davidovich Bronstein:
—birth, 1; deported to Siberia, 16; at
Nicolayev, 31; on Lenin, 38; escapes
from Siberia, 45; at Second Congress,
54-58; supports Martov, 55-56; controversies with Lenin, 57, 64-65, 122-
123, 131-132, 259; his part in 1905
Revolution, 77-79, 156, 161, 186, 438;
on expropriations, 99, 126-127; at

Third Congress, 107, 109; and elections to Duma, 108; his position on split in Social-Democracy, 116, 122, 128; advocates "Europeanisation," 122; on awakening in Russia, 129; calls Congress at Vienna ("August Bloc" 1912), 131; goes to Balkans, 133; at Brussels International Congress, 137; and the War, 141, 147-148
—in the Revolution: returns to Russia, 160; attitude to Revolution, 161; with Lenin in Revolution, 161-162, 249; in "July Days," 165-166; elected to Bolshevik C.C., 169; President of Petrograd Soviet, 170, 180; organises insurrection, 173, 175, 177, 180-184, 189; and Democratic Conference, 174; leads Military Revolutionary Committee, 179; on Politbureau, 179, 265-266, 289; and formation of Bolshevik Government, 191-195, 198; attacked by Gorky, 195-197; and National Question, 199-206; and agrarian question, 206, 208; and Constituent Assembly, 209, 211-212; and Brest-Litovsk peace, 213-219; domestic policy, 221; and world revolution, 233, 262-263
—in Civil War and after: his rôle in Civil War, 222-223, 225, 227, 234, 235, 239, 241, 243-244, 246-247; and the Military Opposition, 226, 228-232, 236, 242, 245; confirmed on C.C., 240; relations with Lenin, 250, 267, 285; and Red Terror, 252-253, 258; and compulsory labour, 259-260; value of his testimony, 267; and Trade Union discussion, 268-273; and Kronstadt rebellion, 274, 278-279; and War Communism, 275, 296; and the N.E.P., 279-280; on Thermidor, 283, 413, 455, 474-475; on Stalin, 287, 294; and the Comintern, 290, 304, 365-368; Stalin and early opposition to T., 291, 298-299; upholds trade monopoly, 304-305; and Lenin's struggle against Stalin, 308-312; on economic planning, 309, 324, 400
—in Left Opposition: the troïka against, 321, 325-329, 331-335, 337, 339-344, 346-349, 358-364, 369, 371, 374-376, 381-382, 385-387, 392; on Soviet economy, 323-325, 414; and German Revolution, 336; and Lenin's death, 335; at Thirteenth Congress, 360-364; his Lessons of October, 377-380, 383; ousted from Council of War, 381; Stalin on T.'s rôle in Revolution, 383-384; and the peasants, 390, 424; remains on Polit-

bureau, 411; on Stalin's rôle, 412-413; his tactics, in Opposition, 414, 417-418, 427, 433, 435, 437, 439-440, 445, 452, 460; on Anglo-Russian Committee, 428; dismissed from Department of Economics, 434; signs capitulations, 436, 453; removed from Politbureau, 436; on Chinese Revolution, 443, 446; at E.C. of the Comintern, 449; removed from C.C., 449-450, 457-459; expelled from Comintern, 456; on Five Year Plan, 460, 493, 495-497; and November 1927 demonstration, 461-462; expelled from Party, 465, 469
—in exile: deported to Siberia, 472; compares self to Babeuf, 473; and crushing of Opposition, 476-477; exiled to Turkey, 492; and capitulators, 495, 581; on Russian economy, 541-542; on State socialism, 570, 673; and Literature, 574; compared to Stalin, 583; and Kirov's murder, 594; and Moscow trials, 626, 629, 632, 633, 635, 652, 653, 655; on bureaucracy, 674; fails to make appraisal, 676
—mentioned and quoted passim
"Trotskyism" (v. also Opposition, Left), 345, 359, 375, 378, 379, 381, 382, 386, 387, 392, 401, 414, 418, 426, 436, 438, 452, 476, 533, 581, 607, 618, 627, 630, 652
Troyanovsky, Alexander, 136
Tseretelli, George, 42
Tseretelli, I. G., 81, 108, 117, 150, 155, 160, 164, 204, 205, 301
Tsintsadze, Alipi (called Koté), 100, 102, 103, 203, 301, 492, 581
Tskhakaya, M. G., 71
Tugan-Baronovsky, M. I., 35
Tukhachevsky, Marshal M., 227, 247, 617, 629, 633, 657, 662
Turgenev, Ivan, 20, 47

Uglanov, N. A., 388, 411, 484, 488, 496, 497, 634
Ulianov, Alexander Ilyich, 28
Ulianova, Anna (Elizarova), 51, 656
Ulianova, Maria, 51, 656
Unschlicht, I. S., 360, 374, 517, 634
Uritsky, M. S., 161, 179, 217, 227, 248

Vandervelde, Emile, 137, 300
Vardin, M., 387, 388, 594
Vereshchak, 111-114, 133
Veressayev, V. V., 574
Verkhovsky, General, 179
Victor, v. Taratuta
Volodarsky, V., 161, 221, 248

Voltaire, 20, 103, 546, 562
Voronsky, A., 334, 574, 639
Voroshilov, Klimenti, in Civil War, 221, 222, 224; leads Military Opposition, 225, 226-230, 232; falsifies history of Civil War, 235, 236, 243, 245, 247; on Revolutionary Council of War, 333, 360; Commissar for War, 398; supports Stalin, 404, 411, 438, 448; and Right Opposition, 480, 482, 484; Stalin's hold over, 486-487; orthodox Stalinist, 518; his evidence on famine, 552; becomes marshal, 617
Vorovsky, V. V., 66
Voytinsky, V., 126, 155, 181
Vyshinsky, Andrei, 606, 626, 632

Wang An-shih, 558-559
Wang Ching-wei, 444, 450
War Communism, 254, 275, 296, 325, 332, 390, 480, 484, 495, 500, 506, 566
War, Crimean, 68, 146, 566
War, Russo-Japanese, 68, 86, 146, 149, 541, 566
War, 1914-1918, 139-141, 143, 149, 152, 162, 179, 188, 280, 541, 566
Washington, G., 59, 77, 283, 413, 461
Witte, Count S. J., 541, 542
Wrangel, General P., 247, 457
Wu Pei-fu, 441, 442

Yagoda, Henry, and Right Opposition, 484, 486; directs G.P.U., 501, 572, 588; and Kirov's murder, 598; aids Stalin's purge, 608, 613, 624, 631, 632; falls into disgrace, 628, 629; in trial of "Rightist-Trotskyist Bloc," 632, 633, 652, 654, 656, 657; closest colleague of Stalin, 593, 659
Yaroslavsky, Emilian, 130, 147, 372, 378, 380, 476, 517, 533, 660
Yegorov, Marshal, 617, 635, 657
Yenukidze, Abel, 4, 60, 71, 606, 628, 632, 637, 659, 660
Yermolov, Viceroy of the Caucasus, 14
Yermolov, A., 11
Yevdokimov, 403, 404, 436, 594, 626
Yezhov, Nicholas, 606, 608, 624, 628, 629, 631, 632, 635, 650, 656, 657
Yuan Shih-kai 441
Yudenich, General, 237, 241, 243
Yurenev, 268, 328, 635
Yvon, 665

Zalutsky, 387, 403, 404, 413, 453
Zamiatin, E., 574

Zasulich, Vera, 27, 30, 36, 55, 593
Zatonsky, V. P., 274, 596, 620, 637
Zavarzin, General P., 136
Zemlya i Volya, 21
Zetkin, Clara, 126, 247, 366, 439, 514
Zimmerwald Conference, 146, 155, 158
Zinoviev, Gregory Yevseyevich, 99, 116, 209, 370, 432, 433, 477, 496, 497, 646
—during the reaction, 117; and elections to Duma, 119; alleged falsifications, 126; his History of the Party, 130; in Galicia with Lenin, 137; and the War, 146, 148; inclines to Kamenev's view of April Theses, 154; in hiding with Lenin, 165; opposes seizure of power, 173, 176; on Politbureau, 179, 265; opinion on European revolution, 185; and formation of Bolshevik Government, 191, 194; and Brest peace, 213; at Eighth Congress, 240; on Trotsky's defence of Petrograd, 243; Lenin on, 249, 306, 505; Trotsky on, 267, 287; joins Stalin and Kamenev against Trotsky, 285, 291; President of Petrograd Soviet, 288
—in troïka against Left Opposition, 299, 321, 363, 364, 365; self-aggrandisement, 303; on freedom of criticism, 317; and German Revolution, 335-336, 455; on Lenin, 356; on "social-fascism," 369; and the peasants, 372, 390, 424; against "Trotskyism," 377-383; urges imprisonment of Trotsky, 381; breaks with Stalin, 383, 385-388, 391-392, 396, 398; on "Socialism in One Country," 394-395, 414
—leads Leningrad or New Opposition, 400-401, 403, 405-407, 409-411, 416, 447; in Opposition Bloc, 415, 417-418, 425-430, 436-437, 439, 452, 459; considers capitulation, 440-441, 469; and the Chinese Revolution, 443; excluded from C.C., 449-450, 453, 457; and Nov. 1927 demonstration, 461-462; expelled from Party, 465
—capitulates, 470; denounces comrades, 472; and Bukharin-Kamenev interview, 482, 483; self-abasement and confessions, 489, 498; on education, 514; denounces Bukharin, 518; exiled again, 535; imprisoned after Kirov affair, 594, 598; his defeat, 597; in trial of "Trotskyite-Zinovievite Centre," 626-627; will write no memoirs, 659-660